TExES™ SOCIAL STUDIES 7-12 (232)

TEXAS EXAMINATIONS OF EDUCATOR STANDARDS™

Dean Ferguson, Ph.D.
Professor of History
Texas A&M University-Kingsville

Contributing Author
Alexander Heatherley, M.S.
Associate Professor of Education
Del Mar College

 Research & Education Association

Research & Education Association

258 Prospect Plains Road
Cranbury, New Jersey 08512
Email: info@rea.com

TExES Social Studies 7–12 (232) Book + Online

Published 2021

Copyright © 2018 by Research & Education Association.
All rights reserved. No part of this book may be reproduced in any form without permission of the publisher.

Printed in the United States of America

Library of Congress Control Number 2018935813

ISBN-13: 978-0-7386-1228-7

ISBN-10: 0-7386-1228-6

For all references in this book, TExES is a trademark in the U.S. and/or other countries of the Texas Education Agency (TEA). All other trademarks cited in this publication are the property of their respective owners.

The Social Studies Test Objectives presented in this book were created and implemented by the Texas Education Agency and Pearson Education Inc., or its affliate(s). For further information visit the TEA website at tea.texas.gov.

Cover image: ©iStockphoto.com/monkeybusinessimages

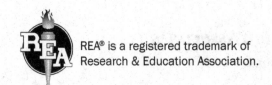

Contents

About the Author v

About the Contributing Author v

About REA vi

Chapter 1
Getting Started 1
   How to Use This Book + Online Prep 1
   An Overview of the Test 3
   TExES Social Studies 7–12 Study Schedule 7

Chapter 2
Proven Tips and Test-Taking Strategies 9

Diagnostic Test .... *www.rea.com/studycenter*

Chapter 3
Domain I: World History 13
   Competency 001: Ancient World Civilizations 13
   Competency 002: World History from 600 to 1450 CE 37
   Competency 003: World History from 1450 to 1750 CE 54
   Competency 004: World History from 1750 CE to the Present 72

Chapter 4
Domain II: U.S. History 101
   Competency 005: Exploration and Colonization 101
   Competency 006: Revolutionary Era and the Early Years of the Republic 124
   Competency 007: Westward Expansion, the Civil War, and Reconstruction 146
   Competency 008: The United States as a World Power 162
   Competency 009: Political, Economic, and Social Developments from 1877 to
      the Present 185

Chapter 5
Domain III: Texas History 211
   Competency 010: Exploration and Colonization 211
   Competency 011: Independence, Statehood, Civil War Reconstruction and Aftermath 231
   Competency 012: Texas in the Twentieth and Twenty-first Centuries 261

Chapter 6
Domain IV: Geography, Culture, and the Behavioral and Social Sciences 289
Competency 013: Physical Geography Concepts, Natural Processes, and
   Earth's Physical Features 289
Competency 014: Global and Regional Patterns of Culture and Human Geography 307
Competency 015: Interactions between Human Groups and the Physical Environment 333
Competency 016: Sociological, Anthropological, and Psychological Concepts
   and Processes 339

Chapter 7
Domain V: Government and Citizenship 347
Competency 017: Democratic Principles and Government in the United States 347
Competency 018: Citizenship and Political Processes in the United States 395
Competency 019: Types of Political Systems 421

Chapter 8
Domain VI: Economics and Science, Technology and Society 441
Competency 020: Economic Concepts and Types of Economic Systems 441
Competency 021: Structure and Operation of the U.S. Free Enterprise System 482
Competency 022: Science, Technology and Society 511

Chapter 9
Domain VII: Social Studies Foundations, Skills, Research, and Instruction 539
Competency 023: Social Studies Foundations and Skills 540
Competency 024: Sources of Social Studies Information; Interpreting and
   Communicating Social Studies Information 560
Competency 025: Social Studies Research 587
Competency 026: Social Studies Instruction and Assessment 600

Practice Test 1 (also available online at *www.rea.com/studycenter*) 623
Answer Key 650
Detailed Answers 651
Self-Assessment Guide 689

Practice Test 2 .... *www.rea.com/studycenter*

Index 691

ABOUT THE AUTHOR

Dr. Dean Ferguson is Professor of History at Texas A&M University-Kingsville, where he has been based since 1998. He earned his master's degree in History from Central Michigan University and his Ph.D. in European History from Purdue.

Dr. Ferguson is an old hand at the TExES exams. He served as a content reviewer for the test developer, ETS, and developed a program at Texas A&M-Kingsville to prepare teacher candidates for success on the social studies and history certification exams.

He has worked extensively with the College Board's AP World History program since its inception in 2002. He served on the College Board's AP World History Test Development Committee from 2008 to 2014. In that capacity, he wrote and reviewed test items. He was Chief Reader for the AP World History free-response reading from 2012 to 2014.

In 2015 he joined the College Board's AP Insight project, developing digital teaching materials and practice-exam questions while heading up committees creating materials for both the AP U.S. History and AP World History courses.

Dr. Ferguson has taught at both the high school and university level, with courses spanning United States History, World History, and Western Civilization, as well as Early Modern European Social and Cultural History, The Renaissance and Reformation, The French Revolution and the Napoleonic Period, Private Life in Early Modern Europe, and Work and Poverty in World History.

A child of missionary parents, he lived in Burundi until age 18. It was a teacher, Nancy Proctor Grimes, who kindled his love for history in the seventh grade.

ABOUT THE CONTRIBUTING AUTHOR

Alexander Heatherley is Associate Professor of Education at Del Mar College in Corpus Christi, Texas. He earned his bachelor's degree in Anthropology from the University of Tulsa and his master's in Curriculum and Instruction from Texas A&M-Corpus Christi.

His diverse experience includes serving as a reader for the College Board's AP European History exam, imparting fish-farming techniques in the Democratic Republic of the Congo, as well as teaching pre-AP Human Geography, AP European History, and AP World History to Texas high school students. In addition, he has taught IB World History and IB Japanese.

Mr. Heatherley is also a former teacher certification test preparation consultant for Education Service Center-Region 2 in Corpus Christi.

ABOUT REA

Founded in 1959, Research & Education Association (REA) is dedicated to publishing the finest and most effective educational materials—including study guides and test preps—for students of all ages. Today, REA's wide-ranging catalog is a leading resource for students, teachers, and other professionals. Visit *www.rea.com* to see a complete listing of all our titles.

REA ACKNOWLEDGMENTS

Publisher: Pam Weston

Editorial Director: Larry B. Kling

Technology Director: John Paul Cording

Managing Editor: Diane Goldschmidt

Senior Editor: Alice Leonard

Copy Editors: John Kupetz, Karen Lamoreux

Indexer: Terry Casey, Casey Indexing and Information Service

Composition Services: Caragraphics

Cover Design & File Prep: Jennifer Calhoun

Getting Started

Congratulations! By taking the TExES Social Studies 7–12 (232) test, you're on your way to a rewarding career teaching social studies to secondary students in Texas public schools. Our book, and the online tools that come with it, give you everything you need to succeed on this important exam, bringing you one step closer to being certified to teach in Texas.

This TExES Social Studies 7–12 test prep package includes:

- **A targeted review** covering all the domains tested on the exam

- **An online diagnostic test** to pinpoint your strengths and weaknesses and focus your study

- **Two full-length practice tests (1 in the book and online, 1 exclusively online)** to simulate the complete test-taking experience with true-to-format questions

HOW TO USE THIS BOOK + ONLINE PREP

About Our Review

The review chapters in this book are designed to help you sharpen your command of all seven domains assessed on the TExES Social Studies 7–12 test. Our content review is designed to reinforce what you have learned and show you how to relate the information you have acquired to the specific competencies on the test. Studying your class notes and textbooks together with our review will give you an excellent foundation for passing the test.

Here are some of the important features you'll find in our review:

✓ We keep the focus on the standards that inform what makes the test tick. The test's seven domains embrace a series of **competency statements** and **descriptive statements**. A competency statement is *broad-gauge*, framing generally what you need to know and be ready to do as you enter the field of social studies in Texas public schools. A descriptive statement is *narrow-gauge*, detailing discrete skills assessed on the TExES test. Competency and descriptive statements correlate with the Texas curriculum standards (TEKS). The book fully integrates these statements into the relevant review to help you make the right connections, and become an effective test-question analyzer and a high-scoring test-taker.

✓ Our **key questions**, interspersed throughout the review, help you cut through the stacks of facts inherent to the study of history and the social studies. The key questions are linked to the TEKS and designed to help you pick out major themes, trends, and connections that will allow you to perform well—particularly on a wide-ranging test like the TExES Social Studies 7–12.

✓ **Periodization** references follow each descriptive statement in the history chapters. With half your score on the line with the test's history items, familiarizing yourself with critical chronological divisions in history will help you spot the correct answers with ease by dealing head-on with the distractor choices. (Bear in mind that from the test developer's standpoint, good distractors are response options that the test-taker who is unfamiliar with the material finds appealing for the wrong reason.)

About Our Practice Tests

We know your time is valuable and you want an efficient study experience. At the online REA Study Center (*www.rea.com/studycenter*), you will get feedback right from the start on what you know and what you don't to help make the most of your study time.

Here is what you will find at the REA Study Center:

• **Diagnostic Test**—Before you review with the book, take our online diagnostic test. Your score report will automatically pinpoint topics for which you need the most review, to help focus your study.

• **Two Full-Length Practice Tests**—Get a complete picture of your performance. After you've reviewed with the book, see what you've learned by taking a true-to-format practice test. You'll find Practice Test 1 in the book as well as online, and Practice Test 2 exclusively online. Our online exams not only simulate the computer-based platform of the actual TExES test, but also come with these features:

✓ **Automatic scoring**—Find out how you did on your test, instantly.

✓ **Diagnostic score reports**—Get a specific score tied to each competency, so you can focus on the areas that challenge you the most.

✓ **On-screen detailed answer explanations**—See why the correct response option is right, and learn why the other answer choices are incorrect.

✓ **Timed testing**—Learn to manage your time as you practice, so you'll feel confident on test day.

AN OVERVIEW OF THE TEST

What is assessed on the Social Studies 7–12 test?

The TExES Social Studies 7–12 test measures the knowledge and skills a beginning educator in Texas public schools must have to teach the subject matter. Because it's a computer-administered test, the exam is available throughout the year at numerous locations across the state and at select locations nationally. To find a test center near you, visit *www.tx.nesinc.com*. Candidates are limited to five attempts to take any of Texas' teacher certification tests.

The Test at a Glance

(Approx. domain percentages)

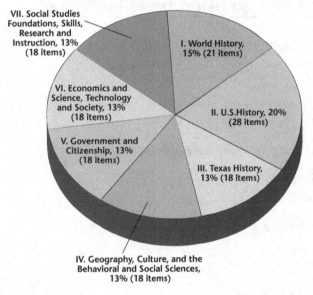

VII. Social Studies Foundations, Skills, Research and Instruction, 13% (18 items)

I. World History, 15% (21 items)

VI. Economics and Science, Technology and Society, 13% (18 items)

II. U.S.History, 20% (28 items)

V. Government and Citizenship, 13% (18 items)

III. Texas History, 13% (18 items)

IV. Geography, Culture, and the Behavioral and Social Sciences, 13% (18 items)

What is the test format?

You'll have 4 hours and 45 minutes to answer a total of approximately 140 multiple-choice items, a few of which may not be scorable because they're being field-tested. You won't know which is which, so they surely aren't worth worrying about. Your final scaled score will be based only on the scorable items.

What types of questions can I expect?

Though all the questions on the test are multiple-choice, they may not all be the type of multiple-choice question with which you're familiar. The majority of questions on the TExES Social Studies 7–12 test are standard multiple-choice items. The questions are not intended merely to test your command of facts or your talent for recall but also your critical-thinking skills. For example, you may be asked to analyze information and compare it with knowledge you have, or make a judgment about it. To acquaint yourself with all the detail on the standards and competencies covered on the test, be sure to consult the latest test framework for TExES Test Code 232 at *www.tx.nesinc.com*.

Some multiple-choice questions are self-contained while others are clustered, relating to a common stimulus. Each question will generally have four choices: A, B, C, and D. (It's possible that an occasional question will have five options.) In addition, the test may sometimes present non-traditional formats for multiple-choice items, both to present the information and to allow you to select the best answer. The test developer, Pearson, reserves wide latitude to use what it terms unfamiliar question types. A rundown of these new formats follows.

What do unfamiliar question types look like?

There are several unfamiliar question types that may show up on your TExES test. First, let's look at the kind of question that asks TExES test-takers to identify more than one correct answer.

Example

1. Which of the following led to the American Revolution?
    A. the French and Indian War
    B. the Intolerable Acts
    C. the French Revolution
    D. Options A and B

Answer and Explanation

Option (D) is correct. In other words, options (A) and (B) are both correct. The French and Indian War (A), fought from 1754 to 1763, served as a powerful vehicle by which the British Empire extended its reach in North America. The British sought to impose taxation on the colonists to finance the defense of the newly acquired territory, which aggravated growing discontent with

British governance. The Intolerable Acts (B) embraced measures enacted by the British Parliament in 1774 to strike back at the colonists' defiance (e.g., the Boston Tea Party in 1773) of British rule. The move backfired, spawning the First Continental Congress later that year. Simple chronology helps you root out the French Revolution (C) as an incorrect option. The French Revolution, fought from 1787 to 1799, is an anachronistic response that could not have led to the American Revolution, which ended in 1783.

According to Pearson, the test may use interactive questions that may include audio or video clips instead of, say, a static map or reading passage. Item formats may ask you to select the correct answer(s) by any of these means:

- Click on a sentence or sentences, or on parts of a graphic representation, such as a map, chart, or figure—sometimes dubbed a "hot spot."

- Drag and drop answer options into "target" areas in a table, piece of text, or graphic.

- Use a drop-down menu.

More than anything, these innovative item types require that you read the instructions carefully to be sure you are fully responsive to the question. The TExES Social Studies 7–12 test is scored based on the number of questions you answer correctly. With no penalty for guessing, you won't want to leave any item unanswered.

When should the test be taken?

The TExES Social Studies 7–12 test is generally taken during your junior or senior year. Teacher preparation programs typically determine when their candidates take the required tests for teacher certification. These programs also clear you to take the examinations and make final recommendations for certification to the Texas State Board for Educator Certification (SBEC). For traditional undergraduates, this Social Studies 7-12 test is usually taken before students begin their student teaching assignments. For alternative certification program (ACP) candidates, passage of the content-area test is required before a teacher candidate can be accepted into the program.

An entry-level candidate seeking social studies certification may take the TExES 232 test at such time as his or her Educator Preparation Program (EPP) determines the candidate's readiness to take the test, or upon successful completion of the EPP, whichever comes first. A traditional EPP (four-year college or university) will make these determinations and make recommendations for when students should take the test.

How do I register for the test?

To register for your TExES test, you must create an account in the Pearson online registration system. Registration will then be available to you online, 24/7, during the regular, late, and emergency registration periods. Visit Pearson's TExES website at *www.tx.nesinc.com* and follow the instructions.

To address issues that cannot be resolved at the teacher preparation program level, you can contact the offices of SBEC at (888) 863-5880 or (512) 469-8400. You must pay a registration fee to take the TExES tests, and you will also incur late fees if registering after the scheduled date.

What's the passing score?

Your TExES exam score is reported on a 100–300 scale. A scaled score of 240 is set as the minimum passing score. To put this in context, you want to be confident you can answer between 70% and 80% of the questions correctly.

As you work your way through our practice tests, scores in this range will suggest that you are sufficiently mastering the test content. The actual test may include some questions that are being field-tested and thus will not be scored.

When will I receive my score report?

As part of the registration process to take TExES examinations, test candidates set up an account with Pearson in which they are assigned a username and password. Use this account to access your score report information on Pearson's TExES website. Score reports will be posted by 5 p.m. CT on the score reporting date.

What if I don't pass the test?

If for some reason you don't do well on the test, don't panic. You can retake the test up to four times, for a maximum of five attempts. After the fifth attempt, you still have the option of requesting special dispensation from the Texas Higher Education Coordinating Board to retake the test; however, approval is not automatic. There is a 30-day waiting period for any retakes.

How should I prepare for the test?

It is never too early to start studying for the TExES. The earlier you begin, the more time you will have to sharpen your skills. Do not procrastinate. Cramming is not an effective way to study, since it does not allow you the time needed to learn the test material. It is important for you to choose the time and place for studying that works best for you. Be consistent and use your time wisely. Work out a study routine and stick to it.

When taking our practice tests, be sure to simulate the conditions of the actual test as closely as possible. Turn your television and smartphone off, and go to a quiet place free from distraction.

Read each question carefully, consider all answer choices, and pace yourself. As you complete each test, review your score reports, study the diagnostic feedback, and thoroughly review the explanations to the questions you answered incorrectly. But don't overdo it. Take one problem area at a time; review it until you are confident that you have mastered the material.

Give extra attention to the areas giving you the most difficulty, as this will help build your score. In addition, be sure to take the time to review the relevant state curricula (Texas Essential Knowledge and Skills, or TEKS) for grades 7–12 available at *http://www.tea.state.tx.us.*

TExES Social Studies 7–12 (232) Study Schedule

Time Period	Activity
Week 1	Take the online Diagnostic Test at the REA Study Center. Your detailed score report will identify the topics where you need the most review.
Weeks 2–3	Study the review chapters. Use your score report from the Diagnostic Test to focus your study. Useful study techniques include highlighting key terms and information and taking notes as you read the review. Learn all the competencies by making flashcards and targeting questions you missed on the diagnostic test.
Week 4	Take Practice Test 1 either in the book or online. Review your score report and identify topics where you need more review.
Week 5	Take Practice Test 2 online. Review your score report and return to the review chapters in this book to restudy any topics you are still struggling with.

Are there any breaks during the test?

Although there is no designated break during the test, you do have some time to use for the restroom or snacking or stretching outside the testing room.

Bear in mind the following:

- You need to get permission to leave the testing room.

- The overall test clock never stops.

- Consult your test admission materials for further details, including updates from Pearson and the Texas Education Agency.

What else do I need to know about test day?

The day before your test, check for any updates in your Pearson testing account. This is where you'll learn of any changes to your reporting schedule or if there's a change in the test site. On the day of the test, you should wake up early after a good night's rest. Have a good breakfast and dress in layers that can be removed or added as the conditions in the test center require. Arrive at the test center early. This will allow you to relax and collect your thoughts before the test, and will also spare you the anguish that comes with being late. As an added incentive to make sure that you arrive early, keep in mind that no one will be admitted into the test center after the test has begun.

Before you leave for the testing site, carefully review your registration materials. Make sure you bring your admission ticket and two unexpired forms of identification. Primary forms of ID include:

- Passport

- Government-issued driver's license

- State or Province ID card

- National ID card

- Military ID card

You may need to produce a supplemental ID document if any questions arise with your primary ID or if your primary ID is otherwise valid but lacks your full name, photo, and signature.

Without proper identification, you will not be admitted to the test center. Strict rules limit what you can bring into the test center to just your ID; we recommend that you consult the Texas Education Agency's "Texas Educator Certification Registration Bulletin" for a complete rundown. You may not bring watches of any kind, cellphones, smartphones, or any other electronic communication devices or weapons of any kind. Scrap paper, written notes, and books and other printed material are prohibited.

No smoking, eating, or drinking is allowed in the testing room. Consider bringing a small snack and a bottle of water to partake of beforehand to keep you sharp during the test.

Good luck on the TExES Social Studies 7–12 test!

Proven Tips and Test-Taking Strategies

2

HOW TO APPROACH YOUR TExES TEST

Here are 14 strategies to help you perform your best on test day.

1. Guess Away

One of the most frequently asked questions about the TExES Social Studies 7–12 test is: Can I guess? The answer: absolutely! There is no penalty for guessing on the test. That means if you refrain from guessing, you may lose points. To guess smartly, use the process of elimination (see Strategy No. 2). Your score is based strictly on the number of correct answers. So answer all questions and take your best guess when you don't know the answer.

2. Process of Elimination

Process of elimination is one of the most important test-taking strategies at your disposal. Process of elimination means looking at the choices and eliminating the ones you know are wrong, including answers that are partially wrong. Your odds of getting the right answer increase from the moment you're able to get rid of a wrong choice.

3. All in

Review all the response options. Just because you believe you've found the correct answer—or, in some cases, answers—look at each choice so you don't mistakenly jump to any conclusions. If you are asked to choose the *best* answer, be sure your first answer is really the best one.

4. Choice of the Day

What if you are truly stumped and can't use the process of elimination? It's time to pick a fallback answer. On the day of the test, choose the position of the answer (e.g., the third of the four choices) that you will pick for any question you cannot smartly guess. According to the laws of probability, you have a higher chance of getting an answer right if you stick to one chosen position for the answer choice when you have to guess an answer instead of randomly picking one.

5. Use Choices to Confirm Your Answer

The great thing about multiple-choice questions is that the answer has to be staring back at you. Have an answer in mind and use the choices to *confirm* it.

6. Watch the Clock

Among the most vital point-saving skills is active time management. The breakdown and time limits of each section are provided as you begin each test. Keep an eye on the timer on your computer screen. Make sure you stay on top of how much time you have left for each section and never spend too much time on any one question. Remember: Most multiple-choice questions are worth one raw point. Treat each one as if it's the one that will put you over the top. You never know, it just might. The last thing you want on test day is to lose easy points because you ran out of time and focused too much on difficult questions.

7. Read, Read, Read

It's important to read through all the multiple-choice options. Even if you believe answer choice A is correct, you can misread a question or response option if you're rushing to get through the test. While it is important not to linger on a question, it is also crucial to avoid giving a question short shrift. Slow down, calm down, read all the choices. Verify that your choice is the best one, and click on it.

8. Take Notes

Use the erasable noteboard provided to you to make notes to work toward the answer(s).

9. Isolate Limiters

Pay attention to any limiters in a multiple-choice question stem. These are words such as *initial, best, most* (as in *most appropriate* or *most likely*), *not, least, except, required,* or *necessary.*

Especially watch for negative words, such as "Choose the answer that is *not* true." When you select your answer, double-check yourself by asking how the response fits the limitations established by the stem. Think of the stem as a puzzle piece that perfectly fits only the response option(s) that contain the correct answer. Let it guide you.

10. It's Not a Race

Ignore other test-takers. Don't compare yourself to anyone else in the room. Focus on the items in front of you and the time you have left. If someone finishes the test 30 minutes early, it does not necessarily mean that person answered more questions correctly than you did. Stay calm and focus on *your* test. It's the only one that matters.

11. Confirm Your Click

In the digital age, many of us are used to rapid-clicking, be it in the course of emailing or gaming. Look at the screen to be sure to see that your mouse-click is acknowledged. If your answer doesn't register, you won't get credit. However, if you want to mark it for review so you can return later, that's your call. Before you click "Submit," use the test's review screen to see whether you inadvertently skipped any questions.

12. Creature of Habit? No Worries.

We are all creatures of habit. It's therefore best to follow a familiar pattern of study. Do what's comfortable for you. Set a time and place each day to study for this test. Whether it is 30 minutes at the library or an hour in a secluded corner of your local coffee shop, commit yourself as best you can to this schedule every day. Find quiet places where it is less crowded, as constant background noise can distract you. Don't study one subject for too long, either. Take an occasional breather and treat yourself to a healthy snack or some quick exercise. After your short break—5 or 10 minutes can do the trick—return to what you were studying or start a new section.

13. Knowledge is Power

Purchasing this book gave you an edge on passing the TExES Social Studies 7–12 test. Make the most of this edge. Review the sections on how the test is structured, what the directions look like, what types of questions will be asked, and so on. Take our practice tests to familiarize yourself with what the test looks and feels like. Most test anxiety occurs because people feel unprepared when they are taking the test, and they psych themselves out. You can whittle away at anxiety by learning the format of the test and by knowing what to expect. Fully simulating the test even once will boost your chances of getting the score you need. Meanwhile, the knowledge you've gained will also will save you the valuable time that would have been eaten up puzzling through what the directions are asking As an added benefit, previewing the test will free up your brain's resources so you can focus on racking up as many points as you can.

14. B-r-e-a-t-h-e

Anxiety is neither unusual nor necessarily unwelcome on a test. Just don't let it stifle you. Take a moment to breathe. This won't merely make you feel good. The brain uses roughly three times as much oxygen as muscles in the body do: Give it what it needs.

Now consider this: What's the worst that can happen when you take a test? You may have an off day, and despite your best efforts, you may not pass. Well, the good news is that this test can be retaken. Fortunately, the TExES Social Studies 7–12 test is something you can study and prepare for, and in some ways to a greater extent than other tests you've taken throughout your academic career. In fact, study after study has validated the value of test preparation. Yes, there will be questions you won't know, but neither your teacher education program nor state licensing board (which sets its own cut scores) expects you to know everything. When unfamiliar vocabulary appears or difficult questions loom, don't despair: Use context clues, process of elimination, or your response option of the day (i.e., choose either A, B, C, or D routinely when you need to resort to a guess) to make your choice, and then press ahead. If you have time left, you can always come back to the question later. If not, relax. It is only one question on a test filled with many.

Take a deep breath and then exhale. You know this information. Now you're going to show it.

Domain I: World History

The TExES Social Studies test's World History portion may be one of the most difficult sections to prepare for. There is so much to cover, in so little depth! On the test, there will likely be only about 21 questions—approximately five questions from each competency in Domain I—to assess your grasp of World History from the Neolithic Period to the present. In your test preparation, it is important that you *not* just accumulate the facts and details included in this chapter by defining concepts or memorizing names, dates, or other factoids. Instead, put these facts into a wider context and think about how and why the test writers would ask a particular question.

COMPETENCY 001 (ANCIENT WORLD CIVILIZATIONS)

The teacher understands significant historical events and developments in ancient world civilizations, factors influencing the development of ancient world civilizations and major characteristics and contributions of ancient world civilizations.

> **Competency 001 Descriptive Statement A.** The beginning teacher: Analyzes the influence of various factors (e.g., geography, processes of spatial exchange [diffusion], development of agriculture) on the development of early and classical civilizations.

Key Question

How did the development of agriculture and cross-cultural interactions resulting from migration, conquest, and trade lead to the development of regional civilizations before 500 BCE?

The emergence of distinctive regional civilizations and cultures in Southwest Asia (the Middle East), China, India, the Mediterranean, the Americas, and Africa continue to help explain much of the modern world's cultural diversity. The role of technological development and the diffusion of technology and knowledge through cross-cultural interactions is an emphasis.

Periodization: Ancient World Civilizations—8000 BCE to 3000 BCE

Competency 001 combines three very different eras into one era called "Ancient World Civilizations." These three eras include the Neolithic agricultural revolution, the development of early civilizations, and the "classical civilizations." The Neolithic period is usually said to last from around 8000 BCE to roughly 3000 BCE. Early civilizations then developed before 500 BCE in regions where early agricultural development occurred. These regional cultures developed their classical form in the period after 500 BCE. The dominant political entities of the period of the classical era were the Greek city-states and the Hellenistic empire, the Persian Empire, the Roman Republic and the Roman Empire, the Mauryan and Gupta empires in India, and the Han dynasty's Chinese Empire.

Hunter-Gatherers in Human History

Hunter-gatherers who live primarily on wild plant and animal food are only a small proportion of the world's population today. In 10,000 BCE, on the eve of the transition to agriculture, the Earth was populated with some 5–8 million hunter-gatherers. Hunter-gatherers lived in small bands of rarely more than 50 individuals and took advantage of the resources around them to meet their needs. Hunter-gatherer societies had relatively unsophisticated technology and few material goods.

Hunter-gatherers exploited their natural resources very efficiently, often spending only a few hours a day hunting, fishing, or harvesting nuts, berries, roots, and other wild crops. Most hunter-gatherer bands had a healthy diet of around 2,400 calories per day, with sufficient meat and protein. Because women nursed infants and cared for young children, they were most often responsible for gathering, while men contributed by fishing and hunting. For most hunter-gathering societies, the majority of calories were gathered by women, as success in hunting was a less predictable and regular source of calories. Fish, shellfish, and other aquatic food sources were also more important to hunter-gatherers' survival than hunting. When not acquiring their subsistence needs, hunter-gatherers spent much of their time maintaining or fashioning rudimentary tools, socializing, relaxing, telling stories, adorning themselves, and fashioning ornaments.

The Neolithic Revolution (8000–3000 BCE): Independent Origins and Diffusion of Agriculture

Why would hunter-gatherers, who were able to meet their basic needs and still have time for leisure and culture, "choose" to become farmers, given the increased labor demands and poorer diet of agriculturalists? Hunter-gatherers had long familiarity with the many uses to which plant and animal products could be put. Whenever hunter-gatherer bands settled, even for short periods of time, they chose areas where certain useful plants were available. As hunter-gatherer bands remained in the same place to be close to desired food sources they began, knowingly and by chance, to shape the environments around them by selecting seeds and cuttings, and eventually planting gardens.

When hunter-gatherer bands remained on the move, it made little sense not to share their bounty, whether from a kill or a berry-laden bush. But with the growth of sedentary settlements, families could support more than one child at a time, resulting in faster population growth. Also, as individual bands became more sedentary, a greater sense of personal and familial property replaced the ethos of sharing common to hunter-gatherers. Increased population densities and a growing feeling of ownership of land ultimately contributed to the cultivation of a small number of staple crops and the domestication of the animal species that still provide the preponderance of calories necessary for human survival.

Agriculture

Evidence supports the view that agriculture developed independently but at different times in a number of world regions.

Origins of Agriculture

Location	Date	Staple Crops	Domesticated Animals
Southwest Asia	ca. 9000 BCE	barley, wheat, lentils	goats, sheep, cattle, pigs, donkeys, camels, horses
China	ca. 7000 BCE	rice, millet, soybeans, rice	pigs, chickens, water buffalo
Mesoamerica	ca. 5000 BCE	squash, maize, beans	none
South America	ca. 3000–2000 BCE	potato, sweet potato, manioc, quinoa	llamas, alpacas, guinea pigs
Sub-Saharan Africa	ca. 3000 BCE	sorghum, millet, rice,	cattle
North America	ca. 2000 BCE	squash, sunflower	none
Southeast Asia and New Guinea	Uncertain	taro, yams, sugar cane, coconut, citrus fruits, rice	pigs, chickens

Southwest Asia

Among the first places where evidence of animal and plant domestication has been found are sites in modern-day Turkey, Palestine, and southern Syria. As early as 15,000 years ago, wild precursors to wheat and barley growing on hillsides of the region encouraged year-round settlement. As early as 8000 BCE in the Jordan River valley, farmers using stone tools began to intentionally plant and harvest wheat. At about the same time in Syria and Iraq, barley was being similarly exploited. At least as early as 4000 BCE the first fruit and nut trees began to be cultivated in the region. Plants were not the only early domesticates. Sheep and goats began to be protected from predators, claimed by human owners, and then bred to accept human control. Sheep and goats soon were providing milk to human consumers. Soon cattle, donkeys, horses, and camels were added to the list of animal domesticates, with the added advantage that they could serve as beasts of burden. Between 5000 and 4000 BCE, wool-bearing sheep also began to have their wool harvested to make textiles. By at least 4000 BCE, farmers in the Tigris-Euphrates River valley were using plows pulled by oxen. The Southwest Asian catalogue of agricultural techniques spread to other regions, including more arid highland zones and forested regions, and began to spread into Europe, the Mediterranean coastline of Africa, and much of Asia. The complex of Southwest Asian domesticates then provided the agricultural foundation for the emergence of civilizations in the Mediterranean, the Indus River valley, and the Nile River valley.

China

Two staple crops were cultivated in China. Rice, which has a much higher yield than barley or wheat, was cultivated perhaps as early as 7000 BCE in the Yangtze River valley in southern China. However, rice cultivation requires much higher labor inputs and more careful regulation of water supplies and land usage. As a result, rice did not become China's dominant staple crop until after 200 CE. Instead, in the Huang He (Yellow River) valley, millet, soybeans, and domesticated pigs formed the foundation of China's agricultural civilization. As early as 5500 BCE in this northern region of China, farmers using hoes and digging sticks began to cultivate the soft and fertile loess soils of the region.

Southeast Asia and New Guinea

An entirely different form of agriculture developed in the tropical regions of Southeast Asia and New Guinea. There, hunter-gatherers settled along the shores of lakes and streams where there were plentiful supplies of fish, shellfish, and other aquatic foods. Hunter-gatherers quickly appreciated the ease of planting and harvesting tubers, like taro roots and yams, and cultivating tree crops. Root crops and fruits were not stored for later use, but left in the ground or on the branch until needed. As a result, there was less need to produce pottery or baskets for storage or granaries to hold the harvest. Political systems and states consequently did not develop as quickly. Early rulers and religious leaders demanded grain as either a tax or tithe, and merchants and artisans traded for the surplus by providing trade goods in exchange. Similar opportunities for taxation and trade were less available in Southeast Asia and New Guinea.

West Africa and the Sahel

The Sahara has not always been the forbidding desert it is today. As the regional climate dried out after 4000 BCE, hunter-gatherers in the Sahara adapted by planting sorghum and wild millet in the moist soils of shrinking lake and stream beds. They also began to herd cattle as a source of milk and protein. As the Sahara expanded, they drove their livestock into the savanna grasslands, known as the Sahel, that reach across Africa from present-day Senegal to Ethiopia. As they moved farther south, however, they encountered tropical forest zones in West and Central Africa that were not suitable to the production of grain crops. There, they developed dependency on root crops and slash-and-burn farming.

The Americas

Three separate regions of the Americas independently developed sedentary agriculture: central Mexico, the high plateaus of the Andes Mountains, and the tropical lowlands of South America. In central Mexico, maize, beans, and squash served as the staple crops. Cultivation of this trio began more than 5,000 years before the present. Shortly after, in the high plateaus of the Andes Mountains (modern Bolivia and Peru), farmers began to cultivate potatoes and quinoa. These same farmers also domesticated llamas, alpacas, and guinea pigs. In tropical lowlands of South America, root vegetables like manioc and sweet potatoes provided the dominant staple calories. In the American Southeast, another combination of crops were domesticated. Gourds and sunflower seeds were cultivated there by at least 2000 BCE. Maize, squash, and beans spread from their place of origin in central Mexico and by 1200 BCE and had become the staples of the southwestern United States, supplanting sunflowers and gourds in the Southeast.

Early Civilizations (3000–500 BCE)

Most world regions where early agriculture developed correspond to emerging urban civilizations. Agriculture contributed to population growth and to the production of surpluses that provided resources to sustain populations of artisans, merchants, and religious and political leaders.

Mesopotamia

Perhaps because agriculture first developed in Southwestern Asia, one of the earliest civilizations flourished nearby in Mesopotamia, between the Tigris and Euphrates rivers. The Tigris-Euphrates floodplain provided exceptionally fertile cropland. Unpredictable flooding and the fact that the rivers frequently shifted course made this an unstable environment. Initially, Mesopotamian society began as a land of small farming villages and towns. Gradually, a number of these towns grew into cities, whose control extended over the surrounding agricultural lands. While most people continued to live as farmers, city dwellers amassed power and wealth and created political and religious institutions. They also controlled the increasingly complex networks of canals, dikes, draining systems, and levees.

Sumer. The first civilization to emerge in southern Mesopotamia was Sumer. The Sumerians arrived in the region by at least 5000 BCE and settled among Semitic-speaking peoples from the southwest. Sumerians took up the Southwest Asian complex of domesticated plants and animals while also cultivating onions, garlic, and date palms. They developed the wheel, the potter's wheel, glass, a type of seed drill to plant grain crops, and cuneiform writing. Cuneiform originated, as did most early forms of writing, as a system of record-keeping. Sumer was not a single state or empire, but was divided into numerous city-states, each controlling a small territory. The high point of Sumerian civilization was during the third millennium BCE. Sumerian culture was attractive to surrounding populations. One of these, the Akkadians, a Semitic-speaking people under the leadership of **Sargon**, conquered the Sumerian city-states and established an empire that lasted from 2370 BCE to about 2125 BCE. After a brief revival of Sumerian civilization, other regional powers established empires in Mesopotamia.

Hammurabi (ca. 1792–1750 BCE). One of the regional powers that established empires in Mesopotamia were the Amorites, or Old Babylonians. Their most famous king, Hammurabi, is known for the law code he ordered compiled. The code reveals a hierarchical society with nobles, commoners, and slaves, with very different treatment for each class. Punishments for crimes were harsh, based on the principle "an eye for an eye." The institution of law, as draconian as it appears to our eyes today, served to reduce retributive violence between families. Previously, violent crime often led to the offended family taking revenge on the offender's families.

Ancient Nomadic Charioteers

The Hittite Empire (1650–1200 BCE). Around 1650 BCE, Babylon was sacked by the Hittites, who had settled in modern-day Turkey. The Hittites were one of many groups of nomadic charioteers that used the advantages of mobility to conquer widely in the ancient world.

The Hittites threatened Mesopotamia and Egypt, settling in Anatolia. Indo-European invaders from the Caucasus migrated into Iran and Northern India. The Shang settled in northern China. The Dorian invaders, also from the Caucasus, settled in Greece.

Iron Metallurgy. Iron metallurgy was one of the most important technological innovations of the ancient world. Iron ore is found in abundance across the planet and once the knowledge of smelting iron was understood, the technique diffused widely. The first iron smelting operations took place in eastern Anatolia (modern-day Turkey) around 1200 BCE and spread across Eurasia. There is some evidence of independent invention of iron smelting in western Africa but by at least 600 BCE iron metallurgy was introduced into sub-Saharan Africa.

The Assyrians. One of the most-feared empires to arise in ancient Mesopotamia were the Assyrians. The Assyrians rose to prominence after 1100 BCE. Their homeland was centered in what is now northern Iraq. The Assyrians established an empire that lasted until 612 BCE. One technique employed by the Assyrians was to relocate many of their conquered peoples to territories far from their homeland. In 722 BCE, the Assyrians defeated the Jewish kingdom of **Israel** and exiled many of its leaders.

In 612 BCE, another Mesopotamian kingdom, the **Neo-Babylonians,** defeated the Assyrians and sacked Nineveh. The Babylonians would also conquer the Jewish kingdom of **Judah,** with its capital of Jerusalem, and force the kingdom's elite into exile.

Mesopotamian Religion

Mesopotamian religion was characterized by **polytheism**. Each Mesopotamian city-state had its favored deities but acknowledged that the gods were many and that other city-states and empires' deities had power and influence and could not be ignored. Many of these deities, with different names, would be adopted by other regional civilizations. These gods and goddesses were **anthropomorphic** (human in form and psychology, though immortal and gifted with superhuman powers).

Origins of Judaism

The Hebrews were a Semitic-speaking people that may have settled in the southeastern corner of the Mediterranean as early as 1600 BCE. By 1100 BCE, the Hebrews began to emerge as an identifiable political entity. The Hebrew-speaking peoples who had settled in Canaan (modern-day Palestine and Israel) and established the Kingdom of Israel (later divided by civil war into Israel and Judah) during their exile in Babylon developed a **monotheistic** faith that was quite different from their neighbors' faith. As they endeavored to maintain their cultural identity while in exile, they recorded what had been largely to that point orally transmitted narratives. These would become the Torah, literally "the instruction," which was comprised of the first five books of the *Tanakh*, or Hebrew scriptures. A central tenet of the Jewish faith was a commitment to the belief that there was one true god, the God who had chosen the Hebrew people. Jews were then required to worship in the temple in Jerusalem (once the Jews were returned to their homeland) and abide by the many dietary and other restrictions that made up Jewish law. These dietary restrictions and the practice of male circumcision served to differentiate them from the polytheistic peoples that surrounded them. With the conquest of the Neo-Babylonians by the Persians, the exiled Hebrews returned to Palestine. The former kingdoms of Israel and Judah did not regain their independence. They were made provinces first of the Persian Empire, and later the Hellenistic and Roman Empires. Despite being subject to these foreign empires, the Jewish population maintained their traditions and the practice of temple worship in Jerusalem. Many Jews also lived outside Palestine during the Roman period. Following a rebellion in 70 CE, the Roman empire would expel most of the Jews from Palestine, creating a **diaspora** (from the Greek for "scattering" or "dispersion") of Jews across the Mediterranean and Middle East. This diasporic community would make Judaism prominent in the merchant communities in Greek, Roman, and Persian cities and contribute significantly to the later spread of Christianity and Islam.

The Nile River Valley

In the Nile River valley, a different and less volatile civilization emerged at around the same time as civilization in Mesopotamia. This civilization relied on the same Southwest Asian complex of domesticated plants and animals. Just as the Tigris and Euphrates rivers provided the environmental basis for Mesopotamian civilization, the Nile River would shape the Egyptian civilization that emerged along its banks. The Nile River flows northward from the interior of Africa. Ancient Egypt, however, extended alongside only 750 miles of the Nile, from the First Cataract to the 150-mile-wide Delta where the Nile flows into the Mediterranean in three rivulets. Average annual rainfall in this corner of Africa amounts to less than one-half inch. As a result, Egyptian civilization emerged within a 10-mile zone on either side of the river. The river's predictability and the fertility of the flood plain alongside the Nile meant that Egypt was not as frequently disrupted by natural disaster as was Mesopotamia. This had important effects on the politics and society of ancient Egypt. The harsh desert environment to the west and the Sinai to the northeast protected Egypt from most outside invaders, further insulating the kingdom from the kind of uncertainty that was commonplace in other early civilizations.

By 3100 BCE, Upper Egypt and Lower Egypt united into a single kingdom. The ruler, or *pharaoh*, was considered a descendant of the Sun God, and was charged with maintaining the divine order of the cosmos. Perhaps the greatest evidence of the success of the Egyptian social and political system was its longevity. Though there were periods of decline, Egypt's pharaonic system of government lasted, with few interruptions, from 3100 to 30 BCE, when the Roman armies of Antony and Cleopatra were defeated by the Roman emperor Augustus.

Egyptians, like most Mesopotamians, were **polytheists**, though the Pharaoh Akhenaten, who ruled from 1353 BCE to ca. 1334 BCE, tried to introduce a quasi-monotheistic worship of the Sun God, Aten. Egyptians did not accept the innovation and quickly returned to their previous worship of multiple gods that appeared in numerous forms, as animals, humans, and natural phenomena. The Egyptians, unlike the Mesopotamian cultures from whom we inherited the concept of hell, believed in a serene afterlife, much like their own relatively stable and prosperous lives. The practice of mummification and provisioning the deceased with grave goods appropriate to their station illustrates the Egyptians positive view of the afterlife.

Like the Sumerians, the Egyptians developed a writing system, initially for record-keeping purposes. Unlike Mesopotamia, however, Egyptian **hieroglyphics** depended on a pictographic system of symbolic images. This system would evolve, however, into a script, known as the **demotic** script, that was more easily mastered by a wider populace.

Sub-Saharan Africa

In addition to the African civilizations that developed around the Mediterranean Sea and in the Nile River valley, sub-Saharan Africa also experienced a number of important developments in the period before 600 CE.

The influence of Egypt extended down the Nile into Africa, and sub-Saharan African peoples, commodities, and cultural influences reached northward into Egypt. Egyptians traded with and occasionally controlled the **Kingdom of Kush,** a kingdom in what is now Sudan, from as early as 2000 BCE. The trade items acquired from this kingdom included three trade goods that were central to much trade between Africa and the outside world for many centuries: gold, ivory, and slaves. Kush would be one of several kingdoms that developed along the Nile before 600 BCE. The kingdoms of **Meroe** and **Aksum** (in modern Ethiopia) were also influenced by the Nile River valley civilization of Egypt and later by the Greco-Roman world. In addition to the trade in gold, ivory, and slaves, these African kingdoms were important sources of perfumes, oils, exotic animals, hides, ostrich feathers, and many other items. The commodities of the Horn of Africa were highly sought in India, the Arabian Peninsula, and the Mediterranean.

The spread of iron metallurgy is a feature of another important sub-Saharan African story: the **Bantu migrations.** In much of southern Africa, most people speak one of over 400 languages from the Bantu language family. The origin of these languages has been traced to an area on the border of Nigeria and Cameroon. Beginning about 1000 BCE peoples speaking a proto-Bantu language began migrating from the area, moving in small bands southward through the tropical forests of the Congo or eastward through the grasslands of what is now the Central African Republic and South Sudan into East Africa. These small bands had two advantages over the hunter-gatherers in the region: iron tools and the practice of slash and burn agriculture. As groups settled across the southern subcontinent, they either intermingled with existing populations or gradually pushed them into less hospitable areas like the Kalahari Desert. The wide variety of Bantu languages reflects the length of this migration; it took nearly 1,500 years before the migration was complete and Bantu speakers were present throughout central, southern and eastern Africa.

Indus River Valley Civilization

Another region that benefited from the diffusion of Southwest Asia's complex mix of domesticated plants and animals was a civilization that developed in the Indus River valley flood plain. The Indus floods twice yearly, first in the spring with the snow-melt from the Himalayan Mountains, then during the summer's monsoon rains. By 3000 BCE, agricultural villages in this area were cultivating barley and wheat and penning goats and sheep for their milk, meat, and wool. Other Southwest Asian crops (date palms, sesame, lentils, peas) were part of the Indus River valley inhabitants' diet. Trade with Sumer likely resulted in the diffusion of such technologies as bronze metallurgy, glass fabrication, and the potter's wheel.

But Indus River valley agriculture also benefited from influences from Southeast Asia. The water buffalo and Indian elephant, domesticated in Southeast Asia and India respectively, served as beasts of burden. Cotton, a crop that was first cultivated in India about 5,000 years ago, provided an important fiber. From India cotton would later spread into China and Southwest Asia.

Between 2900 and 1800 BCE, an urban civilization flourished in the region. The civilization is often called Harappan civilization, as the first urban site discovered in the 1920s was near the village of Harappa. Artifacts from the Indus have been excavated at sites in Mesopotamia and in Bahrain in the Persian Gulf, as well as in Iran, southern India, and Central Asia, indicating that Harappan civilization was connected through extensive trade relationships with these other early civilizations.

The technological sophistication and civil engineering evident in the Harappan civilization is often noted. The cities were carefully organized in a grid pattern of streets and avenues. Private houses and public baths were serviced by an elaborate system of drains, sewers, and fountains. Nearly every house had latrines and access to running water, likely used for ritual bathing as well as consumption. A number of features of Harappan culture seem to have influenced later Indian cultural practices and religious symbols.

Sometime around 1800 BCE, the Indus civilization disappeared. There is some evidence that environmental catastrophe, either unusual flooding or earthquake damage, precipitated its decline. Outside invaders may also have contributed to its decline. By 1500 BCE, the presence of Indo-Aryan migrants into the region was clear. By 1700 BCE, the Indus civilization had ceased to exist and had reverted to small-scale village agriculture.

The **Indo-Aryan** warriors that arrived in the region and then spread over the Indian subcontinent gradually imposed themselves on the Indus and Ganges watersheds. The term *Aryan* does not signify, as it was once thought, lighter skin color, but status. The warriors called themselves *Aryas,* which meant "noble" or "free-born." The Indo-Aryans brought new religious ideas and values with them and as they settled on the land and established a **caste system** to control the conquered agriculturalists already there. Initially the caste system distinguished between the warrior (noble), priestly, peasants and craftsmen, and servant castes. Over time the caste system became more complex. Today India has some 3,000 castes with many more sub-castes.

The period of this Indo-Aryan invasion in 1500 BCE until around 500 BCE is often called the **Vedic Age,** and the culture known as the **Vedic culture,** after the sacred texts known as the *Vedas.* The *Vedas* were transmitted orally and put into written form only after 700 BCE. While the *Vedas* are considered sacred Hindu texts, Hinduism as a religion was very fluid and did not achieve any sort of doctrinal coherence until after 200 CE. Hinduism adopted the belief in reincarnation into the Vedic religion. This belief made the caste system less onerous, as everyone believed they had the opportunity to advance to a higher position in a future life.

China

Just as in Southwest Asia, urban civilization in China took some time to develop after the beginnings of sedentary agriculture. China's earliest urban civilization did not emerge until well after farmers in the Yangtze and Huang He rivers had begun to cultivate rice and millet nearly 9,000 years ago. The first distinctive Chinese civilization only emerged between 2205 BCE and 1050 BCE.

Chinese historians have divided their history by dynasties. The first historical dynasty, the **Shang,** ruled over a territory centered along the Huang He River. This dynastic period lasted from ca. 1766 BCE to 1050 BCE. The Shang are known for the independent discovery of bronze metallurgy and the development of early Chinese writing. The monopoly of bronze weapons by the Shang aristocracy also permitted the development of a rigidly hierarchical society. The Shang, like other Eurasian civilizations, developed a writing system. For the Shang, as for other civilizations, early writing served a number of purposes. The first, and most likely, purpose for writing was keeping commercial and tax records. The Shang also employed writing for divination purposes.

In 1050 BCE, the Shang kingdom was overrun by a Bronze-Age people from the west who established the **Zhou Dynasty**. Because the Zhou had overthrown the Shang, a new rationale was needed. They argued that because the Shang had been wicked, Heaven had withdrawn its support for the Shang. This concept became known as the Mandate of Heaven. Later, Chinese rulers claimed their right to rule from the Mandate of Heaven.

Warring States Period

During the last few centuries of Zhou rule, feudal states within the kingdom were constantly at war. The period from 475 to 221 BCE is therefore known as the "**Warring States Period**." Though remembered for chaotic violence, this period of intense internal competition was also a period of creative development. The dominant philosophical schools of thought: Confucianism, Daoism, and Legalism, developed from the intellectual competition that characterized the period. Similarly, the Warring States Period necessitated the development of a number of political institutions, including more efficient bureaucracies, police systems, diplomatic conventions, and legal traditions. Technologically, this period was also very important: the horse-drawn plow and the crossbow were but two of the technologies developed during the Warring States period. The defeat of all the rival states and the establishment of the Chinese empire in 221 BCE ended this period of conflict.

Early Civilizations in the Americas

The Americas had been populated by Paleolithic hunter-gatherers migrating from Asia between 30,000 and 13,000 years ago. Sedentary agriculture developed, somewhat later than in Eurasia, in three distinct regions: the southeastern United States, central Mexico, and the Andean highlands. In these zones of agricultural development, distinctive cultures emerged, as well as states and urban civilizations.

In the Andes on the coast of modern Peru, as early as 3000 BCE, a society known as the **Norte Chico** appeared with links to farming communities inland. Some of the features of this society would be transmitted to later regional societies. The discovery of the Norte Chico civilization has pushed back the timeline of complex civilization in the Andean region. Prior to this discovery, the **Chavín** society that flourished between 900 and 200 BCE was thought to be the earliest complex civilization in the region.

In Mesoamerica, as early as 1500 BCE in Mexico and the central American nation of Guatemala, a civilization called the **Olmec** flourished. The Olmec civilization developed a distinctive monumental architecture featuring pyramids and colossal sculpted heads, a form of writing, a calendar, and other cultural characteristics that would influence later Mesoamerican civilizations, such as the **Maya** and **Aztec**.

By 400 BCE, the Olmec civilization had declined. The Maya would develop from this precursor society around 200 BCE and thrive between 250 and 950 CE.

> **Competency 001 Descriptive Statement B.** The beginning teacher: Demonstrates knowledge of individuals, events and issues that shaped the development of early and classical civilizations.

Key Question

In what ways did the classical civilizations of the Mediterranean region (Greece and Rome), the Middle East (Persia), and Asia (India, China and Japan) influence religious, political, and economic development of these world regions in later periods?

The TEKS makes clear that the intent of the curriculum is to understand the legacy of each of the world's classical civilizations on subsequent developments in each of the world's regions. Students (and prospective teachers) are required to understand, for example, how Greek political institutions provided a model for later Western conceptions of democracy, and how Confucianism in classical China would contribute to values and morality in contemporary China or Japan. The unstated intention of this emphasis is to connect the rise of the West (Europe and the United States) to intellectual and cultural traditions that derive from Greece and Rome; in particular, republican institutions, democracy, and Christianity. Conversely, the eclipse of Asia and Africa by the West can be partially explained by the influence of the intellectual and cultural traditions of Confucianism, Zoroastrianism, Hinduism, and Buddhism that flourished in classical China, Persia, and India. Though it is important to understand the historical developments in each of the world's classical civilizations on their own terms, it is vital that prospective teachers fully understand the arguments that are used to explain how classical values and institutions contributed to later differences between distinctive world regions.

Periodization: Classical Period—500 BCE to 600 CE

The classical period in world history as established in the TEKS extends from 500 BCE to 600 CE, a period dominated by large world empires and by the emergence of what are called "axial age" religions and philosophy. The creation of these large empires and the development of the axial age religions are intertwined and central to understanding the importance of this period.

The period of classical antiquity was first associated by European historians exclusively with the histories of Greece and Rome. A number of events around the turn of the sixth century BCE seemed to mark an important watershed in the histories of both Greece and Rome. The Athenians celebrated the overthrow of a tyrannical government in 510 BCE and the establishment of the rule of the people, or *demos*. Thus, Athenian democracy is then said to date from 510 BCE. Additionally, the first of the Greco-Persian Wars began in 499 BCE, ultimately resulting in many of the Greek city-states gaining their independence from Persia and embarking on a period of cultural and economic prosperity. The Romans dated the establishment of their *res publica* or republic to 509 BCE.

Events from other regions of Eurasia also support a periodization that begins the classical era in or around 500 BCE. For example, world historians point to the establishment of the Achaemenid, or first Persian Empire, around 550 BCE. Additionally, the lives of Confucius and Siddhartha Gautama, the Buddha, both of whom lived and taught around the turn of the fifth century BCE, are indicators of the significance of changes taking place across Eurasia during this period.

The TEKS, however, rather than follow a traditional classical periodization that dates from 500 BCE to 500 CE, dates the end of the classical period in 600 CE. The end of the classical period was initially associated with the decline of the Roman Empire, the sacking of Rome by a Germanic tribe in 410 CE, or the crowning of the Germanic "King of Italy" in 476 CE. Rounding up to 500 CE provided for a nicely balanced 1,000-year period of classical antiquity. Ending the classical period in 600 CE illustrates a decision to identify the key turning points that end the classical era with other world historical events. Among these was the collapse of the Gupta Empire in India in 550 CE. Additionally, the life of Muhammad, who began his teaching in 610 CE, serves as another signal turning point. Additional turning points occurred in East Asia, following the fragmentation of the Han Chinese Empire in 220 CE, the reestablishment of the Chinese Empire under the Sui (581–618 CE) and Tang Dynasties (618–907 CE).

An Age of Empires

An *empire* is a state where political authority has been established over a large territory formerly comprised of other once-independent states or over previously independent ethnic or linguistic groups. Though the earliest political entities in Southwest Asian civilizations had been city-states, Akkad, Babylon, the Hittites, and Assyria could be defined as empires. The most important and largest empire established in Southwest Asia, before Alexander the Great's conquests, however, was the Persian Empire.

The (Achaemenid) Persian Empire (550 BCE–331 BCE)

Nomadic peoples speaking Indo-European languages had migrated into the mountains and plateaus east of the Fertile Crescent, in what is the modern nation of Iran, as early as 1000 BCE. In 550 BCE under the leadership of the king, Cyrus II (ca. 600–530 BCE), these peoples, who became known as Persians, expanded eastward to the Indus River valley, northward to the Caucasus region, and as far west as the Aegean Sea and Straits of the Bosporus in modern Turkey. By the reign of Darius I (ca. 550–486 CE) the empire included Egypt and parts of northern India as well as many Greek-speaking cities on the Aegean.

The Persians established a much more benign rule than had the Assyrians, who had a deserved reputation for cruelty. Conquered peoples were allowed a degree of self-rule, so long as they continued to provide tribute to the Persian capital. The Persians practiced a religion known as Zoroastrianism, but the many religions practiced throughout the empire were accorded an unusual degree of tolerance for the period. To enable greater control over their empire, the Persians built extensive road networks, used standardized coinage, and employed numerous government officials to oversee taxation and the Persian armies. The defeat of the Persians by Alexander the Great initiated a period during which the influence of Greek culture was the defining feature of life in Southwest Asia and the Mediterranean region.

Classical Greece

The ancient Persian Empire's principal rivals in the eastern Mediterranean were the many Greek-speaking city-states scattered on the southern tip of the Balkan Peninsula and on the shores of the Aegean Sea. These cities built on earlier regional civilizations that the Minoans had developed on the island of Crete around 2000 BCE and on the memory of the Mycenaean civilization that had collapsed around 1100 BCE. One factor in the collapse of Mycenaean civilization was the invasion of Indo-European nomads, speakers of the proto-Greek Dorian language, who settled in the peninsula.

Following a "Dark Age" that lasted until after 800 BCE, a new Greek civilization emerged, with the *polis,* or city-state, serving as its dominant institution. This new Greek civilization remained a collection of rival city-states until Alexander "the Great" of Macedonia united the Greeks under his leadership, defeated the Persians, and established a short-lived Hellenistic or Greek Empire.

The Greek *polis,* or city-state, formed a corporate body made up of citizens (adult males), citizens lacking political rights (women and children), and non-citizens (resident aliens and slaves). Adult male citizens were entitled to equal treatment before the law and the right to participation in a variety of civic and religious rituals. This expanded notion of citizenship is an important contribution of Greek political life to later European society. The Greeks developed this idea of citizenship as a result of population growth and economic expansion throughout the eastern Mediterranean in the eighth century. City residents' success in commerce and agriculture led to demands for greater political voice from the traditional landed aristocracy descended from the Dorian invaders. Another factor contributing to increased political power of city populations was Greek reliance on *Hoplite* infantrymen who fought in a coordinated fashion, in a formation known as the *phalanx,* using iron shields, swords, and long spears. Previously, Dorian warriors with expensive bronze weaponry, fought from chariots or in hand-to-hand combat designed to result in single exploits of bravery. As the Hoplite infantry became the bulwark of Greek fighting forces, the commoners who composed these armies demanded greater political influence. The widening of citizenship identities also resulted from the efforts of tyrannical rulers to appeal to the interests of the poor and lower-social status groups, bypassing the traditional aristocracy.

Though the Greek city-states were often bitter rivals, a number of cultural features provided a common framework for a shared civilization.

Sparta and Athens

The two most important Greek city-states for TExES Social Studies 7–12 examinees to know are Sparta and Athens.

The Spartans ruled over a conquered and enslaved populace. As a result, they established a militarized society which nonetheless is esteemed for the values of bravery and selflessness, a radical equality shared by male citizens, respect for elders, and a rejection of luxury. The term "Spartan" today is a synonym for frugal, strict, stern, or austere. Spartans were also known for their courage in battle, most famously displayed against the Persians at the battle of **Thermopylae** (480 BCE) where a small band of Spartans sacrificed themselves to stop the Persian advance into Greece.

Athens stood in stark contrast to Sparta. Athens was a maritime commercial city, trading throughout the Mediterranean, establishing colonies as far away as the Iberian Peninsula and the Black Sea. As a result, Athens, as early as the seventh century BCE, developed a system of government which allowed freeborn adult male citizens to attend an annual assembly where city magistrates were selected. Many Athenians in the seventh century found it increasingly difficult to survive economically in the more mercantile economy of the period. Political competition coupled with economic dislocation threatened to erupt into civil war. To avoid that eventuality Athenian elites turned to **Solon (640–558 BCE)** to devise a more equitable system of government and laws. Solon's revisions protected Athenians from being sold into slavery to pay their debts, and distributed office-holding throughout the society. Solon's reputation as an ancient "law-giver" rivals that of Hammurabi. Despite Solon's reforms and Athens' reputation as a democratic society, Athenians also experienced significant periods in which they were governed by *tyrants.* Many Athenians, including the philosopher Plato, favored *aristokratia* or the rule of the best, over *demokratia,* or the rule of the people.

The Athenians and Spartans along with most other Greek city-states united to combat the Persians in the lengthy **Greco-Persian Wars (499–449 BCE).** With the end of the Persian threat, Athens entered a golden age. The Athenians in this period practiced a form of **direct democracy** in which citizens ruled directly rather than through elected representatives. However, Sparta and Athens soon began to rival one another for dominance within the region. This rivalry erupted into outright conflict in the **Peloponnesian War (431–404 BCE).** Sparta emerged the victor, but the long-term consequence of the conflict was the creation of a power vacuum into which stepped the kingdom of Macedonia.

Hellenistic Empire

Macedonia is located in the rough, mountainous region to the north of Greece proper. The Macedonians, though Greek speakers, were looked down upon as country cousins of the more cultured Athenians. King Philip II of Macedonia (382–336 BCE) created a powerful army to secure his frontier and then turned on the Greek mainland, ending the independence of the Greek city-states. When Philip II was assassinated, his son **Alexander the Great (356–323 BCE)** expanded on his father's successes and invaded the Persian Empire, rapidly creating an empire that would stretch from Greece to the Indus River. Alexander "the Great," died of a fever before he was able to administer his vast conquests. Because he had not provided for his succession, Alexander the Great's empire was divided among three of his generals.

Hellenistic Culture

The greatest contribution of Alexander the Great's conquests was the spread of Greek culture across the Mediterranean and Southwest Asia, where Greek culture and learning interacted with the cultures and ideas of Mesopotamia, Egypt, Persia, and India to create a vibrant and creative blend of societies. This Hellenistic world—*Hellenistic* means "from the Greek"—witnessed significant scientific and technological development, the flourishing of trade and urban growth, remarkable artistry marked by more realistic sculpture and painting styles, and new forms of philosophical speculation. This Hellenistic culture would be an important cultural inspiration for Romans.

Rome: from Republic to Empire

Rome was the other classical Mediterranean society to strongly influence European development in later centuries. The city of Rome has been continuously occupied from about 1400 BCE. In the seventh century, the **Etruscans** ruled the region but were strongly influenced by interactions with Greek traders and colonists. From the Greeks, the Etruscans adopted their pantheon of deities, and adapted the Greek alphabet to Latin.

Roman Republic (509–27 BCE)

The Romans date the establishment of their republic to 509 BCE, when the Etruscan monarchy was overthrown, and a *res publica*, literally a "public thing," or a "commonwealth," was established. Romans despised the idea of monarchy from this date forward. The symbols of monarchy were consequently disdained well into the latter years of the empire. Rome's republic was governed by the city's wealthiest citizens, the landed aristocracy that dominated the Roman **Senate**. The Senate decided most matters of importance in Rome. The main administrative functions during the republican period were the responsibility of two *consuls* who shared power but alternated monthly in exercising their duties.

Between 509 and 275 BCE, Rome secured its own independence and gradually became a power on the Italian peninsula. Rome offered conquered peoples the possibility of limited citizenship and the right to intermarriage and trade. All defeated states were required to provide manpower for Roman armies. Conscripted soldiers and volunteers served for as long as 25 years but received rewards in spoils and land creating incentives for military service. After securing control over the Italian peninsula, Rome confronted Carthage, a Phoenician city that controlled much of North Africa and the Iberian Peninsula.

Punic Wars

Beginning in 264 BCE, Rome and Carthage fought a series of three wars. In the second of these conflicts, the famous Carthaginian general, **Hannibal**, led an army across the Italian Alps threatening the capital and laying waste to the Italian countryside. But, by 146 BCE, Rome controlled all of Carthage's western Mediterranean dependencies and had destroyed the city of Carthage itself. Rome also extended its influence over the Greek world, fighting a series of wars with the Kingdom of Macedonia and with an alliance of Greek city-states. By the beginning of the first century BCE, Roman rule had spread over Italy, Spain, Gaul, Greece, with major outposts in Africa and Asia Minor.

Rome's expansion brought wealth and power, but it also severely strained Rome's republic. Economic inequalities were exacerbated as wealthy elites acquired the largest share of conquered lands, which were held as enormous plantations worked by slaves. Italian peasants could not compete with this slave labor and frequently lost their lands and were forced to live in Rome, often depending on handouts. Land reform proposals by populist leaders frightened Rome's elites. A number of slave uprisings also threatened the republic. But the greatest threat to the republic proved to be the growing influence of military commanders like Julius Caesar, which ultimately led to the end of the Roman Republic. While the Roman Republic came to an end in 27 BCE, the idea of a republic may be the most significant legacy of Roman political history.

Roman Empire

The Roman Republic came to an end for many reasons, but the role of **Julius Caesar** and his adopted heir, **Gaius Julius Caesar Octavianus**, figured prominently. Julius Caesar made his reputation in the conquest of Gaul. Following a four-year civil war (49–45 BCE), Caesar was granted the title "dictator for life" by the Roman Senate. He then enlarged the Senate, rewarding his allies with positions, began a series of building projects to provide employment for Rome's populace, expanded distribution of bread to the poor, and otherwise used his personality and patronage to expand his power. Rivals in the Senate, opposed to Caesar's accumulation of power, plotted to assassinate him and restore the republic. In 44 BCE, they were successful, stabbing Julius Caesar to death on the Senate floor. But the republic could not be reestablished.

After a lengthy civil war, in 27 BCE, Gaius Julius Caesar Octavianus took the title Augustus Caesar and established the Roman Empire. By 150 CE, the empire extended from the British Isles and Iberian Peninsula in the west, along the banks of the Rhine and Danube River in the north, across North Africa to Egypt in the south, and to the borders of a weakened Persian Empire in the east.

Through the first two centuries of the Roman Empire, Rome maintained peace at home and dominance abroad despite the rule of emperors that were by turns unstable (Nero, Caligula, Claudius, and Tiberius for example) or capable leaders (Trajan, Hadrian, or Marcus Aurelius). The empire flourished as a result of the capable bureaucracy that collected taxes, supervised public works projects, and ensured the free flow of commerce. A comparatively small army, at its largest perhaps only 250,000 men, defended the empire's borders and put down internal dissent. With the Mediterranean serving as a vast highway of commerce in wheat, olive oil, wine, luxury goods, etc., urban life flourished across the empire. Rome itself by the fourth century had a population of 1 million people. Not until the 19th century would Europe boast a city so large. Roman cities were well-supplied with running water and public fountains, amphitheaters and arenas for public entertainments, private villas for the wealthy and cramped apartments for the poor, all connected by a road network still visible across Europe. The Roman Empire also had a well-developed legal tradition and protections for Roman citizens and their property. To encourage social stability, Rome also distributed daily bread rations and welfare to the urban poor. It must also be said that Rome's prosperity was also dependent on vast numbers of slaves. Slaves worked on the large agricultural estates of the Roman elite, and they also worked as artisans, cooks, sex slaves, gladiators, and many other, often important, positions.

Christianity

One of the important legacies of the Roman period was the spread throughout the Mediterranean of the Jewish sect of believers in **Jesus of Nazareth (ca. 6 BCE–ca. 24 CE)**. Jesus of Nazareth was born in the Roman province of Judaea during the reign of Caesar Augustus. As a young man, he began to speak in the tradition of the Jewish prophets. His message and his following were threatening to Roman rule, as he preached the coming of a messiah and the establishment of a kingdom of God. The term *messiah* means "anointed one" and recalls the ancient practice of anointing the kings of Israel and Judah with sacred oil. This language reflected long-held Jewish opposition to rule by outside powers and longing for a Jewish state. Jesus attracted his widest following from among the poor of Judaea who had suffered heavily under the economic change brought about by the Roman conquest and by high taxation. Jesus's success in focusing the unrest of the poor provoked the hostility of the Jewish elite and religious establishment that had made profitable accommodations with Roman authorities. As a result, Jesus was turned over to the Roman authorities as a dangerous rebel against the Roman empire. His death sentence, crucifixion, was commonly administered to those found guilty of the charge of rebellion. Jesus's following was limited to the Jewish communities in Syria and Palestine until the conversion in 35 CE of Saul of Tarsus, who took the name Paul as an indicator of his change of belief.

Paul of Tarsus (ca. 5 CE–ca. 67 CE)

It is Paul of Tarsus who developed an identifiable Christian theology. Unlike Jesus, Paul came from a Hellenized Jewish family in a Mediterranean port city. Whereas early converts to Christianity remained Jewish and adhered to Jewish law, Paul and other Hellenized Jewish converts considered Christianity an entirely new religion which did not require continued observance of Jewish dietary prescriptions or circumcision. Paul's theology made Christianity more palatable to Roman authorities and attractive to Greek-educated pagans. The simplicity of early Christian ritual, centering largely on baptism and the *Eucharist* (or communion), proved attractive to poor and uneducated urban residents. Additionally, early churches had little in the way of formal organization. Socially and politically, Paul's theology was also less revolutionary than had been the teachings of Jesus of Nazareth. He urged slaves not to resist their masters, women to be subservient to their husbands, and Christians to obey their authorities.

Persecution and Triumph of Christianity in Rome

Despite Paul's success in adapting the message of Jesus to non-Jewish audiences, Christians were often misunderstood and persecuted by Greco-Roman society. Because Christians refused to participate in Roman civic religion, Christians were accused of being atheists. They were accused of incest and cannibalism. Roman political authorities also occasionally targeted Christians for persecution.

During the first and second centuries, Christian communities developed important institutions. One of these was an **episcopal** organization. Each Christian community had a single bishop, or *episkopos*, which means "overseer," assisted by elders and deacons. Gradually, the Bishop of Rome, or Pope, would assume primacy among Christian bishops. Christians also developed belief statements, or **creeds**, which served as professions of faith. A final institution of importance was the **canon**, or list of sacred texts. By 367 CE, the New Testament was complete in its current form. By 405 CE, the Bible had been translated in its entirety into Latin.

By 312 CE, Christians composed perhaps 10 percent of the population of the Roman Empire and had attracted followings among the Roman elite as well as the urban poor. In 312 CE as the Roman ruler **Constantine (r. 306–337 CE)** prepared for battle, according to legend, he had a dream in which he was told that if his soldiers fought under a Christian sign, they would win. According to tradition, when his army won, he had his soldiers immediately baptized and he himself adopted Christianity. Constantine then granted Christians the right to freely worship, own property, and receive certain tax advantages. His conversion also meant that Christian leaders now had opportunities for social advancement that were formerly denied to them. Though Constantine did not make Christianity the official religion of Rome, Constantine's conversion did put new pressure on Christians to resolve theological disputes, as these were no longer simply doctrinal matters internal to the Catholic Church, but were increasingly matters of political significance. In 325 CE Constantine called for the **Council of Nicaea** to meet and decide once and for all many of the thorny theological differences that had divided Christians. In 380 CE, the Emperor Theodosius declared

Catholic Christianity the official religion of the Roman Empire. Paganism and heretical forms of Christianity were outlawed.

Competency 001 Descriptive Statement C. The beginning teacher understands major political, economic and developments in and interactions among the civilizations of Africa (e.g., Egypt, sub-Sahara), the Mediterranean basin (e.g., Greece, Rome), Mesoamerica (e.g., Maya), Andean South America (e.g., Inca tradition), Middle and Near East and Asia (e.g., China, India, Japan).

Key Question

The TEKS emphasize the importance of Classical Greece and Rome (discussed earlier), but also identify other classical civilizations as important comparatives. The question underlying this descriptive statement is: how did classical civilizations outside the Mediterranean compare with the classical Greek and Roman civilizations?

Mauryan and Gupta India

During the period known as the "Vedic Age" (ca. 1500 BCE–ca. 500 BCE), populations speaking Indo-Aryan languages moved into northern India, settling after a period of rivalry and warfare with existing populations, most of whom spoke languages from the Dravidian language family. While Indians today speak many languages, those in the northern states speak languages derived from the Indo-Aryan Sanskrit, and many in the southern states speak languages from Dravidian origins. The *varna* system, which would gradually be solidified into the caste system, was also established during this period. Politically, India was fragmented into numerous territorial states, which between 600 BCE and 400 BCE were consolidated into some 16 large states, four of which predominated. One of these the kingdom of Magadha in the fourth century BCE began to aspire to be an imperial power.

Alexander the Great's march along the Indus River in 326 BCE and his territorial conquests in the region created a power vacuum in northwest India into which the Magadha ruler, **Chandragupta Maurya** (r. 322–297 BCE), rapidly expanded. His primary aim was to control the important east-west trade routes that extended from the Ganges to the Indus rivers. With a well-developed system of tax collection, census and statistics offices, and a large army with an infantry numbering in the tens of thousands and a large cavalry and elephant force, Chandragupta Maurya extended Magadha's control over much of northern India. Chandragupta's empire, known as the **Mauryan Empire**, would expand to its largest size under his grandson, **Ashoka** (r. 269–232 BCE). After gaining control of the empire following a civil war that led to the death of all but one of his brothers, Ashoka expanded the empire southward, conquering a neighboring kingdom in a battle that Ashoka later regretted for its carnage and loss of life. Consequently, Ashoka converted to Buddhism and sought to rule more humanely. It was under the reign of Ashoka that Buddhism reached its greatest influence in South Asia.

Buddhist shrines, or *stupas,* were sponsored throughout the country. Throughout the empire, Ashoka ordered that pillar and rock inscriptions spread the ideals of Buddhism and the laws of the empire. Ashoka's public works programs illustrate the influence of Buddhist principles. Ashoka established hospitals and veterinary centers, provided free medicines to the sick, planted banyan and mango trees along all major roads to shade and feed pilgrims and travelers, and had public wells dug in villages across the empire. He also discouraged meat-eating at royal feasts and reduced the significance of animal sacrifice in Indian worship practices. Under the rule of Ashoka, the Mauryan capital, Pataliputra (modern day Patna), housed over 1 million residents. When Ashoka died, it didn't take long before rivalry among his successors resulted in India being once again divided into many regional kingdoms and territorial states. This is an important pattern in the political history of India. Strong and effective rulers, like the Mauryans (and later the Gupta and Moghul dynasties), would consolidate the subcontinent under a singular rule only to have it fragment into smaller territorial states.

Buddhism

During the period from 900–500 BCE, Indians began to speculate philosophically about the nature of reality, the cycle of life and death, and about human moral obligations. Where the Vedic religion had been concrete—demanding specific forms of ritual and sacrifice to satisfy the gods—Indian thinkers in this period began to de-emphasize ritual in favor of understanding and begin to reevaluate the nature of existence. They understood the nature of existence to be an endless cycle of birth, death, and rebirth. Escape from this cycle requires that in one's actions, or *karmic behavior,* good behaviors and thoughts outweigh bad behaviors and thoughts. If the weight of good behaviors is greater than that of bad behaviors, rebirth as a higher form of life, and ultimately escape from the cycle of life and death, becomes possible. To live one's life rightly implies living according to the *dharma,* or fulfilling one's moral obligations within the context of one's particular station, place in the life cycle, etc. This understanding subtly sustained the *varna* system. Other thinkers, particularly those who rejected the social implications of this doctrine, believed it was possible to escape the cycle of birth, death, and rebirth by becoming a wandering hermit or yogi and renouncing the burdens of life entirely, usually through the practice of extreme asceticism.

Buddhism represented a middle path between the conscientious—but often fruitless—attempt to live in exemplary fashion and thereby cycle through the interminable cycles of life and death hoping to achieve escape in some distant future; and the extreme asceticism of those who selflessly and rigorously renounced all desires, attachments, and social attachments to achieve liberation.

According to legend, **Siddhartha Gautama (ca. 566 BCE)** was born near modern Nepal in a princely family. When for the first time, after living a sheltered life, he encountered death, disease, and suffering, he left his home to find answers to the questions that haunted him about the meaning of life. He first studied with famous teachers, then began a regime of penance and self-negation. He then turned to yogic meditation. During one of his meditative sessions, he achieved a state of full enlightenment and release and vowed to help others experience a similar escape. According to the Buddha (the Sanskrit term for one who has achieved enlightenment), the middle path between abject renunciation and slavery to the cycle of life and death involved a realization of the "Four Noble Truths": (1) life is suffering; (2) suffering results from desire; (3) cessation of desire ends suffering; and (4) cessation of desire comes only through an eightfold process of right thought, action, mindfulness, livelihood, concentration, effort, understanding, and speech. This simple (yet personally demanding) practice would allow anyone to escape karmic bondage.

Buddhism spread throughout northern India and found particular support, as we have seen, under the rule of Ashoka. Between 500 and 1500 CE, it was largely absorbed into Hindu practice. Buddhism found its greatest following first in Southeast Asia, and then—following the trade routes from India through Central Asia to China—in Tibet, Mongolia, Vietnam, Korea, and Japan.

Hinduism

Hinduism centers mostly on the development of devotional cults connected to the prominent deities in the pantheon of Indian gods and goddesses, rather than on the philosophical speculation associated with Buddhism. Over time, beginning in the Indus River Valley civilization, the population of India accumulated a number of gods and goddesses. Some animal or nature deities date back to Harappan civilization. Others were incorporated in Hindu practice with the arrival of the Indo-Aryan migration between 1500 and 1000 BCE. Still others belonged to the "little tradition" of the Dravidian language speakers that predated Indo-Aryan arrival. Hinduism therefore brings together various strands of religious tradition. The attributes of the gods and goddesses are regarded as important and provide multiple manifestations of the divine; however, it is the practice of devotion to one or more gods, expressed through proper reverence and temple worship, pilgrimage, and practices of ritual purity that ultimately define what it means to be devout.

The Gupta Dynasty

The fragmentation of India after the collapse of Mauryan rule would last until 320 CE when a new empire developed. The new ruler even took the name **Chandragupta (r. 320 CE–330 CE)** in an effort to connect to the heritage of the earlier Mauryan ruler. The Gupta Dynasty, however, would experience its greatest significance under Chandragupta's son and grandson. Many of the features of later Indian culture were established in this period, in particular the emergence of the religion of Hinduism. Unlike Ashoka, who fostered the promotion of Buddhism, the Guptas supported Brahmanic traditions and the development of what will become classical Hindu religious life.

China under the Qin (221–206 BCE) and Han Dynasty (206 BCE–220 CE)

China, like classical India and Greece and Rome, developed into a large empire during the classical period. In the second half of the third century, the kingdom of *Qin*, from which the word China is derived, united the warring states of China in 221 BCE. The founder of the Qin Dynasty, rather than take the title of king described himself as "first emperor," or **Qin Shi Huangdi (r. 221 CE–206 BCE)**. To put an end to the territorial rivalries that had characterized the Warring States Period, Qin Shi Huangdi destroyed fortifications of rival kingdoms, eliminated the territorial states, and replaced them with provincial governments governed by appointed bureaucrats rather than feudal lords. He standardized coinage, weights and measures, and Chinese script in an effort to rationalize government. He also built a network of roads connecting China's market towns and improving internal commerce. Qin Shi Huangdi is best known for beginning two great building projects, the Great Wall that would extend from the Pacific Ocean across China's northern border, and his own mausoleum in which he buried a whole army of terracotta warrior sculptures amid a life-size replica of his palace.

Han China

With Qin Shi Huangdi's death, the princes that had once ruled China's territorial kingdoms rose up against his successors. An enterprising general who took the dynastic name **Gaozu** successfully consolidated power and claimed the title of emperor, establishing the **Han Dynasty**. The Han Dynasty ruled China from 206 BCE to 220 CE with only a brief interruption. The high point of Han rule came under the rule of **Han Wudi (r. 141–87 BCE)**. During Wudi's reign, the Chinese faced continued threats from the Xiongnu, nomads who raided and traded along China's northern boundary. Various attempts were made to pacify the Xiongnu, with little effect. In part as an effort to neutralize the Xiongnu, Wudi sent armies into the steppe lands south of the Gobi Desert. The outposts established to secure this territory extended Chinese influence into Central Asia and became the foundation of the **Silk Road,** enabling trade and cross-cultural influences to extend from the Chinese capital to Rome.

After the reign of Han Wudi, the empire went into a period of decline caused by unpopular administrative reforms that alienated merchants and large landowners, flooding that destroyed irrigation systems in northern China, and renewed attacks by the Xiongnu. In 23 CE, rebellion cost the sitting emperor his life. The Han Dynasty was restored (through a related family line), and until the end of the first century it was led by effective rulers and military commanders. After 88 CE, however, the later Han emperors were less capable and caught up in court intrigues exacerbated by the power of palace eunuchs and conspiratorial family members. Large landowners were successful in avoiding taxes, and peasants either were reduced to serfdom or fled to the south to also avoid taxation. Others escaped into Buddhist or Daoist religious movements. Additionally, new waves of nomadic peoples again invaded and in some cases established their own small states within boundaries of the empire. Natural disasters and epidemic disease further undermined stability in the empire. By 220 CE, the Han emperor had been deposed and the empire was again fragmented into a number of territorial kingdoms.

Cause and Effect: Comparing the "Decline and Fall" of Classical Empires

Why did the Roman, Han Chinese, and Gupta empires collapse between the beginning of the third century and the end of the sixth century CE? This has been an important question for world historians and an opportunity to make comparisons about the consequences of the rise and fall of empires.

1. **Barbarian Threats:** Populations of mobile or nomadic warriors (which each settled civilization perceived as particularly barbaric) threatened each empire. Germanic tribes (Lombards, Visigoths, Franks) both migrated into the Roman Empire from the second century onward, or invaded the Roman Empire outright in the fourth and fifth centuries. Many of the Germanic tribes that entered into the Roman Empire in the late fourth and fifth centuries were fleeing the Huns, nomadic horsemen from Central Asia. The Chinese faced comparable threats on their northern and western border from the Xiongnu and from Turkic-speaking nomads. The Xiongnu were related culturally and linguistically to the Huns. The Gupta Dynasty in India also faced outside invasion from the Huns, who by 550 CE had established a kingdom in western India.

2. **Internal Fragmentation:** The success of external invasion was in part predicated on already existing internal weaknesses in each of these empires. In India and China as imperial power weakened, territorial states and kingdoms with earlier histories reclaimed their authority and political power was fragmented. In the western Roman Empire, gradually, Germanic rulers assumed power over significant swathes of Roman territory; while in the eastern Roman Empire, emperors managed to maintain control.

3. **Commercial Decline:** As internal instability and threats of violence increased, commercial activity across Eurasia went into steep decline. This was most noticeable in the western Roman Empire.

4. **Epidemic Disease:** Urbanization, a feature of each classical empire, had the consequence of creating large demographically vulnerable populations. Classical empires also encouraged mobility along trade routes, or accompanying advancing armies, which resulted in the spread of disease both within empires and between the classical empires. It is difficult to identify the lethal epidemics spoken of in sources from the period, but a number of epidemic diseases so increased urban mortality across Eurasia that cities began to decline in population unless surplus rural populations resupplied them.

5. **Environmental Degradation:** Deforestation across the Mediterranean and in the Chinese river valleys that had long sustained these civilizations resulted in reduced agricultural surpluses. In the Huang He valley, the breadbasket of China's empire before widespread adoption of rice cultivation, deforestation contributed to increased runoff, which in turn led to frequent flooding of the Huang He and destruction of the elaborate irrigation systems that had increased farm yields for centuries. The soil erosion that followed also made it difficult to sustain populations in many heavily farmed regions. The "Fertile Crescent," for example, experienced such salinization in

many areas of the Tigris-Euphrates river valley that many parts of the region became virtually uninhabitable.

6. **Cultural Changes:** In China, weaknesses of the Han Dynasty and gradual decline in confidence in traditional Chinese values went hand in hand with the expansion of Buddhism in China. Though this would have its greatest impact in later centuries, it was one symptom of Han decline. In the Roman Empire, Christianity was one of a number of "mystery religions" that emphasized a personal salvation over the collective civic religion of Roman paganism. The degree to which these changing values undermined the authority of traditional social and political systems is debatable, but it has often been cited as both cause and symptom of the decline of classical civilizations.

COMPETENCY 002 (WORLD HISTORY FROM 600 TO 1450 CE)

The teacher understands the significant historical events, developments, and traditional points of reference in world history from 600 to 1450 CE.

> **Competency 002 Descriptive Statement A.** The beginning teacher demonstrates knowledge of individuals, events, issues, and traditional points of reference that shaped the development of world civilizations from 600 CE to 1450 CE (e.g., Mongol conquests, the founding of Islam, Charlemagne, the Norman Conquest, Silk Road).

Key Question

What were the turning points in the history of the Middle Ages?

Periodization: The Middle Ages—600 to 1450 CE

The period from 600 to 1450 CE is often called the Middle Ages, or the medieval period. The Middle Ages itself is usually subdivided between the Early Middle Ages (600–1000 CE) and the High Middle Ages (1000–1450 CE). In European history, the early medieval period is usually seen as a period of stagnation following the collapse of the Roman Empire. From a global perspective, however, this period witnessed the emergence of Islam and the expansion of Islamic society, hardly a sign of general decay. Additionally, beginning in 600 CE, China began a process of reunification and growth. This would come to full fruition with the Song Dynasty. The High Middle Ages underwent significant economic growth and cultural borrowing, largely a consequence of increased commercial and cultural linkages that connected Afro-Eurasia.

Rise of Islam and the Development of an "Islamic World"

Islam developed in the pilgrimage center and commercial city of Mecca in the Arabian Peninsula. The dominant powers to the north of the Arabian Peninsula, the Zoroastrian Persian Empire and the Christian Byzantine Empire, maintained client kingdoms in the peninsula, including states that practiced Christianity and Judaism. As a consequence, Christianity, Judaism, and Zoroastrianism had long histories in Arabia. Outside the cities, pagan tribal nomads herded their camels, sheep, and goats from oasis to oasis, to water and graze their herds.

Muhammad (ca. 570–632 CE)

Muhammad was an orphan from a minor family in Mecca. As a successful middle-aged merchant, Muhammad grew increasingly dissatisfied with the growing inequality in western Arabia and the disregard for morality and religious devotion that he saw in Mecca. He began to withdraw into meditation and contemplation. According to tradition he experienced his first revelation in 610 CE when the Angel Gabriel appeared to him. Muhammad taught a strict monotheism. Muhammad also emphasized the moral and ethical responsibility of believers to submit to God. *Islam* means submission, and a *Muslim* is one who submits to God. Muhammad's social message emphasized the moral duty to defend the orphan, the beggar, the weak, the unprotected. He preached against hoarding wealth and loaning money at interest. Muhammad had few early converts. Threatened by influential Meccans, in 622 CE (year 1 of the Islamic calendar), Muhammad fled Mecca to a town later renamed Medina. There, Muhammad developed key practices later followed by devout Muslims: five times daily prayer, dietary prescriptions, regulation of marriage and divorce, fasting during the month of Ramadan, etc. In Medina, as well, Muhammad defined many of the practices associated with Muslim governance, in particular the practice of granting Jews, Christians, and other "people of the Book," who accepted Islamic rule, the right to continue practicing their faith, in return for paying a tax. Between 622 CE and Muhammad's death in 632 CE, Muhammad had acquired a wide following. He returned to Mecca in triumph, uniting the tribes of the Arabian Peninsula into an Islamic *umma,* or community, sworn to allegiance to Muhammad and to the tenets of Islam.

The Islamic Caliphate

Muhammad died without a designated heir. After a brief period of uncertainty, the community selected a *caliph*, or successor. The first four *caliphs,* known as the "Rightly Guided," were close advisors or kin of Muhammad. Under their leadership, control over the Arabian Peninsula was consolidated and, beginning in 634 CE, Arab armies swept out of the peninsula and conquered Egypt, Iran, and the Fertile Crescent. By 651 CE, the Persian Empire had been entirely incorporated into the Caliphate and the Byzantine Empire significantly reduced. Between 661 and 711 CE, Arab armies expanded across North Africa and invaded the Iberian Peninsula. By 751 CE, the Caliphate extended from the Pyrenees and down the Atlantic Coast of North Africa in the west to the Amu Darya (Oxus) River and Indus River in the East. Until the Mongols conquered most of Eurasia, the Islamic Caliphate stood as the largest world historical empire.

As the Arab empire grew, the loose tribal structure of Arab society was transformed to more closely resemble the Persian and Byzantine empires they absorbed. The **Umayyad Dynasty (661–750 CE)** rose to power, moving the capital from Medina to Damascus in Syria. Though the Umayyad oversaw much of the expansion of the empire, dissatisfaction at their rule would have a lasting effect. Muslims who believed that the *caliph* should be chosen from the descendants of Muhammad's cousin Ali and his wife, Muhammad's daughter Fatima, believed the Umayyads to be usurpers. The split between these **Shi'ites**—Shi'ite is shorthand for the party of Ali—and **Sunni Muslims**—who argued that leadership of the empire rested in the hands of those chosen by the community faithful without reference to kin ties to the prophet—remains a fundamental divide among Muslims to this day. The Shia also criticized the worldliness of the Umayyad leaders and considered them to have diverted from the religious zeal of the first generation of Islamic leaders. In 750 CE, a new Arab dynasty, the **Abbasid Dynasty (750–1258 CE),** overthrew the Umayyad and moved their capital to Baghdad. As a result, whereas the Byzantine influence had been greater under the Umayyad, Persian cultural influences increased during the Abbasid period.

Battle of Tours (732 CE)

In Western Europe, the expansion of the Islamic world confronted the Carolingians, a Frankish dynasty on the rise. The Carolingian family began their rise as councilors to the King of the Franks, and by the early eighth century had become the power behind the throne. In 732 CE, a Muslim army crossed the Pyrenees and marched northward across the old Roman province of Gaul. The advance was halted at the **Battle of Tours (732 CE)**. This represented the northernmost advance into Europe of Arab forces. The leader of the Frankish armies in this battle, the Carolingian Charles Martel, gained both in reputation and in opportunities to distribute rewards to supporters. His son **Pippin "the Short"** deposed the Frankish king and took the title for himself. He did so by seeking an alliance with the Pope, who recognized his usurpation, and commanded by "virtue of his apostolic authority" that Pippin be king.

Charlemagne (r. 768–814 CE)

Charlemagne, Pippin's successor, conquered much of western Europe save the British Isles and the Iberian Peninsula. His annual military campaigns also spread Roman Catholic Christianity to pagan German tribes. Charlemagne continued his father's close alliance with the papacy. On Christmas Day in 800 CE, Pope Leo III crowned Charlemagne emperor of what would later be called the Holy Roman Empire. Charlemagne's coronation was a recognition of the Roman Emperor in Constantinople's lack of real authority over events in western Europe. It also contributed to the growing divide between the Eastern Orthodox and the Roman Catholic Church.

Norman Conquest (1066 CE)

The British Isles were never incorporated into Charlemagne's Holy Roman Empire. The British Isles developed differently from countries on the continent because Britain had largely been left exposed to invasion by the Germanic Angles, Saxons, and Jutes following the Roman Empire's early fifth-century withdrawal from Britain. A unified Kingdom of England was established under the rule of Alfred the Great (r. 871–899 CE), and the English adopted Roman Catholicism. Even so, by the ninth and tenth centuries, Britain's development was more influenced by events across the North Sea than by those across the English Channel because of successive waves of invasions from Scandinavia. This changed with the invasion in 1066 CE of **William of Normandy**, who sought to lay claim to the English throne. He defeated the Anglo-Saxon claimant at the **Battle of Hastings** and was crowned King of England. He surveyed his new realm, commissioning a tax census known as the ***Domesday Book***, famed as a thorough accounting of his subjects' wealth. He also imposed continental feudalism on England, granting estates to his warriors and making vassals of Anglo-Saxon landholders. An important cultural consequence of the invasion was the introduction of many French words into the English language. Because William maintained the Duchy of Normandy as well as the Kingdom of England, England would also be drawn increasingly into European continental politics.

Magna Carta

William "the Conqueror's" successors remained Kings of England and maintained extensive holdings in what is modern France. Their adventures in continental Europe and the crusading of **Richard II, "the Lionhearted" (r. 1189–1199 CE)** proved costly and entangled the English monarchy in disputes with the English nobility and religious authorities resistant to his high taxes. **King John I (r. 1199–1216 CE)** reaped the consequences of his brother's policies. High taxation, King John's dispute with the papacy over the pope's appointment of the Archbishop of Canterbury, and costly defeats at the hands of the French resulted in an outright rebellion of the English nobility and high clergy. The nobility forced John to sign a document, **the Magna Carta (1215 CE)**, or Great Charter, which would later be seen as a lynchpin of the English legal tradition. It limited the powers of the monarch and ensured that the privileged had representation in the most important deliberations of the kingdom.

Mongol Conquest

The eastward advance of the Arab Caliphate had been halted in 751 CE, but it faced its most pressing existential threat with the arrival of the Mongols who sacked the Abbasid capital of Baghdad in 1258 CE. The sacking of Baghdad put an end to the possibility of a unified Muslim empire, though the thought of restoring the Caliphate continues to motivate some Muslims even today.

The Mongols were a military confederation formed from a number of distinct and often rival pastoral nomadic tribes and united by **Genghis Khan (ca. 1162–1227 CE)** in the early 13th century. They swept from their ancestral homelands in the Mongolian steppes to establish the largest empire in history. Under Genghis Khan's successors, the Mongol Empire reached from China and Korea in the East across Central Asia to include parts of Eastern Europe, Russia, and Southwest Asia. Though the Mongol conquest was accomplished through extensive violence, the Mongol Empire united China with the rest of Eurasia and contributed to the spread of many Chinese technologies to the West. Among these were Chinese painting techniques, printing, navigation using the compass, gunpowder weaponry, techniques of Chinese shipbuilding, and many other innovations.

Silk Road

The Silk Road served as a link between East Asia and the Mediterranean from at least the Han and Roman periods until the 18th century, if not later. It was not precisely a road. Instead, it was a series of connected caravan routes that extended across central Asia and connected to ancient Persian road networks linked to the Mediterranean Sea. In the desert regions of this trade route, oasis cities facilitated the trade and nomadic kingdoms rose and fell along the routes. Much of the westward-bound trade consisted of silks, porcelain, lacquerware, jade, cottons, and other luxury items. In exchange, horses, wine, and woolens were traded eastward to China. Many cultural practices and technologies were exchanged along these trade routes. Islam, Buddhism, and Christianity were transmitted along the Silk Road by missionaries, merchants, and monks. Guns, gunpowder, stirrups, the heavy plow, horse collars, printing, and paper were only a few of the technologies that were diffused from China to the West along these routes. Epidemic diseases also spread along the Silk Road. The bubonic plague, or **Black Death,** that decimated Eurasia in the 14th century is just the most famous example of an epidemic traveling along these routes.

> **Competency 002 Descriptive Statement B.** The beginning teacher demonstrates knowledge of major developments in and interactions among the civilizations of Africa (e.g., Egypt, sub-Sahara), Mesoamerica (e.g., Aztec tradition), Andean South America (e.g., Inca tradition), and Asia (e.g., Islamic civilization, China, India, Japan).

Key Question

To what degree does the history of the "Middle Ages" represent a "Dark Age"? How did the regional civilizations that developed following the collapse of the classical civilizations (Greco-Roman, Indian, and Han Chinese) creatively build on the legacies of those civilizations?

Periodization: 600 to 1450 CE

The period 600 CE to 1450 CE corresponds roughly with what is often called the Middle Ages or the medieval period. Humanist scholars from the Italian Renaissance were the first to differentiate the period that began after the end of the Roman empire as a Dark Age between the glory of the classical period of Greek and Roman cultural achievement and its rebirth in the Renaissance. This negative perception of the Middle Ages ignored the many accomplishments of medieval Europeans, the flourishing Islamic world, the technological accomplishments of Song China, and India's diverse but vibrant society. This era also witnessed the high point of pre-Columbian Mesoamerican and South American civilizations.

African Empires

A number of large empires developed in West Africa between roughly 500 and 1600 CE. West Africa had participated in trans-Saharan trade to the Mediterranean from Roman times. The introduction of the camel to North Africa and the introduction of Islam to the region resulted in an expansion of this trade and the growth of a series of states that profited from the trade. The commodity most in demand was gold from West Africa, as well as ivory and slaves. In exchange, West Africans received cloth, dates, salt, and a variety of manufactures from North Africa and the Mediterranean world. The first empire in the region, **Ghana**, was established in the late eighth century but flourished until the 11th century. The empire of **Mali (ca. 1230–ca. 1600 CE)** succeeded Ghana, expanding its territory from the Senegambia region on the coast of the Atlantic Ocean across West Africa to beyond the great bend of the Niger River. The population of Mali adopted Islam and became an important outpost in the expansive Islamic world of the 13th and 14th centuries. The wealth of its most famous ruler, or **Mansa, Musa Keita I (c. 1280–1337 CE)**, caused a sensation when on a pilgrimage to Mecca, the alms he distributed to the poor in the form of gold dust and gold coins created a localized inflation. Europeans, hearing of Mansa Musa, were inspired to explore the coast of West Africa. The empire of **Songhai (1464–1592 CE)** was the final of these West African empires. As the coastal trade with European merchants and slavers increased, the trans-Saharan trade routes were supplanted by new linkages to the rest of the world, and the West African empires declined.

The Swahili Coast and Southern Africa

Elsewhere in Africa, trade and cross-cultural relations with the Islamic world contributed to a similar flourishing. East Africans, like their West African counterparts had long traded with the outside world. With the expansion of Islam, trade to East Africa increased and communities of Arab and Persian merchants settled along the coast of East Africa. These merchants intermarried with the Bantu-speaking peoples living there and converted most to Islam. Between 1000 and 1500 CE, this **Swahili** culture flourished in independent city-states that dotted the coastal region. These cities acquired goods from Africa's interior (ivory, gold, exotic animal hides, and sometimes slaves, among other trade goods), exchanging porcelain and silk from China, cotton cloth from India, and spices from Indonesia. The language, **Swahili**, was a trade language that combined Bantu terms and grammatical structures with many Arabic, Persian, and Hindi words, reflecting the cosmopolitanism of the region.

Islamic Civilization

From its beginnings in the Arabian Peninsula, Islam spread rapidly through Arab conquests. It made even wider inroads through trade and missionary activity. Merchants espousing the tenets of Islam established themselves along the Silk Roads and into China, and settled in Persian Gulf and

Arabian Sea commercial centers as well as along the coast of India. Muslim merchants also carried the religion as far east as the Indonesian archipelago. During the medieval period, Islamic medicine, scientific knowledge, mathematics, astronomy, architecture, poetry, and calligraphy reached a peak of creativity. Much of the ancient Greek learning lost to western Europeans was familiar to Arab scholars.

China after the Fall of the Han Dynasty

After the breakdown of the Han Empire in 220 CE China experienced three centuries of disorder and division much akin to that experienced in the aftermath of the collapse of Rome. Between 589 and 618 CE, China was reunited under the **Sui Dynasty**, but their leaders' cruelty led to rebellion and the rise of a militarily powerful family that established the **Tang Dynasty (618 CE–907 CE)** during this period, merchants from Central and Southeast Asia, Iran, and India traded in China's principal cities. Central Asian hairstyles, music, entertainments, ceramics, and poetic styles were widely adopted by Chinese elites. Patronized by the court and appealing to many Chinese peasants, Buddhism also flourished. Buddhist monasteries and temples acquired vast land holdings and provided essential services for the populace. Despite the widespread impact of these foreign influences, the Tang period also saw a resurgence of Confucian scholarship and literature. The extant poetry, commentaries on the Confucian classics, and other literary works from this period dwarf comparable literary output from western Europe during the same period. Beginning in the middle of the eighth century, Tang China experienced a number of significant setbacks and instability. In 751 CE, a Tang army was defeated in western Asia at the **Battle of the Talas River** by an Arab force. This would mark the furthest westward expansion of Chinese territory. An uprising four years later that swept across northern China resulted in the sacking of the Tang capital. The Tang grew progressively weaker until in 907 CE, the dynasty fell.

The Song Dynasty (960 CE–1279 CE)

The Song Dynasty reunified China in 960 CE. Though the Song would eventually be defeated by the Mongols in 1279 CE, under the Song Dynasty China had the most developed economy in the world. Under the Song, peasant landowners, enabled by tax and inheritance systems, gained ownership rights to their land that approximated those that developed later in the rest of the world. Rather than owing labor services or taxes in kind (grain or other crops), and as tax burdens became fixed, Chinese peasants were able to benefit directly the sale of their produce and were incentivized to invest in fertilizers and technologies that would improve their harvests. As a result, Chinese peasants, unlike peasants in Europe's manorial system, were often willing to take risks adopting new techniques and crops. Tea, cotton, and new varieties of rice were introduced and widely adopted.

India

From 550 CE to ca. 1000 CE, India was divided among competing territorial states. During this period, however, the cults of the Gods Vishnu and Shiva experienced an increase in devotion that would be important to the later development of Hinduism. India also continued to be a center for Buddhist practice, attracting monks from China, Southeast Asia, and Japan to study and transcribe ancient Buddhist texts. One of the most important new cultural influences on the Indian subcontinent during this period, however, would be Islam. Muslim merchants settled along the western coast of India and in its southern cities. In the 13th century as well, Turkic and Afghan Muslims expanded Muslim power over northern India, establishing a Muslim Sultanate centered in Delhi. These Muslim states would lay the groundwork for the eventual conquest of India by the Mughals (descendants of the Mongols).

Japan

Japan, which had developed in relative isolation prior to 600 CE in the period from 600 to 1450 CE, was greatly influenced by Chinese culture. Japanese envoys, monks, and students traveled to China, borrowing widely. The Japanese adapted Chinese characters to the Japanese language. Buddhism and Confucianism flourished in this period as well. This admiration for things Chinese soon influenced the Japanese king who began to adopt Chinese institutions, including the title of "heavenly emperor." A new capital was established, laid out in Chinese fashion. The Japanese also adopted a Chinese-style bureaucracy and tax system. An area of difference was its military system that relied on soldiers who volunteered in exchange for remittances of their taxes. These soldiers were known as *samurai* from the Japanese verb, "to serve." *Samurai* provided their own armor, horses, and weapons. Finally, Japanese traditional religious practices were increasingly formalized into what was called Shintoism.

Mesoamerica and South America

Mesoamerica between 600 and 1450 CE sits astride the Classic Period (ca. 100–900 CE) and the Post-Classic Period (ca. 900–1521 CE). The Classic Period is seen as the high-point Mayan culture in modern Guatemala, the Yucatan Peninsula, Belize, and parts of Honduras and El Salvador. The Maya in this period were a literate civilization with sophisticated mathematical capabilities, which included being among the first cultures to develop the concept of zero. Their astronomical calculations and observations were sophisticated. During the Classic Period, Mayan cities approached as many as 50,000 to 70,000 inhabitants, but no single city predominated. Beginning in the ninth century, Mayan civilization began to decline. Around 900 CE, a new people, the Toltecs, began to influence the region. The Toltecs migrated from northern Mexico as would the Aztecs in the early 13th century.

In South America, a number of precursors to the Inca Empire were located in modern Bolivia, Peru, and Chile. The Inca would build on the foundations established by these states.

Competency 002 Descriptive Statement C. The beginning teacher knows how new political, economic and social systems evolved in western Europe after the collapse of the western Roman Empire (e.g., feudalism, manorialism).

Key Question

Why did feudalism and manorialism develop in the aftermath of the breakdown of Roman institutions, and how did these political and economic institutions differ from the later development of free market economies and systems of representative government?

Periodization: Development of Medieval Institutions

The development of medieval institutions reflects a long process of evolution that dated from the last centuries of the Roman period. It is difficult to precisely pinpoint the development of feudalism and manorialism as they were part of a gradual response to the collapse of Roman political institutions, agricultural and trade networks systems and to the slow development of new institutions influenced by the Germanic warrior societies that had entered into the western Roman empire.

Roman to Medieval Political and Social Systems

Between 400 and 600 CE in the western Roman Empire, gradually the old Roman provinces were replaced by small kingdoms governed by Germanic rulers. The Roman Empire had been able to thrive because of the respect for written law and because of the efficiency of the administrative bureaucracies and provincial governments. The new Germanic kingdoms were extensions of the Germanic tribal groups that had either migrated into the Roman Empire, often at the invitation of the empire, or invaded outright as the Roman state weakened. Germanic kingdoms were established in the former province of Gaul by the Franks and the Burgundians, in northern Italy by the Lombards and the Ostrogoths, in the Iberian Peninsula by the Visigoths, and in north Africa and Sicily by the Vandals. The Roman province of Britannia by the mid-sixth century had been divided into a number of rival Anglo-Saxon kingdoms.

As we have seen under the leadership of the Carolingians, an effort was made to restore the Roman Empire under Frankish rulership. But Charlemagne's empire was broken up after his death when a civil war erupted between three of his grandsons. The civil war ended in 843 CE with the **Treaty of Verdun** that divided Charlemagne's empire among the three claimants. One lasting significance of this treaty was that it divided the empire roughly along linguistic lines. The East Frankish Kingdom corresponded roughly with the German-speaking region of Europe. The West Frankish Kingdom corresponds roughly with modern France. The territory between these two kingdoms would eventually fragment into multiple independent duchies, kingdoms, and territorial principalities.

Viking, Magyar, and Muslim invasions

Threats from outside western Europe also undermined any hope of a restored western Roman empire. Germanic seafaring peoples from Scandinavia known variously as Norsemen, Northmen,

Danes or Vikings raided throughout western Europe beginning as early as 793 CE. Their long-boats were sturdy enough to permit long ocean voyages. These raiders terrorized the coastlines of Europe as far south as the Mediterranean and followed river systems through Russia as far as the Black Sea. The Vikings went in search of treasure and slaves that could be sold in the slave markets of north Africa and Constantinople. They also settled in Normandy, Russia, and England establishing kingdoms. Another threat, the Magyars, arose in eastern Europe, like the Vikings, often in search of slaves to sell in Constantinople. Lastly, Muslim sailors in the ninth and 10th centuries threatened the coasts of southern Europe.

Feudalism and Feudal Society

With the disintegration of the Carolingian empire, power became increasingly decentralized. The Carolingians had granted land to their warriors to gain their loyalty and to provide them with the means to supply their armies. As the Carolingian empire disintegrated, these estates became independent power centers with their own customary law and their own military forces. The feudal system developed as a way to raise an army and govern territory without an efficient bureaucracy and monetized tax system. It was a system based on mutual obligations. A **lord** granted a **benefice** or **fief** to a **vassal** who swore an oath of **fealty** or loyalty to the lord. The oath of fealty was a very public ceremony, often sworn on a Bible or religious relic, in which the vassal agreed to serve his lord by providing military service himself or by providing soldiers under his command. The lord was required to provide a "maintenance," which in practice was a land grant, though occasionally it could mean the control of a toll bridge, toll road, or other resource to exploit.

In addition to providing military or other service for one's lord, the fief implied lordship over that estate or benefice. The lord of each fief was charged with keeping the peace and resolving disputes on the fief provided. The base of the feudal hierarchy was the mounted knight. During the Middle Ages armored cavalry became the backbone of all European armies. The feudal system developed largely to meet the expense of training and maintaining a contingent of horsemen. This feudal system of governance was fundamentally based on personal relationships and lacked the institutional permanence of bureaucratic systems of government.

Manorialism

Medieval European society was divided between those who prayed (the clergy), those who fought (the aristocracy), and those who worked (commoners). The fief promised a vassal by his lord included the peasantry that cultivated the agricultural lands. The vast majority of all western Europeans were peasants. Most were serfs. **Serfs** were bound to the land and unable to legally move from place to place, but were not slaves that could be bought and sold. Serfs typically lived in villages on the **manor** of a feudal lord. Serfs had labor duties on the lord's land but also worked their own lands, which they did not own outright, but held from the lord, in exchange for certain customary dues and obligations. These varied widely from estate to estate. In addition, peasants paid **tithes** of one-tenth of their harvest to the church. Aristocrats often had multiple manors and traveled from one estate to another living on the surplus of each estate.

Commercial Revolutions and the Rise of Towns

In the 11th and 12th centuries, well over 90 percent of Europeans lived in the countryside. Few towns had populations greater than 1,000 people. The largest cities were located in Italy and most established cities dated to Roman times. After the year 1000 CE, however, there was an unmistakable increase in the size and importance of cities. In part, this growth of urban life reflected increases in population that occurred with increases in agricultural productivity brought about by new technologies such as the heavy plow, horse collar, and the three-field system. In addition, a global warming trend and longer growing seasons contributed to increased yields. Finally, the invasions that had wracked Roman and then early medieval society had largely subsided.

New towns and cities were granted charters that guaranteed their residents a social status and independence that was quite different from that of the peasantry. These grants were usually given by feudal lords interested in acquiring new sources of revenue from the merchants that came to the towns, or by kings' intent on seeking allies against the feudal nobility. Serfs dissatisfied with their lot might flee to these towns, finding work as a craftsman or laborer. This outlet also encouraged western European noblemen to give more favorable terms to the serfs who remained on the land. Thus, the increase in urbanization improved the lot of the peasantry in the West.

Towns also served as important market places for luxury items as well as staples from the surrounding countryside.

Medieval cities and towns also developed new governing institutions. Towns were often governed by councils composed of leading townsmen. The terms **burghers** (German) or **bourgeoisie** (French) identify townspeople who had the privilege of citizenship in the new towns of medieval Europe. Artisans, craftsmen, and merchants also established **guilds**, self-governing associations organized around specific crafts or trade goods. Medieval cities and towns provided an outlet for excess rural populations or for those dissatisfied with conditions in the manorial economy and served as an alternative to the feudal political system dependent on the manorial economy.

> **Competency 002 Descriptive Statement D.** The beginning teacher: Understands the influence exerted by the Roman Catholic Church and the Eastern Orthodox Church in medieval Europe.

Key Question

Although this descriptive statement appears at first to be a straightforward comparative, it actually poses an underlying question: In what ways did the development of Roman Catholicism in western Europe contribute to the separation of church and state in the West, but not in the East?

Medieval Christianity

Christianity provided a unifying framework for Europeans, much as Buddhism did in East Asia. Across western Eurasia, most people believed in the teachings of Christianity. Doctrinally, however, eastern and western Europeans were deeply divided. In the West, Roman Catholic practices and doctrine predominated. In the Greek-speaking Byzantine Empire (the successor state in the eastern Mediterranean to the Roman Empire) and in most of the Slavic-speaking eastern Europe, Eastern Orthodoxy predominated. Eastern Orthodox religious practice and political structure differed in few important ways from the organization of the Roman Catholic Church. Both differentiated between the **secular clergy** (who ministered to the community) and the **regular clergy** (who withdrew into monastic life). In the West, the "Bishop of Rome," the Pope, ruled over archbishops and bishops who oversaw parish priests. In the East, the Patriarch, the "Bishop of Constantinople" had an analogous role to that of the papacy, and supervised "metropolitans" and "archbishops" in their oversight of rural and urban parishes.

Eastern Orthodox Christianity and the Byzantine Empire

The Byzantine Empire, to a much greater degree than in the West, maintained significant continuities with the Roman Empire. Unlike in the West, Roman roads, taxes, military, bureaucracy, court, and legal system continued largely unchanged for much of the medieval period.

The Eastern Orthodox Church, as it had from the reign of the emperor Constantine, served to legitimize the power of the emperor. Moreover, the emperor had much greater direct control over the Eastern Orthodox Church than was the case in the West. The term for the fusion of imperial and religious authority in the Byzantine Empire has been called *caesaro-papism*, implying that in the Byzantine Empire, the powers of the pope and the emperor were united. The emperor and pope were not, in fact, united in one person; but the emperor had enormous power over the church, appointing the patriarch (akin to the pope in the West), calling church councils to debate doctrine and administrative issues, and even making the final decision on fine points of theology. Perhaps because political and religious power were so tightly linked, doctrinal disputes and theological issues proliferated in the East.

Orthodox Christian missionaries spread Byzantine religious culture to Slavic-speaking populations in the Baltic and into central and eastern Europe. To communicate this textual religion to nonliterate populations, the missionaries developed an alphabet for Slavic languages based on Greek letters known as the **Cyrillic alphabet**. Byzantine economic and cultural prominence in the region contributed to the eventual conversion of Russians and other Slavic populations to Orthodox Christianity. Princes like Vladimir of Kiev, observing the grandeur of Constantinople's many Orthodox churches, and desirous of political and economic alliances with the Byzantine Empire, made the decision to adopt Orthodox Christianity. Along with the adoption of Orthodox Christianity, Russians borrowed Byzantine architectural styles, monastic traditions, and the tradition of close ties between the Orthodox Church and political leaders. After Constantinople fell to the Ottoman Turks, Russian Orthodox religious and political leaders would declare Russia the successor to Byzantium and referred to Russia as the "third Rome." The Russian imperial title **Cza**r (or Tsar), which means *Caesar*, is just one indication of the relationship between Byzantium and Russia.

Roman Catholicism and Western Christendom

By contrast with the Byzantine Empire, where the Byzantine Emperor and the Roman bureaucracy maintained their authority, the fragmentation of the western Roman Empire left few institutions capable of providing social cohesion or order. The Roman Catholic Church stepped into this void. The church had a religious message that encouraged a populace frightened by the pace and violence of cataclysmic change. Its belief statement and rituals of communion and baptism provided a socially unifying framework for everyday life. The bishops and parish priests stepped into many of the administrative functions and roles once fulfilled by Roman bureaucrats. In the countryside, monastic communities served as missionaries, playing a particularly important role in converting Anglo-Saxon and Germanic populations to Roman Catholic Christianity; and contributing to the preservation of Roman learning and scholarship.

During the early Middle Ages (500–1000 CE), the parish priests and local clergy that administered to the needs of a largely rural poor often lacked basic literacy and training. As a result, both parishioners and clergy often shared only a rudimentary understanding of the doctrinal complexities of church teaching. Consequently, in the West, very unlike the Eastern Church where abstract theological debates were commonplace even among the poor, Christians shared a more concrete faith. After the ninth and 10th centuries, however, religious reformers in western Europe contributed to raising the level of religious understanding of both lay people and clergy.

In the eastern Roman Empire, the emperors treated the church essentially as an arm of the state, whereas in the West, the popes maintained an independence from secular power quite unlike that granted to the Patriarch of Constantinople. The pope, or Bishop of Rome, asserted a primacy over other bishops, and even claimed that the authority of the papacy superseded that of kings and other secular authorities. This would result in a number of struggles for power between religious and secular leaders. The most important of these was the **Investiture Controversy** that pitted the Holy Roman Emperor Henry IV against Pope Gregory VII. In 1075 CE, Pope Gregory condemned lay investiture, or the practice of secular leaders making appointments to bishops or other clerical positions. A compromise was eventually reached giving popes the right to appoint to high church offices, while secular rulers maintained the right to nominate and invest bishops with the lands and estates that came with their clerical positions. Similar struggles for power occurred in England (Henry II and the Archbishop of Canterbury, Thomas à Becket), France (Pope Boniface VIII and King Philip IV). The details of these controversies are less important than the fact that they contributed in the West to the development of distinct spheres separating the exercise of religious and secular power.

TExES SOCIAL STUDIES 7–12

Schism between Eastern Orthodoxy and Roman Catholicism

In 1054 CE, a definitive split occurred between the Eastern Orthodox and Roman Catholic churches. This division resulted from a number of causes. Some of these were doctrinal; for example, differences over the precise nature of the Trinity. Others were differences in practice. In the Roman Catholic Church, Latin was the language of worship; in the Eastern Orthodox, Greek was the liturgical language. The Eastern Orthodox Church permitted clerical marriage for parish priests, while the Roman Catholic Church came to insist on clerical celibacy. The eastern church used leavened bread in the Eucharistic ceremony, while in the West, unleavened bread was eaten. The two branches of Christianity also disagreed on the role of images or icons in worship. Finally, however, the ultimate factor resulting in the divorce between Eastern Orthodox and Roman Catholic traditions was the Roman papacy's claim to primacy over the Eastern Orthodox patriarchs. Twice this rivalry led to pope and patriarch excommunicating one another.

Competency 002 Descriptive Statement E. The beginning teacher: Compares social, political, economic, and religious aspects of medieval Europe with previous civilizations.

Key Question

This descriptive statement prompts test-takers to consider the differences primarily between medieval European social and political institutions and those of the Hellenistic world and the Roman Empire. As we have seen already, it is clear that medieval Europe shared a great deal with Greek and Roman civilization and also had significant differences. The short list that follows identifies a few comparisons but hardly does justice to the many ways in which medieval Europe differed and yet owed a significant cultural debt to ancient Greece and Rome.

Comparing Political Institutions

Where Greek social and political life revolved around the *polis* (city state) and the Roman around first the *res publica* (republic) and later *imperium* (empire), medieval social and political life revolved around the *gens* or *gentes,* a Latin term that meant "family members descended from the same male ancestor," but in the Germanic context might be more accurately translated as "clan" and "tribe."

Medieval Europe, unlike the Roman state, relied on family ties and personal loyalties, rather than written law and impersonal bureaucracies. Custom and tradition guided decision-making. The Germanic warrior-kings were surrounded by followers who fought alongside them, pledged their loyalty, and agreed to serve their ruler in exchange for share in the plunder of war, grants of land, or other forms of support. These Germanic kingdoms (Franks in Northern Gaul, Visigoths in the Iberian Peninsula, Lombards in Northern Italy, Anglo-Saxons in England) would be precursors to later nation-states.

Despite this very different form of political association, medieval Europeans employed Roman terms in their political hierarchy. The many terms that indicated noble title or possession of a fief derived from Roman military or political titles. For example, the title "Duke," derived from the Latin word *Dux,* a military rank in the Roman empire roughly corresponding to a general. The land claimed by a duke was then a *duchy.* Similarly, a Count, from the Latin *comes,* which means "companion," designated a lesser military rank. A count had lordship over a county. Other titles of nobility had similar origins. Medieval knights claimed a connection to the *equestrian* class of Roman cavalry. This heritage is seen in the words *caballero, cavalier,* and *chevalier,* meaning "knight" in Spanish, English, and French respectively.

Comparisons of Religious Life

Most basically, Greek and Roman religion was polytheistic, and medieval Christians, whether in the Byzantine Empire or in western Europe, were devoutly monotheistic. In addition, Christianity promised a personal salvation and emphasized human equality before God, whereas Roman and Greek paganism recognized no such equal status and perceived religion as more of a civic responsibility than a personalized salvation. Medieval Christians also valued withdrawal into monastic life. This was antithetical to Roman values of civic life.

Christianity should be remembered as a medieval inheritance of the Late Roman Empire. Christians in the West worshipped in Latin. In the East, they worshipped in Greek. Roman Catholics acknowledged the Bishop of Rome as the Pontifex Maximus, a Roman office. In the East, the Greek Orthodox Patriarch held the See of Constantinople (the Roman capital after 324 CE).

Economy

The medieval agricultural system of manorialism, like so much in the Middle Ages, had roots in the breakdown of late Roman conditions. The classic Roman farm was a centralized and efficient form of production: a huge landed estate, or "villa," worked by slaves growing crops for urban markets. In the aftermath of the Germanic invasions and the breakdown of the Roman urban economy, this system ceased to be profitable. Slave labor was too expensive for the limited returns promised from shrinking urban markets. In response, villa owners farmed out agricultural work, diffusing the land of the manor and the risks of production, to peasants who were no longer slaves but were not free either.

Many cities in western Europe were Roman or Greek cities. Lyon, France, was Lugdunum. London, England, was Londonium. Marseille in southern France was Massalia, a Greek settlement overtaken by the Romans. Additionally, many of the roads used in medieval Europe to travel from city to city were of Roman construction.

> **Competency 002 Descriptive Statement F.** The beginning teacher: Demonstrates knowledge of the political, economic, religious, and social impact of the Crusades and other religious interactions.

Key Question

The TEKS include the Crusades among a list of events that contributed to the end of the medieval period. This is particularly true if the Crusades "and other religious interactions" are seen primarily as significant for how they introduced medieval Europeans to the scientific, technological, and cultural advances visible in the Islamic world at the time.

Periodization: The Crusades—1095 to 1492

The Crusades, strictly speaking, lasted from 1095 CE with the launching of the First Crusade, to 1204 CE at the end of the Fourth Crusade. Historians often also group the Spanish "Reconquista" (which ended in 1492 with the defeat of the last Islamic state in the Iberian Peninsula) among the Crusades. It is for this reason that the end of the Crusades in 1492 is often said to be one more historical event marking the end of the medieval period and the beginning of the modern.

The Crusades

In the late 11th century, the Seljuk Turks began to encroach on the Byzantine capital in Constantinople, prompting the Byzantine Emperor to request aid from Western European Christians. The Seljuk Turks originated in Central Asia on the periphery of the Islamic world. In the 10th and 11th centuries, they gradually settled across Southwest Asia, adopting Islam and establishing territorial states. In the 11th century, they moved into Anatolia, threatening the Byzantine Empire.

Even though the Eastern Orthodox and Roman Catholic churches had only in 1054 CE split over doctrinal and political differences, **Pope Urban II (r. 1088–1099 CE)** called on the nobility of Europe to aid fellow Christians faced with this new threat from Islam. The Crusades that resulted were a series of "holy wars" fought by Christian armies from Western Europe energized to regain the "Holy Land" for Christendom. In the First Crusade, three large armies, motivated by religious zeal and the desire to gain land or plunder in the Middle East, mustered in preparation for an invasion of Seljuk lands. The religious enthusiasm surrounding preparations for these crusades also resulted in anti-Jewish riots and purges of suspected heretics. In 1097 CE, the three armies united in Constantinople and began to march through Anatolia towards Jerusalem, defeating the Turkish armies along the way, besieging and taking Jerusalem in 1099 CE. They divided the territory that they conquered from the Turks into separate "Crusader states." Within a few years, these isolated Christian enclaves within the Islamic world were themselves under siege. Most of the land was retaken by the great Turkish ruler **Saladin (r. 1174–1193 CE)**.

A second crusade was called, but it failed to dislodge the Turks. The Third Crusade may be the most famous, often called the Crusade of the Three Kings, because it was led by the English King Richard the Lionhearted, France's Philip Augustus, and the Holy Roman Emperor Frederick Barbarossa. The Third Crusade (1189–1192 CE) also failed to retake the "Holy Land" for the Christian cause. The taxes raised to fund the enterprise in England and to ransom Richard the Lionhearted created such resentment among the English nobility that it contributed to the revolt of the English barons in 1215 CE and the signing of the Magna Carta. A Fourth Crusade (1202–1204 CE) failed to even reach the Middle East, after the Crusaders decided to sack Constantinople instead, further damaging relations between Eastern Orthodox and Roman Catholic Christians.

Effects of the Crusades

While the Crusades made little lasting impact on the Islamic world, Europe was profoundly influenced by interaction with the Middle East. The crusaders returned from the region with a taste for Asian luxuries, spices, silks, and other commodities. Genoese and Venetian merchants learned how to produce sugar, and they were soon establishing plantations worked by slaves in the Mediterranean. European thinkers were exposed to Muslim scholarship and science. Aristotelian philosophy, long studied in the Islamic world but largely lost to the West, was reintroduced to important effect in Europe. European armies also learned techniques of fortification and siege warfare from Muslim commanders. The Crusades embarked Europeans on an era of technological borrowing. Asian technologies like the magnetic compass, lateen sail, sternpost rudder, gunpowder, paper, and print would all prove instrumental to European successes between 1450 and 1750 CE. Not all of these were acquired as a result of the Crusades, but Europeans' increased interaction with the Byzantine and Islamic worlds opened up the West to technological advancement.

Spanish Reconquista

The re-conquest of the Iberian Peninsula by Christian monarchs was completed only in 1492 when the Islamic Kingdom of Grenada was defeated by the Spanish monarchs Ferdinand and Isabella. Historians often associate the centuries-long struggle by Christian rulers to regain control of the peninsula with the Crusades and the crusading spirit encouraged by Pope Urban II in his call for a Holy War against the Seljuk Turks. Crusading zeal contributed to Portuguese exploration along the coast of West Africa, and to Spanish justifications for exploration and conquest in the Americas. The expulsion of the last Islamic state in western Europe in 1492 is sometimes associated with the end of the Middle Ages and the beginning of the early modern period.

COMPETENCY 003 (WORLD HISTORY FROM 1450 CE TO 1750 CE)

The teacher understands significant historical events, developments, and traditional points of reference in world history from 1450 CE to 1750 CE.

Competency 003 Descriptive Statement A. The beginning teacher demonstrates knowledge of individuals, events, issues, and traditional points of reference that shaped the development of world civilizations from 1450 CE to 1750 CE (e.g., the fall of Constantinople, Martin Luther, the Black Death, Leonardo da Vinci).

Key Question

What were the turning points and events that signaled the beginnings of the early modern world? This descriptive statement asks that test-takers demonstrate knowledge of events, issues, etc. that "shaped the development of world civilizations" during the period 1450 to 1750 CE. The examples identified, however, are traditionally associated with the events and developments that signaled the end of the medieval period in European history and the beginning of the modern period.

Periodization: Early Modern Period—1450 to 1750

The period from 1450 CE to 1750 CE is often called the early modern period. The date 1450 CE is an arbitrary date that has been accepted by many world historians as a reasonable place to begin the modern period. The end of the 100 Years' War, officially brought to a close in 1453, may be said to signal the end of the medieval period in Europe. Additionally, the conquest of Constantinople by the Ottoman Empire puts a definitive end to the last vestiges of the Roman Empire. As importantly, in 1452, Portugal began minting gold coins from gold that Portuguese explorers had acquired in West Africa. The trade in African slaves had also begun by 1450. The age of European expansion thus is often dated to 1450. Other world empires originated around this same period or experienced important landmarks at this time. The end date of 1750 CE also provides a good round number at which to date the end of pre-industrial societies and the beginning of new economic and political revolutions.

The Black Death (1348–1351 CE)

The Black Death marked a turning point in the economic and demographic growth of the Middle Ages. As European populations grew from the 10th to the 14th centuries, pressure on agricultural resources became acute, leading to a series of generalized famines in the early 1300s. Then in 1347, the bubonic plague reached European ports on the Mediterranean following the trade routes from Asia. In successive waves the plague, called the Black Death because of its symptomatic discoloring of those afflicted, swept across Europe striking nearly every part of the subcontinent. By

1350, according to some estimates, nearly one-third of Europe's population had perished. Later epidemics continued until the early 1700s. The social and economic effects of these epidemics helped undermine many medieval European institutions. For example, a shortage of farm laborers led many landlords to commute peasant labor services in favor of money wages. The high mortality of urban artisans resulted in price increases for manufactured goods and encouraged some peasants to leave rural areas for city work. Europeans also began to regulate family sizes by marrying later in life, which reduced pressure on land resources and made greater savings possible. Skepticism of authority grew in the wake of physicians' and the Church's inability to respond effectively to the disease. This contributed potentially to the emergence of the Scientific Revolution. Alternately, many Europeans sought spiritual solace leading to a flourishing of lay piety, increased bequests to the Church, and a new demand for spiritually authentic experience. This saw its culmination in efforts to reform church and society.

The Fall of Constantinople (1453 CE)

Another watershed moment in the transition between the Middle Ages and the modern centuries was the defeat of the Byzantine Empire by the Ottoman Turks and the fall of Constantinople. The fall of Constantinople marked the definitive end of the Roman Empire. Many Byzantine scholars fled to Italy encouraging the development of Renaissance humanism. Additionally, Muslim control of Constantinople encouraged Western Europeans to seek new trade routes to the East, contributing to the Portuguese exploration of Africa and ultimately of Columbus's interest in a westward route to China and India.

Leonardo da Vinci (1452–1519 CE)

Leonardo da Vinci represents the ideal of the "Renaissance Man" or universal person, a master painter, sculptor, military engineer, scientist, and humanist. Leonardo da Vinci represents to later generations a new kind of intellectual, very different from the medieval scholastic.

Martin Luther (1483–1546 CE)

Martin Luther was an Augustinian monk who, in 1517, issued a challenge at his university church to debate the scriptural authority of the Roman Catholic practice of granting indulgences. This very medieval behavior, defending a thesis before an audience of fellow scholars, initiated a political and religious reformation that shattered the unity of medieval Christendom.

> **Competency 003 Descriptive Statement B.** The beginning teacher demonstrates knowledge of major developments in and interactions among the civilizations of Africa (e.g., Egypt, sub-Sahara), the Americas (e.g., Inca, Aztec, Maya), Western and Eastern Europe, Middle East, and Asia (e.g., China, India, Japan).

What European institutional and cultural developments help explain why Europe beginning in 1450 began to expand into other world regions, rather than the reverse?

Competency 003 emphasizes the development of European cultural and institutional characteristics as the primary explanation for European expansion and imperialism in this period. In order to understand the impact of these European developments, it is critical that teachers also understand the conditions and developments in other world regions into which Europe would expand between 1450 and 1750.

Africa

Africa, before the arrival of Portuguese explorers on the African coast, was characterized by a remarkable diversity in languages, political institutions, and religious beliefs and practices. Small territorial kingdoms such as the kingdoms of Benin, the Kongo, Ethiopia, Rwanda, Buganda, Burundi, Ife, and Edo, existed alongside large empires like Mali and Songhai, and city-states along the East African coast. In addition, there were numerous stateless societies that populated the interior of Africa. In other instances, nomadic populations settled along the peripheries of established states, trading with, and when opportunity presented itself, raiding settled societies.

The Americas

In 1450, the Americas remained untouched by the tightening trade and cross-cultural links that connected the Afro-Eurasian world. Two large complex civilizations dominated Mesoamerica and the Andean regions of South America. Elsewhere, smaller-scale agricultural societies were shaping their environments and trading luxury items and other commodities across the region. Perhaps as many as 100 million inhabitants populated the Americas. By 1750, the Americas had undergone a monumental transformation

Mayan Civilization

By 1450 CE, the Mayan civilization that had flourished between 300 and 800 CE had long collapsed. Between 800 and 900 CE, the Mayan people abandoned their principal city in the southern Yucatan and returned to small-scale village agriculture. The focus of Mayan civilization then shifted northward to the city of Chichén Itzá, which would remain a key Mayan trading and ritual center until the 13th century. When the Spaniards arrived in the Americas and advanced along the coast of the Gulf of Mexico, they encountered little of the urban civilization that had once dominated the region. Mayan civilization was reduced to small villages and agricultural settlements that maintained local trade, but by the early modern period, had comparatively little trade outside the region.

Aztec Civilization

The area of modern-day central Mexico, however, was the site of a powerful, urban civilization: the Aztecs, who dominated Mesoamerica from 1428 until the empire was conquered by Hernán Cortés's Spanish conquistadores, allied with an army of Native Americans.

The Aztecs referred to themselves as the *Mexica*. According to their founding legends, they were a nomadic people from the mythical Lake Aztlán in the American Southwest. According to legend, in 1325 CE they settled on the island on which the city of Tenochtitlán was built. By 1428 CE, the Aztecs had become the dominant power in the region and established an empire that would demand tribute from most of the surrounding area. The capital of the Aztecs, Tenochtitlán, was larger than any city in western Europe at the time, with perhaps as many as 300,000 residents. The city was built on islands and landfill in Lake Texcoco. The Aztecs were able to sustain such a large population in part through widespread trade and tribute acquired from across Central and North America and the Caribbean. The Aztecs also fed their population from floating gardens that bordered Tenochtitlán, known as *chinampas*, which were among the most high-yielding agricultural systems in any pre-industrial society. This intensive form of agriculture sustained both a city the size of the Aztec capital and a population in central Mexico of perhaps as many as 25 million inhabitants.

Inca Empire

At almost the same time that the Aztecs were extending their control over central Mexico, an empire stretching along the three-thousand-mile length of the Andes mountain range was developing. At its height, it may have had a population of perhaps 12 million people. Its capital, Cuzco, housed perhaps 200,000 residents. According to Inca legends, the Inca people settled in the Valley of Cuzco around 1200 CE after migrating from the south. After surviving threats from surrounding populations, the Inca established a kingdom and began to expand, but without much success until the early 15th century. Under the leadership of three successive Inca rulers between 1438 and 1527, the kingdom expanded, leaving the Inca in control of the Andes from modern Ecuador to central Chile. For the Inca, like the Aztecs, the Sun God was the supreme deity and the Inca was the Sun's earthly representative.

The Inca depended upon a conscript army, trained within each village and required to serve for two years. Conquered areas were resettled by Quechua language speakers who transmitted the culture and language throughout the realm. A vast road network with bridges and causeways connected the empire culturally and economically, and allowed rapid transit of troops. Runners conveyed messages and information throughout the empire along these roads. The *quipu,* a series of colored strings made of llama or alpaca hair or sometimes cotton, was used to transmit information. While the Inca did not have a system of writing, the *quipu* allowed information to be reliably passed from way station to way station, and from person to person. The Inca also depended upon tribute from their subject territories, but, unlike the Aztec, they exacted this tribute in labor rather than trade or luxury items. The required labor, often carried out on temple lands or in building and mining projects, was known as *mita*. Each village was required to take turns providing this labor. The women of subject regions were required to weave woolen cloths.

Conquest of the Aztecs and Incas

The Aztec and Inca empires both met the same fate at the hands of Spanish conquistadors. In 1518 Hernán Cortés commanded an expedition of some 500 soldiers to the coast of the Gulf of Mexico where Cortés made alliances with local populations dissatisfied with Aztec demands for tribute and control. He then marched to Tenochtitlan, the Aztec capital, where he was met by Montezuma, the Aztec ruler. After an initially pacific diplomatic encounter, the Spaniards determined to hold the Aztec leader hostage and rule through him. A rebellion followed, and the Spaniards and Aztecs fought a number of pitched battles before the combination of epidemic disease and siege warfare forced the Aztecs to surrender. Cortés claimed the Aztec Empire for New Spain and became the governor of the territory.

In 1532 **Francisco Pizarro** led a small contingent of Spaniards into the Inca empire where he confronted an army led by the Inca **Atahualpa.** Atahualpa had recently defeated his brother in a civil war for the rulership of the kingdom. This civil war, and the spread of epidemic disease in advance of Spanish arrival, had weakened the Inca. Nonetheless, Atahualpa had an army of over 6,000 men when he met Pizarro at a location called Cajamarca. Despite being greatly outnumbered, Pizarro carried out an ambush using gunpowder weapons and a cavalry force. Atahualpa was captured and his bodyguard killed. No Spanish soldiers died in the ambush. The Spaniards kept the Inca captive while they looted Inca gold, silver, and other precious jewels, and later had him executed. Despite the chaos that followed the death of their ruler, the Inca fought a protracted war lasting nearly forty years in an effort to regain their independence.

The Middle East

The Middle East in the early modern period was transformed by the same "gunpowder revolution" that had given Europeans such an advantage in the Americas. In the eastern Mediterranean, the Ottoman Empire took advantage of artillery and firearms in their **Janissary Corps**, a disciplined army of slaves from around the Ottoman's vast empire, to expand their power over the Balkans, the Arabian Peninsula, and the Arabian Sea. The height of the Ottoman Empire was during the 16th and 17th centuries.

Another "gunpowder empire" in the Middle East was the **Safavid Persian** empire that ruled over much of Iran, Iraq, and parts of Afghanistan and Pakistan between 1501 and 1736 CE.

China

China, during the period from 1450 to 1750 CE, was ruled by two dynasties: the **Ming Dynasty (1368–1644 CE)** and the **Qing Dynasty (1644–1911 CE)**. Though the Ming were ethnic Chinese and the Qing were Manchu foreigners, both ruled in similar ways and relied on key institutions that had continuity with dynastic rule dating back to the Han Dynasty. Over the course of the period, China would experience significant population growth, from 60 million in 1368 CE to 125 million in 1644 CE, to approximately 300 million by 1800 CE.

Between 1405 and 1433 CE, the Ming commissioned a number of diplomatic missions to display to the fullest extent China's power and economic might. The commander of these naval expeditions was a Muslim eunuch, **Zheng He (1371–1435 CE),** who ranks alongside Columbus and Vasco da Gama as an ocean explorer. In fact, Zheng He was less an explorer than the admiral of a vast fleet of vessels sent around the China Sea and Indian Ocean to expand China's economic and military might. His flagship dwarfed the Columbus ships, and his entire fleet had over 28,000 sailors, soldiers, and merchants. His expeditions sailed as far away as the southern coast of East Africa. In 1435 the Ming emperor ordered an end to these expeditions, faced with renewed threat from the Mongols to the north and of Japanese piracy along the Chinese coast.

The Qing Dynasty, though it did not take up the Ming naval expeditions, was not as insular as once claimed. Instead, the focus of Qing expansionism was to the west and south. The Qing expanded into Tibet, held off Mongol threats, and even negotiated territorial boundaries with the Russian empire. The Qing also encouraged a westward settlement that rivaled 19th-century American pioneer movements westward.

Both the Ming and the Qing dynasty engaged Western European missionaries and merchants. The Chinese at first welcomed new trade partners until the early 18th century when they began to closely regulate European merchants out of alarm at efforts by individual European trading companies to monopolize trade and enforce disadvantageous terms of trade.

Tokugawa Japan

The early modern period in Japan opened with a period of intense internal warfare pitting territorial lords against one another. This period, known as the Warring States era (1467–1600 CE) ended in 1600 when **Tokugawa Ieyasu (r. 1600–1616 CE),** after an earlier effort to unify the island kingdom, seized power, took the title of **Shogun,** and established his capital at **Edo** (Tokyo). He disarmed the peasantry and pacified the territorial landlords, instituted new legal codes, and regulated the behavior of the *samurai.* Ieyasu instituted a policy of seclusion designed to exclude merchants and imports from Europe and Asia. No foreigners were permitted into Japan, and Japanese were forbidden from going overseas. This policy was in place until the arrival of an American fleet in Edo Harbor in 1853.

> **Competency 003 Descriptive Statement C.** The beginning teacher understands the importance of the European Renaissance and Reformation eras in shaping the modern world.

Key Question

 Why did the West rise to a position of technological and economic predominance after 1750?

The roles of the Renaissance and the Protestant Reformation are critical to answering this question. The Renaissance represents the beginning of European modernity and the creation of a unique European cultural identity. Specifically, the Renaissance led to the adoption of a new spirit of curiosity and scientific inquiry. The Renaissance, then, is directly linked to such later developments as the Age of Discovery, the Scientific Revolution, and the Enlightenment. Additionally, the Renaissance is often said to have fostered a new sense of individualism, opposed to medieval Europeans' emphasis on collective identities. The Reformation is also seen as contributing to this emerging European cultural identity. Perhaps the most influential thinker to make this connection was Max Weber, who published his *The Protestant Ethic and the 'Spirit' of Capitalism* in 1904. Simplified, Weber's thesis attributed the development of European capitalism and the Industrial Revolution to what Weber considered uniquely Protestant values that emphasized thrift, hard work, and associated accumulation with God's blessing.

Periodization: Early Modern Period—1450 to 1750

The periodization 1450 CE to 1750 CE, as already noted, is often called the early modern period. That periodization does not fit well with this descriptive statement's emphasis on the two intellectual developments known as the Renaissance and the Reformation.

The Renaissance was well underway by 1450. Many of the most important writers of the Renaissance lived and died in the 14th century. The cultural "rebirth" represented by the Renaissance started well before 1450 CE and could be seen as less the opening act of the modern centuries than the closing act of the Middle Ages. However, the fact that the Renaissance is included here as evidence of the beginning of the modern era should lead test-takers to ask, "What is modern about the Renaissance?" The answer to this question is often given by linking the Renaissance to later intellectual movements, such as the Scientific Revolution and the 18th-century Enlightenment.

The Reformation has a readily identifiable beginning: Martin Luther posting his *95 Theses* on the Wittenberg church door in 1517. While few of Luther's theological positions were new, this initiated a religious and political revolution that shattered the unity of Roman Catholic Christendom and contributed to political upheaval across Europe. Just as the beginning of the Renaissance is difficult to identify, the end of the Reformation is not without competing possibilities. The Peace of Westphalia that concluded the Thirty Years' War (1618–1648) is often seen as introducing a new realism to great power politics in Europe, and bringing to a close a period when religious zealotry often guided European international relations. England, at that time, however, was in the midst of its own religious civil war and rule by Puritan reformers. Only with the peaceful overthrow of James II in the "Glorious Revolution" of 1688 could it be said that the Reformation in England was definitively brought to an end. It is fair to say that by 1700, much of the impetus for the Reformation had ended.

Italian Renaissance

Why the Renaissance began in Italy requires explanation. Italy in the 14th and 15th centuries experienced a period of flourishing cultural and intellectual creativity that has become known as the Italian Renaissance. Renaissance means "rebirth," and the Italian Renaissance represented a rebirth in interest and imitation of classical Greek and Roman art and literature. The Renaissance began in Italy for a number of reasons:

1. Italian cities benefited from their position as traders connecting Europe and the Islamic world, as a result it had more urban centers than did the rest of Europe at the time.

2. The vibrant economic life of the Italian peninsula enriched the merchant classes and guild members at the expense of the landed aristocracy. Often, this rivalry was expressed through patronage of the arts, architecture, and literature.

3. Rivalry among the many Italian city-states contributed to the development of new political ideas and institutions.

4. Italian scholars, artists, and writers who were dissatisfied with the art and literature of the Middle Ages could look to the history and art of ancient Rome and Greece for inspiration.

Humanism

Study of the ancient classics was known as the *studia humanitatis,* or humanism. Italian writers like Leonardo Bruni, Francesco Petrarch, Dante Alighieri, and Giovanni Boccaccio challenged the basic assumptions of medieval knowledge as they turned to classical Greek and Roman texts, collecting and studying ancient manuscripts. Unlike the scholastic philosophers of the Middle Ages, humanists were interested in studying the ancient manuscripts directly and drawing their own conclusions rather than relying on interpretations of religious authorities. Humanists also encouraged a new kind of education based on classical models. Where the medieval ideal had emphasized asceticism and an otherworldly focus, a Renaissance humanist education combined the study of literature, language, and history, with military, musical, and athletic training. The aim of this education was secular rather than spiritual; its objective was the creation of a well-rounded, cultured leader, or "Renaissance Man."

Renaissance Art

Medieval artists had largely employed religious subject matter to convey spiritual ideals not to attempt to represent the individuality of their subject matter. Renaissance artists did not reject religious subject matter—think of Michelangelo's Sistine Chapel frescoes or Leonardo da Vinci's *Last Supper*—but they employed classical techniques to depict their subjects in more realistic fashion. Painters began to employ **perspective**, a technique classical artists had used to give the impression of three-dimensionality. Sculptors revived classical forms, including free-standing nude sculptures. Painters and sculptors sought to capture individual detail and personality in their art forms. Leonardo da Vinci's portrait, *The Mona Lisa*, provides just one example of Renaissance artists' ability to represent individual identities. Architects drew on classical styles, rather than the Gothic style of the Middle Ages.

Northern Renaissance

After 1500 CE, the Renaissance center of gravity shifted from Italy to France, Germany, the Low Countries, and England. French and Spanish rulers invaded the Italian peninsula and undercut the prosperity of Italian cities. The prosperity of Italian cities also diminished as the axis of European trade shifted westward from the Italian-German spine of Europe towards Atlantic seaports of France, Spain, the Netherlands, and England. Renaissance style and cultural influence then spread from Italy to influence European artists and writers. William Shakespeare in England, Rabelais in France, Cervantes in Spain, and others took up the mantle of Italian Renaissance writers and added their own style. European monarchs, like the Italian Renaissance princes, patronized the arts, sometimes importing Italian painters, sculptors, and architects to give their courts the culture that they witnessed in Italy.

Printing Press and the Print Revolution

One of the most important technologies contributing to the cultural influence of the Renaissance and Reformation was the printing press. The Chinese had by the seventh century CE used paper rubbings of stone and metal engraving as an early precursor to printing. By the eighth century, they were employing "block printing" to create multiple copies of a text. The Chinese were also using movable type as early as the early 11th century CE.

The first western European printing press was set up around 1450 CE by **Johannes Gutenberg.** Before Gutenberg, manuscripts were reproduced by hand, often by teams of scribes. These books were expensive and often contained errors in transcription. At first, Gutenberg's press used movable, metal type-face in an attempt to reproduce exactly the hand-written page.

The effect of printing was revolutionary. Previously, learning occurred through oral communication and on-the-job training. Since students in medieval universities lacked books, they listened to readings, or lectures. After Gutenberg, gifted students could acquire books and gain knowledge directly. Printed texts were standardized and allowed knowledge to spread in a more uniform fashion across Europe. Literacy rates rose across Europe. Reading also became a more private and intimate activity, silently done, rather than a public act done out loud, as was the case before printing. Memorization became less important, as one could possess a library of information and simply recall information by going to the relevant text. Without widespread expansion of printing technology, it is doubtful that the Protestant Reformation, the Scientific Revolution, or the Enlightenment would have developed as they did.

Protestant Reformation

Western Christianity fragmented in the 16th century, and a religious revolution known as the Protestant Reformation redefined what it meant to be a Christian. This revolution has been called the Protestant Reformation, but those who took the identity of Protestants were not the only reformers. The Catholic Church itself also undertook significant reforms.

Martin Luther (1483–1546)

The Protestant Reformation began when Martin Luther in 1517 posted his objections to the practice of granting indulgences. An indulgence was the transfer by the Pope of superfluous merit accumulated by Christ, the Virgin Mary, and the saints to remit some or all of the penance required by Christians who died without full absolution for their sins. The sale of indulgences had become a lucrative practice, and Luther and many other Catholics objected to it. Luther objected because the practice implied that one could be saved through the intercession of others. Luther held that humans receive salvation as the gift of God's grace granted to those who have faith. Luther's main objection, however, was that he could find no support for the practice in scripture. Luther held that the Bible was the sole source of religious truth. Though Catholics believed in the primacy of scripture, they also held that papal decrees, rulings of church councils, and other decisions of the Roman Catholic Church provided guidance on matters of doctrine and belief and that a reading of scripture alone was insufficient guidance for the typical believer. Luther went further, rejecting all but the sacraments of baptism and communion as scripturally required, and denying the pope's infallibility in matters of doctrine. In 1521, he was declared a heretic at the **Diet of Worms** (an assembly of the Holy Roman Empire), but was protected by Frederick, the Duke of Saxony for political as well as theological reasons. When in March 1529, the Catholic majority in the Holy Roman Empire called on all Germans to condemn Luther's teachings, a minority of princes and town governments in Germany "protested" that they would not act contrary to God's will, the Bible, or their consciences. This is where the term "Protestant" comes from.

Jean Calvin (1509–1564)

Other religious thinkers quickly adopted a number of Luther's doctrinal positions. The most important of these figures was Jean Calvin. Calvin was a humanist-trained scholar who believed in divine predestination and the necessity of establishing a society that adhered to God's law. He fled his native France in 1536 CE and established a Protestant government in the city of Geneva, Switzerland. In Calvin's Geneva, strict moral discipline was enforced as Calvin, the city's pastors, and church elders established a religiously-based society following strict Protestant moral prescriptions. In addition to the city of Geneva, Calvinist theology gained the widest following in the Netherlands, England, and the Puritan colony of Massachusetts.

Religious Warfare

From 1524 CE until 1555 CE, the Holy Roman Empire experienced a series of rebellions and civil wars that divided the empire between Protestants and Catholics. The **Peace of Augsburg (1555 CE)** temporarily resolved this conflict by establishing an important principle: *cuius regio, eius religio,* granting the ruler of a territory the right to determine the religion of the land. Lutheranism was thus recognized as a legal religion in many parts of the Holy Roman Empire. However, this agreement only recognized the rights of Lutheran and Catholic princes, not those of Calvinists, who by 1555 were an increasingly important minority. This would result in further outbreaks of sectarian violence elsewhere in Europe. Each of these conflicts combined religious competition with dynastic power struggles. The French Wars of Religion (1562–1598 CE) pitted the Huguenots (Calvinists) against Catholic loyalists. In the Netherlands, Protestants in 1564 revolted against the Catholic Habsburgs, the dynasty ruling both the Holy Roman Empire and the Spanish Empire. The Dutch would finally have their independence acknowledged only in 1648 CE. The English under Queen Elizabeth I (1558–1603 CE) engaged in a protracted conflict with Spain in a war with important religious overtones. Finally, the Holy Roman Empire was convulsed by a religious conflict, the Thirty Years' War (1618–1648 CE), in which all of Europe's powers played a part.

Henry VIII and the English Reformation

The Protestant Reformation was introduced into England largely as a result of Henry VIII's (r. 1509–1547 CE) desire to be rid of his wife, Catherine of Aragon, the daughter of Ferdinand and Isabella of Spain. Pope Clement VII was at the time controlled by the Habsburg ruler, and Catherine's nephew, Charles V. Consequently, the pope could not grant the annulment Henry requested. Henry simply declared himself England's spiritual leader, and head of the Church of England. Between 1529 and 1534 CE, the "Reformation Parliament" enacted a series of laws that secured Henry's authority over the church. He immediately divorced his Spanish wife and married Anne Boleyn, his pregnant mistress. Henry's break with the Catholic Church did not result immediately in significant theological reform of the Church of England. It was only under Henry VIII's son, Edward VI, that the English adopted many of the tenets of Protestantism. With Edward VI's premature death and the accession of Mary Tudor (daughter of Catherine of Aragon), Catholicism underwent a brief restoration in England. Only with the reign of Elizabeth I (r. 1558–1603 CE) was the Protestant Reformation secure in England; though over 80 years later, James II, a secret Catholic, was peacefully overthrown by the British parliament in what was called the Glorious Revolution.

Catholic Reformation

The impulses that gave rise to the Protestant Reformation had counterparts within the Roman Catholic Church. Throughout the late Middle Ages and into the 16th century, reformers had criticized the worldly power of the papacy, sought to encourage new forms of piety, and exhibited a missionary zeal in support of a vibrant Roman Catholicism. These reform efforts were rejoined with enthusiasm in response to the development of Protestantism.

Ignatius of Loyola and the Jesuits

Ignatius of Loyola (1491 CE–1556 CE) represented the most important of the Catholic reformers. Loyola organized an order structured along military lines called the Society of Jesus, or Jesuits, in response to the spread of Lutheranism. Over the course of the following centuries, the Jesuits sent out thousands of missionaries and took the lead in establishing Catholic educational institutions across the world. Demanding strict obedience to the papacy and to the tenets of Roman Catholic orthodoxy, the Jesuits were a strong counter to the spread of Protestantism.

The Council of Trent (1545–1563)

In response to the Protestant Reformation, a general council of the church met in Trent in northern Italy beginning in 1545 CE. The papacy introduced a number of reforms to address the criticisms that had been directed at the church by both Protestant and Catholic reformers. Simony, or the selling of church offices, was forbidden. Priests and bishops were required to reside in their parishes or dioceses, reducing absenteeism and pluralism (holding more than one office at the same time). Seminaries were established in each diocese to ensure a better-trained, more professional, and strictly celibate clergy. On most of the theological objections identified by Protestants, however, the council stood its ground, refusing to adopt any of the Lutheran or Calvinist positions on either doctrine or Catholic practice.

Scientific Revolution

One outgrowth of the intellectual ferment of the early modern period was the Scientific Revolution. The Scientific Revolution called for the application of experimentation, empirical observation, and reason while rejecting the view that received authority or religion must guide human inquiry. That the Scientific Revolution took place in Europe and not in China or the Islamic world, given the superiority of Chinese, Indian, and Arab science and technology before 1450, raises the important question: why Europe?

One reason was the well-developed medieval university system that counted over 100 European universities by 1500 CE. A second reason for Europe's Scientific Revolution was that Europeans after 1450 began to accumulate knowledge from across the globe as explorers, merchants, and intellectuals took in the variety of ideas from Asia, the Americas, and Africa. The printing press further encouraged the widespread dissemination of new ideas and texts. As a result, Europeans developed a tradition of scientific inquiry that after 1500 CE was applied first to astronomy and navigation, then to medicine, botany, chemistry, and so on. Much of the scientific knowledge accumulated had direct practical use, for military affairs, agriculture, mining, etc.

Nicholas Copernicus (1473–1543)

The field of astronomy was one of the first to undergo a Scientific Revolution. Nicholas Copernicus in his book *On the Revolution of the Heavenly Spheres* in 1543 proposed the theory that the Earth and the other planets revolved around the Sun. The primary support Copernicus offered for this theory was that the mathematics of his system worked better to explain observed phenomena than did the complicated mathematics needed to make the Ptolemaic system make sense.

Tycho Brahe (1546–1601) and Johannes Kepler (1571–1630)

Copernicus's view gained support from the work of Tycho Brahe and Johannes Kepler. Brahe's careful observations of planetary movements and his tables recording these observations came into the possession of Johannes Kepler. Kepler concluded that to keep the Sun at the center of the Copernican system, Copernicus's belief that the planetary orbits were circular had to be abandoned. Brahe's observations provided the answer. The planetary orbits were elliptical.

Galileo Galilei (1564–1642)

Copernicus's heliocentric theory received additional support with the discoveries of Galileo Galilei, whose improved telescope identified mountains on the Moon, undermining the view that the heavens were not subject to geological change. He also discovered moons orbiting around Jupiter, thereby disproving that the heavenly spheres circled the Earth.

Isaac Newton (1642–1727)

The final piece of the puzzle putting together a basic understanding of the physical universe was provided by the English scientist Isaac Newton. Newton's work provided an explanation for the elliptical orbits of the planets in the theory of universal gravitation. The view that the heavens and the Earth were distinct, and that the motion of heavenly bodies were likewise governed by natural laws and not supernatural forces, was truly revolutionary. Newton's universe was one that did not require a divine explanation for its normal operation, a universe that, like a machine, was self-regulating. Furthermore, knowledge of the universe could be arrived at through observation.

Alongside and contributing to these astronomical discoveries was a new emphasis on empirical ways of knowing, the development of the scientific method, and the institutionalization of science in Western Europe. As a result, Newton's understanding of the cosmos could be applied to other areas of human knowledge. For example, human anatomy could similarly be understood. **William Harvey (1578–1657)**, relying on anatomical dissections, rather than on ancient authorities, described how the heart worked as a pump circulating blood throughout the body. In the 18th century, insights derived from the Scientific Revolution were then employed to explain political and economic conditions.

The Enlightenment

The ideas of the Scientific Revolution spread to the wider reading public of Europe. As importantly, the Scientific Revolution's approach to knowledge, skepticism of ancient authorities, and faith in human reason and scientific discovery were applied to social, political, and economic thinking.

The Age of the Enlightenment is usually associated with the 18th century. A number of 17th-century philosophers, however, laid the groundwork for the ideas of the Enlightenment *philosophes*, as the 18th-century philosophers were known. **John Locke (1632–1704 CE)** hoped to develop a Newtonian-type synthesis of the study of human knowledge and human political institutions. Newton rejected the view, long held by European thinkers, that humans were born with certain innate ideas. He contended that humans were born a "blank slate," and that human knowledge developed as the individual mind experiences the sensory world. Rather than beings flawed by original sin, humans need not experience an act of God's grace to improve themselves. Locke also argued that rulers are bound by natural laws (akin to those discovered by Newton) and did not have absolute power. Moreover, sovereign power was granted to legislators and rulers in order to protect the rights of subjects to life, liberty, and property. In the 18th century, French philosophers, *philosophes*, took up Locke's ideas. **Voltaire (1694–1778 CE)** argued that human society could be improved through the application of reason and science. He also argued for religious toleration and an end to judicial torture and cruel and unusual punishments. **Montesquieu (1689–1755 CE)** employed a scientific approach to politics, contending that the best protection against absolute power was to establish checks and balances by dividing legislative, judicial, and executive political functions. **Adam Smith (1723–1790 CE)**, approached the economy with a Newtonian mindset, arguing that the mercantilist system of government regulation be abolished and that natural market forces be allowed to operate. Smith argued that the selfish economic behavior of individual consumers and producers, left unimpeded by government, would lead to economic expansion to the benefit of all.

Competency 003 Descriptive Statement D. The beginning teacher: Understands the causes of European expansion and the effects of that expansion on European and non-European societies (e.g., Columbian Exchange, Atlantic slave trade).

Key Question

Before 1450, Europe was hardly at the global core politically, culturally, or economically. China and India produced the vast majority of the world's manufactured goods. The world's trade was largely in the hands of merchants from the Islamic world. By many measures of cultural advancement—production of written texts, number of known writers and literary figures, degree of literacy, the proportion of the populace with basic education, the richness of advanced science, and many others—western Europe remained well behind. By 1750, this state of affairs was well on the way to being reversed. The essential question to be posed then is: "Why did this reversal take place?" and "What prompted European exploration and colonization from 1450 to the 1660s?"

Periodization: European Expansion—1420 to 1820

The period of European expansion may be divided into two stages: an early period of European exploration, discovery, initial conquest and settlement beginning as early as 1420 and a period of colonial trade rivalries that dated from the mid-1660s to perhaps 1820.

What motivated European exploration, discovery, conquest and settlement before the 1660s? There are a number of theories that have been proposed to explain the timing of Europeans' early expansion.

1. **A "Great Man" Theory**

   Once it was common to offer as explanation for European expansion a theory that stressed the heroic efforts of explorers (**Columbus, Vasco da Gama, Henry Hudson, etc.**), conquistadors (**Hernán Cortés, Francisco Pizarro, etc.**), and leaders (**Ferdinand and Isabella, Prince Henry the Navigator, etc.**).

2. **Political Causation: European State Rivalries**

   An important explanation often given for why Europe succeeded on the global stage after 1450 was that the development of the European state system characterized intense competition between rival states of relatively equal military and economic power. Because no single European state could gain enough advantage to create a pan-European empire, and the competition within Europe was ruthless, European states developed efficient bureaucratic and military machines capable of exerting power outside of Europe, primarily in the Americas before 1750 and in Africa and Asia after 1750. A factor driving European expansion was the inexhaustible need for new sources of revenue to pay for the costs of militaries that had adopted gunpowder weaponry and required expensive mercenary armies.

3. **Technological Determinism**

   Another explanation concentrates on technological advance. Europe benefited from the adoption and adaptation of a number of technologies of Asian origin that would prove critical to European expansion. **Gunpowder**, cannons, and, to a lesser degree, small arms gave European explorers and conquerors insurmountable advantages in their encounters with Amerindians. The **caravel**, a small, maneuverable vessel developed in the 1450s, utilized the **lateen sail** (originating in the Indian Ocean) and **square-rigged sails**. The triangular lateen sail allowed vessels to sail close to the wind and tack into the wind, while the square-rigged sails gave the vessels great speed when sailing with the wind. The caravel was the oceangoing vessel that explored the Americas and took Vasco da Gama around the Cape of Good Hope to India. Other advances included the compass and astrolabe. One could also point to the widespread dissemination of knowledge as a result of the **printing press** as a factor in encouraging exploration.

4. Cultural Causation (the Renaissance and Reformation)

Cultural explanations often relate European expansion to European curiosity about the world fostered by humanistic drive to challenge ancient truths and push the boundaries of received wisdom. Humanists were also more concerned with this world than the next. It is no surprise that many of the early explorers came from the Italian peninsula, the home of the Renaissance. **Prince Henry "the Navigator" of Portugal (1394–1460 CE)** also exemplified this spirit. He brought together mapmakers, astronomers, mathematicians, and explorers, and funded expeditions to explore the coasts of Africa. He was interested of course in commodities that were known to come from West Africa (gold, ivory, and later slaves). He also hoped to find a route to India around Africa's Cape of Good Hope. But, in part, his and other explorers' motives included a scientific interest. European states also were motivated by religious impulses, particularly after the onset of the Reformation as Catholics and Protestants alike sought allies and increases in numbers of adherents. Jesuit priests accompanied many Spanish expeditions. The **Kingdom of the Kongo**, in western Central Africa, accepted Portuguese missionaries, and its ruler and chief nobles converted to Roman Catholicism in 1491. Part of the drive to discover was motivated by religious impulses.

5. Rivalry with the Islamic World

Much of Europe's initial expansion was carried out in response to feelings of inferiority and dependence upon the Islamic world. Muslim superiority in evidence with the Ottoman conquest of Constantinople prompted Western Europeans to long for new trade routes that would lead directly to China and India without depending on Muslim traders.

Portugal under the leadership of Prince Henry the Navigator began sponsoring voyages down the coast of Africa in the early 1400s. Henry was primarily interested in identifying the source of the gold that had been traded across the Sahara for centuries. By 1452, Portuguese ships had begun trading for gold mined in West Africa. By 1490, **Bartolomeu Dias** had reached the southern tip of Africa; in 1498, **Vasco da Gama** had sailed to India.

Christopher Columbus, a Genoan sailing under the Spanish flag, similarly in search of trade routes to the Indies, sailed westward across the Atlantic, "discovering" the Americas. The first voyage in 1492 was largely a fact-finding mission, but in 1494 Columbus returned with 17 ships and a force of nearly 1,250 soldiers. His intent was to colonize in the Caribbean islands and trade for precious metals or enslave Indians to mine for gold. Other Spanish explorers then laid claims to much of the rest of South and Central America for "New Spain" in the process conquering the Aztecs, Incas, and many other indigenous populations.

French, Dutch, and English explorers and colonizers followed suit, rapidly laying claim to much of the American coastline. Often these explorers were as interested in plundering the Spanish fleets bearing gold and silver from mines in Mexico and Bolivia as they were in establishing permanent settlements.

CHAPTER
3

Effects of European Expansion

1. Spread of Epidemic Disease

One immediate consequence of European arrival in the Americas was the spread of diseases from Afro-Eurasia. Swine flu, measles, smallpox, the Bubonic Plague, chickenpox, and many other diseases for which Amerindians had no natural immunities wiped out millions of Native Americans. Estimates of mortality range from 50 to 80 percent of the population.

2. The Columbian Exchange

Corn (maize), potatoes, tomatoes, squash, tobacco, chili peppers, avocados, beans, and manioc were only a few of the New World crops that spread widely in the Eastern Hemisphere after 1492. Some of these would have immediate impacts on the demography of the Old World. Potatoes and corn provided important new sources of calories in China and later in northern Europe. Potatoes could be grown on smaller plots, permitting earlier marriage and longer fertile life spans for women. This had a positive impact on populations across the Old World.

Old World plants and animals also were transmitted to the New World. The European honeybee, pigs, sheep, cattle, horses, and many other animals were introduced to the Americas. Coffee, sugar, bananas, apples, and many other Old World crops were soon being cultivated in the New World.

3. The Atlantic Slave Trade

Portuguese traders and explorers first began sailing along the coast of Africa in the early 1400s. Initially, they sought gold, spices, ivory, and other commodities. The first African slaves imported into Europe arrived in 1441 CE. When the Spanish and Portuguese began to develop sugar plantations the demand for slaves increased. Once sugar production began in earnest in Brazil and the Caribbean islands, between 1550 and 1600, the slave trade became the dominant commerce in the Atlantic. Between 1500 and 1850, a total of perhaps 12.5 million Africans were exported to the Americas. Brazil received the largest proportion, perhaps 5 million; the combined Caribbean colonies of the British, French, Dutch, and Danish imported a comparable number. The British colonies in North America received only 500,000. The Atlantic slave trade had a detrimental effect on the demography of Africa. By 1850, the regions in West Africa most affected by the slave trade had half the population they might have had there been no slave trade.

Competency 003 Descriptive Statement E. The beginning teacher analyzes the impact of political, economic and cultural imperialism (e.g., conquest of the Aztec, expansion of the Ottoman Empire) on both colonizers and the colonized.

Key Question

Underlying this descriptive statement, and the expectation outlined in the TEKS, is a comparison between western European exploration and colonization and the impact of the Ottoman Empire's own contemporaneous expansion.

Ottoman Expansion

The Ottomans descended from many Turkic-speaking populations that had migrated from central Asia and served the Arab and Persian rulers as soldiers and administrators. After the Mongol invasion of Southwest Asia in 1243 CE, the Ottomans, named after one of their early leaders, Osman, established a state in Anatolia in modern Turkey. The Ottomans alternately fought and allied with the Byzantine Empire over the course of the next two centuries while also expanding into the Balkans. In 1453, led by **Mehmed II "the Conqueror" (r. 1444–1481 CE)**, Ottoman armies using gunpowder technologies and siege cannons breached the defenses of Constantinople and brought an end to the Byzantine Empire's last hold on power. In this regard, the Ottomans employed the same gunpowder weaponry and military organization to defeat their enemies as would the Conquistadors in Central America. After a paroxysm of looting, Mehmed II set about rebuilding the city now renamed Istanbul as a Muslim capital. The **Saint Sophia Cathedral** was transformed into one of the most magnificent mosques in the Islamic world. The city's defensive perimeter was rebuilt, its aqueducts and fountains refurbished, and its many bazaars reopened.

Istanbul soon began to attract merchant ships from throughout the Mediterranean and Black Sea, becoming the primary conduit of Afro-Eurasian trade into western Europe. Spices from the Indies, ivory and slaves from Africa, slaves from central Europe, Persian carpets, coffee from Ethiopia and Yemen, and silks and porcelain from China could all be found in Istanbul's markets.

Ottoman expansion relied on military conquest and enslavement, but it was also a new society that welcomed converts and offered them opportunities for advancement. It also succeeded by rewarding Islamization and encouraging widespread use of the Turkish language. By 1550, the Ottoman Empire incorporated most of the land surrounding the eastern Mediterranean, reaching as far west in North Africa as contemporary Algeria. It included Egypt, the western coast of the Arabian Peninsula, and the Tigris-Euphrates River Valley. Most of the Black Sea coastline, including the Crimean Peninsula were incorporated into the empire. The Ottoman Empire threatened Europe directly from the 16th to the 18th century, besieging Vienna in 1529 and again in 1683. In 1571, Ottoman naval dominance of the eastern Mediterranean was ended when its fleet was defeated at the **Battle of Lepanto**, one of the most decisive sea battles in world history. It nonetheless remained the dominant power in the eastern Mediterranean until the early 19th century. It would last until 1923, finally collapsing in the aftermath of World War I.

COMPETENCY 004 (WORLD HISTORY FROM 1750 TO THE PRESENT)

The teacher understands significant historical events and developments in world history from 1750 to the present.

> **Competency 004 Descriptive Statement A.** The beginning teacher demonstrates knowledge of developments, events, issues, and interactions that shaped the development of world civilizations from 1750 CE to the present (e.g., the Great Depression, the Holocaust, decolonization).

Key Question

This descriptive statement, though it appears to demand an encyclopedic knowledge of "events, issues, and interactions" from 1750 to the present, is really asking the test-taker to support an assessment of how the modern period should be defined. The underlying question can be summarized as follows: Is the modern period defined primarily by such events as the political liberalization associated with the Enlightenment and Atlantic Revolutions and the technological and scientific improvements of industrialization? Or, conversely: Are the modern centuries characterized principally by the rise of nationalist and totalitarian governments, such as Nazi Germany or Stalinist Russia; gross human rights violations from the Reign of Terror in the French Revolution to the Holocaust and the Rwandan Genocide; and failings of industrial economies, as occurred in the Great Depression? For the test-taker, this is an open question. In order to effectively answer the questions likely to be asked on the TExES Social Studies 7–12 Test, you will need to marshal the facts and information given below.

Periodization: Modern Period—1750 to the Present

The modern period in World History dates from 1750 CE to the present. To understand the modern centuries, it is best to divide them into three more manageable periods, as outlined below.

The Long 19th Century—Revolution, Nationalism, and Imperialism

Three principal themes defined the "long 19th century" from 1750 to 1914: (1) industrialization; (2) political reform movements that overturned monarchical governments across the world and established new governments often founded on Enlightenment principles; and (3) European imperialism that both provided raw materials and markets for the new industrial economies of Europe and America, and spread Western cultural and political values.

The Short 20th Century—Crises of Liberalism and Capitalism

During the "short 20th century" from 1914 to 1989, two global wars undermined faith in the liberal institutions established in the previous century; a worldwide economic crisis shook confidence in the ability of free-market institutions to meet basic needs and provide for equitable distribution of resources; African, Asian, and Latin American nations sought successfully to regain their political and economic independence from Europe; and the Soviet Union offered an alternative to the Western model of political liberalism and free-market capitalism.

The Post–Cold War World

Since 1989 and the end of the Cold War's bipolar confrontation between the Soviet Union and the United States, two conflicting trends have largely defined the political and economic environment. The first has been a massive acceleration of economic integration and demographic mobility made possible by new mass-communication technologies, like the Internet, and by speedy means of transportation. This global economic integration has also been facilitated by international institutions and liberal global trade policies. These trends have been collectively described as globalization. Countering these globalizing trends have been the return of ethnic nationalism (Hutu power, Serbian nationalism, Russian and other eastern European nationalism) and religious fundamentalism.

> **Competency 004 Descriptive Statement B.** The beginning teacher analyzes the causes and effects of major political revolutions and independence movements of the 18th through the 20th centuries (e.g., the American Revolution, the French Revolution, Napoleon, Simón Bolívar, Latin American wars of independence, Russian Revolution).

> **Key Question**
>
> How did the Atlantic Revolutions (the American Revolution, French Revolution, and Latin American Wars of Independence) differ from one another, and how did these "liberal" revolutions differ from the radical Marxist revolution in Russia (and by implication China and Vietnam)?

Periodization: First Wave of "Liberal" Revolutions and Independence Movements—1750 to 1825

The first wave of "liberal" revolutions and independence movements, influenced most clearly by the ideals of the Enlightenment, took place between 1750 and 1825 CE. These political revolutions are often juxtaposed to the revolutionary movements in Europe and elsewhere after 1830 CE. Revolutionary movements after 1830 more often exhibited the influence of Marxist criticisms of capitalism.

Atlantic Revolutions

Atlantic revolutions, though on occasion exhibiting some evidence of the social leveling called for in later revolutions and independence movements, did not challenge property rights and social inequalities to the degree that took place in European and anti-imperialist revolutions after 1830. With varying degrees of success these revolutions instituted protections for property holders and established constitutionally limited representative governments.

American Revolution (1775–1783)

The first world region to give expression to these revolutionary ideals were the British North American colonies that would become the United States of America. Britain's Atlantic colonies rebelled in 1775 primarily in response to Britain's effort to impose new taxes and trade regulations. Prior to the 1760s, the British government had granted its colonies in North America great latitude. The debt crisis triggered by Britain's global struggle with France led Britain's parliamentary leaders to impose new taxes and trade controls on their colonies. Britain's tightening of administrative control and increased taxation did not apply only to the 13 North American colonies; but represented a new phase in Great Britain's extension of its imperial authority. These measures infuriated many of the American colonists and encouraged the spread of an American rather than an English identity. The ideas of the Enlightenment—popular sovereignty, natural rights, consent of the governed, the right to revolt, constitutionalism—provided an easily accessible language with which to resist encroaching British power. Enlightenment ideals featured prominently in American founding documents like the Declaration of Independence, the United States Constitution and its Bill of Rights.

A social revolution accompanied this independence movement. American colonial society, even before the Revolution, had exhibited greater democratic tendencies than did European societies of the same period. With independence, the new nation-state began to gradually expand political participation and extend the principles of equality announced in the Declaration of Independence to all white men. Though the United States during the 19th century would be the world's most democratic nation, extending civil rights to all adult white males, the expansion of democracy did not at that point extend to slaves, African Americans, or women.

The American Revolution would inspire revolutionaries from 19th-century Latin America to 20th-century Vietnam. The U.S. Constitution would likewise offer a model for later efforts to establish governments based on Enlightenment principles.

French Revolution (1789–1799)

The inspiration of the American Revolution, which the French monarchy supported, soon spread to France. The ideals expressed in the American Declaration of Independence invigorated revolutionaries across the Atlantic. French aristocrats, urban merchants, and professionals were already agitating for reforms that would restrain a monarchy that claimed absolute authority.

French peasants also demanded land reform and reductions in their tax burden. But the monarchy's indebtedness, much of it accumulated in support of the American revolutionaries, added to a series of bad harvests, ultimately forced **Louis XVI (r. 1774–1792 CE)** to negotiate reforms in exchange for new loans or sources of revenue. The notables called to Versailles as a representative body known as the **Estates General** (a long-dormant parliament) declared itself the representative of the nation and began to demand greater reforms than the king had anticipated. When it appeared that the king was readying to disband the Estates and use force to disburse them, the Parisian **sans-culottes,** or working poor, rose in support, famously storming the **Bastille**, a symbol of royal authority. The revolutionaries at first established constitutional limitations on the monarchy and then in 1792 abolished it altogether, vesting sovereignty in successive national legislative bodies. Louis XVI and Queen Marie Antoinette were executed. The violent turn of the French Revolution, most notably in the **Reign of Terror**, saw many French nobles and others guillotined, as various factions among the revolutionaries struggled for power. The French Revolution also resulted in a series of wars with neighboring powers as French revolutionaries endeavored to protect the gains of the revolution from European kingdoms fearful that revolution and regicide might infect their populace.

Napoleon Bonaparte

The French Revolution's influence spread largely as a result of conquest carried out under the leadership of **Napoleon Bonaparte (r. 1799–1814 CE)**. Napoleon is often credited with both bringing an end to the instability of the revolution and contributing to the spread of revolutionary principles. In 1799, Napoleon established a military dictatorship and restrained the democratic impulses of the revolution. He maintained a number of features of the revolution: its secular legal system, guarantees of religious liberty, and a meritocratic military and bureaucracy. Between 1799 and 1812, Napoleon extended France's territorial boundaries and made dependent states out of many of France's neighbors. French invasion and Napoleonic reforms of European governments would contribute to nationalistic reactions and the desire for greater national unity.

Haitian Revolution (1791–1804)

The Haitian Revolution was one direct result of the French Revolution. Haiti, a French colony, had in the 18th century been the richest colony in the world, producing nearly 40 percent of the world's sugar and half of the world's coffee. The enslaved population vastly outnumbered the island's white population and handful of free people of color. Influenced by the rhetoric of the French revolutionaries and under the impression that the king had already declared the end of slavery, Haitian slaves in 1791 rose in rebellion, burning plantations and killing their former owners. The former slave **Toussaint Louverture** successfully led the Haitian revolutionaries in creating their own independent state and in defending it from successive efforts by French and other European powers to reestablish control over the island. In 1804, the Haitians formally declared their independence. This is the only completely successful slave revolt in history.

Latin American Wars of Independence (1810–1825)

The last of the Atlantic Revolutions took place across Spain and Portugal's Latin American colonies. The French Revolution played an important role in the timing of the Latin American independence movements. Revolutionary and Napoleonic warfare in the Iberian Peninsula destabilized the Portuguese and Spanish governments, making it difficult for the Portuguese and Spanish monarchy to function effectively in New Spain and Brazil. As in North America and Europe, Enlightenment political ideas provided the rhetoric of revolution, though the more radical example of the French Revolution—anti-clericalism, regicide, and egalitarianism—did not have the same appeal in Latin America. In part, this reflected the prominence of the Creole elites (Spaniards born in the Americas) in these independence movements. American-born Spaniards had, over the course of the 18th century, bridled at the monopoly of power maintained by the Spanish monarchy and by *peninsulares,* or Spanish-born administrators. The Spanish colonies had never been granted the autonomy that the British North American colonies had been given. As a result, the Creole population took the leadership in the independence movement without encouraging the radical restructuring of Latin American society that took place over the course of the French Revolution. Moreover, the outcome of the Haitian Revolution, for Creole populations, particularly in the Caribbean, was an outcome to be avoided. The specter of slave rebellion made Latin American elites hesitant to engage in political experimentation. One consequence of this conservativism was a weakening of republican institutions in many of the Spanish territories that gained their independence. For example, the rebellion against Spanish control that erupted in Mexico in 1810 divided over the issues of land reform and legal and social equality for Indians and mestizos. Though Mexico managed to successfully throw off Spanish rule, it struggled to secure a republican form of government during its first century of independence. While the thirteen British colonies in North America had managed to set aside their differences and establish a unified government, regional differences and political power struggles resulted in the proliferation of new nation-states in Latin America. There would be no United States of Latin America.

Simón Bolívar

Perhaps the most noted figure among Latin American revolutionaries was Simón Bolívar. In 1810, Bolívar, a wealthy Creole, took the leadership of a revolt against the Spanish centered in Caracas, Venezuela. His military skill and commitment to independence led contemporaries to liken him to George Washington. Between 1817 and 1822, Bolívar commanded his armies to victories in Venezuela, Colombia, and Ecuador. Bolívar's aspiration was to establish a united nation-state like that developing in the United States. By 1830, Venezuela, Colombia, and Ecuador were united in a nation called *Gran Colombia*. The hope of even this unification was unrealized in the end.

Russian Revolution (1917)

The Russian Revolution began as a liberal reform movement akin to those in France and the United States. It overthrew an established monarchy and threatened status-based social hierarchies.

Like the Atlantic Revolutions, Enlightenment ideas provided some of the inspiration for the reform movements. Russia, however, at the beginning of the 20th century, lagged behind Western Europe in a number of important ways. Serfdom had only been outlawed in 1861. In the 1890s Russia had begun to encourage industrialization, largely fostered by state intervention and foreign investment, which had by the early 20th century begun to pay dividends, though primarily in Russia's few large cities. Educated elites and industrial workers began to demand greater power to reflect their increased economic role in the country. A small number of these reform-minded Russians gravitated towards Marxist socialism. When World War I broke out, Russia was woefully unprepared, and soon the monarchy was increasingly viewed as ineffective.

The Russian Revolution of 1917 was in fact two separate revolutions. The first was a liberal revolution in the same vein as the earlier Atlantic Revolutions, seeking modest reforms that secured representative institutions, voting rights, and legal protections similar to those experienced by most western Europeans. A second revolution called the **October Revolution** followed immediately on the heels of the earlier "February Revolution." This revolution was led by the **Bolshevik Party**, a Marxist-Leninist political party aligned with the industrial working classes of Russia's largest cities. Promising "Bread, Peace, and Land" the Bolsheviks promised an end to participation in World War I, welfare for the urban poor, and land reform for the Russian peasantry. Following a lengthy civil war, the Bolsheviks established the first Communist nation in world history.

> **Competency 004 Descriptive Statement C.** The beginning teacher understands the impact of political, economic, and cultural expansion (e.g., rise of the British Empire, Japanese imperialism).

Key Question

 How did imperial expansionism of industrializing nations differ from the imperial expansion of maritime empires of the early modern period? What were key turning points in the expansion of colonial empires in the 19th century?

Periodization: Industrialization and Global Integration—1750 to 1914

In the early modern period, most European empires were either trading post or maritime empires (like the Dutch in Indonesia or the British at the Cape of Good Hope) or settler colonies like British North America, or plantation-based colonies like those in the Caribbean. In the 19th century, particularly after the end of the slave trade in 1807, colonial expansion shifted from a mercantilist to an industrializing objective.

European imperialism between 1750 and 1914 is divided into two distinct phases: before the **Indian Rebellion of 1857** (sometimes known as the **Sepoy Mutiny**) and afterwards. The former phase was marked by indirect control of colonial empires carried out by state-sponsored companies and the latter by direct control of colonies by European governments. The latter period also featured what has been characterized as a "scramble" for colonies, most evident in efforts to carve up Africa.

European Imperialism

Before the 18th century, Portugal, Spain, the Netherlands, England, and France established trading-post empires along the coasts of Africa and Asia, while creating settler colonies in the Americas. In many cases, these trading-post empires were controlled by state-sponsored corporations (like the Dutch East India Company or the British East India Company). Additionally, "settler colonies" populated by immigrants from the colonizing power were established in the Americas (and in Australia, New Zealand, and South Africa) by the countries of Spain, Portugal, the Netherlands, France, and England. As we have seen, the Atlantic Revolutions resulted in many of these "settler colonies" establishing their independence from their European power.

Before 1857, in most of Africa and Asia (with the exception of South Africa, Australia, and New Zealand), European empire-building continued to be carried out by state-sponsored corporations like the British East India Company and the Dutch East India Company. These quasi-independent businesses relied on state support and often had state powers (armies for example), but operated as profit-seeking, joint-stock companies. Competition among European nations was largely carried out by proxy as these private companies competed with one another. After the Indian Rebellion of 1857, a new era of direct European control and competition developed as European nations competed directly to control large territories of Africa and Asia, or in the case of China, to create "spheres of influence" through unequal treaties enforced through gunboat diplomacy.

Perhaps the most notable example of the new European imperialism after 1857 was the so-called **"Scramble for Africa"** when leading European nations divided up nearly all of Africa into colonial territories claimed by Britain, France, Germany, Belgium, Portugal, Spain, and Italy. This scramble was largely driven by European patriotic fervor and nationalistic rivalries. Key to European success in dividing up Africa after nearly 400 years of trade and cross-cultural interaction were three technologies: **quinine,** which made it possible for Europeans to reduce mortality caused by malaria; **the maxim gun**, or early machine gun, which made it possible for small numbers of European soldiers to defeat much larger armies with small-arms and primitive weaponry; and **railroads,** which made it possible to penetrate more deeply into Africa. Each of these advantages were products of Europe's Industrial Revolution.

The colonies established in the 19th century were seen as necessary sources for raw materials needed by European factories, and as captive markets for the manufacturing products and consumer items produced in the "metropole," or mother country. Often the unequal economic and political relationships established between colony and metropole were justified by European racial and cultural categories that characterized the colonized peoples as racially and culturally inferior.

British Empire

The British Empire in the 19th century extended across the globe. It was often said that "the Sun never sets on the British Empire." The British Empire was composed of settler colonies with large European populations, like Australia, New Zealand, and Canada; tropical dependencies where a small administration of Englishmen oversaw large populations of non-Western peoples; and trading cities where the English maintained favored, or even monopoly, status.

The 19th-century British empire was built through a variety of diplomatic and military efforts. Following the 1808 abolition of the Atlantic slave trade, British naval vessels patrolled the world's oceans and gained control of a number of forts and ports along the coast of Africa.

In India, called the "Jewel of the Crown" by British imperialists, the British had defeated the French and regional Indian states in the 18th century, gaining commercial and military control of much of northeastern India for the British East India Company. Between 1757 and 1857, the company dominated large areas of India until the Indian Revolt of 1857.

In China, British ironclad gunboats in the **Opium Wars (1840–1842 CE)** coerced the Qing dynasty to open up treaty ports to British commerce, including vast quantities of opium that British exported from territories controlled by the British East India Company.

Britain before the 1850s was largely unable to penetrate Africa and had only trading posts, coaling stations, and military forts on the coast of Africa, preferring to engage in trade with local African rulers. This changed as a result of competition with the French who began in the mid-19th century to take a greater interest in expansion into Africa. British missionaries such as **David Livingstone** and explorers like **Sir Richard Burton** began to explore Africa. Soon, British colonial troops and expeditions began to move up the Nile and Niger rivers into Africa, and to make their way into southern and eastern Africa.

The British governed their other colonies through a mix of direct and indirect measures. In each of these colonies, notions of **white racial supremacy** justified European control of local administration. Like most European colonial governments, the British employed a variety of coercive measures to encourage greater production of raw materials and export production by colonial subjects. Head and hut taxes were imposed, which could only be paid in commodities such as coffee, tea, palm nuts, rubber, or other crops valued by British exporters. The British were not as brutal in this regard as the Belgians in the Belgian Congo, where villagers who didn't meet certain quotas had their hands cut off.

The British Empire after World War I experienced a number of stresses that ultimately led to its dismemberment. The first territories to gain independence were the settler colonies that remained "Dominions" of the British Empire, swearing loyalty to the monarchy but remaining largely independent politically. Beginning in 1948 with the Indian independence movement led by **Mohandas K. Gandhi**, Britain's other imperial possessions began to separate from the empire.

Japanese Imperialism

In 1853, a squadron of American ships sailed into Tokyo harbor threatening war if Japan didn't open up its trade to American commerce. Prior to 1853, Japan had kept tight control over all interaction between the island nation and the outside world. By 1868, however, Japan had begun to adopt Western-style industrialization and political reforms. After the humiliation of 1853, Japan was able to avoid being carved up and subjected to European and American control like most of its neighbors. Instead, the Japanese embarked on their own imperial expansion. Wars against China and Russia in the late 19th and early 20th centuries made it clear that it was a formidable military power. It gained control of Taiwan, Korea, and parts of Manchuria. It built up a formidable navy to project its power. Japan became a model for other Asians, though it was difficult for Japan's neighbors to replicate its experience. In the 1930s and 1940s, Japanese imperialism resulted in brutal wars in China, and the conquest of much of Southeast Asia. Japanese nationalists encouraged the idea that Japan was merely liberating Asians from a history of European control.

> **Competency 004 Descriptive Statement D.** The beginning teacher analyzes the causes and effects of the Industrial Revolution.

Key Question

As the reference to the relevant TEKS makes clear, this descriptive statement prompts questions about the relationship between science, free market economic mechanisms, and technological innovation. The TEKS make clear that the Industrial Revolution is to be understood primarily as: a) an outgrowth of the Scientific Revolution; b) driven by technological developments initiated in the "leading sector industries" of textiles, steam power, and iron production; and c) a complex of social and economic advancements made possible by free market economic conditions.

Periodization: Industrial Revolution—1750 to 1914

The Industrial Revolution is often divided into the First Industrial Revolution and the Second Industrial Revolution.

The First Industrial Revolution (1750–1850)

The first Industrial Revolution, centered in Great Britain, developed around innovation in the textile, iron, and transportation industries; the invention of steam-powered machinery; and the beginnings of factory labor in small firms, usually relying on individual ownership or partnerships.

The Second Industrial Revolution (1850–1914)

The second Industrial Revolution spread to the European continent (most notably northern France, Belgium, and Germany). as well as to the United States and Japan. New industries emerged (for example, the chemical and steel industries), and old industries were transformed by industrial production techniques. Coal-driven steam power still predominated, but electricity and petroleum contributed new sources of energy. Additionally, rather than small family-owned firms or limited partnerships, the second Industrial Revolution was characterized by much larger firms, or corporations, capitalized through sales of stock or other financial instruments. The end date of 1914 does not suggest conclusion in the processes of innovation and economic growth unleashed by the Industrial Revolution. Instead, the outbreak of World War I in 1914 is often seen as the beginning of a new era in global relations marked less by the potential for social and economic progress brought about by industrialization than by conflict linked to rising nationalism and imperialistic competition for territory and resources.

Causes of the Industrial Revolution, or "Why England?"

There are many complex explanations for the emergence of industrialization in Europe. For the purposes of the TExES Social Studies 7–12 exam, your focus should be on why the Industrial Revolution began where and when it did: in England after 1750. The answer is complex but usually answered by reference to the following five variables:

1. **Accessible Mineral Resources:** England had abundant and easily accessible reserves of coal and iron.

2. **Colonial Capital and Markets:** England's colonial empire provided an infusion of capital—from profits made in the interlocking trades in sugar, slaves, tobacco, tea, opium, and other colonial products—that were reinvested in England's leading sector industries. England's colonial empire also provided calories and raw materials that encouraged population growth and enabled its own labor-force to be redirected from agriculture to industry. England's colonial empire also served as a market for English manufactured goods.

3. **Property Rights and Protections:** The "Glorious Revolution" of 1688 freed entrepreneurs and inventors to profit from a political environment that encouraged entrepreneurial risk-taking. More reliable tax rates, legal protections for property rights, and policies that protected entrepreneurs encouraged investment. British manufacturers were protected from external competitors by a high tariff regime.

4. **Practical Scientific Knowledge:** Scientists in England engaged practical and mechanical problems, disseminating new knowledge in ways that promoted technological innovation. Early benefits from the application of scientific knowledge to agriculture (scientific breeding, fertilizers, crop rotation) reduced the demand for agricultural laborers and forced many landless agricultural workers to seek factory labor.

5. **Expanding Transportation Networks:** Ever-tightening networks of communication across Great Britain and the British empire (roads, canals, railroads, telegraph, etc.) contributed to growing trade and specialization. These networks encouraged the flow of raw materials and consumer goods, as well as information and capital.

Textiles

Before 1700, European weavers and cloth merchants primarily produced woolens and linen textiles. French, English, Dutch, and German manufacturers struggled to compete in quality and price with high-value Chinese silks and Indian cottons. A number of technological innovations improved efficiencies and made European textiles price competitive. Each successive innovation both created new bottlenecks and spurred further innovation. For example, before the invention of the **"flying shuttle"** in 1733, three or four spinners worked to provide thread for one weaver. The flying shuttle doubled weavers' speed, increasing incentives for innovation in spinning. In 1764, James Hargreaves invented the **spinning jenny**, a spinning wheel capable of spinning eight threads at once. Spinning was further improved with the **water frame**, which used water power to spin thread. In 1771, Richard Arkwright installed his water frame in what would be one of the first factories to process cotton from raw material to finished thread. The **power loom**, designed in 1784, mechanized the weaving process, making handloom weavers obsolete, while increasing output and lowering prices for mass-produced cloth. A final piece of the puzzle was the **cotton gin,** invented in 1793. It made possible the expansion of cotton production in the American South, which supplied the vast majority of England's mills with their raw materials.

Factory Organization

Prior to the Industrial Revolution, most manufacturing in Europe was done by skilled craftsmen working in their own shops or in what has been variously called the "putting out system," or "cottage industry." Before the second half of the 18th century, artisanal production was heavily regulated by the guild system. In the 17th century, merchants interested in breaking free of this system began to rely on rural households to carry out increasingly varied manufacturing tasks. Each household had an individual role in the production process, in effect creating a dispersed assembly line. With the introduction of water and then steam power to textile production, the first factories were established bringing all the processes once disbursed to households under one roof. The modern factory depends upon significant capital investment, substantial technological inputs, and a workforce disciplined to the rigors of a factory regimen.

Iron, Coal, and Steam

A second cluster of inventions united the harnessing of fossil fuels, improvements in iron metallurgy, and mechanization. The use of fossil fuels freed human beings from reliance on their own or draft animal's muscle power. Peat, wood, or charcoal had been used for millennia across the world to provide warmth, process foodstuffs, or refine sugar, brew beer, or make bricks. But, these fuels provided limited reserves of energy. By comparison, coal allowed human beings to tap into much greater stocks of stored energy. Coal's potential uses had been known for some time. Coal deposits along the coasts of England, northern France, Belgium, and the Ruhr Valley in Germany provided an important source of energy for the Industrial Revolution. Britain would be the first to take advantage of these reserves, in part because deforestation had by the end of the Middle Ages so reduced fuel sources. In the 18th century, demand for coal in England increased with the discovery in 1709 that a byproduct of coal—coke—could be used to smelt iron. Coal consumption then increased, fueling greater iron production than would have been possible relying on charcoal. Increased demand for coal meant that deeper seams of coal had to be accessed. To pump groundwater from these deeper mines, colliers employed rudimentary coal-fired steam engines, using the virtually free coal available at the mines' pitheads. The Scottish inventor **James Watt (1736–1819 CE)** in 1781 improved on existing steam-powered pumps, designing a machine that vastly increased steam engines' power and efficiency. With reductions in coal prices it soon became practical to employ coal and steam engines in transportation and in many other industries. Increased railroad mileage in turn necessitated more iron and steel production, and further coal mining. As the technologies of the First Industrial Revolution spread, Scotland, Germany, northern France, Belgium, and later the northeastern United States, followed the same trajectory of industrial development.

The Second Industrial Revolution: Coal, Steel, Railways and Telegraphs, Chemicals and Electricity

Between 1850 and 1914, the center of gravity of the industrial world shifted from Great Britain to Germany and the United States. This shift was accompanied by increased importance of new growth sectors in steel, chemicals, communication, electricity, machinery, and railway production. And, where the First Industrial Revolution took place in relatively small family-owned firms or partnerships, the Second Industrial Revolution relied on giant corporations, whose advantages derived from significant economies of scale. These giant corporations required investment banking, widespread sales of stock, and other financial instruments to generate the capital needed. Such large corporations also depended on new management techniques that required a whole new "middle class" of white-collar professionals and managers to oversee operations.

Science and the Industrial Revolution

The TEKS ask students to "explain how 17th and 18th century European scientific advancements led to the Industrial Revolution." The connection between the Scientific Revolution and the Industrial Revolution's early technological developments, however, is not immediately apparent. Most inventors were artisans and craftsmen and not scientists. Neither did these inventors or entrepreneurs have great access to scientific knowledge, which was in any case, less than practical.

Scientific discoveries contributed to industrial growth first in agriculture. In the 18th century, landowners in England and elsewhere in Europe began to employ new farming methods and applied scientific methods to improvements in agriculture. Among these methods was a new method of crop-rotation where turnips, clover, or other cover crops were planted in rotation to return nitrogen to the soil. New, more efficient plows and other farm implements were introduced. Animal manure, green manure, and even human waste were collected to fertilize worn soils. Later, chemically-synthesized fertilizers were developed. Selective livestock breeding was used to improve animal stock, increasing wool or meat yields. As a result of new scientific methods, agricultural output in Europe (most notably in England and northern Europe) grew faster than population size, reducing the need for agricultural workers and making surplus farm workers available for industrial production.

Science did play a role in industrialization in Great Britain. British scientists emphasized an empirical approach to practical problems that relied on observation, experimentation, careful measurement and mechanical innovation. The **British Royal Society**, founded in 1660, was established to promote "useful knowledge" and did so by widely disseminating scientific discoveries that entrepreneurs and inventors could employ. Continental Europeans and American soon followed suit with the establishment of scientific societies, magazines and journals that spread scientific and practical knowledge, and after 1850 the professionalization of engineering as a career. The role of science was most clearly seen in the Second Industrial Revolution. Scientists and engineers began to systematize invention in research labs and corporations began to actively fund research and development. Universities in Germany and the United States also began to take lead roles in scientific discovery, applying those scientific discoveries to practical and technical problems.

> **Competency 004 Descriptive Statement E.** The beginning teacher demonstrates knowledge of the impact of totalitarianism in the 20th century (e.g., fascist Italy, Nazi Germany, Soviet Union).

Key Question

The TEKS indicate that totalitarianism in the 20th century should be understood as a key cause of World War II, as well as an impact of that war.

Periodization: The Rise of Totalitarian States—1917–1991)

Totalitarian states developed across the globe in response to the crisis of confidence in democratic institutions following World War I and in reaction to the failure of global free-market institutions to resolve the economic crises of hyper-inflation in Germany in the 1920s and the worldwide depression of the 1930s.

Between 1919 and 1945 a new political ideology known as **fascism** spread across Europe, Asia, and Latin America. With the surrender of Nazi Germany and Nationalist Japan in 1945, this ideology lost its credibility across most of the world. Soviet-style Communism represented a second response to the crises of the 1920s and 1930s. Soviet Communism, however, lasted through most of the 20th century as an alternative to the West's democratic governments and free-market economic system. Communism would remain a challenge to the West until the collapse of the Soviet Union in 1991.

Totalitarianism

Totalitarianism is a system of government that vests all decision-making power in the hands of a supreme political body or individual dictator and subjects all aspects of individual life to the state, leaving no aspect of life in the hands of private decision-makers. Individual liberty and/or individual property rights are subordinated to the needs of the state. In the 20th century, totalitarianism has been most often associated with the rise of fascism in Italy, National Socialism in Germany, and Communism in the Soviet Union and China.

Fascism in Italy

Fascism gained its first successes in Italy. Italy had only been a unified state since 1870; representative institutions were still in their infancy. The nation was also divided by both class and regional rivalries. Unemployed veterans of World War I and nationalists unhappy with the terms of the Treaty of Versailles nursed grievances that would be exploited by fascist leaders. The economic instability following World War I resulted in a wave of strikes and social unrest led by the communist and socialist parties and trade union organizers. This social environment led many middle and working-class Italians to turn to a strong man to restore order. Fascist governments called for the creation of a "corporate" economy in which productive property remained privately held but management and labor worked together to promote the interests of the Italian nation-state.

Benito Mussolini (1883–1945)

Benito Mussolini was a former journalist and socialist with a charismatic presence who promised to make Italy great again and afforded the international respect it deserved. He promised to overcome partisan political division and rebuild the nation's economy. Mussolini's fascist movement depended on violent intimidation, recruiting veterans and the unemployed to join his "Black Shirts"—a private army Mussolini used to assault political opponents and attack striking workers. Italy's business owners sided with Mussolini because he promised to restore order and end worker strikes. His adamant anti-communism also appealed to business interests. Mussolini came to power constitutionally in 1922 but rapidly used his secret police and Black Shirts to destroy any opposition while also changing Italy's laws to consolidate his power. By 1927 Mussolini had established himself as a totalitarian dictator of a one-party state. Economically, the Fascist Party established a "corporate state" which subordinated business and labor interests to the state. Mussolini encouraged Italy's Catholic culture, legally establishing Catholicism as Italy's national religion. He promoted traditional Italian family values and stressed women's maternal roles.

Nazi Germany

Nazi Germany also emerged from political and economic chaos following World War I. With the collapse of the German Empire at the end of World War I, a new elected government, **the Weimar Republic**, led Germany after the war. This government was blamed for signing the Treaty of Versailles and enforcing it. Traditional German elites and many in the German military contended that Germany had been betrayed by the republic. They also blamed socialists, communists, and Jews for the nation's loss. The German economy experienced hyperinflation in 1923 that destroyed middle-class Germans' life savings as the German government struggled to pay back war debts. Then, in the 1930s, the Great Depression hit Germany very hard. In 1932, the unemployment rate topped 30 percent. The National Socialist Party, or Nazi Party, gained new life in this economic environment, though it had received few votes in the 1920s. Many Germans found socialist and communist alternatives appealing. In the 1932 elections, the Nazi Party won 37 percent of the vote in parliamentary elections.

Adolf Hitler (1889–1945)

In January of 1933, Adolf Hitler, leader of the Nazi Party, was legally installed as chancellor and asked to form a government. Hitler's message was one of strident nationalism and racial supremacy, anti-Jewish hatred, and anti-communism. Just as Mussolini had played on Italian resentment at the results of the Treaty of Versailles, Hitler repudiated the terms of the agreement and cultivated German bitterness at the treaty. And, like Mussolini, Hitler promised to restore German military prowess and rebuild the economy. Established in power, Hitler rapidly expanded his own and the Nazi Party's control of Germany. In March of 1933, declaring a state of emergency, Hitler pushed through an amendment to the Weimar Constitution called the **Enabling Act** that granted Hitler power to rule without input from the Reichstag (the German legislative body). Civil liberties and the right to habeas corpus had already been suspended. Opposition parties were quickly banned, labor unions outlawed, and the media was placed under state control. Despite these harsh measures, Hitler's leadership remained popular, in part because the Nazi government's massive investments in public infrastructure and military spending reduced unemployment.

The Holocaust

Once in power, Hitler inaugurated a relentless attack on German Jews. He found the Jews to be a focus for a variety of resentments. The Jews were characterized as socialists and communists who weakened the German people with their international ties. Alternately, they were castigated as greedy capitalists, more interested in their bottom lines than in national well-being. Traditional anti-Semitic stereotypes dating to the medieval period were also employed to stigmatize and dehumanize Jews. They were forced to wear a yellow Star of David to mark them. Their stores and synagogues were shut down, and they were harassed in the streets. After 1940 and the outbreak of war on the Western Front, Hitler set out to eliminate German, and then European, Jewry.

Soviet Union (Union of Soviet Socialist Republics—U.S.S.R. 1918–1991)

The Soviet Union was established after the Russian Revolution of 1917 and the overthrow of the Romanov Dynasty. From 1918 to 1924, the Soviet Union was ruled by the Russian Communist Party headed by Vladimir Ilyich Ulyanov (better known by his alias, **Lenin**). Under his rule, the Soviet Union became a one-party state. After a series of debilitating strokes, Lenin died in 1924, leaving behind a power vacuum into which Joseph Stalin stepped.

Joseph Stalin (r. 1928–1953 CE)

Under Joseph Stalin, the Soviet Union embarked on a program of industrialization designed to allow the U.S.S.R. to compete with the West economically and militarily. This program involved strict government planning of the economy and severe restrictions on basic consumption as the Soviets developed heavy industry and military equipment. The Soviets forcibly collectivized the agricultural sector, killing 5–10 million "Kulaks" (farmers that owned their own land) as the government took possession of the nation's farms. All land became national property, and farmers became paid labor on government collective farms. Under these conditions, Russia's agricultural society was transformed into an industrial power. In the industrial sector, Russia's considerable iron, coal, petroleum, and other resources were also nationalized and the government directed all industrial production. The Soviet Union's planned economy, under Stalin's rule, became an industrial powerhouse, second only to the United States in industrial output. The Soviet Union's industrial turnaround was accomplished only at enormous human cost. Stalin purged all political opposition, real or imagined. Millions died as a result of starvation in the first years of agricultural collectivization. Millions were deported to Siberian prison camps. Whole ethnic populations were resettled away from their homelands, often with great loss of life. When Stalin died, the Communist Party under Nikita Khrushchev repudiated Stalin's brutality and secrecy, but largely continued with many of Stalin's economic and military policies.

> **Competency 004 Descriptive Statement F.** The beginning teacher analyzes the causes and effects of World War I and World War II.

Key Question

Behind this straightforward descriptive statement are judgments about the differences between proximate and ultimate causes. The ultimate causes of both World War I and World War II may be found in imperialist competition; struggle for power in first the theater of European, and later the world, state-system; and the rise of nationalism in Europe and then Asia after the Revolutionary and Napoleonic wars. The proximate causes relate to the ways in which alliance structures, nationalistic propaganda in democratic contexts, the nursing of historic grievances, and arms races contributed to the inevitability of hostilities. The effects of both wars, of course, are still being felt.

Periodization: The First and Second World Wars—1914 to 1945

Simply put, World War I and World War II extended from 1914 to 1945. However, the causes and effects of these critical conflicts extend backward and forward in time. In the case of World War I, the causes have roots in the early 19th century in the rise of nationalism, imperialist competition, and industrialization; but the more immediate causes date to the late 19th and early 20th centuries. The most important effects of World War I would be those that led Europeans to repeat the experience in World War II, though immediate actions and reactions of political actors in the 1930s ultimately explain the conflict.

Causes of World War I

World War I (1914–1918)

World War I broke out as the result of the assassination of Archduke Franz Ferdinand, the Austrian heir to the Habsburg throne, by a Serbian nationalist. The Austrian response to this act of terrorism, combined with other European powers' involvement, turned what was essentially an unhappy local incident into a worldwide conflict.

1. Imperial Rivalry

World War I grew out of long-standing rivalries between European powers within Europe and across the globe. France and England had for decades been in a competition to acquire colonies in Africa and Asia. Germany also sought to acquire colonies in Africa and spheres of economic interest elsewhere. France and Germany had been bitter enemies since the Franco-Prussian War (1870–1871) when Prussia had easily defeated France, going so far as to declare Germany's unification in the palace of Versailles. Austria-Hungary, the last remnant of the Holy Roman Empire, had aspirations of restoring its power and influence in the Balkans and Central Europe. Russia also sought to expand its influence in Central Europe and the Black Sea region. The Ottoman Empire, though in a period of long decline, still maintained significant territory in the Middle East and the eastern Mediterranean.

2. Nationalism

One of the legacies of the French Revolution and Napoleonic Wars in Europe, which had only grown over the course of the 19th century, had been the rise of nationalism. This was evident in the assassination of the Austrian archduke by a Serbian nationalist unhappy at Austria's continued control of Bosnia. The assassin was part of a group intent on creating a united Slavic-speaking nation. Nationalistic fervor also infected other European nations: British citizens, proud of their vast empire gloried in British civilization. The French, resentful at German slights, ached for revenge. Germans, proud of their new nation and its industrial might, hoped for international respect and colonial territories to match. These sentiments were fueled by political rhetoric and electoral politics in each of the great powers. Newspapers and popular culture contributed to heightening tensions.

3. Arms Race

Between 1871 and 1914, European powers engaged in an intense arms race. Total military spending by the European powers increased fourfold in the period. As Germany's naval capacity increased, the British felt compelled to respond, increasing the number and capabilities of its fleet. Naval arms races also developed between other powers. The size of peacetime armies also grew. General staffs in all major powers also planned for the eventuality of war, and prepared to mobilize large numbers of troops as quickly as possible. This increased the likelihood of war as being late to mobilize for war could easily spell defeat.

4. Alliance System

The assassination of the Austrian Archduke could lead to a world war largely because of the alliance system. By the 1890s, Britain, France, and Russia had formed an alliance known as the **Triple Entente**, expressly to confront the alliance of the **Central Powers**, which included Germany, Austria-Hungary, and Italy. Italy would ultimately enter the war in 1915 on the side of the British and French. In Italy's place, the Ottoman Empire made up the final great power aligned with Germany and Austria-Hungary. Only in April 1917 did the United States join on the side of the Triple Entente.

With the killing of Franz Ferdinand, Austria-Hungary issued an ultimatum to the Serbs threatening imminent attack. Germany agreed to support Austria-Hungary. Russia promised to aid the Serbs, and France vowed to back Russia. When Austria declared war on Serbia, Russia's mobilization alarmed Germany. Germany's war plans called for its armies to defeat France before turning on their Russian allies. Germany then preempted a French and Russian attack by declaring war on both nations on August 1, 1914. Britain was the last to join three days later. The alliance system led to a domino effect of cascading conflict.

Technology and Tactics of Warfare in World War I

World War I was carried out on multiple fronts: in eastern Europe, where Germans and Austrian troops confronted Russian armies; on the Italian-Austrian border; in the Ottoman Empire; in sub-Saharan Africa; at sea, where U-boats (submarines) hunted military and civilian shipping; and on the Western Front.

After the first frenetic weeks of the war in what was known as the Western Front, World War I was largely fought in northern France along a stagnant line of trenches where millions of men confronted one another in **trench warfare.** Artillery capable of hurling two-ton shells distances of as far as 70 miles, pounded the trenches, softening up enemy armies in advance of an attack. Over the course of the war, machine guns, barbed-wire fences, tanks, poison gas, and biplanes were only a few of the technologies that made the fighting particularly lethal. In a number of months-long battles, casualties on both sides often counted over a million dead.

To produce the needed war materiel and to man the enormous armies, the industrial and human capacity of each belligerent nation had to be mobilized. To accomplish these aims, governmental power in each nation increased markedly, with whole industries taken over by the state. Historians use the phrase **Total War** to describe the way in which European governments devoted their nations' entire productive capacity to winning the war. Governments on all sides also silenced dissent, censored the media, and mobilized propaganda to encourage support for the war. World War I was also a war fought by many colonized peoples. French troops along the Western Front were augmented by troops from France's West African colonies. The British used soldiers from Australia, New Zealand, and India.

Woodrow Wilson's Fourteen Points

Shortly after the United States entered the war in 1917, President Woodrow Wilson outlined the war aims and principles for peace negotiations at the war's conclusions. This 14-point proposal drew on progressive principles and addressed Wilson's understanding of the underlying causes of the war. Wilson's Fourteen Points called for reductions in trade restrictions, an end to secret treaties, and the right to national self-determination. Wilson also argued for arms reductions, freedom of the seas, and territorial adjustments of colonial boundaries. To resolve future international issues, Wilson called for the establishment of the **League of Nations**, a precursor institution to the United Nations.

Treaty of Versailles (1919)

Hostilities ended in November 1918. The war was formally ended in 1919 with the Treaty of Versailles. German negotiators had expected the Fourteen Points to guide the terms of the treaty. But France and Great Britain insisted on much harsher terms for the Germans. Germany's losses were significant: 13 percent of its European land and all of its colonies outside of Europe. It was forced to accept the "War Guilt Clause" that blamed Germany as the aggressor nation causing the war. Its military and navy were vastly reduced, and Germany was forced to pay reparations to the victors. The terms imposed on Germany helped create the conditions that would lead to World War II.

Effects of World War I

Redrawing the Map of Europe

The aftermath of World War I saw the creation of a number of new nation states, carved out of the German, Russian, Austro-Hungarian, and Ottoman empires. These new nations fulfilled one of Wilson's Fourteen Points: the right to national self-determination. Poland, Finland, Latvia, Lithuania, Estonia were carved out of the Russian Empire. Czechoslovakia, Yugoslavia, and Hungary gained independence from Austria-Hungary. Britain and France gained control of large, oil-rich territories in the Middle East from the Ottoman Empire.

The Mandate System

A number of German colonies and Ottoman territories were placed under British, French and Belgian governance as part of the mandate system. German East Africa and German Southwest Africa were granted to Great Britain. France acquired German colonies in West Africa. The mandate system seemed to violate the principle of national self-determination called for by Woodrow Wilson. European powers justified this by arguing that Africans lacked the requisite traditions of self-governance to transfer power to them as was done in eastern Europe. Instead, the mandate system was justified as an intermediate step towards full independence. Similar conditions were imposed on territories carved from the Ottoman Empire. The modern nations of Iraq, Syria, Jordan, Israel and Palestine were created as mandates under British and French control.

World War II (1939–1945)

World War II should be seen as an extension of World War I, played out over a much wider world stage. When seen strictly from a European perspective, the conflict began in 1939 and lasted until 1945. However, fighting began in Asia much earlier with a Japanese attack on Manchuria, a province in northern China. Western reaction to this expansion of Japanese influence led Japan to pull out of the League of Nations and to align with Fascist Italy and Nazi Germany. This trio joined to form the **Axis Powers**. The **Allied Powers**—which included the United Kingdom, the Soviet Union, France, and after 1941 the United States—formed a united front to defeat the expansionist aims of the Axis powers.

Causes of World War II

The war in Europe followed from German efforts to reverse the Treaty of Versailles, and from a failure of European powers and the United States to challenge these efforts. In 1935, Adolf Hitler ordered a massive rearmament program, in violation of the treaty. In 1936, German troops were sent into the Rhineland, which the Treaty of Versailles had demilitarized. In 1938, Austria was annexed without international objection, followed by German acquisition of German-speaking areas of Czechoslovakia. European powers, war-weary from the previous conflict, had little stomach for risking a renewal of war with Germany and hoped that this policy of **appeasement** would satisfy the dictator. It had the opposite effect. In 1939, Germany attacked Poland, leading Britain and France to reluctantly declare war. After consolidating its victory in Poland, in May 1940, Germany turned toward France, quickly defeating the French and driving the British from the continent. A year later, the Germans attacked Russia.

In Asia, the causes of World War II reflected the consequences of Japanese nationalism and imperialism confronted with international efforts, led by the United States, to maintain trade openings in China. Japan felt it had been slighted as an imperial power in the decades after World War I. A series of international treaties had limited Japan's naval expansion. Anti-Japanese immigration policies in the United States and Europe reinforced Japanese resentment at historic Euro-American racial policies. Japan was also dependent on the United States for a number of strategically important resources, including oil, copper, scrap iron, etc. Additionally, European and American control of resource-rich Asian territories—the Dutch in Indonesia, the United States in the Philippines, France in Southeast Asia, and Great Britain in India, Burma, Malaysia and Singapore—meant that Japan was easily cut off from resources and markets it needed to realize its imperial ambitions. Japanese nationalists, feeling encircled by hostile powers, determined in 1941 to strike preemptively to acquire the resources the empire needed. The Japanese attack on **Pearl Harbor**, December 7, 1941 was followed by a Japanese offensive that dispossessed the European and American powers of their colonies and replaced those colonial powers with Japanese military rule.

Key Figures of World War II

Where World War I has often been portrayed in impersonal terms, World War II has more easily been turned into a confrontation between historic villains and heroic defenders of Western democracy. While this perhaps simplifies matters, it does provide a dramatic narrative. It also reflects the terms with which the confrontation was understood at the time.

Benito Mussolini (r. 1922–1943)

Benito Mussolini was the leader of the Italian Fascist Party, and Prime Minister of Italy from 1922–1943. Mussolini's appeal to the Italian populace included promises to regain a global empire. To this end, in 1935, Italy attacked the independent African state of Ethiopia. Mussolini also hoped to regain territories held by France with historical Italian ties, like Savoy, Corsica, and Nice. In 1936 Mussolini and Adolf Hitler signed an agreement of cooperation. Mussolini called this agreement the Rome-Berlin Axis, coining the term "Axis Powers." The treaty became a military pact in 1939. Mussolini accordingly (though not without vacillation) led Italy into war with France in 1940. By 1943, American and British armies had fought through North Africa and invaded southern Italy. Mussolini was forced to resign his position as Prime Minister of Italy, but remained a puppet of German interests in Italy until April 1945 when he tried to escape to Spain. He and his mistress were identified, arrested, and summarily shot, their corpses hung on display in Milan.

Hideki Tojo (r. 1941–1944)

Hideki Tojo, a military general, served as the Prime Minister of Japan for much of the war. Tojo served in many capacities in the Japanese government before taking the position of Prime Minister. He identified strongly as a nationalist, a fascist, and a military hard-liner. He was consequently a strong supporter of the pact between Japan, Germany, and Italy. Though Tojo had already resigned his ministerial position when Japan surrendered in 1945, he was ordered arrested. Before this could be accomplished, Tojo shot himself in the chest, missing his heart. He was revived and forced to stand trial on charges of ordering wars of aggression, violating international law, and ordering and permitting inhumane treatment of prisoners of war. The war crimes tribunal executed him in December 1948.

Joseph Stalin (r. 1928–1953)

Joseph Stalin ruled the Soviet Union from 1928 until his death in 1953. He had been a Communist leader during the Russian Revolution in 1917. During World War II, Stalin was one of the "Big Three," as the leaders of the Allied Powers were known. Before the war began, however, Stalin had signed a non-aggression pact with Nazi Germany in which the two powers agreed to divide Poland. Stalin also took the opportunity of Germany's invasion of Poland to retake the Baltic states of Lithuania, Estonia, and Latvia, which had gained their independence after World War I. In June 1941, Germany violated the non-aggression pact and invaded the Soviet Union. Stalin then turned to Great Britain and the United States for assistance. Stalin met with Winston Churchill and Franklin Delano Roosevelt (or their successors) in three important wartime summit meetings in which war aims and strategy were outlined. Stalin insisted throughout the war that the Soviet Union regain territories in eastern Europe that had formerly belonged to the Russian Empire. He also bitterly blamed Roosevelt and Churchill for delaying the opening of a western front.

Franklin D. Roosevelt (r. 1933–1945)

Franklin Delano Roosevelt was president of the United States for much of the Great Depression and World War II. In the 1932 presidential election, Roosevelt defeated the incumbent president Herbert Hoover. He immediately set about using federal legislation and executive orders to respond to the Great Depression. As World War II raged in Europe, Roosevelt tried to maintain American neutrality while also helping supply Great Britain and the Soviet Union with assistance against the Nazis. When Pearl Harbor was attacked, Roosevelt led the United States into the war, using the power and resources of the federal government to maximum effect. And, just as Woodrow Wilson had sought to take the lead in shaping the post-World War I world, Roosevelt's administration developed many of the institutions of the post-World War II world, though he died before the war was concluded.

Winston Churchill (1874–1965)

Winston Churchill was the Prime Minister of the United Kingdom during World War II. He had a lengthy, prominent political career in British politics before the war but is best known for his courageous leadership of the British people during the darkest period of the war when Great Britain stood, largely alone, against the German air force. His speeches and radio broadcasts steeled English resolve. After the war, Churchill became a vocal opponent of the spread of communism in Europe, perhaps best remembered in this light for his "Iron Curtain" speech urging Western resolve in the fight against communism.

Effects of World War II

Human Costs

World War II was the costliest war in human history in terms of loss of human life; over 35 million died, 20 million in the Soviet Union alone. The Japanese killed 300,000 in the city of Nanjing alone. The United States' firebombing of Tokyo resulted in 80,000 deaths in a single raid. And the atomic bombing of Hiroshima and Nagasaki resulted in perhaps as many as 150,000 and 75,000 casualties, respectively.

Postwar Settlement

Following World War II, the United States took the lead in reconstructing the postwar world. The **Marshall Plan** was instituted to rebuild the badly damaged Western European nations. To ensure that the monetary crises that had destabilized the global economy in the interwar years were avoided, the **International Monetary Fund** was established. The **World Bank** was also founded as a vehicle to encourage economic development and growing markets in "third-world" countries. The **United Nations**, a successor organization to the League of Nations founded after World War I, was created with full support and membership of the United States. The United Nations has provided an important institution in the struggle to reduce international conflict.

A Nuclear Age

With the bombing of Hiroshima and Nagasaki in August of 1945, the world entered the nuclear age. Initially, only the United States had "the bomb." But in 1949, the Soviet Union entered the nuclear club, followed successively by Great Britain, France, and China.

> **Competency 004 Descriptive Statement G.** The beginning teacher understands significant events related to the 20th-century spread and fall of communism (e.g., Cold War, Korean War, Vietnam War) and the post–Cold War world (e.g., globalization, radical Islamic fundamentalism, terrorism).

> **Key Question**
>
> What have been the challenges to the values of Western Civilization since World War II, and how have the United States and its allies faced those challenges?

Periodization: This descriptive statement differentiates clearly between events between 1945 and 1989 — the Cold War — and after 1989 — the post–Cold War world.

The existential challenge facing Western Civilization before 1989 was the threat of global communism. The end of communism as a credible threat to western democracies and free-market institutions has resulted in new challenges and opportunities posed primarily by the growing integration of the global economy and by the threat of terrorism.

Spread of Communism

Before World War II, the only nation with a communist government was the Soviet Union. After the war, communist regimes came to power across the globe. Communism had its political and philosophical roots in the writings of Karl Marx, who argued that the class struggles associated with industrialization would inevitably give rise to working-class revolutions. In the end, the western industrial economies that Marx viewed as most likely to undergo such a transition, adopted many social and political reforms and did not experience the class conflict and revolution he imagined. Instead, communism found the most fertile ground in nations that lagged behind the West in terms of industrialization. By the 1970s, fully one-third of the world's population lived under communist regimes. Eastern Europe had been incorporated into the communist world as the Soviet expanded its military presence and restricted the political and economic independence of eastern Europeans. China had experienced its own communist revolution in 1949. As the Cold War unfolded, communist states were established in Korea, Vietnam, Cuba, Angola, Mozambique, Ethiopia, and many other developing nations. Communist insurrections were also active in many Latin American and Asian nations. Communist parties even had significant voting presences in France, Greece, Italy, and other European nations.

Cold War

Between 1945 and 1989, the world experienced a bipolar power struggle pitting Western capitalist countries led by the United States against communist states led by the Soviet Union. In 1949, the United States organized the **North Atlantic Treaty Organization (NATO)** as a political and military alliance against Soviet aggression. In response, the Soviet Union established the **Warsaw Pact**. Though these treaty alliances called for conventional military defense, the United States employed a nuclear deterrent as the ultimate guarantee of protection. When in 1949, the Soviet Union announced that it also had nuclear weapons, both blocs relied on what would become the policy of **Mutually Assured Destruction (MAD).** Balancing on the edge of nuclear war paradoxically reduced the likelihood of a shooting war between the two superpowers. There were a number of crises in which the possibility of war was heightened, most notably the **Cuban Missile Crisis**, when the Soviet Union threatened to place nuclear missile sites 90 miles off the coast of the United States. Much of the direct competition between the two powers took place in such arenas as sport and culture. The two rivals also competed against one another in what would become known as the "**third-world**," developing countries that were neither part of the industrialized West, the "**first-world**," nor the communist world, the "**second-world**." During the Cold War, the Soviet Union promoted revolution in nations allied with the United States, and the United States promoted revolution in Soviet-allied countries. For example, the United States was implicated in the overthrow of elected leaders of Iran (1953), Guatemala (1954), and Chile (1973) while in 1978 the Soviet Union fomented a Marxist revolution in Afghanistan. The United States propped up dictatorships, like Mobutu Sese Seko in Zaire and the Shah of Iran, while the Soviet Union propped up their own dictators, for example, Fidel Castro in Cuba.

Korean War (1950–1953)

Korea had been ruled by Japan from 1910 to the end of World War II. The Soviet Union had played little role in the war in Asia but in 1945 liberated the northern part of the Korean Peninsula. North and South Korea then established separate governments, the North supported by the Soviets and the South by the United States. In 1950, the North invaded the South. The United States led a force under United Nations' auspices to halt this northern aggression. Later, the Chinese would enter in support of the North. The war then came to a stalemate, and in 1953 an armistice, or ceasefire, was negotiated. Since no peace treaty has been signed since then, North and South Korea are technically still at war today.

Vietnam War

The Vietnam War stemmed from the long-held aspiration of Vietnamese nationalists to gain independence. Vietnam had until the Japanese invasion of Southeast Asia in 1941 been a part of French Indochina. Vietnamese nationalists led by **Ho Chi Minh** fought during World War II against the Japanese with the expectation that independence would follow. The French, however, reasserted colonial control. Vietnamese nationalists then turned their insurrection against the French in 1954, forcing the French to withdraw from Vietnam.

The United States supported the French in their colonial war, viewing the French as an important ally in the fight against communism. As a result, Ho Chi Minh sought Russian assistance, confirming American suspicions that the Vietnamese nationalists were communist-inspired. When it became clear that in 1956 Ho Chi Minh would win a national election, the United States intervened. It divided Vietnam into North and South Vietnam, and propped up successive South Vietnamese governments. From 1956 until 1975, North Vietnam fought a guerrilla war against South Vietnam and the United States, eventually forcing the U.S. withdrawal.

Communist Reform Movements

In the 1980s, both Communist China and the Soviet Union began to reform their political and economic systems. In China, the government dismantled collective farms, permitting Chinese peasants to once again own land. State-owned industries were exposed to global competition and foreign investors and management encouraged to act like private owners. China experienced enormous growth as a result. The Communist Party retained political control, but China embraced many of the principles of free-market capitalism.

The Soviet Union did not as successfully transition away from doctrinaire communism. In the mid-1980s, **Mikhail Gorbachev** became the leader of the Soviet Union. He recognized that economic stagnation, corruption, and popular cynicism about the political apparatus threatened the Soviet experiment. Additionally, Gorbachev understood that the Soviet Union could not compete with the massive military buildup begun by the United States under Ronald Reagan. Gorbachev argued that the Soviet Union needed greater openness, or **glasnost,** and **perestroika,** or restructuring. Unlike China, however, openness and political restructuring did not strengthen communism in the Soviet Union. Instead, the Soviet Union went into a deep decline from which it and its successor state, the Russian Federation, has yet to recover.

The "Miracle Year"—1989

One consequence of Gorbachev's reforms was the weakening of Soviet control over Eastern Europe. In 1989, demonstrations erupted across Eastern Europe and in rapid succession communist dictatorships in Poland, Hungary, Bulgaria, Czechoslovakia, and Romania were swept aside. Perhaps the lasting symbol of this "miracle year" were the demonstrations at and dismantling of the Berlin Wall, itself a potent symbol of the "iron curtain" separating the democratic and capitalist West from the communist East.

Post–Cold War World

The end of the Cold War left the United States without military challengers and few economic rivals. As the 20th century came to a close, the United States faced renewed economic competition from Asia, particularly China and India; a rebuilt Europe; and low-cost producers around the world. Then, in 2001, the United States found itself confronted with what many perceived as a new existential threat in radical Islamism.

Globalization

Globalization represents ever-tightening webs of economic and cultural linkages made possible by improvements in technology and institutions that have promoted expansion of world trade.

A great deal of the globalization between 1945 and 1989 took the form of American penetration of world markets with American commodities, culture, and business investment. The spread of American fast food, soft drinks, movies, television shows, automobiles, etc. represented one phase of post-World War II globalization. Before the end of the Cold War, such cultural and economic interconnections were often constrained by barriers to trade and communication imposed by both national governments and the communist bloc nations.

With the end of the Cold War and reforms to Eastern European, Chinese, and Russian economies, and with the growth of vibrant economies in South Korea, India, Malaysia, Taiwan, etc., the United States and Europe encountered new competitors and new partners in global trade. The expansion of the internet, cell phone service, and television networks, plus the breakdown of barriers to capital transfer and financial investment resulted in a global economy that was more tightly interconnected than ever before as commodities and cultural innovations flowed rapidly around the globe. This interconnected global economy resulted in both positive and negative consequences for consumers and workers worldwide. Low-priced consumer items from clothing to cell phones improved standards of living around the world. However, factory workers in the United States and Europe faced increasing competition from lower-paid laborers in manufacturing centers in the developing world.

Radical Islamic Fundamentalism

Religious fundamentalism is often expressed as the defense of tradition in the face of change. The power of global consumerism, secular science, and liberal democracy that has characterized modern society has often made devout believers of many religious traditions uncomfortable. Fundamentalism represents a religious response to these impersonal forces of change. The term *fundamentalism* originated among Christians unhappy with secular modernity. Parallel responses to modernity exist in Hinduism, Judaism, and Islam. Islamic fundamentalism has emerged in the first decades of the 21st century as the most significant challenge to the West's and the United States' leadership of globalizing modernity. The original target of Islamic fundamentalism's dissatisfaction was not the West, but secular states within the Islamic world (Egypt, Algeria, Iran, etc.) that pursued Western-style economic and political development. The establishment in 1948 of Israel, and its continued protection, in the heart of the Islamic world, provided Muslim religious reformers and political leaders an additional target for dissatisfaction. Given the United States and Western nations' support for the unpopular political leaders in these nations, and their support for the state of Israel, it is not surprising that the United States, Great Britain, and France would also become targets of Islamic fundamentalist opposition.

Americans and Western European nations became targets of Islamist anger. Often, this resentment and anger has been expressed through terrorist attacks on American and Western European targets. The first prominent incident of this sort occurred in 1972 with the Palestinian Liberation Organization taking contingents of the Israeli Olympic team hostage at the Munich Olympics. Other acts of terrorist violence against non-combatants have been a feature of this movement. **Osama bin Laden** became the most visible symbol of this movement after the destruction of the World Trade Center. More recently, organizations such as **ISIS**, **Al-Qaeda**, **Boko Haram** (in West Africa), and **Al Shabab** (in East Africa) have attracted adherents seeking to impose a radical version of Islam across the Muslim world and to challenge western values and institutions.

Competency 004 Descriptive Statement H. The beginning teacher analyzes the influence of significant individuals of the 19th and 20th centuries (e.g., Charles Darwin, Mohandas Gandhi, Adolf Hitler, Nelson Mandela, Mao Zedong, Mother Teresa).

Key Question

This descriptive statement calls out a number of key individuals from the modern period as exemplars of citizenship, influential women, etc. Adolf Hitler is discussed in an earlier section.

Charles Darwin (1809–1892)

Charles Darwin should be remembered for publishing *The Origin of Species* in 1859, a book that applied Isaac Newton's and the Enlightenment's mechanistic interpretation of physical nature to the world of living beings. Darwin did not originate the concept of evolution, but did articulate the principle of natural selection that explained how species adapted to their environmental constraints in order to propagate and survive. In 1871, Darwin took the argument a step further, applying the principle of natural selection to explain the origin of the human species. Darwin's theory of evolution was later applied by Social Darwinists to human social relationships and used as a justification for European imperialism.

Mohandas Gandhi (1869–1948)

Mohandas Gandhi was an English-trained lawyer who became a key leader in the Indian independence movement against Great Britain in the early 20th century. Inspired by Hindu principles and writers such as Henry David Thoreau, Gandhi practiced nonviolent resistance to peacefully undermine British rule in India. In 1948, the British government granted India its independence. Gandhi represents a radically different approach to anti-colonial resistance than that exemplified by Mao Zedong, and other revolutionaries who espoused violence. Martin Luther King, Jr. was inspired by Gandhi's example.

Mao Zedong (1893–1976)

Mao Zedong was one of the founders of the Chinese Communist Party and the Red Army that in 1949 defeated the Nationalist Party's forces under Chiang Kai-Shek to create the People's Republic of China. Mao Zedong's form of communism differed from early Marxist doctrine in its reliance on peasant agriculturalists rather than the industrial working class. As a result, Maoist communism would have its widest appeal in the developing world. Mao was notorious for his leadership of the Cultural Revolution, a purge of educators, intellectuals, and others deemed "counter-revolutionary" that ultimately led to death toll estimated at perhaps 20 million.

Nelson Mandela (1918–2013)

In 1994, Nelson Mandela was sworn in as president of South Africa. He had earlier spent 27 years in prison after leading a militant campaign to sabotage the South African government and its policies of **apartheid**, a policy of systematically separating the races and denying black Africans political and civil rights. Mandela had initially supported nonviolent resistance to apartheid, but had become convinced that Gandhi's methods simply wouldn't move the white power structure in South Africa. In 1990, Mandela was freed from prison, apartheid was abolished, and a new constitution was written guaranteeing civil equality for all races in South Africa.

Mother Teresa (1910–1997)

Mother Teresa is identified in the TEKS as an exemplar of a woman with a prominent impact in the modern period. Her primary significance comes from her charitable activities and care for outcaste and indigent populations in the Indian city of Calcutta. She moved from her home in Macedonia when she was 18 to begin her ministry to people suffering from AIDS, leprosy, tuberculosis, and other diseases that led to their social isolation. In 2016, Pope Francis II canonized her as a saint.

Domain II:
U.S. History

As many as 28 of the questions asked on the TExES Social Studies 7–12 test assess prospective teachers' mastery of American history. But knowledge of United States history is a prerequisite to answering many of the questions in other domains as well. For example, answers to questions from the domains of geography, economics, or government often rely on the test-taker's knowledge of events in American history. As a result, it is critical that you have both a strong foundation in American history as well as be able to make connections between American history and the concepts of these other disciplines.

COMPETENCY 005 (EXPLORATION AND COLONIZATION)

The teacher understands significant historical events and developments in the exploration and colonization of North America and the development of colonial society.

> **Competency 005 Descriptive Statement A.** The beginning teacher understands the causes and effects of European exploration and colonization of North America, including interactions with American Indian populations.

Key Question

This descriptive statement examines the different colonization efforts in North America and asks that students compare the ways in which different colonization practices used by the various European powers resulted in their different relations with the Native American populations.

Periodization: 1564 to 1609

Colonization efforts in North America began with Spanish attempts to settle Florida and then New Mexico between 1565 and 1609. Along the Atlantic coast, other European powers arrived later, with the French, British, and then the Dutch laying claim to wide swathes of North America's coast and interior.

American Indian Populations in North America before European Arrival

By 1492, the eastern half of what is now the United States had a diverse population of American Indians. Nearly 70 separate languages were spoken, representing five separate language families. Most Native Americans combined settled agriculture with **micro-habitat exploitation** of resource niches of the natural environment. For example, in New England, where a harsh landscape and short growing season limited agricultural surpluses, Indians harvested passenger pigeons during their spring migration; fished for salmon, smelt, eels, sturgeon, and alewives during autumn spawning runs; and harvested moose, caribou, deer, and fur-bearing animals. Indians also carefully managed animal and forest resources for human use.

Farming was done mostly by women who cultivated gourds, squash, maize (corn), and beans, which when combined with their harvesting of game and forest products provided a satisfying and complete diet. A similar combination of settled agriculture and fish-and-game management characterized most Native American settlements across North America. Indians lived mostly in small villages rarely housing more than 300 inhabitants. A typical village combined long homes (mat-covered multifamily structures), food storage pits, religious structures, and places for feasting and dancing, guarded by a wooden stockade. Villages were connected by well-trodden footpaths. Many of these paths later became roadways used by Europeans.

Often, Native American populations that encountered Europeans were already in a weakened state from the impact of epidemic diseases. Contact with Old World diseases often preceded actual arrival of Europeans on the scene, as epidemic diseases made their way along Native American trade routes. The populations of Indians encountered by European settlers frequently were in the process of reorganizing their societies after the decimation of these epidemics. European trade goods also destabilized Native American communities and land-use patterns. In order to acquire European trade goods like ceremonial objects, iron implements, knives, cloths, or even guns, Indians had to increase their acquisition of furs or other items that could be traded. This resulted in increased warfare with other American Indians over contested resources. It also meant greater pressure on populations of muskrat, beaver, deer, and other animals valued for their hides.

European Exploration and Settlement

Spanish Colonization

Though Mexico, Peru, and the Caribbean were the most important regions in New Spain, the Spanish also claimed and explored much of what would become the United States. **Juan Ponce de León** had claimed Puerto Rico and landed on the shores of Florida in 1513 searching for slaves, gold, and the fabled fountain of youth. He was repelled by Florida Indians, but in 1565, a second expedition established forts at St. Augustine, Florida (the oldest continually inhabited European settlement in the United States), and in Georgia. Spanish explorers also made their way up the Pacific coast as far as Oregon. Others marched through the American Southwest and Gulf Region vainly hoping to find riches to compare to those acquired by Hernán Cortés in Mexico or Francisco Pizarro in Peru. It was not until 1598 that serious efforts were made to establish permanent settlements north of present-day Mexico. In 1610, Santa Fe, the capital of New Mexico, became the first permanent European settlement in the Southwest. Neither Spanish Florida nor Spain's southwestern settlements ever reached the same population density or numbers as English settlements along the Atlantic coast.

Spanish relations with the Native American population along the Gulf Coast and in the Southwest were marked by violence and resistance, as Spanish priests, landowners, and administrators attempted to subdue, convert, enslave, exploit, and govern dispersed populations of fiercely independent peoples. To accomplish these sometimes-competing ends, one Spanish strategy was to resettle Indian communities, often after destroying existing villages, the nucleus of which were a **presidio,** or fortress, and a cathedral church. This strategy contributed to breaking down ethnic or tribal identities. These settlements, scattered across Texas to California, were outposts of Spanish culture and language. As Indians became assimilated into this culture, converted to Catholicism, and settled into routines of agricultural labor, the Spaniards became increasingly willing to accept them into Spanish society.

New France

The first of Spain's rivals to begin exploring North America were the French. A French fur-trading company funded **Samuel de Champlain's** founding of Quebec in 1608. The Jesuit priest **Jacques Marquette** and a fur trader named **Louis Joliett** made their way to the Mississippi River. The French would eventually claim from the mouth of the St. Lawrence River down the Ohio River to the length of the Mississippi. French settlement, however, remained sparse throughout the history of New France. In 1754, only 55,000 French men and women lived in France's North American territories.

Because the French were so few in number, and because they were interested more in commerce than resettlement of large numbers of Frenchmen, New France was marked by more cultural intermixing and comparable equality between Indians and whites than elsewhere in the Americas. Particularly in the "middle ground," as the upper Great Lakes region was known, French fur traders began to adopt Indian ways rather than the reverse. Additionally, while the Jesuit missionaries sought to convert the Native American population, the French were much more accommodating of Indian religious practices and permitted Indians much greater independence than did the Spanish.

Dutch Settlement in New Netherland

The Dutch in 1624 established two small settlements in North America, New Netherland (New York) and a small station near Wilmington, Delaware. As late as the 1660s when the Dutch lost the territory to the English, their colonies in North America numbered only 9,000 settlers. Dutch interactions with the Native American populations along the Hudson and in western New York were largely peaceful, as the Dutch were primarily interested in trading for furs with the Indians.

Early English Colonization

English motives for settlement in the Americas, like those of the other European powers, can be reduced to the pursuit of national glory, the hope of profit, and religious zeal. For England, a minor power by comparison to its neighbors France and Spain, acquiring colonies could raise the island nation's profile. As both France and Spain were Catholic powers, and England had recently undergone its Reformation, its colonization effort was often couched as part of an anti-Catholic crusade. English promoters of colonization also emphasized both the many raw materials and consumer products that could enrich the mother country, as well as the new markets that colonization would provide for English manufacturers.

English colonization benefited from far greater numbers of people willing to take the risk of sailing across the Atlantic and settling in often harsh and inhospitable lands. In the first century of English colonization, over 500,000 English men and women left England for lives in Ireland, the West Indies, and North America. The Chesapeake region (Virginia and Maryland) saw an influx of 120,000 settlers between 1607 and 1700. The Puritan colony in New England received only 21,000 settlers, most arriving by 1640. This initial population, because it was composed mostly of family groups, grew rapidly from this small migration. A comparable number of settlers arrived in the Middle Colonies (Pennsylvania, New Jersey, New York).

The desire for land was a critical driver of English colonization that was less pressing for the French, Spanish, and Dutch. Each English colony proceeded from a land grant to either a royal ally or a corporation. For these land grants to be profitable, settlers were required. Additionally, land scarcity in England drove many landless laborers to risk the dangerous passage across the Atlantic. The prospect of acquiring land in the Americas proved an important motivator for many thousands of settlers.

As English men and women began to settle in North America, pressure on the land already claimed by American Indians became the root of conflict in each of the British colonies in North

America. Whereas the Spanish were interested in creating loyal subjects to the crown, exploiting Indian labor, or even marrying the Indians; and the French were content largely to trade with and convert Indians; the English sought to displace the Indians. What few efforts were made to convert the Indians were rarely successful. Trade with the Indians was sporadic and intermarriage rare, except on the farthest frontiers. The story of Pocahontas and the "First Thanksgiving" notwithstanding, relations between the English settlers and the Indians they encountered on the Atlantic coast were largely hostile and marked by repeated conflict.

Roanoke Island—"The Lost Colony" (1585–1587)

England's first attempt to establish an outpost in the Americas came in 1585 when Queen Elizabeth I granted **Walter Raleigh** a license to act as a "privateer," or state authorized pirate, preying on Spanish shipping. Needing a forward base that was sufficiently safe from Spanish counterattack, Raleigh chose Roanoke Island, which lay sheltered behind North Carolina's barrier islands. The Indians they encountered were presumed to be willing to trade, work, and ally with the English. The venture failed, despite several attempts to resupply and reinforce it, in large part because the English damaged relations with Indians on the island. Thus, Roanoke Island's characterization as the "Lost Colony" persists to this day, as the mystery over how the settlement ended up completely deserted has never been solved. Several factors should be taken into account, however.

The soldiers sent to Roanoke in 1587 to set up this outpost in England's war with Spain had military experience fighting the Irish. They saw the Roanoke Indians as savages, much as they deemed the Irish. Lacking supplies, the English at first acquired them peacefully from the Roanoke Indians, who initially welcomed the trade opportunity. But native food supplies were insufficient for both populations, even though the English barely numbered 100 inhabitants. We know that English diseases also began to take a heavy toll on the populace. The Indians considered abandoning the island to the English or alternately to attack and drive them away. After the failure of the Roanoke expedition, the English distrusted Native Americans and abandoned the possibility of successfully establishing alliances or working relations with them.

Jamestown and the Powhatan

In 1607, 20 years after the failure of English-Native American relations at Roanoke, the English would again establish an Atlantic coast settlement at Jamestown on Chesapeake Bay.

Powhatan (1545–1618)

The Indians in the Chesapeake area with whom the English colonists had to deal were the Powhatan. They were led by a man properly known as Wahunsonacock. The English knew him as Powhatan (his title and the name of the Indian tribe). In 1607, he was the paramount chief of perhaps 20,000 Indians living along the Chesapeake Bay. The most famous story of early interaction between the Powhatan and the English centers on Powhatan's daughter Pocahontas's interposition of herself between the captive John Smith and the Powhatan. This was likely a highly-ritualized act of a diplomatic nature in which Smith was ritually adopted into the tribe, rather than a romantic moment. After Powhatan's death, his brother, alarmed at the rapid growth of English settlement, led an uprising in 1622 that killed nearly a quarter of the colonists. English reprisals reduced the Indian population to less than 2,000 people who were forced to move to a reservation a distance from Jamestown.

Plymouth Rock, Squanto, and Thanksgiving

Perhaps the most remembered example of English-Native American interaction centers around the Thanksgiving story. In 1620, the *Mayflower* landed at Plymouth on Cape Cod with over 100 English men and women. After surviving their first winter, thanks in no small part to the help of Nauset and Wampanoag Indians, the Pilgrims held a feast of Thanksgiving to which the Indians were invited. Plymouth Colony was built on a site of a Patuxet Indian village wiped out by European diseases between 1616 and 1619. One of the central figures in the drama was Squanto. Squanto was one of the last living members of the Patuxet tribe. He could speak English because he had been abducted by an English trader sailing under the command of John Smith (of Jamestown fame). It was through Squanto's assistance that the Pilgrims were able to grow native crops and trade with surrounding Indians.

Pequot War (1637)

A second group of English settlements were established in New England after 1629. The Native American population in New England likely reached 100,000 at the time of English arrival in the area. Between 1629 and 1641, over 20,000 settlers arrived in the Massachusetts Bay Colony. Indian land came under increasing pressure as these settlers fanned out over the landscape. Following a Pequot Indian killing of a fur trader in 1637, Puritan militia, accompanied by Indian allies, attacked a Pequot village at Mystic, Connecticut, setting it on fire and massacring those who tried to escape. Few Pequot survived, and those that were captured during the war were sold in the West Indies in exchange for African slaves. Puritans saw their success as evidence of God's blessing on their enterprise, and conversely, as judgment on the "heathen" Indians. Between the Pequot War and the 1670s, however, Puritans in New England had few conflicts with the native population.

King Philip's (Metacom's) War (1675–1678)

In 1675, New England's Indian population was scarcely 10,000, compared to over 80,000 English men and women. Despite this imbalance, a coalition of Indians attacked along a wide frontier of the Puritan colony. The assaults destroyed 12 Puritan villages and forced many Puritans to flee to coastal strongholds. Puritans considered the unexpected success of the Indian assaults to be evidence of God's judgment on the second generation of Puritans for failure to live up to the religious purposes of the colony's founding.

Quakers and Native Americans

The Quakers who settled Pennsylvania, led by William Penn, represented one of the few English groups to sustain peaceable relations with the Indian populace. Quakers believed that each human being contained within them the presence of the Holy Spirit, what they described as the "Inner Light." Quakers were also pacifists. In 1682, William Penn signed a "Quaker Peace" with the Delaware Indians near Philadelphia. This would last until 1756 when the Quakers withdrew from leadership of Pennsylvania in the face of growing demand within the colony for war against Pennsylvania's Indians.

The Carolinas

The establishment of an English colony in the Carolinas occurred in a region where the surrounding Indian population had been decimated by European diseases. Initially, Carolinians had provided weaponry to Carolina's Indians, encouraging them to attack the Spanish colony in Florida. Other Indians were enslaved and often shipped to the West Indies. In fact, during the first 50 years of the colony, fewer Africans were imported into Carolina as slaves than Indians exported as slaves.

French and Indian War (1754–1763)

By the 18th century, hostilities between European colonists and Native Americans were sporadic. Indians along the Atlantic seaboard had been so reduced in numbers that they had come to realize that direct confrontation with English arms was suicidal. Additionally, few Europeans lived west of the Appalachian watershed. Indians in the trans-Appalachian west were successful in playing one European power against another, exacting better trade terms in the process. After 1750, however, Scots-Irish and German immigrants and Virginia planters increasingly began to encroach on Indian lands. The Ohio Company, a land-speculating company in Virginia whose membership included George Washington and other key Virginia leaders, gained a charter to a large land grant in Ohio. When Washington crossed into Ohio to survey the grant, he sparked a war between the English settlers, who were supported by the English government, against the Indians and their French allies. This would become a worldwide conflict known as the Seven Years' War. Following the French surrender in 1763, the Indians of the Ohio Valley and Great Lakes Region would carry on fighting the expansion of English settlement in a short-lived conflict known as **Pontiac's Rebellion**.

> **Competency 005 Descriptive Statement B.** The beginning teacher demonstrates knowledge of individuals, events, and issues that shaped the development of colonial society, including interactions among Europeans, Africans and American Indians.

Religious Fervor and American Exceptionalism

Early in British North America's colonial history there developed a sense of American exceptionalism: the view that the colonists, and later the United States, had a vital role to play in history. This was first defined largely in religious terms and only later in secular, political, and economic terms.

The Puritans in New England first expressed this sense of mission, viewing their colonization effort as a God-guided crusade to establish in the American wilderness a model Biblically-based society that would be an example for England, and ultimately for other European nations.

John Winthrop (1587–1649)

The first governor of Massachusetts Bay Colony was John Winthrop, an English Puritan lawyer. In a sermon that outlined the principles that would guide the Puritan colonists, Winthrop famously characterized the New England colony as an "Errand into the Wilderness," and a "City upon a Hill." This language has been often recalled by American political figures who have seen the United States as exceptional, charged with a higher purpose, and an example for other nations. For Winthrop, the Puritan colony in New England was to be a Bible Commonwealth founded upon Biblical principles as understood by Puritan ministers and magistrates. The institutions of government in Puritan Massachusetts were designed, above all, to stop sin. There were laws against adultery, drunkenness, failure to properly discipline and educate one's children, and many other behaviors that the Puritans deemed both sins and crimes.

The Salem Witch Trials (1692–1693)

The Salem Witch Trials represented one of the last paroxysms of the European Witch Craze. In 17th-century Europe and colonial America, witchcraft was a capital crime, and early modern Europeans and Americans believed widely in astrology, magic, and witchcraft. In Puritan New England, belief in the diabolical and in the powers of witches ran deep. In 1692 and 1693, numerous villagers from the town of Salem were accused of witchcraft. Twenty were executed and five others died in prison. When the accusations proliferated and even upstanding citizens began to be named as potential witches, faith in the judicial processes of uncovering witches was discredited and the extraordinary court disbanded.

Religious Tolerance

Another important American value that emerged in many of the colonies was the ideal of religious tolerance, despite the fact that many colonies had an established religion. In Virginia, New York, and the Carolinas, the Anglican Church was the official religion. Massachusetts, New Hampshire, and Connecticut established the Congregational Church as the official religion. The first place where the impulse toward religious tolerance developed was the Massachusetts Bay Colony, in response to the restrictive theology of the Puritans. The Puritans insisted on religious conformity and even executed heretics or those who had different religious beliefs.

Roger Williams (1603–1683)

There were those within Winthrop's Massachusetts Bay Colony who disagreed about how precisely such a Bible Commonwealth should be organized. Roger Williams was a Puritan theologian who was expelled from the colony by Massachusetts officials. Williams objected to Puritans' restrictions of colonists' freedom of conscience to practice their faith as they saw fit. He founded the settlement known as Providence Plantation (later Rhode Island) in 1636. Williams advocated religious tolerance and is also known for encouraging more humane and fair interaction with Native Americans. Rhode Island consequently had no established state church.

Anne Hutchinson (1591–1643)

A second figure whose religious convictions resulted in conflict with Puritan leaders was Anne Hutchinson. She charged the majority of Puritan ministers with preaching a "covenant of works" rather than a "covenant of grace," criticizing them for a legalistic interpretation of scripture. Because she led Bible studies in her home, which proved so popular that women began to bring their husbands, Hutchinson was accused of stepping out of her proper role as a woman. She was banished from Massachusetts in 1637, but found refuge in Rhode Island.

Middle Colonies

Religious tolerance also developed in the Middle Colonies (Pennsylvania, New York, and New Jersey, but less as a reaction to restrictions on religious freedom than as a reflection of the reality that the Middle Colonies were populated by residents from varied religious traditions.

The New Netherlands (New York) had originally been founded by the Dutch West India Company, and officially followed the Dutch Reformed tradition. Jews, Quakers, and Lutherans, were granted the right to settle and practice their religion without persecution, in part because the West India Company desired their investment and economic contribution. The terms agreed to when the British acquired the colony from the Dutch in 1664 guaranteed that the English would not trample on the religious beliefs of the diverse populations in New York.

William Penn (1644–1718) and Pennsylvania

The foundation of Pennsylvania in 1681 by the Quakers further contributed to the development of attitudes of religious tolerance. William Penn, the founder of Pennsylvania, believed strongly in religious freedom. Though the Pennsylvania **Charter of Liberty** insisted that only Christians could serve in public office, Pennsylvania had no established church, and its inhabitants were free to practice their beliefs as they chose. In Massachusetts, church attendance was mandatory; in Pennsylvania, it was entirely voluntary.

The Great Awakening (1720s–1760s)

An important movement that contributed to the growing importance of religion in American life was a revival known as the Great Awakening. The movement began in the 1730s, among the Dutch Reformed and Congregational churches of New Jersey and Massachusetts. One of the iconic sermons triggering this revival was Jonathan Edwards' *Sinners in the Hands of an Angry God*, which captured the fear of damnation and the necessity of an emotional conversion that the evangelical revivalists called for. An English itinerant preacher, George Whitfield, who preached in every American colony, further enflamed religious enthusiasm. This revival particularly appealed to the frontiersmen, the poor, and to African Americans who found the staid religiosity of the established churches to be too formal and too supportive of the social hierarchy. The Great Awakening was one of the first movements to touch each of the colonies. It also encouraged many colonists to challenge their religious and political authorities.

The Integration of the Colonies and the Atlantic Economy

One factor contributing to the creation of an American economy and culture resulted from the increased integration of the colonies with the Atlantic economy after the first wave of colonization.

Navigation System (1650s to 1776)

Colonial trade activity under the British government was largely guided by mercantilism. The regulations that the British parliament employed to regulate colonial trade were collectively known as **Navigation Acts** or the **Navigation System**. The Navigation Acts, although they did also provide some benefits to colonial trade, were often despised by American merchants, who violated them with impunity. Here are four main principles of the Navigation Acts.

1. These laws limited all imperial trade to British ships, defined as those with British ownership whose crews were three-quarters British. These laws not only contributed to Great Britain's rise as Europe's foremost shipping nation, but also helped build up an American merchant marine.

2. The Navigation Acts forbade export to foreign nations of a variety of goods, including tobacco, rice, furs, indigo, and naval stores, unless they first passed through England or Scotland. American producers did, however, have captive markets in England for many of these items.

3. Parliament provided incentives for American production of silk, iron, dyes, hemp, and lumber, which Britain would otherwise have had to import. The system also raised protective tariffs to protect American manufacturing.

4. Americans were forbidden from competing with British textile and steel manufacturing. As a result, Americans failed to establish a profitable textile industry until well into the 1800s. Instead, in the textile industry and many other industries, American colonials were dependent on access to British goods.

The Consumer Revolution

A result of the growing interconnectedness of the Atlantic economy between 1650 and 1775 was an increase in consumerism in the American colonies. American newspapers and shops advertised a wide range of British consumer items: tea service, ceramics, glassware, linens, woolen cloths, coffee, tea, sugar, paper, etc.

Much of the trade in these items flowed through the handful of colonial cities that developed in the late 17th century. Philadelphia, Boston, New York, and Charleston were small port cities that facilitated the trade in these consumer items, in exchange for the produce (mostly slave-grown) of American cash crops. The cities of Philadelphia, Boston, and New York, though they depended upon their surrounding countryside for food and building supplies, were heavily dependent on the "carrying trade" between the Caribbean and American South, Europe and Africa, what has often been called the triangular trade. For example, New England ships often acquired molasses (partially refined sugar), which was distilled into rum in New England, and then exported to England or used to acquire slaves in West Africa, who were sold in the West Indies.

The Frontier and American Individualism

One of the important features often ascribed to early American culture was a penchant for individualistic thinking and behavior. The frontier provided an outlet for Americans lacking land and opportunities in the established Atlantic coast communities. The frontier encouraged a mobility that was rare in Europe. Additionally, men and women on the frontier often neglected, or were unable, to maintain adherence to the norms and cultural expectations common to English men and women in Great Britain and along the Atlantic Coast. Frontiersmen like Daniel Boone, for instance, are often held up as exemplars of American individualism.

> **Competency 005 Descriptive Statement C.** The beginning teacher analyzes political, economic, religious, and social reasons for establishment of the 13 colonies.

Key Question

 In what ways did the economic, religious, social, and political reasons for the establishment of the 13 colonies contribute to the emergence of regional cultures (such as New England, the Middle Colonies, and the Southern colonies) and to the development of particular colonial identities specific to what would later become the original states of the union? This descriptive statement suggests that a comparative framework is necessary in characterizing the development of the 13 colonies.

Periodization: 1607 to 1642

English colonization and settlement of North America occurred in two separate waves. The first colonies (Virginia, Massachusetts, Rhode Island, Connecticut, Maryland) were established between 1607 and 1642. The English Civil War and the Interregnum (period between the reigns of Charles I and Charles II) put a momentary end to British colonization in North America. After the restoration of the Stuart monarchy to the throne in 1660, colonization began again in earnest with the founding of Carolina (later divided between North and South Carolina), New York, New Jersey, and Pennsylvania. These colonies are known as the restoration colonies. Delaware, Georgia, and New Hampshire made up the final three British colonies to be granted royal charters.

The Chesapeake

British colonial settlement began on the banks of the Chesapeake Bay with the establishment of the colonies of Virginia and Maryland.

The colony of Virginia was established primarily as a money-making venture, in the hope that the English could duplicate Spanish experience in central Mexico and the Andes mountains. Maryland was founded as a haven for England's persecuted Roman Catholics.

Virginia Company of London (est. 1606—dissolved 1624)

In 1606, James I granted a charter to the Virginia Company of London, a joint stock company formed to establish a colonial settlement in North America. A **joint stock company** in 1607 was a novel form of ownership in which shares of company stock entitled the owners to receive dividends from company profits. The territory identified in the charter extended from the mouth of the Chesapeake Bay westward and northward to Long Island Sound. The settlers who ventured across the Atlantic were motivated primarily by the desire to get rich, either by searching for gold, acquiring Indian slaves, or exploiting the area's natural resources.

Jamestown (est. 1607)

In April 1607, three ships carrying 104 settlers sailed up what the English later named the James River. The colony they named after Queen Elizabeth I (remembered as the Virgin Queen because she never married). The pioneers built a stockade and set about to secure their position. Few of this contingent had agricultural or construction experience. A third of them were "gentlemen," or aristocrats, and another third were their servants. In the first year, disease and starvation cut their numbers in half. Reinforcements, including two women, arrived in 1608, but the winter of 1609–1610 decimated the population. The 65 settlers still alive set sail for England but were convinced to return by the arrival of a new contingent of colonists. Jamestown, despite its inauspicious start, would be Virginia's capital until 1699.

Headright System

To attract colonists to Virginia, particularly in the aftermath of its disastrous start, the Virginia Company of London offered incentives to attract settlers. The headright system granted 50 acres of land to settlers who paid their own or another settler's voyage across the Atlantic. A later encouragement offered grants of additional land to landowners who brought indentured laborers to Virginia. None of these proved sufficient. By 1622, Virginia still only had barely 1,200 colonists.

John Smith (1580–1631)

One key to Virginia's survival was the discipline instilled by John Smith, who insisted that only those willing to work would be allowed to eat. Smith was a former mercenary and lacked the stature of other key leaders in the expedition. He narrowly escaped being executed for mutiny on board ship in 1607. The expedition, and subsequent resupply missions, arrived without sufficient provisions, but with new mouths to feed. Smith negotiated with and threatened the nearby Indian populace to acquire needed food supplies. Smith's harsh measures to control his unruly settlement population and his often-strained relations with the Powhatan Indians earned him the distrust and enmity of both. His leadership of the Jamestown colony, though critical to its early survival, did not last long as a result.

John Rolfe (1585–1622)

John Rolfe came in the third resupply of Jamestown, arriving in 1609. He is best remembered for his marriage to Pocahontas, daughter of Powhatan. However, it was Rolfe who transformed

Virginia by developing a strain of tobacco that appealed to English tastes. After the first export of Rolfe's variety of tobacco, Virginia rapidly began to produce the crop for export.

Indentured Servitude

The turn to tobacco production resulted in an immediate demand for an adequate labor force. This demand was met at first by relying on indentured servants. An indenture was a contract that bound a worker to the owner of the contract for a period of time (usually 4–7 years) in repayment for the price of passage to the Americas. Indentured labor would be a prominent feature of the colonial labor system until the American Revolution, though in the plantation economies, slavery would surpass the indenture system as a way to supply plantations with workers. Of the 120,000 English men and women who came to Virginia during its first century as a colony, 75 percent came as indentured servants. Indentured servants went through a **"seasoning time"** during their first year as they acclimated to the environment and the heavy agricultural labor. Many died of disease and overwork. Indentured servants were not property and could not be bought and sold. They were, however, exploited much as were slaves. Before the 1660s, they often ran away with slaves, shared living quarters with slaves, slept with them, drank with them, and in other ways shared the hardships of life on tobacco plantations with African slaves. Gradually, however, legal and social barriers to such interaction were constructed that contributed to the development of racial antipathy between poor whites and the enslaved. The major disadvantage of a system of indentured labor was that every year, the labor force needed to be replenished as indentures expired. Equally threatening to the plantation system was the fact that the former indentured laborers found themselves disadvantaged and pushed to Virginia's frontier with the Indians.

Bacon's Rebellion (1676)

The turn from indentured laborers to African slaves in the Chesapeake region was precipitated by a rebellion in which former indentured servants figured significantly. Poor whites sought to acquire land by encouraging a war with Indians on Virginia's western frontier. However, Virginia's governor, Sir William Berkeley, and the "grandees," as wealthy landowners were disparagingly called, profited from the fur trade with the Indians and didn't wish to see this trade diminished. A brash and ambitious newcomer to Virginia, **Nathaniel Bacon**, saw an opportunity to gain politically by taking the leadership of a movement of small farmers, indentured servants, and a handful of Africans. He raised an army of the disgruntled poor to attack the Indians and to intimidate the governor into legitimizing the assault. Berkeley fled Jamestown, leaving the town to Bacon's army, which proceeded to ransack the town before being dispersed by the arrival of English naval vessels intent on restoring order. Though Bacon's Rebellion failed, Virginia's elites increased importation of slaves. Between 1670 and 1750, Virginia's slave population rose from 6 percent to nearly 50 percent of the population. Virginia's elite well understood that they could more easily control an enslaved populace than the many indentured laborers who were annually freed into a society in which they had few opportunities.

Maryland

Maryland was initially established as a haven for Catholics. Cecil Calvert, Lord Baltimore, was the first proprietor of Maryland. In 1632, he acquired a charter to establish Maryland as a haven for English Roman Catholics on the banks of the Chesapeake River. As a **proprietary colony** (compared to a **corporate colony** like Virginia), Maryland was a land grant to Calvert alone. Calvert hoped to settle the area with Catholics. Despite its establishment as a sanctuary for Catholics, however, the majority of the settlers were Protestant indentured servants who worked tobacco farms. Like Virginia, after initially experimenting with a plantation economy worked by indentured labor, Maryland also turned to enslaved Africans as a labor force.

Plantation Economy in the Chesapeake

In Virginia and Maryland, a plantation economy developed that was dependent first upon indentured labor and then on enslaved persons. The plantation system encouraged both a keen sense of hierarchy and a strong sense of individualism. The wealthy landowners of Virginia styled themselves on the British aristocracy and expected the deference of their inferiors. The individualistic ethos of the plantation economy was evident in the construction of isolated farmsteads (as opposed to urban or village centers as developed in New England) scattered across Virginia. Contributing to the individualistic ethos of the colony, settlement along the Chesapeake River was largely undertaken by young, single males. Men outnumbered women by a 4:1 ratio until well into the 18th century.

New England

Colonization in New England was motivated primarily by a desire to establish a society based on the Biblical interpretation of religious reformers known as Puritans.

Puritanism

Puritanism was a religious reform movement of English Protestants determined to rid the Church of England of elements of Catholicism.

Separatists, the *Mayflower,* and the Plymouth Colony

Some Puritans concluded that it was necessary to leave or separate from the Church of England by leaving the country, despairing at reforming the church from within. The Plymouth Colony was founded by separatists who had in 1608 fled England to settle in Holland. Seeing their children adopt Dutch culture, these **Pilgrims** acquired permission from Charles I to settle in Virginia, which at the time was sorely in need of colonists. Some 107 settlers sailed in 1620 to Virginia but were blown off course and landed in Massachusetts where they established the Plymouth Colony.

Massachusetts Bay Colony

In 1629, the Massachusetts Bay Company was granted a charter to establish a settlement near Plymouth. The merchants who formed the company hoped to provide a haven for Puritans who were increasingly harassed by Charles I.

The "Great Migration"

Between 1629 and 1642, in one of several **"Great Migrations"** in American history, 21,000 Puritans emigrated to Massachusetts. This migration is unique by comparison to most historic migrations in several respects: it was composed primarily of family groups; it had an even balance between male and female settlers; rather than being made up largely of young men, there were young and old among the settlers; and it had many reasonably prosperous migrants. Even though this wave of migration stopped in 1642, natural demographic growth and a more hospitable climate resulted in rapid population growth. By 1700, Massachusetts' white population outstripped that of Virginia and Maryland.

Because the Puritans were distrustful of the individual isolated from a godly community, Puritans established **nucleated villages** across the New England landscape. These villages were characterized by the centrality of the town meeting and the Congregational Church to their social and political life. The town meetings became an important laboratory for early democracy in America.

New England Colonies: Connecticut, Rhode Island, New Hampshire

The other early New England colonies were either founded by refugees from Massachusetts Bay Colony or by Puritan farmers in need of new land. Rhode Island was established in 1636 as a haven for religious dissidents from Massachusetts. Connecticut was settled by Puritan pioneers dwelling in the Connecticut River valley and along the coast between 1633 and 1639.

The Carolinas

South Carolina (North Carolina would separate from its southern counterpart in 1715) was founded in 1663 as a barrier between Virginia and Spanish Florida. Many of its proprietors had ties to the sugar island of Barbados, and conceived of the colony as an opportunity for their sons unable to establish themselves on the small island. The proprietors hoped to recreate a feudal society led by a hereditary aristocracy, but the need to settle the colony necessitated the establishment of a representative government and religious toleration.

After briefly attempting to attract indentured servants from Virginia and Maryland to settle in the colony, the colonists turned to the slave trade (first exporting captured Indians) as a source of income, and then to acquire African labor. African slaves were employed in rice and indigo cultivation as well as cattle herding. With the development of the plantation economy Carolina began to prosper and grow. It also became a colony that was characterized by a majority population of African slaves. Because of the proportion of recent African arrivals, Carolina slaves retained much of their African culture.

The Middle Colonies

The Middle Colonies—New York, New Jersey, Delaware, and Pennsylvania—differed significantly from the southern colonies (characterized by dependency on plantation economies and eventually slavery) and the New England Colonies (established initially for religious reasons).

New York

New York, which had earlier been a part of the Dutch Empire, in 1664 was acquired by Great Britain and given by King Charles II to his brother, James the Duke of York. Under the Dutch, the New Netherlands had been an extremely diverse colony with a religious mix that included Catholics, Lutherans, Dutch Reformed, Mennonites, and many other Christian churches, as well as a population that came from a variety of ethnic and linguistic backgrounds. This diversity would persist after the English took control. The old Dutch landowning families who had settled along the Hudson River Valley continued to have significant influence. Well into the 19th century, Dutch would be spoken throughout the state. The city of New York, though hardly the metropolis it would become in the 19th century, became an important trade and financial center for the North American colonies well before the American Revolution.

New Jersey

In 1664, the Duke of York divided his grant, which included land between the Hudson and Delaware Rivers, which became New Jersey. The New Jersey colony was granted to two of the Duke of York's friends, who found it difficult to enforce their rights as proprietors. Like New York, the diversity of religious and national origins in New Jersey meant that it was difficult to establish a state church, as was the case in New England and southern colonies.

Pennsylvania

Pennsylvania was established as a haven for Quakers, a persecuted minority sect that had developed out of Puritanism. Most Quakers were people from the middling ranks of English society: artisans, farmers, and landless laborers. Quakerism had a strong egalitarian emphasis that attracted lower-class membership and proved an irritant to England's elites. Quakers had no formal order of worship and allowed all, women as well as men, who felt led to speak as the Holy Spirit guided them in worship services. This disregard for social hierarchy enraged English men and women. Many Quakers were jailed and even killed during persecutions in the 1660s and 1670s.

One of the few well-heeled Quakers was William Penn, who came from an aristocratic family with close ties to King Charles II. When Penn requested a haven for Quakers to be established in America, Charles II saw this as an opportunity to rid England of what had become a worrisome group of religious dissenters. In 1681, Penn was granted a charter and 45,000 square miles of land. This new colony would be called Pennsylvania. Penn did not establish the colony for religious reasons alone; he also hoped to profit from the sale of much of this land. English Quakers jumped at the opportunity to escape persecution in England and establish their own community in the colonies. Quakers also appealed to other persecuted religious sects in Germany, France, Holland, Sweden, and elsewhere to come worship freely in the new colony. As a result, like New York and New Jersey, Pennsylvania would have a religious and ethnic diversity that was unmatched in New England or the southern colonies. The Quakers, however, maintained control of the colony until the American Revolutionary period.

Georgia

Georgia was a buffer zone between the British colonies and Spanish Florida and was occupied by the Yamasee people until South Carolinians and their Indian allies attacked them in 1715–1717 and forced them from the area. In 1732, James Oglethorpe, a social reformer and Member of Parliament, acquired a royal charter to establish a colony there to be populated by English men and women who had been confined to debtors' prisons. It was not a "penal colony" per se where prisoners were to be transported as part of their punishment. As a result, slavery was not initially permitted by Georgia's directors. When the ban on slavery was overturned in 1749, however, Georgian planters, like those in South Carolina, began to import large numbers of slaves from rice-growing regions of Africa. By 1775, slaves outnumbered white residents in Georgia.

> **Competency 005 Descriptive Statement D.** The beginning teacher demonstrates knowledge of the foundations of representative government in the United States (e.g., ways in which the Mayflower Compact, the Iroquois Confederacy, the Fundamental Orders of Connecticut, and the Virginia House of Burgesses contributed to the growth of representative government).

Key Question

How did the colonial experience of self-rule contribute to a uniquely American culture of representative government? A related question is to what degree was the American culture of democratic values an outgrowth of a developing American identity or the persistence of English values in the Americas?

Magna Carta (1215)

English men and women traced the concept of rights of Englishmen to the Magna Carta, which accorded "all free men" of the English kingdom certain rights, including the right of *habeas corpus* and property protections against judicial seizure without due process.

Virginia House of Burgesses (1619)

In an effort to attract more settlers to Virginia, the Virginia Company of London reduced the powers of its appointed governor and issued a "charter of grants and liberties" that included the creation of the House of Burgesses, the first elective assembly in colonial America.

Mayflower Compact (1620)

The *Mayflower*, with 107 settlers aboard, was blown off course from its original destination of Virginia Colony. As they lacked authorization to settle on Cape Cod, in present-day Massachusetts, the Pilgrims drew up their own charter establishing first their right to self-rule, and then determining that decisions would be based on democratic principles, with the proviso that women and children had no voting rights. The document was signed by the adult males aboard ship and represents the first written framework for self-government in what is the United States.

The Massachusetts Body of Liberties (1641)

The Massachusetts Body of Liberties was ratified by the Massachusetts General Assembly in 1641 and represents the first written legal code in New England. The text outlined significant protections for many categories of individuals. For example, married women were protected by law against domestic abuse or disinheritance. Religious refugees were guaranteed certain protections. Even animals "usually kept for man's use" were protected from cruel treatment. There were guarantees that slavery and serfdom were forbidden, though the protections against human enslavement were so defined as to allow it in practice. The Body of Liberties, however, also commanded capital punishment for those who worshipped any god other than the Christian god, or who was convicted of witchcraft, or who blasphemed.

New England Town Meeting

One of the most important institutions in the early development of American traditions of democracy was the New England town meeting. From the establishment of Massachusetts Bay Colony, most local decisions were made in a process of direct democracy in which townsmen voted for town officials, determined tax rates, awarded land allotments to resident families, established schools, and in other ways regulated daily life. The town meeting proved to be an important schoolhouse of democratic behavior. Most adult males during their lifetime would at some point serve as an elected officeholder.

Iroquois Confederacy (or Iroquois League)

The Iroquois Confederacy was made up of the Mohawk, Onondaga, Oneida, Cayuga, Seneca, and, after 1722, the Tuscarora of the Great Lakes region. The confederacy existed before European arrival, though precisely when is debated. The confederacy was formed to put an end to inter-tribal conflict. Europeans recognized that they needed to trade with this confederation to facilitate land acquisition and access to the fur trade. The creation of the Iroquois Confederation Council, some historians argue, provided a model for a number of features of U.S. constitutionalism. Benjamin Franklin held up the Iroquois Confederacy as a model for the Americans at the Albany Congress in 1754.

Fundamental Orders of Connecticut (1639)

Connecticut claims the nickname "The Constitution State," largely in reference to the adoption of the Fundamental Orders of Connecticut in 1639. Connecticut residents claim this document as the first Western-style constitution. In English and previous Western European history, constitutions did not imply a singular, written document as we understand the term constitution to suggest today. Instead, a constitution was merely the laws, edicts, judgments, and customs that *constituted* the institutions of government at that historical moment.

The Glorious Revolution (1688)

Political events in Great Britain did not go unnoticed in Britain's North American colonies. In 1685, James II acceded to the throne. When James II, a Catholic, announced his heir would be baptized Catholic, Parliament peacefully overthrew the king, turning the throne over to the Protestant and Dutch Prince William of Orange and his English wife, Mary.

James had been for 20 years the proprietor of New York. When he became king, he advocated revoking all colonial charters and placing the colonies under direct royal authority. In 1684, he had annulled the Massachusetts Bay Charter of 1629. Similar policies were enacted in Connecticut, Rhode Island, and New Jersey. James ordered that a single administrative unit, **The Dominion of New England**, be constructed, combining all of New England, New York, and New Jersey. A close ally, James Andros, was appointed governor of this new dominion. It seemed clear to the colonists that James II planned to undermine all local authority and to impose a religious settlement that was unsatisfactory to New England's Puritans.

The Glorious Revolution precipitated a series of revolts in the colonies that presaged the American Revolution nearly a century later. In New England, a committee of merchants and Puritan ministers arrested the governor and placed him aboard a ship to England. His supporters were jailed. Participation in this rebellion encouraged greater popular political consciousness. Similar uprisings took place in New York and Maryland.

English Bill of Rights (1689)

The Bill of Rights were presented by Parliament to William and Mary as conditions under which the new monarchs would find their powers limited following the Glorious Revolution. Among the requirements of this Bill of Rights were free elections, regular parliamentary meetings, and freedom of speech in parliament. Individuals were protected from cruel and unusual punishments, and the right for Protestant subjects to bear arms in their self-defense was guaranteed. The document also insisted that the monarchy govern through Parliament and that the populace be represented by Parliament. The articulation of these rights in written form and the tradition of parliamentary representation would be vital to later American conceptions of political power.

> **Competency 005 Descriptive Statement E.** The beginning teacher analyzes the influence of various factors on the development of colonial society (e.g., geography, slavery, processes of spatial exchange [diffusion]).

Key Question

 What role did geography, slavery, and migration play in creating different colonial societies in New England, the Middle Colonies, and the South?

Geography

The geography of the colonies influenced the kinds of settlements that flourished and the ways in which the colonies developed.

New England Colonies

Though New England's rocky soil and short growing seasons did not make for great farmland, small family-run farms were the backbone of the agricultural economy. Because the farms were small, much of the farming was subsistence farming with only small surpluses available for the market. New England's coastline offered numerous sheltered harbors where fishing communities developed. Its forest lands provided timbers for ship-builders both in New England and for the British navy.

Middle Colonies

Pennsylvania was known as the "best poor-man's country," because of the ready availability of land. Wages or terms of indenture were more favorable in these conditions than elsewhere. Though most of the populace lived in close proximity to Philadelphia, Scots-Irish immigrants and German immigrants in the 18th century found the rich farmland of central Pennsylvania hospitable starting places for farms devoted to producing grains for the market. The farther west settlers moved, however, the costs of transport meant that it was more cost effective to distill grain into whiskey. The frontier settlers of Pennsylvania and New York also depended on the fur trade for income. Similar land grants along the most fertile river valleys also left less agricultural land accessible to settlement by small landowners. In the Middle Colonies, nonetheless, grain farmers on much larger farms than those in New England produced food for the urban markets of Philadelphia and New York City.

Southern Colonies

The climate and rich soils of the southern colonies encouraged the growth of profitable cash crops for export. Tobacco, rice, indigo, and later cotton would provide the dominant source of revenue for plantation owners in the region. A key consequence of this kind of mono-crop agriculture, however, was rapid depletion of soil nutrients. Without chemical or other fertilizers, the soil rapidly tired and yields declined. As a result, acquiring new sources of land was an imperative. The dependence on slave labor also resulted in reduction in white settlement in those areas where the plantation economy was most profitable. Poorer whites were as a result shunted off to less fertile soils in the Appalachian foothills or later into Kentucky and Tennessee. And, because most of the profits of the plantation economy accrued to the families of large land holders, the South never developed the same base of consumers who made possible economic growth in the Middle Colonies and New England. Wealthy landowners purchased their clothing, household furnishings, and other amenities from England, while poorer white settlers increasingly turned to subsistence agriculture on less fertile land.

Slavery and Racial Hierarchies

One of the important features in all the American colonies was the reliance (to varying degrees) of each colony on enslaved labor. The importance of slavery to the British colonies in North America had a critical role in shaping American culture.

The first African slaves arrived in Virginia in 1619. Over the course of the slave trade an estimated 500,000 enslaved persons would be imported either directly from Africa or through the West Indies to British North America. Each British colony in North America relied on enslaved labor or on profits from the slave trade.

Northern Slavery

Rhode Island shippers, for example, every year in the middle of the 18th century, outfitted 18 ships for voyages to West Africa where they traded rum, cloth, and other wares for African slaves. Other northern colonies depended less on the slave trade itself, but did rely on slaves. New Netherlands, New Jersey, and Pennsylvania all employed slaves to clear the land, build fortifications, and lay out the streets for towns and farmsteads. As the colonies became more established, northern cities of New York, Boston, and Philadelphia each had significant minorities of slaves working on the docks, in manufacturing, and as domestic labor. Rural farmers in the North also employed slave labor, though not as extensively as was the case in the South.

Southern Slavery

The southern colonies of Maryland, Virginia, North Carolina, South Carolina, and Georgia had much larger numbers of slaves than did the northern colonies. In 1750, the population of slaves in the five southern states numbered over 204,000 out of a total population of nearly 515,000 people. In some southern colonies, as late as the middle of the 18th century, slaves outnumbered the white population. South Carolina, for example, over 70 percent of residents were enslaved in 1750. In Virginia, at mid-century, 44 percent of the population were of African descent, the vast majority of them slaves.

From the outset, racial distinctions were used to separate slaves from indentured servants and other white laborers. But, the racial categories that supported the slave system did not develop immediately. Free blacks could own land and even purchase indentured servants' contracts, or even slaves. Blacks and whites worked alongside one another and shared much of their daily life. Gradually, however, legal divisions were established to separate blacks from whites.

Laws were established that gave a child born of a free parent and an enslaved parent the status of a slave. This reversed European practice and made it profitable for slave owners to take sexual advantage of slave women. Other laws made clear that a slave's conversion to Christianity had no effect on his social status, decriminalized physical abuse, even murder of a slave by its owner, outlawed miscegenation (interracial marriage), and in other ways established a separation of the races. These laws were most rigorously enforced in the southern colonies, but a persistent racial divide developed throughout the colonies.

Spatial Exchange (Diffusion)

Spatial exchange refers to the processes whereby ideas, products, or cultural traits spread from one region to another. In colonial America, these processes were ongoing, ubiquitous, and complex.

With the arrival of European settlers, the folkways, technologies, building styles, clothing, and many other traits were transported from Europe to the Americas. Something as obvious as the spread of the English language to the Atlantic coast colonies represents diffusion. More specific examples also abound. For example, many of the cultural features associated with New England derived from a particular region in England from where many of the earliest Puritan settlers came. The distinctive New England accent—for example, think "Pahk the cahr in Hahvuhd Yahd," for "Park the car in Harvard Yard"—is a derivation of what in England was called the "Norfolk Whine," an accent from East Anglia in England. New Englanders often built salt-box or Cape Cod-style houses, a building style often seen in East Anglia.

The American South also had distinctive folkways with roots in England (and Africa). Virginia's distinctive drawl and pronunciation patterns, which differed markedly from those in New England and the Middle Colonies, had roots in the English counties along its English Channel coast. The influence of Irish, Scots, and Scots-Irish culture on the culture of poorer whites living in the foothills of the Appalachians from South Carolina to Pennsylvania is another example of cultural diffusion. The frequency of dueling in this population may have been a carryover of Irish dueling clubs and the duty in these Celtic cultures of settling disputes in this fashion. The music that would become bluegrass reflects traditional Celtic musical styles.

Southerners were also, not surprisingly, influenced by African folkways and language. The contribution of Africans and African Americans to the development of an American colonial culture should receive mention. Many English language terms derive from African languages, such as *banana*, *okra*, *yams*, and other terms associated with food and folkways, as well as many other words. African agricultural know-how was instrumental to the success of the southern plantation economy. Rice and indigo were crops that Africans knew well; South Carolina planters purposefully sought to purchase slaves from rice- and indigo-growing regions of Africa. The first "cowboys" were Africans. Africans were familiar with open-range cattle herding, a form of husbandry not practiced in England. And, because African men were often referred to, in a demeaning way, as "boys," therefore, cattle herders in the Carolinas were known as "cowboys."

COMPETENCY 006 (REVOLUTIONARY ERA AND THE EARLY YEARS OF THE REPUBLIC)

The teacher understands significant historical events and developments of the Revolutionary Era and the early years of the Republic, including the foundations of representative government in the United States.

Periodization: 1754 to 1814

The Revolutionary era and the early Republic extend from 1754 to 1814. This is the period during which Britain's thirteen North American colonies gained independence from Great Britain and established the United States of America. Seventeen fifty-four would appear to be an early date at which to begin the Revolutionary Era. It was the start of the French and Indian War, (also known as the Seven Years' War) which would last until 1763. The cost of this war for the British Empire and the sense of accomplishment gained by American colonists during the war would be important contributing factors leading to the American Revolution. The end of the War of 1812, which confirmed the new republic's independence from its "mother country," represents a useful bookend of the period.

The period from 1754–1838 can be subdivided into five eras, each marked by its own issues and events.

1754–1763: The French and Indian War (known in Europe as the Seven Years' War)

1764–1775: Crisis of Anglo-American Relations

1775–1783: **Revolutionary War**

1781–1789: **Government under the Articles of Confederation** (and Constitutional Crisis)

1789–1824: **The Early Republic**

1828–1840: **The Age of Jacksonian Democracy**

Competency 006 Descriptive Statement A. The beginning teacher demonstrates knowledge of individuals, events, and issues that shaped the development of U.S. society during the Revolutionary Era and early years of the Republic.

Key Question

The focus of this descriptive statement is on the "development of U.S. society during the revolutionary era and early years of the republic." What were the changes in American society during this period and how did those changes come about?

Periodization: 1763 to 1824

This period can be divided as follows: a period of revolutionary change from 1763 to 1789, followed by a period (1789–1824) in which the United States, under a new constitution, wrestled with the implications of the new society and political culture that had developed during the Revolutionary Period.

Enlightenment Ideas

An important current of change that affected educated Americans were the ideas of the European Enlightenment. Enlightenment thinkers believed that science and reason, rather than religion, provided the best method to explain natural phenomena and human social behavior. The most prominent Americans influenced by Enlightenment thought were Thomas Jefferson and Benjamin Franklin, both of whom reached wide audiences with their published works. Enlightenment thinkers had important influences on the development of American government. Montesquieu, a French political philosopher held, for example, that the power of monarchy could best be checked by a **separation of powers** between executive, legislative, and judicial branches. Enlightenment thinkers from John Locke to Jean-Jacques Rousseau argued that political power was derived from a social contract between the ruler and the people, and not from divine ordination. A corollary of this view was that if a ruler had violated the terms of that social contract, the people could justly rebel against him. Enlightenment thinkers challenged the use of judicial torture or cruel and unusual punishments, a feature of the United States Bill of Rights. Religious toleration was also a hallmark of Enlightenment belief. Many of the American founding fathers also believed, as did most Enlightenment thinkers, in Deism. This is the view that God, like a watchmaker, created the cosmos at the beginning of time, but no longer intervened directly or in a prophetic sense in the workings of the cosmos, leaving it to operate according to natural laws of science. In the realm of economics, the works of Adam Smith, a Scottish Enlightenment figure, played an important role for Americans who read his *The Wealth of Nations*. Smith argued that the free market, rather than government or corporate monopolies, best met the needs of the widest number of workers, consumers, manufacturers, and the society as a whole.

Constitutionalism

As each of the 13 colonies ended its traditional allegiance to Great Britain, each adopted a new written constitution. As they had rejected monarchical authority, these constitutions founded **republics**. These republics varied in terms of their structure and the degree of popular participation that the constitution encouraged. For example, Pennsylvania had a one-house legislature, near universal manhood suffrage, and constitutional guarantees of free speech and religion. Most other states designed constitutions that maintained significant property qualification for voters and officeholding. Despite these differences, the various states shared the common practice of constructing written constitutions to secure basic liberties, which has become a key feature of American political traditions.

Voting Rights

During the Revolutionary Period and the Early Republic, the right to vote was widely extended. By the 1780s, most taxpaying, property-owning white males were eligible to vote. During the period from 1814 to 1824, the suffrage (right to vote) expanded still further. By the 1830s, in most states, universal white male suffrage was the norm. And, perhaps surprisingly given the poor voter turnout in modern elections, Americans eligible to vote did so in high proportions.

Egalitarianism

A spirit of egalitarianism had infected the American colonies since well before the beginning of the American Revolution. It was only heightened by the events of the Revolution and the Early Republic. During the Revolution, as colonial elites sought the support of citizens for the patriotic cause, demands for social and political equality were increasingly realized. This showed up in refusals to address social betters with titles or demonstrations of deference. Rather than refer to someone as "His Honor," or "Gentleman," or "My Lord," Americans increasingly used the designations "Mr." or "Mrs." Another feature of growing egalitarianism was the abolition of **primogeniture,** or the practice of granting the bulk of an inheritance to the first-born son. This practice, common in Europe, was thought to lead inexorably to an aristocracy. Instead, Americans adopted **equal inheritance,** or granted to parents the right to divide their inheritance as they wished.

Religious Toleration

While Pennsylvania and Rhode Island had long encouraged religious toleration, on the eve of the American Revolution, they were unique. Most of the colonies both supported churches from the public coffers, and refused voting rights and officeholding to Catholics, Jews, and some Protestant denominations. The United States' alliance with the French, a Catholic nation, and the many Catholic Europeans (from France, Poland, and elsewhere) who joined the American cause, encouraged greater tolerance of Catholics. Americans influenced by Enlightenment ideas, like Thomas Jefferson and Benjamin Franklin, also began to agitate for an end to state sponsorship of religion, and for a disestablishment of church and state. In most of the state constitutions written during the period, the free exercise of religion was increasingly permitted.

Free Labor and Free Trade

The revolutionary celebration of liberty soon extended to concerns about the varieties of coerced, or "unfree," labor. This included the labor of enslaved persons, but also of domestic and indentured servants. By 1800, indentured servitude had largely been eliminated across all of the United States. Even domestic servants began to claim greater rights. Servants would demand the right to eat with the family, saying they were as good as anyone and "it's a free country." Others refused to call their employers "master" or "mistress." The Dutch word *baas,* which ironically meant "master," anglicized to "boss," was used instead.

Traditional early modern European and American notions of trade and manufacturing operated on the assumption that local and national governments had a responsibility to regulate prices, ensure the quality of manufactured products, guarantee that bakers, butchers, and grocers did not adulterate their products. During the Revolutionary Era and the period of the Early Republic, much of this regulatory purpose was rejected. Freedom of commerce and freedom of movement for laborers became a feature of American economic life (except, of course, for enslaved African Americans).

The Contradiction of Slavery

The contradiction between revolutionary demands for equality and liberty, and the presence in the American colonies of 500,000 enslaved persons, fully 20 percent of the population, was evident then and now. Before the revolution, there had been only a handful of ardent opponents of slavery and the slave trade in the Americas, though opposition to slavery had prominent voices in England. During the revolution, however, Americans had to confront this contradiction.

Abolition of Slavery in the North

In 1777, Vermont wrote the first constitution banning the practice of slavery. In 1780, Pennsylvania passed a law that authorized the gradual emancipation of slaves born after that year. The

Massachusetts Supreme Court in 1783 declared slavery unconstitutional. New York, New Jersey, and the remaining northern states by 1804 had abolished the institution of slavery. Because most of these laws called for gradual emancipation, however, as late as 1830 there were 3,500 people of African descent still enslaved across the North.

Competency 006 Descriptive Statement B. The beginning teacher analyzes causes of the American Revolution (e.g., mercantilism, British policies following the French and Indian War).

Key Question

The causes of the American Revolution, though complex, can be divided into two categories: (1) **immediate causes**, including British policies between 1763 and 1775 and the American colonists' reaction to them; and (2) **proximate causes**, or underlying factors that contributed to both why the British made the policy decisions they did and why American colonists reacted to them as they did. This descriptive statement requires test-takers to understand the immediate causes.

Periodization: 1763 to 1776

The immediate causes of the American Revolution can be identified in the changes in British policy after 1763 and the American colonists' reaction to those policy changes between 1763 and 1776.

Mercantilism and British Imperialism

Before the 1760s, colonial Americans had largely appreciated the benefits of belonging to the British empire. The collection of laws governing trade within the British Empire, known as the Navigation System, were designed to both encourage trade between Britain and its colonies and to ensure economic growth in the colonies. Though the Navigation System had not been entirely welcome, the British colonies in North America had prospered under the "salutary neglect" of the British government. The colonists' taxes were not high; they had developed a comparatively high standard of living; and they were not unhappy at the state of their relations with the monarchy. Beginning in the 1760s, however, the British parliament began to tighten controls over the empire. Specifically, the parliament sought to assert its sovereignty or authority over the colonies, to regulate more carefully their economic development, and to shift some of the burden of paying for the empire onto the colonies. The guiding economic theory that dictated this policy change was what has been called **mercantilism.**

Mercantilist economic policies were designed to shape colonial economies to benefit the economy of the "mother country." The southern plantation economy and the British sugar islands of the West Indies suited the British mercantilist model. Sugar, tobacco, rice, indigo, and other lucrative cash crops were exchanged for British manufactures. These commodities were marketed in Britain or re-exported to other European buyers, thereby improving the balance of trade between Great Britain and its competitors. Urban economic developments in the seaport towns of Boston, Philadelphia, and New York, however, were increasingly competitive with British manufacturing and shipping. Restraining these developments was one aim of British colonial policy. Local agriculture was reorganized to produce stable crops for Britain to process, rather than mixed cropping for local consumption and sale. American ship manufacturing and the carrying trade by American vessels also were seen as competition to British shipping.

The objective of British colonial policy after 1763 was to redirect the colonial economy to benefit Great Britain. The resulting increases in tension with American colonists would be one factor in the growing distrust and then outright rebellion directed by colonials towards the British monarchy.

British Policy After 1763

The economic policy of the British Empire after 1763 underwent a profound change that would greatly weaken the ties between the American colonies and the Kingdom of Great Britain.

British Policy After 1763

The French and Indian War (1754–1763)

In 1749, the government of Virginia, which claimed the Ohio territory, granted over a half-million acres of land in Ohio to the Ohio Company, whose stockholders included the Governor of Virginia, George Washington, and many other wealthy Virginians. Ohio was claimed by Virginia, but also by French Canada. In 1754, George Washington was sent into the territory to survey the land and to protect the claim from French fur traders. When he was routed from Ohio and a contingent of British Redcoats were also forced to surrender, this American conflict spread to Europe, where it was known as the Seven Years' War, and into the Caribbean, the Atlantic Ocean, and even into Asia. France and Great Britain, along with their respective allies, fought what many historians have called the first truly global war. The fighting officially ended in 1763, with Great Britain the clear victor. Under the terms of the **Treaty of Paris of 1763**, French Canada was awarded to Great Britain. The British, while victorious, saw their national debt double. The cost of British administration and defense of their North American colonies rose to nearly 400,000 pounds per year.

Crisis of Anglo-American Relations (1764–1775)

The American colonies basked in the victory of the British Empire in the Seven Years' War and fully expected to reap the rewards of the victory. It is doubtful that anyone could have imagined that a decade later, the 13 North American colonies would be on the brink of declaring their independence from the mother country. Though there were significant underlying issues causing the American colonies to begin to resent British authority, the immediate causes of the American independence movement were the missteps of the British government, compounded by the ferocity of the American colonists' response.

Proclamation Act of 1763

To keep the peace with Indian populations west of the Appalachian Mountains, the parliament sought to restrain colonial settlers from encroaching on Indian lands. The Proclamation Act of 1763 therefore forbade settlement west of the Appalachian watershed. Colonial Americans, eager to profit from the victory over the French, and their Indian allies felt the spoils of war had been denied them. The British also stationed 10,000 soldiers in North America, most of them on the frontiers, to protect the colonists from likely Indian attack and to keep settlers from crossing the Proclamation Line. This had the doubly negative effect of increasing the cost of British administration and angering the colonists.

Writs of Assistance

One way to improve tax collection was to tighten administration, and most immediately, to improve enforcement of the navigation system. One of the means to enforce laws that required the colonies to pay certain taxes on imported items, or forbade the colonists to trade in other consumer items were Writs of Assistance. Writs of Assistance were search warrants used to find smuggled goods. Though widely opposed by Boston and Rhode Island merchants, they did significantly increase the yearly collection of duties.

Sugar Act (1764)

The Sugar Act was designed to raise needed revenue, as opposed to the usual purpose of the Navigation Acts to regulate and direct trade patterns. Legislation aimed at raising revenue for the British represented a new and worrisome precedent. In addition, the intent of the Sugar Act was to protect sugar producers in the British West Indies from competition. It reduced the tax per gallon on French West Indian molasses, which New Englanders refined into rum to exchange in Africa for slaves, or re-exported to England, marked as a product of the British Empire. But because the reduction in the tax rate was coupled with more stringent anti-smuggling measures and with requirements that the tax be paid in specie, merchants were more likely to pay the lower rate than they had the earlier tax. Customs officials were also permitted to seize cargo with only the flimsiest of probable cause, which further angered American merchants.

Stamp Act (1765)

The Sugar Act did not raise enough revenue to help defray the costs of British administration and defense of the colonies. The British Prime Minister, **George Grenville**, then proposed the passage of a **direct tax** on paper goods. Stamps were affixed to newspapers, books, legal documents, licenses, playing cards, etc. The Stamp Act specified that the proceeds would go directly to pay the salaries of British officials and the costs of defending the American frontier.

"No Taxation without Representation"

The Stamp Act angered colonists because it was a **direct tax**. Prior to 1765, taxes on the colonies introduced by Parliament were largely **indirect taxes**, like those on imports and exports of commodities. Colonists objected that direct taxes should only be imposed on entities that had direct representation in Parliament. British parliamentarians contended that all British subjects, including those in the colonies, were **virtually represented** by parliamentary members. The objection **"No Taxation Without Representation"** became a rallying cry for patriots who objected that Parliamentary power over the colonies was denying colonists their basic liberties. Patriots like John Dickinson likened the situation of those taxed without representation to that of slaves.

Stamp Act Crisis

Widespread resistance erupted in response to the Stamp Act. Colonial elites in Boston, New York, and Philadelphia mobilized the **Sons of Liberty**: artisans, tradesmen, dock workers, and others on the lower ranks of the social ladder who used threats and violence to intimidate Loyalists and attacked customs posts and British officials. Merchants and consumers signed **Non-Importation Agreements**, agreeing to boycott British goods. The Sons of Liberty were often called out to threaten storekeepers and shoppers who didn't abide by these agreements. Each colony also sent representatives to the **Stamp Act Congress** to coordinate colonial response to British policy. In the end, the Stamp Act was rescinded.

Declaratory Act (1766)

Parliament backed down on the Stamp Act in the face of widespread unrest and opposition, but with the Declaratory Act of 1766, it reasserted its authority to pass legislation for the American colonies "in all cases whatsoever."

Townshend Act (1767)

Because the colonists had objected so vehemently to the Stamp Act as a direct and internal tax, a new series of "external" or indirect taxes were raised by Parliament and named after the new Prime Minister. These taxes were levied on luxury items (glass, lead, paint, and paper) and on tea, which was at this time a staple of the English diet, a delivery system for the sugar produced in Great Britain's island colonies, and an important source of calories for Americans. In response to the Townshend Acts, there were renewed attempts to boycott British goods and to intimidate British authorities.

Boston "Massacre" (1770)

The deadlock between the colonists and English authorities resulted in the stationing of four regiments in Boston to keep the peace. These "redcoats" were seen as "occupation by a standing army" and deeply resented. The poorly paid troops also moonlighted, creating further hostilities. Additionally, the 29th Regiment of Foot (infantry) had a contingent of former slaves from the West Indies. Their presence added a racial element to the tension that was opened up with the flogging of white troops in Boston's public square by four black soldiers. In March 1770, a riotous crowd gathered at a sentry post. Soldiers fired into the crowd, killing five people. This proved to be a public relations disaster. Americans came to perceive the British forces not as an ordering presence, but as an imperialistic occupying force.

Somerset v. Stewart (1772)

This decision, while not as well-known as other events in the lead-up to the American Revolution, deserves mention primarily for its role in heightening tensions in the southern colonies. The presiding judge in this case determined that in England (though not in the colonies) slavery was so "odious" that it could not be established where it did not exist except by "positive law"—in short, by a Parliamentary enactment or royal decree. Southern slaveholders saw this case as an important corroboration of their fear that Britain was being increasingly influenced by abolitionist politics. Many slaves also heard news of the decision, leading some to run away in the hopes of making their way to freedom in England.

Tea Act (1773)

This legislation was enacted to protect the British East India Company (BEIC) from economic difficulties at the expense of the American colonies by allowing the company to sell directly to American consumers and granted tax rebates to the company, making it possible for the company to undercut colonial merchants and tradesmen, even those who smuggled Dutch tea into the colonies.

Boston Tea Party (1773)

Everywhere in the colonies but Boston, shipments of BEIC tea were refused entry, but in Boston the Massachusetts governor owned the trading company with the concession to sell BEIC tea. He was determined to have the cargos of tea unloaded. Radical patriots dressed as Indians dumped 46 tons of tea worth the substantial sum of £9,659 (over $4 million today) onto the frozen surface of Boston harbor.

Coercive Acts (1774)

In response, Parliament passed a series of laws to punish Massachusetts residents for their continued acts of rebellion. The first of these laws restricted the power of the Massachusetts General Assembly and of town meetings in Massachusetts, in effect suspending Massachusetts self-government. The second closed Boston's harbor until the BEIC was repaid the damages. A third law ordered Massachusetts residents charged with rebellion to be tried elsewhere in the colonies, denying them the right to a trial by their peers.

Massachusetts' response to these orders was to force royally appointed judges to resign their positions, prevent local courts (under British authority) from convening, and to start developing new institutions of government; in short, to initiate a revolution. In Philadelphia and Virginia, similar acts of rebellion occurred.

First Continental Congress

Conservatives who feared the eruption of mob violence called for a meeting of representatives from each colony to propose a solution to the British for the constitutional crisis in which the British government and the colonists found themselves. The First Continental Congress met in Philadelphia in the fall of 1774. Rather than developing a conciliatory or moderate proposal to resolve matters, Patriot representatives hijacked the convention and instead offered an overt challenge to the authority of the British Parliament and British law. By the beginning of 1775, Patriots had control of the countryside from Georgia to New Hampshire. Claims by the British governors of British sovereignty over the colonies were belied by the situation on the ground throughout British North America. A practical revolution had already been accomplished, as local institutions were largely in the hands of Patriots who favored outright independence from England. Though the First Continental Congress met initially with the intent of coordinating negotiation with the British government, in the end it moved the 13 colonies toward an outright break with England.

Common Sense

American colonists debated widely in taverns, households, and on the public square the grievances and injustices they felt at the hands of the British government. Increasingly, they began to employ the language of John Locke and the Enlightenment, claiming "natural rights," "equality," and "liberty" as justification for their pursuit of independence. Perhaps the most widely read articulation of American objections to British rule was **Thomas Paine's** *Common Sense,* which appealed to a wide reading public and sold some 150,000 copies. Paine's writing galvanized many Americans to join the Patriot cause.

Declaration of Independence

In July 1776, the Continental Congress met to declare the United States' independence. Thomas Jefferson was charged with writing this document. It began with a preamble that expressed the purpose and origin of government as the protection of natural rights to life, liberty, and the pursuit of happiness. It declared that rebellion is justified if these protections are no longer guaranteed by governments. The preamble identified in general terms the justifiable reasons for rebellion. The list of grievances that composed the remainder of the document outlined the case for why the American 13 colonies were justified in entering into a revolution.

> **Competency 006 Descriptive Statement C.** The beginning teacher understands significant political and economic issues of the Revolutionary Era (e.g., taxation without representation, enforcement of the Navigation Acts, Lexington, Concord, winter at Valley Forge, Treaty of Paris of 1783).

Key Question

What factors contributed to American success in the Revolutionary War?

Periodization: 1775 to 1783

The Revolutionary War began with the opening of hostilities in April 1775, well before the writing of the Declaration of Independence. The war took place in three separate acts. The first occurred in New England from 1775 to March 1776, when the British forces withdrew from Boston. The next theater of operations was in New York and New Jersey, as the British attempted to divide the Southern colonies from New England. The Continental Army confronted the British in New York, Pennsylvania, and New Jersey between 1776 and 1778. From there, the British turned their attention to the South, playing out the remainder of the war in Virginia and the Carolinas between 1778 and 1781.

Lexington and Concord (April 1775)

The Governor of Massachusetts, General Thomas Gage, in the spring of 1775 was ordered to suppress illegal Patriot assemblies, to capture their leaders, and to use force if necessary to disarm them and dispossess them of ammunition and military supplies. The unsuccessful attack on Lexington and Concord was repulsed by **"Minutemen,"** amateur soldiers of the colonial militia. Their success energized New Englanders to march on Boston to force the withdrawal of the British regulars and the governor, and the restoration of Massachusetts' General Assembly to its former authority. The success of the militia in this skirmish emboldened Massachusetts residents to take the reins of government and to besiege the British troops in Boston. After American cannons were positioned on the heights overlooking Boston in March 1776, the British withdrew from Boston and took up new headquarters in New York. Washington's army would follow.

Lord Dunmore's Proclamation (November 1775)

In the South, the British attempted to regain control by playing on racial division. In November 1775, the Virginia governor, Lord Dunmore, issued a proclamation that guaranteed freedom to slaves who joined the British. Within months, over 1,000 slaves had fled to the British. Over the course of the war, estimates are that as many as 30,000 slaves in Virginia alone fled their masters. The purpose of Dunmore's proclamation was intended primarily to sow fear in the hearts of southern slaveholders and encourage them to find a settlement with the British. Dunmore had earlier taken the gunpowder and other weaponry from Virginia's arsenal, removing it from the Virginia militia's control. These two actions had the opposite effect from what Dunmore had expected. Virginians became ever more committed to the Patriot cause.

Battle of Saratoga (October 1777)

The Battle of Saratoga was a critical victory for the American forces in the Revolution. A British army advancing southward along the Hudson River from Canada to reinforce British forces in New York City, was surrounded and forced to surrender. American morale was momentarily improved, and more importantly, this victory encouraged the French to assist the Americans in their independence movement. Two days after news of Saratoga arrived in Paris, the French and Americans concluded an alliance that would prove pivotal to American success. France gave formal recognition to the new American republic and agreed to provide war materiel and troops to aid the American cause. Without French assistance, it is doubtful that the Americans could have defeated the British regular army.

Valley Forge (1777–1778)

After the British withdrawal from New England, Washington's army had followed the British Redcoats to the Middle Colonies. But, after a series of indecisive battles, the army had dropped to fewer than 12,000 soldiers. During the bitter winter of 1777–1778, that number dropped further as Washington's men holed up some 20 miles northwest of Philadelphia. The men were ill-equipped for winter, many lacking proper shoes or coats. The Continental Congress failed to provide sufficient food or supplies. Thousands of soldiers died of typhoid, dysentery, smallpox, and other epidemic diseases. More deserted and went home. Half of the soldiers who stayed with Washington were recent immigrants and African-Americans, as well as landless laborers who had no incentive to return to their homes.

Loyalists (Tories)

It might be said that the American Revolution was both a war for independence and a civil war pitting fellow American against one another. Loyalists were found in every state, but New York, Pennsylvania, and the Carolina and Georgia backcountry had the largest populations of Loyalists. Many were convinced that British rule was better than the rule of what Loyalists considered "the mob." Minority populations, like French in Massachusetts, Scots in North Carolina, or Catholics also remained loyal because they considered the British government more likely to protect their rights than would the American majority. Often the determination to remain loyal to the British (or join the Patriot cause) had less to do with British policy than with local animosities. For example, when leading families in New York's Hudson Valley sided with the Patriots, tenant farmers on their land favored the Loyalist cause. In North Carolina, many residents of the western part of the state refused to join with easterners who favored the Patriot movement. Estimates are that between one-fifth and one-third of the colonial population were Loyalists. Among the terms of the Treaty of Paris, the Americans agreed that Loyalists would not be persecuted and that their property would be restored. Nonetheless, many Loyalists migrated to Canada or to British colonies in the West Indies.

Battle of Yorktown (1781)

After 1778, the British shifted their attention to the American South, hoping to exploit tensions between back-country Loyalists and the patriots. Fighting in South Carolina and in the foothills of the Appalachians grew so fierce—characterized by guerrilla warfare and atrocities on both sides—that the British commander, Lord Cornwallis, moved north into Virginia, where he took up a position on a peninsula extending out into the Chesapeake. This was a fateful mistake. Washington's army, assisted by an equal force of French soldiers, cut off Cornwallis on this promontory and awaited the arrival of a French naval fleet. Cornwallis was trapped and after a 17-day siege was forced to surrender. This defeat cost the British government any public support for the war and forced the British to begin peace negotiations soon after.

Treaty of Paris (1783)

The negotiations to resolve the American Revolutionary War took place in Paris. John Adams, Benjamin Franklin, and John Jay were the American delegates. The terms of the treaty confirmed the independence of the 13 colonies, granted to the United States all the land between the Appalachians and the Mississippi River, from Florida to the Canadian border. This treaty made the United States the first independent nation in the Western Hemisphere.

> **Competency 006 Descriptive Statement D.** The beginning teacher demonstrates knowledge of the foundations of representative government in the United States (e.g., the Articles of Confederation and issues of the Philadelphia Convention of 1787, such as major compromises and arguments for and against ratification).

Key Question

What factors led to the failure of the United States' first constitution, the Articles of Confederation, and the need for the Philadelphia Constitutional Convention to revise that constitution? How did the Constitution address the shortcomings of the Articles of Confederation?

Periodization: 1776 to 1789

The Articles of Confederation provided the framework of government for the United States of America from 1777 (though it was not formally ratified until 1781) until March 4, 1789, when the United States Constitution went into effect.

Articles of Confederation

The Articles of Confederation was the first constitution written to provide a framework of government for the new United States of America. Its primary author was John Dickinson, who wrote it in 1776 shortly after the writing of the Declaration of Independence. The Continental Congress approved the Articles in 1777 and ratified it four years later in 1781. The Articles of Confederation then served as the law of the land until 1789 when George Washington and a new Congress were sworn in.

The Articles of Confederation were largely a political response to the need for a union against Britain. It also reflected the deep suspicions that each of the states had at the development of a strong national government that might in the future trample on the rights of the individual states.

The powers of government were held by Congress, to which each state sent delegates. A state could send as many delegates as it wished, but each state had only one vote. There was no independent executive branch, nor a federal judiciary. The powers granted by the states to the Congress under the Articles of Confederation were quite limited: Congress had the right to declare war or negotiate peace treaties, administer the lands west of the Appalachians, and regulate weights, measures, coinage, and the mail system. The Articles of Confederation also required that for all bills relating to apportionment of tax burdens, and for foreign policy questions, a supermajority of nine of the 13 states had to be in agreement. And, to amend the Articles of Confederation, all 13 states had to be in agreement.

Other than these limiting constraints, the Congress was hamstrung by several weaknesses:

1. Congress could not regulate interstate or foreign trade.

2. Congressional laws did not supersede state laws and Congress lacked the power to enforce laws in the states.

3. Congress had no authority to tax; it could only rely on requisitioning revenue from the states, which then determined how and to what extent to tax their own citizens.

Congress under the Articles of Confederation did engineer a number of important successes: it successfully conducted the war with Great Britain and developed an alliance with France. It also passed a series of ordinances known as the **Northwest Ordinances,** which established a process for incorporating western lands into the union on equal footing with the original 13 states.

The inability of the Congress to raise sufficient revenue was a perennial problem. This made it difficult for the government to repay its debts to the French and to wealthy bondholders. Congress was also unable to protect American commercial interests and travel along the Mississippi. This significantly limited the appeal of western settlement as there was little guarantee that farmers in the Ohio country or in the Mississippi territory would be able to get their goods to market. Finally, the eruption of a rebellion by farmers in western Massachusetts, known as **Shays' Rebellion (1786),** (and similar unrest in other states) and the inability of state governments to guarantee order, resulted in pressure to amend the Articles of Confederation.

James Madison and **Alexander Hamilton** observe the weaknesses of the central government under the Articles of Confederation. They grew fearful that the new republic would soon falter and at a meeting held in September 1786 in Annapolis, Maryland, proposed that a convention be called to amend the Articles of Confederation. The date and location for this convention was set for the summer of 1787 in Philadelphia.

Philadelphia Constitutional Convention (1787)

Rather than amend the Articles of Confederation, however, the delegates to the convention decided to do away with it altogether. As the deliberations were bound to be controversial, the delegates also decided that the meetings would be carried out without public discussion or intrusion.

Among the items that the delegates agreed to without great debate were that the system of government would be a republic, and that it would consist of legislative, executive, and judicial branches designed to serve as a check and balance against unfettered power. The **Virginia Plan**, composed by Edmund Randolph and James Madison, called for a two-house legislature, with representation determined by the state's population. A counterproposal, introduced by William Paterson, known as the **New Jersey Plan**, maintained a **unicameral** (single-house) legislature with each state receiving equal representation. In the end, a compromise known as the **Great Compromise** resulted in the establishment of a **bicameral** legislature: representation in the lower house, or House of Representatives, was determined by population; while each state received equal representation in the upper house, or Senate.

The delegates to the convention then deliberated the process of selecting members of government. The convention was split on the value of direct election. Many feared the encouragement of "too much democracy" and called for indirect election of congressional representatives and the President. Madison considered it necessary to "broaden the base" of the government by having at least the lower house elected directly by the people. This was decided on. However, Senators and the president would be elected by state legislatures and the Electoral College respectively.

The counting of enslaved persons in calculating representation in the lower house then became an issue. States in the North with few slaves objected that slaves, who were technically property, should not be included in the calculation of population. Southern delegates, where slaves represented between 25 and 43 percent of the population, argued that slaves should be counted on an equal footing with other residents of the states. In the end, the Constitution included the language of the **Three-Fifths Compromise**, which drew on the method for apportioning taxes under the Articles of Confederation. Only three-fifths of a state's slave population would count for purposes of representation. This compromise greatly increased the South's influence in the House of Representatives. And, because of the creation of the **Electoral College**, a feature of the Constitution introduced by South Carolina's delegation, slave owners in the South would gain further influence in the election of the president. Eleven of the first 16 presidents were southern slaveholders.

Ratification Fight

The Constitution stipulated that it would go into effect when ratifying conventions in 9 of the 13 states had voted to approve the document.

John Jay, Alexander Hamilton, and James Madison wrote a series of essays under the pen name Publius, that were collected into a book called the **Federalist Papers**. These essays explained to the populace why the new Constitution was an improvement on the Articles of Confederation and why the Constitution was not a threat to American liberties, but rather a guarantee of them.

Supporters of the new Constitution were called Federalists; opponents were **Anti-Federalists.** Among the opponents of the Constitution's ratification were such leading revolutionaries as Patrick Henry, Samuel Adams, and John Hancock. These critics argued that too much state and local power was being lost to the national government. They also contended that the new government would be too easily swayed by private commercial or financial interests, and would not represent the people. In order to assuage the fears expressed by the Anti-Federalists, a number of amendments were proposed to the Constitution that would provide greater protections for individual rights and state authority. This **Bill of Rights** protected against Congressional infringement on religious freedom, freedoms of speech and assembly, the right to bear arms, and right to a fair judicial process, among others.

> **Competency 006 Descriptive Statement E.** The beginning teacher understands the origin and development of the American political system and political parties (e.g., Federalists, Democratic-Republicans, Jacksonian democracy, Whigs, Democrats). (1789–1836)

Key Question

In what ways was the Constitution interpreted and transformed as a consequence of the practical realities of governing?

Periodization: 1789 to 1836

The era of the Early Republic dates from 1789 to 1836 and the end of Andrew Jackson's term. The period from 1789 to 1814 is often seen as a period of significant political rivalry as two different interpretations of the Constitution coalesced into very different political parties. This early experimental period ended with American survival in what has sometimes been called the Second War for Independence, or the War of 1812. This early period, characterized by political rivalry and disagreement, was followed by an era known as the "Era of Good Feelings" between 1814 and 1824, during which overt political party competition was at a minimum. Then in 1828, a new political party system formed, which would last until just prior to the Civil War. The period from 1828 to 1836 is associated with the rise of a new democratic sensibility and the rise of the Democratic Party, led by Andrew Jackson.

The Constitution and Political Parties

The Constitution did not reference political parties, and the founders were opposed to the emergence of political parties, considering them to be a divisive force representative of special interests rather than the national good. George Washington, in his farewell address, an open letter to the American public, warned against the "spirit of faction," by which he meant the political parties that were already forming in preparation for the election to choose his successor. Washington's determination to resign the presidency following his second term would establish an important precedent, but his warning against the emergence of political parties would have much less impact.

Federalists

The Federalist Party was the first American political party, established by Alexander Hamilton, who was Secretary of the Treasury under George Washington. Hamilton had been instrumental in promoting the ratification of the Constitution and had been present at the convention, though was less vocal there. The Federalist Party favored a strong national government, the establishment of a national bank to stabilize the nation's currency and promote private investment, and protective tariffs to enable America's young manufacturing sector to compete with England's industrial economy. Hamilton considered England—an urban, industrializing nation—as the proper model for the future of the young United States.

Hamilton's plan for establishing American greatness included having the federal government assume the unpaid debts accumulated by the states during the Revolutionary War. This would create a new national debt that would be securitized by offering interest-bearing bonds to wealthy creditors. This would have the dual effect of binding the nation's elites to the new government and creating a new foundation for the nation's monetary system. The **Bank of the United States**, a privately held bank, issued bank notes and served as the central government's bank. Hamilton proposed to raise the revenue needed to service the interest on the debt and to pay for governmental functions by raising new excise taxes, notably on whiskey.

Democratic-Republicans

In opposition to Hamilton's vision of America, Thomas Jefferson and James Madison took the lead in creating a second political party, at first known as the Jeffersonian-Republicans, and later the Democratic-Republicans. Jefferson and Madison feared the concentration of financial and political power in a strong central government and favored a system that granted the states much greater political power. The Jeffersonian party, strongest in the South, mirrored earlier concerns about the powers of a central government to threaten states' rights.

Jefferson and Madison considered the ideal republic to be one composed of yeoman farmers (landowning small farmers), plantation owners, and independent craftsmen. They considered a citizenry composed of wage earners to be unlikely to long remain a republic. Jeffersonians considered the establishment of a National Bank as an unconstitutional overreach by the federal government, as there was no specific power granted to Congress to establish such a financial institution. This view, known as a **strict constructionist** interpretation of the Constitution, holds that only those powers explicitly granted to the federal government can be exercised by the federal government. All other powers remain in the hands of the states. Federalists argued that the Constitution granted Congress broad powers to "provide for the common defense and **general Welfare** of the United States."

Jefferson and Madison agreed to a compromise with Hamilton in 1790 that accepted the main features of Hamilton's proposals, in exchange for creating a permanent capital between Maryland and Virginia (the District of Columbia). This compromise ensured that the financial and political centers of the new republic were distinctly separated.

In addition to domestic issues, foreign policy concerns also divided the Federalists and the Democratic-Republicans. Jeffersonians saw a kindred spirit in the French revolutionaries, but the growing radicalism of the French Revolution after 1793 led Washington, Hamilton, and the Federalists to fear the possibility of similar social revolution in the United States. After 1793, the outbreak of hostilities between France and England (allied with Europe's other leading monarchies) complicated American independence. England engaged in a blockade of French ports, denying American ships the freedom to trade with the French, and seizing American ships trading with French sugar islands. The English, always in need of sailors, used the practice of **impressment**, essentially kidnapping sailors, even American citizens, and forcing them into the British Navy. In 1794, John Jay negotiated a treaty to resolve this and other difficulties dating back to the conclusion of the Revolutionary War. Democratic-Republicans objected, seeing the treaty as aligning the United States with the interests of the British monarchy and against the principles of liberty shared by the French and Americans.

In 1796, John Adams was elected president, following a particularly bitter contest that divided the nation along almost purely regional lines. New England, New York, and New Jersey voted for Adams; the South, with Pennsylvania, that perpetual swing state, voted for Jefferson. In foreign policy, Adams managed with difficulty to remain neutral. But in domestic affairs, Adams stirred greater partisan controversy with the passage of the **Alien and Sedition Acts (1798)**. These laws first reduced immigrants' ability to gain citizenship rights and authorized detention and prosecution of immigrants perceived as dangerous. Secondly, the series of laws authorized prosecution of those who criticized the government or slandered the president. These measures designed to silence Adams' opposition in the end backfired. Thomas Jefferson, in opposition to Adams' candidacy, ran on the slogan: "Jefferson and Liberty."

Among the landmarks of Jefferson's presidency was the court ruling in *Marbury v. Madison* in which Supreme Court Chief Justice John Marshall established the federal judiciary's power of "judicial review," that the Supreme Court has the power to determine whether Congressional legislation violates the Constitution. Jefferson also negotiated the purchase of the **Louisiana Territory** from France, doubling the size of the United States. The Constitution makes no mention of the federal government's power to buy territory from a foreign government. Jefferson's decision to authorize the purchase illustrates his view that the American republic could only thrive if it had a growing territory on which to settle a growing population of yeoman farmers and plantation owners.

During Jefferson's term, the United States struggled to remain uninvolved in the Napoleonic Wars that were paralyzing most of Europe. In response to both France and England's interference in American trade, Jefferson pressured Congress to ban all American shipping to Europe, believing that the **embargo** would force Europeans to trade fairly with United States merchants. The policy backfired and Jefferson left office in 1809, with the nation and the economy suffering. James Madison, elected in 1808, rescinded the general embargo and promised to use an embargo selectively against any European power that threatened American shipping. As Britain's navy dominated the seas and the French were unable to leave port, the British blockade of France also restricted American commerce. In response to British infringement on the principle of free trade, and with the hope of annexing Canada and Florida, the United States in 1812 declared war against Great Britain, beginning what has frequently been called the "Second War of Independence," or the **War of 1812.**

Between 1814 and 1828, the political party rivalry that characterized the first two decades of the early republic had faded. Opposition to the War of 1812 had resulted in the national discrediting of the Federalist party, which ceased to compete for national office. By 1824, even John Quincy Adams, son of the only Federalist president, concluded that there was no prospect for winning the presidency and had become a Democratic-Republican. He followed in his father's footsteps, but not as a Federalist.

Jacksonian Democracy

Between 1814 and 1824, a number of factors contributed to greater democratization of the nation. Increasingly, voting was done by ballot, rather than in a public division. Pushed by developments in the western states, property requirements for voting were gradually reduced. Campaigning for office, using stump speeches and signage or attracting voters to clambakes, musical concerts, etc., became commonplace. Additionally, while initially only a few states determined their Electoral College vote by giving the statewide winner of the popular vote all the electoral votes, by 1832 South Carolina alone relied on the state legislature to choose their Electoral College voters. This increased campaigning by presidential hopefuls or their subordinates for the popular vote.

In 1824, Andrew Jackson lost to John Quincy Adams, despite winning a plurality of the nationwide popular and Electoral College vote. The presidency was decided in the House of Representatives. Jackson complained that Adams' election was a result of a "corrupt bargain" done in the House. Though the election followed constitutional process, Jackson nonetheless claimed a popular legitimacy.

Jackson ran again in 1828, and definitively earned both popular vote and Electoral College majorities. Jackson won 56 percent of the popular vote. More significantly, over 1 million voters cast ballots in 1828, nearly quadrupling the vote total in 1824. This turnout was encouraged by a new style of overt campaigning and personal appeal. Jackson's victory was clearly a democratic victory or evidence of majority rule. His inauguration was a demonstration of his populist support, as Washington, D.C., was overrun with celebrants from the trans-Appalachian West and the lower and middle classes. The Washington elite were more than a little shocked at the democratic spirit of the inauguration.

Jackson's policies reflected his perception of the democratic nature of his legitimacy. Jackson employed the **spoils system** to fill cabinet and other positions in his administration. Rather than choosing widely respected officeholders, Jackson rewarded loyal supporters. Jackson also opposed "internal improvements" or infrastructural investments, arguing that such spending simply rewarded special interests. He opposed protective tariffs for the same reason. Jackson opposed the Second National Bank of the United States (chartered in 1816 after Hamilton's bank's charter had lapsed). Though Jackson, like Jefferson, favored a smaller federal government, Jackson nonetheless vastly increased the power of the executive branch, using the veto more than all his predecessors combined. Even this increase in presidential power, Jackson argued, was justified as the president was the only national political office chosen by the whole of the people.

The Second American Party System

The competition between Federalists and Jeffersonians, or Democratic-Republicans, between 1796 and 1814 has been called the **First American Party System.** The Second American Party System lasted from 1828 until 1854. It pitted the Democratic Party against the Whigs. These two political parties faced off primarily over economic and social issues raised by the expansion of the market economy and by issues that emerged in competition between eastern, southern, and western states.

Democratic Party

The Democratic Party, founded by Andrew Jackson and Martin Van Buren, feared the growing power of banks, merchants, and land speculators who were viewed as "special interests" intent on using government for their own enrichment at the expense of farmers, craftsmen, and laborers. Democratic party politicians opposed government involvement in the economy, largely because they considered government intervention as fraught with opportunities for corruption. Instead, they favored strengthening the free market and promoting competition, as well as westward expansion. Support for the Democratic Party was strongest in the trans-Appalachian West and the Southeast. The Democratic Party coalition included Southern planters, poorer farmers, and urban workers, particularly immigrant laborers like the Irish, and small business owners suspicious of larger corporate interests. Most slaveholders voted the Democratic ticket, believing the Whigs to be less committed to the institution.

Whig Party

Whigs, for their part, believed that the government should help foster the modernization of the economy. They favored steep tariffs to protect American manufacturing, a strong national bank to provide a stable money supply, and federal assistance to infrastructure projects, like the National Road, canals, and railroads. Support for the Whig Party was strongest in the Northeast. The Whig constituency included established industrialists, bankers, and farmers connected to the market.

> **Competency 006 Descriptive Statement F.** The beginning teacher analyzes the challenges confronted by the government and its leaders in the early years of the Republic and the Age of Jackson (e.g., economic programs and tariffs, court system, expansion of slavery, foreign relations, Indian removal).

Government Investment, Tariffs, and Economic Growth

Political leaders in the early years of the Republic and in the Age of Jackson differed, as we have seen, on what the role of the federal government should be in the economy. Despite those disagreements, the federal government and state governments played an important part in the development of the American economy before 1840.

In 1802, Congress authorized the construction of a turnpike from the Potomac to the Ohio River. Though congressional funding ran out and the road never reached its intended destination of St. Louis by 1837, the National Road was important to opening up the Trans-Appalachian West to settlement. State governments also funded significant "internal improvements" in canal building. By 1840 there were more than 3,000 miles of canals, most of them in the Northeast. Steam travel also benefited initially from government monopolies that granted steam boat companies concessions to control transport along certain stretches of western rivers, though this practice was declared unconstitutional restraint of trade in 1824. Railroad construction also benefited from private-public partnerships. State legislators provided subsidies, monopoly charters, and land grants to rail lines and the banks that financed them, resulting in the production by 1860 of a rail network with over 30,000 miles of track.

For the most part, however, these efforts were undertaken at the state level, as Congress and most early presidents hesitated to commit the federal government to large-scale infrastructure projects. Henry Clay, who advocated what he called the **American System**, called for a federal government that promoted banking, manufacturing, and transportation improvements that would integrate the economy to such a degree that sectionalism would be overcome and a truly unified nation created. The American System faced significant resistance from Andrew Jackson, as well as politicians from the Southeast and Trans-Appalachian West. As we have seen, Jackson and his supporters did not support the National Bank or federal bills for infrastructure improvements. They considered these to be threats to the federalist system of states' rights and a form of crony capitalism that benefited financiers, bankers, and established businessmen at the cost of the rest of American taxpayers.

Indian Removal

Expansion westward into the Trans-Appalachian West resulted in significant resistance from Native American populations squeezed by white settlement. In the Northwest Territories, relations between Indian peoples in Ohio and Indiana had remained relatively peaceful from the 1790s to the 1810. Increasing encroachment by white settlers, however, led to tensions with the Shawnee leaders Tecumseh and Tenskwatawa. The governor of the territory, William Henry Harrison, led an army to northwestern Indiana to disperse the Shawnee settlement there, leading to a bloody battle at Tippecanoe Creek and the eventual flight of the Shawnee from the area. When the War of 1812 erupted, the Indians of the Northwest Territory largely sided with the English. With the American victory, many Indians in the region moved farther west, or fled to Canada, opening the land to further settlement.

In the Southeast, Indian relations were similarly guided by treaties with the area's Indian nations signed after 1790. Andrew Jackson, who negotiated many of these treaties after the War of 1812, believed the Indian population to be subjects of the United States and could not conceive of Indians maintaining their sovereignty within the territorial boundaries of the nation. The Choctaw, Chickasaw, Cherokee, Creek, and Seminole were among the most culturally assimilated native populations. The Cherokee, for example, had developed their own written language, had established a written constitution, developed representative institutions, owned slaves themselves, and had adopted many white folkways. The government of the state of Georgia in 1826, had claimed, despite former treaties that it had the right to take possession of Cherokee land, and when Jackson became president, he agreed. The Cherokee sued in federal courts to secure their property rights and independence. In *Worcester v. Georgia,* the Supreme Court affirmed the Cherokee nation's existence as a sovereign entity within the state of Georgia and that Georgia's laws had no authority over them. Jackson, nonetheless, continued to push for the Cherokee's removal. In 1838, most of the Cherokee were forcibly removed and marched to northeastern Oklahoma. Along the way, more than a quarter of the population died from hunger, exposure, and exhaustion. The Seminole, Chickasaw, Creek, and Choctaw were also removed. The land made available by Indian removal rapidly was incorporated into the growing empire of cotton. With the expansion of cotton production, slavery received a new lease on life.

Expansion of Slavery

Before cotton could be fully exploited by slave labor, however, an important technological innovation, the **cotton gin**, was required. Before the invention of the cotton gin, a single laborer might take an entire day to clean a single pound by hand. The high cost of labor, whether that of slaves or hired hands, made the expansion of cotton production a difficult prospect. The cotton gin, which Eli Whitney patented in 1793, could clean over 50 pounds of cotton in a single day. With an increasingly integrated American marketplace, the cotton gin to process the raw cotton, and the available lands and fertile soils of the Southeast, cotton production rapidly became the most important American export, and the source of untold riches—and sorrows. Between 1815 and 1860, slavers exploited lands vacated by the Indians by marching over 1 million enslaved African Americans from areas with surplus laborers, like Virginia, Maryland, Alabama, Mississippi, Louisiana and later Texas, to everywhere that "cotton fever" spread.

The slaves endured this march chained in coffles, just as Africans had been driven from the interior of Africa or aboard ships in a repeat of the Middle Passage.

COMPETENCY 007 (WESTWARD EXPANSION, THE CIVIL WAR AND RECONSTRUCTION)

The teacher understands significant historical events and developments related to westward expansion, the Civil War, and Reconstruction.

> **Competency 007 Descriptive Statement A.** The beginning teacher demonstrates knowledge of westward expansion and its effects on the political, economic, cultural and social development of the nation.

Key Question

What factors drove the expansion of the United States, and how did American expansion contribute to the development of sectionalism and the coming of the American Civil War?

Periodization: 1750s to 1820

From the beginning of European settlement along the Atlantic coast, English men and women (and other European settlers) were driven by a land hunger. Before the American Revolution, however, most settlers remained east of the Appalachians. Americans began to move into the Trans-Appalachian West in the 1750s. They were met with fierce resistance by Native Americans, during the French and Indian War, Pontiac's War in 1763, the Revolutionary War, and between 1790 and 1814 across the region. Competing claims by other European powers, and even competing claims to western lands by the different colonial governments, made establishing ownership of land a complex proposition before 1790. Additionally, the hardships of establishing a commercially viable farm or land claim discouraged settlement beyond the Appalachians. After the Revolutionary War the United States claimed most of the continent east of the Mississippi. However, until the 1820s, it was difficult for Americans to lay effective claim to this land as it was largely outside the reach of markets and settlements.

Westward Expansion (1790–1820)

After the settlement of colonial (now state) land claims in 1781 and the conclusion of hostilities with Great Britain in 1783, American settlement of the Trans-Appalachian West began in earnest. For the territory north of the Ohio River (Ohio, Indiana, Michigan, Illinois, and Wisconsin), the **Northwest Ordinances** provided the framework for such settlement.

The Northwest Ordinances

A series of Congressional ordinances between 1784 and 1787 established the process whereby western lands would be permitted to join the confederation of the original 13 colonies and later the United States of America. Among the provisions of these ordinances were: (1) slavery was prohibited in the territory; (2) the process for applying for statehood was approved; and (3) the territory would be divided into from three to five states. The land was surveyed for sale (at $1 per acre to be sold in lots of 640 acres), with one section of 640 acres in each township to be reserved to fund public education. These ordinances therefore linked westward expansion and the principle of self-government.

Transportation Revolution

After 1800, a revolution in transport and communication technologies made western expansion into the Trans-Appalachian West a viable economic prospect, and Americans began to flood into the region. A network of roads and canals, and steamboat, railroad, and telegraph lowered transport costs, making it easier for markets to develop, and for rural producers to sell their goods. With these developments, settlement west of the Appalachians exploded.

Turning points in this revolution included the authorization of the **National Road** in 1806, which by 1838 had reached central Illinois; Robert Fulton's improvement of the **steamboat** in 1807 that opened up the Ohio and Mississippi rivers to commerce; the building of the **Erie Canal** between 1819 and 1825 that opened up the Great Lakes region to settlement by New Englanders and New Yorkers; and the creation of a vast network of railroads that by 1860 had grown to 30,000 miles of track.

Western states saw a corresponding growth in population. The Southern states of Alabama, Mississippi, and Louisiana, for example, had 117,000 white settlers in 1810. But enslaved African Americans swelled the states' collective population to 1,897,000 by 1850. Similarly, Ohio, Indiana, and Illinois saw their populations balloon from 268,000 in 1810 to 3,819,000 in 1850.

The Cotton Economy and Expansion

The growth of cotton production after 1790 explains much of the western expansion south of the Ohio River. Eli Whitney's invention of the **cotton gin**, combined with the industrialization of England's textile industry and the emergence of textile factories in New England, resulted in a vast increase in demand for raw cotton, which the southeastern states of Alabama, Georgia, Mississippi, and Louisiana were uniquely suited to fill.

After the War of 1812, Indians across the southeast were forced to cede their lands and move westward to Oklahoma (Indian Territory). Their lands were then taken up by cotton planters who monopolized the best land while poorer white farmers found land available in the hills of Georgia, Kentucky, Tennessee, or Arkansas. The large cotton plantations then were supplied with "surplus" slaves from Virginia, Maryland, and South Carolina who were marched in coffles, chained together, to the Deep South. Over 1 million enslaved persons between 1800 and 1860 made this forced migration.

Cotton production grew as a result. In 1793, the United States produced 5 million pounds of cotton. By 1830, that total had increased to nearly 170 million pounds. By 1860, cotton made up nearly 60 percent of all American exports. As southerners were wont to repeat, "Cotton was King."

Integration of the American Economy

After 1814, the United States economy became increasingly integrated by transportation and trade networks. Northeastern textile mills were supplied by raw cotton from the southeast; its shoe factories got their by hides from the Great Lakes region; its workers were fed with corn and wheat sent by rail or canal from the Midwest. Farmers in New England and along the north Atlantic coast turned away from grain growing and instead turned to dairy farming, vegetable gardening, or fruit orchards, while higher quality and cheaper grains were imported from the Great Lakes and Midwest. The steam engines were fashioned from iron ore from Pennsylvania, or as far away as Wisconsin and Michigan. The railway lines were laid on beds of gravel from Indiana and Illinois while whole forests of white pines from the Great Lakes were cut to make railway ties. These ties also included financial ties. Midwestern farmers and southern planters alike relied on credit extended from eastern banks and insured their farms and slaves with eastern insurance companies. At first glance, it would appear that the transportation revolution of the early 19th century brought the nation's varied regions closer together. However, westward expansion also contributed to a rise in sectional interests and division.

> **Competency 007 Descriptive Statement B.** The beginning teacher understands the political, economic, and social roots of Manifest Destiny, and the relationship between the concept of Manifest Destiny and the westward growth of the nation.

Manifest Destiny

Westward expansion and settlement were justified by many Americans by reference to what was known as **Manifest Destiny**, the belief that the United States had a divinely-inspired mission to expand territorially, spreading American prosperity, republican ideals, and white, European civilization. The phrase was coined by John L. O'Sullivan, in 1845, but the sentiment had roots in Thomas Jefferson's conception of the American republic as an "**Empire of Liberty**." Jefferson's marriage of empire and liberty combined two concepts that classical republicans considered incompatible. Republican thinkers had long considered expansionism to be a threat to freedom. Jefferson instead considered American expansion to be necessary for his republic of yeoman farmers, planters, and artisans. The West, in Jefferson's view, represented American independence, both individual and collective. Without growth, Jefferson feared the nation could not long sustain a citizenry that could make independent choices and provide the virtuous citizenry needed for office-holding. Jefferson's combination of these terms exemplified American "exceptionalism," that the United States, in expanding, offered to the world, and most immediately to the American Indians and later the Mexican population in the Southwest, the promise of representative government and a free market.

Americans were not unique in holding views that supported imperial expansion. Europeans during the early 19th century were making similar claims about the benefits of European imperialism. For many Americans, however, Manifest Destiny was seen as a means for the United States to avoid becoming a land of wage-earning factory workers, dependent upon their employers for survival and living without land in urban slums. The West provided an outlet and an opportunity, and it represented the American dream in an early form. For other Americans, westward expansion offered a mission field to spread Protestant civilization. With the Second Great Awakening, a religious revival of the 1820s and 1830s, American Christians gained enormous confidence in the superiority of their own religious convictions and a determination to spread American Christianity around the world. The American West provided a fertile field for missionary activity, despite the fact that the Hispanic population of the region was Roman Catholic and the Native American population had their own religious beliefs.

> **Competency 007 Descriptive Statement C.** The beginning teacher identifies the territorial acquisitions that formed the United States and explains the factors that influenced these acquisitions.

Westward Expansion (1820–1860)

Between 1820 and 1860, westward expansion and settlement turned increasingly to the Trans-Mississippian West, as American settlers moved farther west. One of the consequences of this wave of westward expansion would be the growth of sectional division as northern non-slaveholding states and southern slaveholding states struggled to define the nature of the republic, and more immediately, struggled to control the reins of power in the United States Congress and the Presidency.

Territorial Acquisitions

Between 1790 and 1860, the United States nearly tripled in size from the territory claimed by the original 13 states and the western territories that made up the nation following independence.

Louisiana Purchase

In 1803, Thomas Jefferson acquired from France a territory extending from the mouth of the Mississippi to its headwaters westward to the Rocky Mountains for a sum of $15 million. The territory had been ceded by France to Spain in 1762 and then reacquired in 1800. Jefferson feared that French control of the Mississippi would mean that farmers and plantation owners in the Northwest territories and in Kentucky, Tennessee, and Mississippi would be unable to get their produce to market. The Louisiana Territory doubled the size of the United States, but as importantly, guaranteed that westward settlement east of the Mississippi would be profitable.

Florida

Florida was from 1513 to 1763 a territory of New Spain. During the Seven Years War, however, Great Britain had acquired it and held it as part of its North American territories until the American Revolutionary war. During the Revolution, Floridians had remained loyal to Great Britain, and as part of the Treaty of Paris concluding the war, it reverted to Spain. From 1783 to 1821, however, few Spanish settlers moved into the colony; instead English Americans and Scots-Irish settlers began to migrate into the Florida Panhandle. In 1810, in rapid succession these settlers would first rebel against Spain and establish their own "Republic of West Florida" before being annexed by James Madison. In response to Seminole Indian raids into Georgia, and to the frequent flight of slaves to Florida, between 1817 and 1821, the United States fought two wars on Spanish territory against the Seminole Indians. As Spain could no longer defend its interests there and the Spanish population was sparse, in 1821 Florida ceded the territory to the United States.

Texas Annexation (1845)

Texas gained its independence from Mexico in 1836. A year later, the Texas Congress voted for annexation to the United States. The lesson of Missouri's application for statehood, however, led

Andrew Jackson and Martin Van Buren to table the matter, fearing the kind of sectional division that had erupted in 1820. James K. Polk, a Democrat, however, in 1844, ran for president on a platform of annexation of Texas and acquisition of **Oregon Territory**. Polk's victory ensured Texas' annexation, despite the fears of northern congressmen that annexation of Texas might lead to the establishment of perhaps as many as five slaveholding states.

The Pacific Northwest had a number of claimants. Russia, Great Britain, and the United States all made a case. In 1818, the United States and Great Britain had agreed to joint ownership, and permitted open settlement by both British and U.S. citizens. In 1833, however, missionaries from the East hurried to the region, spurred by a call to minister to the region's Indian population. When news of the area's natural beauty was reported back to the East Coast, settlers began the long trek along the Oregon trail from Missouri. Over 350,000 settlers would make their way along this treacherous path. In 1844, James K. Polk had run on a slogan of "Fifty-four Forty or Fight," demanding all of the Pacific Northwest, from California's northern border to Alaska. Polk had issued this demand mostly as a sop to northern Democrats, who wished to gain a counter to the acquisition of Texas, for which Polk had also campaigned. Rather than demanding the entire territory in negotiations with Great Britain, Polk agreed to a compromise that divided the Northwest along the 49th parallel, well short of Alaska's southern border.

The Mexican Cession (1848)

The Mexican Cession in the **Treaty of Guadalupe Hidalgo (1848)** ceded California, New Mexico, Arizona, Nevada, and Utah to the United States. Mexico also relinquished any claim to Texas.

The territorial acquisition amounted to 529,000 square miles. Only the Louisiana Purchase and the purchase of Alaska were larger. For southern plantation owners, this territorial acquisition promised further land into which the cotton and plantation economy could expand. However, the territory's true riches turned out to be mineral resources.

Before the Treaty of Guadalupe Hidalgo was finalized, however, gold was discovered in California. Settlers flooded into the territory to lay claim to the gold and to mine it. Joining in the rush were many hundreds more who hoped to set up restaurants, barber shops, taverns, brothels, and boarding houses, or to work as cooks, laundresses, and in other ancillary trades assisting the miners. From a population of 15,000 non-Indian residents, California ballooned to more than 360,000 inhabitants. These "placer" operations required little capital. A mule, pan, shovel, and other tools, plus hard work and persistence were all that were required. People came from the world over: Irish, Germans, and Italians arrived, as did many thousands of Chinese immigrants, making the boomtowns of California exceedingly diverse. Mexico's territory was not only a source of gold. Silver, bauxite, copper, and many other precious mineral resources enriched the United States.

Gadsden Purchase (1853)

The final piece of the puzzle in the continental map of the United States, a 29,670 square-mile corner of New Mexico and Arizona, was purchased by treaty in 1853. The objective of the purchase was to build a railroad connecting New Orleans to southern California. This particular tract of land allowed that route to run south of the mountainous terrain of the Rocky Mountains. Franklin Pierce's administration negotiated a purchase price of $10 million for the territory. The railroad, however, was not built until well after the Civil War.

Competency 007 Descriptive Statement D. The beginning teacher understands major issues and events of the United States-Mexican War and their impact on the United States.

Mexican War and Mexican Cession

President James K. Polk's territorial ambitions, evident in his 1844 campaign commitment to annexation of the Oregon Territory and the Republic of Texas, did not stop with these two acquisitions. He also hoped to bring California into the Union. Initially, Polk hoped to accomplish this aim by purchasing California from Mexico. But when the Mexican government rebuffed monetary offers, Polk sent American soldiers to Corpus Christi, Texas, and ordered them into the Nueces Strip, the land between the Nueces River and the Rio Grande. Mexico claimed the northern boundary of its territory to be the Nueces. The United States held that Mexico's northern boundary was the Rio Grande. When Mexican troops killed 11 and wounded six Americans in a skirmish north of the Rio Grande in April 1846, Polk had justification to launch a war against Mexico.

The war drew criticism from a significant minority of northern politicians and writers. Henry David Thoreau, for instance, wrote his essay "On Civil Disobedience" in response to what he felt was an unjust war of territorial aggression. As an Illinois congressman, Abraham Lincoln also objected to the war. Northern politicians not only objected to the injustice of such a war; they also feared that acquisition of significant territory in Mexico would lead inevitably to a growth in the number of slaveholding states and an increase in the political power of the slave states.

The war proceeded on three fronts. Californians led by John C. Frémont rebelled against the Mexican authorities in California and declared a short-lived independent republic. It was rapidly annexed by the United States. A contingent of American troops marched to Santa Fe, New Mexico, and occupied the province for the United States. The war in central Mexico lasted from January 1846 to March 1848 as forces from the United States marched towards the capital of Mexico City.

The war with Mexico exposed important sectional fault lines before and during the conflict. Most Americans supported the war, and those who did not hesitated to speak out lest they be labeled unpatriotic. Northerners were not quite so committed to the war as Southerners. Southerners immediately saw the acquisition of Mexico's northern states as a boon for their economy and for the spread of plantation slavery. The Missouri Compromise had seemed to forestall expansion of slavery northward into the Louisiana Territory; this new expansion provided an outlet. Southerners also saw the possibilities for trade in the Pacific increase and hoped to rapidly connect Southern cotton fields to the West Coast with the construction of a rail line across the Southwest. Some Whigs objected vociferously that the war was an act of territorial aggression and complained that territory taken from Mexico would inevitably increase the "Slave Power's" hold on Congress and the presidency. Nativists also objected to this expansion, fearing that annexation of northern Mexico would mean that a large population of Spanish-speaking and Roman Catholic citizens would alter the culture and linguistic makeup of the nation.

> **Competency 007 Descriptive Statement E.** The beginning teacher analyzes ways in which slavery and other political, economic, and social factors led to the growth of sectionalism and to the Civil War.

Key Question

How did American expansion after 1820 result in the growth of sectional division rather than the unification of the United States?

Periodization: 1819 to c. 1854

The growth of American settlement in the Louisiana Territory first exposed the republic to questions about the way in which slavery's expansion threatened the political balance between northern and southern states. This was first evident in 1819–1821 and the Missouri Crisis. The crisis averted the same questions would then re-emerge with Texas' independence and the move to annex the Lone Star State between 1835 and 1845. The annexation of Texas and the Oregon Territory, and then the Mexican-American War further heightened these tensions between 1845 and 1850. Finally, controversies over the settlement of the Louisiana Territory returned after 1854 to divide the nation. The question of what to do about Kansas and Nebraska triggered the final rupture between North and South as it became clear that plantation economies that relied upon slavery had very different economic and political needs than did an economy that was based on wage labor, industrial development, and market-oriented small farmers. The struggle for power between these two economies was carried out in Congress as a struggle for control of the legislature and the presidency.

Sectional Division and Slavery

Sectional distinctions have been a feature of the United States since before the American Revolution. During the colonial period, each colony developed along its own trajectory, depending upon different forms of labor systems and developing distinctive political institutions. The regional distinction that most separated the colonies turned on the divide between slave-holding colonies with plantation economies and consequently large populations of slaves and slave-holding colonies (for all 13 original colonies relied to some degree on slavery) dependent on trade and small farms with fewer enslaved residents.

Abolitionism

The anti-slavery movement had deep roots before the American Revolution in England and in colonial America as Quakers, Methodists, and other religious and political figures argued that it was an inhumane institution. During the early years of the American republic the movement seemed to stagnate, with the clearest voices calling for its end being in the free African American community in northern cities. Until the 1830s, calls for an end to slavery often emphasized the corollary that African Americans could not hope for equality or citizenship rights and that emancipation necessitated repatriation or return to Africa. This was called the **colonization movement**. Freed blacks objected to this linkage, though Liberia was established with freed slaves. After the 1830s, however, abolitionism became more strident, pushed by free blacks who claimed their right to an American identity. **William Lloyd Garrison** and a small number of other abolitionists began with the publication of Garrison's weekly abolitionist newspaper, *The Liberator*, to take a much more uncompromising stance, demanding an end to the internal slave trade and to slavery, characterizing it as the national sin. In 1833, the **American Anti-Slavery Society** was founded. Soon, northerners were joining it and similar organizations. Many northerners were not attracted to the radical doctrines of the abolitionists, fearing that it would lead to disruptions of the immense profits associated with slavery, particularly in banking, insurance, and commerce. But a growing minority from 1830 to 1854 became animated by the issue of slavery and a deep desire to end its spread.

With the growth in the North of anti-slavery fervor, southerners began to mount their own defense of the "peculiar institution." A **Pro-Slavery Ideology** emerged that defended slavery along several fronts. Southern slavery apologists argued that (1) slavery was biblical; (2) slavery was constitutional; (3) slavery had been practiced historically in most societies, both ancient and modern; and (4) blacks benefited from the benevolent character of American slavery, and otherwise would remain unconverted and primitive in Africa.

Missouri Compromise

In 1819, Missouri became the first territory from the Louisiana Purchase (other than Louisiana) to apply for statehood. Because many of the settlers in the region had moved from Kentucky and Tennessee, the plantation economy was already well-established, and over 10,000 slaves already lived in the state. Fearing an expansion of slave-owning states' political influence and motivated by opposition to slavery, James Tallmadge, a New York congressman, proposed an amendment to the legislation authorizing Missouri's application for statehood that outlawed the further importation of slaves into Missouri and the freeing of the children of slaves already resident after they reached the age of 25. The controversy over Missouri's statehood divided Congress and the nation over the next 2 years before a compromise was struck that prohibited slavery in the territories of the Louisiana Purchase north of Missouri's southern boundary, but which allowed Missouri to enter the Union as a slave-holding state. Maine was also admitted, maintaining the balance between slave-holding and free states for the time being.

Wilmot's Proviso

As the nation considered the status of the land acquired from Mexico, David Wilmot, a Pennsylvania congressman proposed that slavery be forbidden in all land ceded by Mexico. His "proviso," as the amendment was called, passed the House of Representatives, dominated by Northern interests, but was blocked in the Senate, where Southern senators had greater weight. The debate surrounding Wilmot's Proviso further indicated the divide between Northern and Southern interests. The **Compromise of 1850** resolved the matter of what to do with Mexican lands; California entered as a free state, while the remainder of Mexican land acquired would await a later decision.

The Fugitive Slave Act

As part of the compromise, the Fugitive Slave Clause in the Constitution was reinforced by the Fugitive Slave Act that reduced protections that allowed alleged fugitives some due process, and required local law enforcement and citizenry to assist fugitive-slave hunters in the recapture of slaves. Despite these efforts, abolitionists in a number of widely reported cases helped slaves escape their captors. The **Underground Railroad** increased efforts to help escapees make their way to Canada, out of reach of masters, slave catchers, and the federal law.

Kansas-Nebraska Act (1854)

Within the lands of the Louisiana Purchase, Missouri (1821), and Iowa (1846) had acquired statehood by 1850. The extensive territories of Minnesota, Nebraska, and Kansas had not yet applied. According to the Missouri Compromise, slavery was not to be allowed above Missouri's southern border. Kansas and Nebraska both were situated north of this boundary. **Stephen A. Douglas**, an Illinois Senator who aspired to be president in 1854, proposed a bill allowing Kansas and Nebraska to establish territorial governments in preparation for statehood. Southern congressmen were uninterested in either Kansas or Nebraska becoming states, given the terms established by the Missouri Compromise. Douglas appealed to their interest by proposing that **popular sovereignty** or **majority rule** be the principle determining whether these states would be slave or free. The Kansas-Nebraska Act passed, but at the cost of destroying the Second Party System. The Whig party collapsed. The Democratic Party was divided, with members unhappy with the slave power's influence joining the remnants of the Whig Party to form the Republican Party.

CHAPTER
4

Bleeding Kansas (1854–1859)

Soon after the passage of the Kansas-Nebraska Act, the challenge of controlling the ballot box in Kansas went out to both Northern abolitionists and pro-slavery advocates across the South. Aid societies in New England were founded with the aim of settling Kansas with anti-slavery advocates. Thousands of pro-slavery Missourians began to cross the border with the opposite intent. In the first election to decide matters, nearly twice as many ballots were cast as there were eligible voters. The pro-slavery victors set about to write a constitution that not only permitted slavery but prohibited abolitionists from holding office or even publicly supporting the anti-slavery cause. Helping a runaway slave was a capital crime. Free-staters, however, established their own parallel government. A civil war soon broke out, a prelude to the war that divided the Union only 5 years later.

Dred Scott Decision (1857)

The slave Dred Scott, his wife, Harriet, and their two children sued for freedom in 1846, arguing that the family's time lived in Wisconsin and Illinois, where slavery was not permitted, entitled them to their freedom. The Supreme Court's decision, rendered in 1857, ruled that Dred Scott's rights had not been violated because he was not a citizen of the United States and that African Americans had "no rights which the white man was bound to respect." Additionally, his status was determined by that of his owner, a Missourian, where slavery was legal. Finally, Chief Justice Roger B. Taney concluded that Congress lacked the authority to regulate slavery in territories under congressional control.

Republican Party (est. 1854)

A new political party had been founded in the context of the debate over the Kansas-Nebraska Act. The Whig Party and the Democratic Party had been rapidly fragmenting in the years after the Compromise of 1850. The Republican Party was founded on the principle that slavery must be confined to the South and forbidden in the territories beyond the Mississippi. The *Dred Scott* decision gave further credence to the view that the South and the planter class was conspiring not just to extend slavery in the territories, but to make it a national institution. Abraham Lincoln was a key voice in the Republican Party. With his election in November of 1860, many Southerners concluded that they had little to gain by remaining in the Union.

Competency 007 Descriptive Statement F. The beginning teacher demonstrates knowledge of individuals, events, and issues of the Civil War (e.g., Abraham Lincoln, Jefferson Davis, the Emancipation Proclamation, Lee's surrender at Appomattox Court House).

What factors contributed to the victory of the Union over the Confederacy during the Civil War? Was a Northern victory inevitable given the resources and population available to the Union, or was it the power of political leadership and will that resulted in the North's victory?

Periodization: 1861 to 1865

The American Civil War lasted from April 1861 to April 1865. Before January 1, 1863, it could be said that the war was being fought primarily to save the Union from disintegration. After the Emancipation Proclamation's issuance, however, the war became a crusade to free the slaves and to transform the Southern economy and society.

Secession

During the winter of 1860–1861, Southern state after Southern state voted to secede from the United States of America. South Carolina led the way on December 20, 1860, followed by 10 other slaveholding states (in order of their secession: Mississippi, Florida, Alabama, Georgia, Louisiana, Texas, Virginia, Arkansas, North Carolina, and Tennessee). Not all slaveholding states followed suit, however. Delaware, Missouri, Kentucky, and Maryland remained in the Union. The western 50 counties of Virginia refused to leave the Union when Virginia seceded, and in 1863 were accepted into the Union as the state of West Virginia.

Confederate States of America

The seceding states of the Lower South formed the Confederate States of America (or Confederacy) in February 1861, before Lincoln's inauguration, and were joined by Virginia, Arkansas, North Carolina, and Tennessee after fighting began with the siege of Fort Sumter, South Carolina, in April 1861. The Confederacy wrote a constitution that mirrored the United States Constitution in most regards, while explicitly protecting the institution of slavery, the internal slave trade, and the right to own slaves in any territory of the Confederacy. The Confederate Constitution also more carefully circumscribed the powers of the Confederate Government over the states.

A comparison of the capacity of the Union and the Confederacy to wage war suggests that the South faced significant disadvantages as the two sides entered into conflict. The Union had 71 percent of the nation's population, 91 percent of the nation's industrial capacity, 97 percent of its firearms manufacturers, 94 percent of iron production, and many other advantages.

Despite these disadvantages, Southerners entered the war confident of success. They characterized Northerners as "blue-bellied shopkeepers," lacking in the manly fortitude and martial experience to defeat them. Southerners also believed that they were fighting for their lands and their way of life, and therefore had greater incentive than Northern volunteers, who they considered a mercenary army fighting without commitment to a higher cause. Finally, when comparing economic capacity, Southerners believed that their cotton supply would prove to be decisive, as foreign exchange with which to purchase needed supplies and armaments. They also considered it likely that Great Britain, the dominant world economic power, would intervene on behalf of the South, the primary supplier of its vital textile industry.

Jefferson Davis

Jefferson Davis was a respected politician from a Mississippi planter family. He had graduated from West Point, served in the Mexican-American War, represented Mississippi in the United States Senate, and had been Secretary of War. His military and political experience made him a popular choice to lead the Confederacy. He proved less than capable as president, however. His confidence in his military experience led him to intervene often in strategic and tactical military decisions, to the frustration of his own commanders. His tendency to harshly criticize his opponents undermined his leadership. Perhaps more important than his personality deficiencies, however, was the fact that the Confederacy placed significant limits on executive power, leaving Davis hamstrung to use extraordinary measures to win the war in the way that Lincoln could and did.

Robert E. Lee (1807–1870)

One of the advantages the South could claim at the beginning of the war was a higher proportion of the professional officer corps. There was no better example of this than Robert E. Lee, a pedigreed Virginian, whose estate lay just across the Potomac from the nation's capital. He turned down Lincoln's offer to command the Union armies, instead resigning his commission and offering his services to the Army of the Confederacy. Lee for much of the war proved to be a more capable commander than his Union counterparts. He was also surrounded with a strong staff. Nonetheless, a number of Lee's tactical errors—the most notable being the Southern invasion of the North, which ended in disaster at Gettysburg—weakened Confederate forces.

Abraham Lincoln (1809–1865)

The Union was led by President Lincoln, who by comparison to Jefferson Davis was an inexperienced neophyte who hardly inspired a great deal of confidence. His political experience was largely confined to 8 years in the Illinois House of Representatives, one term in the U.S. House of Representatives, and a failed Senate run in which he earned notoriety for his debates with the eventual winner, Stephen Douglas. He had almost no military or administrative experience. His electoral victory reflected more the divided state of the Union than any great confidence in his leadership abilities. In the end, however, Lincoln's leadership would prove decisive.

Lincoln's leadership stands out in a number of areas. His ability to eloquently communicate to the Northern public the significance of the crusade upon which the nation had embarked was critical to the Union's success. The **Gettysburg Address** and the **Second Inaugural Address** stand out among the most stirring speeches in the English language. Lincoln also, despite his lack of military experience, had a keen strategic understanding, which often clashed with his more cautious general staff. Lastly, Lincoln's strategic sensibility and recognition of the potential deciding role that might be played by the infusion of African American soldiers in the Union Army and the destabilization of the South if large numbers of Southern slaves began to gain their freedom, contributed to Lincoln's decision to transform the war from a war to preserve the Union into a war of black liberation.

Lincoln's Second Inaugural Address, given hardly a month before the Confederate surrender, proposed a conciliatory path towards the nation's healing. His words, "With malice towards none; with charity for all; with firmness in the right, … let us strive to finish the work we are in; to bind up the nation's wounds," illustrated his deep wish to rebuild the fractured nation. Lincoln accordingly offered easy terms to the South, without demanding the wholesale reform of the Southern states. Unfortunately, his plan did not provide for the extension of full citizenship and civil rights to freed slaves, nor did it provide adequately for giving assistance to slaves, either in the form of physical protection, rights to property, or economic and educational support. Lincoln's assassination on April 15, 1865, left the presidency to Andrew Johnson, a Tennessean and slave owner who had even less interest in a true reformation of the South.

Ulysses S. Grant (1822–1885)

Perhaps Abraham Lincoln's most important military decision was to appoint Ulysses S. Grant commander of the Union armies. He did so after observing Grant's success in the western theater of the war, where Grant led northern armies southward along the Mississippi, splitting Arkansas, Louisiana, and Texas from the Confederacy. Few other military commanders so well understood the nature of total warfare. Lincoln gave him command of the Union army in Virginia in March 1864. Grant immediately pressed the Confederate army in a series of battles that were memorable for their ferocity and loss of life, which, because they were advancing, was greatest on the Union side. Grant nonetheless continued to pressure Lee's army, knowing that despite losing double the men, the Confederate army could not replace its losses while Grant could. For this reason, Grant's detractors often called him a "butcher."

Emancipation Proclamation (January 1, 1863)

Abraham Lincoln, in his first inaugural address, had stated that he "had no purpose, directly or indirectly, to interfere with the institution of slavery in the States where it exists. I believe I have no lawful right to do so, and I have no inclination to do so." Gradually, however, the war was transformed into a war of African American liberation. The length of the war and the number of casualties pushed Lincoln to declare the emancipation of the South's slaves as "a military necessity, absolutely essential to the preservation of the Union." The Emancipation Proclamation promised freedom to all slaves in those states still in rebellion; it did not free the slaves in the Union states (Missouri, Kentucky, Maryland, Delaware, and West Virginia) where slavery was legal. Lincoln did not wish to antagonize these border states. The Emancipation Proclamation in many ways simply reflected conditions on the ground wherever the Union armies were close by. Enslaved African Americans from the beginning of the war had sought to make their way to Union lines in the hopes of gaining their independence. This declaration only hastened the degree to which Southern slaves "voted with their feet," freeing themselves and joining the Union armies as "contraband" but also becoming increasingly important to the Northern war effort. By the end of the war, the Union army employed over 180,000 African American soldiers, many of whom played increasingly important combat roles in the last year of the war.

Lee's Surrender at Appomattox Court House (April 9, 1865)

From February 1865, when William Tecumseh Sherman struck northward from Savannah, Georgia, following his "March to the Sea" toward Virginia, and Grant's army continued its relentless war of attrition against Lee's army, the rebellion rapidly came to a conclusion. By April, Lee, trapped between Sherman and Grant, abandoned the Confederate capital, Richmond, Virginia. Jefferson Davis fled, reestablishing a capital in Montgomery, Alabama. As the Confederate Army fled it fired on the city, destroying large areas. African American troops, to the chagrin of the residents, featured prominently in the city's liberation. A week later, after a desperate flight with Grant close on his heels, Lee's army could no longer continue. On April 9, 1865, Lee surrendered at Appomattox Court House, Virginia. Grant's terms required Lee's men to disarm, though they were permitted their private sidearms and the use of their own horses to return home. They were also required to publicly agree not to take up arms against the Government of the United States. With Lee's surrender, the few remaining Confederate soldiers still in the field also gave up, and the war came to an end.

Competency 007 Descriptive Statement G. The beginning teacher analyzes the effects of Reconstruction on the political, economic, and social life of the nation.

Key Question

In what ways did Reconstruction fail to bring resolution to the sectional divisions that had led to the Civil War, and why did Reconstruction fail to extend to freed men and women the full fruits of citizenship and equality?

Periodization: 1865 to 1877

Reconstruction lasted from the end of the Civil War until 1877. Reconstruction, however, developed in phases, with what has been called Presidential Reconstruction (1865–1867) and an era known as Radical Reconstruction (1867–1877).

Presidential Reconstruction (1865–1867)

Andrew Johnson, the Tennessean who succeeded Abraham Lincoln, promised to ease the South back into the Union on the best possible terms. Nearly all white Southerners who swore an oath of loyalty to the Union were admitted, save Confederate leaders and wealthy planters. Even many of them soon were given pardons. White-elected conventions were called to establish loyal governments, and Johnson permitted them wide latitude to govern statewide affairs.

Southern state governments immediately set about reestablishing a form of slavery through **Black Codes** that mirrored closely the South's slave laws before the war. While slaves' freedom was acknowledged and they were granted the rights to marry, own property, and use the courts, service on juries, service in state militias, voting, and other rights were denied. White planters, in need of a labor force, used the Black Codes to compel ex-slaves to work. They were forced to sign annual labor contracts. Those who failed could be arrested as vagrants and then hired out as prison-labor.

Radical Reconstruction

In 1865, Radical Republicans in Congress, many of whom had been abolitionists prior to the war, called for the new Southern governments to be disbanded and the Black Codes abrogated. Among the more radical proposals these congressmen called for was the confiscation of land in the South to divide it among freedmen in the hopes of creating a class of black yeoman farmers. Moderate Republicans, believing strongly in the protection of property rights, objected and proposed other solutions. One of these was what would become the **Fourteenth Amendment**, which guaranteed citizenship to anyone born in the United States, assured citizens of equal protection before the law, thus forbidding passage of Black Codes. The amendment, however, did not secure voting rights for black citizens.

Faced with the continued intransigence of Southern governments, Congress in March 1867 divided the South into military districts occupied by federal troops, and called for new elected governments, with black men allowed to vote. Freedmen in the South registered to vote in large numbers. New state constitutions were written, for the first time with black representation and influence. Over 2,000 African Americans were elected to office during Radical Reconstruction, fourteen of whom were elected to the U.S. House of Representatives. Two African Americans were elected to the U.S. Senate. From 1875 until 1967, no other African American would be elected to the U.S. Senate. These Reconstruction-era governments have been often pilloried as ineffectual and corrupt. However, their accomplishments far outweigh their weaknesses. Southern state governments elected with African American votes established the South's first public school systems, open to black and white students. In New Orleans, the schools were integrated. State colleges and universities were established, though in most cases there were separate institutions for white and black students. Orphanages, mental health institutions, and a more humane prison system were established. Cruel punishments like public whippings were abolished. Railroads, hotels, and other public institutions were forbidden to discriminate by race or color.

Reaction to Reconstruction

These new governments faced strong opposition from the South's planters and merchants. Most white Southerners could not stomach the sight of former slaves voting, holding office, and demanding equality. In response, a reign of terror was unleashed against blacks and their Republican allies. Secret societies like the **Ku Klux Klan**, effectively a militia arm of the Democratic Party, began a coordinated campaign of terrorist violence designed to silence African Americans. At the same time, northern Republicans were increasingly divided and losing interest in reforming the South. With the election of Rutherford B. Hayes in 1876, and with Democratic politicians winning back the South, beginning in Texas, North Carolina, and Tennessee (states where African Americans had smaller voting blocs), the **Redeemers**, as Southern Democrats called themselves, began to reclaim the South for white supremacy. Violence was an important means by which this was accomplished. In 1877, President Hayes agreed to recognize Democratic control of the South and promised an end to federal intervention in the South. Federal troops were ordered to withdraw to their barracks.

COMPETENCY 008 (THE UNITED STATES AS A WORLD POWER)

The teacher understands significant historical events and developments related to the emergence and role of the United States as a world power and the effects of major decisions and conflicts on the United States.

> **Competency 008 Descriptive Statement A.** The beginning teacher understands factors and events that contributed to the emergence of the United States as a world power between 1898 and 1920 (e.g., imperialism, Panic of 1893, acquisition of Hawaii, Spanish-American War, U.S. involvement in and effects of World War I).

Key Question

How and why did the United States, which prided itself as a republic without international or territorial ambitions, acquire an empire that stretched across the globe, and how did it become an influential power in Europe, Asia, and Latin America?

Periodization: 1898 to the Present

The story of the United States' foreign policy history is divided in the TEKS into three distinct periods, 1898–1920, 1920–1945, and 1945 to the present. This descriptive statement surveys the first phase in America's rise to world power, a period when the United States grew into a global rather than a continental power.

American Rise to World Power (1890–1914)

Four primary factors underlay the growth of American international involvement between 1890 and 1914: (1) fears about the consequences of the closing of the American frontier; (2) the need for new markets and resources in an industrializing economy; (3) missionary impulses; and (4) strategic and political considerations.

Manifest Destiny, the "Closing of the Frontier," and Imperialism

In many ways, American entry onto the global political stage was simply an extension of Manifest Destiny. The drive to possess the land between the Atlantic and Pacific oceans, seen as a God-given right and responsibility to bring American values and republican institutions to the West, was easily adapted to a similar drive for markets, resources, and political influence across the Pacific or in Latin America. Many American political thinkers, influenced by Frederick Jackson Turner's "Frontier Thesis," worried that the nation's vigor and democratic character would be stifled with the closing of the frontier. New frontiers, new adventures, and new outlets were needed.

Manifest Destiny had many parallels with European justifications for imperial expansion. The English argued that they had a responsibility to spread English civilization to Africa and to Asia. Rudyard Kipling had called this duty the "White Man's Burden." French imperialists wrote about the "*mission civilatrice*," or civilizing mission. United States expansion from "sea to shining sea" and then beyond into the Pacific or Latin America, like the justifications offered by these European powers, presumed the racial and cultural inferiority of Native Americans, Mexicans, Filipinos, Hawaiians, Cubans, and Haitians.

Industrialization and Imperialism

Between 1865 and 1898, the United States had undergone an Industrial Revolution that also, to a large degree, contributed to America's rise to world power. Like all the great industrial powers, as the United States grew industrially, and as it became a more urbanized nation, new overseas markets became ever more critical to the success of American industry. American business interests also required new sources of raw materials. Commercial interests then were an important driving factor in American territorial acquisitions and economic imperialism.

Panic of 1893

The Panic of 1893, an economic depression that lasted until 1897, confirmed for many business leaders that the American economy required new outlets for American productivity. They proposed a "glut thesis," as explanation for why the economy went into a downturn in 1893. The "glut" resulted from an excess of supply (rather than under-consumption resulting from low wages and lowered purchasing power of American workers) and that without new international markets for America's industrial output, the U.S. economy would continue to experience financial panics.

Business leaders consequently became advocates for American imperial expansion, particularly into Asian markets.

Missionary Impulses

Religious and moral considerations also played into the United States' increased presence outside North America. American missionaries from mainline Protestant denominations (Presbyterian, Methodist, Episcopal, and Baptist churches) combined a Christianizing mission with a belief in the superiority of American institutions as they established missions in the Pacific, Asia, and Africa. These missionaries argued that white Protestant Americans had a Christian duty to spread the Christian gospel and American civilization to the less fortunate populations of the world.

Strategic and Geopolitical Considerations

The North's use of naval power in the American Civil War to blockade the South and cripple its economy contributed to American political leaders' conviction that the United States needed a significant naval buildup to compete globally. The writings of Alfred Thayer Mahan strengthened their viewpoint when he contended that naval power was critical to a nation's military and commercial might. Between 1889 and 1893, the United States Navy grew from the 15th-largest navy in the world to the seventh-largest. Ironclad steamships required coaling stations located at strategic intervals for power to be projected abroad. As a result, one of the first strategic objectives in the Pacific was to acquire naval bases at which to resupply American naval vessels.

Expansion in the Pacific

American businessmen and political leaders had, even before the conclusion of the Mexican-American War and the acquisition of California, seen as a primary objective the opening up of commercial markets in China and Japan. In 1844, U.S. diplomats had gained the right to trade in a number of Chinese ports and the United States would after 1899 be a strong advocate for free trade in China, a policy that became known as the **Open-Door Policy**. As we have seen, Japan had been opened to American business interests by Commodore Matthew Perry's "gunboat diplomacy" in 1853.

After 1856, the United States acquired a number of islands scattered across the Pacific. The Midway Islands were acquired in 1867. In 1872, the U.S. gained the right to establish a base in Samoa. In 1899, the United States established a protectorate over eastern Samoa.

In 1867, the United States had purchased Alaska from Russia, an acquisition that was widely lampooned as "Seward's Folly," as the Secretary of State William Seward had organized the buy. While primarily seen as a means to acquire more territory and to encircle British Canada, the purchase of Alaska increased American presence on the Pacific Rim and provided potential coaling stations and commercial entry points to Asian markets.

Acquisition of Hawaii

The most important acquisition in the Pacific before 1898, however, were the Hawaiian Islands. The acquisition of Hawaii illustrates each of the driving impulses behind American imperialism in the Pacific before 1920. The Kingdom of Hawaii was originally founded in 1795 and by 1810, it composed the entire island chain in the middle of the Pacific. Before 1850, the kingdom had been beset by French and British efforts to exert control over the islands. American missionaries established a significant presence on the islands beginning in the 1820s, converting many Hawaiians to Christianity. The United States after 1850 sought to protect the islands from being controlled by another industrial power. By 1887, American business interests had accumulated vast land grants on the island that were devoted to sugar and later pineapple production. When in 1890, U.S. tariff policy increased duties on imports from Hawaii, white settlers on the island—which included a combination of missionaries and their children, as well as businessmen—urged the United States to annex the islands. When the Hawaiian monarch, Queen Lili'uokalani, in 1893 opposed the takeover of her kingdom, American settlers assisted by the U.S. Navy in Pearl Harbor arrested the queen and declared Sanford B. Dole (brother of the Dole pineapple magnate) the head of a provisional government, the Republic of Hawaii. To free her imprisoned followers and save many from execution, Queen Lili'uokalani abdicated the throne. After Grover Cleveland's initial refusal to recognize this illegal coup, Hawaii was annexed in 1898 in the middle of the Spanish-American War. Hawaii would acquire statehood only in 1959.

Latin American "Sphere of Influence"

The United States diplomatic interest in Latin America, though not its territorial expansion, dated to the establishment of the **Monroe Doctrine,** which opposed European colonialism in the Americas. This policy, issued in a statement by President James Monroe in 1823, was an assertion that the United States would oppose efforts by European powers to take control of any independent state in the Americas. Effectively, the United States with this doctrine identified Latin America as within the United States' sphere of influence.

Spanish-American War (1898)

United States' intervention in Latin American affairs began in earnest with the Spanish-American War. Because the war was also fought against the Spanish in the Philippines, the Spanish-American War also contributed to vastly increasing American military and political influence in Asia as well.

A combination of humanitarian, geopolitical, and commercial factors drew the United States into the conflict. Spanish oppression of the Cuban independence movement after 1895 received wide publicity in the American press and resulted in Americans putting pressure on the U.S. government to intervene. The role of **yellow journalism,** which sensationalized the atrocities of the Cuban government, galvanized American support for the Cuban independence movement.

American businessmen who had invested heavily in Cuba's sugar plantations were also alarmed at the instability on the island. The United States entered the war in 1898 when the *U.S.S. Maine*, a U.S. Naval vessel dispatched to Havana to protect American citizens in Cuba, was blown up, killing 266 sailors and officers. The United States declared war on Spain, sending an expeditionary force, which included the **Rough Riders** led by Teddy Roosevelt, to Cuba, and a naval force under Admiral George Dewey to the Philippines. The Spanish forces in Cuba were easily defeated, and the Spanish fleet in Manila harbor was forced to surrender.

With the short war's end, Spain granted Cuba its independence, but the United States gained possession of Puerto Rico, the Philippines, and Guam, as well as a naval base at Guantanamo Bay.

Like the Cubans, Filipinos had for some time been fighting for their own independent nation-state. With the United States' occupation of the Philippines, the insurrection mounted against the Spanish turned against the new imperialist power. Between 1899 and 1902, a brutal guerrilla war was fought by Filipino nationalists against U.S. forces. More than 4,000 Americans and over 200,000 Filipinos lost their lives as a result. Only in 1942 would the Philippines finally gain its independence from the United States.

Latin American Intervention

Though the United States had not annexed Cuba and accepted Cuban independence, a regime friendly to the United States was installed. At American insistence, an amendment known as the **Platte Amendment** was added to the Cuban constitution. The amendment allowed the United States to intervene militarily whenever instability threatened the Cuban government. The United States would send troops to Cuba in 1906, 1912, and 1917. This pattern of American intervention in the Caribbean and Latin America would become a feature of American policy through much of the 20th century.

Panama Canal

Perhaps the most significant American intervention in Latin America occurred in 1901 when President Theodore Roosevelt encouraged the revolt of Panamanians in order to secure rights to build and control a canal between the Atlantic and Pacific oceans. This was seen as a necessity for the United States to maintain its two-ocean navy and global commercial interests.

World War I

Though the United States was a global power by 1914, it was not drawn initially into what Americans called the "European War." In part, American neutrality reflected the populace's own divided loyalties. German-Americans were the single largest minority population in many states. The horrifying reports of trench warfare confirmed many Americans' view that this was not a war worth fighting. President Woodrow Wilson ran for reelection in 1916 on a campaign that touted "He Kept Us Out of the War."

Nonetheless, in April 1917, the United States entered the war on the side of the Allied Powers. The stated reasons for entering the war included: (1) Germany's efforts to encourage Mexico to attack the United States in return for regaining New Mexico, Arizona, Texas; and (2) Germany's declaration of unrestricted submarine warfare in February 1917.

Other factors contributed to U.S. entry. British wartime propaganda played up German atrocities, as well as the German assault on the neutral nation of Belgium. As the British blockade did not allow American or other neutral vessels to reach Germany or other Central Power nations, the United States, though neutral, was increasingly committed to an Allied victory to avoid enormous commercial losses. Moreover, with the Russian Tsar's withdrawal from the war in early 1917, Woodrow Wilson could claim that the war pitted the autocratic empires of Germany, Austria-Hungary, and the Ottoman Empire against the constitutionally limited governments of the United Kingdom and France.

U.S. entry into the war turned the tide for the Allied Powers. Though American troops arrived in Europe in significant numbers only in the summer of 1918 and played a major role in only two significant battles, American participation destroyed any hope Germany had for a victory on the Western Front. The Americans' most important military campaign during the war occurred during the Meuse-Argonne offensive, which lasted from September to November 1918 and involved 1.2 million American soldiers. Much of the fighting of this offensive occurred in the difficult terrain of the Argonne Forest. American arrival, however, probably had the greatest effect on the German populace, which was demoralized by the likelihood that an American force of over 4 million could be called into action. Very quickly after the arrival of American troops, the Germans began to pursue negotiations with the United States and the Allies.

The United States emerged from the war the clear victor among all the powers. France, Great Britain, Germany, Russia, and the Ottoman Empire were devastated by the prolonged fighting and loss of life. The United States had lost over 100,000 soldiers to combat, but by comparison to the other powers, this was a very small loss. Morale in all the belligerent nations was low. The economic and financial stability of each nation had also suffered. At the close of the war, the United States had surpassed Great Britain in industrial output and was the world's largest creditor. Woodrow Wilson was now poised to lead the United States to a position on the world stage it had not previously known.

> **Competency 008 Descriptive Statement B.** The beginning teacher analyzes how national and international decisions and conflicts between World War I and World War II affected the United States (e.g., the Fourteen Points, isolationism, reasons for U.S. involvement in World War II).

> **Key Question**
>
>
>
> How did American failure to take a leadership role in international politics in the interwar years contribute to the eventuality of World War II, and how was the United States pulled from isolationism into a second world war?

Periodization: 1918 to 1945

Between 1918 and 1945, United States foreign policy was guided first by the idealism of Woodrow Wilson as he led the nation into World War I (1914–1918) and then by a period of isolationism as Americans withdrew from European and international affairs (1921–1933). After the election of Franklin D. Roosevelt as president, the United States was gradually drawn into the global conflict that would eventually erupt in 1939 as the Second World War. The United States would only enter after December 1941, but entry into World War II put a permanent end to U.S. isolationism, and soon Americans found themselves as the unchallenged world leader.

Fourteen Points

Well before American troops had arrived in Europe in numbers, President Wilson declared the terms that he believed should shape the postwar settlement. Wilson's announcement came as a surprise to his European allies and was not immediately welcome, but it did illustrate the new position of the United States as an important power broker on the world stage. Wilson's Fourteen Points outlined a plan that called for free trade, open alliances, disarmament, the right to national self-determination, and the establishment of a League of Nations where international disputes could be refereed and acts of aggression could be met with collective rather than unilateral responses.

Treaty of Versailles (1919)

The Germans were encouraged by Wilson's Fourteen Points, recognizing that they would not receive such favorable treatment from the French or British who had borne the brunt of Allied casualties over the course of the war. Britain and France instead wanted to punish Germany, blaming the Germans for starting the war, as well as for the use of such weapons as the submarine and mustard gas, both of which the Allies considered unconscionable. The Treaty of Versailles, which ended World War I, did not, however, reflect Wilson's magnanimity toward the Germans. They were forced to sign a "war guilt clause," pay $33 billion in reparations to the Allies, limit their army to 100,000 men, scuttle all naval vessels over a certain size, maintain an air force, and give up significant German and colonial territories. The principle of self-determination resulted in the establishment of a number of new European nations (e.g., Czechoslovakia, Yugoslavia) and the re-creation of some ancient kingdoms (e.g., Estonia, Latvia, Lithuania, and Poland).

League of Nations

The League of Nations represented one of Woodrow Wilson's most important contributions to international relations. Unfortunately, Wilson's postwar plan was even more poorly received in the United States. Americans had soured at the prospect of being involved in European affairs and a spirit of **isolationism** had already begun to grow across America. In particular, Wilson's critics objected to the League of Nations' requirement that the United States (and other world powers) were required to defend the territory of other League members that were victims of territorial aggression. The United States Senate refused to ratify the Treaty of Versailles. Consequently, the United States did not then join the League of Nations.

Isolationism

A feature of American isolationism in the 1920s resulted from fear that the Bolshevik spirit that resulted in the Russian Revolution in 1917 might spread to the West and to the United States. This largely unfounded paranoia coupled with existing anti-immigrant sentiment resulted in a **"Red Scare"** that targeted recent immigrants, labor union activists, and socialists and accused anarchists.

Isolationism was also evident in an immigrant quota that limited the number of immigrants allowed into the country to 357,000 and privileged immigration from northern and western Europe rather than from southern and central Europe.

The strength of isolationist sentiment was evident even as late as 1941, well after Japan had invaded Manchuria and then mainland China, and after Germany had annexed Austria, parts of Czechoslovakia, and then invaded Poland. Millions of Americans, including the American aviation hero Charles Lindbergh, supported the **America First** movement that called for the United States to stay out of the war already raging across the globe.

Reasons for U.S. involvement in World War II

The United States entered World War II largely in response to the crippling attack on Pearl Harbor by a force of Japanese aircraft. The attack destroyed much of the Pacific fleet stationed in Hawaii and briefly gave Japan the window of opportunity needed to unleash assaults on the British in Singapore and Malaysia, the French in Southeast Asia, the Dutch in Indonesia, and the United States bases in the Philippines. Additionally, the Japanese created a Pacific perimeter of defended islands that would make defeating Japan a difficult task.

Competency 008 Descriptive Statement C. The beginning teacher analyzes how national and international decisions and conflicts from World War II to the present have affected the United States (e.g., decision to use the atomic bomb, Cold War).

Key Question

From World War II to the present, American society and domestic conditions have been more heavily impacted by events abroad than perhaps at any time in American history. This descriptive statement asks test-takers to be able to analyze the impact on American domestic conditions of these international decisions and conflicts.

The Home Front during World War II

The industrial capacity of the United States was never more in evidence than during the Second World War. The United States produced over 300,000 airplanes, 100,000 tanks and armored cars, 141 aircraft carriers, and over 1,000 naval vessels of all sizes. Mobilizing the nation's industrial might in this fashion involved unprecedented degrees of federal government intervention in the economy. At the beginning of the war, Roosevelt established the War Production Board to aid in the transition from producing automobiles to making tanks, armored personnel carriers, and airplanes, and in steering resources necessary to the war effort away from consumer production.

With 12 million men under arms, wartime industries desperately needed an increased labor pool. Women provided an important source of new industrial workers. By the end of the war, nearly 20 million women worked outside the home. Another pool of labor critical to the war effort was African Americans who moved in significant numbers to northern cities, continuing a trend begun during World War I. To reduce the possibility of labor unrest that would slow down production, the National War Labor Board was revived from the days of World War I to settle disputes over wages, working conditions, and hours. Strikes were prohibited. Nonetheless, labor union membership nearly doubled during the war.

Paying for the war also increased the size and impact of the federal government on the American economy. Though taxation only paid for 45 percent of the increased cost of government, increased taxes on corporate income and the wealthy helped fund the war effort. In addition to increased taxation, the war was funded by borrowing. From $42 billion in 1940, the national debt ballooned to over $251 billion in 1945. Much of this debt was funded through the sale of war bonds, often sold in small denominations to encourage private saving. These war bond drives were wildly successful, in part because there were few consumer items available for sale, as the Office of Price Administration imposed rationing on sugar, butter, coffee, meat, gasoline, and hundreds of other consumer items.

Minorities and the War

Minority populations experienced the war years somewhat differently that did the majority population. For both Hispanic and African Americans, the wartime economy created an unprecedented opportunity for employment in industrial occupations. Nonetheless, discrimination continued to limit their access. African Americans led by A. Philip Randolph sought to challenge these discriminatory practices. A campaign known as the **Double V campaign** was begun demanding "democracy at home and abroad." Randolph threatened Truman that he would lead a March on Washington to pressure the government to change hiring practices in defense industries and to end segregation in the military. The former was accomplished, at least in law, with the establishment of the Fair Employment Practices Committee, which forced companies with federal contracts to make jobs available regardless of "race, creed, color, or national origin." Only after the war, however, did Harry Truman desegregate the military.

Hispanic Americans also found new opportunities for employment in agriculture and industry. The **bracero program** used over 200,000 workers from Mexico, brought in as guest laborers to meet the shortage of agricultural workers. Large numbers of Mexican Americans worked in the shipyards and industrial plants producing war materiel. Over 300,000 Hispanic Americans served in the military, many with distinction. Despite their military and workplace contributions to the war effort, Mexican Americans faced hostility and discrimination. The **League of United Latin American Citizens (LULAC),** which had been founded in 1929 in Corpus Christi, Texas, by veterans of World War I, saw a revival of enthusiasm after World War II when veterans from the war returned to face continued discrimination, despite their willingness to sacrifice themselves for the country.

Japanese American Internment

Of all minority populations, Japanese Americans perhaps suffered the most from discrimination during the war. President Roosevelt, fearing that Japanese Americans might harbor spies, ordered their internment in camps far from their homes. Over 100,000 Japanese Americans—two-thirds of them native-born U.S. citizens—were forcibly removed to camps mostly in the American interior West. The 1944 case *Korematsu v. United States* upheld the internment. In 1988, a formal apology was issued, and survivors were given $20,000 each in reparations.

The "Bomb"

In August 1945, the United States became the first, and to the present, the only nation to use nuclear weapons in combat. For the next four years, the United States had a monopoly on nuclear weaponry, but in 1949, the Soviet Union acquired the technology and a nuclear arms race followed. Rapidly, both powers had the capability to unleash unimaginable horror on the other side. The deterrent effect of this stalemate became known as **Mutually Assured Destruction,** or **MAD**. America's nuclear deterrent also permitted the United States to maximize its projection of power at comparatively lower human and economic costs. The cost of maintaining a conventional army with sufficient artillery and tank resources to fight a war against the Soviet Union was significantly higher than that of building a nuclear arsenal. The United States could shield its allies under a "nuclear umbrella" much more cost-effectively than it could with conventional weapons and armies. As a result, while the defense budget during the 1950s held steadily below $40 billion, Americans could devote their efforts to producing consumer items like cars, televisions, and other goods, rather than maintaining a massive army, giving it an advantage over the Soviet Union, which had to employ a large conventional army to control Eastern Europeans unhappy at being incorporated into its empire. This came at a psychological cost, however. In the 1950s and 1960s, Americans lived in fear of a nuclear holocaust. Children in schools were required to conduct drills to prepare for a nuclear assault. When both sides developed intercontinental ballistic missiles (ICBMs) that could strike the enemy heartland in 30 minutes, fears of nuclear annihilation became even more frightening.

The Second Red Scare

Fear of the spread of communism infected American domestic policy almost immediately following the end of World War II. The **House Committee on Un-American Activities,** or **HUAC,** which had been established in 1938 to investigate potentially subversive organizations, was employed beginning in the late 1940s to uncover private individuals and government officials who were suspected of having communist sympathies. In 1947, the Truman administration began investigating federal employees and identifying organizations that were feared to be "Communist front organizations." A number of political figures saw this "Red Scare" as an opportunity to make their political fortunes. In 1948, Richard Nixon rose to fame investigating a State Department official named Alger Hiss, whom Nixon accused of being an agent of the Soviet Union. The hysteria around the spread of communism increased in 1949, when news that the Soviet Union had the atomic bomb led to fears that spies within the U.S. government had passed secrets to the Soviets. That same year, the Chinese Revolution under Mao Zedong resulted in China adopting a communist government. American missionaries and political figures lamented the "loss of China," again seeking to lay blame on secret communist sympathizers within the U.S. State Department. While the degree to which the spread of nuclear technology or the "loss of China" could be blamed on communist sympathizers in positions of power is debatable, the **VENONA Files,** only made public in 1995, confirmed many of the fears of treasonous American activity, including most notably the role of Julius Rosenberg, who was executed for his role in a Soviet spy ring.

> **Competency 008 Descriptive Statement D.** The beginning teacher demonstrates knowledge of significant individuals who shaped U.S. foreign policy from 1898 to the present (e.g., Alfred Thayer Mahan, Theodore Roosevelt, Woodrow Wilson, Franklin D. Roosevelt, Henry Kissinger).

Key Question

How have key foreign policy actors guided U.S. foreign policy, and what has motivated their direction of American foreign policy?

Four important schools of thought have influenced American foreign policy actors since the 1890s: **Isolationism, Globalism, Idealism,** and **Realism. Isolationists** have been cautious of involvement in world affairs, seeing alliance systems and collective security agreements as likely to draw the United States into unnecessary conflict. Often, isolationists have perceived international agreements as undermining American sovereignty. George Washington's farewell warning against entering into "entangling alliances" is often cited as an important source for these sentiments. **Globalists**, in contrast, have supported policies that increased global integration, often with the stated objective of reducing the potential for international conflict resulting from nationalistic competition and rivalry. Since the 1940s, American foreign policy has, to varying degrees, pursued globalist agendas, taking leadership in promoting open markets, free trade agreements, and multi-lateral organizations like the United Nations as means of reducing international tensions. Frequently globalists have taken an **Idealist** position on foreign policy. **Idealists** contend that instead of acting on the basis of narrowly defined national interest, the United States should use its power and influence to promote the spread of democracy, human rights, representative institutions, or worker rights or free market institutions, etc. In contrast, **Realists** argue that in the anarchic world of international politics, the United States, like other nation-states, must project military and political power in the pursuit of specific and identifiable national interests.

Periodization: 1898 to the Present

American foreign policy from 1898 to the present is divided into three distinct periods: America's Rise to World Power (1898–1945); the Cold War (1945–1989); and the Post–Cold War Period (1989–present).

Alfred Thayer Mahan (1840–1914)

Alfred Thayer Mahan was the author of *The Influence of Sea Power on History, 1660–1783*, a history of Dutch, English, French, and Spanish imperialism between 1660 and 1783. Mahan argued that global political and commercial power depended on naval strength. Mahan's treatise provided support for United States' construction of the Panama Canal, the acquisition of coaling stations on the islands of Hawaii, Guam, Midway, and elsewhere in the Pacific, and the expansion of the American navy. His theories particularly influenced Theodore Roosevelt. The U.S. Navy was expanded significantly after 1890, and the nation turned outward from its historical continental focus to a worldwide involvement.

Theodore Roosevelt (1858–1919)

Theodore Roosevelt was a proponent of a vigorous international American presence, led by a strong executive branch, in pursuit of American national interest. He was a strong advocate of the use of American naval power. In support of this aim, when Colombia refused to accept an American offer of $10 million up front and annual rent payments of $250,000 for a canal zone across the Isthmus of Panama, Roosevelt encouraged and protected a Panamanian rebellion. The new government in Panama immediately accepted the terms that had been offered to Colombia, and the canal was built.

Roosevelt also claimed that the United States had the right to intervene anywhere in the Western Hemisphere as an "international police power" to put an end to unrest or injustice in the U.S. sphere of interest. This **Roosevelt Corollary to the Monroe Doctrine** was invoked to justify intervention in Cuba, Nicaragua, Haiti, and the Dominican Republic. This gunboat diplomacy in the Caribbean is only one example of Roosevelt "carrying a big stick," though he was not unafraid to use his bully pulpit to intimidate opponents.

Roosevelt also encouraged greater American involvement in European and Asian affairs, earning a Nobel Peace Prize for brokering a negotiated settlement between Russia and Japan in the Russo-Japanese War of 1906, and mediating a dispute between Germany and France that threatened European peace.

Woodrow Wilson

Woodrow Wilson, who like Theodore Roosevelt was a progressive politician, differed markedly in the role he believed the United States should play in world affairs. Both were globalists, but where Roosevelt employed political power as a realist promoting American national interest first, Wilson was a committed idealist. Wilson disapproved of Roosevelt's approach of "speaking softly and carrying a big stick." This seemed too clearly a form of militaristic imperialism. Wilson, nonetheless, was as active in intervening in Latin America as Roosevelt had been, if not more so; under Wilson, Nicaragua was occupied from 1912 to 1925, Haiti from 1915 to 1934, and the Dominican Republic from 1916 to 1924. Wilson argued that these interventions were necessary to promote representative government in Latin America.

In 1914, to "teach the South American republics to elect good men," Wilson ordered U.S. Marines to seize the port city of Veracruz, Mexico, to force the military dictator Victoriano Huerta out of office. In 1916, Wilson again intervened in Mexico, ordering General John J. "Blackjack" Pershing and 12,000 soldiers into Mexico in an effort to capture the Mexican rebel leader Pancho Villa.

With the outbreak of World War I, Wilson maintained U.S. neutrality, largely on the grounds that neither side in the conflict had just cause for war and that the war pitted autocratic empires against one another. Wilson also insisted on freedom of the seas and trade as a feature of American neutrality. German violation of that freedom of the seas provided one reason for U.S. entry into the war. But, even here Wilson justified U.S. entry into the war to "make the world safe for democracy." Wilson's high-minded and idealistic war aims were also reflected in his **Fourteen Points**. U.S. war aims in this formulation called for such idealistic objectives as the right to national self-determination (at least for European nations), arms reduction agreements, and the promotion of collective security agreements (the League of Nations) rather than secret treaties or alliances.

Although Wilson was not able to fully realize the idealistic objectives of his Fourteen Points, the United States did not entirely withdraw from international affairs in the years between World

War I and the outbreak of World War II. For example, the Washington Naval Conference (signed in 1922), which attempted to reduce competition between world powers to build ever larger navies, demonstrated continued American interest in the kind of idealistic aims Wilson had promoted. Nonetheless, the United States before entry into World War II had increasingly shunned participation in world affairs.

Franklin D. Roosevelt

Franklin Delano Roosevelt, a progressive Democrat in the mold of Woodrow Wilson, had been an idealist and globalist during the 1920s. He argued for U.S. membership in the League of Nations and considered American absence in that body as a blow to world peace. He also criticized Republican imposition of high trade barriers as undermining stability in Europe, believing that reduced trade restrictions could only contribute to greater national cooperation and international stability. With the outbreak of the Great Depression, Roosevelt was forced by political realities to withdraw from this commitment to globalist idealism, despite his conviction that open markets and international organizations like the League of Nations were necessary to promote world peace. Once the United States had entered into World War II, however, Roosevelt's commitment to these ideals would be apparent in his own vision of a postwar settlement.

Roosevelt did institute a very different Latin American policy from his predecessors, describing it as a **Good Neighbor Policy** aimed at offering Latin American nations a "helping hand" while refusing to intervene as Wilson and his cousin Theodore had done earlier. This did not mean that the United States disengaged in Latin America, merely that under Franklin Roosevelt, Latin American relations were guided more by trade policy than by military engagement.

The United States Congress, between 1935 and 1937, concerned that the United States might be drawn into the increasingly likely conflict in Europe, passed a number of neutrality acts that restricted lending money or selling arms to nations at war and authorized the government to issue warnings to American citizens traveling on ships of warring nations.

As Roosevelt observed the increase of German and Japanese power, he was not entirely hampered by American isolationist sentiment. In 1934, Roosevelt authorized the largest naval expansion since World War I. When the war in Europe erupted, Roosevelt pushed Congress to repeal the arms embargo and permit belligerent nations to purchase weaponry, but only on a "cash-and-carry basis." In December 1940, shortly after his second re-election, Roosevelt increased support for the Allies through the **Lend-Lease Program** that allowed Great Britain and later the Soviet Union to receive war materiel on loan from the United States. In Asia, where Japan was securing its control over China's coastline, the United States supported the Nationalist government of Chiang Kai-Shek. Then in 1941, Roosevelt announced a trade embargo on Japan, cutting the Japanese off from critical supplies of oil and scrap iron. This served as an ultimatum: either stop policies of territorial expansion and reestablish normal trade relations with the United States, or up the ante by attacking Southeast Asia, Indonesia, and the Philippines (an American protectorate) in a desperate bid to acquire the raw materials Japan needed. On December 7, 1941, Japan attacked the U.S. naval base at **Pearl Harbor,** making their choice clear.

While fighting the war, Franklin Roosevelt prepared for the peace that would follow. Evident in the postwar settlement that Roosevelt laid out were many of the elements of the idealist program promoted by Wilson and other progressives. Even before the war's conclusion, an agreement was signed in Bretton Woods, New Hampshire, creating the **International Monetary Fund (IMF)**. The purpose of the IMF was to ensure financial and monetary stability across the world economy, an effort to respond to the economic crises that had contributed to the rise of authoritarian regimes in Europe, Asia, and Latin America. The Bretton Woods conference also established the **World Bank,** to provide reconstruction and development loans to nations ravaged by war. Immediately following World War II's conclusion, the **United Nations** was established, initially with 51 member states, and headquartered in New York City, a clear signal that the United States would not be withdrawing into domestic isolation, as it did in the years following World War I. Whereas the IMF and the World Bank addressed the economic crises that had led to World War II, the United Nations reflected an American commitment, shared by most idealists, to the principle that collective security agreements and arms limitations are the best means to preserve world peace. The **General Agreement on Tariffs and Trade (GATT)**, later changed to the **World Trade Organization**, was a final component of the postwar settlement designed in 1947 to encourage open trade and reductions in tariffs and trade restrictions.

George F. Kennan and the Truman Doctrine

Following World War II, as the United States and the Soviet Union's relationship deteriorated and the Soviet Union tightened its grip on Eastern Europe, President Harry S. Truman, the Congress, and the American people were uncertain how to proceed. Few in the United States supported Winston Churchill's call for war against the Soviet Union. After all, the U.S.S.R. had been a critical ally against the Nazis. In February 1946, George F. Kennan, a career diplomat stationed in Moscow, sent a memorandum to the U.S. State Department. In this cable and in a subsequent pseudonymously published article in *Foreign Affairs* magazine, Kennan argued that the possibilities for U.S.-Soviet cooperation were limited. Kennan argued that Communist Russia was motivated by a combination of expansionist geopolitical aims and the desire to spread communism globally. Kennan argued that Soviet efforts to expand Russian influence should be met with a policy that would be later called **containment**. President Truman implemented this policy of containment, or the **Truman Doctrine**. This involved providing financial and military aid to pro-American governments. Truman and his senior policy advisors explained this costly strategy to Americans eager to return to prewar tax and spending levels by invoking the **Domino Theory** of communist expansion. If the United States stood idly by, the theory went, nation after nation would fall to communism, leaving the United States and its economic and military allies isolated. The Korean and Vietnam War were largely fought on the basis of this theory. The influence of the containment doctrine would figure in American foreign policy until 1989.

Richard Nixon

Through the 1950s and 1960s, the doctrine of containment guided American foreign policy. It was premised upon the view that communism represented a monolithic ideological force against which American interests were arrayed. According to this view, communist ideology in the Soviet Union and in China (which became a communist nation in 1949) were equally threatening to the United States and its capitalist allies. Between 1956 and 1961 Chinese and Soviet leaders had increasingly differed ideologically. Despite a reputation for being a hardline anti-communist, Richard Nixon, following his election in 1968, determined to take advantage of this Sino-Soviet divide.

Henry Kissinger, Nixon's national security advisor, was the architect of Nixon's new policy approach. Kissinger is renowned as a foreign policy realist, willing to set aside ideological positions in the pursuit of national interest. In 1971, Kissinger made a secret visit to China, a visit that was followed up by Nixon, very publicly making a state visit to China in 1972. Kissinger made clear that the United States would judge nations, "even countries like Communist China, on their actions and not on the basis of their domestic ideology." The warming of relations with China also resulted in a warming of relations with the Soviet Union. This thaw was called **détente**. A series of strategic arms limitations talks were entered into, reducing the likelihood of a nuclear exchange. Improved relations with China contributed in the long run to Chinese reforms that introduced features of market economies into China. Though relations with both communist superpowers were not without tensions, after 1972, the likelihood of hostilities between the United States and either the Soviet Union or China was gradually reduced.

Competency 008 Descriptive Statement E. The beginning teacher demonstrates knowledge of significant events and issues that shaped U.S. foreign policy from 1898 to present (e.g., Berlin airlift, Korean War, Sputnik I, Vietnam War, Marshall Plan, North Atlantic Treaty Organization, McCarthyism, Cuban Missile Crisis, the Gulf War).

Key Question

What factors contributed to the United States Government's Cold War and post-Cold War policy decisions? Though this descriptive statement asks for test-takers to demonstrate knowledge of events and issues from 1898 to the present, it is clear from the examples that the Cold War and its aftermath is the focus of this descriptive statement.

Periodization: 1945 to 2001

American foreign policy during the Cold War and post–Cold War should be broken down into the following four distinct time periods:

1945–1971. The period 1945 to 1971 was a period of bipolar confrontation between the United States and its allies, and the Soviet Union and its allies. Though the two superpowers did not face one another in direct combat, the possibility for the outbreak of a "World War III" was always close to the surface.

1971–1989. Beginning with the administration of Richard Nixon, the United States and Communist China, as well as the United States and the Soviet Union, began to move towards more peaceful relations, though in either case, there were periods where relations were nonetheless strained.

1989–2001. From 1989 to 2001 the United States was effectively the sole super power as the Soviet Union's control over its empire collapsed and the Russian Federation, which replaced the Soviet state, struggled to restructure its domestic and foreign policy. China and India had yet to rise to the economic significance they would after the turn of the 21st century. As a result, the United States benefited from a brief period of clear global predominance. Its leadership and military superiority was most clearly seen in the First Gulf War.

The Cold War

American policy makers had long considered communist ideology a threat to American values and economic interests. In 1918, the United States had supported anticommunist forces in Russia, even sending troops to help them fight the spread of Bolshevism. During the Great Depression, the United States had seen Soviet-style communism as the clearest alternative and threat to capitalism. After World War II, despite having allied with the Soviet Union during the war against Nazi Germany, American distrust of the Soviet Union increased.

The Soviet Red Army had advanced deep into Germany during the last year of World War II and was left in control of eastern Germany, Poland, Czechoslovakia, Hungary, Romania, and Bulgaria, in addition to the Baltic States of Estonia, Latvia, and Lithuania, which had been annexed during the war. Joseph Stalin, fearing a repeat of invasion from the west, demanded a buffer zone in Eastern Europe and immediately began to impose pro-Soviet, communist governments throughout the region. American foreign policy makers perceived this expansion of Soviet control over Eastern Europe as a prelude to an assault on Western Europe and set about to contain the Soviet Union and the spread of communism. When, in 1949, the Soviet Union tested its own nuclear device, the Americans also faced a nuclear-armed competitor with a conventional force that matched its own.

Marshall Plan

General George Marshall, the World War II military hero and Secretary of State under President Harry S. Truman, proposed a plan to rebuild the war-ravaged economies of western Europe. The Marshall Plan gave to France, Britain, and other western European nations over $13 billion dollars in assistance. This aid was given with few conditions, unlike the loans that had been destabilizing factors in the post-World War I global economy. With this aid, European nations began rebuilding roads, industrial plant, and urban infrastructure. With their strengthened economies, European consumers could also purchase American goods. As a result, the Marshall Plan benefited American producers as much as it benefited Europeans. The Soviet Union declared that Soviet-occupied countries in Eastern Europe were not eligible for these funds, fearing that they would bolster democratic and capitalistic interests in Eastern Europe.

The Berlin Airlift (June 1948–May 1949)

At the close of World War II, Germany was divided between French, British, and American occupied sectors in western Germany and a Soviet-controlled zone in the east. The capital, Berlin, which was located in the center of the Soviet sector, was similarly divided into four zones, with West Berlin under control of the French, British, and Americans. When in 1948, the British, Americans, and French met to organize the reconstruction of Germany, they proposed extending these efforts into West Berlin, hoping to integrate their sector of the capital into the West German economy. Stalin objected, fearing an extension of capitalist and democratic institutions into eastern Europe, and imposed a blockade of the city—by international law, an act of war—closing all land routes to the capital. The Americans, French, and British then organized an airlift to supply West Berlin with food, coal, and other necessities. The airlift supplied the city for nearly a year, flying in between 4,000 and 10,000 tons of supplies a day. The airlift had successfully maintained the freedom and morale of West Berlin's residents.

North Atlantic Treaty Organization (NATO)

The Berlin Crisis illustrated the need for greater coordination between the United States and its allies. In 1949, France, Great Britain, and the United States formed an alliance and were joined by Belgium, Canada, Denmark, Italy, Iceland, Luxembourg, Netherlands, Norway, and Portugal. According to the terms of the treaty, any attack on one or more of the member states would be "considered an attack against them all." The number of member states has continued to grow, and its mission has gradually shifted from being an alliance primarily directed against threats from the Soviet Union to one that also has participated in the "global war on terror." In response to this alliance, the Soviet Union created its own collective security agreement, known as the **Warsaw Pact.**

McCarthyism

Senator Joseph McCarthy is perhaps the best-known figure to have politically profited from promoting a climate of anti-communist hysteria. In a 1950 speech, he held up a list, never actually disclosed to the press or public, on which he claimed he had the names of over 200 communists working within the State Department and elsewhere in the federal government. Following McCarthy, Nixon and J. Edgar Hoover, the director of the Federal Bureau of Investigation (FBI), as well as Americans in all sectors of life began to suspect their coworkers and neighbors of communist sympathies. Hollywood movie studios were investigated; and writers, actors, directors, and producers were called upon to name names of those they felt harbored anti-American sentiments. University professors were forced from their positions, often on the flimsiest of evidence. The "Red Scare" abated somewhat, finally, when McCarthy himself overreached, accusing the U.S. Army of hiding suspected communist sympathizers in its ranks. The U.S. Army's chief legal counsel, Joseph Welch, demanded that McCarthy produce the names on his vaunted list, and when he would not, Welch famously asked, "Have you no sense of decency, sir? At long last, have you no sense of decency?" The Senate censured McCarthy, and the explosive power of such unfounded accusations lost much of its potency.

Korean War

The Cold War in June of 1950 erupted into a shooting war on the Korean Peninsula. Korea, which had been controlled by Japan, had been divided at the close of World War II into two sectors controlled by the Soviet Union and the United States. North Korea's invasion of South Korea in 1950 seemed to confirm fears that there existed a vast plan to establish communist domination across the globe. In response, the United States began a massive military rearmament and received United Nations authorization to come to South Korea's defense. U.S. entry turned the tide of the conflict in favor of the South Koreans. In 1950, as the American forces approached the North Korean boundary with China, Mao Zedong, fearing a U.S. invasion of China (a not unrealistic possibility given the widely reported anti-communist fervor in the United States), ordered the Chinese Red Army to enter the fray. At this point, what had largely been a localized conflict threatened to erupt into World War III. For three years, the Korean conflict raged across the peninsula, finally settling in a stalemate in July 1953. An armistice, or end to hostilities, was agreed to and the conflict came to a conclusion. No peace treaty, however, has been signed, and to this day North Korea and South Korea confront one another across a demilitarized zone along the 38th parallel.

Vietnam War

The United States became involved in a second "shooting war" in Asia shortly after the end of fighting in Korea. France, an important U.S. ally in the Cold War in Europe, had controlled Vietnam as part of its Indochinese colony. The Vietnamese, led by the nationalist leader **Ho Chi Minh** had been fighting French colonization since the end of World War II. The Soviet Union and Communist China had contributed weaponry, training, and other assistance to the Vietnamese. In 1954, when the French were defeated by the Vietnamese, Ho Chi Minh set about establishing a united Vietnam. The administration of Dwight Eisenhower, fearing another victory for communism, intervened by propping up a non-communist leader in South Vietnam and calling for national elections. When it became clear that Ho Chi Minh and his party would win those elections, the elections were canceled at U.S. insistence.

To prop up the unpopular South Vietnamese government, the United States then provided military and financial assistance to combat the **Viet Cong**, as the communist rebels in South Vietnam were known. When John F. Kennedy was elected president, he increased the United States military presence in Vietnam to 16,700 troops. After Kennedy's assassination, with the South Vietnamese government appearing ever more fragile, Lyndon B. Johnson feared that he would be blamed for "losing Vietnam."

In August 1964, reports of an attempted attack on a U.S. destroyer in the Gulf of Tonkin off the coast of North Vietnam gave Johnson a pretext for escalating U.S. military involvement in support of South Vietnam. Congress voted with near unanimity for the **Gulf of Tonkin Resolution**, which authorized Johnson to "take all necessary measures . . . to prevent further aggression." With this open-ended authorization, Johnson ordered 80,000 U.S. troops to Vietnam to fight a war of attrition against the Viet Cong and the North Vietnamese Army. By 1968, more than half a million American combat troops were engaged in Vietnam. In January of 1968, during the celebrations for the Tet New Year, the Viet Cong and North Vietnamese forces struck simultaneously across South Vietnam. Illustrating the difficulties of winning a counter-insurgency war, the battle was a political and public relations defeat, even though the United States inflicted far greater casualties on their enemies and prevented them from holding their objectives. After the **Tet Offensive**, many Americans became convinced that the war was unwinnable and questioned the degree to which continued involvement was in the American national interest. Widespread protests against the war soon became a feature of American political life. The 1968 election became, in part, a referendum on American involvement in Vietnam. Richard Nixon, accordingly, ran for the presidency promising to achieve "peace with honor." His victory, however, did not result in a quick end to the war. While the heaviest involvement of American soldiers ended in 1973, the last American troops were finally withdrawn in 1975. South Vietnam fell soon after. Estimates of the number of casualties vary widely, but the general estimate is that between 1.5 and 3.6 million Vietnamese soldiers and civilians and some 58,220 American soldiers died in the fighting.

Sputnik I and the Space Race

The Soviet Union and the United States not only competed militarily in places like Korea and Vietnam (or in Afghanistan where the United States supported an anti-Soviet insurrection), the two superpowers also competed on the technological and scientific front. In 1957, the Soviet Union tested the first intercontinental ballistic missiles and then placed the first space satellite into orbit, the **Sputnik I**. The military implications were clear. If the Soviet Union could put a satellite in space, it could also launch a missile capable of delivering a nuclear warhead on the American populace. The United States responded immediately, launching its own satellite only three months later. Nonetheless, John F. Kennedy used closing the "missile gap" as one of his campaign promises when running against Richard Nixon. And, when Kennedy became president, he promised to reach the Moon before the end of the decade. Though he didn't live to witness the event, in 1969, the United States, though a late starter in the space race, put the first man on the Moon.

Cuban Missile Crisis

In 1959, 90 miles from the Florida coast, Fidel Castro overthrew the United States-backed military dictator of Cuba. When Castro established a one-party communist government, the first in the Western Hemisphere, first the Eisenhower administration and then the government of John F. Kennedy sought to overthrow Castro. Both feared the spread of communism in the Americas and recognized the strategic threat of a Soviet ally so close to the United States mainland. In October 1962, U.S. spy planes uncovered evidence of Soviet missiles and launching facilities on the island. The diplomatic and military standoff as the United States set up a naval blockade have often been characterized as the closest the two superpowers came to unleashing global thermonuclear war. The Soviet Union stood down, agreeing to remove the threatening missiles from Cuba, in exchange for withdrawal of American short-range missiles from Turkey. One outcome of the standoff was an increased desire on the part of both superpowers to limit the possibility of a similar near-miss in the future.

> **Competency 008 Descriptive Statement F.** The beginning teacher understands the origins of major foreign policy issues currently facing the United States and the challenges of changing relationships among nations.

Key Question

 How have globalization, the "Rise of Asia," and the ongoing crisis in the Middle East posed significant challenges to the United States since 1989?

Periodization: 1989 to 2001

Between the end of the Cold War in 1989 and the attack on the World Trade Center in New York City and the Pentagon just outside Washington, D.C., in September 2001, the United States interacted with a world that had largely accepted American leadership and the value of the American free market systems and representative institutions as models for stability and growth. The attack on the World Trade Center in 2001 illustrated an important challenge to American hegemony, which was followed by important, though less overt, challenges to American leadership represented by growing economies in China and India.

Globalization and the Washington Consensus

Since 1989, and the conclusion of the Cold War, the dominant position taken by American foreign policy leaders has been one that promoted a globalist agenda. The United States shifted from containment of the spread of communism—which had been largely discredited as an alternative to free-market systems—to a U.S. foreign policy driven by a new idealism: the promotion of a set of policy recommendations known as the **Washington Consensus**. These broad recommendations included encouraging developing countries to exercise fiscal policy discipline (avoiding or reducing national debt), tax reform, reductions of protectionist trade measures, openness to foreign investment, privatization of state-owned industries, and widespread deregulation.

Free Trade and Globalization: NAFTA, the WTO

President George H.W. Bush in 1990 had initiated talks to establish a free trade agreement uniting Mexico, the United States, and Canada. His Democratic successor, Bill Clinton, also supported the negotiations and convinced skeptical Democratic congressmen, many of whom went against their union supporters to back the treaty. The **North American Free Trade Agreement (NAFTA)**, signed in 1993, removed tariff barriers restricting trade among the three nations. Clinton later supported the establishment of the **World Trade Organization** to further increase global free trade measures.

Peace Dividend and Global Hotspots

After the Cold War, many politicians said the United States would receive a "peace dividend," as the federal government reduced military expenditures and redirected the millions spent on defense into infrastructure improvements and social welfare spending.

But instead of receiving a "peace dividend," the United States was drawn into a number of global crises. In 1990, the nation of Iraq invaded its small, oil-rich neighbor, Kuwait, in an effort to force Kuwait to forgive debts accumulated by Iraq during its long war with another neighbor, Iran. Fearing that Iraq's actions would also threaten a key American ally in the region, the Kingdom of Saudi Arabia, President George H.W. Bush ordered American troops to the region to force an Iraqi withdrawal. When Saddam Hussein, then president of Iraq, refused to withdraw, the United States invaded Iraq and forced Hussein to leave Kuwait.

The United States has also faced a number of humanitarian crises since the end of the Cold War, often with mixed results. In August 1992, President George H.W. Bush sent U.S. military units into Somalia to respond to a humanitarian crisis caused by an ongoing civil war in this nation on the Horn of Africa. The mission continued into the presidency of Bill Clinton. After a contingent of U.S. Marines came under attack, Clinton withdrew the force from the region. The United States, perhaps as a result of skittishness in the aftermath of the Somalia debacle, then failed to act to put a stop to the Rwandan genocide in 1994, when over 800,000 Rwandan Tutsi were killed by the majority Hutu population in a bloodbath that many people around the world watched unfold on CNN. The response of the United States to such crises has been an ongoing political and humanitarian concern for American political leaders. In 1999, after years of hesitation to put the American military at risk to end an ongoing civil war in the former nation of Yugoslavia, Bill Clinton committed the United States to a bombing assault on Serbia and to supporting the presence of U.N. peacekeepers in the region. Similar crises, which have been an important reality faced by U.S.

politicians, have posed enormous difficulties for policy makers. Between 2013 and 2017, a similar humanitarian and refugee crisis in Syria illustrates the continuing need for United States leadership, sometimes at significant political and economic cost.

The Global War on Terror

Since 2001, the single most pressing foreign policy issue facing successive American administrations has been how to respond to the threat of international terrorism, particularly the threat of terrorism driven by the ideology of Islamic fundamentalism.

The rise of terrorism committed by groups influenced by Islamic fundamentalism has had a number of causes, the first being the ending of the Cold War. With the withdrawal of Soviet and American support for strongmen in the Middle East, like Hosni Mubarak in Egypt and Saddam Hussein in Iraq, and the withdrawal of Soviet troops from Afghanistan in 1988–1989, a power vacuum resulted, into which more radical political voices stepped. Continued United States support for the nation of Israel has also been a sore spot for many Islamic fundamentalists, who claim Palestine as a part of the Islamic world. Osama bin Laden was also particularly radicalized by the United States presence in Saudi Arabia following the Persian Gulf War in 1991.

Osama bin Laden and many other Islamic fundamentalists also saw exposure to American cultural values, film, consumerism, religious tolerance, and challenge to traditional gender roles and sexuality as threats to traditional Islamic beliefs. The presence of American troops and economic influence is perceived as an existential threat to Islam. While very few in the Islamic world support the radical positions and violence taken by fundamentalist Islamists, the impact of terrorism is always disproportionate to the conventional power of the terrorist; indeed, one reason political actors resort to terrorism is a lack of formal and conventional sources of power and authority.

In response to the September 11, 2001, attacks on the World Trade Center and the Pentagon, the United States under George W. Bush attacked the terrorist camps in Afghanistan that provided the logistical support and training for the Al-Qaeda affiliates that carried out the assault on the Pentagon and the World Trade Center. The American presence in Afghanistan has remained important, as both U.S. presidents George W. Bush and Barack Obama endeavored to rebuild Afghanistan following years of civil war in the hopes of ensuring that it would not once again become a haven for terrorists.

The United States has also been involved in proactive efforts to stop the spread of terrorist organizations elsewhere, using drone strikes, special forces operations, and conventional troop deployments in nations around the world to preempt the possibility of future strikes.

In Iraq, the George W. Bush administration embarked on a more expansive program to change the face of the Middle East. The second Bush administration hoped to institute "regime change" in the Middle East, spreading American traditions of representative government and free market institutions in the hope that this might further undermine the attraction of Islamic fundamentalism to many of the disenfranchised and impoverished in the region. To justify an invasion of Iraq, the Bush administration argued that Iraq had a variety of weapons of mass destruction (WMDs) and potentially nuclear weaponry that might fall into the hands of terrorists. Under Bush's doctrine of preemptive strikes on nations that threatened terrorism, in 2003 an army of British and American troops invaded Iraq, rapidly defeating the Iraqi army and capturing Saddam Hussein. A number of democratic regimes have been supported in Iraq by the U.S. government, although the American military commitment has declined, particularly after 2011.

As a result of the decline in direct American military involvement and of the instabilities in Iraq that were exposed by the American invasion in 2003, a fundamentalist group of former Iraqi military figures managed to create what has been variously called the Islamic State in Iraq, the Levant (ISIL), or the Islamic State in Iraq and Syria (ISIS). It is this terrorist organization that has been the successor to Osama bin Laden's Al-Qaeda organization.

COMPETENCY 009 (POLITICAL, ECONOMIC AND SOCIAL DEVELOPMENTS FROM 1877 TO THE PRESENT)

The teacher understands significant political, economic and social developments in the United States from 1877 to the present.

> **Competency 009 Descriptive Statement A.** The beginning teacher understands political, economic and social changes in the United States from 1877 to the present (e.g., in relation to political parties, transportation, labor unions, agriculture, business, race, gender).

Key Question

Competency 009 asks test-takers to demonstrate understanding of the links between social and economic changes and the currents of political change that have transformed the nation from the end of Reconstruction until the present.

Periodization: 1877 to the Present

The social and economic history of the United States since 1877, and its impact on American political conditions may effectively be divided into three periods. The first extends from the end of Reconstruction and the reunification of the country (at the expense of African Americans in the South) to the inauguration of Franklin Roosevelt in 1933. During this period, the rancor that characterized intra-regional rivalries was diminished as the nation set about developing an industrialized economy built on the raw materials of the American Midwest and West, raw cotton and other Southern commodities, and the urban manufacturing of the Northeast and Midwest. The second period, from 1933 to 1980, represents a period during which economic change and the growing power of labor contributed to both an increase of government social spending and an expansion of government in the daily lives of Americans. This period also saw the flourishing of movements to improve conditions and political power of African Americans, women, and other minorities. Finally, with the election of 1980, the nation entered a third phase during which many of the gains of the working classes and the efforts of minority groups to increase their political influence and economic opportunities have both experienced significant success and faced renewed challenges.

Political Party Alignment since 1877

Since 1877, the American electorate has undergone a number of shifts that have changed the electoral map.

At the close of Reconstruction, as we have seen, the South remained solidly Democratic. It would remain so until the 1960s. Republicans dominated the Midwestern and Western states, while the Northwestern states had important Democratic and Republican constituencies. During the Great Depression, Franklin Roosevelt forged a coalition that united the solid South's Democrats, urban workers and union members, and many Midwestern farmers.

This coalition began to fall apart during the 1940s and 1950s as the Democratic Party increasingly supported civil rights for minorities. After Richard Nixon began to pursue the votes of white Southerners dissatisfied with the gains of the Civil Rights Movement, this "Southern strategy" has characterized Republican political strategy since the 1960s. What had once been a solidly Democratic South, was by the 1980s and 1990s, solidly Republican. The Rocky Mountain states also gravitated to the Republican Party as it increasingly painted itself as the defender of Second Amendment rights, an opponent of federal government intrusion in Western land management decisions, and generally a proponent of smaller government solutions. Ronald Reagan's appeal to the Rocky Mountain region also helped solidify these states for the Republican Party.

In the 1960s, another movement emerged that would have a long-lasting impact on American political alignments: the rise of Evangelical Christians as a Republican voting bloc. Before the 1960s, many Evangelical Christians eschewed political activism, preferring to carry out their social role in church, family, and the workplace. With the rise of groups like the Moral Majority, led by Jerry Falwell, evangelicals began to become more involved. One of the first candidates they supported was Jimmy Carter, who openly described himself as a "born-again" Christian. However, the strength of Democratic support among feminists and minorities, and the decision of many Democratic candidates to support *Roe v. Wade*, the Supreme Court decision legalizing abortion, led to an erosion of evangelical support for Carter. When Ronald Reagan ran against Jimmy Carter in the 1980 election, evangelicals voted in large numbers for Reagan and for Republicans nationwide. Since that election, the evangelical community has been one of the most staunch supporters of Republican candidates.

Labor Movement

The labor movement has contributed to many of the significant political and economic changes that have taken place since 1877.

Industrialization between 1870 and 1914 enriched business owners and corporate managers, but often at the expense of industrial workers. Workers had few protections against workplace hazards. Wages, despite rising slowly, hardly met workers' basic needs. Workdays were long, between 12 and 16 hours, and workers were expected to work six days a week. When workers struck for better conditions or higher wages, troops were frequently employed to protect strike breakers and intimidate union organizers. Many industrial workers lived in "company towns" where the corporation owned the housing stock, grocery stores, and other necessities.

Trade Unionism

One of the first nationally organized labor unions was the **Knights of Labor**, an association founded in 1869 in Philadelphia. In 1884–1885, the Knights of Labor helped organize strikes against key railroad companies. When the railroads settled, the Knights of Labor's membership increased from 100,000 to 750,000 members almost overnight.

One of the demands made by labor unions was for an **eight-hour workday**. In Chicago, in 1886, a strike against the McCormick Harvesting Machine Company led to a clash with Chicago police in which four union members were killed. A rally the following day held at Chicago's **Haymarket Square** was interrupted when someone threw a bomb at police clearing the square. Seven policemen were killed, and in the ensuing chaos four workers were killed and scores injured. The disorder of the "Haymarket Square Riot" soured many of the nation's leaders on the union movement. The Knights of Labor were an early casualty of this sentiment, as was a unionism that demanded widespread social change in addition to specific workplace improvements. In response, labor union organizers changed the direction of the union movement. The **American Federation of Labor (AFL)** represented this approach. Expressly rejecting anarchism and socialism, the AFL, a coalition of affiliated labor unions, focused on making incremental changes in working conditions and wages, without engaging in calls for wholesale social change. This approach appealed to middle-class and skilled laborers who had been unsettled by the growing radicalism of the Knights of Labor. It was a path, however, that neglected the gains that had been made in the union movement in bridging racial and gender divides and organizing across racial and gender lines.

Socialism

Radical solutions to labor's difficulties were not entirely silenced. In 1901, labor activists led by **Eugene V. Debs** formed the American Socialist Party. Rather than seeking change in the workplace, the socialists hoped to replace the capitalist system by employing the vote and the democratic system. Eugene V. Debs ran five times for president on the Socialist Party ticket. Never able to garner many votes, Debs did manage to get nearly 6 percent of the popular vote in 1912. Because of his opposition to American involvement in World War I, Debs was convicted of sedition and jailed from 1918 to 1921.

Labor Union Success

In the 1930s at the height of the Great Depression, surprisingly, the labor union movement achieved some important successes. In 1935, Congress passed the **Wagner Act,** or National Labor Relations Act. The Wagner Act protected unions against unfair uses of injunctions that limited their ability to strike. The act also established a labor relations board to hear and rule on union objections to practices that limited their ability to organize and negotiate for better working conditions and wages. A number of strikes in the auto industry then solidified these gains. The United Auto Workers union, which had been formed in 1935, organized a sit-down strike in Flint, Michigan, and successfully fought off police efforts to remove the striking workers from their factory floor, eventually forcing General Motors to bargain with the union. The workers gained a 5-percent increase in wages, but even more importantly, the union gained immediate legitimacy in the eyes of workers and saw membership rapidly balloon to over 500,000 members. This forced Ford Motor Company and other auto companies to negotiate similar working agreements. Given the importance of the auto industry to American industrial growth in the 1950s and 1960s, the power of union membership, both in terms of economic returns to workers and political influence, made the 1950s and 1960s a high point in labor union success in the United States. At the same time, increases in labor union influence also prompted a backlash that began in 1947 with the passage by a Republican-controlled Congress of the **Taft-Hartley Act**, which banned such practices as the "closed shop," which reduced unions' power to require workers to belong to the union. The Taft-Hartley Act was used by many southern states to encourage "right-to-work" laws, which made it difficult for unions to expand across the South. Since the 1960s, the power of labor unions has progressively declined, as memberships have declined and the American industries that were most easily organized by unions have declined in competitiveness, moved to non-union states, or moved abroad to find cheaper sources of labor. Today, fewer than 10 percent of American workers are members of labor unions.

Agriculture

American agriculture has increased in its efficiency and productivity with the growth of mechanization and introduction of chemical fertilizers, insecticides and pesticides, and new strains of crops. Perhaps as a consequence, the number of American farmers and farm families has declined precipitously since 1877.

In 1850, 63 percent of Americans lived on the farm; by 1900, that number had dropped to just above 50 percent. Today fewer than 2 percent of Americans are farmers.

> **Competency 009 Descriptive Statement B.** The beginning teacher demonstrates knowledge of the effects of reform and third party movements and their leaders on U.S. society (e.g., Populism, Progressive Era reforms, New Deal legislation, Susan B. Anthony, W. E. B. Du Bois, George Wallace).

Key Question

How have American political parties and political culture been influenced by third party movements and reform movements?

Though third parties have rarely been successful at capturing national office, third party and reform movements have had a profound effect in shaping American political life nonetheless. Many features of contemporary political life had their roots in these movements.

Populism

In 1850, the farm population made up about 63 percent of the nation's populace. By 1910, the proportion of Americans living on farms had dropped to just over 32 percent of the population. Farm productivity increased in this period, thanks to the introduction of mechanization and improved fertilizers. Farmers, particularly in the South and Great Plains, faced significant difficulties. High yields put downward pressure on agricultural prices, while the cost of mechanization and transport costs increased. Farmers responded to these increased costs by raising their debt levels. Across the South, the persistence of share-cropping further exposed farm families to high economic risks. National monetary policy also affected farmers negatively. After 1873, the federal government placed the nation on a **gold standard**, shrinking the money supply and causing general deflation. This put more downward pressure on farm profits.

In response, farmers began to organize to improve their economic and political influence. In 1892, farmers in Omaha, Nebraska, created the **People's Party**, also known as the **Populist Party**. The Omaha Platform of the Populists called for ending the gold standard and allowing silver to be used as a form of currency, increasing the money supply. The Populists also called for reductions in storage and shipping costs for grain and other commodities. More radical demands included the nationalization of the banking system, a mandatory eight-hour workday, and a progressive income tax system.

The Populist movement spread rapidly across the Midwest and Southeast. In 1892, the People's Party nominated James Baird Weaver for president. Weaver received 8.5 percent of the public vote nationwide, but managed to receive all electoral votes from Colorado, Idaho, Kansas, and Nevada, as well as some electoral votes from North Dakota and Oregon. Following the financial crash of 1893, the prospects of the Populists seemed strong. In the 1896 election, however, the Democratic nominee, William Jennings Bryan, ran on a platform largely reflective of Populist proposals. The Populists then split over whether to support Bryan, who had a greater chance of victory (though he subsequently was defeated), or to support a third-party option. In the South, southern Democrats exploited the racial fears of small farmers to divide the movement, and improved economic conditions in the Midwest also sapped the Populists momentum.

Many ideas promoted by the Populists, however, were later enacted into law: direct election of senators, federal regulation of railroads and freight rates, elimination of the gold standard, and enactment of eight-hour workday legislation.

Progressive Era Reforms

Whereas the Populist movement had provided an outlet for rural dissatisfaction with the Industrial Revolution, and the labor union movement was an urban working-class response to industrialization, Progressivism reflected middle-class and upper-middle-class responses to the social ills of rapid industrialization and urbanization.

Progressives were never a single group with a single objective. While a Progressive political party was formed, it did not in any way encapsulate or unify the progressives under one political umbrella. Progressive reforms included reforms of local, state, and national governments designed to make government more active in responding to social problems and less easily controlled by urban political machines.

Progressive Governmental Reforms

At the local level, one reform was the development of the **commissioner-city manager** form of government. Following the Galveston hurricane of 1900, which destroyed the Texas Gulf Coast city and took between 8,000 to 12,000 lives, the city reorganized local government by dividing governmental responsibilities among a group of commissioners responsible for specific areas of government. The system improved efficiencies by putting many decisions in the hands of professional managers and reduced opportunities for political interests to exploit city government for personal or political ends.

At the state level, new laws were passed to allow more direct popular influence. These included **ballot initiatives, referenda,** and **recall elections.** In some states, nominating conventions, where decisions were made in the proverbial "smoke-filled back rooms," were replaced by more open **primary elections.** The **secret ballot**, which permitted greater anonymity and reduced opportunities for vote buying and intimidation, was widely adopted.

At the federal level, other reforms were introduced. In 1913, the **17th Amendment** authorized direct election of senators. Also in 1913, the **16th Amendment** allowed Congress to impose an income tax, rather than apportioning taxes among the states according to the decennial census.

Coupled with the 16th Amendment, the **Federal Reserve Act** established centralized control of the nation's monetary and banking institutions. This was done in response to the continuing banking panics, which from 1873 regularly threatened the economy. The Federal Reserve System effectively represented a third national bank, which was longer-lived than the banks established in the early days of the republic.

Progressive Business Reform

Progressive reforms of business resulted from three overarching worries: (1) that unless the business excesses of the Gilded Age were not corrected, more radical political positions like socialism would gain greater appeal; (2) that state and local business regulations might create a patchwork quilt of competing regulation that complicated life for nation-wide corporate businesses; and (3) that middle-class consumers might suffer from a lack of regulations in such industries as meatpacking, waste disposal, etc.

Theodore Roosevelt in 1903 called for the creation of a Bureau of Corporations to investigate business excesses. He also prosecuted a number of corporations, including the Northern Securities Company, a conglomeration of three large railroad companies, under the **Sherman Antitrust Act of 1890**, earning the reputation as a **trustbuster**. Roosevelt initiated antitrust action against more than 44 corporations, arguing that big business should not be above the law. Roosevelt also established two cabinet-level positions, the Departments of Commerce and Labor. An additional Progressive policy undertaken by Roosevelt was the establishment of the National Forest Service to oversee more than 200 million acres of public lands.

The Progressive president, Woodrow Wilson, also encouraged greater regulation of business practices, creating the **Federal Trade Commission**, an agency with prosecutorial as well as investigative powers. Despite these progressive efforts, child labor still persisted, the length of workdays was largely left to business owners, and regulation of working conditions remained spotty.

Progressives and Consumer Protection

One area where progressive business reform received widespread public notoriety was in consumer protection. In 1906, the **Pure Food and Drug Act** and the **Meat Inspection Act** were enacted to guard against unsanitary conditions in food processing plants, and against the adulteration of foods and drugs. These regulatory laws were largely written in response to widespread disgust at the conditions described by **Upton Sinclair** in his book *The Jungle*, an exposé of the meatpacking industry. Sinclair was a **muckraker** journalist, using sensationalized reporting to expose corruption, crime, etc. Other muckrakers included **Jacob Riis**, who wrote about how the urban poor and immigrant population lived in American cities; **Ida Tarbell**, an African American woman whose series on the unfair business practices of Standard Oil gained her fame; and **Lincoln Steffens,** who examined the corruption of big-city political machines.

Women's Rights

Temperance Movement

Middle-class reformers had from the 1820s advocated to end the consumption and sale of alcohol. Business leaders argued that alcohol consumption undermined efficiency and the moral uprightness of their workers. Reformers witnessed men drinking away their pay, leaving women and children in poverty. The **Woman's Christian Temperance Union**, formed in 1874, led women into the streets against the vice of drunkenness. Middle-class women's involvement in the temperance movement served as a training ground for political activism.

Suffrage Movement

The women's rights movement benefited from women's experience in the Anti-Saloon campaign of the 1870s to 1890s. Women's rights activists before the American Civil War had split over the extent to which women should benefit from the Fourteenth Amendment, which had granted civil rights to African American men.

Susan B. Anthony (1820–1906) was one of the early activists prominent in the Woman's Suffrage movement. She was active in the anti-slavery and temperance movement; however, faced with open discrimination even in these progressive movements, Susan B. Anthony and Elizabeth Cady Stanton formed the American Equal Rights Association as well as the National Woman Suffrage Association. Anthony would later take a key role in the National American Woman Suffrage Association.

Before 1920, as a result of the activism and legal challenges mounted by Susan B. Anthony and others, women had full voting rights in 14 states and could vote in presidential elections in 11 states. Texas and Arkansas permitted women to vote in primary elections only. West of the Mississippi, women had greater voting rights, while most states in the East and Southeast did not allow women to vote. To promote the expansion of the suffrage to women, the **National American Woman Suffrage Association (NAWSA)** and the **National Women's Party (NWP)** were founded in 1890 and 1913 respectively. The state-by-state approach of the former had contributed significantly to Western states' increasing voter rights for women. The NWP instead used more provocative means. Alice Paul, founder of the NWP, employed civil disobedience, public protests and marches, and lengthy hunger strikes to publicize the cause of women's rights.

Early Civil Rights Movement

The Civil Rights movement of the 1950s and 1960s emerged from a long history of African American struggle. After Reconstruction, during the last third of the 19th century, African Americans were excluded from the vote across the country, but most systematically in the Southern states; forced to use segregated public amenities; and denied educational opportunities. These "Jim

Crow" laws received Supreme Court endorsement with the court case ***Plessy v. Ferguson*** in 1896, which upheld racial segregation on the principle that "equal but separate accommodations" did not violate 14th Amendment guarantees of equal protection of the laws. Repression of African American rights rested on overt violence as well. Over the course of the 1880s and 1890s, over 2,000 reported lynchings of black men and women took place across the South. The African American response to this repression was varied and vigorous. One approach was to offer an accommodationist response. **Booker T. Washington** represented this approach, arguing that the best way for African Americans to improve their position was not by demanding political and civil rights, but by **self-improvement** and economic progress. Others rejected this spirit of compromise and, like **Ida B. Wells**, who led a widespread anti-lynching campaign, demanded an end to violence against men and women of color.

W.E.B. DuBois (1868–1963)

An important opponent of accommodation was W.E.B. DuBois. DuBois, a Harvard-educated sociologist who rejected Booker T. Washington's approach. In 1905 he founded the **Niagara Movement**, which called for universal suffrage and complete civil equality. DuBois also took a leadership role in the founding of the **National Association for the Advancement of Colored People (NAACP)** in 1909. The NAACP's greatest contribution to the Civil Rights movement was its support for legal challenges to the principle of "separate but equal" in a number of landmark court cases.

New Deal Legislation

In 1932, with unemployment rates in the United States approaching 24 percent, Franklin D. Roosevelt ran against the Republican incumbent, Herbert Hoover. Roosevelt promised a New Deal for the American people. Roosevelt's landslide victory says more about Hoover's unpopularity than the specificity of Roosevelt's promised reforms. Within his first 100 days, Roosevelt set out to get the nation back to work. The legislation pushed through by Roosevelt in the "First New Deal" included relief efforts for the unemployed, new regulatory laws to boost economic production, and industrial reforms designed to reduce the likelihood of future recessions.

Banking Reforms

Within the first two days of taking office, Roosevelt declared a **"bank holiday"** suspending all banking transactions for an entire week. The financial sector was reeling from a succession of bank failures. The nations' banks were then allowed to reopen only if they were in no danger of failing; those with shaky financial foundations were reorganized. He then enacted the **Emergency Banking Relief Act** which provided federal loans to troubled banks. In 1933, the United States abandoned the gold standard, leading to an increase in the money supply and greater encouragement for investment. In 1933, as well, with the passage of the **Glass-Steagall Banking Act,** investment banking and savings banks were separated, and the **Federal Deposit Insurance Corporation (FDIC)** created to insure bank deposits up to $5,000.

Work Relief

Roosevelt's administration proposed a number of programs to address the nation's unemployment crisis. In March 1933, the **Civilian Conservation Corps (CCC)** was created to employ men aged 18 to 25. By 1935, over 500,000 young men were employed in over 2,600 work camps across the country. They were paid one dollar a day, the wage of an army enlistee, and received their room, board, and a uniform. The CCC built roads, trails, campgrounds, and ranger stations; cleared brush; and planted trees. A huge success, the CCC was only discontinued with the beginning of World War II.

A second more widely-targeted relief program for the unemployed was Roosevelt's **Federal Emergency Relief Administration (FERA)**. The **FERA** was funded with $500 million to disburse to the states for distribution to local charitable agencies to pass on to families without employment. The program also funded jobs programs providing low-skilled jobs in local and state government for the unemployed. The FERA was disbanded in 1935 and replaced by a more robust jobs program, the **Works Progress Administration**. The WPA was funded initially in 1935 with $4.9 billion to employ millions of men (and some women) in a wide range of works projects. Most of those employed found work in construction. Over 120 WPA projects were completed in Texas, including San Antonio's River Walk, the city halls of Houston and Austin, and Dealey Plaza Park, to name only a few. The WPA also provided work for musicians, artists, actors, and filmmakers. At its height, the WPA employed over 3.3 million Americans. All told, over 8.5 million Americans found work with the WPA. Another works project, the **National Youth Administration**, established in 1936, would be a model for many later programs designed to provide young people with job experience. By offering wages for work-study jobs, the program encouraged young men and women to remain in school.

A final works project that would have enormous long-term impact was the **Tennessee Valley Authority (TVA),** enacted into law by Congress in May 1933. The project was designed to address flooding problems on the Tennessee River and bring electricity to the many poor communities of the region. As a result, many isolated corners of the Appalachian region were integrated into American consumer society.

Agricultural Relief

Roosevelt then turned to the agricultural sector with the passage of the **Agricultural Adjustment Act (AAA)**. American agricultural surpluses since the 1920s had placed significant downward pressure on prices, leaving farmers little choice but to increase production still further to keep incomes up. The AAA paid farmers cash subsidies not to plant crops, or even to destroy crops already in the ground. Millions of pigs were slaughtered; millions of gallons of milk left to sour;

and over 100 million acres of land were plowed under in an effort to stabilize prices. One effect of the program was to stabilize farm prices. A second unexpected result was to force large numbers of sharecroppers, many of them African Americans, off the land as farm owners found it more profitable to use the subsidies to update farm machinery and expand their cultivated acreage, rather than rely on sharecroppers.

Regulatory Reforms

Relief efforts addressed the symptoms of the economic crisis. Roosevelt's regulatory changes attempted to address working conditions, labor rights, and industrial practices that had contributed to the origins of the Great Depression.

Roosevelt's **National Industrial Recovery Act (NIRA)**, passed in 1933, was headed by Frances Perkins, the first female cabinet member. It established law protecting workers' rights to organize and bargain collectively with their employers, including a process for setting maximum weekly and daily working hours, minimum wages, and working conditions. When no voluntary agreement could be reached, the president was authorized to impose standards. As a result, the eight-hour day and 40-hour workweek became standard, a long-held desire of the labor movement. Though a national minimum wage was not enacted immediately, it was set in 1938 at 25 cents an hour. NIRA also outlawed child labor.

Social Insurance Reforms

The elderly had been particularly hard hit by the Great Depression, yet few states offered anything in the form of assistance for the elderly. At the same time, hard-earned savings and pensions often went unpaid as banks and pension plans went bankrupt. In 1935, Roosevelt proposed the passage of the **Social Security Act**, a system funded by tax contributions by both workers and employers. The act also established an unemployment insurance program and assistance to dependent mothers and children, the blind, the handicapped, etc. Before its later expansion, the Social Security system covered fewer than half of all workers; domestic laborers and farm workers were ineligible, for example.

Civil Rights Movement and Reaction

The tide of Civil Rights reforms that began in the aftermath of World War II resulted in political reactions from southerners intent on maintaining racial segregation. In the years after World War II a number of notable African Americans broke through the color barrier; Jackie Robinson in baseball is perhaps the most well-known. Many black soldiers returned from the war, much more militant in their resistance to Jim Crow laws, not ready to let "the Alabama version of the Germans kick me around," as one former GI recalled. Truman's 1948 executive order integrating the United States military, coupled with Supreme Court decisions that struck down housing discrimination and "separate but equal" in law school admissions convinced some Southerners that a new party to challenge the Democrats in the South was needed.

Dixiecrats

The States' Rights Democratic Party, more widely known as the Dixiecrats, stood for states' rights and segregation. The party nominated Strom Thurmond, an avowed segregationist, to stand against Harry S. Truman in the 1948 election. The party had no local or state slate of candidates, but Thurmond managed over 1 million votes and garnered the Electoral College votes of South Carolina, Alabama, Mississippi, and Louisiana. Despite failing to compete nationally, the Dixiecrats began the process of fragmenting the New Deal political coalition that united industrial labor, white Southerners, and recent immigrant groups (mainly Catholics and Jews).

George Wallace

A successor to the Dixiecrats, George Wallace, served as governor of Alabama from 1963 to 1967 (and later from 1971–1979). Wallace, like Thurmond, made his name as a segregationist, famously saying in his inaugural address, "segregation now, segregation tomorrow, segregation forever." He also gained notoriety by publicly opposing the integration of the University of Alabama. Wallace, like the Dixiecrats, coupled states' rights and opposition to the expanding powers of the federal government with insistence on Southern states' rights to continue Jim Crow segregation. In 1968, he ran for president, earning nearly 13 percent of the popular vote, and the electoral votes of five Southern states.

Third Party and Independent Candidates since 1980

Third parties have had little impact on U.S. presidential politics, with the few exceptions already discussed. The one significant exception since 1980 came with the candidacy of **Ross Perot**, who ran as an independent in 1992 and again as the Reform Party's nominee in 1996. Perot ran on platforms calling for balancing the federal budget and opposing the North American Free Trade Agreement. Though Perot led in the polls at points during the 1992 campaign and received 18.9 percent of the popular vote spread widely across the country, he failed to win any electoral votes. In 1996, Perot's vote total decreased. Perot and the Reform Party's impact in the end were not significant except as outlets for growing dissatisfaction at Washington politics.

> **Competency 009 Descriptive Statement C.** The beginning teacher analyzes the causes and effects of industrialization in the United States.

The United States was a latecomer to the Industrial Revolution, really beginning to industrialize only after the conclusion of the Civil War. As a result, the United States was a beneficiary of what European historians call the Second Industrial Revolution, usually dated from 1850 to 1920.

Causes and Effects of American Industrialization

1. **Natural Resources and Sectional Divisions**

An important cause and feature of the United States' Industrial Revolution after 1860 was its regionally diversified resource base. While the East Coast cities were the center of industrial manufacturing, they depended upon raw materials from across the country. Cotton, the South's most important contribution to American industrialization, was the country's leading export product from 1810 to 1937, as it had been in the pre–Civil War period, Other raw materials necessary to industrialization came largely from the West and the Midwest. For example, copper (necessary for copper wiring) came from Michigan's Upper Peninsula until the 1890s and afterwards, from mines in Montana and Utah. Iron ore from the Lake Superior region was shipped through the Great Lakes to smelting furnaces in Pennsylvania and Ohio. The Rocky Mountain region would produce more iron, coal, and lead for American factories. Petroleum, first drilled in Pennsylvania and Ohio, after the 1890s became an important source of riches in Oklahoma, Texas, and California. Timber from the Northwest and from Great Lakes forests provided the raw materials for construction and paper production.

2. **Systematic Invention**

In 1911, the United States Patent Office issued its 1 millionth patent. Of those, fully 550,000 had been issued in the previous 20 years. Of these patents, most were not the product of a single inventive mind—an Eli Whitney, Robert Fulton, or Samuel Colt. Most were evidence of a systematic innovation that took place with corporate research and development laboratories, often funded by private and public investment.

Thomas A. Edison and **Henry Ford** are often held up as examples of the inveterate tinkerer who putters around in a garage before making a significant discovery. While both Edison and Ford were exactly that, many of their innovations reflected the new systematic innovation of the modern economy.

Edison, in 1879, produced the first electric lamp. Edison's work was completed in a research lab, "Menlo Park," accompanied by a team of engineers and scientists. Moreover, for Edison's discovery to have real significance required a vast infrastructure for distributing electricity. Electricity required private investment and public regulation. **J.P. Morgan,** a banker who had made a fortune loaning money to the U.S. government during the Civil War, arranged a series of mergers to form General Electric that made Edison's invention profitable. Similarly, the Ford Motor Company depended upon both a network of private investors and vast public spending on road networks that made a private automobile worth buying.

3. New Forms of Corporate Organization and Financing

Large corporations like those that developed in the latter half of the 19th century required substantial investment, more than individuals could effectively raise on their own or with their friends and associates' capital. Instead, they relied on investment banks that pooled the resources of large investors. To avoid losses, investment bankers like **J.P. Morgan** also insisted on reorganizing and consolidating businesses in which he invested, resulting in **trusts** like those that dominated the railroad industry.

In other cases, corporate owners used **vertical** and **horizontal integration** to establish monopoly control over their industries. **Andrew Carnegie**, unlike the railroad magnates who combined with other competitors to control the market, established a vertically-integrated corporation that controlled virtually the entire range of operations necessary to manufacture steel. He owned iron ore mines, acres of coal-mining land, smelting plants, and even a fleet of transport ships. By 1900, Carnegie's companies produced one-quarter of the nation's steel, and he annually earned $25 million (over $900 million today). **John D. Rockefeller** employed horizontal integration to control crude oil refining. He undercut his competitors and bought up other refineries, incorporating them into **Standard Oil (1870)**. By 1881 Rockefeller owned 90 percent of the nation's refining capacity.

Such large corporations represented a significant change from pre–Civil War industries. By 1904, 70 percent of American industrial workers were employed by large corporations. By 1929, fully half of the nation's corporate wealth was owned by 200 companies.

4. Managerial Revolution

Such large corporations required a different sort of management. Corporations employed armies of lawyers, accountants, engineers, mid-level managers, salesmen, secretaries, clerks, as well as the factory workers, both skilled and unskilled. These "white collar workers" represented a new kind of worker, requiring different training and skills than "blue collar workers." The growth in the 19th and early 20th century of American colleges and universities in part was designed to provide the training necessary for this new middle class.

5. A New Industrial Workforce

The late 19th century factory required a large pool of laborers. Some steel mills employed as many as 10,000 men. Many factories had 2,000 workers in their plants. Electricity made it possible to employ two shifts a day in constant production, doubling the demand for labor. This inexorable demand for labor was met by a massive internal migration from the farm. But this rural migration was insufficient. American industrialization depended upon a vast reservoir of immigrants. Between 1860 and 1920, nearly 40 million immigrants found work in the United States.

6. The Role of the State

One feature contributing to American industrialization that cannot be ignored was the role of the federal government in both promoting business interests and protecting American industry. From the Civil War to the Great Depression, despite a belief in the importance of free markets, the United States enacted a wide range of protective tariffs that made it difficult for European producers to enter the American market. Vast tracts of Western lands were opened up to railroad owners who acquired them for pennies on the dollar. The Supreme Court decision in *Santa Clara County v. Southern Pacific Railroad* determined that a corporation could be construed as a "person" with all the rights and entitlements of an individual. At the same time, federal and state laws managed to keep labor unions from having much influence, denying workers the right to incorporate in the same fashion as corporate employers, thereby claiming the rights to negotiate with owners, and allowing corporations to "lockout" employees, use strike-breakers, and private armies to intimidate laborers.

> **Competency 009 Descriptive Statement D.** The beginning teacher demonstrates knowledge of significant individuals who shaped political, economic and social developments in the United States from 1877 to the present (e.g., Jane Addams, Henry Ford, Franklin D. Roosevelt, Martin Luther King, Jr., Cesar Chavez, Betty Friedan, Malcolm X).

Jane Addams (1860–1935)

Jane Addams was one of the most important urban reformers of the late 19th and early 20th century. In 1889, she founded **Hull House**, a "settlement house," a haven on Chicago's west side for recently arrived immigrants and a center for social reform in an urban neighborhood blighted by poverty. Hull House also attracted many upper-middle-class women to work among, teach, and learn from the recent immigrants, many of whom worked in the meatpacking industry. To care for the neighborhood's population, Hull House built the city of Chicago's first public playground and a public gymnasium, provided classes in English language, and provided rudimentary health care. Cultural events were also organized, including ethnic food festivals and art shows. Hull House also became a center for political activism, pressuring the city for child labor legislation, workplace safety laws, immigrant rights, pensions, etc. Hull House would be a model for hundreds of settlement houses around the nation.

Henry Ford (1863–1947)

Henry Ford, perhaps more than any other individual, shaped American lives and lifestyles from the 20th century to the present. Born on a Michigan farm during the Civil War, he migrated to Detroit at age 16 and worked as a machinist, tinkering with watches, engines, and other devices. In 1896, he developed his first self-propelled vehicle, while working for Edison's lighting company. In 1898, he left Edison's employ and established an ultimately unsuccessful automobile company.

After several other failed efforts to establish himself in the automobile industry, Ford in 1903 created the Ford Motor Company. In 1908, he introduced the **Model T**, which cost $850 (the equivalent of over 20 months' salary). In 1910, the Model T cost $950 (22 months of work). By 1924, however, the Model T would cost only $290 (equivalent to 3 months' salary), which put the automobile within reach of most American consumers. Ford's success resulted from efficiencies of the assembly line process he developed. Ford's Highland Park plant in a suburb of Detroit could produce a car once every 93 minutes. By 1929, the United States had over 27 million cars on the road, one for every 4.5 Americans. Automobile production also drove growth in many other industries: rubber, plastics, glass, gas stations, road construction, motels, drive-in theaters, diners, etc. New social interaction also resulted from Ford's innovation; young men and women "dated" freed from parental supervision, rather than "courted" in a young woman's home or at public gatherings.

Franklin D. Roosevelt (1882–1945)

Franklin D. Roosevelt served as president of the United States from 1933 until his death in 1945, leading the nation through the Great Depression and World War II. He was born in 1882 into a wealthy Dutch family with a long history in New York. His began his political career as a progressive reformer and supporter of Woodrow Wilson, who rewarded his support with a position as assistant secretary of the navy. His political career, however, was abruptly interrupted when in 1921 he contracted polio, leaving him unable to walk without assistance, a condition he hid from the public for most of his career. As the Great Depression worsened, and President Herbert Hoover's popularity diminished, Roosevelt was elected in a landslide electoral-college victory. Roosevelt's **New Deal** programs helped bring the country out of the Great Depression. What ultimately restored the nation's economic fortunes, however, was the outbreak of World War II, Roosevelt's second challenge. Before U.S. entry into the war, Roosevelt managed to negotiate a fine line between American isolationism and his own support for the British, French, and Russian alliance against the Nazis. During this period, Roosevelt argued that the United States should defend what he called the **Four Freedoms: freedom of speech, freedom of worship, freedom from want, and freedom from fear**. Defending these freedoms, Roosevelt made clear his view that the United States had an ideological imperative to combat the spread of Nazism. When the U.S. joined the war in 1941, Roosevelt, Winston Churchill, and Joseph Stalin were the "Big Three" who led the war against Nazi Germany and Japan. Roosevelt died April 12, 1945, not quite a month before Germany's surrender. His vice president, Harry Truman, filled out his term, ultimately making the decision to use the atomic bomb on Japan to end the war.

Martin Luther King, Jr. (1929–1968)

Martin Luther King, Jr., at age 26, in 1955, was chosen to lead the **Montgomery bus boycott** in Montgomery, Alabama. The boycott began when Rosa Parks was arrested for refusing to give up her seat on a city bus to a white man. King, a Baptist minister who had earned his doctorate in theology from Boston University was, even as a youthful pastor, highly respected in the Montgomery community. Despite being arrested and having his house firebombed, King and the Montgomery boycott persisted until the federal courts in 1956 ruled bus segregation unconstitutional. King and other ministers then formed the **Southern Christian Leadership Conference** (SCLC) and King was chosen to head the new civil rights organization. King gained nationwide fame as a result of the boycott and became the face of the Civil Rights movement to most Americans. King argued that non-violent protest and peaceful civil disobedience, modeled on Mahatma Gandhi's independence movement in India, rather than violent protest, would eventually result in the end of Jim Crow segregation and voting rights. In 1963, King led a March on Washington for Jobs and Freedom where he gave his most famous address, his "I Have a Dream" speech. He was also prominent at many protest marches, including the "Bloody Sunday" march in Selma, Alabama, in 1965. King also became an important political figure in Washington, meeting with John F. Kennedy, Lyndon Baines Johnson, and Robert Kennedy to promote federal civil rights legislation. As the Vietnam War escalated, King also took a stand in opposition to the Vietnam War. He was assassinated April 4, 1968, standing on a motel balcony in Memphis.

Malcolm X

In contrast to Martin Luther King, Jr., Malcolm X, born Malcolm Little, rejected peaceful protest and civil disobedience, favoring black nationalism and separatism. Where Martin Luther King, Jr. as a Baptist minister attempted to use moral suasion to reach out to whites, Malcolm X argued that white bigotry and violence, as well as the slow pace of reform, necessitated more drastic action. His slogan "By Any Means Necessary" became a watchword for a more radical Civil Rights agenda. Malcolm Little had been a petty criminal in Omaha, Nebraska, jailed from 1946 to 1952. While in prison, Little had been drawn to the teachings of the Nation of Islam, or Black Muslims. In prison he also changed his name to Malcolm X. Malcolm X's widest following came in Northern cities, where racist zoning laws and hiring practices had left many African Americans in poverty and ghetto conditions. After he traveled in Africa and the Middle East, Malcolm X renounced the Nation of Islam, adopted Sunni Islam, and began to reach out to white audiences. He was killed in February 1965 by members of the Nation of Islam.

César Chávez (1927–1993)

Hispanic Americans, whether from Puerto Rico, Cuba, Mexico or elsewhere in the Caribbean and Latin America represented the fastest growing minority in the United States in the 1960s. César Chávez began to organize Mexican-American or Chicano farm workers, forming the **United Farm Workers Association (UFW)** in 1963 to improve working conditions for migrant workers. Like the African American Civil Rights movement, Chávez advocated for nonviolence, appealing to the nation's moral conscience through campaigns that made the public aware of the poor working conditions and living conditions experienced by the people who grew and picked much of the nation's farm produce. Chávez organized a national boycott of grapes to show support for the UFW's demands. Chávez's influence spread to South Texas and to farm workers Michigan, Oregon, Colorado, and elsewhere.

Chicano activism around the issue of fairness for farm workers soon expanded to take on employment and educational discrimination against Hispanic Americans, as well as demands for Spanish language instruction, the teaching of Mexican American history in the schools, and civil equality.

Betty Friedan (1921–2006)

The Civil Rights struggle provided inspiration for American women as well. In 1963, Betty Friedan published *The Feminine Mystique* and three years later was instrumental in establishing the **National Organization for Women (NOW)**. In *The Feminine Mystique* Friedan challenged the expectation that women were fulfilled solely through their domestic roles serving their husbands, raising their children, and subordinating their own satisfaction to that of the family. Friedan captured the dissatisfaction of many suburban, middle-class women who wished for more intellectual and occupational challenge and equal opportunity to realize their goals. The National Organization for Women was founded to combat persistent employment discrimination that favored men in a variety of careers, and held out promotion to positions of responsibility to men only. Friedan has been credited with being one of the founders of "Second Wave Feminism," the suffrage movement being the first.

> **Competency 009 Descriptive Statement E.** The beginning teacher demonstrates knowledge of events and issues that shaped political, economic and social developments in the United States from 1877 to the present (e.g., ratification of the 19th Amendment, Great Depression, passage of the GI Bill, passage of the Civil Rights Act of 1964, urbanization, antitrust legislation, immigration restriction, globalization, terrorism).

Urbanization

A continuity of American history from 1865 to the 1960s has been an increase in the proportion of Americans who live in cities. The growth in cities, however, was most notable during the period from 1870 to 1920. In 1870, only one-fifth of Americans lived in towns and cities with populations over 8,000. In 1870, there were only eighteen cities with more than 100,000 residents. In 1920, for the first time, over half of Americans lived in urban centers, and there were nearly 70 cities with more than 100,000 inhabitants.

Rankings of the largest cities in the country are often important evidence of changes in the economy. From 1870 to 1910, with few exceptions, the largest cities remained the same: New York, Chicago, Philadelphia, St. Louis, Boston, Baltimore, Cleveland, Buffalo, San Francisco, and Cincinnati counted in most lists of the top ten cities. The importance of the automobile industry after 1910 propelled Detroit into the top 10, and until the 1970s, it would be fourth or fifth. Los Angeles appeared on the list of largest cities in 1920, illustrating the growing importance of California's oil and film industries. From the 1950s to 1980, the growing power of the federal government that began with World War II resulted in a population boom in Washington, D.C. Since 1980, however,

Washington, D.C., has declined in importance in the hierarchy of urban centers. Houston, in the 1960s, Dallas in the 1970s, and San Antonio since the 1990s reflect the growth of the Texas oil economy. Other "Sunbelt" cities have risen into the ranks of America's largest cities. On the list of America's largest cities in 2010, only New York, Chicago, and Philadelphia remain from the top 10 cities in 1870. The large northeastern cities have been replaced by Los Angeles, Houston, Phoenix, San Antonio, San Diego, Dallas, and San Jose, illustrating the shift of the American economy from the Northeast and Midwest to the Southeast and Southwestern United States.

Increases in urban population have resulted from both internal migration and immigration. From the 1870s until the present, one constant internal migration has been from the farm to the city. As farms have grown more efficient, demand for farm labor has decreased, and opportunities for more lucrative employment in cities has drawn many farm boys and girls to the city. African Americans moving to the North from southern farms were also important to the growth of northern cities from 1910 to 1980. In part, this migration came about as African Americans sought better opportunities in the factories, particularly during the war years when jobs were plentiful. African Americans also fled the segregated South, beginning as early as the 1890s. More recently, an important internal migration has seen an outflow of population from the Northeast and Midwest towards the South and Southwest, as the so-called "Rust Belt" states have seen declining economic opportunities.

International immigration has also contributed heavily to the demographics of American cities. Before 1880, most 19th-century immigrants came from northern and western Europe. Over 80 percent of newcomers during this era were Irish, English, Germans, and Scandinavians. Between 1880 and 1920, a new wave of immigrants arrived from southern and eastern Europe: Italians, Poles, Russians, a variety of Slavic-speaking eastern Europeans, and Armenians. Immigration laws enacted after World War I, followed by falling immigration during the Great Depression resulted in significant declines in the immigrant population across the country. Since 1965, urban populations have been once again bolstered by immigration, this time from Asia and Latin America.

Ratification of the 19th Amendment (1920)

The 19th Amendment was first proposed in 1878, though women had long demanded the suffrage. With its ratification in 1920, women were guaranteed the right to vote. Women's rights activists had hoped that granting the right to vote to women would result in the enactment of a progressive agenda of reforms. The impact of women's voting rights, however, did not result in wholesale changes. The feared female voting bloc did not materialize. Many women, despite having the right to vote, did not. And those who did, not surprisingly, did not necessarily share the same world view or political interests.

Great Depression

The Great Depression began as a financial crisis—the collapse of the stock market after the long bull market of the 1920s. On October 24, 1929, the New York Stock Exchange experienced a

$3 billion loss in value. Within a week, another $10 billion in stock value had been lost (the equivalent of over $1 trillion in losses today). By Thanksgiving, industrial stock value was cut in half. Stocks continued to freefall until 1932, when stocks worth $87 billion had fallen to one-fifth their value at the stock market's peak.

The Great Depression reflected underlying weaknesses in the American and global economy that the stock market exuberance of the 1920s had only masked. A summary of those weaknesses includes the following:

1. A boom in construction and consumer spending had followed the austerity of the war years. By 1928, the "boom" had slowed as the market reached a point of satiation. As a result, employment had slowed, and by fall 1929, nearly 2 million Americans were out of work before the stock market crash.

2. Corporate profits had not been plowed into higher wages, but had either been reinvested or put into speculative stock market investments, fueling the stock bubble.

3. Dividends from reductions in the federal and state taxes paid by the wealthiest Americans were often plowed into the stock market, again adding to stock values.

4. The stock market boom had also been fueled by purchases made "on margin"—in other words, gambling on future stock price increases to pay off a portion of the initial investment. Stocks purchased "on margin" were purchased by borrowing, in the hopes of paying back the loan with the sale of stocks that had increased in value. When stock prices began to drop, this led to an ever-increasing vicious cycle that created further downward pressure on stock prices as stock purchasers sold their stock to cut their losses, further driving stock prices down.

5. The 1920s economy had relied for much of its growth on rising consumer debt, which by 1929 had risen by 250 percent over the decade. With declining employment, consumers were hesitant to add to their debt, and they began to cut back on purchases.

6. The financial system, which did not differentiate clearly between investment and savings institutions, and combined stock-brokerage with traditional banking, had speculated heavily in the stock market frenzy. Many banks were not in the Federal Reserve System and had substantial uninsured deposits and little regulatory oversight.

7. The Federal Reserve System had kept the money supply growing by lowering interest rates. When in 1929, the Federal Reserve raised the interest rate, investors began to sell off their holdings.

8. Agricultural prices had been low since World War I, and as farmers went bankrupt, so did their rural banks and businesses. In the 1920s, small farmers were still a significant sector of consumers.

9. High tariffs on imports globally discouraged foreign trade, making it difficult for Europeans to sell their goods abroad and thereby afford to purchase American products.

With the economic collapse, banks were shuttered, losing billions of dollars in depositors' savings. Unemployment rose from 3.1 percent in 1929 to nearly 25 percent in 1933. Steel mills, automobile factories, textile works, and railroads operated at minimum capacity. The ranks of the homeless were filled by veterans, families, and young men and women who hit the road in search of work, or simply in desperation. Hunger was commonplace, even for those who had jobs, as earnings fell to hourly rates of less than 25 cents.

The Great Depression was also an ecological disaster, at least across the Great Plains. A **Dust Bowl** extended from North Texas to the Canadian border. In part, this reflected an extended drought. But it resulted ultimately from 60 years of overgrazing and intensive farming that had destroyed the prairie grasslands. During the Great Depression, over 3.5 million people abandoned their farms in Kansas, Texas, Arkansas, and Oklahoma. Some 350,000 "Okies" migrated to California looking for work.

GI Bill (1944)

The Servicemen's Readjustment Act of 1944, better known as the **GI Bill,** provided educational grants, home and business loans, and employment preferences for veterans of World War II. By 1948, about half of all male students in college had their college tuition and expenses paid by the Veterans Administration. The bill was passed, in part to express gratitude for the sacrifices of so many veterans, but it also served the purpose of keeping returning veterans from flooding into the employment markets and driving down wages to prewar levels. In addition, the bill ensured that the men who had been away at war would have skills necessary for the changing economy. This act encouraged an immense expansion of higher education following the war. Along with increases in union membership and low-interest **Veterans Administration Housing Loans**, the GI Bill contributed to the creation of a strong middle class in the postwar years. The GI Bill resulted in an overall reduction in women's college enrollment; however, since 95 percent of GI Bill recipients were male. Veterans also benefited from preferences in hiring that women, many of whom had gained valuable industrial experience during the war, could not claim.

Civil Rights Act of 1964

The Civil Rights Act of 1964 outlawed all discrimination in public accommodations based on color, religion, sex, and national origin. It also forbade unequal voter registration requirements and racial segregation in schools and places of employment. The bill also prohibited sex discrimination in employment, both hiring and promotion. John F. Kennedy had called for its passage, but it was under Lyndon B. Johnson that the bill was finally enacted into law. Enforcement measures in the law included establishment of the Civil Rights Commission with investigative and reporting powers, authorization of the Department of Justice to file suit to enforce the law, and provisions to deny access to federal funding to any government agencies that practiced discrimination.

Voting Rights Act of 1965

Just as the Civil Rights Act of 1964 initiated the end of discrimination by outlawing Jim Crow laws and discriminatory hiring and educational practices, the Voting Rights Act of 1965 initiated the protection of citizenship rights of African Americans and other minorities. One of the primary goals of the civil rights movement had been to dismantle legal and extra-legal efforts to exclude African Americans from the vote. White Southerners directed their harshest reaction at attempts to break their monopoly on political power. The Voting Rights Act of 1965 outlawed poll taxes, literacy tests, or other measures designed to disenfranchise African American voters. With the passage of the bill, the number of African Americans registered to vote in the South soared. In Mississippi, for example, the percentage of African American voters increased from 7 percent to nearly 60 percent.

Suburbanization

Beginning in the 1890s with the expansion of streetcar lines, and continuing in the 1920s with the growth of automobile culture, suburbs had expanded as bedroom communities for middle-class homeowners who worked in America's cities. In the 1950s and 1960s, growth of suburbs exploded. By 1960, more Americans lived in suburbs than in cities, small towns, or in rural areas.

After World War II, returning GIs faced a housing shortage that existing construction methods struggled to meet. **William Levitt,** who had built barracks and other military dwellings during the war, adapted the lessons of the factory and assembly line to housing construction. He built standard-sized prefabricated houses, which were rapidly erected in a series of routinized steps, and then furnished with uniform, mass-purchased amenities. A Cape Cod home (there was no other design) cost $7,900. **Levittown**, a suburban neighborhood on Long Island, had nearly 18,000 Levitt homes built between 1949 and 1951. Similar housing developments went up in suburbs across the country.

The construction of the **National Interstate Highway System** also contributed to suburbanization. Authorized in part to contribute to national defense in the Cold War, the highway system initially called for 41,000 miles of highways to be built between 1956 and 1966. Cheap gasoline, inexpensive automobiles, and a network of roads enabled Americans to move to cheaper suburban lots and drive to urban occupations. Alongside these highways, motels, fast food restaurants, gas stations, and other amenities soon provided new sources of employment and business opportunities.

Immigration Restriction

Between 1870 and the present, there have been a number of efforts to restrict immigration.

In 1882, the **Chinese Exclusion Act** suspended Chinese immigration for 10 years. In 1892, the act was renewed, and in 1902 made permanent. It was only repealed in 1943, at a time when China was an American ally against the Japanese. At the same time, Chinese already in the country were for the first time allowed to become naturalized citizens.

During the "First Red Scare" following World War I, Congress passed the **Emergency Quota Act (1921)** and the **National Origins Act (1924)**. Both laws targeted immigration from eastern and southern Europe, particularly Italians and Eastern European Jews, by establishing quotas that limited the annual number of immigrants from different world regions. These quotas continued to restrict immigration from the targeted areas until passage of the **Immigration and Nationality Act of 1965**.

The Immigration and Nationality Act of 1965, also known as the **Hart-Cellar Act**, ended the quota system from the 1920s, and permitted larger numbers of non-European immigrants. A dramatic increase in immigration from Latin America and Asia followed.

Globalization

Globalization since 1989 has been characterized by the rise of new information technologies that have made possible almost instantaneous communication across the world, including the possibility of rapid transfers of capital and investment to markets with the greatest prospects for profit. There has also been a widespread commitment to reducing barriers between nations. As a consequence, Americans have seen an influx of immigration from Latin America, Africa, and Asia that has changed the demographic makeup of the country. Though this has not been uniformly recognized, this increase in immigration has reflected a growing consensus that the United States is a multicultural nation that benefits from widespread racial, ethnic, and cultural diversity.

Not all Americans have been supporters of globalization. Liberal critics have contended that globalization simply has provided an opportunity for American cultural and economic institutions to be imposed on developing nations. Workers have argued that globalization has resulted in significant job loss for American workers as corporations have taken advantage of free-trade agreements to move factories to low-wage countries. Others object to the increased immigration that goes hand-in-hand with reduced barriers to travel and trade.

Terrorism

Terrorism is not a new phenomenon in American history. During Reconstruction, terror was employed to intimidate African American property owners, voters, and workers. During the late 19th century, anarchists threw bombs at police. The Industrial Workers of the World or "Wobblies" as they were known, called for violent revolution and destruction of public property as a part of their labor radicalism. In Tulsa in 1921, in a violent attack on the city's most prominent black neighborhood, a white mob used terror to drive out the African Americans who lived there. In the 1960s, such groups as the Weather Underground set in motion a campaign of bombings of government buildings and banks. The bombing of the Alfred P. Murrah Federal Building in 1995 by a member of a right-wing militia was, until September 2001, the single most deadly act of terrorism committed in the United States.

The attack of September 11, 2001, on the World Trade Center in New York City and the Pentagon by Osama bin Laden's **Al-Qaeda** network, however, has changed the way Americans approach the threat of terrorism and has focused attention on Islamic groups that commit acts of terrorism. In the immediate aftermath of the event, George W. Bush articulated what became known as the **Bush Doctrine,** which declared that Americans had the right to fight a "preemptive war" on nations and independent entities that threatened the United States. Additionally, the **USA PATRIOT Act** was passed to permit greater surveillance of American citizens and potential foreign threats. Though the act has been criticized from both the political right and left for its intrusiveness, President Barack Obama extended many of its provisions. In addition, both Presidents Bush and Obama used the American military forces to attack terrorist groups affiliated with a variety of Islamic fundamentalist terrorist organizations in countries such as Iraq, Yemen, Somalia, Nigeria, and elsewhere.

> **Competency 009 Descriptive Statement F.** The beginning teacher analyzes the impact of civil rights movements in the United States, including the African American, Hispanic, American Indian, and women's rights movements.

A number of movements in support of greater rights for minority communities proved particularly powerful during the latter half of the 20th century. Most of these movements built on earlier precedents and learned from activists from other minority groups.

African American Civil Rights Movement

African American soldiers returning to the United States after World War II found little to justify their willingness to make the ultimate sacrifice to spread democracy and fight racism abroad. Many vowed to fight for civil rights and equality. Jackie Robinson's effort to integrate Major League Baseball represents an individual act of heroism, but there were many others who began to take smaller, but no less heroic, stands. One such stand was the decision by a group of African American families in Topeka, Kansas, to enroll their children in a whites-only school. When they were denied, they sued. In the landmark decision ***Brown v. Board of Education of Topeka, Kansas***, the U.S. Supreme Court found that segregated educational facilities violated the 14th Amendment and overturned nearly 60 years of precedence in support of the legal position that "separate but equal" facilities were constitutionally acceptable. To make this decision a reality, in the face of massive opposition in the South, the Civil Rights movement began a series of campaigns to see that the implications of *Brown* were fully realized. Sit-ins at lunch counters, bus boycotts, voter registration drives, marches, and many other direct efforts then composed the Civil Rights movement's campaign to hold white Americans to the fulfillment of the words of the Declaration of Independence. These efforts would only intensify over the course of the 1950s and 1960s. Thousands of black—and white—volunteers and activists would risk their lives—and in a number of notable cases, lose their lives—for the cause.

Though the effort to ensure equality, economic opportunity, and justice for African Americans is not yet complete, there have been a number of prominent successes. The Civil Rights Act (1964) and Voting Rights Act (1965) addressed denials of equal opportunity and access and outlawed discrimination against African American voters. Lyndon B. Johnson's "Great Society" programs also endeavored to address the economic disadvantages experienced by poor Americans of all races. In many aspects, the Civil Rights Movement has resulted in remarkable changes. However, while **de jure,** or legal discrimination, has been eliminated, **de facto** discrimination and **institutional racism** continue to undermine the successes of the Civil Rights Movement. American public schools are still heavily segregated by race; prisons are disproportionately filled with African American and Latino men; and poverty and joblessness are still more likely to strike African American communities than white neighborhoods.

Hispanic Civil Rights Movements

The struggle for equality for Hispanic Americans paralleled, influenced, and was inspired by the African American Civil Rights Movement.

Two landmark legal cases brought by Mexican-Americans helped pave the way for the *Brown v. Board of Education* decision of 1954, which actually consolidated five cases under one name (*Oliver Brown et al. v. The Board of Education of Topeka*). In 1946, a number of Mexican and Mexican-American parents in California sued an Orange County School District to stop segregation in the district. The case ***Mendez, et al. v. Westminster School District of Orange County* (1946)** resulted in the repeal of many segregationist features of California educational law. ***Hernandez v. Texas* (1954)**, in the same year as the *Brown* decision, also ruled against racially segregated public schools. Alongside *Brown*, these decisions laid the grounds for the repeal of ***Plessy v. Ferguson* (1896)**, which had sustained Jim Crow segregation for decades.

As we have seen, the rise of the Chicano movement in the 1960s, though initially developing from farm labor activism, rapidly took on the character and tactics of the African American Civil Rights Movement. Nonviolent resistance, protest, sit-down strikes, walkouts from public schools, and voting registration drives all were part of the toolkit of the Hispanic Civil Rights Movement as well. And, just as African Americans like Malcolm X promoted a Black Nationalist agenda when peaceful resistance was met with increasing retaliation and when change seemed to move at a glacial pace, Hispanic Americans also developed a Hispanic Nationalist movement. In the 1970s, Mexican-American voters in Texas grew increasingly dissatisfied with the Texas Democratic Party. At a meeting in Crystal City, Texas, in 1970, a new party, the **La Raza Unida Party,** was formed to run candidates in state and local elections. The party managed to make inroads in the Rio Grande Valley and spread as well to other southwestern states.

American Indian Movement

Though Native Americans had long struggled to secure their rights, in the 1960s they began to employ many of the methods of the African American Civil Rights Movement. Whereas African Americans had claimed "Black Power," Indians shouted "Red Power." A key difference between the Hispanic and African American movements and the American Indian Movement were Native American claims for tribal sovereignty and independence. Many of the methods were nonetheless the same. Native Americans held "fish-ins" rather than sit-ins to illustrate their historic fishing rights in the Northwest. The American Indian Movement (AIM) also set about teaching Native Americans who lived off the reservations about the history and culture of native peoples.

Women's Rights Movements

Civil Rights activism also provided inspiration and strategy for "Second Wave Feminism" as middle-class and upper-middle class feminist activists endeavored to put an end to sex discrimination in the workplace and to increase women's political power. As we have seen, Betty Friedan and others founded the National Organization for Women (NOW) in 1966. By the end of the sixties, women were also using the methods of the other rights movements, staging sit-ins, marching, picketing etc., in favor of greater rights for women.

Domain III: Texas History

TExES Social Studies 7–12 test-takers must demonstrate proficiency in Texas history. As Domain III accounts for 13% of the test's weight, a test-taker should expect between 18 and 20 test questions to center on this subject matter. In order to ensure your success on this portion of the test, however, it is useful to draw connections between the material in this domain and the knowledge of United States history you'll need to draw upon for Domain II. In addition, there are numerous moments when stories from Texas history intersect with the development of United States and Texas government (Domain V), so as you prepare to master the content and historical narratives of Texas history, keep in mind that the Texas story features prominently in these other domains.

COMPETENCY 010 (EXPLORATION AND COLONIZATION)

The teacher understands significant historical developments and events in Texas through the beginning of the Mexican National Era in 1821.

> **Competency 010 Descriptive Statement A.** The beginning teacher understands the important similarities and differences among American Indian groups in Texas including the Gulf, Plains, Pueblo, and Southeastern groups.

Much of Texas had been only sparsely populated by Native Americans before the 16th century. The arrival and spread of Spaniards across central Mexico pushed many American Indians from their native territories into less hospitable lands in northern Mexico and southern Texas. Diseases brought from Afro-Eurasia with the Columbian Exchange also affected native populations, often long before Europeans arrived. The high mortality rates associated with the spread of epidemic disease often required American Indians to reconfigure their communities by joining with other groups in new locations. With the westward advance of English and French colonization in the 17th and 18th centuries, American Indian populations in what would become the United States also were driven from their homelands, either by European arrivals or dispersed Native Americans in search of new hunting territories or farmland. As populations from the forestlands of the Ohio and Mississippi River valleys moved west, they set in motion a domino effect of migrations that increased the Texas populations of American Indians.

Gulf Coast Indians

The earliest written record of the peoples settled along the Gulf Coast comes from the account of Álvar Núñez Cabeza de Vaca, in 1528. The Gulf Coast had the most sparsely settled American Indian populations, struggling to secure their livelihoods in environments that didn't lend themselves to either settled agriculture or pastoral nomadism.

Karankawa

One of the Indian communities located along the Gulf Coast was the Karankawa. The term *Karankawa* designated several hunter-gatherer bands, usually with no more than 30 or 40 members, inhabiting the coast from Matagorda Bay to Corpus Christi Bay. By 1685, French explorers estimated the population of Karankawa at perhaps 500 men. With women and children, the population may have numbered as few as 2,000 inhabitants. The Karankawa migrated frequently to take advantage of coastal resources, often traveling in dugout canoes between the barrier island chains and interior coastline during the fall and winter. During the spring and summer, they shifted their camps to the coastal prairies and scrublands in search of deer, rabbits, game birds, and even buffalo.

The first lengthy interaction between the Karankawa and European settlers occurred in 1685 with the establishment of a French settlement on Matagorda Bay. Although the Karankawa first tolerated the French, repeated theft of canoes and other confrontations left the Karankawa little choice but to drive the French out. Spanish efforts to convert and settle the Karankawa also had little success despite repeated attempts between 1721 and 1821. The Karankawa resisted resettlement in Spanish missions, saw little reason to become settled agriculturalists, and perceived even less advantage in converting to Christianity. With Mexican independence and the arrival of Anglo-American settlers, the Karankawa faced a new threat. Stephen F. Austin perceived the Karankawa's extermination as necessary to his settlement's success and tried to drive them out. The growing Anglo settlement in the region brought reprisals against the Karankawa, and the tribe, already vastly reduced in numbers, fled south into Mexico. Equally unwelcome in Mexico, the Karankawa returned to the Rio Grande Valley area only to be attacked in genocidal warfare and eliminated as a population in 1858 by Texans led by Juan Cortina.

Coahuiltecan Indians

A larger Native American population of possibly 85,000 inhabited the coastline and coastal plains south of the Nueces and Guadalupe rivers deep into northeastern Mexico. The designation, Coahuiltecan, refers to a varied population of as many as 39 separate groups that spoke a common or related set of Coahuileteco languages. Like the Karankawa, the Coahuiltecan Indians were hunter-gatherers who foraged over large territories in search of game animals but also ate lizards, rats, birds, fish, and insects. They also traveled seasonally to harvest prickly pear, roots, nuts, mesquite beans, and cactus. Their technological toolkit was limited, with bows and arrows, a small shield, and nets among the most important tools, and their housing was a simple round hut covered with mats or thatching. In the harsh and inhospitable environment of much of South Texas, they maintained population levels through selective infanticide as well as lengthy nursing periods for young children and taboos against sex with nursing mothers. With Spanish settlement and the establishment of ranching in the region in the 18th century, the Coahuiltecans declined because of Spanish-borne diseases, the reduction and dispersal of deer herds, and raids from other Native American populations. As their lands were appropriated for ranches and cattle grazing, the Coahuiltecans were most often found among the Indians settling near Spanish missions.

East Texas Indians

In the northeastern area bridging Texas' present border with Louisiana, Arkansas, and Oklahoma, a series of confederacies were established by the people known collectively as the Caddo. The Caddo, or Hasinai Confederacy, amalgamated several Native American peoples brought together in the aftermath of the introduction of European diseases into the region. The Caddo called their confederacies *tayshas* or *taychas*, meaning friends or allies. The Spanish pronounced it *Tejas*, and the state's name derives from this term. The Caddo were settled agriculturalists, related to the Mississippian mound builders who had populated large parts of the central United States. They had cultivated maize (corn), squash, beans, sunflower seeds, and tobacco for centuries before European contact. Like other Mississippian cultures, the Caddo lived in settled villages and small towns, usually located near rivers and streams, scattered across the best farmlands of East Texas. The Caddo settlements also took advantages of forest cover, which proved to be good protection against threats posed by the plains Indians who did not relish taking their horses into the tangle of underbrush and forest. The Caddo Confederacy was headed by a ceremonial ruler, known as a *xinesi*, and each smaller community by a *caddi*, or chief. The chief organized communal agricultural responsibilities, served as a judge in cases of internal conflicts, and had some role in military decisions. Caddo political institutions typically approximated those found in European hereditary kingdoms, and they controlled the watershed of the Red River area.

The first European arrival in the area was the expedition of Hernando de Soto in 1542. Europeans did not return until La Salle's landing on Matagorda Bay in 1685. Upon hearing of French interest in the region, Spanish missionaries were sent to the Caddo, largely to re-assert Spanish claims. The Caddo were not immediately hostile to either the French or Spanish, partly because their presence allowed them to acquire trade goods that included the horses and weapons they needed to protect themselves from Apache raiding parties. Even before European settlement in East Texas, the Caddo played an important role in trade between New Mexico and the Mississippi River Valley region. They would continue in this role with the spread of European trade goods across the Southwestern United States.

Plains Indians

From a handful of horses that escaped from Francisco Coronado's and Hernando de Soto's expeditions in the 1540s, the Great Plains were transformed by the spread of horses. By 1750 horses were widely used by American Indians throughout the region. As American Indians gained expertise in horsemanship, they learned better ways to exploit the buffalo herds and other natural resources of the plains. As horse nomads like the Mongols and Huns created empires and threatened settled societies, populations of Great Plains Indians exploited their ease on horseback to create powerful empires that stretched across the plains and into Texas.

The **Comanche** did not exist as an identifiable ethnic community in the early 1600s. They originated in Utah's Great Basin but appear in Spanish records in New Mexico in the 1690s and in the archaeological record before that in southern Colorado and Kansas, having abandoned their homeland, possibly in flight from a smallpox epidemic. Around this same time, the Pueblo Rebellion of 1680 provided a supply of Spanish horses the Comanche purchased from New Mexico's Indians. With renewed Spanish colonization in the Southwest after 1690, the Comanche then acquired European weaponry and trade goods. By the early 18th century, the Comanche had expanded into North Texas in search of wild mustangs and buffalo and traded with the Wichita Indians for French trade goods. The Comanche had once been hunter-gatherers. After adopting horse nomadism, they devoted their energies to acquiring buffalo hides and meat, as well as horses and slaves, which they traded to other Indians for guns, iron tools, corn, squash and fruit.

As the Comanche expanded their territory, they confronted their most threatening rivals, the **Apache**, a semi-agricultural population that combined maize-growing in river valley floodplains with horse culture in the surrounding grasslands. The Apache had been one of the American Indian groups in the southern plains to adopt horse nomadism. Before the 17th century, the Apache had been hunter-gatherers on foot, migrating across the plains, hunting bison and other wild game. When horses were introduced in New Mexico, the Apache acquired them through trade with the Pueblo Indians. The horses gave the Apache an early advantage on the southern plains of Texas. By the 1690s, the Apache were frequently raiding the Caddo and other Texas Indians and driving them eastward.

Through the 18th century the Apache and Comanche fought a series of bloody wars over control of the southern plains. The Spanish tried to block Comanche expansion by providing weaponry and assistance to the Apache, only to see Spanish missions and fortresses become targets of Comanche raids. In the end, most of the Apache would be driven into the deserts of New Mexico and

Arizona, far from their fertile homeland. This left the Comanche a territory of some 250 million square miles of grassland that extended across north and west Texas. Between 1750 and the early decades of the 19th century, the Comanche captured or bought horses from Spanish settlements in Texas and New Mexico, accumulating them in vast quantities and trading them to Plains Indians from Kansas to the Dakotas. They also traded horses to Anglo-American settlers in trading posts from New Orleans to St. Louis, exchanging them for the firearms, powder, and bullets that made the Comanche a formidable threat to Spanish authority in Texas. Comanche also traded for beans, squash, sunflower seeds, and other staples that enabled them to sustain a growing population. To diminish exposure to European diseases, the Comanche avoided traveling to trading centers, relying on trading parties of Indians and Europeans to bring their wares to the Comanche. As a result, the Comanche were among the most populous American Indian societies in the Southwest until well into the 19th century. Comanche dominance in the Southwest would ultimately so threaten Spanish settlement in Texas that their presence was one factor contributing to Mexico's acceptance of Anglo-American planters' petition to settle in the province.

Like the Apache, the Tonkawa had to reckon with the expansion of the Comanche. The term *Tonkawa* (from a Waco Indian term for "they all stay together") designates high-plains Indians who in the late 17th and early 18th centuries, were pushed from the high plains and into Texas by more powerful groups of horse nomads. As they sought haven from raiding Apache and Comanche, they migrated into Central Texas. The Tonkawa were largely hunter-gatherers, originally dependent on buffalo herds. As these herds diminished, they took advantage of other sources of wild game for food and skins. They also gathered seeds, nuts, fruit, roots, and other vegetables. They lived in tepees, originally covered in buffalo hides and later with grass and leaves. As nomadic peoples, they did not have a rich material culture. They ornamented themselves with tattoos and body paint and wore necklaces and earrings made of bone, wood, and shells. The founding of Spanish missions near the Tonkawa in the 1740s resulted in devastating epidemics as well as exposure to threats from Apache attacks. A Tonkawa alliance with the Comanche, and their combined attack on a Spanish mission to the Apache resulted in Spanish hostility and intermittent warfare with Spain until the 1780s. Thereafter, relations with the Spanish, and later Mexican, authorities were characterized by a tenuous peace. After 1820, Anglo-American settlers in Stephen F. Austin's colony relied on Tonkawa help against the Comanche because the Tonkawa had turned away from the Comanche in favor of an alliance with the Apache. After the Tonkawa were relocated in the 1850s to a reservation on the Brazos, they were removed to Oklahoma, where during the Civil War they were nearly wiped out by attacks from other Indian groups. During the Civil War, they returned to Texas and were settled near Fort Griffin in West Texas. They worked as scouts, intermarrying with other Indians and whites. The Tonkawa no longer exist as a distinct population.

The Jumano Indians

The Jumano lived in the southwestern corner of Texas near El Paso. It is not clear whether the term *Jumano* designated a specific linguistic or cultural community, or whether it identified a group who made their living trading goods between New Mexico and the Caddo of East Texas.

Earliest Spanish accounts dating from the 16th century frequently note the role of the Jumano as middlemen trading horses and Spanish goods from northern Mexico and the Hasinai Confederacy. More recent research suggests that the Jumanos descended from the Jornada, an ethnic group in contemporary Arizona and New Mexico. By the mid-15th century, groups of Jornada had settled in the trans-Pecos region at the confluence of the Rio Grande and the Rio Conchos. They settled in small agricultural communities like the pueblos of their New Mexican ancestors. During spring and summer, other Jumano hunted and gathered from temporary camps across the plains, returning in fall and winter to camp near the agricultural villages of fellow Jumano. Perhaps because of their combination of sedentary and nomadic cultures, the Jumano were traders and maintained posts in their settled villages.

> **Competency 010 Descriptive Statement B.** The beginning teacher demonstrates knowledge of the traditional historical points of reference in the history of Texas during the Spanish colonial period.

Periodization: 1685 to 1810

Spanish colonization of Texas proceeded in fits and starts, beginning in earnest after 1685. Before then, the Spanish claim on Texas was scarcely backed by a significant Spanish presence. After 1685, Franciscan friars, military commanders, and Spanish ranchers combined to establish a small presence in northeastern New Spain, which would become Texas. Between 1685 and 1750, the Spanish monarchy tried to secure a buffer zone in Texas between the French in Louisiana and more lucrative areas of New Spain in northern Mexico and New Mexico. After 1750, however, Spanish settlements in Texas languished and suffered from continuing conflict with the Comanche and Apache, making the growth of a secure and profitable colony difficult. Beginning in 1810, the War of Mexican Independence, which in Texas as elsewhere was as much a civil war as a war against Spanish authority, contributed further to Texas' marginalization on the frontier of Mexico.

Texas and the Age of the Conquistadors

The Spanish colonial period in Texas should be understood as part of the Spanish conquest of the New World. Christopher Columbus had begun this process with his second voyage in 1494, bringing with him priests, soldiers, and settlers to lay claim to the riches of the Caribbean Islands and to establish Roman Catholicism in the lands claimed by him for the Spanish crown. On the mainland, he was followed by a generation of *conquistadores,* explorers and conquerors driven by a combination of religious devotion and thirst for gold and glory. Hernán Cortés's conquest of the Aztec Empire in 1521 and Francisco Pizarro's defeat of the Inca in 1532 proved so lucrative that Spanish adventurers set about across the Americas to replicate their successes. Spanish occupation of Texas, however, took nearly a century and a half before Spanish authority was firmly established over the region, and well after the Spanish claim had been secured, Spanish settlement would remain sparse. As late as the 1810s, only 6,000 Spaniards were settled across the vast expanse of Texas.

As early as 1519, the Texas coastline was mapped by Alonso Álvarez de Pineda, though there is little evidence that either Pineda or his crew came ashore. Pineda had been sent on this expedition to explore the area for the Spanish governor of Jamaica and a rival of Cortés for control of the American mainland.

With the Texas coast claimed for Spain, two groups of Spaniards reached the shores of Texas in 1528. One explored north beyond the Rio Grande from a Spanish fort at Pánuco, near the modern city of Tampico. A second group reached Texas in 1528 when a Spanish expedition begun in western Florida led by Pánfilo de Narváez was left behind by the four ships that had transported them. The expedition marched north from Tampa Bay, laying claim to an area that extended from Florida to Tamaulipas in northeastern Mexico and across northern Mexico to the Pacific. Narváez's fleet was ordered to reconnoiter the Gulf Coast for suitable harbors and reconnect with the expedition later, but after a year's search, Narváez and his men could not be found. They had faced continual hostility from Indians as they made their way along the coast. Abandoning their overland march, Narváez and 245 survivors built five makeshift rafts and drifted along the coast of the Gulf of Mexico, passing the mouth of the Mississippi. The currents of the Mississippi and strong wind gusts separated the rafts in November 1528. Each of the rafts made landfall along the Texas coastline, one as far south as South Padre Island where the famished and weakened Spaniards were quickly killed and their gear taken by Indians. Others received better treatment, but ultimately the same result. Only two of the 245 Spaniards made their way back to New Spain: Álvar Núñez Cabeza de Vaca and Estevanico.

In 1541 and 1542, two later Spanish expeditions reached what is now Texas. Led by Francisco Vázquez de Coronado, the first took an overland route from northwestern Mexico through New Mexico in search of the legendary Seven Cities of Gold and the mythical golden kingdom of Gran Quivira. Coronado made his way across the Texas Panhandle region before turning back. The second, under Hernando de Soto, marched westward from Florida to the Mississippi. De Soto died there of a fever, and Luis de Moscoso Alvarado took command, hoping to return overland to Mexico. His party only reached as far west as the Trinity River before being turned back, deciding like Narváez's expedition to build boats and make their way back by sailing along the Gulf Coast. The failure of De Soto and Coronado to find the gold of legend resulted in a period during which the Spanish paid little attention to Texas or the vast territories claimed by these explorers for Spain. Instead, Spanish interest was largely directed at settling among and converting the Pueblo people in New Mexico. Contact with the Jumano people, who served as the conduit of trade between New Mexico and the Caddo in northeast Texas, allowed the Spanish to gain further knowledge of the region, but they still saw little interest in establishing a presence.

Missionaries, Slave Catchers, and Traders

In 1629, a Jumano leader asked that missionaries from New Mexico be sent to his people. According to legend, the Jumanos were said to have been miraculously converted by the appearance of a beautiful woman dressed in blue. She was supposedly the abbess of a convent in Spain and was claimed to have converted the tribes "in ecstasy," though she never traveled to the New World during her lifetime. A Franciscan friar, Juan de Salas, obliged and in 1632 returned with a contingent of Franciscan missionaries and a handful of soldiers to the Jumanos' camps along the Nueces River. Indian requests for missionary help often were coupled with the hope that Spain would be an ally against rival Indian nations. For example, the Jumano Indian leader, known in Spanish as Juan Sabeata, in 1683 asked that priests be sent to his region. He hoped the Spanish would help in the Jumano rivalry with neighboring Apache.

In 1650, a Spanish expedition to the Nueces discovered fresh-water pearls and made contact with the Caddo, leading the Spanish to return four years later, this time acquiring slaves, buffalo hides, deer hides, and other items. A mission to the Jumanos was also established in 1659 near El Paso and would later shelter refugees from New Mexico's Pueblo Revolt in 1680. The missions to the Jumano and other missionary efforts extended Spanish influence into Texas, as information about the Caddo kingdom spread among the Spanish. From the 1650s until the 1680s, the Jumanos and Spaniards carried out a brisk trade in hides. During much of this period, Spanish slave-catchers also were active along the southern border of what would become Texas. The first recorded account of such activity dates from 1655 when soldiers from Saltillo and Monterrey recounted capturing over 70 slaves in a location over 80 miles north of the Rio Grande. Despite increased knowledge of the region, the Spanish presence in what would become Texas was hardly noteworthy.

French Encroachment and Spanish Response

Spanish interest in Texas was significantly increased when its European rival, France, explored the interior of North America and established trading posts from the Great Lakes along the length of the Mississippi River. René-Robert Cavelier, Sieur de la Salle, in 1682 traveled the Mississippi and claimed its watershed, including much of Texas, for France. In 1684, La Salle landed with four ships at Matagorda Bay, where he remained with his one ship (the *Belle*) and 180 settlers. After securing the location, La Salle explored Texas' interior. Returning to the coast, he discovered that the *Belle* had wrecked and set out on foot with 17 men for the nearest French outpost on the Mississippi. Along the way, he was murdered by his mutinous crew, and the settlement on the coast, by that time 20 men and women, was wiped out save for a few French children and adolescents adopted by the Karankawa in the spring of 1689.

La Salle's unsuccessful expedition spurred Spanish interest in asserting control over the region. Between 1686 and 1690, the Spanish monarchy authorized two expeditions to convert the Caddo and secure Spanish governance of Northeast Texas. Miscommunication, cultural insensitivity, and religious differences doomed these missions, and in 1693 the Spanish again withdrew. Only renewed French interest in what is now Louisiana brought the Spanish back to East Texas. In 1716, Domingo Ramón and Father Francisco Hidalgo, a Franciscan missionary who had worked among the Indians of East Texas before 1693, brought a contingent of soldiers and priests and established a *presidio*, or fortress, near Nacogdoches and four missions. The government of New Spain in Mexico City then took further interest in the region. New missions and presidios were founded and combined the purposes of outreach to specific Indian populations with the creation of a chain of outposts and an extensive supply line connecting East Texas to the Rio Grande.

The presidio **San Antonio de Béxar** was founded in 1718 as a midway point to East Texas. Around it four missions were established between 1720 and 1731 to convert the Coahuiltecan Indians and protect them from Apache threats. In 1731, a *villa,* or settled town, was chartered at San Antonio. To supply the southern coastal route to East Texas, a presidio and mission were built in 1721 on the Gulf Coast at La Bahia. This fort was later moved to Goliad and served as an important fort on the southern roadway between the Rio Grande Valley and East Texas. Spanish settlements also sprang up along the Rio Grande, and tracts of land were parceled out to farmers and ranchers. Many of these presidio-missionary complexes succeeded, but others failed, often because Spanish were perceived as threats to the balance of power among American Indian rivals. For example, a mission and fort built in 1757 on the San Saba River ministered to the Apache and was immediately perceived as a threat to the Comanche and their allies. It was attacked and destroyed.

Bourbon Reforms

After 1750, Spanish fears of French encroachment on their Texas claims declined following French cession of their Louisiana territories to Spain at the end of the Seven Years' War (what in American history is known as the French and Indian War). When the United States was formed, it also posed little threat to New Spain's northern frontier. In this climate of relative security, the Spanish monarchy instituted a series of imperial reforms. The **Bourbon Reforms** included reductions in mercantilist regulations of trade and customs duties in the hopes of fostering greater commerce between different parts of the Spanish Empire. For Texas, these reforms took the form of orders to reduce the military presence of the presidios in East Texas and move the provincial capital to San Antonio.

At the same time, the Spanish tried to pacify the Comanche and Apache with a policy that combined a coordinated military presence and careful management of alliances with rival Indian peoples. The mobile and well-armed Texas Plains Indians, however, proved difficult to control. The Spanish government also failed to arm and staff the presidios adequately, leaving them vulnerable and unable to exert control over the Native American populations. Efforts to use trade and gifts to buy off Indian populations or play one band against another also failed because insufficient resources were devoted to these attempts.

Reflecting the influence of Enlightenment anti-clericalism on the Spanish court, Bourbon Reforms also reduced the role of missionary activity as a part of Spanish imperial policy. The Spanish government thus sought to reduce the missionary activity of the Franciscan friars who had played such an important role in the establishment of Spanish culture in Texas by secularizing the missions and turning them over to local landowners. This coincided with local ranchers' interest in acquiring mission lands and cattle and government officials' desire to tax mission property.

> **Competency 010 Descriptive Statement C.** The beginning teacher understands the major causes and effects of European exploration and colonization of Texas.

European exploration and colonization of Texas extended over nearly 200 years, from 1519 until the Mexican Revolution against New Spain in the early 19th century. The causes and effects of exploration and colonization depend upon the time.

Periodization: 1519 to 1750

1519–1628: Exploration and Discouragement

Spanish interest in Texas was largely motivated by an interest in discovering sources of wealth or converts to Christianity. Finding little of either, Spanish interest in the rough terrain of Texas waned, and few Spaniards showed much interest in settlement.

1628–1685: Missionaries, Traders, and Official Neglect

A few fitful attempts to secure a foothold in Texas were mostly carried out by Franciscan friars and other missionaries as well as a handful of adventurers who hoped to engage in trade with the Indian populations who inhabited the area. Although Spain continued to claim Texas as a northern frontier of New Spain, it did not invest much in asserting a real presence.

1685–1750: Establishing a Spanish Presence

Only with the intrusion of other Europeans into North America did the Spanish become interested in securing Texas. This was motivated in part by a desire to reduce Indian raids on northern Mexico, which also would provide European rivals with an inroad into New Spain's richer, more settled territories in contemporary Mexico. Texas was strategically significant as a buffer between the French and later the American challengers.

Claiming Territory and Searching for Riches

In the 16th and early 17th centuries, interest in Texas largely reflected efforts to extend the boundaries of New Spain north. In 1522, Hernán Cortés founded Pánuco in the modern Mexican state of Veracruz, expanding New Spain north from the Aztec Empire's center. The expeditions by Coronado and de Soto represented exploratory efforts to determine what sources of wealth Texas and the rest of the interior of the continent might provide. Passages across Texas found little to offer. By 1565, the Spanish had conquered as far north as Saltillo and Monterey. In 1579, Luis de Carabajal was granted the authority to establish the Kingdom of Nuevo Léon, a territory that took in much of west Texas. Carabajal founded his capital just south of the Rio Grande. In the early 17th century, Spanish explorers and troops were drawn across the Rio Grande in a fruitless search for silver mines and in support of Indian allies. The expeditions into Texas yielded little in the way of riches, but did open up new opportunities for missionary activity in the region.

Trade

Important trade routes predated Spanish and French arrival in Texas. The Jumano and Coahuiltecan as well as a variety of plains Indians had traded with Caddo who lived along the Red River and with other Indians from the Mississippi River region. They exchanged staples, furs, salt, bow wood, and other items for turquoise, silver, and other items from central Mexico and what is now New Mexico. With the Spanish conquest of the Aztecs, Spanish trade goods replaced many of the items formerly sought from Mesoamerica. These included iron tools, weapons, and perhaps most importantly, livestock, the latter acquired as often by raiding rather than exchange. The Jumano and Coahuiltecan Indians rapidly became the middlemen in this trade. This trade and the strategic significance of the region to France's imperial aspirations attracted the French to the region in 1685. Spanish traders entered this commerce. One reason for the establishment of outposts in La Bahía and San Antonio was to secure the trade routes across Texas.

Indian Pacification

Indian raids on Spanish forts and missions in northern New Spain also contributed to Spanish interest in exploring and settling in Texas. For the entire period of Spanish control over the territory of Texas, Indian raids would be a problem. Initially the Coahuiltecan, Apache, and other tribes positioned in northern Mexico were drawn to the Spanish missions and presidios as sources of trade items. Failing that, they were sources of items of plunder, which could be exchanged in the interior of the continent. In the 18th and 19th centuries, Comanche, Apache, Kiowa, and other Indian peoples found the sparse Spanish-speaking settlements tempting targets for raids designed to acquire horses that would bring profitable sums when sold to the French or Americans. The system of military forts and missions established in Texas were intended to stop the raids and pacify the region. Because so few settlers and soldiers were willing to move there and because not enough was invested in Texas, that effort had mixed results.

Missionary Impulses

Efforts to bring Christianity to the region contributed to Spanish exploration and colonization. The first mission activity occurred in West Texas when some Jumano Indians asked for religious teachers. In 1629, Father Juan de Salas established a mission among the Jumanos. Later missionaries to the region established missions at Presidio, Texas, and at San Antonio de la Isleta, the site of El Paso today. In the 1680s, Franciscans also tried to convert Indians in the San Angelo area, establishing a mission that had to be abandoned after attacks by Apaches. Another effort to establish a missionary presence in West Texas failed in 1758, when the San Saba mission was attacked and burned. Much of West Texas then was largely left free of Roman Catholic missionary activity. In South, Central, and East Texas, missionaries had better results.

The French Threat

Spain's real interest in Texas began largely for defensive reasons. In 1685, Robert Cavelier, Sieur de la Salle, founded a short-lived colony on Matagorda Bay. His aim was to secure a series of trading posts along the Mississippi River and claim the interior of North America for France. The settlement, which disintegrated before the Spanish could militarily expel it, nonetheless alerted the Spanish to the vulnerability of their northern borders and to commercial opportunities in trade with Texas Indians. The French were better positioned. Their presence in New Orleans and their long history of positive trade relations with the Great Lakes and Mississippi River Indians threatened Spanish control over Texas and the Spanish claim in North America that extended from Florida across the Southeast to Texas. To confront the French threat, the Spanish established a post across the Mississippi from the French trading post in Louisiana in the Caddo Indian settlement of Nacogdoches. Until 1803, Spanish interest in Texas lands was largely carried out in a defensive posture as the Spanish sought to secure a buffer zone between its more prosperous territories and the European interlopers.

> **Competency 010 Descriptive Statement D.** The beginning teacher understands how significant individuals, events and issues shaped the early history of Texas from the Spanish Colonial Era to the Mexican National Era (e.g., Álvar Núñez Cabeza de Vaca, José de Escandón, Fray Damián Massanet, Francisco Hidalgo, Alonso Álvarez de Pineda, Moses Austin).

Several important figures shaped the early history of Texas and reflected the successive importance of conquistadors and explorers, Franciscan missionaries and priests, and Anglo-American impresarios. This descriptive statement directs prospective teachers toward key figures in the Spanish Colonial Era and their impact on the Texas history.

Alonso Álvarez de Pineda

In 1519, Alonso Álvarez de Pineda was sent by the Spanish governor of Jamaica, Francisco de Garay, to search the American coastline. America was still conceived of as a large island off the coast of Asia, and the search was for a strait that would allow passage to Asia. Pineda mapped much of the coastline of the northern and eastern shores of the Gulf of Mexico, becoming the first European to explore the Texas coast. Pineda's voyage showed that the Gulf of Mexico was surrounded by a large land mass and that no water route to Asia existed from Florida to the Yucatan Peninsula.

Álvar Núñez Cabeza de Vaca (ca. 1488–ca. 1560)

Álvar Núñez Cabeza de Vaca, the treasurer of the Narváez expedition, was one of only two survivors of the ill-fated effort. He and his raft with 40 emaciated men washed ashore on Galveston Island in the fall of 1528. A second raft also made landfall on the island, and the two groups were reunited with the aid of local Indian bands. The Indians first helped the Spaniards, feeding them and building back their strength during the harsh winter of 1528–1529. In return, however, the Indians required that the Spaniards work, assigning them the tasks of digging for roots, hauling firewood and other tasks usually done by Indian women. After four years of what effectively amounted to enslavement, the Spaniards were reduced to five survivors, including Cabeza de Vaca, a North African slave named Estevanico, and Lope de Oviedo. In 1532, Oviedo chose to remain, and Cabeza de Vaca and the others escaped. They traveled south, hoping to reach the closest Spanish fort located at Tampico. Along the way, Cabeza de Vaca acted as a healer. After crossing the Rio Grande, however, the group did not progress south to Tampico but went north and west, reaching what is now El Paso before making their way across northern Mexico to the Spanish outpost of Culiacán near the Pacific Ocean. Only Cabeza de Vaca and Estevanico survived the ordeal. Along the way, Cabeza de Vaca heard tales of fabulous wealth to be had in the American Southwest. His stories inspired the Spanish authorities to dispatch an expedition guided by Estevanico to search for the fabled Seven Cities of Gold supposed to be found in New Mexico.

Fray Damián Massanet

Fray Damián Massanet was chaplain of a company of Spaniards sent out in March 1689 to confront the French settlement established by Sieur de la Salle. The leader of the expedition was Captain Alonso de Léon. As the contingent advanced into Texas, they named the Frio, Hondo, Nueces, Medina, and Léon (San Antonio) rivers. As the Spaniards approached the French settlement, they learned that La Salle had left, and the French had been killed by coastal Indians. Massanet promised an Indian leader with whom he established a relationship that he would return to the area to minister to the Caddo people. In 1690 Massanet and Léon founded the mission of San Francisco de los Tejas to minister to the Caddo. The mission had little success because the soldiers accompanying the mission caused difficulties and Spanish cattle destroyed Caddo crops. The Caddo also saw little reason to convert to Christianity. The mission was abandoned three years later, and the Spanish withdrew from East Texas for the next 19 years.

Francisco Hidalgo (1659–1726)

Francisco Hidalgo, perhaps the most important missionary to colonial Texas, contributed much to Spain's return to Texas after 1694. Hidalgo had accompanied Father Massanet in 1690 and tried unsuccessfully several times to get approval from Spanish authorities for a return to East Texas. In 1713, when a French outpost was established at Natchitoches in western Louisiana and French traders established a presence as far west as the Rio Grande, Spain again took an interest in the region. Capt. Domingo Ramón was dispatched to secure a buffer between the French and the remainder of New Spain in East Texas. Hidalgo was with him. Ramón established a *presidio* near present-day Nacogdoches and four missions. Hidalgo remained in East Texas working with the Caddo until 1719.

José de Escandón (1700–1770)

A Spanish soldier who had gained notoriety stopping Indian revolts in central Mexico in the 1720s and 1730s, José de Escandón in 1746 was given the responsibility of surveying and pacifying the northern frontier of New Spain beyond the Rio Grande. Between 1748 and 1755, Escandón led a series of expeditions, surveying South Texas between the Rio Grande and San Antonio rivers and establishing some 23 settlements along the Rio Grande. These included Laredo and Dolores within the current boundaries of the state. As an incentive, settlers were given generous land grants to be held in common as well as money for relocation and 10-year abatements on taxes. For some time, ranchers living south of the Rio Grande had grazed their herds on its northern bank. Escandón granted titles to these informal land claims, including 329,000 acres in what are now Webb and Zapata counties, on which vast herds of cattle, horses, mules, and donkeys were soon grazing. Similar extensive *haciendas* were granted to ranching families across South Texas. Escandón's administration of this far region of New Spain contributed much to establishing Spanish control over what had largely been an ignored part of the empire.

Adams-Onís Treaty (1819)

The Louisiana Purchase in 1803 made it imperative that the boundaries of New Spain and the United States be clarified because they had been a matter of speculation and diplomatic controversy. Almost immediately, encroaching Anglo-Americans created controversy with the Spanish in Texas. Diplomatic discussions lasted until 1819, when both parties agreed to establish the eastern boundary of Texas along the Sabine River to the 32nd parallel, from where it extended north to the Red River. It then followed the course of the Red River upstream to the 100th meridian, then due north to the Arkansas River. From the headwaters of the Arkansas River, a boundary line was established and reached to the 42nd parallel, in what is now Wyoming. Spain and the United States then agreed that the northern boundary of New Spain extended west to the Pacific along the 42nd parallel.

Moses Austin (1767–1821)

Moses Austin was born in Connecticut to a prominent merchant family with commercial branches and lead mines in Virginia. When the businesses failed in 1795, Austin heard of rich lead mines in what is now Missouri, then a part of New Spain. He acquired permission in 1797 from the Spanish ambassador to the United States to relocate to a grant of land located in Missouri. From 1799 to 1819, Austin prospered in Missouri, which in 1803 was passed to the United States. The Panic of 1819, however, wiped out all his wealth, and he turned to Texas to renew his fortunes. He traveled to San Antonio by horseback, arriving in December 1820. As a former subject of the Spanish empire, he requested the right to settle in the country. The Spanish government approved his proposal to lead the settlement of 300 Catholic families from the United States in Texas. In return, he was to get a significant grant of land. During his return to Missouri, Austin fell ill and died soon after returning home. His son, Stephen F. Austin, would fulfill the terms of his father's agreement, though it would require renegotiation with the newly independent Mexican government.

Stephen F. Austin (1793–1836)

Stephen F. Austin was 27 when his father died, leaving to his responsibility the establishment of the settlement in Texas. As early as the fall of 1821, colonists were entering Texas in fulfillment of the Austin agreement. The newly independent Mexican government, however, did not recognize the agreement. Stephen Austin then went to Mexico City and waited five months before any action was taken. The contract was finally approved in March 1823, but the Mexican emperor, Augustín de Iturbide, was overthrown, requiring Austin to enter further negotiations with the new government. By the summer of 1824, Austin had secured title to his colonial land settlement, relocated to Texas the 300 families promised by his father, and established a settlement on the Brazos River.

State and National Colonization Laws (1824 and 1825)

Under Spanish law, the provinces of New Spain were to be populated by Spanish settlers or native inhabitants. Foreign immigration was severely restricted, and thus the California, Texas, and New Mexico territories had few settlers. Many Mexicans felt that the northern provinces of New Spain and later the independent nation of Mexico needed to attract settlers, both to protect the northern provinces from encroachment by Anglo-Americans living illegally in Texas as well as from the growing threat of Comanche and Apache raids. To encourage internal migration and immigration into these northern provinces, a series of national and state laws were passed. The first was the Imperial Colonization Law of 1823, which had served as the initial framework for Moses, which Austin's colonization scheme. The 1823 law specified that colonists brought into Texas had to be Catholic but had few other stipulations. This law had not gone into effect because of the overthrow of the imperial government.

In 1824, a liberal and federalist Mexican Congress issued a revised statute that authorized individual states of Mexico to regulate immigration if their immigration laws did not violate the national constitution. The newly formed state of Coahuila y Tejas' law, enacted in 1825, stated that foreign immigrants should be Christian and that they must abide by national laws. Colonists were allowed free exercise of their religion if they did not disturb the public peace. Slavery also posed a problem. Mexican national and state laws banned the African slave trade. The colonization law of Coahuila y Tejas remained vague, and local and state officials turned a blind eye to the importation and sale of slaves.

Empresario Contracts

The national colonization law also established a procedure for negotiating with "empresarios," or land agents, to secure land for larger groups of settlers. Between 1821 and 1835, 41 empresario contracts were signed, most with Anglo-American land speculators. Each empresario pledged to bring a specified number of colonists in exchange for title to grants of land. The largest was granted to John Lucius Woodbury in 1826 and reached from Comal County, just north of San Antonio, to Brewster County and the Big Bend area. Few of the empresarios succeeded in supplying the required number of families, but this system brought significant numbers of Anglo-Americans to Texas.

> **Competency 010 Descriptive Statement E.** The beginning teacher understands the impact of major geographic features of Texas on American Indians and settlers, and how various groups altered the natural environment through the beginning of the Mexican National Era.

Geographic Regions of Texas

Texas is composed of five physiographic regions: the Gulf Coastal Plains, the Central Lowland region, the High Plains and Plateaus region, the Basin and Range region, and sitting along the New Mexico-Texas border near El Paso, a small promontory of the Rocky Mountains. Within these five physiographic regions, different climate and precipitation characteristics as well as vegetation and animal life further contribute to the diversity of the state's resources. The length of the growing season decreases while moving from South Texas into the Texas Panhandle region, varying from 300 days to fewer than 180 days on average. The average annual rainfall decreases east to west. Jasper County in the southeastern corner of the state gets an average of nearly 61 inches, while El Paso gets less than 10 inches. These extremes of temperature, rain, plant life, and growing season resulted in different conditions for Native Americans and settlers.

Each arrival of Native Americans and settler populations transformed the Texas environment and adapted it to their own uses and culture.

American Indians Shape the Environment

Native Americans in Texas were adept at exploiting their environment but also helped shape their environment to maximize the availability of resources. The perception persists of Native Americans as "ecosystem people" living in harmony with nature, rarely upending the balance between humans and their natural environment. By contrast, European settlers are often considered distinct from their environment, turning it to their own ends with advanced technology and profit-driven efforts. Descriptive Statement E asks teachers to consider how the environment both shaped American Indian and Spanish settler culture as well as how American Indians and Spanish settlement changed the natural environment of Texas.

Plains Indians and Grassland Ecology

The Comanche and other plains Indians provide an important demonstration of how Native Americans were shaped by and, in turn, shaped their environments and how the introduction of the horse transformed both Indian cultures and their environments. Before they emerged as an identifiable ethnic population, proto-Comanche hunted bison and used domesticated dogs to carry loads of up to 60 lbs. balanced on a *travois*, an A-shaped frame pulled by dogs and later by horses. Like the Kiowa, Wichita, and other Texas plains Indians, they were hunter-gatherers who depended upon a range of sources of protein and vegetable calories. After the Comanche acquired horses, they and other plains Indians shifted the bulk of their effort toward accumulating horses and harvesting meat and hides from the seemingly endless herds of bison on the southern plains. During the 18th century and increasingly after 1800, the southern Plains Indians ceased to be "ecosystem people" relying on their local surroundings for subsistence and maintaining a balance within that ecosystem. Instead, Texas' Plains Indians hunted bison, not just for their own consumption, but to sell the meat, hides, and other by-products to other Indians and to French and Spanish settlers. They also acquired vast herds of horses to meet the needs of a market that extended across the American Midwest. Southern Plains Indians numbering no more than 30,000 people, accumulated by the first decades of the 19th century between 250,000 and 500,000 horses, which meant between 10 and 14 horses per person. In addition to these herds, 2 million wild mustangs grazed the same territory. Southern Plains Indians also regularly rounded up these mustangs to sell in this market. Because of the Comanche and other Plains Indians transforming from subsistence-driven hunter-gatherers to market-driven horse nomads, enormous pressure was put on the bison herds of the American West well before the arrival of Anglo-American buffalo hunters. Competition for herds, grazing lands, and horses also fueled much of the violence across the Great Plains before the 1850s.

Caddo Trade Routes and Mound Building

The Caddo people in the Red River basin in East Texas shaped their environment in a different way. By 800 CE the Caddo had developed a distinctive culture, dependent upon maize, squash, beans, and sunflower seed cultivation. Abundant game also provided food sources for the Caddo. The Caddo lived in towns amid their surrounding fields. They also shaped their environment through networks of trade that reached from East Texas to the Jumano in the Big Bend region and the Coahuiltecans who lived from Central Texas to the foothills of the Sierra Madre Oriental. When Spanish missionaries, merchants, and government officials later built roads to connect their vast province, they often built along the same pathways that the Caddo had used to exchange trade goods.

The most distinctive feature of Caddo material culture is perhaps their large burial mounds for family or clan members. Carvings, ceramic pottery, copper engravings, tools, masks made of shells, and other items were buried in these mounds. The mounds were often from 5 feet to 10 feet high, though some reached more than 30 feet and would have required the removal and transport of large quantities of mud and dirt. Mound-building reached its peak some 300 years before European arrival in the area, but accounts of French and Spanish explorers mention these landmarks.

Texas and the Columbian Exchange

After Columbus, the arrival of Spanish explorers, conquistadors, missionary priests, and planters would transform the American environment in what has often been described as the Columbian

Exchange. Like the importance of the spread of horse culture on the Great Plains, the introduction of cattle, sheep, and goats would have a similarly significant effect on Texas landscapes. Less obvious elements of the Columbian Exchange also have changed the Texas environment. The European honeybee is one invasive species that flourished wherever Europeans went. Native Americans living along the Atlantic Coast called the honeybee the "English fly" and knew its presence indicated the pending arrival of Europeans. Spanish explorers described few trees and scrub brush as native to the southern plains. A key introduction to the region, the mesquite tree, would transform much of the landscape.

Other crops of the Columbian Exchange would have a delayed impact on New Spain's northeastern frontier of Texas. Cotton varieties from Mexico would provide the raw material of the American Southeast's cotton industry, making their way west to Texas. Sugar cane was also introduced from Southeast Asia, through the Arab world, into Europe, and because of European exploration and expansion, to Texas. Many of the grasses that would eventually cover the coastal plains and replace native prairie grasses, were weeds transported on explorers' clothing and more likely via the bowels of grazing animals.

Missions, Presidios, and Villas—Spanish Administration and the Texas Environment

The establishment of Franciscan missions across Texas had important consequences for its environment. While Spaniards planted missions in many locations, the most successful missions were in East Texas, along the Gulf Coast, and in San Antonio.

Supplying these scattered missions proved difficult throughout the history of Spanish settlement. To become self-sufficient, the missions often located near rivers where they could divert water to surrounding fields. The irrigation canals, or *acequia* (an Arabic word reflecting the Arab impact on the Iberian Peninsula), that Franciscan friars had their Native American converts dig often transformed barren landscapes into rich farmlands. For example, along the Rio Grande south of El Paso, 3,000 acres of orchards and vineyards grew and were watered by a series of irrigation canals. Nearly all missions tried to create such irrigation networks. The best-known *acequia* networks supplied the mission and villa of San Antonio. Beginning in 1718, a 6-mile canal watered 900 acres of land belonging to the Alamo Mission. Irrigated land not owned by the missions was divided among settler populations by a lottery system with accompanying title to the water needed to turn arid land into gardens. Mission pasturelands, burial grounds, and compounds with a mission church became landmarks of Spanish settlement across Texas.

Presidios were the military garrisons that accompanied the spread of Spanish authority into Texas. They combined a military function with other roles. Soldiers were often sent out to capture runaway mission Indians, sometimes even kidnapping Indians and bringing them to labor on the missions. Carpenters, blacksmiths, stone-masons, and other ancillary occupations accompanied the soldiers. Independent settlers and traders often congregated near these fortresses.

Apart from the missions, farming did not flourish in Spanish Texas. Land grants of only 170 acres were too small for profitability and too large for a single family's labor. Cattle ranching and trade proved more lucrative, and few laborers were willing to carry out the backbreaking work of clearing the land. Subsistence rather than commercial agriculture characterized Texas' farms. Only where settlers could take advantage of mission irrigation and the Indian labor that dug the canals did farmers grow more than their basic needs.

Only four authorized towns were chartered by the Spanish monarchy before the end of the 18th century: Nacogdoches, La Bahia (Goliad), San Antonio, and Laredo. The population of these towns included military families, artisans, traders, seasonally employed ranch laborers, and local figures who met the townspeople's needs. San Antonio was the largest chartered town, with fewer than 1,500 people in 1800. Town planning in Texas reflected Spanish roots with the orientation of the city around the plaza, a town square at the heart of the street grid. These plazas usually were bordered by the town church, government offices, and storefronts as well as boarding houses. Prominent members of the town usually lived nearby, while the poorer townspeople built homes farther away, usually from makeshift materials, mesquite wood or adobe with grass thatching.

Cattle Ranching and the Texas Environment

Cattle were among the most important livestock of the Columbian exchange to affect the Texas landscape, even to this day. In 1493 Columbus left cattle on the island of Hispaniola, and they spread to other Caribbean islands. By 1521, cattle had been transported to Mexico. Cattle ranching followed, but only in the 17th century. In 1689, Alonso de León's expedition brought 200 cattle, 400 horses, and 150 mules. Like a Noah in reverse, de León released a pair of each species on the banks of every river he crossed on the way back to northern Mexico. Other explorers continued the practice. As these cattle grew feral, instead of herding them on foot as generations in the Old World had long done, the Spanish relied on horses to round up stock and drive cattle to grazing lands. Wild horses later provided the Comanche and other plains Indians a stock of horseflesh that could be sold to Indians farther north or to Anglos in the southern United States. These herds also encroached on the grasslands of other native species, transforming the Texas landscape as they spread. The plains west of San Antonio soon saw grazing herds of thousands of cattle and mustangs competing for grass with the native stock. A key factor in the decline of plains buffalo herds, even before the arrival of buffalo hunters with repeater rifles, was the spread of Texas longhorn.

> **Competency 010 Descriptive Statement F.** The beginning teacher demonstrates knowledge of significant cultural and economic developments in Texas history through the beginning of the Mexican National Era.

Periodization: 1685 to the late 1700s

After 1685, Spanish settlement placed a clearer stamp on Texas culturally and economically. Before then, Spain had a claim but little authority or impact on Texas. Texas became Hispanic gradually, but by the late 1700s, the influence of Spanish cultural and institutional structures was transforming the region.

Key Question

Which features of Texas' cultural and economic heritage owe their origins to Spanish settlement and frontier mixing with Texas Indians?

Culturally, Texans combined sparsely settled Native American and Spanish populations that melded together in a frontier setting far from the administrative centers of New Spain. A look at a census of 1777 is suggestive. The census lists 3,103 people in Texas under the authority of the Spanish government, with 957 listed as Spaniards, or *Espanoles*. Elsewhere in New Spain, these descendants of Spanish settlers were often called *creoles*. It lists 111 *mestizos,* of mixed Indian and Spanish descent and counts 669 inhabitants as *colores quebrados* or (broken colors) suggestive of the degree of the cross-cultural and interracial melting pot that Spanish Texas had become. It also lists 871 Indians, converts to Christianity who were associated with the different missions. In addition, a large contingent of Canary Islanders were in San Antonio. Not 20 years later, a second census shows a similar diversity, listing Spaniards, Indians, mestizos, mulattoes, Negroes, Europeans, and men and women of other castes in a population of 2,990. Noticeably absent were Spaniards from the Iberian Peninsula, or *peninsulares*. Spanish Texas was a culturally and ethnically mixed society with a relatively level social hierarchy. Spanish Texas had class divisions, however. They were most evident in San Antonio and in the *presidios*. In San Antonio, the Canary Islanders declared themselves the "first settlers" and guarded their rights as *hidalgos*, or gentlemen. In the military installations, such hierarchies had a military function.

A look at census data from Spanish Texas provides a picture of a relatively undifferentiated economic hierarchy. Many Spaniards who came to Texas lived as peasant farmers, landless laborers or merchants. Servants, muleteers, carpenters, blacksmiths, tailors, shoemakers, masons, and other artisans comprised a significant minority. These men and women lived in the few towns and provided needed services for the royal officials, soldiers, missionaries, and priests. The real wealth of the colony as late as the 1820s was found in its cattle, and thus a significant proportion of Texans were cattlemen. Even the small farmers depended on their herds. Because ranching was critical to Texas' economy, it is worth noting how herding cattle shaped the culture.

Cattle Culture

As noted, an important feature of Texas' early economy was open-range cattle ranching. From the late 17th century, after Spanish settlement began in earnest, Texas developed a unique "cattle culture" that would be later adapted by Southern cattlemen. Although their origin is debated, cattle breeds that eventually became the Texas Longhorn seem to have descended from Iberian cattle with genetic roots in North Africa. The archetypical cowboy derived from these early Spanish cattle herders. The vocabulary used to describe the tools of the cattle trade illustrate the Hispanic origins of the Texas cowboy. The lariat, a stiff rope used to capture cattle, derived from *la riata* or rope. Chaps used to protect cowboys' legs and lower garments, came from the word *chaparajos*. *Bandanna*, *corral*, *rodeo*, and *remuda*, are other terms that show the relationship.

Hispanic Architectural Traditions and Material Culture

As we have seen, Spanish missions, towns, and military installations shaped the Texas environment in lasting ways. The use of roof tiles, Moorish arcades or columned porticos, whitewashed façades, and wrought-iron gates and windows show Spanish influence on Texas building styles. The adobe structures that surround a tiled patio or courtyard are also Hispanic design elements that persist across the American Southwest. Adapted from these designs, the "ranch style" house is akin in Texas to the prominence of the Cape Cod or saltbox houses of New England in that both reflect their European origins. The Hispanic influence was also evident inside Texas homes. Rather than importing fine porcelain china, a sign of family wealth in Eastern homes, Spanish and Mexican-era homes in Texas used brightly colored *majolica* glazed pottery and tiles. The latter were used to decorate façades, fountains, shrines, etc. Rough-hewn cedar or cottonwood tables, chairs, and other household furnishings reflected the simplicity of mission influence. With candles and crucifixes as well as depictions of the saints, household shrines are often found in Texas homes of all ethnic groups. This feature of Roman Catholic practices today has become common even in Protestant and Anglo homes.

The culture of Spanish Texas shaped and continues to shape Texas to the present in many other ways.

COMPETENCY 011 (INDEPENDENCE, STATEHOOD, CIVIL WAR RECONSTRUCTION AND AFTERMATH)

The teacher understands significant historical developments and events in Texas from 1821 to 1900.

> **Competency 011 Descriptive Statement A.** The beginning teacher demonstrates knowledge of the individuals, issues and events related to Mexico becoming an independent nation and the impacts of this event on Texas.

Mexican War of Independence (1810–1821)

Resentment among residents of New Spain had grown with the Bourbon Reforms and with increased Mexican dissatisfaction with the Spanish monarchy's colonial and tax policies. However, the Mexican War of Independence began largely because of the political crisis precipitated by

Napoleon Bonaparte's occupation of Spain in 1808. In 1810, an open revolt led by Miguel Hidalgo y Castillo erupted. It combined rebellion against rule by *peninsulares*, the Spanish-born colonial authorities, with a social revolution against the inequalities and injustice of New Spain's mercantile and political system. Hidalgo's army of enthusiastic but poorly trained peasants frightened both royalists and the Creole population who dominated Mexico. Although they marauded unchecked at first, the peasants were defeated when faced with a professional army. Hidalgo was captured and executed, but his banner was taken up by others. Sporadic but bitter fighting with revolutionary armies continued until 1820 when Agustin de Iturbide, a prosperous Creole who initially favored the royalist cause, concluded that the only way to stop the socially revolutionary forces unleashed by Hidalgo was to establish an independent, yet staunchly Roman Catholic Mexico, dominated by Creole landowners and the military. To gain power, Iturbide aligned with **Vicente Guerrero (1781–1831).**

Vicente Guerrero was born near Acapulco in southern Mexico into a mixed-heritage or *mestizo* family. His "El Negro" nickname hinted at rumors of African ancestry. Whatever his parentage, he started poor, earning his living as a muleteer. In 1810, Guerrero joined with Father José María Morelos' revolutionary army. After Morelos was executed, he became the leader of Morelos' forces in southern Mexico. Despite their different visions of the future of Mexico, Guerrero and Iturbide in 1821 succeeded under the Plan of Iguala, or the Plan of the Three Guarantees—to defend the Roman Catholic faith, political independence from Spain, and unity founded on social equality for Mexico's social and ethnic groups. They gained Mexican independence and established the Empire of Mexico under Iturbide's authority. This empire lasted until March 1823, when Iturbide was overthrown and exiled.

After the fall of Iturbide's short-lived empire, liberal politicians devised a new constitution for a federal republic. Unsurprisingly, the **Constitution of 1824** resembled the U.S. Constitution written 37 years earlier. Politically, the Constitution of 1824 represented a momentary victory of the Federalists over the Centralists. The Mexican government would be a republic rather than a monarchy and a federation of states rather than a unitary and centralized government. The Mexican interpretation of federalism, however, differed from how federalism was understood by the Anglo-Americans accustomed to its U.S. version. In the American system, the states pre-existed the national government and invested the central government with its powers, maintaining to themselves their own spheres of autonomy. In the Mexican system, the national government created the states—along historical lines, to be sure—and delegated powers to the states. This different version of federalism would contribute to the misunderstandings that led to the Texas Revolution. However, when Texans contemplated resistance to the Santa Anna government, they did so under the banner of restoring the Constitution of 1824, rather than rejecting Mexican authority outright.

A key figure in the divide between Texas and Mexico was Vicente Guerrero. After independence, Guerrero served in the Iturbide regime as well as the republic that followed. He ran unsuccessfully for president in 1828 and contended that the election had been fraudulently lost. Guerrero and General Antonio López de Santa Anna engineered a coup, naming Guerrero president in

April 1829. Perhaps the most important legislation from Guerrero's time in office was the Decree of September 15, 1829, which freed Mexico's slaves. Though the decree was rescinded for Texas in December 1829, Mexico's apparent unwillingness to guarantee slavers' property rights would be a worry for Texans and a contributing factor in the Texas War for Independence. Guerrero's rule was short-lived, however, and conservative politicians overthrew him in December 1829. After trying to regain the presidency, Guerrero was captured and in February 1831 was executed.

Guerrero's overthrow and execution shocked the young Republic of Mexico and tainted the legitimacy of the junta that had overthrown him. After several years of instability, Mexico elected Santa Anna as president in April 1833. He found the responsibility of governing tedious and turned much of it over to his vice president, a political liberal who sought significant reforms of the army and the Roman Catholic Church. When conservatives objected to these reforms, Santa Anna agreed and called for the repeal of the liberal reforms. He dissolved the Congress and formed a new conservative government, with a centralizing rather than federalist impulse. The Constitution of 1824 was set aside and a new constitution, "The Seven Laws," was promulgated. Santa Anna had established himself as a military dictator. In response, 11 states rebelled, but only Texas would gain its independence.

> **Competency 011 Descriptive Statement B.** The beginning teacher demonstrates knowledge of important individuals, events and issues related to the Texas Revolution (e.g., the Law of April 6, 1830, Fredonian Rebellion, Battle of Gonzales, Surrender at Goliad, Battle of the Alamo, Battle of San Jacinto, George Childress, Juan N. Seguín, Antonio López de Santa Anna, William B. Travis, James Fannin).

Causes of the Texas Revolution

The Texas Revolution had multiple causes and partly reflected the context of power struggles within Mexico itself, where the political elite were deeply divided in the early years of its republic between centralist and federalist factions. In 1833, Santa Anna had removed a centralist faction from power, proposing himself as a federalist. But he soon took a more centralist approach and accumulated dictatorial powers Several Mexican states rose against this change in policy, and the Texas Revolution itself was an outgrowth of the rebellion in 1835 of the Mexican state of Coahuila y Tejas, of which Texas was a department. The wider rebellion against Santa Anna triggered the Texas Revolution, but other underlying causes should get equal consideration.

Anglo-American Immigration and Cultural Differences

From 1521, when Spain first established its claim over Texas, the Spanish had only settled 4,000 people in the area, a pattern continued by the fledgling Mexican republic. By comparison, in the decade since Moses Austin had acquired his land grant, English-speaking inhabitants had arrived in such numbers that Texas' non-native population had quintupled by 1830.

Before Austin had acquired his concession, Anglo-American migration into Texas and encroachment on Mexican land had also been underway. In 1801, Spanish authorities caught Philip Nolan, who claimed to be searching for horses to sell in Louisiana, deep in Texas territory. Military and scientific expeditions to determine the western boundaries of the Louisiana Territory also caused diplomatic incidents in 1806. In 1819, investors who were convinced that the Louisiana Purchase had included extensive territory in Texas backed an effort by "filibusters," an irregular and unauthorized military force, to claim land coveted by Southerners eager to expand their cotton and sugar plantations. The government of Mexico understandably looked with some apprehension at the illegal encroachment on its territory and feared the possibility that the goal of Anglo-American settlers was to annex Texas to the United States. With the rapid growth of Anglo-American settlement, these fears increased and were exacerbated by the frequent Anglo-American disregard for Mexican law and culture. An important example of this occurred with the so-called Fredonian Rebellion of 1826.

Slavery

The role of slavery among the causes of the Texas War for Independence has often been under-emphasized. The expansion of cotton production and slavery into Mexico faced deep ambivalence on the part of authorities in the new Mexican republic. Mexico, and Tejanos specifically, encouraged the spread of cotton cultivation brought by Anglo-American settlement and saw it as critical to the development of Texas. But anti-slavery reformers in Mexico City, cognizant of the inconsistency of the practice with the values of the republic, openly objected to chattel slavery and sought its end. Debates about slavery in the Mexican press and in the legislature as well as efforts to restrain its spread contributed much to Texans' push for independence. These factors undoubtedly contributed to the eventuality of the rebellion, but the Texas Revolution, like most such uprisings, developed gradually from a series of decisions and missteps. Both Texans and Mexican authorities made them.

Fredonian Rebellion (1826–1827)

In 1825, an *empresario* contract was granted to Haden Edwards, a pioneer settler and land speculator, to bring 800 Anglo-American families to East Texas. The grant extended from northwest of Nacogdoches, west to the Navasota River, and south to a line just north of Galveston Bay, with an eastern boundary approaching the Sabine River. The grant also stipulated that the land claims of Hispanic residents who had lived since the 1780s in the Nacogdoches area were to be respected by Edwards and his Anglo-American colonists. But many Spanish-speaking residents lacked written deeds to their land. Arriving in Nacogdoches in October 1825, Edwards sought to dispossess Hispanic farmers and ranchers of their land unless they provided proof of ownership or paid him a purchase price. Edwards also sought to deprive Anglo squatters who had also lived in the area for decades of lands for which they had no written titles. Complaints of Edwards' heavy-handed and culturally insensitive efforts to drive these residents from their land were taken to San Antonio for adjudication. Edwards' contract was canceled, and his settlers were ordered to leave Texas. In response, Edwards and his brother, Benjamin, seized the *alcalde,* or magistrate, of Nacogdoches and declared their colony the **Republic of Fredonia**. The brothers encouraged several Cherokee Indians to join them in their insurrection, but the Indians ultimately refused. When a contingent of soldiers from San Antonio, including militia from Stephen F. Austin's colony, arrived in January 1827 to suppress the uprising, Edwards fled to Louisiana.

The rebellion alarmed Mexican authorities and Anglo-American settlers. Although Edwards' tactics were seen, even by fellow *empresarios*, as a threat to good relations with the Hispanic populace and the Mexican government, Anglo-Americans were alarmed that a contract could be so easily abrogated. Mexican leaders meanwhile were alerted to the potential threat to their authority that was posed by the many Anglo-Americans that were settling in Texas territory. An official inspection tour of the state by Manuel de Mier y Terán was ordered. Terán concluded that Anglo-American assimilation into Mexican culture was unlikely and that Anglo-American loyalty could not be trusted. He recommended a new law governing the Anglo-American presence.

Law of April 6, 1830

One result of Terán's recommendation was the passage of the Law of April 6, 1830. The law reflected Mexican fears that a rebellion of Anglos like the Fredonian Rebellion might provide a pretext for the United States to annex the region in much the same way that Western Florida, which extended into present-day Mississippi and Louisiana, had been acquired by the United States in the early 1800s. The law therefore sought to limit Anglo-American immigration, requiring all arrivals to have a passport authorizing them to settle in already well-established colonies like Stephen F. Austin's. Significantly, the law also forbade the immigration or importation of slaves. To enforce these laws, troops were stationed in Nacogdoches and at other border posts. Special tax exemptions granted to immigrants had also expired, and tariffs thus were imposed to fund the troop installments. These taxes on imports were especially burdensome on pioneering Anglo-Americans who relied on imports through the port of Galveston to resupply.

The Guerrero Decree (Sept. 15, 1829)

An additional factor contributing to the unease of Texan slavers was the decree of President Vicente Guerrero in September 1829 abolishing slavery in the Mexican republic. Ramón Músquiz, the political chief of Texas, refused to enact the decree because it violated the terms of the colonization acts of 1824 and 1825. But the law still alarmed Texans, who felt that it would end to the rapid development of the cotton economy. Anglo-American settlers who had entered the state with slaves also expressed concern for the security of what they said was their property. In the end, Texas was granted an exemption from the law, but many Texas slaveholders remained concerned that abolitionist sentiment in Mexico might one day threaten their interests.

Antonio López de Santa Anna (1794–1876)

Santa Anna has been perhaps the most vilified of any Mexican leader, both in Texas and in Mexico. Texans despised him as a tyrant, and many Mexicans scorned him for losing Texas and the Mexican-American War and for shamefully selling parts of Mexico to the United States in 1853. Santa Anna joined the Mexican independence movement in 1821, building his reputation as a revolutionary by liberating his own home province. He was elected president of Mexico six times, serving 1833–1835, 1839, 1841–1844, 1846–1847, and 1853–1855. His victories at the Alamo and in stopping Spanish and French invasions are overshadowed by the disaster at San Jacinto and the loss of half of the nation's territory to the United States in 1848. He is often used as an example of the classic South American *caudillo*, or military strongman. Often remembered as a dictator and tyrant, Santa Anna has more recently experienced a measured rehabilitation by scholars.

Battle of Gonzales (Oct. 2, 1835)

Following Santa Anna's order to disarm state militias across Mexico, the military commander of San Antonio ordered the Texans living at Gonzales to return a small cannon issued to them by the Mexican government to help the Texans defend against Indian attacks. The Gonzales residents refused and sent out a call for volunteers to join them. A force of cavalry was sent to retrieve the cannon but was not authorized to seize it. Unable to ford the rain-swollen Guadalupe River, the cavalry camped across the river from a force of 18 Texans and tried to negotiate the cannon's return. On the morning of Oct. 2, 1835, the Texans skirmished briefly with Mexican forces. After a brief respite and negotiations between the commanders of the Mexican cavalry and the assembled Texans, a defiant banner was raised with the words "COME AND TAKE IT," repeating the Spartan response given at Thermopylae when the Persians demanded they lay down their arms. This "battle," which those present remembered as the "fight at William's place," was later labeled the "Battle of Gonzales" and was called the "Lexington of Texas" to refer to the opening shots of the American Revolution. One or two Mexican soldiers were killed, and this "battle" represented a watershed in the relationship between Texas republicans and the Mexican government.

Consultation of 1835

A gathering of Texans met Nov. 4, 1835, at San Felipe de Austin, where Stephen F. Austin headquartered his colony. Despite the recent fighting at Gonzales, the gathered Texans were divided. A "War Party" pushed for an immediate vote of independence, but a majority proposed that Texas remain a part of Mexico if the Mexican Constitution of 1824 was followed. The "Peace Party" prevailed, and a declaration was drafted, restating Texans' loyalty to Mexico and to the Constitution of 1824. Despite this decision, a plan for a provisional government was adopted, and officers were chosen, with each to swear an oath to support the Constitution of 1824. The gathering also voted to reconvene March 1. The Consultation of 1835 has often been likened to the meeting of the Second Continental Congress in Philadelphia in 1775. With the latter, the battle of Lexington and Concord had already taken place, and with the former, the Battle of Gonzales, the "Lexington of Texas," had already occurred.

Convention of 1836

When the proposed meeting convened in March 1836, the Alamo was under siege, and troops from Santa Anna's right flank were marching up the coast road toward Goliad. The revolution was underway. The Consultation of 1835 had been divided on whether independence from Mexico should be sought. Meeting at Washington-on-the-Bravos, the Convention of 1836 had lost most of this ambivalence. The delegates were younger, more recent arrivals to Texas than those at the earlier consultation. Moreover, events had rapidly outpaced the delegates. After convening March 1, the convention the following day adopted the Texas Declaration of Independence. Much like the American Declaration of Independence, it laid out the grievances and justification for rebellion against the lawful authority of the Mexican government. **George Childress**, who had arrived in Texas in 1834, was named chair of the committee to draft the Texas Declaration of Independence. The convention also chose an interim government under President David G. Burnet. While creating a constitution, the interim government got news of Santa Anna's victory at the Alamo. With Santa Anna rushing toward Washington-on-the-Brazos, the interim government fled, leading Santa Anna on a chase that would end at San Jacinto.

Battle of the Alamo (March 6, 1836)

After the successful skirmishes at Gonzales and Goliad, volunteers rushed to San Antonio to besiege the presidio and missions there. Between Dec. 5 and Dec. 11, Texans fought a house-to-house campaign forcing the Mexican commander to surrender the city. By early February 1836, Santa Anna had entered Texas territory as the head of an army of 6,000 soldiers, many of whom were poorly trained draftees. He arrived outside San Antonio by the end of February. He was faced by a force of some 240 to 260 Texas volunteers under the leadership of William Barret Travis and James Bowie, holed up in the mission known as the Alamo. After a brief siege, on March 6, Santa Anna's army began the assault on the mission. Relying on effective artillery and the sharpshooting of the Tennessee riflemen, among them Davy Crockett, the Texans laid down withering fire on the Mexican troops. The Mexicans experienced significant, though not surprising casualties, given the nature of the assault on a fortified position. They eventually overwhelmed the Texan defenses, killing all but a handful of those in the mission. Some 257 Alamo defenders died, and estimates of the number of Mexican casualties rise to as high as 600, though most historians agree today that some 200 Mexicans were killed and another 200 were injured.

William B. Travis (1809–1836)

One of the Texans who died at the Alamo was William Barret Travis. Born in Georgia, Travis had lived a checkered life before coming to Texas. He was a teacher in Alabama before studying law in Claiborne, Alabama. While apprenticing under a local lawyer, Travis also dabbled in newspaper publishing. Although he opened a law practice in 1829, he fell into increasing debt and attracted few clients. After he was publicly humiliated by his creditors and faced with an order for his arrest, Travis set out for Texas in 1831, leaving his pregnant wife and two children behind. He acquired land from Stephen F. Austin and again opened a law office in Anahuac. He was a leading figure in the Anahuac disturbances and in February 1836 joined the Alamo defense with a small contingent of regular soldiers. With James Bowie's health failing, Travis became the commander of the Alamo shortly before its fall. Travis' letter "To the People of Texas and All Americans in the World," written during the siege of the Alamo, calling for American reinforcements and proclaiming "Victory of Death," served as a rallying cry among Texans as well as in the United States in support of the Texas revolutionaries.

Surrender at Goliad

While Santa Anna's army was facing the rebels at the Alamo, a second Mexican force, led by General José de Urrea, advanced along the coast from Matamoros. After surprising a small contingent of Texans at the Battle of San Patricio, killing 16 and taking 24 prisoners, Urrea's troops then defeated another force of Texans at Agua Dulce. Urrea next advanced on the Presidio la Bahía in Goliad, which the Texans had claimed in early October 1835. A force of Texans led by **James W. Fannin** waited there, and Fannin retreated, facing a shortage of supplies and Urrea's superior numbers. The Texans were surrounded by the Mexican force at Coleto Creek, surrendering after a two-day battle, "the battle of the prairie." Of the 342 who surrendered, all but around 30 were summarily executed, including Fannin. The brutality of this treatment of prisoners of war enraged and alarmed Texans and reduced the possibilities of a negotiated political settlement. The combined massacres at Goliad and the Alamo, though dispiriting, soon proved rallying cries for the Texans who now saw no alternative but independence.

The Runaway Scrape

As the disasters at Goliad and San Antonio unfolded, **Sam Houston** was given command over the Texan troops, who were now united in opposition to Santa Anna's armies. With a small force of only 500 men, Houston withdrew toward Louisiana, perhaps hoping for U.S. intervention. Whether a tactical decision or not, the retreat led to a pell-mell flight of Texas settlers with their slaves, scared of possible Mexican reprisals as well as Indian assaults on their unprotected farmsteads. Bad weather contributed to the chaos. The flight toward Louisiana was remembered as the "Runaway Scrape."

Battle of San Jacinto

While Texas settlers fled the advancing Mexican armies, Santa Anna and his army of fewer than a thousand men set out to eliminate the Texas government and confront Houston's forces. After continuing his retreat and infuriating many of his men as well as Texas interim President David G. Burnet, Houston, on April 16, 1836, saw an opportunity to turn and face the Mexican forces. During the night of April 19, Houston marched his men to a crossing of the San Jacinto River, where they confronted Santa Anna's army of nearly 1,200 with a force of 900 men. After some skirmishes, late in the afternoon of April 21, after Santa Anna had concluded that no attack was imminent that day, Houston ordered his men to advance in a surprise assault. The battle was over in 18 minutes. Nine Texans were killed, while more than 630 Mexicans died in the battle. Another 730 were captured. Santa Anna escaped but was captured the following day. Houston resisted calls by Texans, infuriated by the Goliad and Alamo defeats, to execute the Mexican president. He forced Santa Anna to sign an agreement to end hostilities and to withdraw his armies from Texas.

Juan N. Seguín (1806–1890)

Juan Seguín was born to a prominent San Antonio family. His father had served in the Mexican Congress in 1823–1824, and Seguín himself had been elected to several posts in San Antonio, finally being chosen the *alcalde,* a position akin to city mayor, of San Antonio in 1833. In this position, he also served as acting *jefe,* or political chief, of the Department of Bexar. A staunch federalist, Seguín saw the expansion of the national government's power under Santa Anna as a usurpation. Seguín thus took a prominent role in the Texas independence movement, both as a military and political leader. He was elected to the Texas Senate, serving in three successive Congresses. He is often used as an example of the diversity of the Texas independence movement. He also continued to participate in political activity within Mexico. After serving in the Texas Senate, he was elected mayor of San Antonio, serving in this capacity from 1841 to the spring of 1842. He grew increasingly exasperated at the mistreatment of Hispanic residents by Anglo-Texans. He was suspected of undermining Mirabeau Lamar's scheme of expanding into New Mexico and incriminated for his communication with Mexico before its invasion of San Antonio in 1842. His role in Mexican efforts to regain Texas and his participation with the Mexican army during the Mexican-American War also harmed his reputation with Anglo-Texans. However, he held several political positions during the second half of the 19th century. In 1874, years after his death and burial in Nuevo Laredo, Mexico, Seguín's remains were returned to the town of Seguín, Texas, to acknowledge his role in the Texas Revolution.

> **Competency 011 Descriptive Statement C.** The beginning teacher demonstrates knowledge of important individuals, events and issues related to the history of the Republic of Texas and early Texas statehood (e.g., Stephen F. Austin, Lorenzo de Zavala, Sam Houston, Joshua Houston, Mary Maverick, Mirabeau Lamar, the Córdova Rebellion, the Council House Fight, the Santa Fe Expedition, United States-Mexican War).

Stephen F. Austin

Stephen F. Austin has been introduced as *empresario* and founder of Anglo settlement colonies in Mexican Texas. His role in the Texas Revolution has also been mentioned. Given his establishment of the state, Austin's role in the early years of the Republic of Texas was less than might be expected. When news of Sam Houston's victory at the Battle of San Jacinto was relayed to him in New Orleans, Austin returned to his Texas estate and announced his plans to seek the presidency.

His election seemed assured until Houston announced his candidacy. Austin finished a distant third behind Houston and Henry Smith. Houston appointed him secretary of state, which suited his diplomatic skills, but he died two months later, single and childless. To honor Austin's significance, Houston proclaimed him "The Father of Texas."

Lorenzo de Zavala (1788–1836)

A leading figure in the Mexican independence movement, Lorenzo de Zavala published several revolutionary newspapers and served as a state governor and national assemblyman during his Mexican political career. He had the unique experience of drafting both the Federal Constitution of the United States of Mexico in 1824 and the constitution of the Republic of Texas in 1836. A liberal, Zavala favored a federal system modeled on the United States for Mexico's new republic. He opposed a monarchy and a centralized government as well as slavery. In 1829, after the overthrow of the Mexican republic, Zavala was arrested and went into exile. He traveled throughout the United States and wrote about its political system. While in the United States, Zavala also formed the Galveston Bay and Texas Land Co., hoping to attract U.S. settlers to Texas. The Colonization Law of April 6, 1830, curtailed any hopes of profiting from this opportunity, and de Zavala became one of the law's most outspoken critics. In 1833, after Santa Anna consolidated his power in Mexico, Zavala moved to Texas, settling his family in Harris County. Zavala threw his lot in with the Texas independence movement, arguing that the centralizing government of Santa Anna had violated the Constitution of 1824 and thus gave the states of Mexico, including Texas, no choice but to rebel. Zavala hoped that Texas would stay connected to its Hispanic and Mexican heritage after gaining independence. He argued that Spanish should be the official language and had the constitution issued in both English and Spanish. Zavala also served as the first vice president of the Republic of Texas. Zavala has also been wrongly credited with designing its flag.

Sam Houston (1793–1863)

Born in Virginia, Sam Houston emigrated to Tennessee at the age of 13 after his father's death. Two years after moving to Tennessee, Houston ran away from home and lived among the Cherokee Indians for three years. While among the Cherokee, he was informally adopted by a Cherokee leader, Chief Oolooteka. This experience gave him a sympathy for Native Americans, often missing in other white people of his time. He served in the U.S. Army during the War of 1812, rising rapidly through the ranks. He fought under future president Andrew Jackson at the Battle of Horseshoe Bend and gained his patronage and support. Houston then embarked on a political career that saw him elected to the U.S. Congress as a representative from Tennessee, and he was chosen in 1827 as the Tennessee governor. After this auspicious beginning to Houston's political career, personal failure drove him to Texas.

After an eleven-week marriage and a painful and humiliating separation, Houston resigned his governorship and fled to Indian Territory to live with his adoptive Cherokee family. He then fought depression and alcoholism. He also participated in Cherokee affairs and was granted Cherokee citizenship. After marrying a Cherokee woman (who became his second wife), Houston again participated in American political life. After an altercation with a U.S. representative from Ohio on the streets of Washington, Houston went west again, moving to Texas in 1832. He soon became embroiled in debates about Texas statehood and independence, favoring war with Mexico and immediate Texas independence. In November 1835, Houston was appointed the commander of the Texas army. After leading a strategic though undisciplined retreat from Gonzales, Houston led the Texas forces that defeated Santa Anna at the Battle of San Jacinto in 1836.

Houston's victory at San Jacinto ensured the independence of the Republic of Texas and gave him a reputation as the "Texas Liberator," often mentioned with such other American revolutionaries as George Washington and Simón Bolívar. Houston rode this wave of acclaim to a runaway election victory as Texas president over Henry Smith and Stephen F. Austin. Houston would twice serve in this office, the first time from 1836 to 1838. The Texas Constitution did not permit a president to succeed himself but allowed nonconsecutive terms, and he served again from 1841 to 1844.

Houston supported U.S. annexation of Texas, but when this did not take place, he helped build the institutions of a new republic. In 1836, the settlement of Houston was founded as the new republic's capital. But the Republic of Texas lacked the wealth or commerce to fund a new government. Its wealth was in land and slaves, neither of which the government wanted to use as the basis of taxation. Despite Houston's frugal government, Texas' national debt had risen to $2 million by the end of his first term. Houston tried to reduce expenditures by gradually furloughing much of the army and trying to maintain peace with the Native American population. This proved unsuccessful, and the Córdova Rebellion, which united Indian and Mexican grievances, threatened the stability of Houston's efforts to secure peace between the white settlers and Texas Indians. During his second term, Houston again faced severe financial constraints, this time worsened by Mirabeau Lamar's failure to exercise fiscal restraint during his brief tenure as president. Houston tried to sell the Texas Navy's four ships, make treaties with Indian bands in Texas, and avoid a costly war with Mexico, even after two Mexican incursions into the republic in 1842.

After his second term and following the annexation of Texas in 1845, Houston served the state as a U.S. senator between 1846 and 1859. As senator, Houston earned a reputation as a Unionist, opposed to the sectional divisions that increasingly characterized the nation's political discourse. Though a slave owner, Houston was committed to the Union and supported the 1820 Missouri Compromise, and the Compromise of 1850. He opposed the Kansas-Nebraska Act because he feared the effect of allowing slavery to be settled by majority vote. When his positions proved unsupportable in the Texas Legislature, which appointed the state's two senators, it was clear that Houston would not be returned to Washington. He then twice ran for governor of Texas. In 1859, he was elected and assumed office in December. Houston thus was Texas governor in 1860 when Abraham Lincoln was elected U.S. president. Houston opposed secession, arguing that a civil war would follow and that the North would win, resulting in the destruction of Southern institutions and culture. Despite his warnings and his refusal to call a special session of the Texas Legislature, the only body that could convene a convention, a Secession Convention was called under a cloud of unconstitutionality and met in early 1861. Houston accepted the inevitable but refused to swear an oath of allegiance to the Confederate States of America. He was then removed from the governorship. Houston left Austin and moved to Huntsville, where he died at age 70 in 1863.

Joshua Houston (1822–1902)

Joshua was born a slave on the plantation of Temple Lea in Perry County, Alabama. When Temple Lea died in 1834, Margaret Moffette Lea inherited the 12-year-old boy. In 1839, Sam Houston, the hero of the Texas Revolution and former president of the Republic of Texas, visited Alabama in search of investors for a planned community he was developing. When Houston and Margaret Lea met, they fell in love and were married in 1840. Through the marriage, Sam's third, Joshua became Sam Houston's property, taking the Houston surname and serving Houston until 1863, when Houston died. Although literacy was discouraged for slaves, Joshua learned to read and write. He was also leased to a stage-coach company and allowed to keep some of his earnings. After the Civil War, Joshua took his earnings and opened a blacksmith shop and built a home in Huntsville. He became prominent in the local Baptist Church and was twice elected a county commissioner. In 1888, he was a delegate to the Republican National Convention.

Mary Maverick (1818–1898)

Mary Maverick was born Mary Ann Adams, daughter of a wealthy Alabama family with roots in Virginia. She married Samuel Augustus Maverick in August 1836. In 1838, she moved with her family and some 10 slaves to San Antonio. She later claimed to have been the first U.S.-born woman to settle in San Antonio, though this is doubtful. But her second child, Lewis Antonio Maverick, was the first Anglo-American born in San Antonio. Maverick participated in a several battles with Texas Indians, including the massacre of a delegation of Comanche at the Council House Fight in 1840. She included accounts of these battles in her memoirs. Her diaries and memoir provide an important source of San Antonio's history. After the Civil War, Maverick would be a prominent in San Antonio's Historical Society and the Daughters of the Republic of Texas. She was an important civic booster of San Antonio and a leader in efforts to restore the Alamo.

Mirabeau Buonaparte Lamar (1798–1859)

Sam Houston is the more remembered president of the Republic of Texas, but the Texas leader who had the greatest impact on the new republic may be Mirabeau Lamar. Lamar was born in Georgia in 1798 into a family descended from French Huguenots (Protestants) who had emigrated from France to Maryland in the 17th century. Lamar had been unsuccessful in business in Georgia before serving as the state governor's private secretary as well as editor of a Georgia newspaper. When his wife died in 1833, Lamar made a short trip to Texas, then returned to join Sam Houston's army, fighting with distinction at the battle of San Jacinto. He was elected to the Texas vice presidency in 1836 and two years later was chosen as its second president.

After the United States rejected annexation, Lamar sought diplomatic allies and commercial partners for the new republic. He established diplomatic relations with England and France, but failed to gain formal recognition from Mexico, which still claimed its former northern state. Lamar began a program to develop the republic's natural resources, started a system of public education, and established a new capital city at Austin. Lamar also hoped to expand Texas' boundaries, sending an expedition of volunteers and traders to Santa Fe, New Mexico. This expedition ended in disaster. However, Lamar did expel the Cherokee from East Texas following the Córdova Rebellion and led attacks on the Comanche and Kiowa in West Texas. Lamar's ambitious plans for economic development coupled with the costs of expansionism and frontier defense placed the new republic in difficult financial straits. Forced to borrow heavily, Texas saw its paper currency drop in value and faced an existential crisis. Lamar in 1844 supported U.S. annexation, though he had opposed it early in his presidency. After annexation, Lamar served under General Zachary Taylor in the Mexican-American War before retiring to his plantation in Richmond, Texas. In 1857, he was appointed ambassador to Nicaragua, where he was tasked with negotiating a treaty that would have given the United States a protectorate over the Isthmus of Panama. Failing to secure a site for a canal, Lamar was recalled in 1859 and died soon after.

Córdova Rebellion (1838)

The Córdova Rebellion was an organized conspiracy centered in Nacogdoches. The rebellion combined Anglo-American settlers disgruntled at the influx of recent migrants, Hispanic residents still loyal to Mexico, and Cherokee Indians who had been promised secure land titles in exchange for their neutrality during the War for Independence. The central figure in the conspiracy was Vincente Córdova, a prominent Nacogdochian. A group of Nacogdoches residents were searching for escaped horses when they came upon a party of some 100 armed Mexicans. Some 300 Cherokee Indians later joined the band. Córdova issued a proclamation outlining the group's grievances. The conspiracy was quashed well before its true dimensions could be determined. But in August 1838 a Mexican spy was killed near the Red River and was found with a diary and papers that revealed the Mexican government's plan of inciting East Texas Indians to attack Texans across the territory. Then, in May 1839, more evidence of a conspiracy was found on the body of Manuel Flores. The leader of a group of Mexicans and Indians, Flores had died fighting the Texas Rangers as the leader of a group of Mexicans and Indians, and he was found with evidence of a much wider conspiracy to encourage Mexican and Indian cooperation against the Texas Republic. Partly in reaction to this potential coordinated uprising of Indians and Hispanic Texans, President Mirabeau Lamar concluded that the Cherokee must be removed from the republic.

Santa Fe Expedition (1841)

The presidency of Mirabeau Lamar also included a failed expedition to Santa Fe in Mexico's northern state of Nuevo México. The Republic of Texas claimed that the Rio Grande served as the boundary of Texas "from source to mouth," extending the territory of the state far beyond its current limits. With this western boundary, Texas' western border included roughly half of the contemporary state of New Mexico and significant portions of Colorado as well as parts of Oklahoma, Kansas, and Wyoming. Santa Fe, the capital of Nuevo México, was included in the claim. Nuevo México also was supplied with commercial items through a series of trade routes that extended from Mexico City or the Pacific into the territory. To secure this claim and to divert at least some of the lucrative Santa Fe trade to Texas, Lamar in 1841 tacitly authorized an expedition that combined commerce — over $200,000 worth of trade goods were transported in ox-drawn wagons — with military support. The merchants and their goods were protected by a military force led by Hugh McLeod. The party encountered hostile Indian forces along the route, had not brought sufficient food or water, and were at one point abandoned by their Mexican guide. By Oct. 5, 1841, the entire group of Texans were broken physically and surrendered to Mexican forces who marched them to Mexico City as prisoners. In April 1842, most were released, but the expedition and its aftermath had caused a diplomatic incident involving Texas, Mexico, and the United States.

The Council House Fight (March 19, 1840)

Faced with widening Texas Ranger attacks and threats from other Native American tribes, the Penateka clan of Comanche in 1840 sought to negotiate a peace with Texas officials. Return of all white captives was among the demands made by Texas negotiators. When a Comanche delegation arrived in San Antonio March 19 to return their captives and complete negotiations, a young white girl, Matilda Lockhart, described her abuse by the Comanche. She also said the tribe still held captives. The Texans did not accept the Penateka explanation that the captives Lockhart referred to were held by other Comanche bands over which the Penateka had no authority. Texas soldiers were called into the Council House, and the Comanche delegation was told they would be held as hostages until all captives were released. The Comanche inside tried to fight their way out of the Council House, while the Comanche outside fought to rescue them. In the fight, 37 Comanche were killed, and 27 became hostages, while one Comanche woman was released to secure the release of the white captives in exchange for the 27 Penateka leaders. The Comanche regarded this breach of protocol as heinous treachery, and the Penateka under Chief Buffalo Hump acquired a special hatred of Texans. They increased attacks on Texas settlements and farmsteads.

Jack Coffee Hays (1817–1883)

Following the Battle of San Jacinto, Jack Coffee Hays arrived in Texas in 1836 and enlisted in the Texas Rangers, which then was dedicated to meeting the Comanche threat. He was later commissioned as a captain and earned his reputation in numerous battles with the Comanche and other Indian tribes. He and his Rangers are best remembered for their introduction of the Colt revolver, which allowed the Rangers for the first time to match the rapid fire and accuracy of the Comanche bow and arrow. Hays is also remembered for cultivating a close relationship with the Lipan Apache in Kerr County, and with Flacco, the Lipan Apache chief. Hays would later spend time in

California, serving as a sheriff of San Francisco County, helping to found the city of Oakland, and participating in state Democratic politics until shortly before his death in 1883.

United States–Mexican War (1846–1848)

The U.S. War on Mexico culminated a campaign of imperial expansion often explained by Manifest Destiny. The United States instigated the war to end Mexico's claim to Texas and acquire by force as much Mexican territory as could be defended. The immediate pretext of the war was the defense of "disputed" territory between the Nueces River and the Rio Grande. The progress of the war showed the superior firepower and numbers available to the American forces.

The Texas Rangers played a notorious role in pacifying northern Mexico, which by 1847 had become a war zone characterized by atrocities and reprisals on both sides. To reduce the resistance, a volunteer force of 700 Texas Rangers was armed with rifles, revolvers, and Bowie knives and sent into the Mexican countryside. They first were to act as scouts but soon were turned loose to raid villages, shoot or hang Mexican citizens, and otherwise subdue any opposition. They acquired such a reputation for lawlessness that Mexicans called them *Los Diablos Tejanos* (the Texas Devils), and General Zachary Taylor at one point threatened to arrest the entire company in reaction to a massacre of 25 unarmed civilians at Rancho Guadalupe.

> **Competency 011 Descriptive Statement D.** The beginning teacher demonstrates knowledge of important individuals, issues and events of the Civil War and Reconstruction in Texas (e.g., Jack Coffee Hayes, John Bell Hood, John Magruder, the Battle of Galveston, the Battle of Palmito Ranch).

Periodization: 1861 to 1865

The Civil War began April 12, 1861, with the attack on Fort Sumter in South Carolina and lasted until April 9, 1865, when Robert E. Lee surrendered at Appomattox Court House. Confederate forces in Texas, however, did not surrender until nearly two months later.

Key Question

The American Civil War was largely fought east of the Mississippi. Texas was never a significant war front. This statement poses this question: Why did Texas secede, and what role did Texans—and Texas—play in this central drama of American history?

Texas Secession

Although Texas was a slaveholding state with an economy dependent upon the labor of enslaved African Americans, it was not a foregone conclusion that Texas would join the secession with other

Southern states. Although a slave holder and opposed to abolition, Sam Houston in 1859 campaigned as a unionist who favored remaining within the United States. When the Texas Legislature voted to secede from the Union in 1861, Houston would not accept the legality of this action and was forced from office for refusing to swear his allegiance to the Confederate States of America. Opposition to secession was not confined to Sam Houston. A sizable contingent of Unionists could be found in pockets across Texas. Support for the Union cause was strongest in the German counties of the Texas Hill Country. Although most Spanish-speaking Texas residents who fought in the Civil War did so with the Confederacy, a significant contingent of Tejanos joined the Union cause, and most were suspicious of the direction a Confederate victory would take the state.

Texas was the only Southern state to put the question of secession to a popular referendum. Texans voted in a landslide, 46,153 for to 14,747 against, to secede. The Secession Convention that had called for the popular vote then reassembled, affirmed the decision to secede, and rewrote the state constitution to enshrine slavery in state law.

Texans at War

Texas' role in the Civil War as a supplier of Confederate troops has often been noted. Texans provided significant troop contingents to the Confederacy. Although an estimated 65,000 to 90,000 Texans saw service in the Confederate military, two-thirds spent the war defending the state from Union forces and Indian raids or making expeditions into New Mexico Territory. Confederate officials and commanders often demanded that Texas contribute larger numbers to the fighting in the Confederate heartland. But Texas Governor Francis Lubbock resisted sending too many young men to fight in Virginia or the Civil War's western front and instead formed "frontier regiments" to protect against Indian attacks.

Maintaining control of the Texas coastline was unquestionably the most important strategic victory of the Confederate forces in Texas. Union efforts to take ports at Corpus Christi and Galveston were rebuffed, and the Texas coastline was often defended against Union attacks. At war's end only Brazos Island was held by Union forces. Maintaining control of key ports along the coast permitted blockade runners to continue shipping Texas cotton to world markets, providing a vital source of foreign exchange. Along the Rio Grande, Union successes in 1863 first cut much of the trade between Texas and Mexico. But Confederate troops under John S. Ford regained Brownsville and reopened this gateway to Mexico in summer 1864. Texas troops also played important roles in combat in Louisiana and Arkansas.

An important Texas presence was felt in battles far from the state's borders as well. Generals Albert Sidney Johnston at Shiloh and John Bell Hood at Chickamauga were among the most prominent Texas commanders during the war. The Texan presence in Confederate cavalry units was often noted, with their superior horsemanship also recognized. Following a rapid rise in the ranks, Hood was appointed brigade commander of a force that would be known and respected as Hood's Texas Brigade. Hood acquired a reputation as a brave but often reckless commander, known for leading his troops personally into assaults on enemy lines.

John Bell Hood (1831–1879)

Gen. John Bell Hood may be the most recognized of Texas' Civil War commanders. His reputation was such that his name graces Fort Hood, the largest military base in the world, between Austin and Waco. Born in Kentucky, Hood came to Texas after 1856 when he was stationed at Fort Mason, on the frontier with the Comanche and where he received his first of many battle wounds. Hood resigned his U.S. military commission after Fort Sumter, but because Kentucky remained neutral, he joined the Confederacy as a Texan. Hood's Texans fought in many of the most important engagements, including Antietam and Gettysburg. At Gettysburg, Hood was severely wounded, losing use of his left arm. After recuperating from this wound, Hood was sent to Tennessee to rejoin his division where he fought at the Battle of Chickamauga. Hood was again wounded severely, and his leg was amputated just below his hip. Nonetheless, he returned to battle, wearing a cork prosthesis bought by the Texas Brigade. Hood was eventually given command of the Army of Tennessee, despite Robert E. Lee's misgivings about his brash and risky nature. Hood was blamed for losing Atlanta to the advancing William Tecumseh Sherman, partly because he tried a diversionary advance on Sherman's rear, leaving the way open for Sherman to march forward with few impediments. Nonetheless, Hood is a revered figure in Texas Civil War lore.

Battle of Galveston (December 31, 1862)

Galveston in 1860 was Texas' second largest city. Two-thirds of Texas' cotton crop was exported to global markets through its port. The port itself was prized, as it provided a protected harbor for the Union's fleet of blockading ships. In July 1861, the USS *South Carolina* was sent to Galveston to enforce the blockade of the port. The civilians fled, fearing that the city would be shelled and invaded. The Confederate troops guarding the port were also forced to withdraw. The Union's naval power, however, failed to hold Galveston. Major General **John B. Magruder** was sent to take charge, and in the Battle of Galveston, his forces retook the city. They held it until June 2, 1865, a full six weeks after Lee's surrender at Appomattox.

John B. Magruder (1807–1871)

Gen. John Bankhead Magruder earned a reputation as an effective military tactician in Virginia's Peninsular Campaign in 1862, but after a less than impressive showing in the ensuing Seven Days Battles, Magruder was relieved of his command in Virginia. He was sent to Texas to command the District of Texas, New Mexico, and Arizona. Magruder repaired his reputation at the Battle of Galveston and with his defense of the Texas coastline.

Battle of Palmito Ranch (May 12, 1865)

The Battle of Palmito Ranch, on the north bank of the Rio Grande, was the last battle of the Civil War, fought nearly a month after the surrender at Appomattox. The battle saw 800 Union troops led by Colonel Theodore Barrett try to take a Confederate encampment east of Brownsville.

Colonel John "RIP" Ford defeated the Union forces. The battle is of little significance other than its taking place well after the war had ended. The Confederate soldiers most likely fought because they doubted the veracity of reports of the surrender. The number of casualties on both sides as well as how captured Texans were treated by the Union army are subjects of historical debate.

> **Competency 011 Descriptive Statement E.** The beginning teacher understands the major effects of Reconstruction on the political, economic, and social life of Texas.

Reconstruction is said to have lasted from the end of the war in 1865 until 1877 when federal troops were withdrawn from the South under false assurances that Southern state governments would protect African Americans from retribution and violence. Without enforcement, efforts to reform the South and transform its economy ended. Over the next 20 years, Southern legislatures gradually erected what would by 1896 be a developed system of segregation, known colloquially as "Jim Crow," and an economic system of share-cropping and tenant farming that held both blacks and poor whites in economic subservience.

Periodization: 1865 to 1877

1865–1866: Presidential Reconstruction—A period of relative leniency toward the ex-Confederates followed the lead of President Andrew Johnson, a Tennessean and former slave owner.

1867–1875: Congressional or Radical Reconstruction—A period of enforced reform was led by Radical Republicans in the U.S. Congress. The period saw increased political participation by African Americans as well as military occupation of the South and the passage of the Reconstruction Amendments (13th–15th).

1873–1877: Redemption—A period of retrenchment and political reaction by Southern Democrats coupled with Northern withdrawal in the aftermath of the economic recession beginning in 1873.

Key Question

How did white Texans re-establish the racial and economic hierarchies that sustained the post–Civil War cotton economy and hold former slaves in a new form of bondage?

On June 2, 1865, nearly two months after Appomattox, Confederate Gen. Edmund Kirby Smith surrendered in Galveston, ending the Civil War in Texas. What surrender would mean for Texans was unclear.

Andrew Johnson, who succeeded Abraham Lincoln as president, had proposed a plan for Reconstruction that required former Confederates to take an oath of allegiance to the United States in exchange for presidential pardon. On June 17, President Johnson appointed Andrew Jackson Hamilton as provisional governor of Texas and issued a proclamation empowering the governor to call a convention composed of Texans who had sworn an oath of allegiance to the United States.

Juneteenth

On June 19, 1865, Union occupation forces under the leadership of General Gordon Granger arrived in Texas and immediately issued General Order No. 3, which declared all slaves in Texas free. The order enforced the Emancipation Proclamation of 1863, and its terms laid out what freedom meant to former slaves. It gave them the same personal and property rights as whites and ensured that the labor relationship between former masters and former slaves would be the same that existed between employers and hired labor. June 19 is therefore remembered annually by African Americans in Texas as the end of slavery in the state.

With the end of slavery, Texas enslavers lost what had been to them vital property and a source of capital. The wealthiest 7 percent of Texans owned some 72 percent of Texas' slaves, and the value has been estimated at over $400 million. The labor value in 2017 terms is more than $2 trillion. Texas landowners still had cotton and sugar plantations and feared they could not make a profit growing cotton, sugar, and other crops without a labor force. How Texas resolved its labor question after slavery's end would set in place a system of labor relations that would persist into the Great Depression.

White Resistance

One provision of Reconstruction required each Confederate state to revise its constitution. In 1866, Texas had adopted a constitution and elected a government. James W. Throckmorton was elected governor, and a convention met to revise the constitution.

Throckmorton and the Texas legislature sought to reinstitute "black codes" designed to control African American labor and to limit their political influence. He also requested that the U.S. Army units stationed in Texas be redirected towards the threat of Indians on the frontier, rather than the protection of the states' freedmen.

This demand was denied, and Throckmorton was removed from office as an "impediment to Reconstruction." Now controlled by radicals unhappy with the leniency of President Johnson's plan, the U.S. Congress refused to recognize the new state constitution. Congress also objected to the passage of a series of laws known as Black Codes. These laws were designed to control the black labor force and provided ample evidence of the unreconstructed nature of the Texas government.

When Congress passed its own plan for Reconstruction in 1867, it demanded that Texans ratify the 13th Amendment ending slavery, renounce secession, and repudiate the state's Confederate war debt. Most Anglo Texans objected to these provisions, which threatened their economic interests and undermined their political control of the state. Vigilante violence and such groups as the Ku Klux Klan proliferated.

Black Codes

Whites did not accept blacks' insistence on their full freedom. In Texas, these codes were almost immediately put in place. The codes were designed to keep African Americans in a subordinate position and to ensure that a black labor force was readily available to continue meeting the needs of Texas' plantation economy. The Texas law granted blacks basic property rights as well as guarantees against discrimination in criminal law. However, they could not hold office, vote, serve on juries, or testify in cases involving whites. They were also forbidden to marry whites. Separate accommodations and segregated public facilities were enshrined by law, as was denying access to public schooling and public lands to black people. Black codes also employed measures to give white landowners immense coercive power over the black labor force. An "apprentice law" let landowners ask the courts to require court-ordered apprenticeships for many minors. Laws also enshrined new forms of labor contracts that gave landowners the power to deduct wages for time-wasting, theft, property destruction, or absences. Vagrancy laws gave courts the right to arrest African Americans defined as idle and to contract them to landowners. While African American men and women were no longer held in bondage, the Black Codes kept them politically powerless and economically constrained while ensuring that the labor force needed by white landowners was still available.

Freedmen's Bureau

The Freedmen's Bureau, as the U.S. Bureau of Refugees, Freedmen, and Abandoned Lands was known, was established in 1865 by Congress to help ex-slaves and poor whites in the South make the transition to the political and economic conditions shaping the South after the Civil War. The Freedmen's Bureau helped former slaves settle on lands confiscated or abandoned during the war. It also provided legal assistance, documentation for marriage and birth records, medical and housing assistance, and schooling for freed blacks. Texas was divided into some 58 subdistricts extending across the eastern half of the state. The bureau was chronically underfunded and faced intimidation from white vigilante organizations. It was active only until 1872 when Congress discontinued it in the face of pressure from Southerners. The Freedmen's Bureau was only marginally successful in improving conditions for African Americans, but without the bureau's presence, former Texas slaves would have faced even greater difficulties in securing even a modicum of freedom.

Joseph B. Kiddoo (1840–1880)

At 26, Joseph B. Kiddoo was appointed assistant commissioner of the Freedmen's Bureau in Texas in May 1866 after a meteoric rise from enlisted man to general. Following Kiddoo's arrival in Texas, he toured the state, talked with planters, and gauged the willingness of Texas' white population to accept African Americans' freedom. He recorded prejudicial attitudes toward African

Americans and bitter resentment at what Texans viewed as the "unconstitutional confiscation" of white property. He also observed that white Texans would re-enslave African Americans if offered the opportunity. Kiddoo thus viewed the Freedmen's Bureau as the African American populace's "guardian and protector." Kiddoo objected to the Black Codes as a subterfuge designed to re-enslave African Americans and recommended that Freedmen's Bureau agents be allowed to abrogate contracts based on the 1866 Black Code. Kiddoo also worked with religious organizations and freedmen's organizations to enable blacks to gain title to land as well as to establish schools for the freedmen's children. He worked with the American Missionary Association to recruit teachers for black schools and protect the teachers from slander, abuse, and intimidation, all of which were common concerns. Kiddoo's program is credited with teaching some 10,000 blacks to read and write. His ability to protect African Americans, however, was severely limited. Given the area under his authority, the paucity of troops to enforce protections of African Americans, and the virulence of the hostility that black men and women faced, Kiddoo failed to accomplish many of his aims. Within a year, Kiddoo had grown frustrated and by January 1867 had been replaced at the helm of the Freedmen's Bureau.

African American Office-Holding

During Radical Reconstruction, Republicans, including many African Americans, served as legislators and officeholders across the South. In Texas, nine African Americans were delegates to the 1867 constitutional convention, and 19 were elected to the Texas Legislature between 1870 and 1876. By comparison to the numbers in such states as South Carolina or Mississippi, which had greater African American populations, the black legislative presence was less significant in Texas. In addition, Texans did not elect any African Americans to the U.S. House or Senate during Reconstruction, as was the case in several Southern states.

A New Labor Regime

In Texas, the Freedmen's Bureau got off to a slow start in 1865, as its appointed head arrived some six months after the end of the war. His absence enabled white former slaveholders to define the new labor regime with little intervention from the Freedmen's Bureau. Prices for cotton and other agricultural products had reached wartime highs in 1865, making it imperative that the crops be harvested. Gen. C.C. Andrews, the military commander of Texas before a provisional government could be put in place, required African Americans to stay with former masters who would treat them as freedmen and encouraged them to contract their labor to others if their former masters were unwilling to pay them a wage. Andrews believed that a fair "share" of the crop—he proposed one-tenth—would be an equitable wage, as most masters could not afford to pay money. Across the South, sharecropping would become the new system of agricultural labor throughout the states. This was true of sharecropping in Texas, although it did not develop immediately from Andrews' administration.

A form of semi-coerced wage system immediately emerged instead. Andrews required freedmen to agree to labor contracts he deemed reasonable. When African Americans refused to accept what he considered fair terms, he authorized the military to compel them to work. Other commanders perpetuated the old pass system, modeled on the passes that slaves had been forced to carry, and required former slaves not to be out and about without their employer's permission. This made it difficult for former slaves to offer their services to anyone but their former masters. Planters then tried to bind their former slaves with signed contracts that offered them wages and established their working conditions. Contracts usually required a five-and-a-half-day work week, at 10 hours a day. Workers were housed, clothed, and fed as they had been under slavery, but with the cost of their maintenance deducted from their wages. Many contracts also required that the former slaves get their employer's permission to leave the plantation. Some contracts established the planters' rights to use physical punishment to ensure hard work. In many ways, this system reproduced slavery and the slave economy.

Despite the threats from the U.S. military and the planters' vigilante violence, a significant labor shortage in 1865 forced planters to accept sharecropping rather than contracted gang-labor. The shortage occurred because many freedmen refused to sign the coercive contracts. They were enabled in this by smaller farmers who had lacked the resources in the antebellum period to buy slaves. After the war, these farmers could afford to hire freedmen. Adding to the labor shortage was the increasing tendency of African American women to refuse field work. Because of the growing labor shortage, cotton planters offered higher wages. But freedmen and women opposed these wage contracts because they replicated the slave system. Instead, they preferred an arrangement letting them farm a plot of land in return for a share of the harvest. In these arrangements, the landowner provided land, a residence, draft animals, tools, seed, and cash advances. The freedmen—and soon enough poor white farmers—provided the labor. At year's end, the laborer kept a quarter to half of the crop, which could then be sold. The landowner got the rest. By the end of 1865, landowners across Texas had adopted the sharecropping system.

> **Competency 011 Descriptive Statement F.** The beginning teacher understands the major causes and effects of the expansion of settlement along the frontier in Texas and of the conflicts between some settlers and American Indian groups (e.g., Quanah Parker, Texas Rangers, Buffalo Soldiers).

Descriptive statements E and F are two sides of a single coin. Descriptive statement E asks beginning teachers to understand how Native Americans after 1865 were rapidly driven from their home ranges by a combination of Texas volunteers and Texas Rangers and most importantly by a coordinated series of military campaigns that fortified the frontier and harried the Comanche, Apache, Kiowa, and other plains Indians into surrender. Because of Indian removal, Texas and the federal government opened a wide swathe of fertile land for cattle grazing and cotton farming. Railroads, stagecoaches, and white farmers rapidly intruded into these now economically accessible and pacified lands, building on the cotton and cattle economies that had marked Texas since the arrival of Austin's settlers in the 1820s.

Key Question

How did Texans open the frontier to economic development at the expense of American Indian groups?

Indian Removal

As an independent nation and then as a part of the United States, Texans expanded into Indian lands via what can be characterized as a policy of ethnic cleansing that gradually (over some 50 years) forced most Indian peoples out of the state.

As an independent nation, of course, the Texas government could establish Indian policy without interference or restraint by the U.S. government. With Texas as its own country, Indian nations also could not do what the Cherokee had done—although unsuccessfully—and appeal to U.S. courts for redress and protection. Unlike the other territorial governments of the West, Texas after U.S. annexation also had unique authority over its lands with little federal oversight. Only after the Civil War did the federal government play a significant role in mediating between Texas' Indians and the increasing Anglo-Texan population.

Despite claims by the Mexican government and then the Texas republic, most of Texas in the 1830s was controlled by Indian peoples. As settlers moved up the Trinity, Colorado, Brazos, Nueces, and San Antonio rivers, they encountered well-established Native American populations. As white settlers encroached on Indian lands, they engaged in widespread violence to drive Indians from their territories. For example, in the 1850s two reservations were established on the upper Brazos when a campaign was started by John R. Baylor, nephew of the namesake of Baylor University, in his newspaper *The Whiteman*. It called for expelling the Indians from the reservations and exterminating those who resisted. A vigilante campaign ensued, and despite efforts by Indian agents and federal troops to defend the reservations, federal officials determined the better part of valor required removing the Indians from their reservations and sending them to the Indian Territory (Oklahoma). More than 1,000 Comanches, Caddos, Wichitas, Shawnees, Delawares, and Tonkawas were forced to leave their homes to be settled across Oklahoma. The Indian agent who tried to avoid this eventuality was murdered in cold blood by Patrick Murphy, a vigilante leader.

Instead of establishing peace, the removal of these reservation Indians made the frontier a much more violent and dangerous place for white settlers. The lawlessness engendered by vigilantism also provided cover for other violence as well as banditry, horse rustling, and flight from law enforcement. Much violence on the frontier had little to do with Indian raids. Indian raids also often provided a pretext for federal reprisals. The Civil War also increased the violence on the frontier. With the end of the war, as white settlement increased and the bison herds diminished, Comanche and Kiowa Indians on the southern plains were driven to increased desperation. A more violent generation of Indians, who didn't trust the promises of federal Indian agents, struck in a vengeance at ranchers, farmers, and buffalo hunters who entered the *comancheria*, as the Comanche territories were known. Led by Gen. William Tecumseh Sherman, the U.S. Army set about to end these attacks. The Comanche and Kiowa faced an adversary unlike any they had encountered. The tactics used in the "Red River War," mirrored the total war strategy Sherman used against the South during the Civil War.

Quanah Parker (1845–1911)

Born in 1850, Quanah Parker was the son of a Noconi Comanche chief and Cynthia Ann Parker, a white girl taken captive during a raid on Parker's Fort, Texas. In 1860, his mother was recaptured and his father was killed, leaving Quanah orphaned and a refugee to the Quahada Comanches. The Quahada refused to accept the Treaty of Medicine Lodge in 1867, and Parker became one of the leaders of the fugitive bands of Comanche who were unwilling to accept the strictures of reservation life. He stands as one of the most important Comanche leaders following the Civil War, and the Quahadas essentially controlled the southern Great Plains for seven years. He raided into Texas and Mexico, attacking buffalo hunters and avoiding capture by the U.S. Army from 1867 to 1875. Parker and his band eventually surrendered at Fort Sill, Oklahoma, not long after a disastrous raid on a group of buffalo hunters at Adobe Walls. The band was then confined to a reservation in the southwestern corner of Oklahoma, and Quanah was named chief of the Comanche. Parker's ability to cross cultural boundaries helped the Comanche. Parker counseled a degree of cooperation and assimilation as a means of survival. Parker also became quite rich through a series of careful investments in railroad stock and leasing agreements with cattlemen. Despite his apparent assimilation, Parker nonetheless remained polygamous, rejected Christianity, wore his hair long and braided, and continued to use peyote in religious rites.

Buffalo Soldiers

During the Civil War, more than 180,000 African American troops fought in the U.S. Army. Following the war, while most segregated units were disbanded, two regiments of cavalry and six regiments of infantry were retained. The 9th and 10th U.S. Cavalry and the 24th and 25th U.S. Infantry regiments then played an important role across the West during the Indian Wars of the 1860s and 1870s. The plains Indians called these troopers "buffalo soldiers," a sign of respect and a comment on their curly hair. Black regular army soldiers served from 1866 to the 1890s across the frontier, notably in Texas.

Texas Rangers

The Texas Rangers trace their origin to a group of "rangers," or irregular fighters, hired by Stephen F. Austin in 1823 to carry out a raid against a group of Indians accused of stealing from Austin's settlement. The term was used again in 1826 when Austin tried to defend his colony against Indian attacks. A force of 20 to 30 Rangers were to be kept ready. Whether this force was raised is unclear, but clear evidence shows a unit known as the Texas Rangers in late 1835. During the Texas Revolution, three companies of Texas Rangers were established to guard the frontier, mostly against Indian incursions, showing the first purpose of the Rangers was to protect Texans from Indian attacks. They served little role in the fighting of the Texas Revolution. This relative inactivity continued until Mirabeau Lamar's election and the start of more bellicose frontier policy. The Texas Rangers were called upon to carry out much of this policy. Their number was increased, and they were directed against the Comanche and Cherokee as well as other Indian groups. Following their success in these "Indian Wars," they were also charged with repelling the Mexican invasions in 1842.

During the Mexican War, the Texas Rangers received national interest as a fighting force. Following the Mexican War, however, the Rangers were largely a volunteer force and raised when needed. For example, when Juan Cortina took the city of Brownsville in 1859, a group of Texas Rangers joined with the vigilante group known as the Brownsville Tigers to end the uprising. During the Civil War, the Rangers were again called upon mainly to protect the frontier from Indian attacks. Following Reconstruction, the Texas Rangers were called upon to address continued threats on the frontier and end the increased lawlessness in the state. The Rangers then became more involved in law enforcement. During this period, the Rangers arrested such criminals as the gunslinger John Wesley Hardin and the bank robber Sam Bass.

During the early 20th century, the Texas Rangers earned a reputation along the Mexican border as a repressive force that routinely carried out extra-judicial killings and intimidated the state's Hispanic population. Some 5,000 Mexicans and Mexican Americans may have been killed in South and West Texas between 1914 and 1919. In response to complaints about the Rangers' brutality along the border, the force was reorganized and efforts were made to recruit more professional staff.

During the 1920s, the Rangers were called upon to enforce Prohibition and bring order to the oil boom towns in addition to their traditional law enforcement. During the Depression, the Rangers ended several important crime sprees, most famously that of Bonnie and Clyde. However, because of the Rangers' partisan politics during the 1930s, their professionalism and nonpartisanship were again questioned. Only through a series of reforms that increased their professionalization and resources did the Texas Rangers regain their reputation as an elite, nonpartisan, and professional law enforcement agency.

> **Competency 011 Descriptive Statement G.** The beginning teacher demonstrates knowledge of the impact of major economic and technological developments in Texas in the period 1821 to 1900.

Cotton and Slavery in Texas

Southern-style slavery arrived in Texas with its first Anglo-American *empresario*, Stephen F. Austin. The cotton-producing regions of antebellum Texas were in its Southeast region, which thus had the state's heaviest concentration of slaves. The slaves represented a vital source of labor for the state. Without the labor of the enslaved, the state's early prosperity is hard to envision. The slaves cleared land, tilled the soil, and planted and picked crops. Although slaveholders represented only a third of the state's farmers, their plantations produced more than 90 percent of its cotton. By 1860, the state produced nearly one-half million bales of cotton. Given the profitability of slaveholding, the number of slaves in Texas grew. In the first year of statehood, Texas had 31,099 slaves. By 1855, that number had grown to more than 105,000, almost a quarter of the population. Slaves were more than a labor force. The assessed value of enslaved Texans in 1855 was just over $53 million. By comparison, the assessed value of all the land in productive use in the state was $58.7 million. As property, mortgaged slaves also served as the collateral behind much of the state's economic expansion before 1865.

Cotton Country after the Civil War

Cotton continued to be king in Texas well after the Civil War. By 1900 the state produced more than 3.5 million bales of cotton. While cotton crops relied on enslaved labor through the Civil War and then on African American sharecroppers during Reconstruction, the new cotton lands were worked by European immigrants or migrants from the Deep South who worked as tenant farmers or sharecroppers, buying their supplies, foods, tools, and other items on account and settling their debts at the end of the growing year. This crop-lien system remained the practice until the Great Depression.

Transportation

Texas' transportation infrastructure developed slowly over the 19th century. The first settlers followed Indian and game trails through the forests and prairies, and the Spanish developed two arteries that connected the Rio Grande to East Texas. The El Camino Real linked East Texas to the Rio Grande Valley through San Antonio. This same route reached farther south to Mexico City. A second route, also known as the Camino Real, passed through Goliad to the Sabine River. By the mid-19th century, several roads linked the interior with coastal towns and connected much of the eastern half of the state. Despite the development of these roads, the state was underserved by effective transportation arteries until the last few decades of the 19th century.

An effort to improve statewide communication and connect East Texas to El Paso as well as New Mexico and California was the brainchild of Henry Skillman. He acquired a contract with the U.S. postmaster general to develop a passenger and mail service from Indianola on the Gulf Coast through San Antonio, with two routes that converged in El Paso. Although Skillman lost his contract, he formed a partnership with George H. Giddings to create a network of horse-drawn coaches, stationed across the state in stages — hence "stagecoaches" — to transport passengers and mail. For heavy and bulky cargo, Texans used mule- or ox-drawn carts.

Rail construction lagged behind the rest of the country. The first rail line began in 1853, connecting Harrisburg and Richmond along 30 miles of track. In 1854, railroad companies were granted 16 sections, roughly 10,000 acres, for each mile of track laid, which proved insufficient incentive. By 1860, Texas had only 400 miles of track, and as late as 1873, not quite 600 miles. In 1876, government land subsidies again were used to encourage investment in rail construction. For laying just under 3,000 miles of rail lines, 40 railroads got more than 32 million acres. One of the largest recipients of these grants, Jay Gould's Texas and Pacific Railroad, now part of Union Pacific, is still one of Texas' largest landowners.

Cattle Ranching

The establishment of rail heads would have much impact on Texas ranching. By 1865, an estimated 5 million head of cattle ranged across Texas. Through the 1860s, however, much of the profitability of cattle production was earned by salting or pickling the beef, selling hides, or rendering the fat for tallow. The market for beef existed in East Coast cities, but the difficulty was getting beef to market. Joseph G. McCoy, however, had convinced a railroad entrepreneur to establish a cow town with pens, corrals, and other amenities in Abilene, Kansas. McCoy believed that by directing Texas cattle to Abilene, they could be redirected to the cities whose residents were hungry for beef. Cattle valued at $5 a head in South Texas could be sold for between $30 and $85 in northern cities. Between 1867 and 1871, an estimated 1.5 million head of cattle were driven to Abilene. Between 1872 and 1875 more than 1 million were driven to Dodge City. Some 10 million head of cattle may have been driven north from Texas between 1867 and 1890. But too many cattlemen or would-be cattlemen as well as overstocking, over-grazing, drought, and more refined tastes resulted in a gradual diminishment of open-range cattle herding and cattle drives. Ranchers, such as Mifflin Kenedy and Richard King, who fenced their lands to protect grazing lands and water rights, soon secured both finance capital and legal protections. This enabled large ranchers to dominate the Texas grasslands.

> **Competency 011 Descriptive Statement H.** The beginning teacher understands the impact of major geographic features of Texas on migration, settlement patterns and economic development and how various groups altered the natural environment.

Texas is composed of several geographical regions, each having helped shape migration, settlement patterns, and economic development. The state's development during the late 19th century, however, mainly represented an extension of the pre–Civil War cotton and ranching economy, with consequences for the natural environment.

Southeast Texas

East Texas, divided from West Texas at the 98th meridian, was settled first and is still home to two-thirds of the state's population. The earliest Anglo-American settlers moved most easily into the area's coastal plains, where cotton flourished. To the west, in what would become known as the Texas Sugar Bowl, vast sugar cane and rice fields provided additional economic growth and incentive for migration.

North of the coastal plains, in the Pine Belt, another source of wealth became available with the development of rail lines through the state. Before the 1870s the Pine Belt was exploited locally, except where access to a waterway permitted timbers to be floated to water-powered saw mills. When railroads cut through East Texas, lumber producers in the area sold over 1 billion board feet of wood, valued at $12 million. Before the discovery of oil in 1901, lumber was the most profitable source of state income after cotton and cattle. By 1900 more than 7,900 men worked in this industry.

North Texas and the Panhandle

The area of North Texas extending east from the Caprock Escarpment along the southern bank of the Red River to the Pine Belt in East Texas proved to be a fertile ground for expanding cotton production after the Civil War. Before the end of the Indian Wars, the area's westernmost part was subjected to Indian attacks that discouraged settlement, but after 1870 an influx of cotton farmers moved north and west into the area. When connected to transcontinental rails, the Fort Worth cattle pens also drew residents. The path of migration into the area was an extension of Southern migration into Texas before the war.

The Panhandle of Texas probably saw its first significant Anglo-American settlement after 1876. Before then, buffalo hunters, soldiers, and the occasional mule team passed through what was Indian country. With the Indians driven out, the Panhandle entered a new phase. Cattle drives brought livestock and cowboys, who at first were just passing through on their way to Kansas railheads. But with the introduction of heavy, cast-iron plows that could break the heavy virgin soils and with the laying of a rail line across the plains, new possibilities for agricultural development were opened up. In 1887, Amarillo was founded and became a cattle-shipping center. The Panhandle was largely settled by Midwesterners, usually transplanted Germans, Norwegians, Russians, and Czechs. Quaker communities from Indiana resettled, as did Catholics from across the Midwest. With their arrival, wheat farming became the primary grain crop, and farmers diversified with sheep, hogs, chickens, and later alfalfa, soybeans, etc.

South Texas

In South Texas, cattle ranching had long been important to the economy and culture, and the Mexican-American War drew more Anglo-Americans into ranching. The most famous Anglo-American ranchers, Mifflin Kenedy and Richard King, for example, had come to the region to supply Zachary Taylor's army. They invested their earnings in ranch lands in the Nueces strip. Kenedy established a sheep ranch in Hidalgo County. King, a steamboat captain, bought a Spanish land grant near the Santa Gertrudis creek. During the Civil War, Kenedy and King supplied English buyers with Confederate cotton, increasing their land holdings with the accumulated profits. When the two parted ways in 1868, it took over a year to round up and divide their respective livestock holdings. Kenedy sold his 242,000-acre holding to a Scottish firm. Before selling,

Kenedy had been among the first Texas ranchers to fence his property. King found a unique way to staff his ranch. On a trip to Mexico to acquire cattle, he convinced some 100 men and their families to move from Mexico to herd his cattle. These *kineños*, or King's men, remained the backbone of the King Ranch operation until recently. The ranch remained in family hands until the 1990s when it became a publicly held corporation.

Competency 011 Descriptive Statement I. The beginning teacher demonstrates knowledge of major cultural developments in Texas in the period 1821 to 1900.

Key Question

What explains the cultural diversity that developed between 1821 and 1900?

Southern Roots

Texans often debate the degree to which Texas is "Southern" or "Western" in its political culture and character. From the establishment of Austin's colony, Texas was settled mainly by Southerners and their slaves and was a slave state and a part of the Confederacy. The first wave of this population growth occurred between 1845 and 1861, when Southerners poured into the state, bringing their slaves and searching for cheap land. Alabama and Tennessee provided most of these settlers. A fourth of white Texans came from these two states, although Tennessee migrants were less likely to own slaves. Tennessee migrants were more often "poor whites" on the make, hoping to change their fortunes by moving to Texas. These migrants settled in the eastern third of the state where the climate and proximity to coastal ports enabled them to both harvest their crop and easily market it.

The Civil War saw emigration to Texas decrease, but after the war, a renewed migration began into the southeastern corner as well as into the grassland ranges of West Texas and the Panhandle. As the Indians were pushed from the region or forced onto reservations, new land was made available for cotton and then winter wheat. The cattle boom of the 1870s and 1880s, coupled with the increase in sheep- and goat-grazing, brought an influx of Southerners to the range lands. They often competed with Mexican herdsmen and former slaves for work.

The Confederate defeat and the long efforts to efface its memory and defend Southern institutions and white supremacy were as important as the Southern migration itself in shaping the state's Southern character. Over the 19th century, Black Codes, Jim Crow segregation, and the remembrances of both the Texas Revolution and the Civil War formed a powerful cultural framework that helped define political and cultural solidarities.

European Immigration

The largest population of European immigrants to Texas came from Germany. Many of the earliest Germans to emigrate to Texas were convinced to do so by Friedrich Diercks, known in Texas as Johann Friedrich Ernst. He got a grant in Stephen F. Austin's colony and wrote to German friends and associates about the abundance and opportunity in Texas. A German association in the Rhineland was established and organized to facilitate emigration to Texas. Most Germans settled in ethnic enclaves across East and Central Texas, with some 7,000 settling between 1844 and 1847. By 1900 more than 48,000 German immigrants lived in Texas. Many Texas towns still bear the cultural imprint of this German immigration. They include Fredericksburg, Castroville, New Braunfels, Groene, and many others that make the so-called German Belt. At one time, German language schools, newspapers, and radio stations flourished.

In the 1840s and 1850s, Irish immigrants fleeing the potato famine also made their way to Texas.

Eastern Europeans also arrived before and after the Civil War. One immigrant group came from Poland. Like the Germans, the Poles spread across Central and Southeast Texas, establishing small towns and farming communities. After the Civil War, many were recruited as tenant farmers by plantation owners to replace former slaves. In 1851, Czechs also arrived, slowly at first and then in larger numbers. The 1900 census counted more than 9,200 Czech immigrants. Other European populations came in smaller numbers before 1900, adding more diversity.

African American Cultural Contributions

As landowners turned to European tenant farmers, African Americans migrated to the peripheries of cities like Dallas, Austin, Houston, Beaumont, and San Antonio. Cities were not immune to Jim Crow segregation and vigilante violence, but as African Americans congregated in numbers, they better enabled their self-defense and created institutions that permitted greater independence and fostered self-respect. In these "freedmen's towns," they built churches, businesses, cooperative and benevolent societies and other institutions. Houston, for example, attracted large numbers of freedmen and women from the sugar plantations in Fort Bend County and from the cotton growing region of East Texas. By 1870, Houston was 40 percent African American. Black neighborhoods sprang up south and west of the city center. Houses were built from cypress trees, streets were lined with brick cobblestones, a black college was founded, and political associations were formed. In response to increased segregation over the 19th century, African Americans in Houston—as they did in other cities—promoted their own culture. When blacks were banned from Fourth of July Festivities, they celebrated Juneteenth with barbecues and music. Excluded from Houston's baseball team, the "Buffaloes," African Americans formed their own team, the Houston Black Buffaloes. These cultural institutions not only sustained the African American community but also enriched the wider society.

COMPETENCY 012 (TEXAS IN THE TWENTIETH AND TWENTY-FIRST CENTURIES)

The teacher understands significant historical developments and events in Texas from 1900 to the present.

Competency 012 Descriptive Statement A. The beginning teacher understands the impact of individuals and reform movements such as the Progressive movement and the Civil Rights movement on Texas in the late nineteenth and twentieth centuries (e.g., Jane McCallum, Lulu Belle Madison White, Manuel C. Gonzales, Oveta Culp Hobby, James Hogg, Hector Garcia).

Key Question

How did Texans participate in the key reform movements of 20th century America, beginning with the Progressive movement and especially with the Civil Rights struggle?

Periodization: 1900 to the Present

James S. Hogg (1851–1906)

James Hogg was the first Texas governor born in the state. He served from 1891 to 1895 and advocated progressive policies. He also pursued anti-trust actions against railway magnates like Jay Gould. Under Hogg, Texas passed what came to be known as the "Hogg Laws," which established the Railroad Commission to regulate railway corporations and included laws to regulate railway financial instruments, limit railroad land holdings, and reduce railroad companies' influence on local and municipal governments. Hogg also promoted and supported the state's universities and teacher-training colleges. Hogg was especially active in seeking to protect public land to invest it in education.

Jane McCallum (1877–1957)

A prominent Texas progressive, Jane McCallum was a suffragist and temperance advocate. After attending the University of Texas and marrying, McCallum was elected president of the Austin Women's Suffrage Association and campaigned for a state constitutional amendment granting women the right to vote. She was also state chairman of the ratification committee on the 19th Amendment to the U.S. Constitution. A member of what became known as the "Petticoat Lobby," McCallum promoted education and prison reform and advocated prohibition of alcohol sales and consumption as well as child labor laws, health care funding, and other progressive causes. She served as Secretary of State from 1927 to 1933 and remained active in Texas politics until shortly before her death. She also wrote books and articles about Texas women.

Lulu Belle Madison White (1907–1957)

In the early 1940s, Lulu B. White complained that the "colored" waiting room in a Houston train station was kept dark much later than the "whites only" waiting room. This vocal protest exemplified how White challenged the Southern system of racial segregation. After a brief career as a teacher, Lulu B. Madison married Julius White, a successful Houston business executive and worked as a community activist. In the 1930s, she became an important voice in the Houston chapter of the National Association for the Advancement of Colored People and later served as a director of the NAACP state branch. Her accomplishments included eliminating the practice of "white primaries." Texas passed a white primary law in 1923 to prevent blacks from voting in primary elections. White led the NAACP struggle against this law, and the Supreme Court in *Smith v. Allwright* in 1944 declared the practice unconstitutional. In 1945, White convinced Heman Marion Sweatt to agree to sue the University of Texas Law School. He had met all requirements for entry but was denied because of his race. Sweatt argued that because no law school existed for African Americans, he should have been admitted. The Supreme Court agreed. Rather than unequivocally open the law school to people of color, the state instead developed a parallel system of legal education for African Americans. But in 1950–51 Sweatt enrolled in the University of Texas Law School. Although this case did not end the doctrine of separate but equal, it helped undermine the legal justifications of *Plessy v. Ferguson*.

Oveta Culp Hobby (1905–1995)

Oveta Culp Hobby in 1953 was appointed by President Dwight D. Eisenhower to be the first secretary of the U.S. Department of Health, Education, and Welfare. During World War II, she had been placed in charge of the Women's Army Auxiliary Corps, later the Women's Army Corps, after studying how women could play a larger role in the war effort. She was awarded the Distinguished Service Medal for her military service, becoming the first woman to be so recognized. These two roles represented the crowning achievements of a long life of service and learning. She had been the Texas House of Representatives parliamentarian, serving while she attended the University of Texas. She was a clerk for the Banking Commission and active in codifying state banking laws. She was a leading Democratic Party campaign organizer, though her only run for elected office ended in defeat. In 1931, she married William Hobby, the 27th Texas governor and the publisher of the *Houston Post*. Throughout her life, she wrote, edited, and helped manage the *Post*, while also assuming many civic duties in Houston and the state.

Manuel C. Gonzales (1900–1986)

A leading early Mexican-American civil rights activist and political leader, Manuel C. Gonzales helped found several Mexican-American civil rights organizations, including the League of

United Latin American Citizens in 1929. He ran for several local and state political offices between 1930 and the 1970s. He also wrote often and in many publications to support Mexican-American rights and was a trustee in San Antonio's Junior College system.

LULAC

The League of United Latin American Citizens was founded in Corpus Christi to bring together several similar Hispanic Civil Rights organizations. Hispanic veterans of World War I led in LULAC's founding. In its objectives and organization, LULAC paralleled the NAACP, but its leaders did not see much advantage in uniting with the African American Civil Rights movement, partly because members feared that defining their cause as racial rather than cultural and linguistic would increase discrimination against Hispanic Americans. Still, LULAC used many methods of African American activists: organizing voter-registration drives, petitioning the legislature, and engaging in legal challenges to segregation. LULAC's support for cases challenging the racial segregation of Mexican-American students—*Del Rio v. Salvatierra* (1930), *Mendez v. Westminster* (1945) and *Minerva Delgado v. Bastrop ISD* (1948)—helped establish precedents that would lead to *Brown v. Board of Education* (1954).

Hector P. Garcia (1914–1996)

Hector P. Garcia was born in Mexico before the Mexican Revolution. His family fled to the United States in 1918, living in the Rio Grande Valley. After attending the University of Texas and then graduating from medical school, Garcia volunteered for the military in 1942 and served until the end of the war. In 1946, he moved to Corpus Christi to open a medical practice. After participating in LULAC, Garcia helped found the American GI Forum in March 1948 to struggle for equal rights for Hispanic Americans. The organization focused first on inequalities in the distribution of benefits through the GI Bill of Rights of 1944. Garcia and the American GI Forum also protested when a funeral home in Three Rivers, Texas refused to do the proper burial of a young Hispanic GI, Private Felix Longoria, who was killed in the Philippines during the last days of World War II. The Three Rivers cemetery also maintained a segregated area for "Mexican" burials. After contacting the funeral home director and the cemetery, Garcia carried out a campaign to contact Texas legislators to redress this injustice. U.S. Sen. Lyndon B. Johnson arranged to have Felix Longoria buried in Arlington National Cemetery. The Felix Longoria affair galvanized Mexican American citizens across Texas. Garcia also participated in Democratic Party politics, coordinating the Viva Kennedy–Viva Johnson outreach to Hispanic voters. His role in the Mexican-American Civil Rights movement and his efforts to improve living conditions for Mexican Americans in South Texas contributed to his reputation as a leading figure in the Civil Rights movement in Texas and the nation.

Heman Marion Sweatt (1912–1982)

The Supreme Court decision in *Sweatt v. Painter* (1950) was among the important cases leading to *Brown v. Board of Education* (1954), which overturned the principle of "separate but equal" established in *Plessy v. Ferguson* (1896). Heman Marion Sweatt, an African American teacher and substitute mail carrier, applied to enroll in the University of Texas Law School in 1946. Despite qualifying for acceptance, he was denied entrance because the Texas Constitution forbade integrated education. The state district court that first heard the case postponed its decision to give the state time to establish a law school for black students in Houston at the Texas State University for Negroes, now Texas Southern University. Rather than accept this remedy, Sweatt, backed by the NAACP, appealed the decision but was denied in the state's appellate courts. Eventually, the case was argued before the U.S. Supreme Court, with Thurgood Marshall serving as one of Sweatt's lawyers. Marshall argued that the resources and faculty of this institution were not equal to those available to white students at the University of Texas. The Supreme Court agreed and overturned the lower court's rulings. In September 1950, Sweatt enrolled in the University of Texas Law School.

Integration in Education and Sports in Texas

Brown v. Board of Education of Topeka (1954) overturned the "separate but equal" principle that formed the basis for Jim Crow segregation of schools. Like most Southern states, Texas fought hard to sustain the practice. Allen Shivers, a vocal opponent of integration, proved so popular that in 1952 he ran for governor as the nominee of both major parties, appearing on the ballot as a Democrat and a Republican, the former defeating the latter. He ran and won again in 1954. When African American students inspired by *Brown v. Board* sued to integrate Mansfield ISD in a Fort Worth suburb, the district became the first in the state to be placed under a federal court order to desegregate. The city mayor and police chief as well as a mob of 300 whites tried to stop three black students from registering in the fall of 1956. Shivers sent the Texas Rangers to support the segregationists and permitted the school district to bus its students to Fort Worth schools, thereby nullifying the effect of the federal court order. Shivers' success inspired Arkansas Governor Orval Faubus to obstruct the integration of Little Rock Central High School in 1957, resulting in President Dwight Eisenhower's ordering the 101st Airborne to enforce the federal law. Additional state and local legislation was passed to delay integration of Texas schools, but many school districts quietly followed the law. Austin, San Antonio, San Angelo, El Paso, and Corpus Christi as well as some 120 smaller districts by 1957 were integrating their schools.

Public and private universities in Texas were important battlefields in the struggle to end segregation. African Americans in Texas before the 1960s mainly depended on historically black colleges and universities (HBCUs) for post-secondary education. The state has nine active HBCUs, with the best known Prairie View A&M and Texas Southern University. The first colleges and universities to integrate their classes were Del Mar College in Corpus Christi in 1952 and Southern Methodist University and Texas Western College (UTEP) in 1955. The University of North Texas and Lamar College followed in 1956.

Sports encouraged wider integration in Texas society. Gil Steinke of Texas A&I, now Texas A&M University—Kingsville, was among the earliest proponents of integrating football. In 1960, Steinke recruited Sid Blanks, the first African American to get a football scholarship from a Texas university. In 1967, Texas A&M (College Station) granted its first scholarships to African American athletes. Two years later, the University of Texas recruited African Americans to the Longhorn football team. One of the most important national events involving the integration of Texas sports teams occurred in 1966 when Texas Western University's basketball team defeated the University of Kentucky basketball powerhouse. Kentucky was coached by Adolph Rupp, who refused to recruit African-American players. Texas Western, now the University of Texas at El Paso or UTEP, was coached by Don Haskins whose integrated team fielded five African American starters in the title game.

> **Competency 012 Descriptive Statement B.** The beginning teacher understands the political, economic, cultural and social impacts of major events in the twentieth century, including World War I, the Great Depression, World War II and the Cold War on the history of Texas.

Texas has boasted a long military tradition, most often associated with the Texas Revolution, Mexican American War, and the Civil War. From these conflicts, Texans developed confidence that Texas soldiers were courageous and capable. This military ethos remains important to many Texans' identity. The conflicts of the 20th and 21st centuries have deepened this conviction. This description also calls attention to Texans involvement in the Great Depression and the Cold War. This book will discuss both.

World War I

Long before Congress declared war in 1917, Texans had been on the front lines preparing for a German-Mexican invasion of the state. The Texas National Guard had been mobilized in March 1916 in response to Pancho Villa's raid into New Mexico. The Zimmermann Telegram, promising that Mexico would regain its lost territories, including Texas, if it joined the war on the German side had outraged Texans and heightened the urgency of the defensive preparations of the National Guard. When war was declared in April 1917, nearly 1 million Texans registered for the draft, and 198,000 Texans saw service in the war. Some 5,170 Texans died in combat, and four were awarded the Congressional Medal of Honor.

As in World War II, Texas would be an important staging ground. Military installations and training facilities were built across the state.

World War I contributed to heightening ethnic and racial tensions in Texas, although many Texans of Mexican heritage and many African Americans from Texas served in the military. Many in the Tejano community volunteered for enlistment. In Kingsville, some 100 Tejano men volunteered upon hearing of the declaration of war. Of the 198,000 Texans who volunteered, more than 5,000 had Hispanic surnames. World War I gave Tejanos an opportunity to serve and claim the full citizenship conferred by service. Many Texans of Mexican descent, however, fled to Mexico to avoid conscription. The memory of recent atrocities committed by the Texas Rangers across South Texas and throughout the Texas borderlands against the Hispanic population soured their willingness to sacrifice for a nation that considered them second-class citizens.

The arrival of African American troops in Texas highlighted the contrast between the ideals for which the nation was supposedly at war and the strengthening of Jim Crow segregation. The construction of Camp Logan near Houston led to one of the most unfortunate incidents of the war. On Aug. 23, 1917, a pitched battle erupted between black soldiers stationed as guards at Camp Logan and white police officers and Houston residents. Twenty people were killed. Secretary of War Newton D. Baker said the fight was caused by Houston's Jim Crow laws. African American soldiers off base in Houston refused to abide by segregation ordinances. Hearing rumors that a mob was preparing to attack the camp, more than 100 African American soldiers armed themselves and attacked residential neighborhoods nearby as well as the police sent to quell the violence. Houston was placed under martial law. After a hurried investigation and series of court-martials, 19 African American soldiers were executed and 41 were imprisoned for life. Scholarship on the riot suggests that many of those arrested and some of those executed were innocent.

The Great Depression

As it was worldwide, the Great Depression in Texas was not simply an economic downturn, It also posed an existential crisis. Texans first felt insulated from the crisis, which seemed distant and limited to the financial sector. The oil boom shielded many Texans during the first two years of the downturn. Tenant farmers and sharecroppers, who had suffered from depressed agricultural prices throughout the 1920s, failed to notice the difference in their condition before and after the 1929 stock market collapse. But by 1932 the Depression had hit Texas, and 400,000 Texans were unemployed.

The Texas Panhandle was devastated by the Dust Bowl. Drought and "black blizzards," as the towering dust storms were sometimes called, ripped the parched topsoil. Between 1935 and 1937, about one-third of families living in the Panhandle left their farms, taking to the open road to look for work in California, Arizona, or elsewhere. They joined the ranks of the "Okies," as these migrants were disparagingly called. This farm exodus transformed Texas from a rural state to one with an urban majority. New Deal policies would exacerbate this migration.

For women, the Great Depression had contradictory effects. As farm prices fell, women in landowning and farming families had to economize. Many women took in boarders or did laundry, earning cash but adding to their household duties. In urban areas, women entered the workforce. A quarter of Anglo and Mexican-American women and more than half of African American women worked for wages. Women were often paid half the wages men got. The iconic wartime image of Rosie the Riveter is most often associated with the rise of women's employment, but the Great Depression may have been as significant in drawing women to work for wages.

For minorities, the Depression was especially harsh. At the start of the Depression, nearly 700,000 Mexicans and Mexican Americans lived in Texas. Many were long-term residents and U.S. citizens. Most lived in its southwestern corner. Most were agricultural workers, either migrants following the harvests across the country or settled Texas farm laborers, but an important minority were employed in manufacturing, service, or the professions. As the Depression worsened, between 200,000 and 250,000 Mexicans and Mexican Americans in Texas were "repatriated" or forcibly deported to Mexico. Conservative estimates suggest as many as 1 million Mexicans and Mexican Americans were expelled from the country. Repatriation and deportation took place without clear coordination from the federal or state government. Instead, local authorities and employers made it clear that workers of Mexican descent were no longer welcome and that relief or charity would no longer be extended to them. Repatriation often meant a county agent's knock on the door and this recommendation: "You would be better off in Mexico. Here are your train tickets." When these measures were insufficient, deportation raids were used to remove Mexicans from Texas. These peaked in 1931 but continued sporadically throughout the 1930s.

World War II

Texas' contributions to the war in World War II effort were significant. Although the state had only 5 percent of the U.S. population, more than 7 percent of U.S. military deaths were Texans, numbering more than 22,000. Nearly 830,000 Texans served. Lt. Audie Murphy and Sgt. Jim Logan were among the most decorated soldiers of the war, and Commander Sam Dealey was the most decorated naval officer. They were Texans, as were 30 other Congressional Medal of Honor winners. Texans were prominent military leaders, with more than 150 generals and 12 admirals. More than 12,000 Texas women served in the Women's Army Corps (WAC) and other women's auxiliary forces. They included Col. Oveta Culp Hobby, the WAC commander. Texas was also home to some 80 military installations, including army bases, airfields, naval air stations, and other training facilities. Some 1.25 million troops were trained across Texas, and many would return to Texas after the war. If not, they contributed their paychecks to the industries that served the troops during the war.

Texans were integrated into the American military, but several divisions had a Texas flavor. The 36th Infantry Division, often called the "Lone Star Division," began as a Texas National Guard unit but was activated in 1940 to prepare for deployment if war started. One battalion, the 131st Field Artillery, which had been dispatched to the Philippines and diverted to Dutch Indonesia on the news of the Pearl Harbor attack, was defeated in Java. Most of the unit were taken prisoner, and the battalion became known as "The Lost Battalion." As prisoners, they were forced to work on the Burma-Siam Railway, made famous in the movie *The Bridge on the River Kwai*. Most of the 36th Infantry Division, however, fought in Europe. Although the 36th was deployed to North Africa, the division played little role in the fighting, instead training and serving as guard for some 25,000 Axis prisoners of war. Its first combat in the European theater was the invasion of the Italian mainland at the Battle of Salerno. The 36th was the first American division to see action in Europe. The division fought in the amphibious landing at Salerno and advanced up the Italian peninsula, participating in the bloody fighting around Monte Cassino and entering Rome in early June 1944. The 36th Infantry then was involved in the assault on southern France and the advance into Germany, fighting for 400 days before being returned to the Texas National Guard in December 1945.

While Texans' combat role has been more celebrated, Texas also played a significant role in arming the nation. Ammunition was produced in the Lone Star Army Ammunition Plants in Texarkana and Harrison County. Airplane factories scattered across North Texas built the P-51 Mustang and B-24 Liberator as well as countless other fighters, bombers, and training planes. Corpus Christi, Houston, Galveston, and Port Arthur shipyards built military vessels, and the Dallas Ford plant produced thousands of jeeps and army trucks. Oil production also was critical to the war effort. The Texas defense industry employed hundreds of thousands of rural Texans who flocked to cities for better-paying employment as well as nearly a half-million non-residents who came to work in Texas. Many stayed after the war.

Domestic contributions to the war effort included the numerous prisoner-of-war camps scattered throughout Texas. At least 24 facilities housed prisoners from the Axis powers, including 50,000 Germans, 5,000 Italians, and 1,000 Japanese who spent time in Texas POW camps.

Hispanic and African Americans in Texas were also affected by World War II.

Before December 1941, Mexican Americans in Texas already were enlisting when the U.S. Army took volunteers. Military service provided honorable employment and advancement Tejanos were often denied. In Texas and nationwide, Mexican American youth served in higher percentages than any other ethnic or racial group. Five Texans of Mexican heritage were awarded the Congressional Medal of Honor.

African Americans also served in large numbers. More than 257,000 black Texans served, with many in segregated units. Among the black Texans who gained acclaim for their heroism was **Dorrie Miller**, a mess man from Waco. He operated a machine gun on the USS *West Virginia* and shot down several Japanese aircraft before escaping the sinking ship. Despite his heroism, he was denied any commendation until protests were published in the African American press. In Texas training facilities and in surrounding towns, African Americans were subjected to the indignities of Jim Crow throughout the war. But black veterans of World War II returned with renewed confidence as well as greater conviction that segregation and racial discrimination must end. Voter registration by African Americans in Texas more than tripled in 1946, and many of these new voters were veterans who refused to accept second-class status after sacrificing for the nation.

Cold War

Unlike the global conflicts of the first half of the 20th century, the Cold War did not result in large-scale fighting between the principal parties, the United States and the Soviet Union. The Cold War began shortly after the end of World War II as the Soviet Union exerted its control over Eastern European nations that had been freed from Nazi control by its Red Army. The United States responded by developing a strategy designed to contain the spread of communism. This led the nation into two "hot" wars, the first in Korea and the second in Vietnam. Texas shaped and was shaped by these wars and their consequences. The state also was shaped by the domestic conflicts engendered by the Cold War.

Texans were divided by the Cold War, even before it began. During the 1940s, many conservative Democrats, whose party dominated state government through the 1970s, grew dissatisfied with the New Deal policies of Franklin Roosevelt and with the Supreme Court decision in 1944 in *Smith v. Allwright* that ruled all-white primaries were unconstitutional. These conservatives, whose movement was called "the Texas Regulars," said the New Deal was "communist-controlled." They said New Deal liberalism, labor union activism, government regulation of the economy, a liberal university professoriate, demands for racial equality, and calls for anti-lynching laws suggested a communist conspiracy. Four years later, in 1948, many conservatives were drawn to the Dixiecrat movement led by Strom Thurmond.

With the "fall of China" in 1949 and with Soviet testing of a nuclear device, a national anti-communist hysteria began in earnest. The "Red Scare" in Texas followed the national panic. In 1946, an investigation opened at the University of Texas to root out Marxist subversion. In the early 1950s, conservative organizations like the Minute Women of Houston pressured the Houston school board, urging the firing of a liberal school superintendent. Even New Dealers like Lyndon Johnson were pressured to emphasize anti-communist credentials. In the climate of anti-communist paranoia, loyalty oaths were required of university professors, public school teachers, and other public employees. The state school system set out to root out subversive teachers and identified one communist among the state's 65,000 teachers. In 1955, Texas undergraduates at public colleges and universities were required to take six hours of U.S. history and six hours of U.S. and Texas government.

The Cold War had unexpected domestic policy implications for Texans. Fears of Soviet invasion contributed to reshaping the Texas landscape. In 1956, Congress appropriated $25 billion for the construction of the Interstate Highway System. The project then was the single largest public works program in American history. The Eisenhower administration justified the expenditure as a part of the national defense. As a result, more than 3,200 miles of expressway were built in Texas. Suburban communities grew along the extension of these highways. Vast quantities of asphalt were needed, as were enormous quantities of oil and gasoline to fuel the commuter vehicles and delivery trucks that traversed the highways.

The Korean War (1950–1953)

As in the other American wars of the 20th and 21st centuries, Texans played important military roles. The Korean War lasted from 1950 until 1953. A cease-fire ended hostilities but did not end the war. Some 289,000 Texans served in this conflict. More than 50,000 Americans and 1,700 Texans were killed. Thirteen Texans received the Congressional Medal of Honor, with 10 receiving it posthumously.

Vietnam War (1955–1975)

Perhaps more than any other state, Texas shaped and was shaped by the war in Vietnam. After all, Lyndon B. Johnson was the president who escalated the American role in Vietnam and defined its significance and meaning. Texans were more enthusiastic about the war's escalation than other Americans and remained committed to the war long after the rest of the country had soured on it. It is difficult to determine how many Texans served in the Vietnam War, though some estimates say as many as 500,000 Texans fought in Vietnam over the long course of the war. Texans who died in this war number 3,415, and more than 102 Texans are still listed as missing in action. Texas again provided an important training ground for the war effort. Fort Sam Houston trained the medics, physicians, and corpsmen deployed to Vietnam. More second lieutenants from Texas A&M University's ROTC program, "the Corps," were casualties in Vietnam than were graduates from any other university in the country.

Over the course of the 20th century, Texans and Texas played important roles in each of the crises that have caused some historians to characterize the century as the "Age of Extremes."

> **Competency 012 Descriptive Statement C.** The beginning teacher understands the political, economic and social impact of major events and individuals in the latter half of the twentieth and early twenty-first centuries on the history of Texas (e.g., Kay Bailey Hutchison, Barbara Jordan, Eddie Bernice Johnson, Henry B. Gonzalez, Lyndon B. Johnson, James Farmer, George Walker Bush, Craig Anthony Washington, immigration, Rustbelt to Sun Belt migration).

Barbara Jordan (1936–1996)

In 1967, Barbara Jordan was the first African American to be elected to the Texas Senate since Reconstruction. Her service in the Texas Legislature led her to run successfully for a seat in the U.S. House of Representatives, and she was the first African American woman from a Southern state to serve in Congress. As a representative, she played an important role in the House Judiciary Committee Watergate hearings and was asked to give the keynote address at the Democratic national convention that nominated Jimmy Carter for president. She became the first woman to give the keynote address at a national convention.

James Farmer (1920–1999)

James L. Farmer of Marshall, Texas, was the son of one of the few African Americans from the South with a Ph.D. in the 1930s. He set out to become a minister like his father, but after getting his divinity degree from Howard University's School of Religion, Farmer chose to work with the Fellowship for Reconciliation (FOR), a pacifist Quaker organization. When World War II began, he applied for conscientious objector status, which proved to be an unnecessary measure because of his divinity degree. While with FOR, Farmer lived in Chicago, where he met many students from the University of Chicago. Some of them, with Farmer, established the Congress of Racial Equality (CORE) in 1942. This interracial, non-violent organization recruited white, middle-class college students as well as African American students to protest segregation across the country. CORE was among the first to apply the principles of Mahatma Gandhi to American civil rights activism. CORE activists pioneered sit-ins, freedom rides, and other direct action. CORE took a lead after the 1954 *Brown v. Board of Education* decision in such protests as the Montgomery Bus Boycott and other efforts to end segregation across the country. Farmer was an important leader in the Freedom Rides of the early 1960s and in the "Freedom Summer" registration of African American voters in Alabama, Mississippi, and Louisiana. Farmer also ran for political office without success but remained a labor and civil rights activist.

Henry B. González (1916–2000)

Born Enrique Barbosa Prince de González in San Antonio, Henry B. González was a prominent and long-serving Texas legislator and civil rights activist. After getting an education at the University of Texas as well as a law degree from St. Mary's University, González served in the military during World War II and was a probation officer in the years immediately after the war. In 1953, he was elected to the San Antonio City Council and earned a reputation as an opponent of segregation. When he was elected to the Texas Senate in 1956, he became the first Mexican American elected to do so. González and another senator filibustered for 36 hours against a series of bills introduced to uphold segregation in Texas in violation of the *Brown v. Board of Education of Topeka, Kansas* decision. He was unsuccessful in campaigns for governor and the U.S. Senate but in 1962 became Texas' first Mexican American elected to a seat in the U.S. House of Representatives. González served in the House from 1961 until 1999. As a representative from San Antonio, González supported most of Lyndon Johnson's Great Society program initiatives and became an important figure in the federal savings and loan crisis of the late 1980s. For his investigative role in this controversy, González won the Profile in Courage Award presented by the John F. Kennedy Library.

Lyndon B. Johnson (1908–1973)

Lyndon Baines Johnson was the first Texas-born U.S. president. Johnson was born near Stonewall, Texas, to Sam Ealy Johnson Jr. and Rebekah Baines Johnson. His father was an ambitious populist elected to the Texas House of Representatives from 1904 to 1908 and again from 1918 to 1924. His mother came from a prominent local preacher's family and was a teacher as well as a writer for local newspapers. Despite his parents' prominence, Johnson grew up with few of the amenities of urban life at the turn of the century. The Johnsons had no electricity, phone service, running water, or indoor plumbing. Johnson would remember the daily household tasks as burdensome. A feature of Johnson's upbringing that would shape him was his opportunity to sit in on front-porch political discussions led by his father and to sit in the gallery—and sometimes on the House floor—of the Texas Legislature as well as act as his father's unofficial page. After high school, Johnson had three years of uncertainty about his future before enrolling in Southwest Texas State Teachers College at San Marcos. To pay for his education, Johnson worked as a school janitor and messenger boy. Although often discouraged by his poverty and checkered academic progress, he would be remembered later by administrators and professors for his assertiveness and energy as well as deference to teachers. Midway through his college years, Johnson left San Marcos to teach in Cotulla, Texas, in a segregated Mexican school. This experience was transformative. All accounts say Johnson gave his students attention that few teachers had afforded them. He organized extracurricular activities, distributed toothpaste, organized a parent-teacher association and encouraged students to believe in themselves. Johnson then returned to San Marcos and got his B.S. in education and history.

After a brief period teaching high school history, in 1931 Lyndon Johnson took an appointment as secretary to U.S. Rep. Richard Kleberg. Kleberg was from the wealthy King Ranch family and introduced Johnson to a standard of living he had never experienced as well as to men of influence and power. Johnson arrived in Washington in the last year of Herbert Hoover's presidency when the Democrats took the majority in the House of Representatives. Kleberg showed little interest in the daily work of the legislature and left Johnson, a 23-year-old former school teacher, in charge of much of his congressional duties. Johnson's unflagging energy and careful attention to the demands of Kleberg's constituents contributed much to Kleberg's legislative successes and to his re-election in 1932. Johnson also convinced Kleberg, despite his privileged upbringing and a personal philosophy that ran counter to Franklin Roosevelt's New Deal, to vote for most of Roosevelt's reform agenda. In 1934, after courting and marrying Claudia Alta (Lady Bird) Taylor, briefly attending Georgetown University's evening law program, and campaigning for the presidency of Texas A&I University in Kingsville, Johnson left Kleberg's staff to become the head of the National Youth Administration in Texas.

After learning the job of a U.S. representative by doing Kleberg's work, Johnson was eager to seek election to the House. In 1937, Johnson ran for the U.S. House of Representatives as an unabashed New Dealer and a "total Roosevelt man." After an aggressive, no-holds-barred campaign, Johnson won a House seat. Johnson served in the House from 1937 to 1949, although he ran unsuccessfully for a Senate seat and was appointed a lieutenant commander in the U.S. Naval Reserve, getting called to active duty despite his congressional position. After the war, Johnson again ran for the Senate, winning in an election best known for allegations of voter fraud in Jim Wells and Bexar counties. Johnson cultivated close relationships with several senior senators and rose in the committee structure and in the Democratic leadership of the Senate. Despite his relative inexperience in the Senate but with his re-election in 1954 as well as the Democratic control of the Senate, Johnson was chosen as its majority leader. He served in this position successfully until 1961. Many historians say Johnson was the most successful Senate majority leader of the 20th century. But Johnson wanted the presidency.

Johnson entered the 1960 presidential race, but when it became clear that Kennedy would win, Johnson agreed to run as Kennedy's vice president. Kennedy needed Johnson to attract Southern voters, and Johnson had reached the limits of his influence as a strictly regional figure. He hoped to raise his profile for a presidential run in 1964 or 1968. Johnson also immediately sought to expand the power of this traditionally weakened office, often acting outside his purview and causing tension with members of the Kennedy family and administration.

On Nov. 22, 1963, John F. Kennedy was assassinated in Dallas. Johnson was sworn into office as president aboard Air Force One hardly two hours later. Johnson immediately set out to push through Kennedy's agenda and build on it. Johnson's first success was to negotiate passage of Kennedy's tax proposal, lowering the highest marginal personal income tax rate from 91 percent to 70 percent and reducing the highest corporate income tax rate from 52 percent to 48 percent. The "Kennedy tax cuts" would provide a model for tax proposals later put forth by Ronald Reagan and George W. Bush. Reduced tax rates did spark exhilarating growth. The GNP rose, median family income increased, poverty rates decreased, and employment reached full levels of nearly 4 percent. Industrial production and corporate profits also increased.

Johnson also pushed through Civil Rights legislation that the Kennedy administration had earlier proposed. Five days after Kennedy's assassination, Johnson defended the Kennedy civil rights bill before a joint session of Congress, arguing thus: "We have talked long enough in this country about equal rights. . . . It is time now to write the next chapter, and to write it in the books of law." Johnson's familiarity with congressional procedures and his ability to strong-arm his former colleagues ensured the passage of the Civil Rights Act of 1964.

As Johnson prepared for the 1964 presidential campaign, he put forth an ambitious program of his own to wrestle with the problems of poverty that had troubled Johnson since his days in Cotulla, Texas. Johnson called his domestic legislative agenda "The Great Society." Its centerpiece was the "War on Poverty." Many of these programs are still prominent parts of the American social welfare system. Johnson's programs included the following:

Johnson's Great Society Programs at a Glance

Economic Opportunity Act	Established the Office of Economic Opportunity to oversee anti-poverty and urban renewal programs.
Job Corps	Provided employment and job experience to disadvantaged youth.
VISTA	Placed volunteers in high-poverty neighborhoods. (modeled on the Peace Corps).
Head Start	Offered preschool programs for underprivileged children.
Upward Bound	Improved college readiness of high-risk and underprivileged youth.
Elementary and Secondary Education Act of 1965	Federal funding for public education, educational research, and help for special education programming.
Bilingual Education Act of 1968	Federal aid to local school districts and children with limited English language proficiency.
Medicare	Funded medical care for the elderly and disabled (Social Security Act of 1965).
Medicaid	Funded medical care for welfare recipients.
Child Nutrition Act of 1966	Introduced the School Breakfast program.

Johnson's Great Society has shaped the contours of the federal government's efforts to alleviate social problems and poverty since the 1960s. Johnson's agenda also included a wide range of additional programs that have contributed to the improved quality of the life of American citizens across the social and economic spectrum. For example, Johnson supported the establishment of the National Endowment of the Arts and the National Endowment for the Humanities as well as the founding of the Public Broadcasting System and Corporation for Public Broadcasting. Johnson also promoted significant improvements in urban mass transit, highway safety, and other transportation improvements. A host of consumer protections were also passed under Johnson's administration. While Johnson's expansive domestic agenda generated significant public support and ensured his victory over Barry Goldwater in the 1964 presidential election, it also generated a significant conservative backlash. Although Richard Nixon concentrated his efforts on international affairs and even expanded upon many elements of Johnson's environmental and educational programs, the presidencies of Ronald Reagan, George W. Bush, and Donald Trump contain efforts to chip away or roll back the legacy of the Johnson presidency.

Perhaps the greatest hindrance to the success of Lyndon Johnson's domestic programs was his escalation of the Vietnam conflict and the protest and social unrest the Vietnam War caused. In August 1964, a few months before the November election, Johnson got a report that two American destroyers had been fired on by North Vietnamese vessels. Johnson feared his Republican opponents would paint him as weak internationally and was convinced that he needed to respond forcefully to ensure an electoral victory and to protect his domestic agenda. Johnson also subscribed to the "Domino Theory" of communist expansion and feared that a communist victory in Vietnam would lead to conflict elsewhere. Johnson thus urged the passage of the Tonkin Gulf Resolution, which authorized him to expand the U.S. presence in Vietnam. Johnson also approved a bombing campaign code-named Operation Rolling Thunder. The number of American military in Vietnam grew from 23,000 in 1964 to nearly 525,000 in 1968. American casualties also increased, as did growing uneasiness in the United States about the war. When the North Vietnamese and the Viet Cong, as South Vietnamese communists were called, unleashed a surprise offensive in 1968, Americans in large numbers turned against the war. The stalemate in Vietnam convinced Johnson not to run for re-election that year.

Johnson's legacy was tarnished by his determination not to be the president who "lost Vietnam." The war cost the lives of some 3 million Vietnamese and more than 54,000 American service members, and—coupled with increased domestic spending on Johnson's many social programs—the war destabilized the American post–World War II economy. Inflationary pressures and ballooning deficits made further spending on Johnson's domestic priorities hard to get through a divided Congress. Although Johnson may have in five years done more to shape the future of the country than any other 20th century president except Franklin D. Roosevelt, he is more often remembered for the blunder of Vietnam than for any of his domestic reforms. In January 1973, Johnson died of heart failure and was buried in a family plot near his birthplace.

Eddie Bernice Johnson (1935–)

Eddie Bernice Johnson of the U.S. House of Representatives, has represented the state's 30th District comprised of parts of Dallas and Dallas County since the district's creation in 1993. Before that, Johnson in 1972 became the first black woman elected to the Texas House of Representatives from the Dallas area. She also is the first registered nurse to serve in the U.S. Congress.

Kay Bailey Hutchison (1943–)

When Kay Bailey Hutchison was elected to the U.S. Senate in 1993, she became the first Texas woman to be elected to that office. Hutchison served until 2009 when she resigned as senator to run against Rick Perry, the incumbent Texas governor in the 2010 election. Hutchison had much support from Republican moderates, but in the aftermath of Barack Obama's 2008 election, Perry rode the wave of opposition to Obama and the rise of the Tea Party movement to defeat her.

George Walker Bush (1946–)

George W. Bush was born into a prominent Connecticut political family but grew up in Midland and Houston. He served as Texas governor from 1995 until 2000 when he resigned to become the 43rd U.S. president. His father was George Herbert Walker Bush, the U.S. president from 1989 to 1993. Before 1988, when Bush worked on his father's political campaign, he had not seemed destined for political success, though he did run for election to the House of Representatives in 1978. Following his graduation from Yale University in 1968, Bush served in the Texas Air National Guard. He also earned an MBA from Harvard in 1975. Bush's career in business included the establishment in 1977 of an oil exploration company that was later absorbed by several other larger corporations in which Bush continued to have leading roles. In 1989, Bush and several partners bought the Texas Rangers baseball team.

Bush defeated the popular Democratic Governor Ann Richards in 1994, running on a slate of campaign promises that would also figure in his presidential platform: welfare reform, tort reform, tax reduction, law and order, and educational reforms. Bush also gained the support of Texans interested in liberalizing the rights of gun owners, promising to allow easy access to permits for concealed weapons. Bush slashed taxes by $2 billion as governor. That success as well as the economic boom of the 1990s helped Bush win re-election in a landslide victory. Before 1975, Texas governors served two-year terms, and Bush's victory in 1998 made him the first Texas governor to be elected to two consecutive four-year terms.

In the 2000 presidential campaign, Bush ran against a full slate of Republican rivals, campaigning as a "compassionate conservative" and attracting a large following of Evangelical Christians. Texas' economic successes shortly after the bursting of the "dot-com" bubble as well as his gubernatorial education reforms made his candidacy attractive. Bush's opponent was Al Gore, vice president under President Bill Clinton.

The election was among the closest campaigns in American history. Bush won the electoral college majority only on the strength of a Florida victory that was so close that a series of controversial recounts were done. A Supreme Court decision, *Bush v. Gore*, assured Bush's electoral victory. Nationwide, Bush lost the popular election by over half a million votes.

Among the most important features of Bush's domestic program was a $1.35 trillion tax cut, among the largest in American history, and the promotion of significant educational reforms, specifically his No Child Left Behind Act. This act sought to reduce the performance gap between rich and poor students via accountability measures and funding incentives.

The defining event of Bush's presidency occurred Sept. 11, 2001, less than a year after he became president, when terrorists flew two airliners into the Twin Towers of the World Trade Center in New York City and a third airliner into the Pentagon. A fourth plane was forced into a Pennsylvania field by passengers who refused to allow the aircraft to be used as a missile. Much of Bush's two terms in office would be shaped by his response to these attacks. The Bush administration restructured the United States intelligence services, authorized more comprehensive intelligence gathering under the USA PATRIOT Act, and set out to destroy the Al-Qaeda terrorist network that had perpetrated the crimes. The most immediate targets were the bases of Al-Qaeda in Afghanistan and Osama bin Laden, the terrorist who planned the attacks. Although unable to capture bin Laden, the U.S. military neutralized Al-Qaeda and the Taliban that supported them in Afghanistan. Bush then turned American military might on Iraq, declaring that the Iraqis under Saddam Hussein had WMDs, or weapons of mass destruction, that should not be allowed to fall into terrorist hands. The war on Iraq became the most controversial of the Bush administration's decisions. Evidence of WMDs in Iraq proved to be false, and Bush was blamed for engaging the United States in a war that seemed to have no effective end.

The costs of the "Global War on Terror," as the multifront conflict came to be known, coupled with the significant tax cuts pushed through during Bush's first year in office, resulted in ballooning debt during his second term. The devastation of New Orleans by Hurricane Katrina in the fall of 2005 also embarrassed the Bush presidency, as relief efforts failed to meet the needs of the devastated city. In addition, the last months of the Bush administration saw the American and global economy experience a severe credit crisis that led to massive layoffs, home foreclosures, and bank failures.

Craig Anthony Washington (1941–)

Craig Anthony Washington was among five minority legislators elected to the Texas House of Representatives in 1972. He, Ben Torres Reyes, George Thomas "Mickey" Leland, Anthony Hall, and Cecil Bush were the first minority representatives in the Texas House since the end of Reconstruction. Washington served in the Texas House from 1973 to 1983 and in the Texas Senate from 1983 to 1989, chairing committees on criminal jurisprudence, social services, and human services as well as chairing the Legislative Black Caucus. As a legislator, Washington took leadership roles with several Texas civil rights issues, fought to see Texas divest itself of investments in companies that did business with apartheid South Africa, and supported legislation to fight poverty and support AIDS research. In 1989, he was elected to the U.S. House of Representatives from Houston's 18th District. He served in this role until 1995 and continues to practice law in Houston.

Immigration

In the 20th and 21st centuries, immigrants to Texas have arrived in a series of waves, each helping to shape the state's economy and culture. The Mexican Revolution of 1910 caused many Mexicans to flee to Texas. These refugees came from all classes, with the poorest soon merging with the Tejano agricultural labor force. Some of the better off immigrants, however, would make names for themselves in Texas. Hector P. Garcia, the Corpus Christi civil rights activist, for example, came from a refugee family, as did Texas congressman Henry B. González.

A demographic study of Texas in 2013 reported that the foreign-born population of Texas was higher than at any time since the state was admitted to the Union. One in six Texans in 2013 had been born outside the United States. The largest number of these immigrants came from Mexico and Central America. Since 2005, the number of Asian residents, largely from India and China, also has ballooned, although Asian immigrants are likely to have moved from another state. Most Asian immigrants are from California, Florida, Illinois, and New York. This group of immigrants represents a highly educated, skilled population.

Rust Belt to Sunbelt Migration

After World War II, and especially since the 1970s, Texas has benefited from the migration of businesses, jobs, and workers from the industrial Northeast and Midwest to the state. The same phenomenon has characterized migration from the "Rust Belt" to the "Sunbelt" across the Southeast, but Texas has perhaps benefited the most. Five explanations have been offered for this migration: (1) a warm climate, perhaps not as pleasant as Florida's, but a more central location; (2) comparatively inexpensive costs of living; (3) a low-wage labor pool with weak union protections; (4) a tradition of limited government regulations, low taxes, and few social services; (5) an influx of immigrant labor, including low-skilled service and agricultural labor as well as highly-skilled professional workers.

Since the state's beginnings, Texas' population has grown faster than the national rate. Migration to Texas has come in four successive waves. The first (1820–1860) witnessed a mass influx of Southerners moving into the state to take advantage of cheap land and the cotton boom. A second began in the early 20th century, again composed of Southerners, this time eager to profit from or labor in the oil patch. With the collapse of the U.S. industrial heartland in the 1970s and 1980s, a third migration took place, bringing factory workers and their families from the Rust Belt. By 1990, after two decades of this migration, one in every five Texans has now come from the Midwest. These Texans left the steel mills, automobile factories, and coal mines of Illinois, Michigan, Indiana, and Ohio for jobs in the Texas oil patch at first and then for employment in the many other industries that developed after 1980. Since 2000 an additional migration has been underway from points across the United States. While undoubtedly opportunities in Texas have drawn Midwesterners to the state, Texas also benefited from the migration of skilled and professional workers. In 1998, nearly two-thirds of Texas' college-educated workforce got degrees elsewhere. The infusion of human capital drawn to the state has contributed to the diversification of the Texas economy.

> **Competency 012 Descriptive Statement D.** The beginning teacher understands the impact of major developments in manufacturing, the petroleum and gas industry (e.g., Spindletop), commercial agriculture (e.g., cotton, citrus, beef and dairy production) and suburbanization and how various groups altered the natural environment from 1900 to the present.

Periodization: 1900 to the Present

Since 1900, the Texas economy has flourished partly because of an abundance of natural resources, most noticeably its reserves of petroleum. The state also has a history of limited regulation and low taxation that has rewarded investors. This has combined with significant stimulus from public investment in infrastructure, human capital and industry since the 1930s.

Competitive Industrial Growth: 1900–1931. The Texas economy was characterized by the expansion of the oil industry alongside its traditional agricultural leading sectors. Starting with the "wildcatting" phase of entrepreneurial risk-taking and cutthroat competition, it shifted after 1916 to consolidation and the emergence of giant petroleum-producing corporations and refining operations.

State-Assisted Corporate Growth: 1933–present. Since the Great Depression, while the mythology of Texas' independent, individualistic, and entrepreneurial economy has persisted, much of the state's industrial growth and diversification has been driven by federal and state investment in defense, aviation, and aerospace firms and in construction of highway systems and air transport facilities as well as investment in universities, health care centers, and other high-tech sectors. An infusion of migrants from other states, often with sought-after skills or credentials, has supported this growth. An increase in the service and construction sectors, often relying on migrants from Mexico and Latin America, has also helped.

Key Question

What explains the transformation of the Texas economy from its agricultural dependence on cotton and cattle into a diversified economy that would, on its own, rank in the top 10 global economies, behind only the United States, China, Japan, Germany, the United Kingdom, France, India, Italy, and Brazil?

Commercial Agriculture

The Texas agricultural economy before 1900 depended primarily upon cotton production and cattle ranching. Although ranching and cotton production remained prominent in the Texas economy, commercial agriculture diversified in several ways over the 20th century.

In 1908, for example, the citrus fruit industry was launched in the Rio Grande Valley. The first orange saplings were planted in 1908. By 1929, more than 5 million citrus trees, most of them grapefruit, grew in the Rio Grande Valley. The Rio Grande also became an important sugar-producing region. Sugar cane had been an important Texas product dating to the establishment of Stephen F. Austin's colony. The coastal region southwest of Houston was described as the "sugar bowl of Texas." In the 20th century, however, the Rio Grande became an important source for cane sugar. To the north, in what is known as the Winter Garden Region north of Laredo, irrigation enabled the growth of onions, spinach, beets, strawberries, and nuts. Small vegetable farms characterized the region until the Great Depression, when price collapses drove many small operators out of business. After World War II, corporate investors came into the area, making the Winter Garden region again an important producer of vegetables.

As in the 19th century, cotton was the dominant Texas agricultural product in much of the 20th century. East and Central Texas remained the heartland that grew most Texas cotton before World War II. South and West Texas, however, saw cotton production grow during the 20th century. The primary threat to cotton crops in the early 20th century was the boll weevil, which in some years destroyed up to a third of the harvest. Cotton prices rose in the first two decades of the 1900s, especially during World War I, but cotton prices dropped steadily after 1920. Farm foreclosures posed significant problems for rural communities well before the Great Depression.

Before World War II, most Texas farmers were tenants or sharecroppers. More than 60 percent of Texas farmers worked someone else's land in the 1930s. Sharecroppers worked a landlord's property, providing their own seed, tools, draft animals, and supplies, while landlords claimed one-third to one-fourth of the crop. Tenant farmers rented land and borrowed against their income to pay their production costs. Although the number of tractors and trucks on Texas farms increased in the 1920s, most farms were undercapitalized and had little mechanization, especially in East and Central Texas, where cotton farming had the longest history. Many Texans were employed as wage-earning agricultural laborers, and the cotton harvest attracted many of them. The 1920s and 1930s saw reductions in their wages. In 1920 cotton pickers were paid as much as $4 for 100 pounds of cotton picked. By the end of the decade, they earned $1 for the same 100 pounds.

Cotton prices and farm wages continued to decline after the "Roaring Twenties," a decade that had hardly been prosperous for Texas farmers. In 1931, cotton prices dropped from 10 cents to less than 6 cents a pound. Corn and cattle prices dropped 50 percent in the first years of the Great Depression. In desperation and despite efforts by the Federal Farm Board and the Texas Marketing Association to restrict cotton production, farmers increased acreage under production and thus increased the downward pressure on prices.

New Deal farm programs sought to address the farm crisis by encouraging farmers to withdraw acreage from production. The Agricultural Adjustment Act, or AAA, sought to restrict cotton, wheat, corn, rice, tobacco, dairy, pork, and beef production. Between 1934 and 1936, as Texans plowed their crops under or cut back on planting, cotton, corn, and beef prices stabilized and increased. By 1940, the federal government's subsidies of more than $3 billion to Texas farmers to reduce harvests had resulted in millions of acres being taken out of production. Texas ranchers also got substantial federal assistance in exchange for cutting the size of their herds.

Ironically, both the Great Depression and the New Deal agricultural policies designed to alleviate the impact of the Depression had detrimental effects on agricultural laborers, sharecroppers, and tenant farmers. Falling prices and reduced wages forced workers to rely increasingly on their entire family's labor in the fields. During the 1930s, opportunities for tenant farming also were reduced. Landowners took farm acreage out of production at the instigation of the AAA, reducing the demand for tenant farmers. Subsidies also made it possible for landowners use subsidy payments to mechanize their farms, reducing the need for sharecroppers or tenant farmers. Poor people thus found themselves pushed off the land because of the combined impact of the Great Depression and New Deal. Increased mechanization, improved pesticides and insecticides and chemical fertilizers improved farm yields, reducing the demand for farm laborers and tenant farmers.

Although agricultural yields increased and farm sizes grew, following World War II, the improvements in efficiency reduced the number of Texans who owned farms or worked in agriculture. By 1960, only 10 percent of Texas's population still farmed, but the size of average holdings nearly doubled. In addition, cotton no longer represented the most valuable crop in Texas. Grain crops surpassed cotton, and vegetables, sugar, peanuts, and other crops had grown in significance to the Texas economy. By the 21st century, the proportion of Texans involved in farming had dropped further. Less than 3 percent of Texans today earn their living in farming.

Several significant trends have influenced Texas agriculture since the 1970s. Family farms, whether sharecropped or owned, characterized agricultural organization before the 1960s, but over the last decades of the 20th century, agribusiness and corporate farming has increased its dominance of agriculture in Texas. In addition, farm subsidy programs like those started in the New Deal have increased their role in the fortunes of Texas agriculture. Between 1995 and 2014, Texas farmers got over $30 billion in farm subsidies. Total farm income in Texas since 2002 has thus grown, though much of that is tied to increases in federal and state subsidies and to growing international demand for Texas farm products because of such trade agreements as the North American Free Trade Agreement, or NAFTA.

Cattle Ranching in Texas

By the end of the 19th century, the era of open-range ranching was over, and South Texas cattle were no longer driven northward to rail heads or to the high plains grasslands. Texas cattle ranching had turned to smaller pasturage with improved scientific breeding programs and careful livestock management. Cattlemen were still subject to the booms and busts of the cattle market. World War I saw a boom in cattle and horse prices, followed by a decades-long depression that saw drought as well as declining prices. Federal efforts to buy and slaughter excess stock offered ranchers the opportunity to reduce their herds and improve their breeding stock. Such federal programs like the AAA paid farmers to take acreage out of cotton production and incentivized Texas farmers to shift to cattle grazing on land formerly used for cotton.

Texas ranchers also oversaw efforts to breed improved stock. By the 1880s and 1890s, Hereford cattle immune to tick fever had already been bred, and Angus herds were also introduced. In the inter-war period, the popularity of the Hereford and Angus continued to grow alongside other dairy and mixed beef cattle. Although Texas is known for beef production, the state by the 1950s also had over 1.5 million dairy cattle. Texas cattle ranchers rank No. 1 nationally and have done so throughout the past century in the number of cattle owned across the state, although dairy production has declined since the 1970s. Texas has also led the nation in the number of farms and ranches and in total farm and ranch land.

The growth of feedlots, slaughter houses, and packing plants is related to Texas' success in raising cattle. As ranchers moved from grazing their herds on the open range to smaller lots, commercial feed become more important and contributed to the growth of soy and corn production. The development of feedlots also became important. Feedlot production, which accounts for just under 50 percent of all cattle and calf sales, is a prominent feature of Texas cattle raising. Commercial feedlots fatten cattle for the slaughter markets, with larger feedlots handling as many as 50,000 head a year. A late 20th century increase in slaughterhouses and meat-packing plants in Texas also is associated with the growth of feedlot production. While some smaller independent slaughterhouses and meat-packing plants are found across Texas, 80 percent of these operations are controlled by a handful of large corporations.

Petroleum and Natural Gas Industry

Although it has been an enormously profitable source of revenue and industrial growth in Texas since 1901, the petroleum and gas industry has also placed the state on a roller coaster of booms and busts.

The first boom began at the turn of the 20th century. In 1901, Capt. Henry F. Lucas, a wildcatter, or speculative oil driller, struck oil at Spindletop, near Beaumont. The well sat atop one of the most lucrative deposits of oil discovered to that point. In less than two years, more than 285 wells had been drilled to profit from the discovery. Beaumont's population exploded, make it one of Texas' first oil boom towns. Spindletop had not been the first oil well in Texas. An earlier well drilled in Corsicana in North Texas had produced over 800,000 barrels a year. But the Spindletop well, financed by Pennsylvania oil men, used new drilling techniques combined to transform the Texas oil industry. In 1901, more than 491 oil companies were incorporated in Texas in search of new sources of profit. As the competition within the oil industry shook out over the next decade, Gulf Oil, Texaco, Humble Oil and Refining (forerunner to Exxon Mobil), Magnolia Petroleum Co., and Sun Oil Co. were among the companies to emerge. The Spindletop well encouraged drilling across Texas, and fertile oil fields were discovered in North and Central Texas before 1925. By 1926 oil speculators were finding new sources of oil in West Texas. From 1896, when Texas had produced only 1,000 barrels, oil production continued to grow. By 1929, the Texas oil industry was producing over 290 million barrels of oil yearly, which was worth nearly $430 million annually. A second phase of the oil boom began in East Texas in October 1930, near Kilgore, Texas, where most geologists thought discovery of oil was unlikely. But this new field spread across 140,000 acres and contained nearly a third of the nation's known oil reserves, offering a new opportunity for profits. By 1933, the East Texas oil field alone pumped 205 million barrels of oil per year. With the prominence of the East Texas oil fields, many oil companies relocated their headquarters to Dallas, making it the undeclared capital of the southwestern oil industry.

In addition to drilling firms, pipeline companies connected the scattered oil fields to refineries that dotted the Gulf Coast. Ancillary industries that developed alongside the oil industry included asphalt producers, tank-car makers, and oil-field equipment manufacturers. New professional opportunities also developed: oil and gas law, petroleum engineering, geological surveying, and other petroleum-related occupations flourished.

Oil fever resulted in the development of unplanned and often unruly boomtowns. Towns grew overnight from sleepy agricultural hamlets of 500 people to towns with 30,000 or more residents. City services could not keep up. Occupational safety was ignored. Fire and health hazards were common. Prostitution, gambling, alcoholism, and violence also created concerns. Even when recognized, environmental threats took a back seat to making enormous profits.

Environmental concerns and fears of overproduction threatened the stability of oil prices, spurring the Texas Legislature to authorize the Texas Railroad Commission to establish limits on the amount of oil that an oil well could pump annually. Although these regulations were hard to enforce and a black market of "Hot Oil" commerce flourished in the 1930s, state and federal law enforcement combined with the growing monopoly power of the major oil producers, who had an interest in curtailing unrestricted drilling, to end unregulated and speculative oil exploration.

With the expansion of America's automobile culture, suburbanization, and increased production of plastics and other petrochemicals in the 1950s, Texas again experienced a flourishing oil and gas industry. The production of crude oil in Texas doubled from 755 million barrels in 1945 to 1.5 billion barrels in 1955. During the 1950s, Texas took in oil revenues of up to $3.2 billion a year. The center of Texas oil production shifted from East Texas to West Texas, with Odessa and Midland becoming the most important oil-producing cities. To export Texas crude, 13 deepwater ports as well as new refineries were built across the Gulf Coast region. The Texas Railroad Commission's ability to establish pumping quotas and thereby determine prices for crude oil was reinforced in 1959 by national legislation that established import quotas on oil. The U.S. car culture and petrochemical industries thus depended on Texas, which had more than 50 percent of the nation's oil reserves.

The 1970s and 1980s saw both boom and bust in the Texas oil industry. Before the 1970s, oil prices had remained stable. In 1973, the Organization of Petroleum Exporting Countries, or OPEC, embargoed oil sales to the United States and Europe in response to the West's pro-Israel policies. Prices for crude oil rose over the decade from $3 per barrel to as high as $40 in 1980. Like other Americans, Texans faced gas shortages and rising prices at the pump, but they also benefited from the rising prices of crude oil. When the price of Texas crude rose, money flowed into the state. While the

American industrial heartland endured profound reorganization and decline, Texas saw real estate prices rise, construction boom, and employment opportunities increase. Auto workers from Michigan and steel-mill workers from Ohio and Pennsylvania swarmed Texas in search of jobs.

The 1970s and early '80s boom ended in the mid-1980s. International conservation efforts, oil drilling by non-OPEC nations, and OPEC's failure to enforce its own production quotas caused a decline in world oil prices. In 1986, crude oil prices dropped to below $10 per barrel. Prices gradually rose through the last decade of the 20th century but never approached the heady days of the late 1970s. State tax revenues, real estate prices, oil-related employment, construction, and financial institutions contracted. The number of Texas banks declined by half between 1986 and 1992. This decline shows the extent of the oil bust.

Manufacturing

In 1900, Texas had little manufacturing. Although the number of manufacturing firms and industrial employees had grown since the end of the Civil War, only 1.5 percent of the population in 1900 earned their living from manufacturing and industry. Most Texas manufacturing firms were extensions of the agricultural sector. Meat-packing plants, flour mills, lumber yards, and cotton ginning represented the largest portion of Texas' manufacturing employment. The abundance of hides made Texas an important center for making boots. The Piney Woods area's timber production led to the manufacture of pulp and paper as well as cedar oils, pine tar, railroad ties, telegraph and telephone poles, fence posts, and other wood products. Before Prohibition, Texas also became known for its distilleries and breweries. When railroads crisscrossed the state after 1865, machine shops were devoted to railroad car production, engine repair, and other rail needs.

With the discovery of oil, refineries also became important to Texas's nonagricultural sector, as did the production of chemicals and petroleum byproducts. Still, between 1900 and 1932, the Texas economy remained largely undercapitalized and geared to low-wage, low-skill, labor-intensive production of nondurable goods in a manufacturing sector that was small compared to the state's agricultural and extractive economy.

The transformation of Texas' economy began with the New Deal policies of Franklin Delano Roosevelt and the vast infusion of federal defense spending the state got during World War II and the Cold War. World War II especially transformed Texas from an agricultural economy into a technologically sophisticated industrial economy. This also meant shifting people from rural areas to cities. During the war, some 500,000 Texans moved from rural to urban areas to work in the defense industry. Many jobs went to women as well as African Americans, Hispanics, and men too old for military service. Another 450,000 workers from outside the state came to work in Texas' war industry.

These investments and the influx of outsiders into the state established the necessary infrastructure, developed human capital, and injected significant reserves into the Texas economy. This helped make Texas one of the prominent "Sunbelt" success stories of the late 20th century and early 21st century. Many workers who migrated to Texas during the war stayed, as did many of the soldiers who had been stationed in the state. Texas' manufacturing economy might best be understood by examining the two most important manufacturing centers in the state: the Dallas-Fort Worth metroplex and Houston.

Dallas-Fort Worth

Dallas was established in 1841 and became an important regional business center in the 1870s when it became the county seat and a railroad hub. Cotton, cattle, sheep, wool, hides, and wheat were transported from Dallas to St. Louis and other cities. Dallas' population then grew from 3,000 in 1870 to more than 40,000 by 1890. The oil boom contributed more growth, as Dallas bankers financed oil exploration and Dallas-area factories produced oil-field equipment. Fort Worth was founded as an army base and became the seat of Tarrant County in 1849. As an important terminus of South Texas cattle drives, the city grew until the early 1870s. The stockyards and meat-packing plants contributed to the city's growth.

New Deal policies and defense spending during World War II transformed the region into a manufacturing and industrial center. Only Los Angeles' manufacturing sector grew more than the Dallas-Fort Worth area between 1932 and 1955. Because 10 railroads, nine major highways, and three airlines converged in Dallas, the area was an attractive location for the defense industry. In addition, the location of big military bases in Texas made the state a strategic location for military contractors. Because Dallas-Fort Worth lacked a port, however, the region was limited to light industry. Texas Instruments was among the successful companies that grew out of defense industry investment. This electronics company began by designing equipment for use in oil exploration, but it entered the defense electronics market during World War II. Defense and aerospace industry companies also were attracted to Texas. Between 1942 and 1994, the Convair corporation, later owned by General Dynamics and McDonnell Douglas, first produced bombers and fighters and later rockets and spacecraft. Convair was perhaps best known during World War II for building the B-24 Liberator. During the war, other aircraft manufacturers relocated to the Dallas-Fort Worth area. Bell Helicopter, Lockheed, Rockwell, and General Dynamics were among the many corporations that benefited from wartime spending. The location of these plants in North Texas would provide the region with a pool of engineers, skilled laborers, and managers needed to transform the area's economy from its agricultural and extractive origins into a retail and high-tech hub. The growth of retail and the electronics, aircraft, and computer industries in Dallas specifically and Texas generally is an important long-term offshoot from the increases in federal government spending and defense sector investment since the 1940s.

Oil: A Buffer to the Depression

Before the 1900s, Houston had been mainly a commercial city through which Texas' cotton and other agricultural products reached world markets. After 1901, however, Houston's growth as a retail and manufacturing center was tied to the oil industry. The Spindletop discovery took place less than 90 miles from the city. Between 1900 and 1930, Houston's population grew from just 44,000 people to nearly 292,000 residents. Because of Houston's connection to the oil industry, the Great Depression did not affect Houston as it did other cities. The discovery of a huge new oil field in the early 1930s helped the city ride out the Depression. In 1940, half the world's oil production took place within a 600-mile radius of Houston, and more than half of all U.S. oil flowed through Houston and the Gulf Coast. Although population growth slowed during the 1930s, the city still increased its population by 31.5 percent during the Depression. Houston was called the "oil capital of the world" well into the 1960s, and Shell, Texaco, Gulf, and Exxon had headquarters there.

Houston was insulated from the Depression, but World War II had a mixed effect on the city. The port of Houston's commercial traffic suffered with declines in international consumer trade. However, the location of the Houston Ship Channel, sheltered from submarine attacks, became a center of production of aviation fuel, synthetic rubber production, and ship building. At manufacturing plants along the ship channel, Houston manufacturers built Liberty Ships, sub-chasers, and naval escorts.

After World War II, Houston's economic growth continued, again heavily affected by manufacturing that grew around the oil industry.

The growth of manufacturing led to Texas' growing population as well as increased urbanization. Between 1950 and 1980, the Texas population doubled. With an estimated population of 17 million by 1987, Texas was the nation's third most populous state after California and New York and holds this rank today. Of that population, a third were born outside the state, most from areas outside the Old South. In addition, two-thirds of the state's college graduates had been born outside Texas. This influx of human capital contributed much to Texas' economic boom between 1950 and 2000. By 1990, more than 80 percent of Texans lived in towns and cities with more than 8,000 residents. In 1930, no Texas city ranked among the top 10 U.S. cities. In 1960, Houston, with over 900,000 residents was the sixth largest city in the country. In 1970, Dallas joined Houston in the top 10. Since 1990, San Antonio, Dallas, and Houston have been among the top 10 most populous American cities.

> **Competency 012 Descriptive Statement E.** The beginning teacher understands the effect of major developments in computer technology, transportation (including aerospace) and medical research on the contemporary economic and social history of Texas.

From the 1960s, Texas underwent a transition that put it near the forefront of the global information and technological economy. One cause of the shift was instability in the petroleum sector. While oil prices were rising as high as $40 a barrel in the 1970s, the industrial Northeast and Midwest were declining. Workers poured into Texas from depressed areas, and real estate prices and construction starts took off. The number of investment banks exploded, eager to lend money to oil investors, but the ensuing 1980s bust in the oil industry forced the economy to diversify. That diversification had several causes.

One contribution came from continuing investment in aerospace and aviation, which combined with defense sector spending dating from the early 1960s. From 1965 to the 1990s, state government also took a greater interest in expanding the number of Texas universities as well as increasing graduate programs and research. Of the state's 37 four-year campuses, 15 have been established since 1965. Many of them emphasize science, technology, engineering and mathematics, or STEM, fields and have been located in historically underserved areas of the state. Texas thus has become a leader in the high-tech revolution that is changing the American economy. Although Dallas and Houston have benefited, Austin may provide the best case study for this recent economic development.

Austin

Dallas and Houston benefited the most from Depression policies and World War II defense spending, while Austin was marginally affected. The city had been bypassed by the early 20th century oil boom and had dropped from its place as the state's fourth largest city in 1900 to 10th by 1920. Certainly Lyndon Johnson's patronage during the Roosevelt administration did benefit Austin. While Dallas had 20 New Deal construction sites and Houston had 10, Austin had more than 40 New Deal projects. However, the New Deal programs only served to stop the city's decline, not reverse it. Military investment during the war also helped sustain the city, but Dallas and Houston benefited from their place at the center of the nation's maritime and overland transportation networks in ways that Austin could not.

Austin's real growth occurred after 1970 and had several causes. One was the rise of the University of Texas into the ranks of America's elite research institutions. Austin also developed a tolerance and diversity, which marked it as unique among Southern cities before 1980. The city also emerged as a center of technological growth and creativity. Austin's reputation as a center of high-tech research was most important. In 1967, IBM moved to Austin to take advantage of the growing number of faculty and students studying computing. Texas Instruments followed in 1969, locating its headquarters in Austin. Motorola arrived in 1974.

In 1984, Michael Dell, a pre-med freshman at the University of Texas, founded Dell Computer, then known as PC's Limited. Dell's personal story shows the convergence of an entrepreneurial spirit and the critical importance of public investment in higher education. Dell exhibited from an early age a keen entrepreneurial sense. By 13 he had formed a mail-order business to sell the contents of his stamp collection. As a high school student, he organized a group of friends to sell the Houston *Post*, by offering free trial subscriptions that would yield thousands of dollars in earnings. After teaching himself how to build his own computers, he bought components and began rebuilding IBM computers to sell them. At the University of Texas, Dell acquired such a reputation for quality products that Austin business executives would come to his dorm room to buy upgraded computer equipment. In January 1984, still operating from his dorm room, Dell was selling over $50,000 a month in rebuilt computers. When he incorporated his company as Dell Computer Corp., his initial investment was $1,000, the fee required to incorporate. After his freshman year, Dell dropped out, hired a local engineer to build the first Dell computer, and sold made-to-order computers for clients, allowing him to maintain a reduced inventory while selling at a high profit. Within two years after its founding, Dell Computer had sales of $60 million. During the 1990s, Dell became one of the first computer firms to take full advantage of the first wave of internet sales. Within the first year of selling Dell computers on-line, the firm earned more than $1 million in internet sales alone. Dell became one of the first to fully comprehend the enormous potential of the internet. Although Dell did not graduate from the University of Texas, many Texas business, engineering, and computer technology graduates have been hired by the company, and Dell has contributed significantly through his philanthropy to programs in the Austin community and at the University of Texas.

Houston: A Hub for Aerospace and Health Care

Texas also benefited from spending on space exploration and medical research, and Houston became a hub for both sectors.

In the 1950s and 1960s, Houston gained the nickname "Space City, U.S.A." for its place in the space race and missile technology industry. In the 1950s, the Department of Defense under Dwight D. Eisenhower's presidency approved plans to send scientific satellites into orbit. The Soviet Union's launch of the first space satellite in 1957 had what has been described as a "Pearl Harbor effect" on the American public. In direct response, the National Aeronautics and Space Administration, or NASA, was established in October 1958. In 1961, the Manned Spacecraft Center was sited 25 miles outside Houston's city center on land donated by Rice University. It would later be renamed the Lyndon B. Johnson Space Center. The selection of Houston represented a choice by John F. Kennedy to reach out to Texas voters before the 1964 election and to ensure Johnson's continued commitment to Kennedy's presidency. The Houston location, which reflected the long reach of LBJ's patronage arm, then attracted an influx of engineers, Ph.Ds., computer scientists, and project managers to the city and its southern suburbs. In the first year, more than 1,000 space center staff had transferred to the area. By 1966, a workforce of more than 5,000 men and women oversaw the development of the U.S. space program. Through the Mercury, Gemini, Apollo, Skylab, Apollo-Soyuz, and space shuttle programs, Houston has served as the headquarters of the nation's space exploration program. Because of the city's leadership in the sector, a host of additional aerospace contracting firms have made their way to the Houston area.

Across Texas, much of the growth of the aerospace, aviation, and other related industries dates to the 1960s and the escalation of the Vietnam War. Following the decision in 1961 to locate NASA's headquarters in Houston and the 1962 decision to award a $6.5 billion fighter project to Fort Worth's General Dynamics Corp., Texas' share of defense contracts rose significantly. By 1965, Texas had risen from 11th to eighth in getting defense contracts. By 1968, it was second, behind only California. In 1966, $2.5 billion was disbursed in defense contracts to Texas companies. At the height of the Vietnam War, Texas refineries sold the Department of Defense millions of gallons of jet fuel. Bell produced over 7,000 of the iconic Huey helicopters that symbolize the air cavalry.

Texas' reliance on the aerospace and aviation industry as well as other high-tech industries has increased since the 1970s. A study in 2014 listed more than 1,323 firms, employing over 153,000 workers who were earning average annual salaries of nearly $81,000. The leading firms have long histories in the state: Lockheed Martin, Boeing, Raytheon, Bell, Pratt & Whitney, SpaceX, Bombardier, General Electric, and many more companies constitute one of Texas' most vibrant economic sectors.

Texas has also become an important center for medical research and treatment. Here again Houston has taken the lead. Banker and cotton trader Monroe Dunaway Anderson, with his brother and brother-in-law, built the world's largest cotton trading company between 1904 and 1939. The firm created the M.D. Anderson Foundation in 1939, funding it with $19 million. Two years later, the Texas Legislature appropriated funding to establish a cancer research and treatment center. The M.D. Anderson Foundation agreed to match the legislative appropriation if the state located the hospital in Houston. A temporary facility was built from unused army barracks, and a permanent facility was built in 1950. The hospital became known for innovative therapies, and was among the first to use radiation therapy when most hospitals prescribed surgery alone. It was also among the first centers to use chemotherapy to attack virulent forms of cancer. M.D. Anderson also developed a reputation for promoting African American nurses and physicians. The center shows the role of state and federal funding, combined with private philanthropy, in encouraging innovation in health care research and technological advancement. In 2015, the Texas Medical Center, which combines the University of Texas M.D. Anderson Cancer Center and the University of Texas Health Science Center, was the largest medical center in the world. The University of Texas Medical system annually contributes more than $14 billion to the state's economy.

CHAPTER 6

Domain IV: Geography, Culture, and the Behavioral and Social Sciences

Domain IV: Geography, Culture, and the Behavioral and Social Sciences, like all the other domains except World History and United States History, makes up approximately 13% of the questions you will encounter on the TExES Social Studies 7-12 test. So, here again is a domain that will have you answer roughly 18 to 20 test questions. It is important to note that this chapter is the first of the "social science" chapters. History is often categorized among the "humanities," though historians have also tried to claim that their discipline is a social science with the same rigor and application of the scientific method as the behavioral and natural sciences. Geography, anthropology, sociology, and psychology, however, more clearly illustrate the impact of the "hard sciences" on their disciplines. Geography combines physical and social science approaches, while the other subjects examine the individual and group behavior of human beings. In preparing for Domain IV, then, you will need to concentrate more directly on vocabulary acquisition and concept mastery, rather than on remembering the different narratives that make up the subject matter of the three historical domains.

COMPETENCY 013 (PHYSICAL GEOGRAPHY CONCEPTS, NATURAL PROCESSES, AND EARTH'S PHYSICAL FEATURES)

The teacher understands basic geographic concepts, natural processes involving the physical environment, and Earth's physical features.

> **Competency 013 Descriptive Statement A.** The beginning teacher understands the concept of physical region as an area of the Earth's surface with related physical characteristics (e.g., soils, climate, vegetation, river systems).

Key Question

What are the processes that have shaped the physical environments of Earth? Specifically, what processes have created the various geographic features found on planet Earth?

Geographic Features of the Earth

Thirty percent of planet Earth is composed of land. The geographic regions of the Earth are unified by shared physical features. Some features of the land surface are based on elevation. These include mountain ranges, canyons, hills, mesas, basins, plateaus, valleys, and plains. Other surface features are effects of erosion, climate, and/or vegetation. These include deserts, rainforests, marshes, and swamps. The other 70 percent of planet Earth's surface is composed of water. The Earth's water features include canals, rivers, lakes, seas, and oceans. The descriptive terminology used to identify these surface features of the Earth are important starting places for the geography teacher.

Basins: A basin is a region of land that is drained by a river and its tributaries or drains into a lake or sea. The Amazon River Basin and the Mississippi River Basin are notable examples. The Congo River Basin depicted below drains into the Atlantic Ocean from the interior of Africa. The Congo River and a host of other smaller rivers flow from the intercontinental divide towards the Atlantic.

Figure 6.1
Congo River Basin

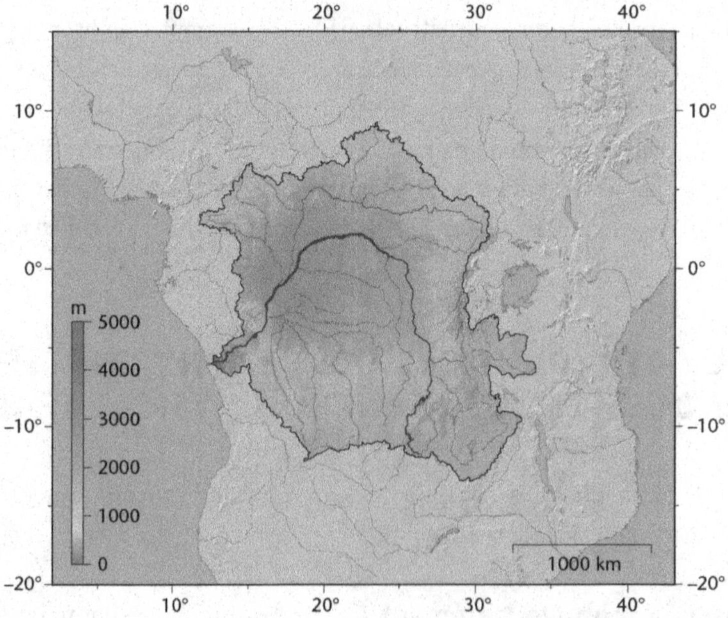

Canals. Canals are man-made passages constructed to connect two larger bodies of water. Such canals are primarily designed to encourage economic development. The canal networks of Mesopotamia were instrumental as irrigation conduits. The ancient Chinese began construction on the Grand Canal that connected the Yangtze River and the Huang He River, enabling transport of grains and consumer items between northern and southern China. More recent examples of commercially vital canals include the Panama Canal (connecting the Pacific and Atlantic oceans), and the Suez Canal (connecting the Red Sea with the Mediterranean Sea). These were the crowning achievements of a 19th-century canal-building boom that saw canal networks created in the United States and Europe.

Deltas. Deltas are triangular areas of land that have been formed by soil and sediment deposited at the mouth of a river. Many deltas have extremely fertile soils, and are important agricultural regions. The Nile Delta, which was the cradle of Egyptian history, is one such example. The marshy Nile Delta region, fed by three channels of the Nile, was the richest agricultural region of the ancient Egyptian kingdom. Similarly, the delta of the Yangtze River sustained one of the most densely populated regions of the pre-industrial world.

Deserts. Deserts are large areas of arid land that receive 10 inches or less of rainfall each year. Notable deserts are the Sahara of northern Africa, the Atacama of South America, the Namib of South West Africa, the Gobi of Asia, the Arabian Desert, and the Outback of Australia. While deserts are sparsely populated, they have not been inconsequential to world commerce. The Sahara, for example, was traversed from ancient times by caravans of donkeys and camels, transporting gold, ivory, and slaves northward to the Mediterranean, as well as cloth, paper, salt, porcelain, and other commodities into West Africa.

Foothills. Foothills consist of hills that are found between mountain ranges and plains. When approaching the Rocky Mountains from the Great Plains region, for example, a traveler first encounters an upland area on the eastern side of the Rockies that extends from New Mexico to Alberta in Canada.

Hills. Hills are a naturally smooth or rounded raised area of land, not as elevated or craggy as a mountain. Most hills rise to an elevation of between 500 and 2,000 feet. Hills are formed by a variety of geographic forces, including faulting, the melting and shifting of glaciers, or through wind and water erosion.

Lakes. Lakes are bodies of water surrounded by land. There are millions of lakes in the world, found in every sort of geographical environment and at nearly all elevations. Most lakes are composed of fresh water, basins for rain, melting snow and ice, and streams. Freshwater lakes are "open," meaning that the water contained in them leaves through an outlet or river. Saline lakes, like the Great Salt Lake in Utah, or the Dead Sea, bordering Israel, the Palestinian Territory, and Jordan, are "closed," in that the water leaves through evaporation. Among the most notable lakes are the Great Lakes of North America; Lake Titicaca of South America; Lake Victoria, Lake Tanganyika, and Lake Malawi of Africa; and Lake Baikal of Asia. The Great Lakes were formed by the withdrawal of glaciers that exposed deep basins as they receded. Lakes Victoria, Tanganyika, Malawi, and Kivu in Africa, and Lake Baikal and the Caspian Sea in Asia were formed as the result of shifting tectonic plates.

Marshes and Swamps. Marshes and swamps are wet lowlands. Swamps are characterized by woody plants, and marshes by non-woody vegetation. Such wetlands are vital to fisheries and bird populations as they provide food sources and cover for a wide range of fish, bird, and wildlife species. Just as importantly, wetland plants absorb nutrients and pollutants through their root systems, acting as a filter that purifies water systems.

Mountains. Mountains are landforms of at least 2,000 feet elevation above sea level, with steep or craggy slopes. Notable mountain ranges, or chains, are the Alps of Europe; the Urals of Europe/Asia; the Himalaya and the Hindu Kush of Asia; the Andes of South America; and the Rocky and Appalachian mountain ranges of North America. These mountain ranges formed when the tectonic plates that formed the Earth's crust collided and buckled upwards. Mountain ranges that formed more recently are marked by sharper, craggier peaks and higher elevations than ranges of older origin.

Oceans. Oceans are the largest bodies of water on Earth. While there is technically only one global ocean, composed of the salt water that covers over 70 percent of the Earth's surface, customarily, geographers have identified four Oceans: the Pacific, Atlantic, Indian, and Arctic Oceans. In 2000, the International Hydrographic Organization counted the "Southern Ocean" that surrounds Antarctica and reaches to 60 degrees latitude among the world's oceans. The world's oceans contain nearly 97 percent of the Earth's surface water. The Pacific Ocean is the deepest ocean, averaging depths of over 15,000 feet, with the Mariana Trench its deepest point, at over 36,000 feet. By comparison, the Atlantic Ocean averages only 10,950 feet deep. Oceans serve a number of important natural functions, including absorbing and storing the Sun's incoming energy. Ocean currents distribute this heat energy, heating the world's surface in winter and cooling it during the summer.

Oceans store the majority of the planet's moisture and energy and heat from the Sun. Surface currents and deep ocean currents circulate that energy between the equator and the poles. Without the oceans, the Earth's surface would suffer much greater ranges of temperature fluctuation, as the oceans distribute heat around the planet.

Plains. Plains are landforms that form regions of flat or rolling land, much lower than other surrounding landforms. Many plains have been formed by river basins over thousands of years, and may have extremely fertile soil. The majority of the world's populations are found in such landforms. Notable plains are the Great Plains of North America between the Appalachian and Rocky Mountain ranges, the Ganges Plain of the South Asian subcontinent, and the plains of China located between the Yangtze and Yellow rivers.

Plateaus. Plateaus are elevated landforms that tend to be level or flat on the top. Plateaus comprise over a third of the Earth's terrain. Though they stand at higher elevations than surrounding landforms, they are different from mountain ranges. The Altiplano of South America and the Tibetan Plateau of Asia are notable plateaus. The Edwards Plateau, seen below, covers some 41 Texas counties. It is the southernmost region of the Great Plains and provided a home for Jumano and Coahuiltecan Indians, before the Apache and later Comanche dominated the area's grazing and farmlands.

Figure 6.2

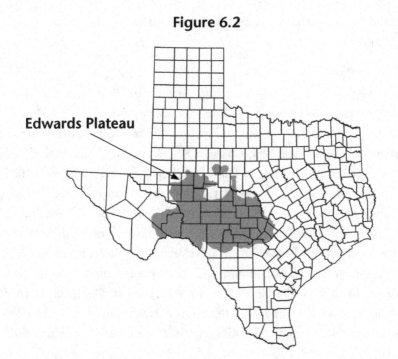

Edwards Plateau

Streams and Rivers. Streams and rivers are bodies of water that have a current and are constantly in motion. Streams and rivers are one of the prominent forces of erosion and deposition of top soil. The source of a stream or river is usually found in high mountains where snows collect and then melt, in high altitude lakes, or in springs, where water erupts from below the surface. A stream or river may have more than one source. The place where two streams join is known as a **confluence.** At the confluence, the smaller of the two joining streams or rivers is known as a **tributary.** The location at which a stream or river enters a larger body of water is known as its **mouth.** Rivers are larger bodies of flowing water formed by melting snow or rainfall that descend from higher elevation to lower elevation. They are often formed by a multitude of streams that join to make up a river. Most rivers empty into a larger body of water, usually a sea or an ocean. River systems consist of large rivers and their many smaller tributary rivers flowing into them. Notable river systems are the Nile and Congo rivers of Africa; the Mississippi River of North America; the Amazon and Orinoco rivers of South America; and the Yangtze, Yellow, Indus and Ganges rivers of Asia.

Divides. Divides are topographical areas that separate landscapes into different water basins. For example, in central Africa, rain that falls on the eastern side of the highlands, which extend from Lake Tanganyika northwards to the southern boundary of the Central African Republic flows into the Nile River. Rain that falls on the western side of this Congo-Nile Divide, descends toward the Congo River. Similarly, rainfall that lands on the western slopes of the Appalachian Mountains flows into the Ohio River and ultimately into the Mississippi. Precipitation that lands on the eastern slope of the Appalachians flows into the Potomac and other rivers that make their way into the Atlantic. This is known as the **Eastern Continental Divide** or **Appalachian Divide.** Similarly, the **Great Western Divide,** which is situated along the Sierra Nevada mountain range, directs precipitation either into the Utah and Nevada basin or into the rivers that descend into the Pacific Ocean through California.

Seas, Gulfs, and Bays. The terms "sea," "gulf," and "bay" are often used with a degree of imprecision. People commonly employ the terms "ocean" and "sea" interchangeably. For example, people make reference to the "high seas" or the "law of the sea" when describing maritime law or ocean passages. Alternately, some bodies of salt water are entirely surrounded by land, and though called "seas" (the Aral Sea, Caspian Sea, Dead Sea, Salton Sea, for example) are in fact counted among the world's lakes. The Earth has over one hundred bodies of water that are called "seas." Seas are large bodies of water, though smaller than oceans, which are nearly surrounded by land or located where the land and the ocean meet. The Mediterranean Sea, the Caribbean Sea, and Sea of Japan are notable seas, partially surrounded by land and bordering oceans. Not all seas, however, border oceans. For example, the Aegean Sea and the Adriatic Sea in the Mediterranean are identified as seas. Additionally, bodies of salt water that might otherwise be identified as seas, the Gulf of Mexico, the Bay of Campeche (within the Gulf of Mexico) or Hudson Bay, which connects to the Arctic Ocean, are large bodies of salt water that are smaller than the oceans but have qualities that in other contexts might result in their being referred to as seas. These terms, therefore, are less reflective of precise geographical denomination than of cultural and historical preferences.

Valleys. Landforms located between hills and mountains are called valleys. Some may have gentle slopes that are suitable for habitation; others may have very steep walls, making farming or homebuilding difficult. Canyons are deeper, narrow, steep-sided valleys, usually with a river carving its way through the valley floor.

> **Competency 013 Descriptive Statement B.** The beginning teacher analyzes ways in which physical processes shape patterns in the physical environment (i.e., lithosphere, atmosphere, hydrosphere, and biosphere).

These spheres of the planet Earth can be analyzed and defined separately; however, they are in constant interaction and influence processes in the other spheres. Water and wind combine to create erosion and weathering of the lithosphere. All interact and influence the biosphere. Even the biosphere has an influence and impact on the others, as it exists within each of the other spheres. Man-made climate change and pollution are two such examples.

Atmosphere. The Earth's atmosphere is the envelope of gases surrounding the planet. This gaseous layer is called the "atmosphere" from the Greek word for vapor or smoke, *atmó*(s). Without this atmospheric layer, life on Earth would not be possible. The atmosphere provides a protective layer against harmful solar rays and most meteorites. It also provides oxygen, water, and warmth. The atmosphere extends only 500 miles from the Earth's surface. There are various layers of the atmosphere that influence weather, climate and life on the surface of the planet. The atmosphere is composed of nitrogen (78 percent), oxygen (21 percent), argon (0.93 percent), carbon dioxide (0.03 percent) and other gases (0.04 percent). The layers of the atmosphere include the *troposphere,* the **ozone layer,** the *stratosphere*, and finally the *mesosphere.* The troposphere, the lowest layer of the Earth's atmosphere, is where most weather takes place. The ozone layer or ozone shield, in between the troposphere and stratosphere, provides a protective shield from the Sun's harmful ultraviolet radiation. The stratosphere begins between 6 and 11 miles above the Earth's surface (except at the poles). Compared to the troposphere, the stratosphere contains little water vapor and weather disturbances. Airplane flights generally seek cruising altitudes in the lower regions of the stratosphere, in order to reduce drag and improve fuel efficiency. Above the stratosphere lies the mesosphere, whose boundaries, like those of the troposphere and stratosphere, vary with the latitude.

Hydrosphere. All of planet Earth's water, including surface water (water in oceans, seas, lakes, and rivers, etc.), groundwater (water in soil and beneath the Earth's surface in aquifers), snow cover, ice, glaciers, and water in the atmosphere (including water vapor, such as clouds and precipitation) all make up the hydrosphere. The Earth's oceans contain 96.5 percent of the planet's water, leaving only 3.5 percent of the Earth's water as fresh water. Moreover, most of the Earth's fresh water is contained in the glaciers and ice sheets of Greenland. While water found in lakes, rivers, etc., is important to transportation, agriculture, and human survival, groundwater is equally critical to agriculture and human survival. For example, the **Ogallala Aquifer,** which extends from West Texas to South Dakota and Wyoming, provides about one-third of the nation's water used for irrigation. The American Great Plains states' wheat, soybean, and cotton production is heavily dependent upon this aquifer for its production.

Lithosphere. The lithosphere is composed of the Earth's surface landforms and landmasses. Though the vast majority of the Earth's surface is covered by water, the landforms and landmasses of the Earth's surfaces serve as the principal location of human habitation. Of the major landmasses, the biggest is Afro-Eurasia. Though often referred to as the three continents of Africa, Europe, and Asia, they in fact make up a single land mass of over 32 million square miles. Only the man-made Suez Canal separates Africa from this large land mass. North and South America are a second land mass only separated by the man-made Panama Canal. In total, the American land mass comprises over 16 million square miles. Antarctica, though hardly hospitable to human habitation as it is covered with ice, is the third largest land mass. Antarctica has an area of over 13 million square miles, nearly as large as North and South America combined. Australia is the smallest of the Earth's continental land masses, with a total area of approximately 3 million square miles. In addition to these continental land masses, there are a number of smaller island land masses: New Guinea, Borneo, Greenland, Madagascar, Baffin Island, Sumatra, Honshu, and Great Britain are the largest of the island land masses off the coasts of the continents.

Biosphere. The biosphere is the zone of life of planet Earth. It is also known as the **ecosphere**. It includes the areas of the lithosphere, atmosphere, and hydrosphere that contain biological living organisms.

Theory of Plate Tectonics

Modern science has developed the theory of plate tectonics. This modern model of the lithosphere consisting of specific plates that move over time helps to explain the movement of continents and the formation of various landforms caused by internal forces of the Earth's mantle. According to this theory, the Earth's core, composed of a liquid outer core and a solid inner core, is surrounded by a mantle composing two-thirds of the Earth's mass. The mantle flows very slowly as heat from the Earth's core results in convection in the mantle. Convection occurs when hotter and consequently less dense matter rises and colder and denser matter sinks under the forces of gravity. This is the power that drives the processes of plate tectonics.

Tectonic plates are sections of the Earth's rigid crust and upper mantle, or Lithosphere. The tectonic plates float on the layer of fluid-like extremely hot rock in the upper layer of the Earth's mantle. Scientists believe that there are currents that flow throughout the upper part of the mantle that carry these tectonic plates. This plate movement over the Earth's history is directly responsible for the continents and many landforms found thereon. There are over 10 different plates; the major ones are referred to as continental and oceanic plates.

Movement of these plates over time results in two different forms of interaction. **Divergence** occurs when plates move away from each other, and **convergence** occurs when plates collide. Divergence of plates can create oceanic rifts at the bottom of the ocean, which results in the formation of new oceanic crust. Above the ocean, divergence creates rift valleys such as are found in eastern Africa. Convergence, or collision of plates, results in formation of fault lines that result in the formation of mountain ranges, volcanoes and earthquakes. These are found on plates' boundaries where plates collide or separate, or even where plates slide past one another.

Subduction is the process when one plate slides beneath a heavier plate at the point of collision. Subduction points can be found on the ocean floor and create deep trenches such as the Mariana Trench.

When plates slide sideways on each other they form major fault lines that are characterized by earthquakes or seismic activity.

Plate movement also contributes to the process of mountain building or **orogeny**. Volcanic activity or plate collisions result in the formation of mountain ranges that are raised above surrounding land.

Weathering and erosion then impact the lithosphere and transform landscapes above sea level. Weathering and erosion is the process of weakening and breaking the landforms of the exposed continental plates. The hydrosphere contributes with rain, ice, and glaciers that over time break down the rocks and mineral of the Earth's surface. Weathering can be either physical or chemical. Physical weathering or erosion can be caused by natural processes, such as the flow of rivers and wind. Chemical weathering is the result of acids in rain and water over time.

Younger mountain ranges are very craggy and broken apart, such as the Rocky Mountains. Older mountain ranges, such as the Appalachian, have been weathered and smoothed over time and are less elevated and craggy.

> **Competency 013 Descriptive Statement C.** The beginning teacher demonstrates knowledge of how Earth-Sun relationships affect physical processes and patterns on Earth's surface.

The location of the Earth in the solar system, it's rotation, revolution and the tilt of its axis, along with its satellite, the Moon, affect global conditions, including the seasons and tides. The Sun, hardly notable by comparison to other stars, dwarfs the other objects in our solar system. The Sun is 500 times the mass of everything else in our solar system. Relative to the Earth, the Sun's mass is 333,000 times greater. It is 109 times the diameter of the Earth. The gravitational pull of the Sun, coupled with the gravitational forces of the other planetary bodies in the solar system exerted on the Earth, keep the Earth orbiting the Sun at a distance that has proven ideal for the survival of life.

Axis. The Earth's axis is an imaginary line that passes through the center of the Earth extending from the North Pole to the South Pole. It is on this axis that the Earth rotates. The axis is tilted in relation to the orbital plane, which results in light from the Sun striking directly on different parts of the Earth's surface as it moves in its revolution around the Sun throughout the year.

Rotation. The Earth requires 23 hours, 56 minutes, and 4 seconds to make a single rotation on its axis. The 24-hour length of an Earth day thus results from this rotation on the Earth's axis. The Earth rotates at the equator at a speed of roughly 1,054 miles per hour. At the poles, however, the speed of the Earth's rotation is nearly zero.

Revolution. The Earth's annual passage around the Sun is known as its revolution. The annual movement of Earth in its orbit around the Sun spans a period of 365.24 days from which we take our calendrical year. By comparison, Venus's revolution or year takes only 226 days; Mars by contrast revolves around the Sun over the course of 687 Earth days, or one Mars year. The Earth's orbit, like that of the other planets, is elliptical rather than circular. This means that at some times of the year the Earth is farther from the Sun than at other times of the year. The Earth is at its farthest distance from the Sun on January 3rd and at its closest distance to the Sun on July 4th.

Moon. The Moon is a natural satellite that revolves around the Earth. The gravitational interaction of these two celestial bodies results in the tidal changes of the Earth's oceans and large lakes. A tide is the rise and fall of large bodies of water. The gravitational pull or attraction of the Moon results in a tidal bulge. As the oceans cycle through these bulges, tides rise and fall. Tidal changes result in vast movements of water that are great potential energy sources.

The rotation, revolution, and tilt of the Earth's axis, combine to influence the climate patterns of the Earth. The seasons of the year are a direct result as the Earth moves in its orbit around the Sun. When the Northern Hemisphere is tilted in the direction of the Sun, it experiences the warmer seasons spring and summer, as the surface temperatures rise. During the same time the Southern hemisphere experiences fall and winter as the surface temperatures cool as it tilts away from the direct rays of the Sun. As the Earth moves in its orbit, the poles reverse and the Southern Hemisphere tilts toward the Sun and experience spring and summer while the Northern Hemisphere experiences fall and winter. Nearer the equator, where the surface of the Earth receives more direct rays all year around, there are two seasons. The rainy, or wet, season, is characterized by an increase in rainfall. The dry season is characterized by a decrease in rainfall. The seasons directly affect all the spheres of the planet Earth, including the atmosphere, hydrosphere, and, especially, the biosphere.

The atmosphere and hydrosphere are affected as different parts of the Earth warm and cool. Air currents develop and change, distributing moisture and precipitation. Ocean currents also warm and cool and have seasonal effects upon weather patterns and surface temperatures. El Niño and La Niña are notable examples.

El Niño and La Niña are among the largest and most important sources of short-term climate change. The cycle, also known as ENSO (El Niño southern oscillation) results in changes in climate that occur over a two- to seven-year cycle. During normal periods, trade winds cross the Pacific Ocean from east to west near the equator. A low-pressure center is situated above the western equatorial Pacific Ocean. The currents warm water in the western Pacific and raise sea levels. Along the coastline of the Americas, the Peru Current takes colder waters northward and then westward along the equator. These cold deep-sea waters bring nutrient-rich water to the surface. In an El Niño year, by contrast, the trade winds either weaken or reverse, blowing toward South America. Warm water from the western Pacific flows across the Pacific and accumulates along South America's west coast. The upwelling of colder, nutrient-rich water is blocked by warmer, low-density water. The decline in nutrient levels reduces plankton populations, the base of the oceanic food web. As a result, fish numbers decrease, as do bird populations. Even humans experience this decline in the fisheries. More importantly, however, the El Niño changes global climate patterns. Rainfall decreases in some regions of North and South America, as well as in the southern United States, and Western Europe. Droughts occur in parts of South America, much of Africa, and southern Europe. This cycle usually lasts one to two years.

The Hydrological cycle is also affected by the Earth-Sun relationship. The cycle of evaporation of water from the ocean due to higher surface temperatures carries water to higher elevations such as mountain ranges. Precipitation falls and forms rivers, or is stored as ice or snow. As the Earth revolves, surface temperatures rise, causing snow and ice to melt. This flows into rivulets and tributaries to rivers and flows toward the oceans once again. The flow of rivers results in erosion changing the landscapes and landforms of planet Earth.

However, due to the tilt of the planet, the two poles remain in extreme cold due to the diffused rays of the Sun striking the poles. This results in continually cold climate and much water remains frozen as ice and snow. Furthermore, the tilt is such that for six months of the year the

Polar Regions will experience either six months of darkness or sunlight, depending on which pole is tilted towards the Sun.

> **Competency 013 Descriptive Statement D.** The beginning teacher analyzes relationships among climate, vegetation, soil and geology to explain the distribution of plants and animals in different regions of the world.

Biomes. A biome is a large community of vegetation and animals that occupy a certain region and are adapted to survive in that region.

Aquatic. Water, which is the largest part of the biosphere, covers nearly 75 percent of the Earth's surface. This biome is home to millions of plants and animal species from the largest to some of the smallest. The aquatic biomes are divided into two subcategories: Freshwater and Marine. Freshwater biomes are found in ponds and lakes, streams and rivers, and wetlands. Freshwater is defined as having a salt concentration usually below 1 percent. The living organisms found in freshwater regions have evolved to thrive in areas of low-salt concentration.

Freshwater Biomes include ponds and lakes, streams and rivers, and wetlands.

Ponds and lakes typically have more limited species diversity as they often develop in greater isolation from other water sources. Freshwater biomes are divided between three different zones associated with the depth of the water and its distance from the shoreline. The *littoral zone* is the region of a pond or lake near the shore and in the shallows. In these warm and shallow waters, the absorption of solar energy supports a diverse range of species, including algae, aquatic plants, snails, insects, fishes, and amphibians. This zone provides abundant food supplies for shore birds turtles, snakes, and many other species. In the open water adjacent to the littoral zone is found the *limnetic zone*. This region is dominated by aquatic plankton and freshwater fish. The plankton serves a vital role for the survival of all species, including human beings. They provide a critical source of nutrients for many other aquatic and other species. As plankton die, they fall into the deep zone of lakes and ponds, the *profundal zone*. Little light penetrates this colder and denser aquatic region.

Streams and rivers change as they descend from their sources to the mouth of the river. Closer to the source are found fish and aquatic species that are adapted to colder, clear, and more oxygen-rich waters. As the river or stream descends it widens, its depth increases, and numerous aquatic species expand the biotic diversity of the river. Then, at the river's mouth, as the river's speed slows and sediments accumulated over its course begin to descend, the water becomes murky, with reduced sunlight and lower oxygen levels. In this part of a river's course, bottom-feeding fish like catfish, carp, or gar find their niche.

Wetland regions are areas of standing water. These include marshes, swamps, bogs, etc. The flora that adapt to this environment include such species as lilies, cattails, sedges, and other similar plant life. Wetlands are characterized by a high level of species diversity. Some wetlands, such as salt marshes with high salt concentrations, are an intermediary zone between marine and freshwater biomes. These support such species as shrimp, shellfish, salt grasses, and other plant and animal species that are adapted to more saline environments.

Marine Biomes are found in oceans, coral reefs, and estuaries. Marine biomes comprise nearly 75 percent of the Earth's surface and contain some 97 percent of the water on Earth. Oceans, coral reefs, and estuaries make up the three most common types of marine biomes. Marine Biomes are critical to the biological diversity and richness of the planet. Algae and tiny marine plants and animals form the basis of the food web on which all life depends. Marine life composes the vast majority of all biomass on Earth. Biomass is the total mass of living organisms. Marine organisms supply food sources and marine plant life that are critical to creation of oxygen.

Forest. Forest biomes make up about one third of the Earth's surface and are biomes that are predominantly trees and other woody vegetation. Forest Biomes are divided into three subcategories: Tropical, Temperate, and Boreal (or Taiga).

Tropical Forest Biomes have the greatest biodiversity of all nonaquatic or terrestrial biomes. Tropical forest biomes are found in the regions directly north and south of the Equator between the Tropic of Cancer (23° N latitude) and the Tropic of Capricorn (23° S latitude). Tropical Forest Biomes are divided between **Tropical Broadleaf Evergreen Forest**, **Tropical Rainforest** (also known as Equatorial Rainforest Biome), and **Tropical Seasonal Forest Biomes** (also known as Tropical Deciduous Forest or Tropical Monsoonal Forest).

Equatorial or **Tropical Rainforests** are generally located on either side of the Equator. Tropical Seasonal Forests are located north and south of the equatorial zone. Tropical forests cover roughly 7 percent of the Earth's surface. Asia contains some 25 percent of tropical forests; Africa has nearly 30 percent; and the Americas hold nearly 45 percent of Tropical Forest Biomes. Tropical Forest Biomes have an abundance of species of plants and animals that make up the biomass of these regions. They are characterized by equal day length, constant heat and moisture levels, and relatively constant temperatures through most of the year. Tropical Forest Biomes require heat and sufficient precipitation to thrive. They are threatened by frost and either frequent or persistent temperatures at or below freezing. While Temperate Forest Biomes are known for their fertile soils, in Tropical Forest Biomes, the soil lacks comparative nutrient richness, as they have only a thin layer of decaying organic matter, and the torrential rains that are commonplace often leach the soil of nutrients. This is one of the reasons that while areas that once were sites of extensive temperate forests (think Ohio and Indiana, for example) yielded rich farmlands, areas in the Amazon or Ituri Forest in the Congo have not been as rich agricultural areas.

Temperate Forest Biomes. Temperate Forest Biomes are situated in the "mid-latitudes" between 40 degrees and 60 degrees latitude. These forests are found most commonly in the eastern United States, west and central Europe, Japan, China, and parts of New Zealand. Temperate Forest Biomes cover approximately 20 percent of the land area of the mid to upper latitudes. The climate of these regions is characterized by seasonal variety and greater temperature variation than that of Tropical Forest Biomes. The trees found in temperate forests are typically deciduous; in other words, they lose their leaves in the winter months. Maples, oaks, lindens, beech, hickory, and sweet gum are commonly found in these forests. Temperate Forest Biomes also have plenty of evergreen trees. Temperate Forests have sufficient rainfall and precipitation over the course of the year, and because of the falling and decaying of leaves annually, the soil in temperate forests is rich and fertile.

Boreal Forest Biomes. Boreal Forest Biomes, also called *taiga*, are found in the high latitudes above 60° latitude. Most Boreal Forest Biomes are located in the northern regions of North America, Europe, and Russia. The vegetation in boreal forests are usually evergreen, cone-bearing trees, like the spruce, pine, and fir species. Temperatures in boreal forests are cold, and these forests experience comparatively less precipitation than temperate or tropical forests. The soil of these forests lacks the nutrient richness of temperate forests because the trees do not drop their leaves, and the cold temperatures slow decomposition processes, even during the short summers of these forest regions.

Grassland. Grassland biomes are dominated by grasses rather than trees and woody vegetation. This biome is divided into two categories, the **Tropical Grassland Biome** and **Temperate Grassland Biomes**. The latter is found in temperate middle latitudes, and the former is found in the tropics. Tropical Grassland Biomes are also known as **Savannas**, while Temperate Grassland Biomes are also called **Steppes**.

Grasses are a family of plants with thousands of different species that share physical characteristics with rushes, sedges, and bulrushes. As a group, this family of plants are flowering, though their flowers (or florets) lack petals and do not attract much attention.

Temperate Grassland Biomes are located in the middle latitudes, in the interior of large continents and between forest and desert biomes. They experience a wide range of temperature variation and are usually found at intermediate elevations, rather than near sea level or at high mountainous altitudes. Below freezing temperatures are common in winter months in the temperate grasslands. Precipitation totals range from 10 to 20 inches annually. The soil of temperate grasslands is rich in nutrient content, as the grasses are typically annuals, completing their life cycle in one year or less, or perennials that live two or more years. Grasslands attract large grazing species that return nutrients to the soil in the form of manure.

Tropical Grassland Biomes are located in low elevations in the tropics where the temperatures experience little variation and frosts are absent. Precipitation in savanna grasslands is usually greater than in temperate grasslands, often varying between 20 and 60 inches a year. These grasslands are found in areas where there is a high-sun rainy season and a low-Sun dry season. By contrast to temperate grasslands, the soil in tropical savanna grasslands is nutrient-poor, leached from tropical rainfall, and acidic. While large grazers and browsers make up a large proportion of the animal population on the savannas, this biome also features many of the world's more threatening carnivores.

Desert Biome. Desert Biomes are found where annual rainfall is less than 10 inches per year. Moreover, in many Desert Biomes, rainfall is not only rare but may come at very irregular intervals. Chile's Atacama Desert, for example, has experienced periods of up to 20 years without rainfall. They make up about 20 percent of the Earth's surface. Desert biomes are divided into four subcategories: Hot and Dry (sometimes simply identified as arid), Semiarid, Coastal, and Cold.

Hot and Dry (Arid) Desert Biomes. Hot and Dry Desert Biomes are often seen as the prototype of desert biomes. As we will see, however, the polar regions are considered deserts, despite looking quite unlike the Sahara or the Gobi deserts. Hot and dry deserts are most frequently located along the tropics. In Africa, for example, the Namib and Kalahari deserts are situated on the Tropic of Capricorn, while the Sahara Desert sits along the Tropic of Cancer. Hot and Dry Desert Biomes are characterized by very irregular and scarce rainfall, little early morning dewfall, significant wind erosion, and wide swings between nighttime and daytime temperatures. Hot and dry deserts are also characterized by little biodiversity of plant and animal species, and limited organic matter in soil that is characterized by low nutrient levels.

Semiarid. The sagebrush deserts of Utah, Montana, and the Great Basin of the United States are among the world's Semiarid Desert Biomes. Like hot and dry deserts, semiarid deserts experience dry and hot summers and winters with little precipitation. Nighttime temperatures, which drop to below 50 degrees in summer, allow plants and animals to reduce moisture loss and concentrations of morning increase semiarid desert's moisture levels. While hot and dry desert soils have higher salt concentrations, soils of semiarid areas are usually shallow, rocky, and gravelly, permitting improved drainage. The dominant plants often feature spiny or woolly exteriors that reduce transpiration, or glossy, silvery leaves that reflect solar radiation. The insect and animal population, like jackrabbits, lizards, snakes, or burrowing owls seek shelter in burrows during the daytime heat.

Coastal Deserts. Coastal Desert Biomes experience cool winters and moderately long, but warm, summers. Temperatures in coastal deserts are moderated by ocean currents that cool the air but also reduce precipitation levels. Average rainfall, like that in other desert regions, ranges from 3 to 5 inches annually. An example of a coastal desert is the Atacama Desert in Chile. The Atacama is the Earth's driest desert. The western Sahara Desert in North Africa is also a Coastal Desert Biome.

Cold Desert Biomes. Cold deserts occur in Greenland, Antarctica, and the Arctic. Unlike most other deserts, Cold Desert Biomes experience greater precipitation during short summers. They also feature long, cold winters. Precipitation averages between 9 and 18 inches of rain or snowfall per year. Animals like jackrabbits, kangaroo rats, and other rats and mice, as well as antelope and ground squirrels, are adapted to the sage brush, spiny cactus, and other low shrubs that dot the landscape.

Tundra. Tundras are treeless plains (from the Finnish word *tunturia*, meaning "treeless plain") and are the coldest of all the biomes. Very little biodiversity is found in tundra biomes. This biome can be divided into two subcategories: arctic tundra and alpine tundra. Tundras experience very low temperatures, low nutrient levels, little precipitation, and very short growing seasons.

Arctic Tundra is found in the regions circling the North Pole. The growing season typically lasts less than 60 days, with winter temperatures averaging below –30° F and summer temperatures only rising to 37°–54° F. Though this growing season lasts less than two months, it is sufficient for the biome to maintain life. Rainfall and melting snow provides annual precipitation of between 6 and 10 inches. The soil consists of a permanently frozen layer of subsoil called permafrost. As melted snow and rainfall accumulates in the upper layers of the soil, bogs and ponds provide nutrients and moisture for plant life. Vegetation, however, is unable to put down deep roots. As a result, shrubs, sedges, mosses, lichens, grasses, and flowers make up the bulk of the flora. This plant life provides sustenance for lemmings, caribou, squirrels, arctic hares, and other herbivores. Arctic foxes, wolves, polar bears, falcons, and ravens live on these herbivores, as well as on abundant cod, salmon, trout and other fish.

Alpine Tundra is a high-altitude biome that develops above the tree line of mountainous regions. Despite a longer growing season, approaching half the year, and with more well-drained soils, the Alpine Tundra Biomes nonetheless have a limited biodiversity, with plant life very similar to that found in Arctic Tundra Biomes.

> **Competency 013 Descriptive Statement E.** The beginning teacher demonstrates knowledge of the patterns and characteristics of the major landforms, climates, and ecosystems of Earth and the processes that produce these patterns and characteristics (i.e., factors that influence physical regions such as elevation latitude, location near warm or cold ocean currents, mountain barriers, and tectonic processes).

Landforms. The form, structure, and character of surface features of the land are known as landforms. A landform consists of a single unit characterized by elevation, slope, stratification, and soil types. These are different from landform regions, which share unifying characteristics that define the surface of a region. Landforms consist of single units such as hills, cliffs, canyons, valleys, mountains, etc.

Landforms result from a variety of natural processes that shape the Earth's surface. Among these are the processes of plate tectonics, erosion, weathering, and deposition. As we have seen in Descriptive Statement B above, plate tectonics give rise to mountain ranges, volcanoes, rift valleys, and other landforms. Glacial movement has also contributed to the development of many distinctive landforms. Glaciers shape the landscape by creating **erosional landforms** or **depositional**

landforms. In erosional landforms, rock and sediment frozen onto the bottom of a glacier act as abrasives, carving deep scratches or glacial grooves into the Earth's surface; this frozen glacier bottom also serves to pluck material from the Earth's surface, creating U-shaped valleys, cirques (scoop-shaped bowls), and other landforms. Depositional landforms occur when glaciers deposit soil, sediment, rocks, and other materials, leaving particles of all sizes in their wake. Wind and water erosion both shape hillsides, river valleys, canyons, etc. The biosphere can also have a direct impact on the development and sustainment of landforms. Plants and trees can affect landforms, such as dunes and marshes.

Finally, of course, human-environment interaction has a very direct and powerful impact on landforms as well. Often, human impact is incremental in its effect and limited to the localized environment. For example, the earliest irrigation canals and water management systems that developed in the Mesopotamian region were small-scale and hardly affected the landforms of the region. But, over time, the effect of poor water management contributed to turning the land between the Tigris and Euphrates River from a region where high yields and fertile soils gave it a just reputation as the cradle of civilization into a region of desolate, barren, and salt-encrusted soil. The Indus River floodplain, the Viru Valley in Peru, and the Salt River region of Arizona experienced similar consequences from the impact of human irrigation efforts. More recently, hydroelectric dams on the Nile, Yangtze, Colorado, Zambezi, and many other world rivers have shaped landforms both downriver and upriver from these projects.

Climate. Climate is the average of weather conditions for a specific location or region over an extended period of time. Weather is the daily conditions of a location, such as temperature, air pressure, wind, and water in the air in the form of humidity or precipitation. Precipitation consists of rain, snow, sleet, or hail. There are three major climate zones that break down into separate more distinct subclimate types. These different types are affected by such varied factors as seasons, latitude, elevation, soil types, annual rainfall, average temperatures, and distance to bodies of water.

Geographers have devised a number of classification systems for categorizing climates. The most widely used of these is the Köppen climate classification system (KCCC) devised early in the 20th century. This system bases its categorization on measurements of monthly and yearly temperatures and precipitation levels. The Köppen climate classification system identifies some 30 different climate types and variants; but for most purposes, geographers distinguish between five different climate zones: Tropical, Moderate, Continental, Polar, and Dry climates. These then are subdivided into more regional climate subtypes. A region's climate, together with its physical characteristics, determines its plant and animal life.

Tropical. A tropical climate in the Köppen climate classification is a humid climate in which all months of the year have average temperatures of at least 64°F. In tropical climates, there are often only two seasons: a wet season and a dry season.

Tropical Wet. Located along the equator, this climate type is characterized by high temperatures and large amounts of rainfall. Average temperature of this region is about 80°F. The average rainfall is around 100 inches, with up to 300 inches per year in some areas. There is no change of season in this climate. Tropical rainforests thrive in these regions, and only cover 6 percent of the Earth's surface, yet they produce 40 percent of the oxygen and support nearly half of all plant and animal species on the planet.

Tropical Wet-Dry. Located on the outer fringes of the Topical Wet climates, Tropical Wet-Dry climates are close to the equator. This climate is characterized by two distinct seasons: wet and dry. The wet, or summer, season is characterized by average temperatures of 77°F, and at least 25 inches of seasonal rainfall. The dry, or winter, season is characterized by average temperatures of 68°F and four inches or less of seasonal rainfall. During the wet season, plant and animal life flourishes, and during the dry season, plant and animal life struggle to survive. The most common vegetation are grasses and shrubs, with a few scattered trees. These types of plants have adapted to long periods of dry weather. The large grasslands are often called *savannas.*

Moderate (Temperate). These climate types generally lie within the tropical and polar regions, in the middle latitudes. Temperatures are moderate and not extremely hot or too cold. Most of humanity lives in the three subcategories of moderate climate.

Humid Subtropical. Found mainly on the east coasts of the Earth's continents, this climate type is found between 20 degrees and 40 degrees latitude. Average temperatures are at or above 70°F, with mild winters. The average rainfall is about 48 inches. Broad-leafed evergreen trees such as ferns and palms are common in these regions. Agriculture and farming are successful, as the growing season is up to eight months.

Mediterranean. Found mainly on the west coasts of the Earth's continents, this climate type is found between 30 degrees and 45 degrees latitude. There are basically two seasons, warm to hot dry summers, and cool mild wet winters. The seasonal changes in these regions are due to ocean currents and nearby water temperatures. This climate type gets its name from the climate around the Mediterranean Sea, which is the body of water that regulates temperature in that part of the world. Fruit trees and vines such as grapes, figs, olives, and citrus fruits grow well here.

Marine West Coast. Found mainly on the west coast of middle latitude locations, this climate type is found between the tropics and the polar regions, and is influenced by the presence of mountains and ocean currents. Ocean currents keep these regions cool in summer and warm in winter though there is comparatively little variation in temperature. Marine west coast climate areas receive regular rain that supports thick forests and a wide variety of plant life, including evergreen trees (conifers) such as spruce, cedar, pine, and redwood. Temperate rainforests are also found in these regions.

Continental. Found in the interior of the continents of Asia and North America, these regions have relatively dry seasons with very hot summers and very cold winters.

Humid Continental. Located predominantly in the Northern Hemisphere between 30 degrees and 60 degrees latitude. This region is characterized by four distinct seasons, a warm humid summer, a cool dry fall, a cold harsh winter, and a warm wet spring. The summers can have temperatures above 100°F and winters have temperatures below 0°F. These areas receive 20–50 inches of precipitation annually, including snow during the winters. These regions are dominated by vast plains called temperate grasslands. This climate is excellent for farming since it has warm summers and regular rainfall.

Subarctic. Found only in the Northern Hemisphere, this region is found in the interior parts of northern continents between 50 degrees and 70 degrees latitude. Located inland, these areas have only two seasons, summer and winter. Far from regulating bodies of water, the temperatures in winter are extreme, as cold as minus 40°F. Summers are short and mild reaching temperatures up to 85°F. Evergreens such as coniferous spruce and pine do well in this region. These forests are referred to as Taiga, and make the largest land biome on Earth, covering vast parts of Canada and Russia.

Polar. These regions are found in the areas surrounding the North and South poles.

Tundra. Found in the Northern Hemisphere, this region is located between 60 degrees and 75 degrees latitude. There are two seasons: cold-harsh winters and cool summers. In the winters, temperatures can reach up to minus 50°F; the summers are 35° to 50°F. The soil below the surface in this area can remain frozen year round, and is called permafrost. The permafrost prevents trees and vegetation from growing in these areas, although lichens and algae survive well.

Icecap. Located at either pole, these regions are the most extreme climates on the planet Earth. There are two seasons, mainly determined by night and day, not temperature fluctuations. The summer, when there is 24 hours of sunlight, temperatures average minus 16°F. The winter, when there is 24 hours of darkness, temperatures average minus 70°F. No traditional vegetation can survive in these regions; however, some rare lichen do.

Dry. These are regions of Earth that receive little precipitation, and the air is dry throughout the year.

Semiarid. These regions are found on the fringes of arid climate regions. They can be found in both hemispheres, and can be cold or warm. These areas can receive some rainfall, but are prone to long droughts that make survival hard. Temperatures depend on location along lines of latitude. Mainly shrubs and grasses are found in these regions.

Arid. Found mainly along the 30-degree line of latitude in both the Northern and Southern hemispheres, arid regions receive less than 10 inches of rainfall annually. Some parts are found in the rain shadow of mountain ranges. There are no regular seasons in these regions, mainly dry hot days, and some very cold nights. Antarctica qualifies as a desert, as it has less than 10 inches of precipitation each year. Little vegetation thrives in these regions unless they require very little water, or can store water. Cacti and certain grasses and scrub bushes can survive.

Highland. Found in high mountain areas, these regions are found on mountains of high elevation or plateaus of high elevation. There are no seasons in highland climates. Elevation along the slopes determines the various differences in climate from low elevation to higher elevations. Precipitation, temperature, and vegetation are all determined by elevation along the slopes or the elevation of the plateau.

COMPETENCY 014 (GLOBAL AND REGIONAL PATTERNS OF CULTURE AND HUMAN GEOGRAPHY)

The teacher understands global and regional patterns of culture, and characteristics and processes associated with different culture regions.

Key Question

What is culture? How does it develop and spread? How do cultural patterns and regions interact and influence human geography?

> **Competency 014 Descriptive Statement A.** The beginning teacher understands the concept of cultural region as an area of Earth's surface with unifying cultural characteristics.

Just as the Earth can be divided into regions based on physical characteristics and landforms that share similarities, such as mountain ranges, desert, or bodies of water, the Earth is also divided into cultural regions. These cultural regions share similar characteristics that allow geographers to categorize human culture into culture regions. Most cultural practices were developed over time through human interaction with the environment in which they dwelled. Until recently, when humanity has achieved a higher level of environmental control, most cultural adaptation of people has been determined by their surrounding environments.

The Earth's culture regions are based on many different characteristics; however, the most common categories are based on religion, language, politics, and standard of living. Thus both geographers and the wider public employ such terms as the "West," which combines the United States, Canada, Australia, and much of Europe in one geographic and cultural category. The term "developing world" is juxtaposed against the "developed world" to designate other cultural and economic categories. Similarly, it is not uncommon for journalists, scholars, and others to refer to the "Islamic world." Such distinctions are not based directly upon climate, landforms, or latitude, but upon human beliefs, activities and institutions. The study of these characteristics within a geographical context is known as the study of human geography.

Human Geography. Geographers not only study the location of landforms and biomes, but also focus on human activities. Culture, language, and religious practices are some of the things geographers focus on; however, any and all human beliefs and activities are part of human geography. Most significantly, human geography studies the ways in which humans across the world and in all cultures adapt to and modify their natural environments. Human geography differs from physical geography in that it focuses on human activities regardless of the culture.

Race. One classification system that has been used as a tool of human geography has been race. Race, as a biological concept, refers to categorizations of people into groups based on shared physical characteristics and genetic ancestry. Most social scientists have increasingly argued that race is a social construct with limited scientific foundation. Racial differences and racial systems of categorization were prominent tools used in the 19th and 20th centuries to sustain imperial expansion, systems of racial inequality, slavery, and immigration restrictions. As a result, race has become a much more problematic category of analysis for social scientists generally and for geographers specifically.

Cultural geography examines the role of culture in adapting to and/or shaping the environment.

Culture. Typically, culture is identified as the shared attitudes, beliefs, language, and way of life that is passed down from generation to generation. As such, it is seen as a system of symbols and meaning shared within a community. These different practices divide peoples of the world into different culture regions. Thus, we can speak of an "American culture," or a "Chinese culture," or a "Samoan culture." This definition, however, understates the degree to which culture is always changing and often contested, even within a community. Moreover, this definition appears to de-emphasize the material or economic influences and features of a culture, while privileging such things as religion, folk beliefs, or ideology. When thinking about "culture," it is worthwhile remembering that "culture" does *not* mean "high culture" in the sense that we say someone is a "cultured person," or that the arts correspond to "high culture." Instead, think of culture as a combination of "material culture" (the tools, homes, transportation, clothing, furniture, and other items of daily life); social institutions (governmental entities, the economy, educational institutions, families and households religious beliefs and practices, and other social communities like tribes, clans, and nations); and language and representational forms (art, music, dance, theater, etc.). Each of these aspects of culture are learned and transmitted through language, but also often contested or reshaped by groups within a wider culture in ways that are not necessarily shared equally by all members of the culture.

There are common to all cultures a number of "cultural universals." These cultural universals include the following:

1. A communication system that employs vocalization of a limited number of sounds and grammatical rules for formalizing communication.

2. Classification systems that rely on gender and age, as well as marriage status and kinship relationships, to differentiate populations.

3. The practice of raising children in family settings and establishing a form of gender division of labor.

4. Rules that govern sexual behavior and establish realms of privacy.

5. A normative system that distinguishes good from bad behavior.

6. A developed leadership structure to determine how community decisions will be made.

7. Aesthetic standards and artistic traditions.

8. Bodily ornamentation or stylistic expressions.

Subculture. This is a group of people within a larger culture who share ideas and beliefs that are different from their main culture, but still retain some of the core values and beliefs of the main culture. Often subcultures are defined by their deviation from the beliefs or practices of the dominant culture. For example, the emergence of youth subcultures since the 1950s has attracted scholarly interest. These subcultures were seen as representing a desire to act out or resist the dominant or mainstream culture. In other cases, subcultures result from the mixing of culture that occurs in complex societies where inhabitants of a region have come from many parts of the world. For example, in the United States, we can speak of subcultural groups such as Vietnamese Americans, African Americans, Mexican Americans, etc. Within these subcultures, elements of these populations' culture of origins are retained alongside features of the wider American culture.

Language. The method of communication, both spoken and written, that humans use to express thoughts and feelings is central to culture. Languages relate to one another in much the same way that family groups do. Language families are descended from a common prehistorical language. For example, there are some 445 Indo-European languages spoken today. These languages are descended from a single Proto-Indo-European language spoken in the Neolithic era, likely spoken in the region north of the Caucasus region of Central Asia. From this Proto-Indo-European language developed a number of sub-groups of languages, including Germanic languages (from which developed English, German, Dutch, Danish, and Swedish, among others), Hellenic and Greek, Celtic languages (from which emerged modern Welsh, Scots Gaelic, etc.) and the Indo-Iranian languages (from which developed ancient Sanskrit and Old Persian, and the modern languages of Hindustani, Bengali, Punjabi, and other South Asian languages.) Similarly, in Africa, most languages spoken in eastern and southern Africa are languages from the Bantu language family.

Just as national identities often congeal around shared language, subcultures are formed around their own exclusionary language. One need only think of the way that scientific jargon serves as a barrier to entry of those not trained in it, or the way in which youth cultures use a specialized vocabulary to keep the older generation at bay to see how language is used both to include members and exclude non-members.

Religion. Religion refers to a belief in supernatural forces or beings that consists of an organized system of rituals, ceremonies, and rules. Religious beliefs help give meaning to a society's perception of the natural world and help order a society's time according to a ritual calendar. Religion also serves to establish ethical and moral guidelines for acceptable behavior. Geographers have developed a method of classifying religions that divides them into two major groups: **universalizing religions** and **ethnic religions**. Universalizing religions seek to proselytize or convert non-members and are thought to have a message and moral teachings that apply to all humans. Ethnic religions are associated with specific ethnic or national groups, and little effort is made to attract new adherents from outside the community. Christianity and Islam are both universalizing religions; Buddhism. Hinduism, Judaism, and Shintoism are ethnic religions, as is Sikhism.

Political systems. Political systems provide another important unit of analysis for geographers. Political geography may in fact be one of the oldest fields in the study of human geography. Political geographers analyze the relationship between spatial perspectives and physical geography and political, cultural, and economic systems. Political systems are the sets of laws, principles, and ideas relating to a form of government. Often a culture's economic system will also be intertwined with its political systems. Political geographers examine the relationship between spatial and geographical settings and local, national, and international politics. However, most often the country, or more formally, the **nation-state** provides political geographers with their focus of study. A **nation-state** is defined as a geographically bounded or defined sovereign (independent) state comprised of citizens sharing a common heritage, cultural identity, and political goals. The concept of the nation-state is a relatively recent development, only arising in 18th-century Europe, with the Enlightenment, French and American Revolutions. Before the emergence of the nation-state as the idealized political entity, most political systems were kingdoms (the hereditary domain of a dynasty) or empires, which combined many different ethnic, linguistic, and national communities under the rule of a single ruler or dynasty.

Standards of Living. A simplistic definition of the concept of "standard of living" essentially conceives the concept as the level of wealth, comfort or well-being of a cultural region or nation-state. In purely material terms, then, this can be simplified to a measure of the sum total of goods and services at the disposal of residents of a region. Often, real Gross Domestic Product (GDP) has been used to measure the standard of living of specific nations or world regions. To gauge the standard of living of individuals in a nation, per capita GDP has served as a useful measure. This measure also provides a means to compare economic growth rates with those of populations to gain a clearer measure of the economic health of a population. Often, the standards of living of a region correlate positively with the natural resource base of a region.

> **Competency 014 Descriptive Statement B.** The beginning teacher analyzes ways in which cultural processes of innovation and diffusion shape patterns in the human environment.

Cultures are not static, unchanging entities. Even societies that are described as "traditional" undergo frequent changes and innovation, and are subject to outside influences that transform them in important ways. A feature of modern society has been both a rapid increase in change brought about by innovation, whether technologically or ideologically driven. Modern societies have also experienced significant increases in the rate of change that occurs as a result of diffusion that takes place as a result of movements of peoples around the globe. In all periods of human history, ideas, technology, and cultural practices have spread from one region to another as a consequence of migration, trade, travel, conquest, missionary activity, and other human interaction. This process of diffusion sped up, first with the development of industrial age transportation and communication techniques such as the steamship, railroad, and telegraph. Today, diffusion is often instantaneous, as an idea expressed in one distant part of the planet can be immediately received elsewhere. I can, for example, find a recipe for Kao Phad Sapparot (a vegetarian Thai dish) posted online by a chef in Bangkok in the morning and be cooking it by lunchtime.

Innovation and diffusion, however, occasionally encounter resistance, adaptation, or syncretism. Novel technologies, ideas, beliefs, or cultural practices are never just adopted wholesale without adaptation.

Resistance to cultural and technological change takes many forms, and most new ideas and technologies face resistance.

Other technologies and ideas are appropriated by those that adopt them, and put to novel uses. The Model T Ford, for example, represented a revolutionary transportation technology. However, farmers across the United States not only used them to travel and transport goods, but also took their rear tires off, attached pulleys or belts to the wheel and then used the vehicle as a power tool to drive wood saws, drills, and other equipment. This was not what Henry Ford had intended. The farmers appropriated the technology and put it to uses unintended by its inventors. This is an example of adaptation.

As ideas diffuse from one place to another they are often changed through processes of **syncretism.** Syncretism is a process that involves the merging of different religions, cultures, or ideas. As Christianity diffused across the Roman, and later the Germanic "pagan" world, Christianity changed as missionaries and converts adapted its message to make sense to new adherents. Many of the features of Christian practice, like the way Christmas and Easter are celebrated reflect practices that derived from pre-Christian societies in Western Europe.

The terminology that cultural geographers and anthropologists use to describe these processes of diffusion, innovation, and change is below.

Spatial diffusion. Geographers are interested in spatial diffusion, or processes spread across geographic landscapes of a variety of phenomena, including technologies, cultural trends, ideas, or even epidemic diseases.

Expansion diffusion. Expansion diffusion occurs when ideas or innovations spread throughout a culture and eventually to other culture regions. This can occur along borders between cultures, through trade, and intermarriage between individuals from different culture groups. Geographers identify two types of expansion diffusion: contagious diffusion and hierarchical diffusion.

Contagious diffusion. Contagious diffusion occurs when ideas or innovations are transmitted over space as a result of person-to-person contact within a given culture or between different cultures. This can occur by word of mouth, person-to-person contact, or via the internet and mobile devices. Epidemic disease, of course, offers a model for such transmission. However, in the modern context when an idea or meme "goes viral," it is fair to say that it is being spread by a process of contagious diffusion.

Hierarchical diffusion. Hierarchical diffusion refers to the spread of ideas or cultural practices between locales that are similarly situated on the hierarchical continuum of urban spaces. There is, for example, a greater degree of diffusion of cultural practices, music, or styles among the cultural capitals of London, New York City, Los Angeles, and Paris than between Paris and rural Brittany, or between New York and small towns in rural upstate New York. Thus, New York and Los Angeles will adopt new styles in music, clothing, etc., before secondary regional urban centers, such as Chicago, Boston, or Cincinnati.

Hierarchical diffusion thus describes the descent of ideas or innovations as they spread from more powerful or influential cultures to smaller or subjugated cultures. This can occur when a group of people is conquered and subjugated by another culture. It can also occur within a culture group when those in positions of power and influence dominate those of less power or influence.

Stimulus diffusion. Stimulus diffusion refers to changes in one culture that are prompted by an innovation or invention elsewhere. The introduction of the stirrup from Asia and the Islamic world to medieval western Europeans in the eighth century, for example, led to a whole host of technological and social innovations. Swords were lengthened to be useful from horseback and the short-blade *spata* used in Roman times was abandoned. A wing was added to the common lance to prevent it from too deeply penetrating when it was driven into a victim by force of the horse's forward momentum. Additionally, the infantry became less critical to medieval armies, perhaps resulting in the emerging of the feudal system itself. As another example, the introduction of block printing in Europe, a technique developed in China, led to the innovation of movable type printing presses.

Relocation Diffusion. Relocation diffusion occurs when ideas or innovation spread through the migration of individuals or groups of people moving from one region to another. These people bring their own ideas and beliefs to new locations and then spread them throughout the new region. Waves of migration to the United States have resulted in successive influences of relocation diffusion. In the late 19th and early 20th centuries, Italian, Polish, Russian, Czech, Irish, and other European immigrants brought new food ways, languages, social conventions, and other influences that helped shape the development of the United States. Since 1965, Latin American, African, and Asian migrants to the United States have again introduced new cultural traditions to the country.

Adaptation. The concept of adaptation as used in cultural geography reflects the influence of the biological sciences and evolutionary theory. Most organisms have adapted to life in a particular environment. Similarly, cultural groups undergo changes in behavior and beliefs based on changing economic, social, political, and environmental conditions. However, rather than stressing the role of heredity or genetic adaptation, in cultural geography, the emphasis on adaptation identifies the ways in which groups develop cultural modifications or learn new techniques in order to adapt to changing environmental, economic, or political circumstances. For example, the Bedouins adapted to take advantage of the desert environment of the Sahara and the Inuit people adapted technologies and social institutions that allowed them to thrive in the inhospitable environment of the Arctic.

Acculturation. Another way to describe expansion diffusion, acculturation occurs when two different cultures come into regular contact with each other. Acculturation, however, usually takes some time to fully develop. When a culture is fully acculturated, it is said to be assimilated into another.

Assimilation. Assimilation refers to the completion of the acculturation process. When two cultures in regular contact with one another result in cultural or behavioral assimilation, it can be said that the ethnic aspects of the two cultural groups have been united functionally. Important measures of the degree of assimilation that exists between two cultures are high rates of intermarriage and eliminations of spatial segregation between the two groups. Often, even with fully assimilated cultures, the persistence of such things as ethnic restaurants, social clubs, or segregated religious institutions indicate the slow progress of assimilation. Assimilation may also be reversed. For example, the movement of automobile factories out of Michigan's urban centers to suburban and then southern states, resulted in a reversal of African American assimilation that had been underway in Detroit, Flint, Saginaw, Lansing, and other Michigan cities since World War I. Economic changes and the rise of nativist sentiments can often reverse processes of assimilation that are well underway.

Extinction. Cultures, like species, can also completely disappear from existence. This can occur due to disease, famine, or warfare. Perhaps the most striking example of cultural extinction resulted from the arrival of Europeans in the Americas after 1492. Whole Amerindian tribes were annihilated by the combined effect of epidemic disease, enslavement, and warfare. Even where there were individual survivors, in the aftermath of disease and widespread death, Native American tribes often had to move, adapt to new environments, and frequently merge with other ethnic groups. Cultural extinction takes place today as well. Often this extinction can be measured by examining the loss of world languages.

Competency 014 Descriptive Statement C. The beginning teacher demonstrates knowledge of locations and cultural environmental features of major world regions and regions of the United States and Texas.

The study of world regional geography necessitates that the world be divided into separate regions for study and understanding. These regions are based on various physical characteristics such as location, climate, landforms, bodies of water, and human characteristics such as development, language, and religion.

North America. North America *as a cultural region* includes the United States and Canada. These two countries share location and geographical features. They share similar languages, religions, and other cultural aspects. Both share a history of colonialism, and are today nations descended from immigrants from other parts of the world, but predominantly Europe. North America is characterized by a high rate of urbanization. Approximately 80 percent of the residents of North America live in urban areas. Both Canada and the United States experience high standards of living in the aggregate. The United States has the world's largest economy. Canada's GDP places it in the top 10 nations. In per capita terms, the United States ranked eighth, and Canada 16th in 2017.

Mexico, Central America, and the Caribbean. Central America (Mexico, Guatemala, Honduras, Costa Rica, Belize, El Salvador, Panama, and Nicaragua) is a cultural region sometimes referred to as Mesoamerica. It is often grouped with the Caribbean island nations found in the Greater Antilles (Cuba, Jamaica, Haiti, and the Dominican Republic) and the smaller island nations of the Lesser Antilles (Saint Kitts, Nevis, Antigua, Barbuda, Montserrat). Mesoamerica is often grouped together for cultural and linguistic reasons. Most of the region was a part of the Spanish colonial empire. Belize, however, was a part of the British Empire. Excluding Mexico, the nations of Mesoamerica form the land bridge between South America and North America, and share many climatic and geographic conditions. Most of the inhabitants of the region also are adherents to Roman Catholicism. The Caribbean, though frequently grouped with the Central American nations, is quite diverse. Spanish is spoken in many nations, but French, Dutch, and English are also national languages. The Caribbean island nations reflect the diverse colonial history of the region. The presence of descendants of African slaves is also more pronounced than in Mesoamerica, though many residents in Costa Rica, Honduras, Belize, and Mexico are also of African descent. The Caribbean received nearly two-thirds of all slaves who were part of the forced migration of Africans to the Americas. With the abolition of slavery, many South Asians were transported to the Caribbean to work as indentured laborers on the sugar plantations. As a consequence, islands nations like Trinidad and Tobago have large populations of South Asians and a culture that combines African, British, and Indian features.

South America. South America includes all of the diverse countries of the South American continent. There is a large variety of climates and landforms, from the cool Andes to the Brazilian rainforest. Levels of development vary throughout the continent with pockets of development and developing regions. These countries also share a history of colonialism from Spain and Portugal. As a consequence, while most of the region is Spanish-speaking, Portuguese is the dominant language in Brazil. The diverse populations of South America also reveal the impact of the slave trade. Fully 35 percent of all enslaved Africans transported to the Americas were taken to the Portuguese colonies of Brazil. In the 19th century, Argentina, Chile, Uruguay, Brazil, and Paraguay benefited from an influx of European migrants, just as the United States benefited from a wave of Italian,

German, and other European immigrants. This migration would persist until after World War II. Along the Pacific Rim of South America, Asian migration contributes to the ethnic and cultural diversity of Peru, Chile, Ecuador, and Bolivia.

Europe. Europe includes all of the countries of western and eastern Europe, as well as Russia. Though Russia spans across Asia, its culture and history are connected to Europe. The climates of western Europe are regulated by bodies of water and warm ocean currents. In central Europe and Russia, the effect of these ocean currents diminishes, resulting in colder winters and greater fluctuations in temperatures. Southern Europe is marked by a Mediterranean climate. Northern and western European nations experience high standards of living and high rates of urbanization. Most European nations also have developed strong social support networks, including socialized medicine in a variety of forms, extensive protections for workers, and generous pension plans. Western European nations also have well-developed traditions of representative government.

Northern Africa, Southwest Asia, and Central Asia. The defining feature of this cultural region is less geographic or climatic, than religious. For most of the region, Islam represents a powerful cultural and religious unifying force. Additionally, though there are other languages spoken throughout the region, Arabic is the predominant language spoken in most of this cultural region. This region includes the Maghreb, or the countries of North Africa, the nations of Southwest Asia (in popular parlance, often called the Middle East), and the former Soviet countries of Central Asia. Climates vary here, but are predominantly hot and dry desert, semiarid, or Mediterranean. Levels of development vary widely in the region. Qatar, for instance, ranks above the United States in per capita GDP; and Israel, Kuwait, the Kingdom of Saudi Arabia, Bahrain, and the United Arab Emirates all experience standards of living on a par with those in Western Europe. The wealth of these nations results from (with the exception of Israel) the presence of vast oil reserves. Other nations in this region, however, rank among the poorest in the world. Uzbekistan, Palestine, Kyrgyzstan, and Afghanistan are in the poorest third of the world's nation-states.

Sub-Saharan Africa. This region includes the many developing countries of Africa located south of the Sahara Desert. Climates are wetter and hotter in this region. Sub-Saharan Africa features large areas of Equatorial or Tropical Rainforest and Tropical or Savanna Grasslands. In the southwestern corner of the continent, the Namib and Kalahari deserts stretch from Angola to South Africa. At the Cape of Good Hope on the southern tip of Africa, one can even find a small region with a Mediterranean climate. These countries share a history of the impact of European colonialism. Indeed, the boundaries of these nation-states reflect European efforts to carve up Africa between the British, French, Belgian, German, and Portuguese empires. Most African political boundaries were drawn with little attention to the ethnic or historical traditions of African peoples. For example, the Maasai people and their lands were divided at the Berlin Conference of 1884–1885 as Germany took German East Africa (Tanganyika), and the British took British East Africa (Kenya and Uganda). Most African nation-states also have many ethno-linguistic groups within their boundaries. More than 200 indigenous languages, for example, are spoken in the Republic of the Congo. Over 520 languages are spoken in Nigeria. Africa, thus, is characterized by enormous diversity, both geographically and culturally.

South Asia or the Indian subcontinent. Within the boundaries of the Indian subcontinent or South Asia are the modern nations of India, Pakistan, Bangladesh, Nepal, Bhutan, and Afghanistan, though an island off the coast of the subcontinent, Sri Lanka should also be seen as part of this cultural region. The geographic boundaries of the region are the Himalayan and Hindu-Kush mountain ranges to the north and west, and the Arabian Sea to the west and Bay of Bengal to the east. South Asia is divided between four primary climate zones. The south of India and Sri Lanka have a tropical rainforest climate. The interior has a tropical climate with varying precipitation levels. Northwestern India, Pakistan, and Afghanistan have dry subtropical climates, and the Himalayan and Hindu-Kush region have alpine climates.

The peoples of the region that settled before 3000 BCE arrived from southeast Asia, Africa, and the Pacific Islands. Since that time, migration has been predominantly from the northwest, through the passes in the Hindu-Kush mountains. The entire subcontinent, with the exception of the period during which it was under British rule, has not been unified in one political system, though much of the region was united under the Mauryan, Gupta, and later Mughal empires. South Asia is reported to have over 400 languages from six different language families. In India alone, nearly 500 million people speak Hindi as their first language; Bengali, Telugu, Marathi, Tamil, and Urdu all have over 50 million speakers. Over 125 million speak English in India; in Pakistan, Sri Lanka, Bangladesh, Bhutan, and Nepal, English is either a co-official or commonly spoken language. This reflects the legacy of the British Empire's rule over the region.

East Asia. This region includes the nation-states of China, North Korea, South Korea, Taiwan, and Japan. Climates vary throughout the region. In southeastern China, for example, tropical climates predominate, while in northern and western China, arid and semiarid climates are common. In northeastern China and North Korea and South Korea, by contrast, humid continental climates predominate. The islands of Japan are divided between humid continental and tropical climates. By contrast with South Asia, with its linguistic and ethnic diversity, East Asia has relative ethnic and linguistic homogeneity. Chinese, Korean, and Japanese are the dominant languages of the region. This comparative homogeneity disguises a greater diversity, however. Chinese speakers speak a number of different dialects, many of them mutually unintelligible. By far the most commonly spoken dialect is Mandarin. China has many residents that speak other languages as well. Japan and Korea are more homogeneous linguistically. Economically, Japan is commonly categorized among the western, industrialized, and capitalistic economies. Taiwan and South Korea have since the 1970s industrialized at a rapid rate and boast high standards of living and social development. The People's Republic of China lags behind Taiwan, Japan, and South Korea (as well as Hong Kong and Macao) in per capita GDP, but since the 1980s has grown into the second largest economy in the world, trailing only the United States.

Southeast Asia. This region lies between India, China, New Guinea, and Australia. The mainland of Southeast Asia contains the nations of Vietnam, Cambodia, Laos, Thailand, Burma, and West Malaysia. Maritime Southeast Asia is composed of the island nations of Indonesia, East Malaysia, the Philippines, Singapore, East Timor, Brunei, and a number of smaller island nations. The region in 2016 had a population approaching 650 million people, made up of a wide range of ethnic and cultural groups. Climates in Southeast Asia are predominantly tropical, with wet-dry and savanna climates. Languages and religions vary throughout the region. Indonesia is the most populous Muslim-majority country in the world. In the region as a whole, Islam counts over 250 million followers. Buddhism predominates in Vietnam, Thailand, Laos, Cambodia, Burma, and Singapore. Christianity is the dominant religion of the Philippines. Historically, Chinese merchants played an important role in the trade of the region, and Chinese influences remain important. Singapore, Brunei, Vietnam, Malaysia, and Indonesia have rapidly industrialized since the 1960s. While per capita living standards still lag behind those in South Korea, Japan, and Taiwan, Southeast Asia has experienced significant commercial and industrial growth.

Oceania. This region includes the larger island nations of Australia and New Zealand, and also includes the many other island nations in the Pacific Ocean.

Regions of the United States. The United States is commonly divided into six regions, based primarily on location, though there are regional cultural traits that bind these areas together as regions as well.

Northeast. The Northeast is usually described as constituting the states that make up New England (Maine, New Hampshire, Vermont, Massachusetts, Rhode Island, and Connecticut) and the Mid-Atlantic states (Pennsylvania, New York, New Jersey, and Delaware). Occasionally, Virginia, Maryland, West Virginia, and the District of Columbia are included among the Mid-Atlantic states, though just as often they are characterized as belonging culturally and historically to the southeastern United States.

New England has a rocky coastal landscape on the Atlantic, which rises in the interior to the Appalachian mountain range. It features cold winters and a short growing season. It is blessed with pockets of very fertile soil and abundant precipitation in the form of both snow and rainfall, with an average of four inches of precipitation per month. New England's coastline has many inlets and coves, which have contributed to a history of fishing and maritime commercial activity. Culturally, though waves of Irish, French, Portuguese, Italian, and other immigrants have changed the ethnic makeup of the region, the reach of the region's first Puritan settlers continues. One feature of this continued legacy may be seen in the characteristic New England accent, which itself originated in the Norfolk whine of the East Anglian region of England where many Puritans came from. The Puritan emphasis on education can be seen in the number of prominent public and private universities that continue to lead American higher education.

The Mid-Atlantic states are bisected by the Appalachian Mountains, which extend through the region from southern Virginia to New England. The coastal plains rise to the ridgeline of the Appalachians, and to the west the Appalachian Plateau extends across western New York, Pennsylvania, and West Virginia into Ohio. The northern states of Pennsylvania and New York experience similarly high amounts of snow and rainfall, and cold temperatures. Maryland, Delaware, and New Jersey, as well as West Virginia, Virginia, and the District of Columbia are plentifully supplied with rain, but do not experience the frigid winter temperatures or quantities of snow. Culturally, the Mid-Atlantic states have historically been characterized by their diversity, both religiously and ethnically. The cities of Philadelphia and New York were conduits of immigration from their earliest days and thus served as gateways to successive waves of German, Scots-Irish, Irish, and later immigrants who shaped the culture of the region. In the western regions of New York and Pennsylvania, many of these immigrants settled on the fertile soils of the Appalachian Plateau. Western New York and Pennsylvania were the first "bread baskets" of the early United States.

Southeast. The southeastern region of the United States is composed of a number of geographic regions. **The Atlantic Coastal Plain and the Gulf Coastal Plain** extend along the Atlantic Ocean and Gulf of Mexico. This region with its subtropical climate, warm temperatures, and abundant rainfall served as the foundation of the plantation economy that developed during the colonial period and extended well into the 20th century. The **Piedmont Region** is an area of rolling hills that separate the Atlantic Coastal Plain and the Appalachian Mountains. This region proved an enormously fertile area for tobacco and later cotton production. Less prosperous, but no less culturally significant to the development of the region, was the **Appalachian Mountain System** which included the Blue Ridge Mountains and Great Smoky Mountains. Because the region was less suited to planting cotton, tobacco, rice, indigo or sugar, it attracted fewer large landholders and instead drew poor white farmers to the region. In particular, Scots-Irish, Scots, and Irish immigrants migrated to the many "hollers," or valleys, that reached into the mountain system. Similar populations moved into the Ozarks in Missouri. A number of marshlands, piney woods, and wetlands flourished across the Southeast and in Virginia, northeastern North Carolina, Arkansas, and east Texas. In each of these regions distinctive economic activities and populations shaped the cultural geography of the Southeast. The climate across the region is generally warm with hot, humid summers and mild winters.

The Southeast has, like the Northeast, developed a distinctive regional culture with its own vocal rhythm and accents, folkways, food ways, vocabulary, etc. One influence on this regional culture was the fact that many of the migrants to Virginia, and later the Carolinas, came from the south and southwest of England, which had its own distinct accent, quite different from the East Anglian heartland of the Puritans. Their "drawl," with its elongated vowel pronunciations (and such distinctive terms as saying "aksed" rather than "asked" or "ain't" rather than "isn't") became a part of Southern speech. The presence of large numbers of Africans also introduced African terms into the regional language. To "sass" when one is disrespectful, to call the plantation owner "massa" (which is not a mispronunciation of "master" but a West African term for chief), or to call your grandma "nana" are but a few examples of the assimilation of African language into southern vocabulary. Southern cuisine (for example, barbecue, fried chicken, gumbo, and okra) and Southern gentility are evidence of the intersection of African and English cultures.

Midwest. The Midwest extends from the border of Ohio and Pennsylvania westward to the western borders of North Dakota, South Dakota, Nebraska, and Kansas. It comprises two smaller regions, the Great Lakes region and the Great Plains region. The Great Lakes region is composed of the six states (Ohio, Michigan, Indiana, Illinois, Wisconsin, and Minnesota) that surround Lake Superior, Lake Michigan, Lake Huron, and Lake Erie. The Great Plains states include Iowa (and sometimes Missouri), as well as the plains states that extend from North Dakota to Kansas. Unlike the Southeast, the Great Lakes and Great Plains are characterized by cold winter months. Both regions are known for their agricultural output, particularly the production of winter wheat in the Great Plains and maize (corn) in the Great Lakes area and Iowa.

Culturally, the Great Lakes were, until the early 1820s, largely settled by migrants from Virginia, Kentucky, and the American Southeast. With the construction of the Erie Canal in 1825, a wave of New Yorkers and New Englanders settled north of a line that extended across the middle of Ohio, Indiana, and Illinois. South of what is now Interstate 70, many of the folkways and values of Kentucky, Tennessee, and the American South persisted. North of that line, the Great Lakes developed in ways more akin to New York, Pennsylvania, and New England. While later migrations of eastern Europeans, Germans, and then African Americans from the South have changed the cultural landscape of the Great Lakes, the divide that was opened with the building of the Erie Canal has continued to some degree.

The Great Plains region culture has been shaped in large measure by the migration into the area in the 19th century of settlers from the Ukraine, central Europe, and Scandinavia. Many of these immigrants brought with them knowledge of winter wheat farming which continues to the present as the most important crop in the upper Great Plains. But, they also contributed in other ways to shaping Midwestern culture.

Southwest. The American Southwest is generally defined as a region spreading westward from Oklahoma and Texas into California. The physical geography of this region is marked by an arid and semiarid climate. The presence of the Rocky Mountains and Sierra Nevada Mountains create a "rain shadow" that limits rainfall east of these mountain ranges. As moisture-bearing clouds rise to make their way over the mountain ranges, they release much of their moisture on the western slopes, leaving the interior plateaus and basins with little precipitation. As a result, the flora and fauna of the region features cacti, shrub pines, jackrabbits, small deer and antelope, and other plants and animals adapted to this harsh environment. This landscape stretches across northern and western Texas and Oklahoma through New Mexico, Arizona, and southern California. The Pecos, Rio Grande, and Colorado Rivers stretch across this landscape, carrying snow melt from the Rockies.

Resource extraction (silver, copper, uranium, petroleum), ranching, and irrigated agriculture have historically provided the principal economic foundations of the region. Since World War II, manufacturing and construction has increased in importance, largely stimulated by government investment in communications, aviation, defense spending, and by government support for the construction of hydroelectric dams and highways that have served the region. Additionally, the region has become an attractive place for retirees and the entertainment business. Phoenix (Arizona) and Las Vegas (Nevada) stand out as hubs for leisure and retirement activities.

Culturally, the southwestern region of the United States has been shaped by Spanish, Indian, and Anglo influences. Most Native Americans are found on the major reservations that dot the region. The original Spanish population that colonized the region has been augmented since World War I by successive waves of Mexican immigration. Since the 1950s, the region has benefited from booming construction and population growth as a consequence of growth in the defense, aerospace, and manufacturing industries, as well as the arrival in the region of a host of "snowbirds" fleeing the colder climates farther north.

Rocky Mountains. The Rocky Mountain region extends from northern New Mexico and Arizona northward through Utah, Wyoming, Idaho, and Montana. This region shares a great deal with the Southwest. This region of the U.S. is one of the most unpopulated parts of the country, though it does boast the cities of Salt Lake City and Denver. The Rocky Mountains serve as the continental divide for North America, and provide water for over a quarter of the country, including the heavily populated cities of coastal California and the Southwest. Though identified with the Rocky Mountains, much of the region is in fact occupied by the Colorado Plateau and Great Basin, and the High Plains of Montana and Wyoming. This region boasts more square miles of national parkland and federally owned territory than any region of the country.

The region, unlike the American Southwest, did not experience significant early Spanish settlement. The first white settlers into the region were Mormons who settled near the Great Salt Lake beginning in 1847. Later settlement was largely driven by gold rushes and other mining booms in Colorado, Idaho, and Montana. Ranching, forestry, and extraction of copper, gold, natural gas, and coal have historically been the foundation of the region's economy. More recently, tourism and skiing have been growing sources of economic activity.

Pacific. The Pacific Coastal Region extends from California along the West Coast and includes Alaska and Hawaii. Southern California shares a great deal with the cultural and physical geography of the American Southwest, while Northern California has more in common with the physical and cultural characteristics of the Pacific Northwest (Oregon and Washington).

The Northwest is a diverse geographic region, with volcanic mountain ranges (the Coast Mountains, Cascade Range, Columbia Mountains, and the Rocky Mountains) and plateaus. The Pacific Northwest has abundant rainfall along the coast and is the home of temperate rainforests with some of the largest trees in the world. Farther to the east, in the Interior Plateau, a largely dry region relies on irrigation to sustain farming activity. The coastline of the Pacific has many bays, inlets, and fjords. Port cities like San Diego, Long Beach, San Francisco, Portland, Seattle, and Tacoma serve the Pacific Rim economy.

The economy of the region is very diversified. The Pacific Coastal region has important agricultural regions. California produces over 400 different agricultural commodities. Over a third of the nation's vegetables and fruits and nuts are grown in California. The San Joaquin Valley produces grapes, raisins, almonds, pistachios, and citrus fruits. Washington and Oregon are producers of cherries, apples, and other orchard fruits. They also produce significant quantities of wheat, potatoes, onions, carrots, etc. Hawaii is an important sugar and pineapple producer. The region is also a prominent fishery for the world. Alaska, Washington, and Oregon are important producers of salmon, herring, and shellfish. The Pacific Coastal region is also the center of the world's semiconductor, software, and computer technology industries. Seattle is the headquarters of Microsoft. The southern portion of the San Francisco Bay area is often referred to as Silicon Valley on account of its role in the development of high-tech industries. California's investment in public and private higher education has attracted many of the world's top minds to the region. Apple, Amazon, eBay, Tesla, Yahoo, Twitter, and many more high-tech companies have benefited from this intersection of public education and innovation.

Culturally, the Pacific Coastal Region is also very diverse. Perhaps this is owing to the fact that its first growth spurt occurred during the San Francisco gold rush of the 1840s and 1850s, which attracted adventurers and profiteers from all over the world. Large numbers of immigrants from China, Japan, and India have arrived at different times in the region's history, mixing with migrants from all over the United States. World War I and World War II encouraged a wave of migration from the American South and Midwest as families moved to West Coast cities in search of jobs in aerospace and defense contracting industries.

Regions of Texas. The regions of the state of Texas reflect primarily physical features or landforms that unify the area.

Coastal Plains. The Texas Coastal Plains extend from the border of Louisiana along the extent of the Gulf of Mexico to the Rio Grande River. The climatic conditions and vegetation across this region are similar to those in the southeastern United States. Not surprisingly, this region attracted many settlers from the American Southeast. As a result, the region's culture bears a strong resemblance to that in Louisiana, Mississippi, and Alabama. This cultural influence diminishes, however, as one moves farther west and south along the Coastal Bend. The most important industries of the region are ranching, fishing, and oil production and refining.

Central Plains. East of the Coastal Plains, the Central Plains extend from the Red River down towards Austin. Dallas, Fort Worth, Wichita Falls, and Waco are the largest cities in this region. The region is mostly grasslands, ideal for cattle grazing, cotton production, and farming. The climate is marked by a hot summer with temperatures often reaching into the high 90s. The region is also prone to drought.

Great Plains. The Great Plains region extends from the Texas Panhandle down to the Mexican border. It has hot, dry summers and winters with more snowfall than other regions of the state. The land is flat and covered with broad grasses and few trees. The Canadian and Pecos rivers drain the area. Though largely grasslands, it is also the site of a number of striking landforms, such as Palo Duro Canyon and the Llano Estacado. Agriculturally, the region supports cotton and wheat production and the cattle industries.

Mountains and Basins. The westernmost part of Texas, sometimes referred to as the Big Bend region, is known as the Mountain and Basin Region of Texas. The Guadalupe, Chisos, and Davis mountains are located in the region. It is arid and semiarid, with plentiful cacti, mesquite, and desert vegetation. It is the driest region of Texas, receiving typically less than eight inches of rainfall per year. It is also the most sparsely populated region of the state, though the city of El Paso is located there.

Competency 014 Descriptive Statement D. The beginning teacher understands how the components of culture (i.e., land use, systems of education, religion, language) affect the way people live and shape the characteristics of regions.

Many regions of the world are determined by location or physical features, such as landforms. However, many regions are influenced by unifying cultural factors.

An excellent example of this is the global region of Northern Africa, Southwest Asia, and Central Asia. There are natural boundaries that could physically separate these different areas of the world. There are many different ethnicities and a variety of languages that could also separate the people of this region. However, this region is unified by human cultural practices. The people of this region are predominantly Muslim, or followers of Islam. The beliefs of Islam shape the lives of the people in this region, and thus unify these people as a region of the world. Daily living, from schooling to diet to courtship, is influenced by the precepts of Islam. The language of Islam, Arabic, also plays a vital role in unifying this region.

Furthermore, the conceptual region of "The West" or "Western Civilization" is also an excellent example of a unifying way of life that creates a large region of the world that does not share contiguous location. The traditions, religions (Judeo-Christian), and philosophies that grew out of ancient Greece and Rome have influenced the cultures and people of Europe and many countries around the world that share these traditions. The United States, Australia, and New Zealand can be included in the same region of "The West" with European countries, even though they do not share physical proximity.

> **Competency 014 Descriptive Statement E.** The beginning teacher demonstrates knowledge of the growth, distribution, movement, and characteristics of world populations (i.e., trends in past world population growth, distribution, push and pull factors affecting major national and international migrations, ways in which physical and cultural factors affect migration, how migration and immigration have affected societies), and understands the benefits and challenges of globalization.

Demography is the study of the growth and movements of populations. Rapid population growth since the second half of the last century has resulted in over 7 billion people living throughout the world.

Birth rates. Birth rate is calculated by the number of children born per 1,000 of the population each year. In 2016, the worldwide average birth rate was 18.5, or 18.5/1000. This average masks significant differences between world regions and within nations. Developing nations generally have much higher birth rates than developed nations. Sub-Saharan Africa, for example, in 2015 had an average birth rate of 48/1000. By comparison, European Union member states had a birth rate of 10/1000, while North America's birth rate was 12/1000. The birth rate should not be confused with the Total Fertility Rate (TFR), which measures the average number of children born to a woman over the course of her fertile life span. As TFR refers to the births per woman, it is a more direct measure of fertility. The countries with the highest total fertility rate in 2016 were the African nations of Niger and Burundi with 6.62 and 6.04 children born per woman, respectively. Singapore had the lowest TFR at .82 births per woman. The United States had a TFR of 1.87 in 2016.

Death rates. The death rate is calculated as the number of deaths per 1,000 of the population per year. The death rate in the United States in 2017 was 8.2/1,000, slightly above the world death rate of 7.8/1,000. The nation with the highest death rate in 2017 was Gabon with a rate of 14/1,000.

Natural increase is the difference between crude birth and death rates. Some populations have a positive increase; others can have a negative increase as their population decreases. This measure does not take into consideration growth from migration. Developing countries typically have a high growth rate of natural increase, while most developed countries have negative or low rates of natural increase. Niger, for example, (which was earlier identified as having a high TFR) in 2017 had a crude birth rate of 44.2 and a crude death rate of 11.8, giving it a natural increase rate of 32.4, among the highest in the world. The United States during the same period had a rate of natural increase of only 5.45. Many nations in Europe actually have negative rates of natural increase. Germany, for example, in 2016 had a rate of natural increase of –2.87.

Figure 6.3
Demographic Transition Model

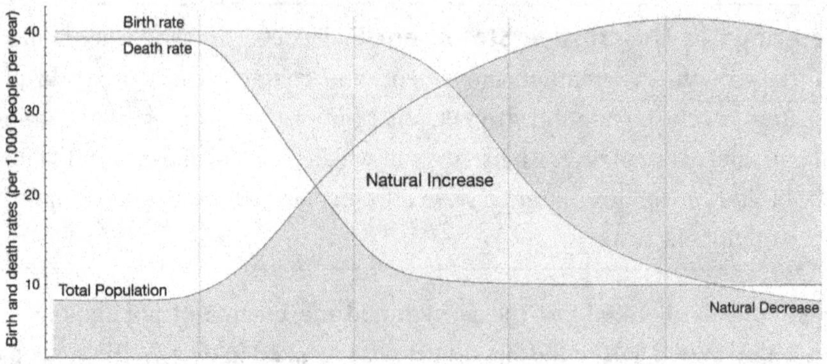

	Stage 1	Stage 2	Stage 3	Stage 4	Stage 5
Birth rate	High	High	Falling	Low	Very low
Death rate	High	Falls rapidly	Falls more slowly	Low	Low
Natural increase	Stable or slow increase	Very rapid increase	Increase slows down	Stable or slow increase	Stable or slow decrease

Courtesy of Max Roser, author, "Our World in Data" website. Reproduced under a CC BY-SA license.

Demographic Transition. The term "demographic transition" refers to the transition from high birth and death rates to lower birth and death rates as a country or region develops from a pre-industrial to an industrialized economic system. The demographic transition model consists of five stages that reflect the overall population patterns of the world over time.

- **Stage one** reflects most pre-industrial cultures throughout history, where birth rates and death rates are high, and the natural increase is stable and slow.

- **Stage two** reflects most modern developing countries or countries in early industrialization. Death rates decrease dramatically, yet birth rates still remain high. The natural increase results in rapid population growth.

- **Stage three** reflects a stabilization of death rates and a decrease in birth rates. Natural increase slows in this stage.

- **Stage four** reflects lower and stable birth and death rates. The natural increase is stable and slow. Most modern industrial nations have transitioned to this stage.

- **Stage five** reflects the demographics that a few industrialized nations have reached today in which the birth rates have dropped below the death rates, resulting in a negative natural increase, or a slow stable decline in population.

Migration. Human migration is the movement by people from one place to another. The movement is often over long distances and from one country to another, but internal migration is also possible; indeed, internal migration is the dominant form of migration globally. Internal migration in mainly from rural areas to urban areas, leading to increased urbanization.

Emigration. Emigration is the process of leaving one's home country to relocate and settle in a different country.

Immigration. Immigration is the process of coming into another country from the outside to settle in the new country.

Push factors. These are factors that force populations to leave their homes to go to new locations. Common push factors are disease, war, famine, or corrupt governments.

Pull factors. These are factors that attract populations to come into new locations. Common pull factors are stable governments, economic opportunity, and higher standards of living.

The world imbalance in rates of natural increase has had a profound effect on patterns of geographic mobility worldwide. Declining natural growth rates in developed nations have produced **pull factors** encouraging immigration, as declining natural growth rates threaten economic growth and undermine the social welfare system. In addition, high natural growth rates in poorer world regions threaten to overwhelm the productive and social welfare systems of developing nations, leading to **push factors** that encourage emigration.

Refugee. A refugee is a person who flees another country to avoid war, natural disasters, and/or persecution. Refugees include asylum-seekers who have claimed a right to international protection as refugees; internally displaced persons (IDPs) who have fled violence, human rights violations, or natural or man-made disasters but remain in their home country; and stateless persons. According to the United Nations High Commission for Refugees (UNHCR), today there are over 65 million forcibly displaced persons worldwide, of whom over 22 million are recognized as refugees.

Globalization. Globalization is the development of a world culture and the increase in the interdependent international world economy.

Competency 014 Descriptive Statement F. The beginning teacher analyzes ways in which political, economic, and social processes shape cultural patterns and characteristics in various places and regions (i.e., analyzing political, economic, social, and demographic indicators to determine levels of development and standard of living in countries).

There are varying economic and political structures found throughout the world. Geographers use many different measurements to determine if countries are developed or developing.

Political systems. The system of laws and government of a nation-state are known as its political system.

    Limited government. A system of limited government is a political system under which the people who make the laws must obey them as well. Democracy is one form of limited government. Constitutions, statements of rights and laws that limit the power and scope of government are common among limited governments.

Unlimited government. A political system that fails to limit the power of the governing classes or rulers is characterized as *unlimited government*. In practice, no governments act without limits. However, in many political systems, the limits upon the government or the rulers of the country are either so weak or unenforced that rulers have few limits on their behavior or decisions. Dictatorships and absolute monarchies are examples of unlimited government.

Economic Systems. An economic system is the system by which people or countries distribute resources and trade goods or services.

Traditional economies. People in traditional economies meet their needs through exchange and barter. Most individuals do the same work their parents did, and there is little change or innovation.

Command economies. Also known as centralized economies, in command economies the government controls all the means of production and distribution. Communism is an example of a command economy.

Market economies. Also known as the free enterprise system, in market economies, individuals and firms determine for themselves what to produce and consume. Under this system supply and demand regulates market prices and the distribution of goods and services.

Mixed economies. In a mixed economy, both the government and the individual decide what to produce and how to distribute goods and services. Most modern countries have mixed economies. Governments regulate businesses and create laws that influence the exchange of goods and services.

Economic activities. There are four levels of economic activity.

Primary activities. Primary activities are the harvesting of natural resources from the Earth. Fishing, farming, and mining are examples of primary activities.

Secondary activities. Secondary activities involve manufacturing or the making of products using the harvested natural resources. Construction, factories, and processing plants are examples of secondary activities.

Tertiary activities. The tertiary sector involves providing services. Retail sales, education, and restaurant services are examples of tertiary activities. The United States has increasingly become an economy dependent on the tertiary sector.

Quaternary activities. The quaternary sector involves gathering of data and information. Research and providing information are examples of quaternary activities.

Standards of Living. The populations of the world live in conditions that can be measured to determine if they have high standards of living or lower standards of living.

Industrialized countries. Also known as developed countries, industrialized countries generally provide higher standards of living. A surplus of goods and services is common in these countries. In industrialized or developed countries, a mixture of all four levels of economic activity is common, though manufacturing, services, and information gathering are increasingly important to the growth and success of these economies.

Developing countries. Developing countries are places where people are not yet industrialized and experience a lower standard of living. Many of the people in these countries produce only enough food for their daily survival. Most economic activity is limited to the primary level in these countries, though it is becoming increasingly common in the globalizing economy that secondary activities start to replace agricultural labor and resource extraction as sources of income.

Gross National Product (GNP). A nation's GNP is a broad measure of a nation's total economic activity. GNP is the value of all finished goods and services produced in a country in one year. The United States has the largest GNP of any of the world's economies. The United States' GNP for 2016, for example, was $18.75 trillion.

Gross Domestic Product (GDP). The gross domestic product (GDP) is one of the primary indicators used to gauge the health of a country's economy. It represents the total dollar value of all goods and services produced over a specific time period.

GDP measures all the income produced within a country by measuring the total expenditures of that nation within a given period. GNP counts GDP but adds income from foreign sources minus the income paid to foreign citizens and firms.

Per capita income. Per capita income, or average income, measures the average income earned per person in a given country in a year. Americans on average in 2016 thus earned $52,194.90. This measure does not capture the degree to which incomes are inequitably distributed. The lowest 20 percent of income earners in the United States during the same period earned only $12,547 while the wealthiest 20 percent of income earners averaged over $202,366 in income.

Life expectancy. Life expectancy is the average number of years that an individual is expected to live in a specific country. Among the measures used to gauge the health and wealth of a nation's citizens, life expectancy provides an important touchstone. The average life span of Americans has risen from 69.77 years in 1960 to 78.74 years in 2015. It has, however, plateaued since about 2010, while the life expectancy in Japan, Germany, and the United Kingdom has continued to rise.

Literacy rates. The literacy rate measures the percentage of a country's citizens who possess the ability to read and write. Ninety-nine percent of Americans can read and write.

Infant mortality. Infant mortality rates measure the number of children in a given country that die before the age of one year out of 1,000 births. Worldwide, the infant mortality rate is 49.4/1,000. The United States has an infant mortality rate of 6.5/1000, or 29th of the 35 developed nations that belong to the OECD. By contrast, many developing countries have infant mortality rates greater than 50/1000.

> **Competency 014 Descriptive Statement G.** The beginning teacher applies knowledge of the history and significance of major religious and philosophical traditions (i.e., Buddhism, Christianity, Confucianism, Hinduism, Islam, Judaism, Realism, and Idealism).

Religion is one of the most common cultural factors that is used to define a cultural group. There are hundreds of sects and branches of religions in the world today, each of which shape the daily lives and activities of people throughout the Earth. As was earlier observed, religions are generally divided between ethnic and universalizing religions.

Ethnic religion. Ethnic religions are practiced by specific ethnic groups in specific areas. They generally do not seek to convert other people to their religious beliefs. Shintoism and Hinduism are examples of ethnic religions.

Universalizing religion. Universalizing religions are not tied to one specific ethnic group. Their beliefs and practices are thought to have broad appeal to different people in different countries. Universalizing religions endeavor to convert as many people to their beliefs as possible. Christianity, Islam, and Buddhism are examples of universalizing religions.

Animism. Animism is the belief that all things have a spirit or soul, including animals, plants, rivers, mountains, stars, the Moon, and even the Sun. There are many varieties of animism found throughout the world and all are ethnic religions.

Buddhism. Founded by Siddhartha Gautama, or the Buddha, Buddhism originated in India and spread throughout the Indian subcontinent and into East and Southeast Asia. Buddhism branched out from Hinduism as a rejection of the caste system of early Hinduism. Followers are called to free themselves from attachment to worldly things and to devote themselves to ending the world's suffering.

Christianity. Christianity was founded by the followers of Jesus Christ, originating in Southwest Asia in the Roman province of Palestine, and has spread throughout the world. Christianity grew out of Judaism. Christians are called to follow the teachings of Jesus Christ found in the New Testament.

Confucianism. Founded by the philosopher Confucius, Confucianism originated in China. There are no gods or priests. Confucianism is a moral philosophy that emphasizes respect for elders, authority, and ancestors. Confucianism has had a tremendous influence on China, Japan, and Korea.

Hinduism. An outgrowth of the Vedic traditions of the Indo-Aryan migrants into South Asia between 1500 and 1000 BCE, Hinduism was established in northern India, and then spread throughout the Indian subcontinent. Hinduism recognizes hundreds of gods and goddesses. The belief in reincarnation is also important to the caste system that was established in India. While Hinduism is a polytheistic ethnic religion, it has proved adept at incorporating into its beliefs and practices the worship of gods and goddesses that originated in other religious traditions. It also developed important philosophical approaches to religious belief that have had widespread impact across Asia and Europe.

Islam. Founded by Mohammed, Islam was established in the Arabian Peninsula in Southwest Asia, and spread through most of the nearby areas. Because it is a universalizing religion, it is now found throughout the world and is the second largest religion in the world, behind Christianity. Followers of Islam live by the teachings of the Koran.

Judaism. Judaism is an ethnic religion that originated in Southwest Asia perhaps as early as the second millennium BCE, though its sacred texts and religious practices seem to date from sometime after the eighth century BCE. It is the first and oldest monotheistic tradition. Followers recognize Yahweh as god, and live by the teachings of the Torah, or Judaic law. Both Christianity and Islam are religions from the Abrahamic tradition established by Judaism.

Shintoism. Founded in Japan, Shintoism is the original ethnic religion of Japan. Shintoism is founded on a belief in, and worship of, *kami*, or the spirits or phenomena of nature or natural forces. As such, it is deeply connected to place. Unlike Judaism, Christianity, Buddhism, or Islam, all of which have identifiable founders, Shintoism does not have a founder. Neither does the religion have a scriptural text per se. The religion emphasizes ritual behavior associated with rites of passage, ancestral veneration, and other ceremonial events. Historically, Shintoism has also been critically connected to imperial power in Japan.

Daoism (or Taoism). Founded in China, Daoism is the native Chinese belief system that adheres to animistic practices and ancestor worship. Daoism, unlike Confucianism, has emphasized the metaphysical and natural harmony rather than ritual responsibility and respect for authority and the elders.

Realism. Realism is the philosophical theory that believes that reality exists independent of our perception of it.

Idealism. Idealism is the philosophical belief that reality is merely a mental construct and there exists no object without an observer.

Competency 014 Descriptive Statement H. The beginning teacher understands the importance of place for populations (i.e., Mecca, Jerusalem, Cuzco, Ganges River, and Shrine of Guadalupe).

Place is the physical and human characteristics that make a location unique. Over time, people inhabit and interact with certain locations, altering the place, and sometimes leading to those locations gaining in importance as symbolic centers of a culture. Religious traditions often play an important role in enhancing the importance of a location so that it grows in esteem and importance to a culture. There are a number of prominent locations worldwide that have such religious and symbolic significance.

Mecca. The most important city and holy center of Islam, Mecca is located in Saudi Arabia. Tradition teaches that the founder of Islam, Mohammad established a shrine in Mecca, supplanting and repurposing an existing traditional pilgrimage site. Millions of Muslims travel to Mecca each year to take part in a pilgrimage called the *hajj*. All Muslims are called to make the *hajj* at least once in their life, if they are able to afford to do so.

Jerusalem. The most important city for both Judaism and Christianity, Jerusalem, is located in modern-day Israel, though the city is also claimed by the Palestinian state as well. Jerusalem has long been considered a holy site for Muslims as well. For Jews, the Wailing Wall, or the last standing wall of the temple of Solomon, is the most revered holy site. The site of the old temple is now the site of the Dome of the Rock, an important holy site for Muslims. Tradition tells that Mohammad ascended into heaven from the site of the Dome of the Rock. Christians also hold Jerusalem as an important holy site. It is the site where Jesus was crucified by the Romans. A church built on the site where Jesus was purportedly entombed has attracted pilgrims since before the era of the Crusades.

Cuzco. Once the most important city for the ancient Inca civilization, Cuzco is located in the Andes Mountains of modern-day Peru. Cuzco was the capital of the Inca. The city was of central importance to the Incan people.

Ganges River. Considered to be a goddess by Hindu worshippers, the Ganges River is located in eastern India. Bathing in the Ganges is an important purifying ritual for Hindus. Additionally, Hindus scatter the ashes of their dead in the river in the belief that this will send their soul to heaven.

Shrine of Guadalupe. Located in Mexico, the Shrine of Guadalupe commemorates the appearance of the Virgin Mary to a peasant in 16th-century Mexico. A shrine was constructed on the site of the vision. The legend of the vision was important to the Spanish Catholic Church in converting Native Americans to Catholicism. The shrine of the Virgin of Guadalupe was built on the location where the pre-Columbian population of central Mexico worshipped the Goddess Tonantzin, a fertility goddess of the Aztecs. This shrine now not only represents Mexican national heritage, but also symbolizes the importance of the Catholic Church in Mexico.

Competency 014 Descriptive Statement I. The beginning teacher demonstrates knowledge of the impact of religion on the way of life in the United States.

Though a secular system of government exists in the United States, religion has played an important role in the founding and daily lives of Americans.

The need to worship without persecution was an influential factor in the colonization of the "New World" or the east cost of the modern United States. A group of English settlers, known as Separatists, or Pilgrims, fled England for the Americas to be free of the state-sponsored religion in their homeland. They wished to worship God in the way that they wanted, and were prohibited from doing so in England. The Pilgrims were able to discover the freedom to worship in their desired way in the new world. They were too far from the influence of the English government and thus free from any mandated governmental beliefs about god.

More and more colonists arrived over time and religious diversity grew. Another earlier group of settlers fleeing religious persecution in England were the Puritans. They were the largest group of Protestants to immigrate to the New World. The Puritan form of Christianity was very strict, and so stern that they often expelled members of their community that did not share their stern religious views. Roger Williams was one such victim. Though a Puritan himself, he was expelled, and went to the found the colony of Rhode Island.

The colony of Pennsylvania was also founded as a result of Puritanical persecution. Another religious group that left England to practice their religious beliefs in freedom were the Quakers. The Quakers view of religions and Christianity were vastly different from the Puritans. This led to conflict with the strict Puritans in the colony of Massachusetts, when they hung the leader of the Quakers, Mary Dyer, for refusing to convert to Puritanism. Pennsylvania then was founded as a refuge for Quakers facing persecution in both England and in Puritan Massachusetts.

The Church of England, or the Anglican Church, was the officially authorized religion in the colonies of Virginia, Georgia, North and South Carolina. Only during the period of the American Revolution was this state-established religion challenged as men like Thomas Jefferson and James Madison, influenced by Enlightenment ideas, called for an end to the establishment of state-sponsored religious institutions.

Maryland was founded by colonists of the Catholic faith that were loyal to Mary Stuart, the queen for whom the colony was named. However, and significantly, the colony's charter made no reference to religion, unlike other charters of earlier colonies.

Eventually the documents of the newly formed United States of America made no reference to a preferred or state-sponsored religion. The first amendment to the American Constitution clearly states that the government may not sanction any religion. This was different from most European nations at the time, and was a departure from the early charters of the American colonies, many of which sanctioned certain forms of religion.

> **Competency 014 Descriptive Statement J.** The beginning teacher recognizes relationships of the arts to the times in which they were created in the United States and world areas.

For almost 1,000 years, the Roman Catholic Church, and its religious views controlled the production of the arts in Europe. Art, music, architecture, everything was designed to glorify god and to consolidate the power of the Catholic Church across Europe.

The Renaissance, or rebirth, was a time of curiosity and learning. This was a "re-discovery" of ancient Greek and Roman civilizations. This new birth led to change in the arts, moving away from glorifying the church and god, to celebrating Humanism and Individualism. Many ideas and innovations of the Renaissance marked the beginning of many modern ideas and philosophies.

Florence was one of the major city-states that led the Renaissance. The De Medici family was very influential. The new wealth that trade brought to certain families and cities led to a flourishing of new arts, literature, music, and eventually the sciences. New methods of painting, architecture, and sculpting were pioneered by the most famous artists of the day. Among them were da Vinci, Michelangelo, Raphael, Donatello, Rembrandt, and Brunelleschi.

Literature also underwent a transformation during this period. Writers such as Erasmus, Boccaccio, Petrarch, and others changed the focus of literature from a focus on god and the church to more secular and humanist themes. The vernacular, rather than the Latin of Church, also grew in popularity. Humanism was the driving force that eventually inspired the works of Shakespeare, Cervantes, and Dante.

The invention of the printing press by Gutenberg helped to facilitate the diffusion of Renaissance ideas throughout Europe, and eventually the rest of the modern world.

In its modern form, the novel also developed as an extension of the Renaissance. The first modern novel is credited to Samuel Richardson, for the work *Pamela, or Virtue Rewarded*. It was the first full-length realistic prose story set in contemporary times. This form of writing grew in popularity and is the basis of much influential literature thereafter.

At the beginning of the 20th century, literature was heavily influenced by realism, and reflected the real struggle of the individual to find a place in a changing and urbanizing world. The alienation felt by many as countries industrialized was reflected in the works of Joseph Conrad, James Joyce, Sigmund Freud, Kafka, Albert Camus, Sartre, and many others. Their writings reflected the themes that the individual struggles to find meaning in life in the modern world, and that many struggle to understand what they are searching for.

Modern theater also has its roots in the early theatrical operettas of the European romantic period. Eventually the traditions of the European music halls, and American vaudeville combined together to create the modern form of theater.

Evolving from various forms of American folk music, popular music of the modern age in America got its start at the beginning of the last century. Early popular music was characterized by a consistent structure. Eventually, after World War II, with the rise of radio, younger Americans started to have a greater influence on music. Many different modern forms of American music emerged: jazz, country, rap, blues, and rock and roll.

COMPETENCY 015 (INTERACTIONS BETWEEN HUMAN GROUPS AND THE PHYSICAL ENVIRONMENT)

The teacher understands the nature and significance of interactions among people, places, and environments.

Key Question

One of the five themes of geography is human-environment interaction. Geographers strive to answer the questions of how environment affects human activity, and how that activity itself has affected not only the local environment, but, in modern times, the global environment as well.

Competency 015 Descriptive Statement A. The beginning teacher analyzes ways in which humans depend on, adapt to, and modify the physical environment in a variety of cultural and technological contexts.

Human populations are dependent upon the location of their settlements and must adapt to the resources and climate of such locations. In turn, human settlement also has a direct impact on the environments in which they settled.

The earliest human populations were controlled by their environments in which they were located. The climate, topography, soils, biomes, etc., all influenced how humans settled and adapted. Over time this has now shifted as human populations have more control over their environments, so much so that modern human activity has had detrimental impacts upon local and even global environments.

The basic needs of all humans, food, clothing, and shelter, were the driving force for how people adapted to their environments. As human populations grew, they spread throughout the world, adapting to the different environments they encountered.

Early humans were nomadic hunter-gatherers. Dependent upon their food sources, they were forced to roam seasonally with the herds they hunted. Human cultural patterns were also influenced by this nomadic lifestyle; portable shelters were created to adapt to it.

The development of clothing allowed humans to explore and adapt to a wider range of climates as they moved from place to place. Clothing allowed humans to adapt to colder environments and to migrate to new places to settle. In colder climates, the development of clothing was crucial to adaption and survival.

Upon the Neolithic revolution, when humans turned toward farming and domestication of plants and animals, settled life brought new challenges to adapting to environments that were suitable for agriculture and animal husbandry. Certain physical environments were conducive to settlement, such as river plains and deltas where soils supported agriculture. However, not all climates and biomes were suitable for human settlements and farming. Humans still needed to adapt to different factors to successfully grow the crops needed to survive. For most of the history of humanity, people depended on the environment to provide food, shelter and clothing.

The Neolithic revolution was the beginning of humans having a direct impact on their environments as they started to gain more control of their surroundings. After the industrial revolution, the table was turned as humanity harnessed power sources and technology to have a greater influence over their environment. Technology has now reached the point where humans can supply food anywhere in surplus, and are able to adapt and travel to any environment on the planet.

However, this has not come without a price. Pollution, deforestation, desertification, and climate change are a few of the detrimental impacts of human technology impacting the Earth's environment.

> **Competency 015 Descriptive Statement B.** The beginning teacher understands and analyzes how people, places, and environments change over time and are connected and interdependent (i.e., impact of different types of natural disasters).

What humans see as disasters are many times just the natural processes of the physical environment. In addition, often what are perceived as natural disasters have a human and political dimension. Human settlement patterns have placed populations in areas where these natural processes pose hardships to the people impacted. However, human industry and technology are also changing the environments and this, too, has had an impact on human populations.

Droughts. Droughts are lengthy periods of low rainfall over a given region. Droughts lead to a decline in agriculture and food production. This can lead to famine, and is a common push factor for the migration of human populations. Droughts also contribute to desertification, which is also exacerbated by human farming techniques.

Earthquakes. Earthquakes are seismic activity that occurs along tectonic plates. Many areas of human settlement are located on fault lines that are susceptible to earthquakes and volcanic activity. Earthquakes can cause significant damage to property and loss of life. Sometimes, tsunamis can also result from earthquakes, leading to more destruction and death. Volcanic eruptions create lava flows and release ash clouds that can threaten human settlements and life.

El Niño/La Niña. The cyclical warming (El Niño) and cooling (La Niña) of currents in the Pacific waters along the western coasts of Central and South America can cause periods of drought or flooding that negatively impact farming and fishing industries in both the Western Hemisphere and Afro-Eurasia.

Hurricanes. Tropical cyclones of the Western Hemisphere, hurricanes form over the warm water near the equator. They move westward and can threaten the Caribbean, the Gulf of Mexico, the western Atlantic, and the eastern Pacific. Hurricanes cause high winds and flooding that can cause severe property damage and loss of life. These are referred to as typhoons in the Eastern Hemisphere (western Pacific).

Monsoons. Monsoons are seasonal winds that blow across South Asia and Southeast Asia. Monsoons carry dry air in the winter and warm air in the summer. Summer monsoons are responsible for large amounts of rainfall and can cause flooding, leading to property damage and loss of life.

Tornadoes. Tornadoes are violent rotating columns of air descending from thunderstorm clouds. Tornadoes, too, pose a threat to property and life.

> **Competency 015 Descriptive Statement C.** The beginning teacher understands types and patterns of settlement and physical and human geographic factors that affect where people settle (i.e., transportation routes, availability of resources) and development processes of settlement over time.

Early human settlements were exclusively founded in relationship to the availability of local resources, and/or access to transportation routes. As humans have taken greater control over their environments, access to resources and trade routes are no longer limited by the natural physical environments.

Transportation routes. Early human settlement was established along natural transportation and trade routes. As a result, most human habitation and urban development took place on rivers, or on the coasts of the world's oceans and seas. After the Industrial Revolution, new forms of transportation facilitated trade and access to resources, opening new possibilities for settlement. Today, transportation systems, such as railways, roads and highways, and air travel and ocean travel, now allow populations to live farther away from natural trade routes, industries, and resources.

Availability of resources. Original human settlements were dependent on the availability of local resources. Water, arable land, minerals and more were crucial to the earliest settlements of humanity. In the modern world, populations are not as dependent upon local resources to survive. Modern technology and transportation facilitates the distribution of resources throughout the world. Furthermore, the construction of dams, man-made lakes, and canals has also brought water resources to locations that were previously limited in natural access to water sources.

> **Competency 015 Descriptive Statement D.** The beginning teacher analyzes the influence of physical and human geographic factors on political, social, cultural, and economic developments and events in World History (i.e., Dust Bowl, opening of Panama and Suez canals).

Events in world and U.S. history have had an impact on human developments. Though unintentionally man-made, the Dust Bowl affected settlement patterns of people in the U.S. and the construction of the Panama and Suez canals influenced trade routes and success to resources that changed the modern world.

Dust Bowl. The Dust Bowl refers to the Great Plains region during the Great Depression. During the 1930s, drought coupled with erosion resulting from over-farming and poor land use, resulted in a series of dust storms that greatly impacted the ecology and farming of the southern Great Plains, stretching from north Texas to Nebraska and eastern Colorado. This ecological crisis was a tremendous push factor affecting American migration toward the West and California. The flood of Dust Bowl refugees, often referred to as Okies, created political, social,and cultural change throughout California.

Panama Canal. The Panama Canal is an artificial waterway 50 miles long that spans the Isthmus of Panama and connects the Atlantic Ocean to the Pacific. A tremendous feat of human engineering, the completion of the canal played a vital role in expanding trade routes and access to resources.

Suez Canal. The Suez Canal is an artificial waterway 120 miles long that spans the Isthmus of Suez, connecting the Red Sea, and thus Asian trade, with the Mediterranean Sea and Europe. This sea-level canal was not as difficult to achieve, yet its impact on global trade routes and availability of resources is as important as the Panama Canal.

Competency 015 Descriptive Statement E. The beginning teacher analyzes the impact of the Neolithic Revolution on human life and the development of the first civilizations.

Besides the later Industrial Revolution, no other change in human lifestyles was more influential on humanity than the Neolithic Revolution.

The earliest human cultures relied on hunting and gathering to meet their survival needs. Due to the movement of herds and seasonal changes, areas where food and resources could be found changed throughout the year. This forced early humans to live a nomadic lifestyle as they moved with the change of seasons, or the movement of their prey herds. This nomadic lifestyle meant that there were no permanent human settlements.

About 10,000 years ago this all began to change. Archaeological evidence points to South West Asia as the origin of this change in lifestyle. People in this area started to settle down and domesticate both plants and animals for their survival needs, eschewing the previous nomadic lifestyle of their ancestors. This transition occurred at different times and places throughout the world, but the area known as the Fertile Crescent, in modern day Iraq and the Levant, appears to be the primary location for this change in lifestyle. Climate, access to water, and fertile soils combined to provide and excellent location for growing crops.

This area is also sometimes referred to as the Cradle of Civilization. As the domestication of plants and animals necessitated permanent settlements, humans started to occupy places year round. This settled lifestyle led to a new way of life centered around the raising of crops and domestication of livestock. This freed up time that would otherwise have been spent hunting and gathering so that people could start to develop more complex societies than nomadic hunter-gatherer bands.

Permanent human settlement led to the development of many of the characteristics of modern human civilization. The development of writing was a major milestone. Furthermore, in order to regulate the growing population centers, the idea of government and a hierarchal structure developed as well. This was also intertwined with the first religious practices and belief systems that developed simultaneously. Laws and government, rituals and religion, writing and record-keeping all mark the beginning of civilized culture and history.

> **Competency 015 Descriptive Statement F.** The beginning teacher demonstrates knowledge of how population growth and modernization have affected the physical environment throughout history.

Ever since the Neolithic Revolution, humanity has significantly impacted the physical environment. Humans settled around and developed natural resources. For a long period of time, human activity had a minimal impact on the physical environment. With the start of the Industrial Revolution and rapid population growth, however, that impact has grown tremendously.

Population growth, which accelerated over the second half of the 20th century, has led to the spread of the world's population over a wider area of the Earth's surface. This larger distribution of population has put pressure on scarce resources, such as inhabitable or arable land. Moreover, growing population has increased the demand for goods and services. All of this has had an impact on the Earth's environment.

Increased use of pesticides and fertilizers to grow food for the Earth's increasing population has led to pollution of waterways and impacted local flora and fauna. The increase in industrialization and the use of automobiles has increased air pollution. Populations building new settlements have been a cause of deforestation and led to the decrease in flora and fauna, producing endangered species. Oceans and coral reefs have seen degradation as well.

All of this activity has led to what many scientists believe to be man-made global climate change, or global warming. Due to high emissions of CO_2, scientists believe there has been an increase in the average global temperatures. This is theorized to be the result of the greenhouse effect that leads to warming. Scientists believe that human impact on the environment is leading to an increase in natural disasters and potential extinction of flora and fauna throughout the Earth.

> **Competency 015 Descriptive Statement G.** The beginning teacher understands factors affecting the location of different types of economic activities and economic issues related to the location and management of key resources.

In the modern world, location next to natural resources is not as imperative as it once was. Modern transportation routes have helped to bring resources to various locations throughout the Earth. However, the increasing industrialization and demand for goods around the world has led to pressures to limit and conserve resources so that they do not disappear due to over-farming, over-fishing, or over-mining. Furthermore, since these economic activities threaten flora and fauna, modern governments strive to preserve and protect certain areas of land.

Economic activities start with primary-level activities. Thus, most settlements have been near these resources. These raw materials are required to support the other levels of economic activities, and towns and cities have developed close to these resources.

Generally, most towns and cities were established around a specific economic activity. A mining town, for example, is usually located near mineral resources. Mill towns, logging towns, and fishing villages were founded in similar was,y with the economic survival of the town or city dependent on a nearby natural resource.

However, if this important natural resource were to be depleted or improperly managed, it could result in an economic disaster for the towns or cities that rely on those resources. Over-fishing is one such example. Whether local, national, or international, governments work to regulate fishing, both recreational and large-scale. If the waters were to be depleted too quickly fish populations would be threatened, thus threatening economic prosperity. Similarly, over-mining, over-farming, over-hunting, and over-logging can lead to the collapse of towns and cities. If the resources they depend on disappear, then so does their residents' livelihood.

This not only threatens local communities; it also puts pressure on a nation's overall economic activities. Many countries' governments have passed laws and regulations intended to manage important natural resources and prevent their depletion. Examples of this range from laws about farming and mining to the preservation of natural reserves to protect natural flora and fauna. In the United States, Yosemite National Park is one such example.

> **Competency 015 Descriptive Statement H.** The beginning teacher understands relationships between physical and human geographic factors and political divisions, relationships, and policies (i.e., ways in which forces of conflict and cooperation influence control of Earth's surface; and the influence of physical and human geographic factors on foreign policies of countries such as Iraq, Israel, Japan, and the United Kingdom).

Conflict over the power to control territory is driven by a need to have access to resources and the ability to transport resources.

The power to control territory is directly related to a government's ability to maintain a stable government and military power, as well as allow for economic development. Additional research and development are key to new techniques to manage vital resources and advance military strength. Conflict and war often arise from the need to control vital natural resources, such as water and energy sources, including petroleum, oil, and gas. Access to resources is tied to control over the territory of the resources, and thus competing claims to territory lead to conflict, such as over petroleum in Iraq, or the struggle over water rights in the Israeli-Palestinian conflict. Trade routes and transport of goods is also vital control for economic development, and control over trade routes can lead to rising tensions among countries, as demonstrated in the case of the United Kingdom vs. Argentina over the Falkland Islands. Today there is rising tension in the South China Sea between Japan and China.

International organizations have been created to serve to mitigate disputes and prevent or respond to war between nations. The UN (United Nations) is the largest organization dedicated to mediating conflict and preventing war. The need to share resources has impacted international relations, leading to trade agreements between nations. NAFTA (North American Free Trade Agreement) is a 1994 agreement to promote trade between the United States, Mexico, and Canada. The EU (European Union) is an economic union of European member states. OPEC (Organization of Petroleum Exporting Countries) is another example of cooperation to ensure mutual benefits.

COMPETENCY 016 (SOCIOLOGICAL, ANTHROPOLOGICAL, AND PSYCHOLOGICAL CONCEPTS AND PROCESSES)

The teacher applies sociological, anthropological, and psychological concepts and processes to understand cultural formation and change, intergroup relations, and individual development.

Key Question

What are the basic ideas of sociology, anthropology, and psychology as they relate to geographic studies of humans and human behavior?

Competency 016 Descriptive Statement A. The beginning teacher understands the role of culture as a foundation of individual and social behavior.

The predominant beliefs and values of a culture determine the traditions and behaviors of that culture. Cultural beliefs are what people of that culture hold to be true. Religion plays a major role in the daily lives of people every day. Beliefs can also be influenced by economic, political, or philosophical ideas. The idea of communism, for example, is an economic belief system that plays a role in the lives of individuals who live in countries that adhere to a command economy.

Cultural values are concepts of right or wrong, or morals, that are shaped by the prevailing cultural beliefs. These values are highly influenced by religious beliefs, and other belief systems as well. In Confucian societies, respect for authority and elders influences the moral behavior of the society. In democratic societies, the individual and individual liberties take precedence over the social expectations of respect for elders and authorities.

The cultural products of a people are a reflection of their beliefs and values. The arts, literature, music, architecture, and fashion, reflect the beliefs and values of a people. These cultural products become part of the heritage of a culture and are passed down from one generation to the next. Thus, cultural values and beliefs are transmitted through time.

> **Competency 016 Descriptive Statement B.** The beginning teacher understands the evolving nature of race and gender relations in the United States and knows how people from various racial, ethnic, and religious groups have adapted to and modified life in the United States and contributed to a national identity.

Race. Race is a classification system that developed in the context of slavery and European imperialist expansion in the 18th and 19th centuries. It was used as a means to describe and categorize groups of people originally from a common geographic location, who generally shared common physical characteristics. Frequently, skin color and facial features were used to determine racial identities. An extensive scientific and pseudoscientific system of observation was used to evaluate and characterize behaviors and cultural traits on the basis of racial categories. There is much controversy surrounding the concept of race in the modern United States. Scientifically, race can be defined by genetic lineage; however, socially the idea of race is much more complex. Self-perception and self-identification may be more important when attempting to understand the challenges of race and race relations.

Ethnic Group. Ethnicity describes a group of people who identify as having a common social background and shared cultural beliefs and values. Ethnic groups tend to preserve their beliefs and values by inter-marriage within their own group. Ethnic groups often share language and religious beliefs. They may exist within a larger culture, thus forming an enclave. Ethnicity is different from race in that people of an ethnic group may share the same physical characteristics of a larger cultural group, but not the same beliefs and values. For example, racial categorizations that attribute certain common social or cultural values to people of African descent often overlook the wide range of ethnic and linguistic differences that divide Africans. Similarly people characterized as Caucasian, "white," or in Texas, "Anglo," frequently share little in the way of cultural similarities.

Gender. While sex refers to the physiological characteristics (biological features, hormonal characteristics, chromosomal differences, internal and external sex organs) that describe men and women, gender references the characteristics that a society or culture defines as masculine or feminine. Increasingly, however, similar to race, self-perception and self-identification has become more important in defining gender and sexuality.

The United States is an immigrant nation, and many diverse cultures immigrated to the New World, and continue to immigrate to the United States today. In the past, these cultures were mainly from Western Europe. These European immigrants were allowed to maintain their cultural beliefs and values, though most were expected to assimilate. Most did so, assimilating to an American culture within a generation or two. America has been somewhat tolerant toward these European immigrants, and their cultures still survive today in Americanized forms. Americans have treated most nonwhite cultures as inferior. For example, Chinese and Japanese immigrants were discriminated against. Africans were enslaved for hundreds of years; even after the end of slavery, African Americans were segregated from white America and discriminated against in many ways. As a result, the process of assimilation for African Americans proved more difficult and lengthy. African Americans have faced substantial obstacles that limited their full assimilation and acceptance in the dominant culture, even though they were historically as prominent in the settlement of the country as Europeans.

More recently, immigrants from Latin America, and new waves of immigrants from Africa and Asia have experienced similar treatment as earlier immigrants. Modern-day activists strive to erase the barriers to full participation in American society for these newly arrived immigrants.

Women have also been treated as inferior for the greater part of American history. However, womens' rights movements have removed many barriers to equality in American culture. In the United States, women make up the majority of college students today and are active in all facets of American economic and political life. This is not to suggest that women have overcome all the barriers to their political and economic influence.

> **Competency 016 Descriptive Statement C.** The beginning teacher analyzes ways in which cultures and societies both change and maintain continuity (i.e., social movements, modernization).

Sociology has defined three different ways that cultures define and maintain expected cultural behavior. These practices are designed to maintain continuity of cultural beliefs and practices from one generation to the next.

Folkways. Folkways are the daily informal rules of behavior, or etiquette. Bowing before elders or shaking hands with a business partner are common practices in different cultures. These are daily expected rituals that maintain civility. Violations of folkways are not seen as illegal or immoral, but improper and uncouth.

Mores. Mores are cultural values that are stronger than folkways in maintaining cultural practices. Mores are basically moral beliefs that stem from expected societal behavior. The results of violating mores are more severe than not following folkways. Cheating on a spouse, for example, is often not illegal, but a violation of cultural mores. To be considered immoral is to be outside the normal values and beliefs of a culture.

Laws. Laws are formal codified rules of cultural values with formal punishments, fines, jail time, etc., for their violation. Laws often reflect the mores of a culture. For example, in some cultures cheating on a spouse is not only immoral but illegal, with formal legal punishments for violators. Laws, which are enforced and maintained by governments, are more formal ways in which societies maintain social beliefs and values. Folkways and mores are less formal, and their enforcement is maintained by members of the various cultural groups.

However, it must be recognized that beliefs and values can change or evolve over time, and these changes will reflect new folkways, mores, and laws. Societal movements, such as the Temperance Movement of the 1920s, the Civil Rights Movement of the 1960s, and the Women's Rights Movement of the 1970s, all changed either temporarily or permanently the beliefs and values of American society.

Furthermore, modernization and globalization have led people in other cultures to adopt similar social movements in other cultures that have resulted in change. An excellent example of this is the social change that occurred during the Meji Restoration of Japan. The Japanese adopted the folkways and mores of Western countries, including European countries and the United States. Many of these values were then codified into law and regulated the behavior of the Japanese in a way that was quite different and new compared to the feudal social norms that existed before.

Competency 016 Descriptive Statement D. The beginning teacher demonstrates knowledge of the theoretical foundations of sociology and basic sociological processes, including those related to group membership, roles, status, values, and stratification.

Social stratification is a natural phenomenon of culture groups that divide their societies into different subgroups based on various characteristics, such as ethnicity, language, religion, family heritage, and socioeconomic standing. This stratification leads to divisions within a culture that may maintain certain levels of wealth or even relegate certain groups to lower economic classes. Roles in a society may be determined by status or group membership.

The early sociologist Max Weber divided the forms of social stratification into three distinct categories: status, class, and party. The way he saw it, these were the three interrelated dimensions in which power is distributed in the community: status based on prestige gained through the social order; class through the economic order; and party through the political order.

Mobility among social classes varies among cultures. In American society, people can move between classes depending on one's economic status. With a shift in politics, political status can also change as well. In the past, social classes were much more rigid, and it was difficult or impossible to move up or down. In the former caste system of India established under Hinduism, almost all aspects of life for an individual were determined by one's birth into a particular caste.

Competency 016 Descriptive Statement E. The beginning teacher understands the role and influence of social institutions in meeting basic societal need (i.e., family, religion, educational system, science, and mass media).

Social institutions serve to reinforce cultural beliefs and values. Human beings have certain needs that, according to psychologist Abraham Maslow, are arranged hierarchically. Among the most basic is Among the most basic is a deep-seated psychological need to belong to a larger class, group, or society. Maslow proposed that the desire to belong is a necessary part of an individual's existence.

Social institutions such as family structure, marriage, religion, and educational systems help to teach and reinforce cultural beliefs and values. These structures vary from culture to culture, but all necessarily exist to help the individual become socialized and fulfill the need to belong.

> **Competency 016 Descriptive Statement F.** The beginning teacher demonstrates knowledge of the roles of men, women, children, and families in historical and contemporary cultures.

According to sociologists, family can be defined as an intimate domestic group made up of people related to one another by bonds of blood, sexual mating, or legal ties. The structure of family varies from culture to culture. These different family structures play an important role in transmitting and maintaining cultural beliefs and values. Social and economic trends have influenced the structure of family over time. The family is also an important economic unit. There are three basic structures of family.

Nuclear family. A nuclear family consists of parents and one or more children living together. The nuclear family has been the predominant form of family structure across most human societies over time.

Single-parent family. A single parent family consists of only one parent living together with one or more children.

Extended family. An extended family is one that goes beyond the nuclear family, including grandparents, aunts, uncles, and other relatives who all live nearby or in one household. One form of extended family is the "stem family," in which multiple generations live under one roof. Another form of extended family brings together the family patriarch and matriarch, aunts and uncles, and younger generations within one household.

> **Competency 016 Descriptive Statement G.** The beginning teacher understands ways in which socialization, cultural values, and norms vary across space and time and influence relationships within groups.

Socialization is the process by which people learn cultural beliefs and values. The important folklore, mores, and laws transmitted to the youth by the older generation. In this way, they learn the expectations of the culture so that they might successfully function within that culture. Socialization occurs through social institutions like the family, religion, and educational systems. The family unit is the most important social institution. As children interact and observe their family, they learn socially acceptable ways to behave within the culture.

Abraham Maslow theorized that socialization is an important part of how the individual fulfills the important psychological goal of belonging and group identity.

Of course, since cultural beliefs and values vary across the globe, socialization tends to occur in different ways in different cultures. Modern globalization and social movements have caused changes to the ways in which cultures socialize over time.

> **Competency 016 Descriptive Statement H.** The beginning teacher demonstrates knowledge of the theoretical foundations and development of psychology.

Psychology is the study of human individual behavior. It grew out of the work of the *philosophes* of the Enlightenment, who took an interest in the internal motivations that shaped human behavior. Prior to the Enlightenment, the intellectual and academic tradition of Western Europe emphasized the role of sin as an explanation for deviant or immoral human behavior. Enlightenment thinkers considered humans inherently rational and sought to find explanations for seemingly irrational human actions. Moreover, they did not lack the confidence in their ability to find explanations for both reasonable and deviant human behavior or beliefs, as they had inordinate faith in the power of human reason, including their own.

The first laboratory dedicated to psychology was established at Leipzig University in 1879 by Wilhelm Wundt. This marks the beginning of the modern field of human psychology. Wundt recorded human reactions under controlled conditions, and this became the first observational study of human behavior. William James was the first to establish a laboratory for human experimental psychology at Harvard University in 1890.

Another influential early psychologist was Sigmund Freud. Freud developed the technique of psychoanalysis, which focused on introspective psychology. Freud is better known than Wundt or James because he discussed sexuality in his work and argued that the role of repressed or subconscious motivations helped explain a variety of human behaviors.

Freud's theories, which relied on personal introspection rather than experimentation, caused a counter-reaction, which led to the foundation of behavioral psychology. Behaviorists believe that psychology should focus on human behavior, rather than on subjective introspections about how the human mind works.

Behaviorism was pioneered by researchers such as B.F. Skinner and John B. Watson. Their studies showed that humans could be conditioned, like animals, to behave in certain ways in response to controlled variables.

Modern psychology continues to build upon this early research and has branched into neural and cognitive psychology today.

> **Competency 016 Descriptive Statement I.** The beginning teacher demonstrates knowledge of behavioral, social, cognitive, and personality perspectives of human identity, development, and learning.

Research by psychologists has had an important impact on education, and thinking about how humans learn. Researchers like Piaget, Dewey, Vygotsky, and Skinner have influenced modern ideas of how we think and how we learn.

Behavioral learning theory. Behavioral psychologists following in the footsteps of B.F. Skinner, study conditioning as a form of learning. Behavioral learning holds that by pairing stimulus and reaction, people learn. As the stimulus becomes associated with a certain reaction, we learn how to behave.

Social learning theory. Social learning theory, championed by Lev Vygotsky, is based on observation and repetition. According to Vygotsky, humans learn by fixing new knowledge to a scaffolding on existing or prior knowledge. They also learn by observation and repetition built on behavior modeled by others. The scaffolding or modeling helps the observer to learn.

Cognitive learning theory. Cognitive learning theory focuses on the individual, his choices, and his awareness of the process of learning. Unlike behaviorism, cognitive psychologists hold that the mind works in specific ways to help it process information. Through focusing on how the brain functions and processes information, cognitive psychology has also contributed to modern computer technology.

Personality learning theory. Personality psychology theory holds that there are different characteristics and types of individual personality. These personality types affect how the individual processes information and learns. Howard Gardner's theory of Multiple Intelligences is a recent work that has had a tremendous impact on the field of education. Gardner theorized that humans have a number of distinct intelligence modalities: musicality, spatial intelligence, linguistic intelligence, logical-mathematical or reasoning intelligence, bodily-kinesthetic intelligence, social intelligence, introspection, naturalistic intelligence, and existential intelligence. Humans do not have each of these abilities in equal parts; thus an individual's intelligence and learning style will reflect each individual's particular aptitudes in these realms.

> **Competency 016 Descriptive Statement J.** The beginning teacher understands basic psychological principles and processes, including those related to motivation, sensation, perception, cognition, personality, relationships between biology and behavior, and relationships between the self and others.

Psychological processes describe the way humans process information and perceptions, and the resulting human behavior. Critical thinking, communication and language use, and cognitive thinking and memory functions are all processes of psychology. They can be conscious or unconscious. Sensation, perception, and motivation are other examples of psychological processes.

Sensation. The information or stimulus we receive through our five senses is referred to as sensation. This is the most basic process humans use to take in information about their environment. Sensation is the starting point for other psychological processes, as input from the environment stimulates individuals to analyze and understand their environment. Reaction to sensory input is driven by other psychological processes.

Perception. This is the first step individuals take as they are stimulated by sensory input. How we perceive things drives our other psychological processes. For instance, one may perceive a dog as a threat or not a threat. Tone of voice can be perceived as harsh or benign. Perception can be different from our sensory input.

Motivation. Motivation is an individual's strong desire toward a certain course of action or a certain goal based on those actions. Basic motivation is represented by a drive to satisfy hunger, or live safely. As one moves toward one's goals, other psychological processes are involved in deciding a course of action and achievement of goals.

Personality. Personality is the sum of an individual's behavior patterns, thoughts, and emotions. Perception and motivation are highly influenced by one's personality. Psychologists study how personality affects perceptions and motivations, and how personality plays a role in learning and thinking.

The relationship of biology and behavior is a growing field of inquiry in psychology. The way the brain functions cognitively and the way memory works affect sensation, perception, motivation, and personality. Neural psychology focuses on the brain and its complex chemical reactions to further understand how the mind works.

How the individual behaves and reacts in relation to other people is the focus of social psychology. How the individual sees themselves and their role in society affects how they interact with their fellow human beings. Perception, motivation, and personality are all affected by an individual's self-concept.

Domain V: Government and Citizenship

The title of Domain V, "Government and Citizenship," is an indication of the two intended emphases that the Texas Education Agency wants social studies teacher candidates to bear in mind. While political science is a social and behavioral science, preparation in Domain V emphasizes mastery of the processes of American and Texas government as well as an understanding of the rights and roles of the citizen. The former requires learning how government works. The latter requires both a historical knowledge of the expansion of civil rights and the changing role of government in both the United States and Texas. Prospective teachers must be familiar with the key documents and legal decisions that have shaped the nature of our governmental institutions and the relationship of citizens to their government. While this domain will ask test-takers to answer approximately 18 to 20 questions, or about 13 percent of the exam, many of the questions will also require an understanding of American and Texas history.

COMPETENCY 017 (DEMOCRATIC PRINCIPLES AND GOVERNMENT IN THE UNITED STATES)

The teacher understands the principles of democratic government and the structure and functioning of government in the United States.

> **Competency 017 Descriptive Statement A.** The beginning teacher analyzes the beliefs and principles reflected in the U.S. Constitution (e.g., republicanism, checks and balances, federalism, separation of powers, separation of church and state, popular sovereignty, individual rights) and other important historical documents (e.g., Declaration of Independence, Federalist Papers, English Bill of Rights).

Key Question

What are the sources of American political values, and how are these values reflected in the "sacred" texts of the American republic?

English Bill of Rights (1689)

The Revolutionary War reflected a variety of grievances shared by American colonists. In rebellion, however, revolutionary leaders invoked their "rights as Englishmen." These rights, reflected in colonial charters, derived from England's "unwritten" constitution, which included a key component called the English Bill of Rights. The English Bill of Rights limited the power of the monarchy and provided safeguards against arbitrary rule. The English Bill of Rights provided a model for individual states' listing of citizen rights, and for the drafting of the American Bill of Rights. Perhaps most importantly, the English Bill of Rights influenced the colonists to view their society as one in which law circumscribed the government's power over the individual. Additionally, the English Bill of Rights featured beliefs about the government's proper exercise of power, which Americans continue to hold today. Americans later claimed other rights laid out in the English Bill of Rights for their own, including the right to petition the government for redress of grievances, the right to freedom of speech (though the English Bill of Rights limited this to political speech in Parliament), the right to a jury trial in certain cases, prohibitions of cruel and unusual punishments or excessive bail or fines, and a limited right to bear arms.

Declaration of Independence

The Declaration of Independence has no force of law. It is not a constitution in itself, nor is it a part of the United States Constitution, despite the frequency with which it has been called the "real preamble to the Constitution." To understand the Declaration of Independence's purpose, a number of important questions must be answered: Who was its intended audience? What did the Declaration in fact declare? And why did the colonists make this Declaration?

The introductory and closing paragraphs of the Declaration identify its audience and purpose. The authors—Thomas Jefferson produced the first draft—made clear that the audience was the world's peoples, or nations, and not just the English crown. The concluding paragraph demands that the world's nations recognize that the 13 "Free and Independent States" had "the full Power to levy War, conclude Peace, contract Alliances. . ." and in every other way act as sovereign states. The first and last paragraphs also identify a second purpose, a listing of the grievances the colonists had against the British government. These were "the causes which impel them [the 13 colonies] to the separation [from the British Empire].

Most of the intervening text lists the many objections to British rule that the colonists had accumulated over the previous decades. Among these grievances were complaints about the Crown's interference in colonial self-government: vetoes of colonial laws, imposition of new officials, intervention in colonial courts, and royal dissolution of colonial assemblies. Other complaints included the maintenance of standing armies in the colonies, interference with colonial trade, encouraging domestic uprisings in the colonies, and more.

The most-referenced paragraph in the Declaration of Independence, and undoubtedly the most inspiring, is the second paragraph. In it can best be seen the beliefs that underlay the American Revolution, and the aspirations that American have been trying to fulfill ever since. In this second paragraph, we see the influence of the English philosopher John Locke and theories of natural rights. Locke contended that all humans possessed inalienable natural rights, among them "life, liberty, and property." Jefferson opened the second paragraph of the Declaration of Independence, with the breathtaking claim, familiar to readers of Locke, "that all men are created equal," and "that they are endowed by their Creator with certain unalienable Rights, that among these are Life, Liberty and the pursuit of Happiness." The purpose of government, according to Locke and Jefferson, was to protect the life, liberty, and property—which Jefferson broadened to "the pursuit of Happiness" —of its citizenry. The contractual nature of the relationship between the state and its citizens is also clear. Contracts are made, but when violated, can be unmade. As Jefferson wrote in the Declaration, when "any Form of Government becomes destructive of these ends, it is the Right of the People to alter or to abolish it." The ideas celebrated in this second paragraph—liberty, equality, individual rights, protections of private property, limited government, the right to self-government, and the right to revolt—are all central to American notions of legitimate government.

Articles of Confederation

The final paragraph of the Declaration of Independence employed language that today might appear either colloquial or strange. The document announces that as a result of the British crown's tyranny, "that all political connection between . . . the united States of America in General Congress, Assembled . . . and the State of Great Britain, is and ought to be totally dissolved." Jefferson did not capitalize "united" for a reason. The 13 states that united in Philadelphia to assert their independence from Great Britain were not yet joined as a single nation-state. They were a confederation of states, each claiming its individual sovereignty. This is most evident in the framework of government that was written at the same time known as the Articles of Confederation. The Articles of Confederation, the first constitution of the independent United States, was adopted during the Revolutionary War. Under the Articles, each state retained its "sovereignty, freedom, and independence."

The Articles established a weak national government often unable to effectively carry out its responsibilities. The unicameral [single chamber] Congress had authority to provide for the national defense and to make treaties with foreign powers and Indian nations. It had the power to request funding, but it did not have the power of taxation. As a result, it was perpetually under-funded. It was supposed to establish a basis for the general economy but lacked the authority to regulate the money supply, or to otherwise interfere in each state's commercial policies. Individual states could negotiate with foreign nations or other states to regulate interstate or international trade. Trade wars and competition between the states, as a result, frequently threatened the cohesion of the government.

To a great degree, the weakness of the government under the Articles of Confederation resulted from the fact that the separate states (and not the nation's people as a whole) were the source of any authority claimed by Congress under the Articles of Confederation. In Congress, each state had one vote in all deliberations. To ensure that states maintained their pre-eminence under the Articles, significant decisions—such as funding requisitions, declarations of war, or treaty ratification—required a supermajority of nine of the 13 states to agree. And, most significantly, any amendment of the Articles of Confederation required unanimous agreement of all 13 states. George Washington lamented at one point that the United States did not deserve to be called a nation. In fact, it was not; it was a confederation of virtually autonomous nation-states.

Though the power of the states relative to the federal government today has certainly diminished, the principles of state sovereignty are still reflected in the federalist system that the Framers developed. This sovereignty is most evident in the 10th Amendment to the United States Constitution, which states that "the powers not delegated to the United States by the Constitution, nor prohibited by it to the States, are reserved to the States respectively, or to the people." To this notion of limited state sovereignty we can trace many of the arguments made over the course of our history for the principle of "states' rights."

Beliefs and Principles of the U.S. Constitution

The United States Constitution, crafted in Philadelphia in 1787, represented a marked departure from the form of government established under the Articles of Confederation.

Popular Sovereignty

"We the people, of the United States," so begins the preamble to the United States Constitution. With these words the Framers situated the locus of sovereignty in the people. In many ways, the government established at the Philadelphia Constitutional Convention removed powers from the control of the original 13 state governments, and thereby reduced the power of direct popular influence. However, this statement reflects the Enlightenment period and the American Revolutionary rejection of monarchy. The term *monarchy* derives from the Greek word *monarkia*, or "rule of one." Instead, the Framers situated the locus of authority in the whole of the nation, or the people. An alternative to the rule of one, of course, is the rule of the people, or the majority. The Greeks called this *demokratia*, which can be translated as either the "rule of the people" or the "rule of the majority." The Framers of the Constitution sought to steer a course between these two systems of government.

The Framers of the Constitution did *not* establish a democracy. As Elbridge Gerry famously remarked at the Philadelphia convention, "The evils we experience flow from the excess of democracy." Most representatives at the Constitutional Convention were hesitant to extend political power to the mass of American citizens. They feared the rule of the majority, which they considered in most ways ill-informed, prone to manipulation, and motivated to serve their own self-interest rather than consider the good of the whole. Indeed, among the complaints directed toward the system of government laid out under the Articles of Confederation was that the powers of the people and of private interests were too great in the state legislatures. As a result, under the Constitution, while sovereignty is said to derive from the people, decision-making power is largely held elsewhere. In some cases, as in the election to the House of Representatives, the people make their voices known directly. In other instances, as in the election of the president, intermediary bodies (the Electoral College) mediates the popular voice.

Nonetheless, the principle of **majoritarianism**, the belief that in determining public policy, or in counting of votes, the majority should prevail, has been an important assumption of American political institutions. The definition of "the people," or those with voting and office-holding power, has gradually expanded over the course of American history, first with the expansion of civil rights to most white males in the period from 1800 to 1836, then through the Reconstruction Amendments, which granted citizenship rights to descendants of slaves, and the 19th Amendment granting women the right to vote. The Civil Rights movement(s) have further expanded those who are entitled to sovereignty.

Republicanism

Instead of a *democracy*, a term that today is often used to denote a representative government, the Framers established a *republic*. In Article IV, section 4 of the United States Constitution, the federal government was also charged with guaranteeing each state a republican form of government.

A republic is a form of government designed to allow majority rule constrained by safeguards for the minority. The Framers worried that a majority often has the tendency to act as a mob, trampling the rights of the few. Republicanism as a form of government places decision-making power in the hands of what are hoped to be virtuous representatives, lawmakers imbued with an enlightened sense of public interest. The Framers feared that a democracy would result in a government driven by the pursuit of self-interest, whether by elected representatives who made decisions motivated by a desire to appeal to the electorate or by voters who chose their representatives on the basis of what would best serve their own private interests. During the heady days of the American Revolution, patriots like John Adams, James Madison, and George Washington thought it likely that a republic would generate virtuous men to lead the nation. What they observed in the early years of the American republic instead was a thriving factionalism or partisanship, driven by self-interested voters and corrupt office-holders.

The Framers who established the representative system of the United States incorporated several provisions designed to keep officeholders at arm's length from popular pressures. The House of Representatives, whose members were up for election every two years, was the most sensitive to popular pressure. United States Senators, by contrast, were appointed by legislatures of their respective states (until the 17th Amendment in 1913). Every two years, a third of the Senate faced reappointment, which further insulated the Senate from popular pressure. The president, as we have seen, was chosen by the Electoral College, its members themselves chosen by the separate state legislatures. Federal judges and justices were appointed and not elected, whereupon they had lifetime tenure, "during good behavior." In each of these ways, the new Republic restricted the likelihood that a determined majority could gain unchecked control of the reins of government.

Separation of Powers

The Framers of the United States Constitution were heavily influenced by the ideas of the Enlightenment. The French political philosopher Montesquieu had a particular influence on the Framers' development of a government marked by a separation of powers. Montesquieu had considered carefully the implications of the Enlightenment's emphasis on liberty. Liberty, he concluded, could not be the right to do whatever one wishes, of course, because that liberty might harm others. Law then provides the only sure restraint that allows us to do what we want without coming to harm or harming others. "Liberty," Montesquieu contended, "is a right of doing whatever the laws permit." But, laws may also be misguided, onerous in their application, or unfair. As Montesquieu noted, when legislative and executive powers are held by the same individual or group, "a monarch or senate" could "enact tyrannical laws, to execute them in a tyrannical manner." Similarly, if the judiciary is not separate from the legislative power, "the judge would then be the legislator," and "the life and liberty of the subject would be subject to arbitrary control." Montesquieu proposed a clear separation of powers between the legislative function, the executive function, and the judicial function of government. It was only in this way that tyranny could be avoided.

The target of Montesquieu's critique was the French monarch, in whom legislative, executive, and judicial functions were melded. For the Framers, the greatest fear was the tyranny of the majority, or a tyranny of a democratically elected faction. To counter the likelihood that a majority would concentrate power to the detriment of others, the American system of government instituted a careful separation of the powers of government along both horizontal and vertical lines. Vertically, state and federal governments were separated in what is called a federal system. In this system, the federal government acted to restrain the states (which the Framers viewed as most susceptible to democratic pressures), and the states acted as a brake on overreaches of federal power. Horizontally, the legislative, executive, and judicial functions were divided. Within the legislative branch, which was envisioned as the first and most powerful branch of government, there was separation between the House of Representatives and the Senate. In this way, the Framers sought to ensure that no majority or faction could capture the government and use it in a tyrannical fashion. The system of checks and balances internal to the separation of powers further provided for limited federal and state governments.

Checks and Balances

If the Framers were concerned that too much democracy resulted in the tyranny of the majority, they were equally concerned that one branch of government might concentrate power to the detriment of the other branches. The Constitution therefore established a system in which the separate institutions of government shared powers and jurisdictions to act as a check and balance against each other.

Thus, while Congress has the power to make laws, the president can veto Congressional acts. The president also recommends legislation, offers budgetary proposals, and can call special sessions of Congress. Presidents also have the power to issue executive orders, which have the force of law. Perhaps as significantly, when the president executes the law he also interprets it, often with different emphases than those intended by Congress. The principle of judicial review, whereby the courts determine the constitutionality of a legislative or executive enactment, provides an important check on the legislative function.

Just as Congressional legislation is subject to judicial review, the courts may also declare decisions of the executive branch and the president unconstitutional. The president's executive power is also limited by the powers of Congress and the courts. The Senate must approve treaties and high-level appointments. Congress's law-making powers impinge on presidential authority. Congressional control over budgets and appropriations forces presidents to align their priorities with those of Congress. Executive actions, such as executive war-making power, in most instances require legislative authorization. The power of impeachment stands out as the most pointed example of Congressional power over the presidency. The process of impeaching and removing a president well illustrates how the system of checks and balances comes into play. The House of Representatives draws up and votes on "articles of impeachment," the equivalent of a formal indictment. The Senate has the responsibility of hearing the case—with the Chief Justice of the Supreme Court presiding over the proceedings—and deciding on the removal of the president.

While individual federal judges have an independence and tenure that shelters them from popular and political pressure, the judicial branch does not act without restraint within the system of checks and balances in the United States. The president appoints federal judges. The president executes court decisions, although sometimes without enthusiasm. The Senate approves judicial appointments.

Federalism

Under the Articles of Confederation, "these united States" as contemporaries referred to the confederation, was a nation in name only. The 13 states and their governments had their own constitutions and their own political culture and identity. The state governments were widely popular with their citizens, who identified first with their state and rarely with their national identity. Most of the delegates to the Philadelphia convention, however, were committed to a stronger, unified nation, not an association of states. The compromise arrived at was a division of sovereignty and a system of government that was soon identified as a federalist system.

A **federalist system** of government divides powers between the central, or national, government and the state. The federal government is charged with matters that have a national scope: defense, international and interstate trade, taxation, and many other powers. States are empowered to address local issues, such as public education, police powers, local infrastructure, licensing, and regulation of the state economy. A **federal** system differs from a **confederacy** in that in the latter the states are sovereign. The government acquires its authority from the states. These two systems can be contrasted with **unitary systems** of government that are common in many governments around the world. In unitary systems, power at all levels of government derives from the national government, whose laws are supreme and binding on the lower levels of government. In unitary systems, often the national government has the power to disband the state or provincial governments.

The institution of a federalist system resulted from the reality that, while the country's political and economic elite were largely in agreement about the need for a stronger national government, the states were committed to defending their individual sovereignty. Supporters of the Constitution, who took the name **Federalists,** argued for the division of powers between state and national governments. They characterized the division between national and local authority as another check against tyranny, on the part of either state or national government.

Separation of Church and State

The First Amendment to the United States Constitution reads: "Congress shall make no law respecting an establishment of religion, or prohibiting the free exercise thereof." This amendment was originally aimed largely at Congress, a branch of the federal government. Before the American Revolution, many of the colonial governments had supported churches with public funds and had discouraged the growth of dissident religious sects. During the Revolutionary period, however, New York, North Carolina, and Virginia had separated church and state in their constitutions. The other nine states, however, maintained a number of provisions for state support of religion. In some cases, ministers were prohibited from holding public office. In others, there were religious tests for office holding.

Many of the Framers of the Constitution, however, were what would later be described as *deists*. Deists abandoned traditional Christian professions of faith. They also increasingly rejected the view that the state should sponsor religious institutions and support them through taxes. Others recognized that religious division could threaten the future of the new republic.

The opening clause of the First Amendment, the **establishment clause**, thus forbids the government from favoring one religion or sect over another, thereby establishing an official religion. Over the history of the republic this clause has resulted in numerous rulings that have restricted mandated prayer in public-school classrooms or official religious displays. The second clause, the

free-exercise clause, prohibits the government from interfering with the exercise of one's religious beliefs.

Individual Rights

Protections for individual rights were largely ignored in the Constitution. The Constitution did forbid Congressional **bills of attainder**, legislative acts that pronounced an individual or a group guilty of crime without benefit of trial; or laws that impeded the fulfillment of legally binding contracts. But, in the main, the Constitution was silent on individual rights. This deficiency became a principal objection of many **Anti-Federalists**, as opponents of the Constitution were known. But, even supporters of the Constitution noticed the absence of a Bill of Rights. John Adams and Thomas Jefferson, both on diplomatic missions at the time of the Convention, thought the absence of a Bill of Rights to be a deficiency. Even men who had participated in the Constitutional Convention, including Elbridge Gerry and George Mason, refused to sign their names to the Constitution because it lacked a Bill of Rights. To ensure ratification of the Constitution, it was agreed that the first meeting of Congress would follow the process for proposing amendments to the Constitution and put forth amendments that would serve as a Bill of Rights that would protect against federal abuses of individual rights.

Congress approved 12 amendments, of which 10 were ratified by the states. These amendments are known collectively as the Bill of Rights. As most states already included within their constitutions their own bills of rights, these 10 amendments were originally applied to the federal government. Only later would their protections be applied to state governments. The individual rights that the Bill of Rights protects may be divided into three broad categories:

1. **Protections of freedoms of expression.** These amendments protect the rights to free speech, freedom of the press, the right to petition your government representatives for redress of grievances, and freedom from state intervention in individual religious belief and practices.

2. **Protections from the federal government's police powers.** These protect against unreasonable search and seizure; provide for the right to due process before the law, including the right to a public trial, the right to mount a defense and to defense counsel, the right to a trial by jury and to a speedy trial; and establish prohibitions against excessive bails and cruel and unusual punishment.

3. **Limiting federal authority over the people and the states.** The last two amendments of the Bill of Rights broadly restrict the federal government from encroaching on rights of the people and the individual states. The Ninth Amendment was written to put the federal government on notice that rights not specifically protected in the Bill of Rights are nonetheless not to be infringed on by the federal government. The 10th Amendment reiterates the view that was explicit in the Articles of Confederation: the states have their own sovereign identities, and powers not granted specifically to the federal gov-

ernment belong by default to the states. This amendment is at the root of many states' rights claims.

In the aftermath of the Civil War, the Constitution was amended in a variety of ways to extend the rights originally articulated in the document. Additionally, these rights continue to be defined and extended as the courts and individual citizens are confronted with new ways in which these rights are both infringed upon or interpreted.

Words Missing from the Constitution and What They Tell Us

Sometimes what is left out of a document is as important as what is made explicit. The United States Constitution is silent on a number of matters that might come as a surprise.

Political party

Noticeably absent from the United States Constitution, given the prominent place of political parties today, is any mention of political parties. Political parties were thought to represent "factions," what we today would call "special interests." In classical republican thought, officials were not to be motivated by self-interest or the interests of a narrow group of constituents, but instead were to make decisions in the interest of the whole. There was a debate about whether politicians should receive payment for their public service, as they might then be motivated more by greed than by philanthropic interests. In the early republic, campaigning actively for votes was thought to be unseemly. Parties were seen as likely to protect selfish and special interests.

Slavery

The Framers did not use the word "slavery" in the Constitution. The only time "slavery" or "slave" appears in the United States Constitution is in the 13th Amendment, which abolished the institution of slavery. However, the 13th Amendment was not added until 1865. Before then, the word "slavery" was excluded from the Constitution. The Constitution of 1789, in fact, protected the rights of slaveholders over their human property and enhanced the political power of the slave-holding states. Exclusion of the word "slavery" in the early Constitution was not at the behest of delegates from the South, as we might think today. Instead, the word was excluded because Northern delegates feared it might cause their states to refuse to ratify the new constitution once their constituents realized how deeply the document implicated slavery.

The Constitution gave Southern states greater representation in Congress and more Electoral College votes, the assurance that federal troops would be deployed to put down slave rebellions if necessary, and a virtual veto power over any Constitutional amendments to which slaveholding states would object. The South effectively dominated the nation's politics from 1788 until 1861. Of the first 16 presidents, 11 owned slaves while in office, or had owned slaves earlier. All of the two-term presidents to hold office were slave owners.

God

The Declaration of Independence and the Articles of Confederation mention God. The Constitution does not. The Constitution of the Confederacy invoked "the favor and guidance of Almighty God" in its preamble. A number of explanations have been offered for this omission of God in the Constitution. One argument suggests that the absence of a direct reference to God did not reflect any irreverence on the part of the Framers. Instead, the authors of the Constitution wished to make clear that the United States government derived from the people's consent, in contrast to most European monarchs who claimed a divine right to rule.

Free Enterprise, Capitalism

There is no mention in the Constitution of the terms "free enterprise system" or "capitalism." These terms would not enter into usage until long after the Philadelphia convention. Capitalism first appeared in print in 1854, and the term "free enterprise" in 1890. Even Adam Smith, the most important theorist of the free enterprise system, did not use either of these terms. Smith described the economic system he envisioned as "the system of natural liberty," while his most prominent biographer employed the terms "free market," "free commerce," and "free competition" to describe the ideals that would later be understood to combine in the free enterprise system.

Neither did the United States Constitution directly address the form of economic system the nation would take. Indeed, one of the most important divisions that emerged in the early republic was between Thomas Jefferson, who considered the Constitution to have been designed to create an economic system based on commercial agriculture, small farmers, merchants, and artisans. He did not consider the prospect, assumed by Alexander Hamilton, of the emergence of a capitalist economy based on wage earners, factory owners, and urbanization to be a positive one.

As we will see in this book's chapter 8, "Economics and Science, Technology and Society," many of the protections that are taken for granted in free enterprise systems are evident in the United States Constitution. However, the features of the American free enterprise system as it has evolved are rooted less in the United States Constitution than in later legislative enactments, court decisions, and customary practice.

The Federalist Papers

The United States Constitution was not immediately accepted as a better alternative to the Articles of Confederation. Despite the august reputations of many of the Framers, reputations that have only increased over time, many in the 13 states, including such patriotic figures as Patrick Henry, were adamantly opposed to its ratification. The essays in *The Federalist Papers* were written largely to address opponents to the Constitution's ratification in New York. Even though nine of the 13 states had already approved the Constitution, it was hard to see how the Union could survive without New York's favorable vote for the Constitution's ratification. Alexander Hamilton, John Jay, and James Madison therefore wrote a series of 85 essays that were published anonymously under the pseudonym Publius, describing in detail how the three branches of government would operate, the relationships between the states and the national government, advantages of a strengthened centralized system of government, and the congruency between the Constitution and republican values.

For constitutional scholars and jurists, the *Federalist Papers* provide one of the best insights into the **original intent** of the Framers at the Constitutional Convention. No outsiders were permitted in the Pennsylvania State House rooms in Philadelphia where the Framers met, and each member was sworn to secrecy. Minutes of the proceedings were not kept and few notes survived, save James Madison's *Notes of Debates in the Federal Convention of 1787*, which were only published after Madison's death in 1836.

> **Competency 017 Descriptive Statement B.** The beginning teacher demonstrates knowledge of the structure and functions of the government created by the U.S. Constitution (e.g., bicameral structure of Congress, role of congressional committees, constitutional powers of the president, role of the Cabinet and independent executive agencies, functions of the federal court system).

Bicameralism

Bicameralism, simply defined, is a lawmaking body that is composed of two legislative houses or chambers. The English Parliament provided the most immediate example for the Framers of the Constitution. Parliament is divided into the House of Commons and the House of Lords. Eleven of the 13 original states had established bicameral legislatures in their own constitutions. Pennsylvania and Georgia had **unicameral** legislatures, considering them more democratic and more attentive to the popular will. Today, only Nebraska has a unicameral legislature. The United States Congress under the Articles of Confederation was also a unicameral body, reflective of its affirmation of the equal sovereignty of each of the states. William Paterson's "New Jersey Plan," which was proposed at the Constitutional Convention, called for the continuation of a unicameral Congress. The Founders chose instead to construct a legislative branch composed of two chambers, the House of Representatives and the Senate.

The Framers' decision to adopt a bicameral legislature reflected a number of considerations. The first was a deep suspicion by the smaller states of the power of the larger states. The House of Representatives would have a proportional representation determined by population size, giving greater power to the more populous states. Smaller states insisted on a second chamber to act as a brake on the power of the more populous states. A second argument in favor of a second legislative chamber reflects a quasi-aristocratic and republican view. The Senate would be smaller with a more select membership, made up of men chosen for longer terms of office. The lower chamber, the House of Representatives, would serve as the embodiment of the popular will, while the upper chamber, the Senate, would act as a check on that democratic but sometimes arbitrary will.

Congressional Committees

Most of the work of Congress is carried out through the standing committee system. There are at present 20 standing committees in the House and 16 in the Senate.

House of Representatives	Senate
Agriculture	Agriculture, Nutrition, and Forestry
Appropriations	Appropriations
Armed Services	Armed Services
Budget	Banking, Housing and Urban Affairs
Education and the Workforce	Budget
Energy and Commerce	Commerce, Science, and Transportation
Ethics	Energy and Natural Resources
Financial Services	Environment and Public Works
Foreign Affairs	Finance
Homeland Security	Foreign Relations
House Administration	Health, Education, Labor, and Pensions
Judiciary	Homeland Security and Governmental Affairs
Natural Resources	Judiciary
Oversight and Government Reform	Rules and Administration
Rules	Small Business and Entrepreneurship
Science, Space, and Technology	Veterans Affairs
Small Business	
Transportation and Infrastructure	
Veterans Affairs	
Ways and Means	

Most of the standing committees also have **subcommittees**; for example, the House Agriculture Committee has six subcommittees: Commodity Exchanges, Energy and Credit; Conservation and Forestry; Nutrition; General Farm Commodities and Risk Management; Biotechnology, Horticulture, and Research; and Livestock and Foreign Agriculture. House and Senate subcommittees have generally about a dozen members.

In addition, there are a number of special and select committees in both chambers, as well as joint committees with membership drawn from both houses.

Each committee has a fixed number of members, with the party in the majority of the respective chamber holding the majority of seats on each committee. Though there is no established rule enforcing this practice, typically the number of seats in a committee held by each party corresponds roughly to the ratio of the party's representation in the full House or Senate. Committee membership is one of the ways in which party leaders reward their members. In the House, members usually serve on two standing committees, while Senators often serve on four.

Each bill introduced in either chamber must be referred by party leaders to the appropriate committee. Each committee is generally chaired by the member of the majority party with the most seniority on that committee. The chair schedules hearings, determines the priority given to a bill's discussion, presides over committee deliberations, and directs committee staff. The chair can also choose to shepherd a bill through floor debate in the Senate or House. Committee chairs have enormous influence on either promoting or hindering a bill.

Since 1995, the role of seniority in the committee system has diminished somewhat. When Republicans took control of Congress in 1995, they instituted term limits on committee chairs as a measure to ensure that the committees pursue the party's priorities, rather than an individual chair's priorities. When the Democrats regained control of Congress in 2007, they kept this system in place. As a result, committees have increasingly reflected the power of the national party apparatus, rather than the sectional or individual interests of powerful chairs.

Presidential Powers

Following the Preamble to the Constitution, Article I outlined the role of the Congress in the United States' system of government. This reflects the priority that the Framers gave to the legislative branch. Article I, Section 8 then delineates in very specific terms the different powers of Congress. By contrast, Article II, which describes the president's powers, does so with much less specificity. As a result, understanding the extent of presidential authority or the limitations on presidential power from a constitutional perspective is much more difficult. To understand the extent of these powers it is useful to divide them into the following categories: powers over foreign affairs; powers vis-à-vis the legislative branch; protective powers; and judicial powers.

Powers over Foreign Affairs

Article II of the Constitution makes clear the president's primary responsibility over foreign affairs. The president is "the Commander in Chief of the Army and Navy of the United States," has the power to "appoint Ambassadors," and has full authorization to negotiate treaties, with the advice and consent of the Senate. Presidential independence is perhaps more important in the realm of foreign policy where flexibility, secrecy, and speed of response are more critical. Nonetheless, the Constitution granted Congress singular responsibility for declaring war and gave the Senate a critical oversight role in approving treaties. Despite Congress's constitutional monopoly of war-making powers, as we will see, presidents have only rarely been hindered from sending American troops into combat out of deference to congressional authority. All of the wars of the 20th and 21st centuries, except World War I and World War II, have been carried out without a congressional declaration. Additionally, using the expedient of executive agreements, presidents have also entered the United States into obligations with foreign nation, without the full advice and consent of the Senate. The power of the Senate to withhold ratification of a treaty, however, has been used to great impact on a number of occasions. For example, the Senate's refusal to ratify the Versailles Treaty ending World War I, and its refusal to permit the United States to be a member nation of the League of Nations severely weakened this international body.

Powers vis-à-vis the Legislative Branch

The Constitution assigns the president a number of functions that feature in the lawmaking process.

Most immediately, the president has the power to approve or to veto Congressional legislation. The **veto power** gives a president enormous power to influence legislation well before a bill reaches a final form. A mere threat to veto a bill often forces Congress to alter or withdraw a proposed law.

Article II, Section 3 tasks the president with the responsibility to "take Care that the Laws be faithfully executed." Congress, thus, delegates duties to the executive branch. Over the course of the 20th century Congress has created a vast bureaucratic system and given executive branch officials significant leeway to enact regulations and punish violators. Congress in 2002, for example, passed into law the Homeland Security Act. The act created a Department of Homeland Security which was given as one of its primary missions to "prevent terrorist attacks within the United States" and to "investigate and prosecute" terrorism. The 187 pages of the legislation then outlined the different responsibilities of the different executive branch agencies required to execute the intent of the law.

Presidents are also able to shape the execution of Congressional legislation through their power of appointment. Presidents appoint (and remove from office) a large number of the principal officers of the United States government. By appointing Cabinet members or other officials in charge of government departments, they are able to stamp their own interpretation on Congressional law. For example, in 2017 President Donald Trump appointed a number of agency heads whose priorities diverged markedly from the Congressionally-legislated purpose of the agencies they oversaw. In this way, Trump sought to redirect the priorities of those agencies to reflect his own legislative and political agenda.

Protective Powers

Presidents have often been called upon during moments of crisis to seize the initiative and act to protect the nation from domestic and international threats. Presidents have used these powers, for example, to intervene in labor disputes. In 1957, President Dwight Eisenhower ordered the 101st Airborne Division of the U.S. Army into Arkansas to enforce the desegregation of Little Rock Central High School. He did so without waiting for a divided Congress to authorize this deployment. Even the notorious internment of hundreds of thousands of Americans of Japanese descent during World War II was upheld by the Supreme Court as a justified emergency measure.

Presidential Immunities and Privileges

Presidential powers include a number of protections and immunities from civil suits deriving from the president's fulfillment of his office. The objective of these immunities is to protect the president from being hindered in the fulfillment of official duties by a wave of litigation. Additionally, presidents have often claimed presidential privilege, for example, when refusing to acknowledge subpoenas from other branches of government. A difficulty arises, however, in that the president must not be seen as being above the law. For these reasons, the primary recourse against a president who commits "high crimes and misdemeanors" is for Congress to lodge charges of impeachment against them. If a president is successfully removed from office after an impeachment hearing in the U.S. Senate, they then become liable criminally or under civil statutes for actions that have violated the law.

Powers Relative to the Judiciary

The president has a number of powers relative to the courts. The most important is the responsibility to appoint members of the federal judiciary. This provides each president with an opportunity to shape the character of the judiciary and the way the courts interpret law. Judges, once appointed, are largely independent of pressures from the executive branch. Judges have lifetime tenure, which insulates them from presidential or popular pressures. Occasionally, judges appointed by a president depart significantly from the philosophical positions of the president who appointed them.

The Constitution authorizes the president to "grant Reprieves and Pardons for Offenses against the United States, except in Cases of Impeachment." The power to pardon was designed to give the president power to check legislative and judicial excesses in punishment. English monarchs had broad powers to grant pardons, as did royal governors in the American colonies. In this realm, the president has similar latitude and no oversight from either Congress or the courts. The presidential power to issue pardons has sometimes been controversial. For example, Andrew Johnson issued four general amnesties pardoning members of the Confederacy and restoring their civil and property rights. In 1974, President Gerald R. Ford granted former president Richard Nixon a pardon that many described as a "corrupt bargain." Nixon had earlier granted a pardon to Jimmy Hoffa, a Teamsters Union boss with mob ties, in what was later described as a deal to free Hoffa in exchange for Hoffa throwing the Teamsters behind Nixon's 1972 presidential campaign. Most often, however, presidential offers of clemency or pardons happen with little public fanfare.

Cabinet and Executive Agencies

The president staffs the executive branch, appointing several thousand executive officials. The executive branch is composed of the **White House, the Executive Office of the President**, and the **Cabinet.**

The **Executive Office of the President (EOP)** was an innovation of President Franklin D. Roosevelt's New Deal administration. The EOP is the nerve center of the executive branch. Each president organizes the EOP to suit their own management style and priorities. The White House Office, the Office of Management and Budget, the Council of Economic Advisors, and the National Security Council have carried over in each administration.

The **White House Office** serves the president as personal assistants, advisors, liaisons to the press and the legislature, and special assistants. The president has the power to fire them at will, and may expand or contract the number of advisors as necessary. Often presidential advisors are among the most powerful people in Washington because they have the ear of the president and can influence policy in ways that few others are able. White House Office positions vary from administration to administration, but usually include the Office of the Counsel to the President, the Office of Legislative Affairs, the Communications Office, the Office of the Press Secretary, and the president's Chief of Staff, among others.

The president's **Cabinet** is made up of the department heads of the 15 executive departments. These department heads also serve at the pleasure of the president, subject to the confirmation of the Senate. Their function includes representing the president's positions and providing leadership to their respective departments. Cabinet-level departments are the following: the Departments of Agriculture, Commerce, Defense, Education, Energy, Health and Human Services, Homeland Security, Housing and Urban Development, Interior, Justice, Labor, State, Transportation, Treasury, and Veterans Affairs. The Cabinet at one time served as the president's most important policy-making forum. Since President Franklin Roosevelt's presidency, however, the White House Office and the Executive Office of the President have replaced the Cabinet as the policy-making centers of presidential administrations. Cabinet members are nonetheless important in communicating policy to departmental officials and in managing the various executive departments.

Federal Court System

The Constitution established the federal court system as a separate, coequal, and independent branch of the federal government. Under the Articles of Confederation, no federal judiciary system was created, resulting in frequent jurisdictional rivalries. The federal judiciary was originally established to adjudicate disagreements between the states or to hear cases involving foreign governments and the United States.

The Supreme Court was created by the Constitution, but the Constitution left to Congress the power to create lower courts, and determine the types and number of lower courts. The Constitution made clear that the president had the power to nominate and appoint federal judges, subject to Senate confirmation. The Constitution also established lifetime tenure for federal judges, freeing them from the pressure to run for office (as is often the case for state judges) and from political pressure by either Congress or the president. Federal judges may be impeached, but few lower court judges have ever been removed through this expedient.

Article III of the Constitution authorizes the Supreme Court to serve as both a court of first instance and to hear appeals from lower courts. Only rarely, however, has the Supreme Court been the first to hear a case. It most often hears cases on appeal. In this role, the Supreme Court does not retry cases on the evidence, but determines whether the court with **Original Jurisdiction**, that heard the case initially, or other appeals courts, have followed proper procedure or applied the law correctly. The Court's jurisdiction involves hearing cases that involve federal law, federal regulations, and international treaties. It also hears cases arising from disputes that cross state boundaries.

Perhaps the most important feature of the Supreme Court's role today, its power of **judicial review**, was not explicitly stated in the United States Constitution. This power to declare another branch of government's actions unconstitutional was only asserted in 1803 in the case *Marbury v. Madison*.

Congress has over time approved a significant expansion of the federal judiciary. Below the Supreme Court in the federal judiciary hierarchy are U.S. District Courts and U.S. Courts of Appeal. There are nearly 100 U.S. District Courts. Texas has four federal judicial districts. Some states have only one U.S. District Court. District courts have original jurisdiction to hear a case for the first time. Cases appealed from the district courts go to a federal appeals court. The United States today has 13 appeals court circuits. These "circuit courts" hear appeals from the district courts in their circuit, which may comprise district courts from between three and six states. Each case in appeals courts is usually heard by a three-judge panel.

> **Competency 017 Descriptive Statement C.** The beginning teacher understands the processes by which the U.S. Constitution can be changed.

Article V of the United States Constitution outlines a two-step process for amending the Constitution, separating the process between proposals for change and the ratification process. There are two methods for proposing amendments. If two-thirds of both houses of Congress agree on the need for a change, Congress can propose amendments. Or, if the legislatures of two-thirds of the States demand it, Congress must call for a convention to propose amendments. Two separate possibilities existed to ratify changes. With the legislatures of three-fourths of the states in agreement, or the approval of ratifying conventions in three-fourths of the states, proposed amendments would be ratified. The latter method for ratification has never been used.

Article V placed two restrictions on the power to amend the Constitution. The first limitation forbade any amendment prior to 1808 that allowed Congress to regulate slave imports. A second provision of Article V banned any amendment that deprived a state of its equal representation in the Senate.

The process for amending the Constitution has resulted in relatively few changes in the document since its original ratification. The Framers intended the process to be a laborious one requiring widespread consensus, making it difficult to amend the Constitution.

The odds of proposing an amendment and seeing it through to addition to the Constitution are slim indeed. More than 11,000 proposals to amend the Constitution have been introduced in Congress since 1789. Of these, only 33 have been approved by the U.S. Congress. Of those approved, only 27 were then ratified by three-fourths of the state legislatures. These include the first 10, known as the Bill of Rights. Since ratification of the Bill of Rights, only 17 changes have been made to the Constitution.

Calls from state legislatures to demand that Congress convene a second constitutional convention have never to this date been successful. On May 4, 2017, the Texas House of Representatives joined the Texas Senate in passing a resolution calling for an "Article V Convention" to amend the Constitution. Governor Greg Abbott signed it, making Texas the 11th state of the 34 needed to require Congress to call an amending convention. The purpose of the convention is to amend the constitution to add Congressional term limits and a balanced-budget requirement to the constitution. Both of these measures would significantly reduce the power of the federal government, making it unlikely that these measures would follow the usual amendment process. There are many questions that arise about how such a convention would work, or whether it is a good idea, but this has been a movement that has been gaining ground during the past two decades.

> **Competency 017 Descriptive Statement D.** The beginning teacher knows procedures for enacting laws in the United States.

The Journey of a Bill

A bill may start its journey in either the House or the Senate except for appropriations bills, which always start in the House. Here are the steps involved in how a bill becomes law.

1. **A bill starts off as an idea,** usually from an interested member of the public, or from a congressional staffer or member of Congress. Often interest groups, industry organizations, labor unions, or other public interest groups contribute to developing ideas

and sometimes even the language for bills. Only members of Congress, however, can introduce a bill onto the legislative floor.

2. **Introducing a Bill.** A bill may be introduced into either the House of Representatives or the Senate. The congressperson who introduces the bill is known as the **sponsor**. Other congresspersons who support the bill are known as **cosponsors**. Once a bill is introduced to either chamber, it is given a number and a title and then assigned to committee where it is sent to the proper subcommittee. Fewer than 10 percent of bills make it out of committee. The full House or Senate can overrule a committee's negative decision and call the bill to the floor of the chamber, but this is a rare occurrence.

3. **Hearings.** A bill that has support will have **hearings** scheduled on its subject matter. A subcommittee will invite lobbyists, experts, administration officials, and others interested in either the bill's passage or rejection to give public testimony.

4. **Mark-Up.** Following public hearings either the standing committee or the sub-committee may hold additional hearings and may **"mark up,"** or revise, the bill.

5. **Floor Debate.** Upon a majority vote in favor of the bill by the standing committee, the bill is referred to the full chamber. Following that, the process varies in the House of Representatives and the Senate.

In the House of Representatives, the **Rules Committee** determines the length of time given for debate on the matter, whether amendments will be allowed—this is called an "open rule"—or whether no changes will be allowed—a "closed rule"—and when a final vote will be taken. Parties in the majority typically seek to limit the changes they will allow in a bill placed before the body as the amending process is a frequently used delaying tactic and method to dilute the effect of proposed legislation. In the House, usually only a few members are permitted to speak on proposed legislation.

In the Senate, the Rules Committee has less power over the process. Instead, the Senate Majority Leader, working with the Minority Leader, schedules floor debate on bills. Unless a three-fifths majority of the full Senate agrees to close off debate by voting for **cloture**, there are no limits on the length of time afforded for discussion on a measure. A vote for cloture reduces the total time allotted for debate to 30 hours. Cloture votes are a means to end a **filibuster**. When a minority of Senators wishes to stall passage of a bill or slow down the momentum of the majority party, they talk until changes are made or those in favor of the bill give in and withdraw it from consideration.

6. **Amending a Bill.** In the Senate, any member can offer amendments of any kind to any bill. This often results in the attachment of **riders**, which appear at first glance to have little to do with the subject of the bill. In the House of Representatives, amendments must be germane to the bill's contents.

7. **Passage of a Bill.** In both the House of Representatives and the Senate, passage of a bill requires only a simple majority of the chamber in which it was introduced. For a bill to become a law, however, requires that the identical version of the bill be passed in both the House and the Senate. For the roughly 10 percent of bills that differ materially from one chamber to the other, this requires that they be sent to a conference committee.

8. **Conference Committees.** Differences between bills passed in the House and in the Senate are **reconciled** in a conference committee formed temporarily to unify the bills into a compromise version of the legislation. Usually, the members of the conference committees are chosen from the standing committees in the House and Senate that heard the bill originally. Once the bills have been reconciled, they go back to both the House of Representatives and the Senate for a floor vote. A bill that has already been through the conference committee may not be amended further during the course of House or Senate deliberations. It may be passed by both houses, defeated in one or both, or returned to the conference committee. Approval by the House of Representatives and the Senate, however, does not enact the bill into law.

9. **Presidential Action.**

   There are three possible presidential responses to a bill that makes its way to the president's desk.

   If the president approves a bill, they may sign the bill into law.

   A president may also exercise a **veto**. If a president vetoes a bill, it is sent back to Congress, with a presidential rationale for the veto. Congress can **override** the veto with a two-thirds vote of each chamber. If Congress overrides a veto, it becomes law without presidential consent. If either or both houses of Congress cannot muster the votes to override the veto, the bill dies.

   If Congress is in session and the president neither signs nor vetoes the bill within 10 days, the bill becomes law without presidential signature. If Congress is not in session, however, and the president does not sign the bill within the 10-day period, Congress must take up the measure from the beginning of the process in the next term. This is called a **pocket veto.**

Competency 017 Descriptive Statement E. The beginning teacher analyzes changes in the role of the U.S. government over time (e.g., civil rights, New Deal legislation, wartime policies).

American Party Systems

America's early political leaders did not trust political parties. George Washington famously warned against the "spirit of faction" in his farewell address. He was warning against the political party system that developed during his second term in office. This suspicion of political parties has been a feature of our republic to the present. Despite these concerns, political parties have been an important component of how American government works, and how it sometimes fails to work. The emergence of parties and later realignments of party systems are among the most important changes that have occurred in the roles of the U.S. government over time.

The **First Political Party System** originated in the competition between Thomas Jefferson and Alexander Hamilton. Jefferson supported states' rights and a federal government that was restricted in its size and use of power, and a society that was composed of small-scale farmers, planters, and merchants. Hamilton promoted a strong national government built on a strong financial, commercial, and manufacturing base. Jefferson's supporters formed a political party, the Jeffersonian Republicans, not to be confused with the Republican Party as it is now constructed. Hamilton's party, the Federalists, took their name from the name given to those who had supported the Constitution during the ratification fight. Jefferson's victory in the election of 1800 was followed by five successive presidential victories for Jefferson's Republicans. Even John Adams' son, John Quincy Adams, saw no future in running under the banner of the Federalists in 1824 and joined with the clearly dominant party. By 1824, the Democratic Republicans had a virtual monopoly on power.

The **Second Political Party System**. Competition within the Republican Party after 1820, however, soon resulted in the formation of a second political party system. Andrew Jackson, after failing to win election in 1824, despite winning a plurality of the popular vote, argued that he represented the majority of the American people, particularly growing populations in the trans-Appalachian West, and in the South. Initially, the party of Jackson was the Democratic-Republican Party, later shortened to the **Democratic Party**. A new opposition party emerged to challenge Jackson's Democratic Party. It initially took the name National Republicans, a reflection of their commitment to a stronger and more interventionist national government, but was soon known as the **Whig Party**. This second political party system did not last long. Sectional rivalry and arguments over slavery divided both parties in the 1850s. The Whig Party fragmented. In 1854, the **Republican Party** was formed to challenge the Democrats, who were also divided by the slavery issue. In the 1860 election, the Democratic Party's northern wing nominated Stephen A. Douglas, and the southern wing put forward John C. Breckenridge. The Republican nominee, Abraham Lincoln, was able to win the presidency despite earning barely 40 percent of the popular vote.

The **Third Political Party System**. Since the Civil War, the U.S. government has been controlled by either the Democratic Party or the Republican Party. The third political party system has been characterized by a number of party **realignments**. The Civil War realignment saw the Republican Party replace the Democratic Party as the majority party. With a secure hold on the more populated and urbanized Northeast and Midwestern states, the Republicans controlled the Congress and the presidency for much of the period lasting between 1865 and 1932. The Great Depression triggered a political realignment that saw many Americans blame the Republicans, Herbert Hoover's party, for its pro-business approach that seemed to neglect the needs of the majority of Americans. Franklin D. Roosevelt's election began a period of Democratic control of the presidency that lasted until 1968, save for Dwight Eisenhower's two terms in the 1950s. The dominance of the Democratic Party was even greater in Congress. Only in 1947–1948 and 1953–1954 did Republicans hold majorities in the Congress.

A third realignment developed over the course of the 1970s and 1980s. Richard Nixon embarked on a "Southern Strategy" to appeal to Southern voters dissatisfied at the Democratic Party's support for the Civil Rights movement. Voters in Northeastern and Pacific Coast states and urban voters have increasingly been drawn to the Democratic Party, as have minority voters; while white, Southern, rural, Midwestern, and Western voters have increasingly become Republican constituencies. This realignment, it seems, persists to the present.

New Deal Legislation

The New Deal had an economic effect, though it did not achieve full economic recovery for the nation; nor did it redistribute the national income, despite a good deal of mythologizing. While it has often been said that the size of the federal government ballooned, the accumulation of New Deal deficits was smaller than the $53 billion deficit in 1943, the first full year of American involvement in World War II. Neither did the New Deal fundamentally challenge private ownership of the means of production. The United States, unlike every other industrial society during the Depression, at no time established significant state-owned enterprises. The New Deal, did however, have significant impacts on the workings of state and federal government.

Roosevelt's New Deal in many ways created the modern presidency. Roosevelt used broad authority granted to him by the Congress to create the **Executive Office of the President** in 1939. Much of the work of the White House takes place under the auspices of this office. The expansion of the EOP is a feature of the growing power of the presidency. Today the agencies within the EOP include the National Security Council, Council of Economic Advisers, Council on Environmental Quality, Office of Management and Budget, Office of Science and Technology, and a number of other important White House agencies. Roosevelt did not perhaps envision the increasing importance of the Executive Office of the President, but its creation in 1939 would set in motion an important increase in presidential power.

The New Deal also had an important impact on the practice of federalism. Many federal enactments required states to change their bureaucratic and legal systems in important ways. In 1932, Congress authorized the Reconstruction Finance Corporation to loan $300 million to state governments to distribute as welfare payments to poor Americans. This sum was quickly distributed, and Roosevelt ordered the newly established Federal Emergency Relief Administration (FERA) to distribute $500 million in additional funding, this time as grants rather than loans to state and local governments. To qualify for these funds, however, the federal government required that state governments create a new bureaucratic agency to manage the distribution of these funds. This represented a novel, though now commonplace, feature of the relationship between the federal and state governments. It represented an example of the federal government compelling the states to create new professional agencies and standards in order to receive funds from the federal government.

The FERA also required that funding be distributed to poor households without regard to race, creed, or political affiliation. Welfare distributions at the state and local levels had often been used as patronage tools or in discriminatory fashion before the New Deal. Many state governors and legislators, though they usually took the money, often complained at the increased power of the federal government in shaping state policy.

Wartime Policies

During times of war, historically, the powers of the federal government expand vis-à-vis the states, and the federal government expands its influence into the economy, family, and private lives of citizens in ways that were not necessarily envisioned by the Framers of the Constitution. Some have even gone so far as to argue that instead of a "welfare" state, we have developed a "warfare" state, echoing the fears raised by President Dwight Eisenhower of the rise of a "military-industrial complex." In each major conflict in our history, we have seen an erosion of fundamental freedoms and an expansion of the power and influence of the federal government.

Civil War

The results of the Civil War altered the American Constitution in important ways. The 13th Amendment ended the enslavement of African Americans across the South. Also, as often happens during wartime, the size and scope of the federal government increased, and individual freedoms were significantly restricted. The order to free the slaves illustrated one use of federal power that is sometimes overlooked. With the stroke of a pen, Abraham Lincoln, and later the 13th Amendment, illustrated the power of the federal government to redefine property rights and to sweep aside the claims of property owners across the South to property worth billions of dollars in value, despite how illegitimate these rights appear to us today.

Additionally, the war resulted in a real loss of individual rights. President Lincoln, for example, in 1861, shortly after the start of the Civil War, suspended the right of *habeas corpus*, an important constitutional limitation on arbitrary detention of a person. *Habeas corpus* (which literally means "to have the body") requires governmental authorities to bring a detained person into court and present their reasons for having the individual in custody. It was a feature of English law used as a bulwark to protect British citizens from arbitrary arrest and detention at the hands of a tyrannical monarch. The U.S. Constitution in Article I, Section 9 provides that "the privilege of the writ of habeas corpus shall not be suspended, unless when in cases of rebellion or invasion the public safety may require it." Lincoln's determination without an act of Congress was controversial, but his action illustrates the broad powers the executive branch often claims in times of war or turmoil.

The imposition of a military draft was another novel expansion of federal power resulting from the war. In March 1863, the first wartime conscription act was passed requiring all males between ages 20 and 45 to make themselves available for the draft.

Federal powers to tax also expanded substantially during the war. Before the Civil War, most federal revenues were derived from land sales, taxes on a variety of goods, and import taxes. In 1862, as the costs of the war mounted, Congress introduced an income tax for the first time. The office of the Commissioner of Internal Revenue (precursor to the Internal Revenue Service) was established with the responsibility of enforcing tax laws and collecting federal revenue. The income tax was repealed in 1872 and only reinstituted in its current form in 1913. Federal borrowing also increased substantially.

Congress also passed a number of "internal improvements" that would significantly increase the federal government's role in the American economy. In 1862, the **Morrill Act** distributed 30,000 acres of federal land to eligible states to establish agricultural, mechanical, and technical colleges across the nation. Before the Civil War, higher education was largely privately funded, and was a concern for state, not federal, governments. Texas A&M, Michigan State University, Purdue University, and many other institutions of higher education originated from this legislation. The **Pacific Railroad Act of 1862** represented another legislative expansion of federal power. Before the Civil War, there was a desire to build a transcontinental railroad, but Congress could not agree on a route. The act authorized the sale of government bonds and the granting of land to railroad companies to incentivize private construction of railways in the West.

World War I

World War I witnessed another period of expansion in the federal government's authority and a similar diminishment of individual freedoms. As was the case during the Civil War, demand for military manpower resulted in conscription. Under the **Selective Service Act of 1917,** more than 2.8 million men were drafted into the military.

The war resulted in an unprecedented increase in government intervention in the national economy. To pay for the war, five bond issues were authorized, with public drives to encourage their purchase. Over $20 billion was borrowed in this way from American citizens. By the end of the war the debt-to-GDP ratio had reached 33 percent. Another innovation introduced during World War I was the institution of the "debt limit." Prior to World War I, Congress had voted individually on every increase in expenditures financed by borrowing. For example, Congress voted to issue bonds to pay for the Panama Canal, or to fund the Spanish-American War. To allow the Department of the Treasury greater ability to raise money, Congress during World War I began simply voting to raise the "debt limit."

A War Industries Board (WIB) was empowered to direct the mobilization of the American economy for the war effort. The WIB established production quotas, directed resources to the manufacture of war materiel, and coordinated purchasing of military necessities. The WIB also intervened in labor relations, stopping strikes and helping to negotiate wage and benefit packages to avoid rapid spikes in both during a period of high labor demand. During the war, the national railway system was even placed under government management.

The Espionage Act of 1917 was enacted to prevent actions deemed to be hindering the war effort or recruitment of military personnel. The Sedition Act of 1918 broadened the Espionage Act by punishing those who in speech or written form made "false reports or false statements with intent to interfere with the operation or success of the military or naval forces"; or who promoted "the success of its enemies"; or who used "disloyal, profane, scurrilous, or abusive language about the form of government of the United States, of the Constitution of the United States, or the military or naval forces of the United States, or the flag of the United States, or the uniform of the Army or Navy." This sweeping attack on freedom of speech during wartime was repealed in 1920. However, the Espionage Act of 1917 is still in effect. Eugene V. Debs, Julius and Ethel Rosenberg, Daniel Ellsberg, and, more recently, Chelsea Manning and Edward Snowden are among those who have been charged with violations of the Espionage Act.

World War II

World War II, which has often been described as a "total war," resulted in even greater changes in the scope and size of the U.S. government. Many of the most widely held beliefs about the nature and function of government were discarded over the course of the war and its immediate aftermath.

Just as in the Civil War and World War I, a wartime draft was instituted to fill the ranks of the American military. At the end of the war there were more than 12 million men in the services. Following the war, though the size of the military shrank, it was not until 1973 that the draft was discontinued. The Selective Service administration and required registration for the draft remain.

The United States also entered into wartime military alliances that have become more or less a permanent feature of our diplomacy, flying in the face of warnings against the dangers of "entangling alliances" issued by the Framers. The "special relationship" with Great Britain dates to World War II and has formed the foundation of later alliances, such as the North Atlantic Treaty Organization.

Spending on World War II dwarfed anything seen in the New Deal policies of Franklin Delano Roosevelt. The "Lend-Lease" program that loaned tanks, trucks, weaponry, ships, and other war materiel to the Allies spent more over the course of the war ($50 billion) than had all the New Deal programs combined ($40 billion). More Americans were affected certainly than had been impacted by the New Deal. Nearly 65 percent of Americans held war bonds, loaning their savings to the federal government to support the war effort. Seventeen million men (and many women) worked in industries supplying the war effort. This figure added to the 12 million or more people who served in the military, plus the number of men and women directly employed in the war effort, more than double the number of men and women employed over the course of the Works Progress Administration's tenure during the New Deal.

The size of the federal government debt exploded during World War II. The debt-to-GDP-ratio reached 113 percent by the end of the war. The total debt had ballooned to $241 billion, approximately $3.24 trillion in 2017 dollars. To pay this debt, the federal income tax became a much greater feature of American life. Few Americans in 1939 paid a federal income tax. It was a tax that fell only on the truly well off. The number of federal income taxpayers rose from 4 million in 1939 to more than 43 million in 1945. The tax rates for all income earners also rose. In 1939, the most poorly paid taxpayers paid 4 percent of their income in federal income taxes. By 1945, the lowest tax rate was 23 percent, while for the highest earners, those making over $1 million, the highest marginal tax rate was 94 percent.

The Global War on Terror

The "Global War on Terror," as the wars in Afghanistan and Iraq have been known, also includes American operations around the world; for example, special operations raids in Yemen and Mali, as well as drone strikes in Somalia, Syria, and elsewhere. Just as World War I and World War II encouraged the growth of government and changes in the distribution of power within the government, the "war on terror" has similarly resulted in the expansion of governmental power and transfers of power from the legislative to the executive branch.

One of these expansions of executive branch power has been known as the "Bush Doctrine." First articulated in September 2002, the Bush Doctrine emphasized the American right to preemptive self-defense. As the document outlining this doctrine makes clear, "We cannot let our enemies strike first." Rogue and threatening states, as well as non-state actors, must be prevented from attacking the United States, its allies, or its interests. Historically, the United States has followed a policy of retaliation and containment of threats. Importantly, the determination to make "preventive war" has been left in the hands of the president of the United States. The United States Constitution reserves to Congress the power to declare war. Critics of the Bush Doctrine, and those who argue that the power of the executive branch has grown too great, argue that this approach violates the fundamental separation of powers established by the Constitution.

The Global War on Terror has also contributed to the erosion of a number of American rights, as has been the case during every major American conflict. The USA PATRIOT Act, passed six weeks after the 9/11 attack, for example, vastly increased the executive branch's surveillance powers, while reducing the requirements that probable cause be proven. The PATRIOT Act also widely increased the kind of information that could be swept up and mined for suspicious information, including business, medical, educational, and library records, Though these expansions of surveillance powers were begun under the Bush administration, they have largely continued with little diminishment in succeeding administrations.

> **Competency 017 Descriptive Statement F.** The beginning teacher understands changing relationships (e.g., Franklin D. Roosevelt's attempt to increase the number of U.S. Supreme Court justices, War Powers Act, judicial review) among the three branches of the federal government.

Key Question

How and why has the balance of powers between the "coequal branches" of government shifted over time? The Framers established a system of shared power marked by distinctive checks and balances between the executive, legislative, and judicial branches. At different times during U.S. history, however, observers have objected to the emergence of an "imperial presidency" or complained about "judicial activism." This descriptive statement asks that test-takers understand how the balance of power among the different branches of government has changed over time.

Judicial Review

The role of the judiciary as a check and balance against the other branches of government was the least clearly specified in the Constitution. This role, known as judicial review, is the power to determine whether actions taken by the executive or enactments of the legislative bodies of federal and state governments violate the Constitution. The Constitution did grant the Supreme Court the power to make judgments on all cases "arising under this Constitution." But nowhere in the Constitution is the power of judicial review specified, even though the majority of state ratifying conventions had expressly claimed that the judiciary branch had this authority to **nullify** executive decisions or legislation that violated the principles of the Constitution. It was only in 1803 with the landmark decision in *Marbury v. Madison* that Chief Justice John Marshall firmly secured the power of judicial review for the courts. Marshall concluded, "It is emphatically the province and the duty of the judicial department to say what the law is." Though the Supreme Court is the final arbiter of constitutionality, the practice of judicial review is not exclusively the province of the Supreme Court. Lower federal courts may also rule on the constitutionality of executive uses of power or legislative enactments.

The power of judicial review, unlike many of the powers held by the president and Congress, is dependent upon widespread and shared belief in the legitimacy of the courts to check the powers of the other two branches. Congress has clearly identified economic power—for example, the power to raise and lower taxes and spending. The president also has clearly identified powers; for example, the powers to wage war and to appoint and fire members of the executive branch. The power of the courts, in contrast, is only enforceable because Congress and the executive branch accept the legitimacy of the Supreme Court and the federal judiciary. Rarely has the legitimacy of the Court's decision been challenged. In 1832, after the Supreme Court, led by Chief Justice John Marshall, found on behalf of the Cherokee nation in the case *Worcester v. Georgia*, which struck down Georgia laws evicting the Cherokee from their land, Andrew Jackson famously said, "John Marshall has made his decision; now *let him enforce it!*" Such refusal to recognize the legitimacy of the judiciary's authority by either of the other branches of government threatens the entire apparatus of checks and balances, which is dependent upon the judiciary's power of judicial review.

FDR's Court-Packing Incident, or "A Switch in Time Saves Nine"

At other times, facing the sting of persistent checks by the judiciary, both the executive and legislative branches have sought to undermine the independence of the courts. Franklin Delano Roosevelt's New Deal programs established a number of new federal agencies, increased the authority of others, and involved the federal government more extensively in the nation's economic affairs than at any time in the nation's history. While Roosevelt's programs had legislative support and wide popular approval, conservative critics of the expansion of federal and executive authority challenged a number of Roosevelt's most important initiatives in the courts. The Supreme Court, tasked with reviewing the constitutionality of New Deal legislation, was divided between four conservative justices, known as the "Four Horsemen," who were bitterly opposed to the New Deal; and three liberals, known as the "Three Musketeers." Chief Justice Charles Evans Hughes and Owen J. Roberts then swung the direction of the Court. With Roberts and Hughes often siding with the conservative justices, in 1935 and 1936, the Court found against the Roosevelt administration in eight of 10 cases involving New Deal programs. The Court voided the Agricultural Adjustment Act, the Railroad Act, and the Coal Mining Act. The Court also struck down the National Industrial Recovery Act, the centerpiece of Roosevelt's New Deal. Roosevelt and New Deal advocates grew increasingly frustrated as each effort to resurrect the American economy was struck down by the Court. New Deal supporters called this an "economic dictatorship."

When Roosevelt won reelection by a landslide in 1936, he quickly introduced a plan for "judicial reorganization." His critics called it "**court-packing**." The measure proposed the addition of a new Supreme Court seat for each justice who did not retire upon reaching the age of 70. As two-thirds of the justices were over the age of 70, this measure would have the effect of immediately expanding the court to 15 members, all of whom Roosevelt would be able to appoint. Even many of Roosevelt's supporters saw this as an unconstitutional threat to the judiciary's independence. Roosevelt's plan never passed the legislature. It nevertheless had his desired effect. In a number of key High Court decisions after 1937, with Roberts and later Hughes switching to vote with the liberals, the New Deal was reaffirmed, and conservative limitations on the power of the federal government were set aside.

War Powers Act

More recently, the power of the presidency has raised concerns about the balance of power between Congress and the executive branch. This imbalance has been most clear in the realm of foreign policy. The decision to go to war is perhaps the most difficult any government must contemplate. The Framers of the Constitution expressly granted to Congress alone the power to "declare war." Since World War II, the United States has been at war in Korea, Vietnam, the Persian Gulf, the Balkans, Afghanistan, and Iraq, not to mention countless other military interventions throughout the world. Each of these wars, large or small, has been fought without a congressional declaration of war. In fact, in the nation's history, only five wars have been congressionally declared: the

War of 1812, the Mexican-American War, the Spanish-American War, World War I, and World War II. This should not be taken to mean that the nation's other uses of military force were entered into unconstitutionally. For example, Congress authorized the use of force in Afghanistan in 2001 and in Iraq in 2002 without formal declarations of war. Also, the escalation of the Vietnam War in 1964 resulted from Congressional approval of the Tonkin Gulf Resolution that gave Lyndon B. Johnson broad powers to conduct the war in Vietnam.

As the Vietnam War effort stalled, and as Americans increasingly soured on the war, many even within Lyndon Johnson's own party argued that he had misrepresented the Gulf of Tonkin incident to escalate the war. After Richard Nixon ordered a bombing campaign of Cambodia in 1970, again expanding the war in the face of widespread opposition, a coalition of Democratic and Republican congressmen moved to restrict the war-making powers of the presidency.

In 1973, the culmination of these efforts resulted in the **War Powers Act of 1973**, which passed over the veto of President Richard Nixon. The act established specific criteria for the use of the American military, required that the president report to Congress within 48 hours after the initiation of hostilities, and placed a time limit of 60 days before a president was required to receive authorization or a declaration of war, and 30 days more to extricate the troops from conflict. Most presidential administrations have agreed with Richard Nixon in objecting to the War Powers Act, seeing it as undermining broad presidential powers to protect the nation in time of attack or emergency.

> **Competency 017 Descriptive Statement G.** The beginning teacher demonstrates knowledge of the impact of constitutional amendments on U.S. society (e.g., 13th, 14th, 15th, 17th, 19th, 24th and 26th amendments).

The constitutional amendments identified above and described in the following, are primarily amendments that widened the meaning of "liberty" and "equal rights" over the course of the period from 1865 to the present. These amendments were added to the Constitution to address inequalities or discriminatory practices.

13th Amendment

The 13th Amendment, which was ratified in 1865, marked the first time the U.S. Constitution referenced slaves or slavery by name. The amendment formally abolished slavery and involuntary servitude (indentured servitude and peonage) throughout the United States. Abraham Lincoln's earlier Emancipation Proclamation was limited to the states under Confederate control during the Civil War. The amendment did not prohibit such forms of involuntary labor as military conscription, jury duty, or convict labor. Unusually, the amendment includes language in section two authorizing Congress to enforce the amendment "by appropriate legislation." Under this authority, Congress has prohibited racial discrimination in contractual and property transactions, legislated against hate crimes, enacted fair-housing laws, and prohibited sex trafficking.

14th Amendment

In 1863, Abraham Lincoln had enacted the Emancipation Proclamation freeing enslaved persons in the states under the Confederacy. In 1865, Congress had passed, and the states had ratified, the 13th Amendment, securing in the United States Constitution an end to slavery. Nonetheless, across the former Confederate states, African Americans after the Civil War were rapidly subjected to infamous "Black Codes" that allowed public officials to use policing powers to coerce ex-slaves to work for their former masters. Other features of these codes forbade African Americans to work in any other employment but agricultural labor without special licenses, and forbade them from renting or leasing land except in towns and cities. The Black Codes effectively operated to re-enslave African Americans and deny them their basic civil and human rights. In 1866, in response to continued efforts by Southern states to subordinate African Americans, Congress proposed the 14th Amendment, which was ratified two years later.

The amendment has had a wide-ranging significance, well beyond that of its immediate context.

The first clause reads: "All persons born or naturalized in the United States, and subject to the jurisdiction thereof, are citizens of the United States and of the State in which they reside." Most immediately, this clause overturned the *Dred Scott* decision that denied African Americans United States citizenship. The "**citizenship clause**," as this portion of the amendment is called, was interpreted in *United States v. Wong Kim Ark* (1898) to extend citizenship to anyone born in the United States, to parents with a residence or permanent domicile, who are not employed in a diplomatic capacity by a foreign power.

The second portion of the amendment reads: "No State shall make or enforce any law which shall abridge the privileges or immunities of citizens of the United States, nor shall any State deprive any person of life, liberty, or property, without due process of law."

The first thing to observe about what is called the "**due process clause**" is that it extended the due process norm from the Fifth Amendment, which applied to only to the federal government, to the states.

Secondly, the due process clause has been expanded to protect a number of groups of people from discriminatory laws. For example, in *Lawrence v. Texas* (2003), a Texas law prohibiting homosexual sodomy which did not also prohibit heterosexual sodomy was found to violate due process protections. Or, more recently, the case *Obergefell v. Hodges* (2015) found that same-sex couples were entitled to the right to marry, because "the right to marry is fundamental under the due process clause," and "the reasons marriage is fundamental under the Constitution apply with equal force to same-sex couples" as to heterosexual couples.

The final clause reads: No State shall, . . . deny to any person within its jurisdiction the equal protection of the laws." This, known as the "**equal protection clause**," sought to address the denial of basic rights of African Americans in the Black Codes and in other legislation that singled out

African Americans for unequal treatment before the law. In *Plessy v. Ferguson* (1896) the impact of this clause was significantly eroded as the court's decision allowed states to circumvent this requirement by providing for "separate but equal" treatment before the law. In 1954, the landmark case *Brown v. Board of Education of Topeka, Kansas* overturned the separate but equal standard, arguing that it violated the equal protection clause. As a result of this decision, the 14th Amendment's due process clause has been more widely applied to other forms of race-based discrimination. In 1967, the *Loving v. Virginia* case ruled that statutes which prohibited interracial marriage were denials of equal protection under the law. Housing discrimination, discriminatory public transportation rules, race-based determinations in jury selection, and many other racially discriminatory practices have been challenged.

Like the other clauses of the 14th Amendment, the equal protection clause of the 14th Amendment has had a much wider impact than in its application to discriminatory treatment of African Americans. In 1971, for example, the Supreme Court ruled that the equal protection clause also protected women from sex discrimination. A number of cases have applied the equal protection clause to end practices that discriminated against gays and lesbians as well as to other minority populations.

15th Amendment (1870)

Simply stated, the 15th Amendment ensures that the voting rights of United State citizens were not to be denied or limited by either the United States government or by individual state governments "on account of race, color, or previous condition of servitude." Before the Civil War, slaves and free blacks alike in the South were denied the right to vote. Northern states, which by 1861 had long done away with chattel slavery, still often denied free African Americans the franchise. During Reconstruction, the Radical Republicans who controlled Congress required that Southern states, before they were allowed re-admittance to the Union, had to include in their state constitutions the right of African American men to vote. By 1869, seven of the 11 Confederate states had complied. The Radical Republicans in Congress feared that once readmitted, Southern states would repeal the suffrage guarantees in their constitutions. The 15th Amendment to the Constitution was proposed to forestall this eventuality. Republicans also had immediate electoral concerns to consider. Most Northern states, despite indignation at Southern disenfranchisement of African Americans, continued to deny African Americans the right to vote. Radical Republicans feared that the Republican majority in Congress was declining. The 15th Amendment's nationwide guarantee of African American voting rights promised to secure the Republican majority in Congress for the foreseeable future. Black voters were presumed to be likely Republican voters. This convergence of humanitarian and political interest resulted in comparably rapid ratification of the amendment.

17th Amendment (1913)

The Framers of the Constitution had granted to the people the right to directly elect members of the House of Representatives. The president, judiciary branch, and the Senate were chosen through a variety of indirect measures. Senatorial elections were the purview of state legislatures. The Founders believed that state legislatures would be filled with men whose education and character would enable them to put the good of the nation and the state above their own private or party interests. Instead, battles in the state legislatures over the choice of U.S. senators became highly partisan contests often marred by corruption that not infrequently left senatorial seats vacant for extended periods. The 17th Amendment was a Progressive Era reform that promised the populace a direct voice in selecting their senators in the hopes that the corrupting influence of bribery, corruption, and machine politics might be reduced.

19th Amendment (1920)

The 19th Amendment gave American women full voting rights with men. Before 1920, it should be noted that women were voting in a number of states, though often with restrictions. For example, there were states that allowed women to vote in school board elections or in primary elections, but not in general elections. Western states were more interested in granting women voting rights, in part because they needed to have enough voters to qualify for statehood. Wyoming (1869), Utah (1870), Kansas (1885), and Colorado (1893) were the first states to grant women complete suffrage. In August 1920, with Tennessee being the 36th state to ratify the amendment, women across the country (except Native American women who, like Native Americans generally, were not granted citizenship until 1923) could vote for the first time, regardless of their residence.

24th Amendment (1964)

The 24th Amendment outlawed the practice of requiring the payment of any kind of tax to vote in federal elections. In 1964, five states, including Texas, required the payment of a poll tax to vote. Poll taxes had been administered discriminatorily across the South as a way to skirt the 15th Amendment and to exclude African Americans from voting. The 15th Amendment requires that voting rights not be limited by "race, color, or previous condition of servitude." Southern states then promptly required that all voters pay a poll tax, which had the effect of excluding the poor from voting, which in the South had a disproportionate effect on African Americans. By 1902, 11 states, all in the South, had poll taxes, which, combined with literacy tests, "whites-only primaries," and outright violence, had the effect of denying African Americans their voting rights. The amendment was proposed during the height of the Civil Rights movement, over the objections of most Southern state legislatures. Texas finally voted to ratify the amendment in 2009.

26th Amendment (1971)

The 26th Amendment was proposed March 23, 1971, and ratified on July 1, 1971, making it the fastest amendment to be ratified. It lowered the voting age from 21 years of age to 18. Among the arguments most often heard in favor of lowering the voting age was that American males were being sent to fight in Vietnam who were old enough to marry, old enough to drink (the drinking age was 18 in most states in 1971), and old enough to be drafted into the military, but they did not have the right to vote.

> **Competency 017 Descriptive Statement H.** The beginning teacher analyzes the interpretations and impact of landmark Supreme Court decisions on U.S. society (e.g., *Marbury v. Madison; McCulloch v. Maryland; Cherokee Nation v. Georgia; Dred Scott v. Sandford; Plessy v. Ferguson; Schenck v. U.S.; Brown v. Board of Education of Topeka, Kansas; Engel v. Vitale; Miranda v. Arizona; Roe v. Wade; Regents of the University of California v. Bakke*).

Marbury v. Madison (1803)

The case *Marbury v. Madison,* decided in 1803, is generally identified with the origin of the principle of **judicial review** in the United States. The case raised the issue of whether the courts had the power to declare federal legislation unconstitutional. William Marbury had been appointed to fill a newly created judicial position by John Adams immediately before Adams left office in 1801. The new judgeship had been created by the Judiciary Act of 1801, which Thomas Jefferson and Congress repealed shortly after taking office. Additionally, in Adams' rush to fill a host of positions before he left office, he had failed to forward the signed commission to Marbury. Jefferson had instructed his Secretary of State, James Madison, not to deliver the commission. Marbury sued to secure his position as justice of the peace.

Supreme Court Chief Justice John Marshall, himself a Federalist and an Adams appointee, had the responsibility of hearing the case. Jefferson and his Republican Party had handily won the election of 1800 and were determined to use their popular mandate to reverse the course that Adams and the Federalist Party had charted. Marshall wished to avoid having the federal judiciary appear to be merely a tool of one or the other party. He recognized that the court needed to maintain its independence from the other branches of government and from the emerging political party system. In his decision, Marshall concluded that, while Marbury was entitled to the commission, the Supreme Court did not have the power to remedy Marbury's complaint because the act authorizing the remedy was inconsistent with the Constitution. Marbury was denied his judicial office, which satisfied Jefferson, but Marshall had asserted the Supreme Court's right to rule on both executive and legislative enactments, giving the Supreme Court and the federal court system a clear claim to the power of judicial review.

McCulloch v. Maryland (1819)

Article I, Section 8 of the Constitution of the United States enumerates the various powers of Congress, concluding with what is known as the "**necessary and proper clause.**" The clause reads as follows: "The Congress shall have Power . . . to make all Laws which shall be necessary and proper for carrying into Execution the foregoing Powers, and all other Powers vested by this Constitution in the Government of the United States, or in any Department or Office thereof." This language grants Congress broad discretion to enact legislation to implement the powers listed in Section 8.

In 1816, Congress chartered the Second Bank of the United States, and enabled it to issue bank notes, which circulated as legal tender, or money. The Bank loaned the federal government and held its revenue as part of its reserves. State banks regarded the National Bank as a competitor, and opponents of the bank considered its establishment a constitutional overreach. In 1818, the state of Maryland levied a tax on banks chartered outside the state, a tax clearly directed at the National Bank's Baltimore branch. The Baltimore branch president, James McCulloch, refused to pay the tax, arguing that the tax was unconstitutional.

When the suit was appealed to the U.S. Supreme Court, Chief Justice John Marshall ruled the Maryland tax constitutional and the charter of the National Bank a constitutionally legitimate act of Congress. He argued that because Congress was empowered to regulate interstate commerce, borrow money, and collect taxes, it had the powers necessary and proper to see to the fulfillment of this responsibility, which included the right to charter a National Bank. Moreover, Maryland's tax was unconstitutional in that it threatened to undermine the authority of federal law.

The case vastly expanded congressional power while reaffirming the superiority of federal law over state law.

Cherokee Nation v. Georgia (1831)

In 1785, the United States government had recognized the Cherokee Indians as a sovereign nation, with all the attributes of sovereignty and nationality, including recognition of their territorial claims to lands in Tennessee and Georgia. A second treaty in 1791 had guaranteed the Cherokee possession of lands also claimed by the Cherokee nation. In 1828, however, the state of Georgia stripped the Cherokee of their rights and ordered Cherokee removal from their territorial lands. The Cherokee sued to retain their property and territorial rights, claiming that the United States had guaranteed the Cherokee nation their land and independence as a separate nation-state. The Supreme Court ruled it had no jurisdiction to decide the case, despite expressing sympathy with the Cherokee people's situation, because Indian nations had a status as foreign nations within the boundaries of the United States. The Court's responsibility to hear suits brought by foreign nations under Article III of the Constitution therefore did not include cases brought by Indian nations. Indians within the boundaries of the United States were thus both stripped of protections guaranteed citizens of foreign nations, and denied protections of citizens of the United States.

Dred Scott v. Sandford (1857)

In 1857, Chief Justice Roger B. Taney issued one of the most controversial decisions in Supreme Court history. The court had ruled 7–2 (including five Southern judges) that the Framers of the Constitution had never intended that African Americans, whether free or enslaved, could claim citizenship in the United States of America. Taney claimed that the Supreme Court in coming to this ruling was following the original intent of the "Founding Fathers." As a result, Dred Scott, a slave suing for his freedom, had no claim to protections under the law as a citizen. Scott had been born a slave in Virginia. His master had moved to Missouri in 1830, taking Scott with him. After his first master's death, Scott had been sold to an army surgeon, Dr. John Emerson. Emerson took Scott with him to the territory of Illinois in 1833. Illinois' state constitution, while abolishing further enslavement, had protected the property rights of slave owners who already owned enslaved persons. When Emerson was then posted to a fort in Wisconsin Territory, Scott again accompanied him. When his second master died, Scott offered Emerson's widow, Eliza Irene Sanford*, $300 for his own and his wife's manumission, or emancipation. She refused, whereupon Dred Scott and his wife sued separately on the grounds that they had spent considerable time in territories and states where slavery was not permitted. With the Supreme Court's decision, not only were African Americans declared ineligible for citizenship in the United States; the decision also invalidated the Missouri Compromise of 1820, which had restricted the spread of slavery north of the 36th parallel, and effectively nationalized the practice of slavery. If a slave owner moved into a "free state," their rights to their property in human chattel were not to be infringed upon.

Plessy v. Ferguson (1896)

Following the Civil War, across many states in the South and in many cities in the North, state and local governments had passed ordinances that separated blacks and whites in public accommodations, theaters, railway cars, streetcars, etc. In 1892, a group of African American leaders in New Orleans, Louisiana, decided to force a test of the constitutionality of Louisiana's 1890 Separate Car Act, believing that it and laws like it violated the equal protection clause of the 14th Amendment. Homer Plessy, a light-skinned African American, volunteered to test the local ordinance by sitting in a train car reserved for whites only. In an act that would be repeated by Rosa Parks in the 1950s, on June 7, 1892, Plessy purchased a first-class ticket and boarded a train in New Orleans where he took a seat in the whites-only car. When the conductor came to collect Plessy's ticket, Plessy reportedly said, "I have to tell you that, according to Louisiana law, I am a colored man." When the conductor asked Plessy to give up his seat and go to the car reserved for African Americans, Plessy refused. He was removed, arrested, and spent the night in jail before being released. His original trial was largely a foregone conclusion, and the Louisiana judge who heard the case found against Plessy and his legal team. The case was appealed to the Louisiana Supreme Court, where the state of Louisiana argued that the state had the right to regulate its railways, and that the 13th and 14th amendments granted civil rights (such as the rights to vote or hold office), but that they did not protect rights to social equality. They also argued that "equal accommodations do not mean identical accommodations." The Louisiana Supreme Court decided against Plessy as well.

With that predictable setback, Plessy was able to appeal to the United States Supreme Court. The Supreme Court that decided *Plessy v. Ferguson* had seven justices appointed after 1886,

---

* The name is spelled "Sandford" in the Court's decision because of a clerical error.

most of whom had been dissatisfied with the direction the court had taken during the period of Reconstruction. The Supreme Court decided by a 7–1 majority that laws like Louisiana's did not constitute a violation of either the 13th or 14th amendment. They judged that laws requiring the separation of the races "did not imply the inferiority of either race." The doctrine of "separate but equal" derives from this case, a legal doctrine that established as settled law the right of state and local governments to institute separations of the races and restrictive legislation based on race. *Plessy v. Ferguson* would only be overturned in 1954 with the case *Brown v. the Board of Education of Topeka, Kansas.*

Schenck v. U.S. (1919)

In June 1917, after the United States' entry into World War I, the federal government passed the Espionage Act of 1917, which in combination with the Sedition Act of 1918, formed the basis for American sedition law until 1948. Charles T. Schenck, the general secretary of the Socialist Party, a critic of United States involvement in the war, had distributed 15,000 copies of an anti-war pamphlet entitled "Assert Your Rights" to draft-age young men. The leaflet argued that conscription subjected draftees to a form of slavery, in violation of the 13th Amendment to the Constitution. Likely draftees were encouraged to refuse to be drafted on the grounds that this denied their constitutional rights. Schenck was arrested and convicted of violations of the Espionage Act. Schenck claimed that his First Amendment right to freedom of speech had been violated. The Supreme Court unanimously confirmed Schenck's conviction, determining that Schenck's freedom of speech had not been abridged. Chief Justice Oliver Wendell Holmes wrote that Schenck's leaflet created a "clear and present danger" threatening the nation's security. Holmes argued that the First Amendment would not protect a man in shouting "Fire!" in a theater and causing a panic. This test of the limits of free speech has become one of the important considerations when the courts have measured the boundaries of acceptable public utterances.

Brown v. Board of Education of Topeka, Kansas (1954)

In 1954, the Supreme Court unanimously ruled in *Brown v. Board of Education of Topeka, Kansas* that racially segregated schools violated the constitutional principle of equal treatment for all citizens. The lawsuit that became known as *Brown v. Board* was a case that combined cases from five separate jurisdictions in Kansas, Delaware, Virginia, South Carolina, and the District of Columbia. Each of the cases resulted from the determination of courageous African American young people and their parents to protest and then legally challenge the inferior teaching materials, lack of bus transportation, poorly paid teachers, and other features of the separate but unequal education that African Americans received across much of the country, most notably in the South. The National Association for the Advancement of Colored People (NAACP) supported the plaintiffs, hiring **Thurgood Marshall** as the lead attorney to argue the case. Marshall would later become the first African American Supreme Court justice. Marshall argued that psychological and sociological studies showed the effects of segregation on black students, and that separate but equal was inherently unequal education. The Supreme Court in its decision unanimously agreed. The ruling stated, "To separate [children] from others of similar age and qualifications solely because of their race generates a feeling of inferiority as to their status in the community that may affect their hearts and minds in a way unlikely ever to be undone." As a result, the court concluded, "that in the field of public education the doctrine of 'separate but equal' has no place." The court then enjoined that school segregation be ended with "all deliberate speed." In response, across the South, white "citizen's councils" rose up to fight integration. Southern governors and state legislatures argued that the decision violated the federalist system that afforded states the right to regulate public education. Leading Southern politicians like George Wallace vowed to fight integration. In 1957, President Dwight Eisenhower sent in the American military to Little Rock, Arkansas, to enforce desegregation. Resistance to school segregation, nonetheless, lasted for much longer.

Engel v. Vitale (1962)

A New York State law required that each school day commence with a recitation of the Pledge of Allegiance and the following nondenominational prayer: "Almighty God, we acknowledge our dependence upon Thee, and we beg Thy blessings upon us, our parents, our teachers, and our Country." Students were allowed to leave the room during the pledge and prayer, but many students felt that this singled them out and exposed them to ridicule. A parent sued on behalf of their child, objecting to the child being required to participate in a mandated public prayer. The Supreme Court ruled 6–1 that the establishment clause of the First Amendment forbids prayers "composed by government officials as a part of a governmental program to further religious beliefs." Later court decisions relying on the precedent set in *Engel v. Vitale* have widened the scope of such prohibitions, on the principle that the establishment clause of the First Amendment has "erected a wall of separation between church and state."

Miranda v. Arizona (1966)

In March 1963, in Phoenix, Arizona, a learning-disabled 18-year-old woman was abducted and raped by Ernesto Miranda. Miranda then released the woman, who reported the crime. While the victim of this crime was able to provide some evidence to identify the vehicle of her abductor, the police did not have enough to conclusively identify her rapist. Eventually, however, a number of clues pointed investigators to Miranda. Miranda was picked up for questioning and placed in a police lineup. The young woman identified Miranda as her abductor. Miranda was then interrogated by two police officers. The police detectives admitted during the course of the trial that they hadn't advised Miranda of his rights to have an attorney present during the interrogation. After two hours of questioning, the officers had a written confession. Before the Miranda decision, precedent from common law maintained only that a confession be voluntarily given for it to be admissible. Earlier court decisions had begun to more carefully measure the voluntariness of confessions. But Miranda had not alleged any coercion. In the 1964 case, *Escobedo v. Illinois*, the Supreme Court had narrowly concluded that police interrogators had to honor a suspect's request for a lawyer's presence during questioning. Miranda's attorney's appeal of his conviction argued that the police had not informed him fully of his rights to remain silent and to have an attorney present. Moreover, because the police had not informed him of his Fifth Amendment right against self-incrimination, Miranda's attorneys argued he had been denied due process. By a 5–4 decision, the Supreme Court agreed. Since the decision, police have been required to "read" suspects their rights. The "Miranda" warning, known as "Mirandizing" a suspect, has become a key feature of police procedure.

Roe v. Wade (1973)

Before the 1860s in America, abortions had been legal. According to both Catholic and Protestant traditions, the soul entered the body after its formation, or "quickening," which was thought to be the moment when a child was formed. Abortions before quickening were not considered criminal. Women who sought an abortion, and the midwives who often performed them, were left the responsibility of determining when "quickening" had taken place. Beginning in the 1820s, as the medical field became increasingly professionalized, medical doctors began to become more involved in managing childbirth. As health care became more professionalized, and midwives and women were increasingly excluded from roles as health care practitioners, the American Medical Association (AMA) and male physicians began to regulate childbirth and abortion practices. The AMA began lobbying for laws ending abortion and excluding midwives from the birthing process. After the 1860s, most states prohibited abortions from conception on, except in cases where the mother's life was in jeopardy. The 1873 Comstock Act, which prohibited distributing birth control or circulating birth control information through the mails, also forbade the distribution of information on abortion. By 1900, all states had enacted legislation penalizing both the woman and the abortionist, and dropping the quickening distinction. Only in the 1960s, with the emergence of the women's rights movement, did new challenges to these laws begin to have success. In the 1965 case *Griswold v. Connecticut,* the Comstock Act's restrictions on the distribution of birth control and on information relating to birth control were loosened. An important part of the *Griswold v. Connecticut* decision acknowledged a right to privacy or right to personal autonomy, based on the Fourth Amendment's protections of individuals' right to make decisions about their bodies or their private lives without governmental interference. This definition of the right to privacy would prove critical to the decision in *Roe v. Wade*, which legal scholars considered a logical extension of the *Griswold* judgment.

In 1970, Norma McCorvey, a Texas resident who had been unable to obtain an abortion in Texas, asked two lawyers, Sarah Weddington and Linda Coffee, both University of Texas Law School graduates, to assist her in challenging the Texas law that allowed abortions only when it was necessary to save a mother's life. Wishing to protect McCorvey's privacy, Coffee fashioned a pseudonym under which to file the case, Jane Roe. The lawsuit then became known as *Roe v. Wade*. (Wade was the name of the district attorney of Dallas County who enforced the law.) Weddington and Coffee argued that the Texas law violated the First, Fourth, Fifth, Eighth, Ninth, and

14th Amendments to the Constitution; that it was vague and unconstitutionally broad; and that it infringed on the right of all women to choose whether or not to have children. On January 22, 1973, the Supreme Court decided by a 7–2 majority that the Texas anti-abortion statute was unconstitutional. The decision noted that while the "Constitution does not explicitly mention any right to privacy," decisions dating back to 1891 have recognized "a right of personal privacy, or a guarantee of certain areas or zones of privacy." The roots of that right, the decision continued, were found in the Bill of Rights and the 14th Amendment, and that "activities relating to" marriage, procreation, contraception, family relationships, and childrearing were protected within those zones or areas of privacy. Furthermore, the decision denied the contention made by the state of Texas that the fetus had a constitutionally guaranteed right to life or personhood within the meaning of the 14th Amendment. The justices observed that the Constitution and the 14th Amendment, written when the "quickening" doctrine was recognized and when legalized abortion was widely practiced, could not reasonably be concluded to have originally intended that the word "person" as used in the 14th Amendment applied to the unborn.

This decision, which acknowledged both a right to privacy and abortion rights for women, has proven enormously controversial. States, including Texas, have endeavored to restrict that right and to limit the opportunities for abortion. The decision has also proven to be a galvanizing factor in the rise of religious conservatives as a political force in American electoral politics.

Regents of the University of California v. Bakke (1978)

Allan Paul Bakke, a 33-year old aerospace engineer, applied to the University of California, Davis, School of Medicine. Bakke had done well on the medical school entrance exam, scoring in the top 3 percent of test-takers. He had already applied to more than a dozen medical schools and been denied admission by all of them. One factor in many of the medical schools' decisions had been his age. At 33, he was older than most applicants or students in medical school. The University of California, Davis, explained that not only was his age a factor in their decision-making process, but Bakke had also been denied admission in part because the medical school reserved a number of places in each incoming class to historically disadvantaged populations. The UC Davis medical school designated 16 places out of the 100 in its incoming medical school class for minority students. As a result, when the medical school made its admission decisions, Bakke was not given a place. Bakke sued, claiming that he had been denied equal protection under the law guaranteed by both the 14th Amendment and the Civil Rights Act of 1964. He argued that he had been unable to compete for the 16 minority-designated positions. He contended that he had been the victim of "reverse discrimination." The case ultimately was heard by the Supreme Court, which rendered a dual judgment in 1978. The first part of the ruling, decided by a 5–4 majority, rejected UC Davis' dual system of admissions. This part of the ruling rejected the use of specific racial quotas in admissions systems. By another 5–4 majority, however, the Court also found that the university could take race into account as one of a number of factors used to make admissions decisions. This part of the decision confirmed the view that schools and universities could continue to promote racial diversity as one of the goals of an institution. As a result of the decision, Bakke enrolled in medical school, received his M.D., completed his residency at the Mayo Clinic, and practiced medicine in Minnesota.

Obergefell v. Hodges (2015)

The Supreme Court case *Obergefell v. Hodges* consolidated the claims made by 14 same-sex couples from Michigan, Ohio, Kentucky, and Tennessee who argued that their 14th Amendment rights to equal protection under the law were violated when they were denied the right to marry or have their legal marriages performed in other states recognized. In each case, the district courts had found in favor of the plaintiffs, but the respective states had appealed in opposition of their claims. The states claimed that recognizing the marriage of same-sex couples would "demean a timeless institution." Justice Anthony Kennedy, who wrote the majority opinion, rejected this argument, arguing that the "right to marry is a fundamental right inherent in the liberty of the person," and that under the due process clause and the equal protection clause of the 14th Amendment, "same-sex couples may not be deprived of that right and that liberty." Kennedy also noted that while marriage has been an institution fundamental to the social order of the nation, it has also undergone legal and social changes. In this regard, he cited ***Loving v. Virginia* (1967)**, which had invalidated laws that prohibited interracial marriage. Kennedy concluded by noting, "As some of the petitioners in these cases demonstrate, marriage embodies a love that may endure even past death. It would misunderstand these men and women to say that they disrespect the idea of marriage. Their plea is that they do respect it, respect it so deeply that they seek to find its fulfillment for themselves. Their hope is not to be condemned to live in loneliness, excluded from one of civilization's oldest institutions. They ask for equal dignity in the eyes of the law. The Constitution grants them that right."

> **Competency 017 Descriptive Statement I.** The beginning teacher understands the relationship between the states and the national government of the United States (i.e., federalism).

The Constitution of the United States established a federal system of government. Federalism, according to the political scientists James Q. Wilson and John DiIulio, Jr., is a political system "in which sovereignty is shared so that on some matters the national government is supreme and on others the states, regions, or provincial governments are supreme."

In a federal system where power and sovereignty are shared in this fashion, each citizen (or territory) is under the authority of more than one level of government at the same time. Each American is at once a citizen of their own state, with rights, responsibilities, and privileges that extend from that state; and a citizen of the United States, with rights, responsibilities, and privileges that are derived from the national government. Local governments (your township, city, county or other governmental body) acquire their authority from the states, and so are under state jurisdiction.

Each level of government has its own realm of authority and powers. Article I, Section 8 of the U.S. Constitution lists the **enumerated powers** of the national government. They include the sole power to mint currency, regulate interstate commerce, conduct foreign policy, declare war, establish post offices, and establish and oversee the army and navy. The **reserved powers** are those not granted to the national government or to the people. These are reserved to the states. The Constitution also establishes **concurrent powers** that are shared by both state and national governments. These include, but are not limited to, the power to tax. Certain powers are prohibited to both federal and state governments. For example, neither the state nor the federal government can establish a state or national religion. Federalism also mandates that neither federal nor state governments can abolish the other. The Civil War was fought over this principle, later confirmed in the case *Texas v. White* (1869). The judgment in the case read that the Constitution had created "an indestructible Union, composed of indestructible States." States could not secede, thereby destroying the Union, and the nation could not abolish the states.

Debates about where the boundaries between state and federal power should be drawn have animated much of American political history. Some describe the period from 1789 to 1901 as the era of "Dual Federalism," characterized by very little collaboration or competition between the national and state governments. From 1901 to 1960, the states and federal government shared many more functions and has been described as an era of "Cooperative Federalism." Since the 1960s, the expanding role of the national government has shifted the power relationship between national and state governments, which has resulted in a backlash as states grow concerned about federal regulations, unfunded federal mandates, and growing intrusion of the national government into areas jealously guarded by the states.

> **Competency 017 Descriptive Statement J.** The beginning teacher demonstrates knowledge of the structure and functions of Texas state government and local governments.

Texas Constitution

Texas' current constitution is its seventh. When Texas joined the Union in 1845, it wrote its third constitution as part of the terms of entering the United States. After withdrawing from the Union, a fourth constitution was drafted under the Confederate States of America. During Reconstruction, the state twice rewrote its constitution, once in 1866, to gain reentry into the Union and then again in 1869. The current Texas Constitution was ratified in 1876. The preoccupations and fears reflected in the 1876 Texas Constitution have played an important role in shaping the state's development.

The resentment felt by Texas Democrats, predominantly white ex-Confederates, at their exclusion from power in the aftermath of the Civil War, left them with a deep distrust of the Republican Party, and of the concept of loyal opposition in general. As a result, from 1876 until the mid-1970s, Texas was effectively a one-party state, with Democrats largely shutting Republicans out of significant office. Anger at the progressive government that had ruled Texas during Reconstruction and suspicion toward strong central government then led Texas politicians to draw up a Constitution in 1876 that was much more specific than the United States Constitution in limiting the government and specifying its powers. Texas in 1876 was a rural society with a deep distrust of corporate, banking, railroad, and big business interests. As a result, the 1876 Constitution emphasized protection of individual rights and rural interests over those of larger propertied interests.

The Texas Constitution of 1876, and many of the later amendments added to the document, reflected efforts to limit unwelcomed federal government involvement in such questions as gun ownership, environmental quality, education, social welfare distribution, and health care.

Limited Government

The Texas Constitution is a case study in restricting the powers of government. It was written to prevent any expansion of governmental authority. The Texas Bill of Rights was placed at the forefront of the document, rather than an afterthought, as was the case with the national constitution. This placement signaled Texas' intent to limit governmental power. The Texas Bill of Rights provides a more expansive list of restraints on state power.

Republicanism

The Constitution of the United States makes it the responsibility of the federal government to ensure that each state has a republican form of government. The Texas Constitution pledges the people of Texas to preserving a republican form of government.

One feature of the "little r" republicanism evident in the Texas system of government is the restriction of the legislature to meeting biennially (every two years) for only 140 days. Classical republican thinkers struggled with the idea of a professional office-holding class or professional politicians. The fear was that professional office-holders soon became more concerned about their own interests and paychecks than they did about the best interests of the republic. Texas legislators are provided a small salary of only $7,200 per year plus a per diem of $190 per day, the legislature is in session. Thus, over a two-year period, a state legislator would make between $33,800 and $41,000.

Checks and Balances

As is the case with the federal government, the Texas legislature, executive branch, and the judiciary exercise restraints on each other. This happens through the legislative power to limit or authorize executive actions or agencies, as well as through the legislative power of the purse. The governor has the authority to veto bills. The judicial branch also the power of judicial review over administrative or legislative enactments.

Federalism

The United States Constitution establishes a federal system of government in which the state and national governments share power. The **supremacy clause** of the Constitution guarantees that the Constitution is the supreme law of the land and that the enactments of the national government, in general, take precedence over those of the states. To the states, however, are given a class of powers known as the **reserved powers**, those powers that are not specifically enumerated as powers of the Congress and national executive branch. Interestingly, the government of Texas as established within the Texas Constitution, is a **unitary government** in which city and county governments are subject to the state and lack the features of independent self-rule common to federalist systems of government.

Separation of Powers

The Texas system of government incorporates a separation of powers similar to that of the federal government, with a legislative branch composed of two chambers, an executive branch headed by the "chief executive officer" or governor, and a judicial branch.

The legislative branch is composed of a lower house (the House of Representatives) and an upper house (the Senate) that enact laws to promote the public welfare and protect public safety. The legislature meets biennially for 140 days over a two-year session. The legislative branch has the power to tax, spend, and grant powers to the executive branch or judiciary.

The executive branch is headed by the state governor. Texas has one of the weakest state governorships in the country. Governors have no cabinet. They may appoint members to a number of boards and commissions with executive functions, but these officials cannot be fired by the governor, and are therefore often beyond the governor's control after their appointment.

One of the most unique checks on the power of the state's governor is the power of the lieutenant governor. He is a statewide-elected official who is independent of the governor. Often it is said that the lieutenant governor is the most powerful Texas politician. The lieutenant governor is the presiding officer in the Texas Senate and controls the budgeting process.

Popular sovereignty

The Texas Constitution, in its preamble, asserts that it is "the people of the state of Texas" that "do ordain and establish" its Constitution. In Article 1, Section 2 of the Texas Bill of Rights, the constitution reiterates the emphasis on popular sovereignty. "All political power is inherent in the people," the constitution states, "and all free governments are founded on their authority, and instituted for their benefit."

Article 1, Section 2 continues with the assertion of the people's "inalienable" right "at all times" to "alter, reform, or abolish their government." In other words, the Texas Bill of Rights restates what was not affirmed in the United States Constitution, but which was a central feature of the American Declaration of Independence: the right to revolution. This right is written into the Texas Constitution, but does not imply a written declaration of Texans' right to rebel against the federal government. What this section of the Texas Bill of Rights does illustrate, however, is an attitude widely shared across the state: a deep distrust in government and a desire to strictly limit both the state's and the federal government's powers.

Individual rights

Texans have always claimed a strong reverence for individual rights and individualism. In part, this reflects the legacy of the American frontier. Texans on the frontier during the state's early years often had to fend for themselves under severe circumstances. It also reflected the fact that Anglo-American Texans, along with whites throughout the South's plantation economies, developed an intensely individualistic value system that juxtaposed the honor that adhered to white planters and yeoman farmers with the degradation of the enslaved and the landless laborer. Protections of a family's homestead, property rights, and the right to bear arms, and prohibitions against imprisonment for debt all reflected a sense of vulnerability of the individual to threats from a variety of sources.

Comparing the Texas and U.S. Constitutions

In comparing the Texas and U.S. Constitutions, one of the first things that stands out is the sheer length of the former. The U.S. Constitution has only 4,400 words. Texas Constitution is more than 89,000 words long. The comparative length of the two documents illustrates a primary difference. The U.S. Constitution's brevity was designed to give the U.S. government a degree of flexibility that enabled it to develop organically and adapt to very different conditions and cultural considerations. The Texas Constitution's length and specificity was designed to accomplish precisely the opposite. The Texas Constitution was designed to hinder just such organic growth by hemming in the Texas legislative and executive branches and carefully limiting them.

Compare the Texas Bill of Rights with the U.S. Bill of Rights

The Texas Bill of Rights begins with a declaration of states' rights emphasizing the "freedom and sovereignty of state." It then asserts popular sovereignty and the people's inalienable right to alter or even abolish their government.

Thereafter, the Texas Bill of Rights has a number of protections that overlap with those in the U.S. Bill of Rights. It guarantees freedoms of speech, press, religion, peaceable assembly, the right to petition, and protects against unreasonable searches and seizures, double jeopardy, and the right to a speedy jury trial. A number of protections do not appear in the U.S. Bill of Rights. For example, the Texas Bill of Rights protects against imprisonment for debt, and against committal for mental incompetence without a medical or psychiatric evaluation.

While the United States Bill of Rights is composed of 10 amendments, there are 34 sections in the Texas Bill of Rights, with the most recent addition incorporated in 2015. This latest amendment illustrates the degree to which the Texas Bill of Rights seeks to codify the rights of Texans, leaving little to the interpretation of the courts. It asserts a positive right to "hunt, fish, and harvest wildlife," spelling out that hunting and fishing are "preferred methods of managing and controlling wildlife." In 2009, public access to the beaches of the Gulf of Mexico was granted as an unrestricted right. The Bill of Rights has a "defense of marriage" amendment, added in 2005, which has since been nullified by *Obergefell v. Hodges*. Indeed, a perusal of the Texas Bill of Rights provides a useful history of the preoccupations of the state's citizens. For example, in 1972, the state included an equal rights amendment and in 1989 added a victims' rights amendment for victims of crime.

Structure and Function of Local Governments

Unlike the federal government, local governments are not independent of the state government, but are understood as "creatures of the state" under the **Dillon Rule.** The Dillon Rule effectively establishes a unitary system of government within the state of Texas, as local governments have no inherent constitutional powers other than those granted to them by the state legislature. Texas has more than 1,200 cities, 254 counties, more than 1,090 school districts, and more than 2,250 special districts. Counties provide governmental services such as road construction, police, jail and courts, and health and welfare functions. They are also charged with voter registration and motor vehicle licensing. Special districts are considered "single purpose" units of government, providing singular functions such as education, water, or hospitals. Cities are divided between "home rule," or larger cities, and "general law cities" with smaller populations. Home rule cities have a charter that outlines the governmental organization of the city. Smaller cities lack a charter and therefore carry out functions only as authorized by the state. The vast majority of the state's cities are "general law" cities.

State Revenues and Spending

Texas state revenues come from a variety of sources. Texas is one of seven states in the country that does not have a state income tax. As a result, the state's coffers are filled by a mixture of sales taxes, licensing fees, and excise taxes. **Figure 7.1** illustrates the amounts and primary sources of revenue for the state.

Perhaps surprisingly, more than one-third of the state's revenues come from the federal government in the form of payments for programs administered by the state. These include Medicaid, funding for the Every Student Succeeds Act (replaced by the No Child Left Behind Act in December 2015), and aid to needy families and other social programs. The extent of federal government spending in Texas is actually understated in this measure, as it doesn't include spending in Texas on social security payments, interstate highway construction, military spending, and other big-ticket federal expenditures that are directly administered by the federal government.

State sales taxes amount to more than a quarter of state revenues. State sales taxes on consumer purchases are capped at 6.25 percent, though most Texans pay higher sales taxes when local sales taxes are added. Nearly 10 percent of state funding derives from licenses, fees, permits, fines, and penalties. A variety of taxes on motor vehicle sales, fuel consumption, oil and natural gas production, alcohol and tobacco taxes, and lottery proceeds, make up the remainder of Texas's state revenue.

Figure 7.1

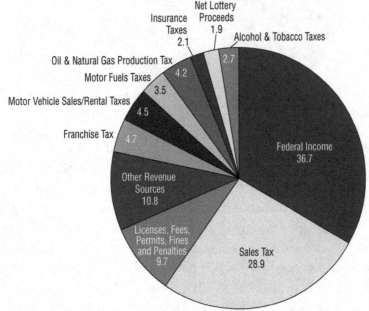

Texas Revenue Sources 2015
(in billions of dollars)

Texas state government expenditures, as seen in **Figure 7.2** are largely disbursed on three categories of spending: pensions for retired state employees, health care for the state's residents, and education. These three priorities make up nearly 75 percent of the state's expenditures. By comparison, the next three areas receiving the highest proportion of state spending—transportation, criminal justice and police protection, and welfare—receive less than 20 percent of state spending. It is worth noting that local governments have a much greater impact on the state's citizens than does the state government. As seen in **Figure 7.3** and **Figure 7.4,** local taxes and spending are more immediately felt than the state's levies.

Figure 7.2

Texas State Government Expenditures, 2015
(in billions of dollars)

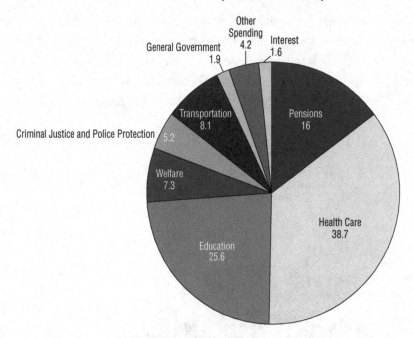

The most important local spending priority, not surprisingly, is public education. More than 59 percent of every local government dollar is devoted to K–12 education and to local community college districts. This amounts to a total of nearly $60 billion. Health care and police protection (including local courts and jails) together amount to nearly 20 percent of local spending. Interest payments on municipal and county debts also make up an important component of local spending that is much reduced at the state level. A not insignificant part of funding school building, local road building, and other infrastructure projects is paid for by issuing bonds and borrowing money. The state government's gross public debt in 2015, for example, amounted to only $48.2 billion; while city, county, and other local districts in 2015 accumulated nearly $260 billion in debt. After spending on transportation infrastructure, local government debt service payments are the fourth-largest single cost to local governments.

Figure 7.3

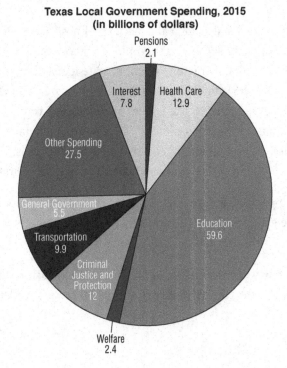

Texas Local Government Spending, 2015
(in billions of dollars)

COMPETENCY 018 (CITIZENSHIP AND POLITICAL PROCESSES IN THE UNITED STATES)

The teacher understands political processes in the United States, and the rights and responsibilities of U.S. citizens.

> **Competency 018 Descriptive Statement A.** The beginning teacher understands the historical and contemporary roles played by political parties, interest groups and the media in the U.S. political system.

As we have seen, the Framers mistrusted political parties. Nonetheless, political parties are important both to the workings of the electoral system that makes possible expressions of the popular will and to the workings of government in the United States.

First and foremost, political parties are associations organized to win elections at the local, state, and national levels. They identify likely candidates for political office, raise money, develop platforms that identify the party's policy positions, canvass for votes, and drum up support for candidates and passage of legislation.

Parties are organized along local, state, and national lines. Most elective offices are local offices. Not surprisingly, most party activists are employed by or volunteer in local organizations. Local parties focus their efforts on mayoral, city council, state legislature, or countywide elections. Local party offices do not have the influence they once could muster, and they rely on large numbers of volunteers during election seasons. Each local party office is organized differently, making generalizations about local party structures difficult. In general, local party offices throughout the country conduct registration drives, conduct get-out-the-vote campaigns, operate phone banks at election time, and otherwise offer assistance to candidates' campaign operations.

The state-level party apparatus, unlike most local party structures, has a paid staff directed by the party chairperson. The state party organization focuses on statewide races (for state governor, U.S. senator, and the state legislature) and on fundraising.

The national political party organizations, headquartered in Washington, D.C., are primarily involved in fundraising, organizing the national party convention, ass well as developing the party platform.

Interest Groups

While individuals exercise civil rights and civic duties, groups influence the political process most often and most effectively. These groups vary widely. In many ways, groups provide a scaffolding for individual identity. Familial, neighborhood, religious, recreational, occupational, and regional groups provide only a fraction of the possible sources of community and social identity. Belonging to a group provides ways in which economic and noneconomic needs are met. Labor unions, business groups, and professional associations all promote the financial interests of their members. Environmental convictions, religious values, ideological beliefs, and rights protection also provide bases for the formation of associations. Each of these kinds of groups can also enter into the political arena to protect their political interests. They then become **political interest groups**. Interest groups share goals and interests, establish institutions and organizational structures, and seek to influence law and public policy. Often, interest groups carry out **lobbying** activities designed to influence legislation.

Political interest groups are not the same as political parties. They have a narrower membership base and are usually more focused on policy, rather than electoral victories. Parties exist to win political contests. Interest groups exist to affect policy decisions. Interest groups do, however, often write legislation (though the author of that legislation is the member of Congress who introduces the legislation on the floor of either the House or Senate). Interest groups provide publicity for pending legislation, either in support or opposition. They lobby for financial support for legislators that support their policy agenda. They attempt to inform the public and government officials about the issues that affect them.

The following are several broad categories of interest groups, with representative organizations.

Economic Interest Groups	National Association of Manufacturers (NAM)
	American Federation of Labor and Congress of Industrial Organizations (AFL-CIO)
	National Education Association
	American Federation of Teachers
	American Medical Association
Public Interest Groups	Environmental Defense Fund
	League of Women Voters
	Center for Democracy and Technology
	American Civil Liberties Union (ACLU)
Government Interest Groups	National Conference of Mayors
	National League of Cities
Civil Rights Interest Groups	Southern Christian Leadership Conference
	National Association for the Advancement of Colored People (NAACP)
	League of United Latin American Citizens (LULAC)
	Mexican-American Legal Defense and Education Fund (MALDEF)
	National Organization for Women
	Aids Coalition to Unleash Power (ACT UP)
Ideological Interest Groups	Americans for Democratic Action (ADA)
	American Conservative Union (ACU)
Single-Issue Interest Groups	National Rifle Association (NRA)
	National Abortion Rights Action League (NARAL)
Religious Interest Groups	The Christian Coalition
	The Interfaith Alliance
	Family Rights Council
	B'nai B'rith International
	Muslim Public Affairs Council
	Council on American-Islamic Relations

Competency 018 Descriptive Statement B. The beginning teacher demonstrates knowledge of processes for filling elective and appointive public offices (e.g., primary system, electoral college).

Political parties control the **nomination** process, which selects individual who will represent the party in a general election. The nomination process until the 20th century was largely controlled by party organizations that threw their support behind candidates who in turn promised that upon election they would steer government jobs, contracts, and other patronage rewards to the party organization. Nominations usually took place in the proverbial "smoke-filled back room," rather than through public or transparent processes.

Primaries and Caucuses

During the Progressive period, to combat the influence of urban **bosses** who controlled the party apparatus, the **primary election** or **direct primary** was introduced across the country. Primaries were more transparent processes that placed power in the hands of party voters. In many states, nominees are chosen in **closed primaries**, in which only registered party members or voters who declare their party identification are allowed to vote in the primary held by their declared party. **Open primaries** permit independents or voters of either party to choose which primary they will vote in, with the proviso that they vote only for candidates in one party. **Blanket primaries**, which are rarely used, allow primary voters to select from Republican or Democratic candidates by office, even in the nominating process.

Primaries reduce party control over candidates and elected officials. Candidates are effectively appealing to the voting public rather than to the party leaders. Additionally, candidates largely fund their campaigns themselves and through donations, further reducing party control.

Electoral College

The Electoral College reflects a number of the Framers' preoccupations. First, it reveals their deep suspicion of the electorate. The Framers had no faith that the populace would have the needed information to make important decisions, and feared that they would be easily swayed by appeals to their self-interest over the needs of the nation as a whole. Second, the Electoral College illustrates the Framers' continuing conviction that the states (and not the people) were the locus of sovereignty. The Electoral College was to be chosen by the states through their respective legislatures, rather than by the people of the states. The decision to establish the Electoral College reflected Southerners' conviction that no Southerner could hope to become president if the office was chosen by popular election. The number of enslaved persons in the Southern states reduced the relative number of voters in the South in presidential elections. As James Madison acknowledged, "The right of suffrage was much more diffusive in the Northern than the Southern States; and the latter could have no influence in the election on the score of the Negroes."

Today, electors are no longer chosen by state legislatures, but instead reflect the vote of the electorate in each state. Voters in presidential elections are actually selecting a slate of electors in the Electoral College. The number of electors from each state mirrors the number of U.S. senators and representatives each state has. With the exception of Maine and Nebraska, the popular vote winner in each state receives all of a state's Electoral College votes.

To win a presidential election, then, requires a majority of the electoral votes, or 270 of the 538 Electoral College votes. A presidential candidate can win a majority of the nation's popular votes cast and still not earn the majority of Electoral College votes. Until the 2000 election, this had happened only twice over the course of American history, in 1876 and 1888. In the 2000 election, Al Gore had more than 40,000 votes than did George W. Bush. In 2016, Donald Trump won the Electoral College vote while receiving more than 3 million fewer popular votes than did Hillary Clinton.

If no candidate takes a majority of the Electoral College votes, the election is thrown into the House of Representatives, which selects the president. There, the state delegation determines how each state's one vote will be cast. The 1824 and 1876 elections were the last presidential elections to be settled in the House of Representatives.

> **Competency 018 Descriptive Statement C.** The beginning teacher demonstrates knowledge of processes for making policy in the United States, the impact of technology on the political process, and ways in which different points of view influence decision making and the development of public policy at the local, state, and national levels.

Public policy, simply defined, is any decision made by government designed to accomplish a particular result. Public policy decisions can be made to promote or regulate economic activity, to influence and improve public health outcomes, to improve the level of educational attainment of American young people; in short, public policy decisions impinge on all aspects of American life.

The public policy process involves three stages: problem recognition, policy formation, and policy implementation. The best way to illustrate how the public policy process works is to examine a specific public policy problem and how a variety of policies have been implemented to address it.

Recognizing a Policy Problem

While dieting for cosmetic purposes has been a feature of American life since before the Great Depression, it was only in the 1980s, with the development of the Body Mass Index, that physicians, epidemiologists, and social scientists began looking closely at the problem of obesity as a health care issue in the United States. In 1985, the National Institutes of Health classified obesity as a disease, and BMI risk categories for Americans were defined. The scope of the health problem, which had been developing for a number of decades, only began to elicit policy proposals and careful scientific study during the 1980s and 1990s. In the early 2000s, the U.S. Department of Health and Human Services alerted the public that more Americans were clinically obese than were underweight.

Recognition, of obesity as a social and health crisis took some time to develop. This is not always the case with public policy issues, which can sometimes arise quite quickly. The problem of international terrorism, for example, became apparent immediately after the coordinated attacks on the U.S. homeland on September 11, 2001, and American public policy makers began to focus their energies and resources on the problem.

Developing Policy Solutions

A series of studies by the National Institutes of Health and the International Obesity Task Force resulted in the development of a number of **policy formations** to address the problem of obesity. One proposal was to require new labeling requirements to inform consumers of the nutrient and calorie content of the food products they purchased. The Food and Drug Administration proposed the study of fat substitutes that could be used in snack foods. The Department of Health and Human Services developed a series of health promotion and disease prevention programs designed to inform the public of the dangers of obesity and ways that the threat of obesity could be reduced.

Developing policy solutions typically involves a wide-ranging combination of industry groups, government agencies, public service organizations, lobbying groups, and congressional or executive-branch officials. Politicians typically are the least informed of policy developers. They are often reliant on the white papers, news releases, scientific policy papers, and lobbying efforts of other groups that are more closely connected to the problem than are congressmen or executive branch politicos. Policy solutions often are enacted into law. However, because laws are so often difficult to pass and become embroiled in political struggles, policy proposals are frequently implemented in much more incremental fashion within administrative agencies.

Policy Implementation

Once a policy has been adopted, it has to be implemented. Often, the implementation of a policy fails to live up to the policy's goals. For example, among the many policy proposals that were implemented to address the issue of obesity was the development of government–industry partnerships to change the range of choices available in restaurants, public school meal plans, and grocery stores. In addition, these proposals called on a wide range of publicity measures to communicate to parents and children the dangers of childhood obesity and strategies to address the problem. Some of these programs worked in that they made parents aware of the threat of obesity to young children. The huge fast-food chain McDonald's, as a part of the government–business effort, increased the number of salads and diet-conscious offerings available for consumers. They were not alone. Unfortunately, these measures did not contribute significantly to reducing childhood obesity, particularly among the working and the working poor. The process of policy evaluation revealed that in many cases, poor and working-class populations lived in what have been described as "food deserts," where affordable and high-quality fresh foods were unavailable due to a lack of grocery stores, farmers markets, and other sources of fresh foods. As a result, families were left only with a range of highly processed foods. The recommendations made by government agencies also failed to recognize the time constraints associated with home preparation of more healthy foods.

Policy implementation requires both putting a policy in place and assessing the successes and failures of the policy.

> **Competency 018 Descriptive Statement D.** The beginning teacher understands rights guaranteed by the U.S. Constitution, including each amendment in the Bill of Rights (e.g., due process, equal protection), and its role in protecting individual liberties.

The Constitution of the United States, as composed at the Philadelphia Constitutional Convention, focused largely on the organizational structure and principles of representative government: federalism, separation of powers, bicameralism, representation, the amendment process, and other practices of republican governance. The first 10 amendments to the Constitution, known as the Bill of Rights, were enacted to respond to critics of the Constitution who argued that the states and individuals needed greater protections against the power of the federal government. James Madison then proposed a list of changes to the Constitution that were compiled into a list of amendments. These 10 amendments were ratified by the states and became the Bill of Rights.

These amendments to the Constitution were initially applied only to the federal government. However, in a process known as **incorporation**, various portions of the Bill of Rights have been gradually extended to the states through the 14th Amendment. Most of this process of incorporation has taken place since 1940.

First Amendment

> "Congress shall make no law respecting an establishment of religion, or prohibiting the free exercise thereof; or abridging the freedom of speech, or of the press; or the right of the people peaceably to assemble, and to petition the government for a redress of grievances."

The First Amendment is perhaps best understood as four separate protections from federal government encroachment on individual rights. Over time, these protections have been incorporated against the states and are now understood to protect individuals from state governments' infringements on these same rights.

The Establishment Clause

During the colonial period, the Church of England and the Congregationalist (Puritans) church were the authorized, or established, churches in the Southern colonies and New England, respectively. The states of Delaware, New Jersey, New York, Pennsylvania, and Rhode Island did not have an established church.

The Constitution made clear that the national government had no power to legislate the establishment of a national church or to impose a state-sponsored religion on the states. In 1947, the establishment clause was applied to the states under the equal protection clause of the 14th Amendment. The language of the majority opinion in *McCollum v. Board of Education of School Dist. No. 71, Champaign County* (1948) perhaps best describes the meaning of the establishment clause:

> "Neither a state nor the Federal Government can set up a church. Neither can pass laws which aid one religion, aid all religions, or prefer one religion over another. Neither can force nor influence a person to go to or to remain away from church against his will or force him to profess a belief or disbelief in any religion. No person can be punished for entertaining or professing religious beliefs or disbeliefs, for church attendance or nonattendance. No tax in any amount, large or small, can be levied to support any religious activities or institutions, whatever they may be called, or whatever form they may adopt to teach or practice religion. Neither a state nor the Federal Government can, openly or secretly, participate in the affairs of any religious organizations or groups and vice versa."

Cases that have arisen under the establishment clause include questions about the constitutionality of public funding for religious schools or other activities carried out by religious institutions; concerns about government-sponsored prayer or other services; and governmental use of religious symbols. The Supreme Court in *Reynolds v. United States* (1878) and in *McCollum v. Board of Education*, among other cases, has invoked the metaphor, used by Thomas Jefferson and James Madison, of a "wall of separation" that must be maintained between church and state.

The Free Exercise Clause

A second clause in the First Amendment that pertains to religion is known as the free exercise clause. The free exercise clause protects people from being jailed, fined, or otherwise penalized for practicing their religion. This does not entitle an individual to harm others in the course of exercising their own religious beliefs. These practices can be regulated. Prior to 1940, the free exercise clause was only applied to the federal government's ability to limit or regulate religious practices, and its enforcement was not extended to the states. After 1940, most cases have involved attempts by the state to regulate or restrict certain religious practices. For example, in 1943, in *West Virginia Board of Education v. Barnette,* the Supreme Court heard the case of a number of Jehovah's Witness children who were expelled from school for refusing to salute the flag and recite the Pledge of Allegiance. The Court overturned the expulsions, both on free exercise grounds and on establishment grounds, arguing that mandatory pledge recitations were unconstitutional for all children. In later cases, the Court required that the only justifiable reason a state agency or organization could give for enacting legislation that burdened the practice of an individual's religion was if it had a "compelling state interest" and if the legislative or administrative enactment: (a) had a secular legislative purpose; (b) did not have a primary effect of advancing or inhibiting religion; and (c) did not result in "excessive government entanglement" in religious practices. On these grounds, the

Supreme Court struck down displays of the Ten Commandments in county courthouses and ruled unconstitutional Alabama's mandate that schoolchildren be required to honor a moment of silence each day "for prayer and voluntary meditation."

Freedoms of Speech and Press

Freedom of the press, the Framers called the "bulwark" of liberty. It was seen to act as a fortress protecting all other rights and privileges. Each of the state constitutions written before 1787 also included protections against infringements on the freedom of the press. The First Amendment in the same section also protects freedom of speech. In most cases, these two freedoms have been seen as inseparable. In other words, both the media and private individuals are protected from efforts of the state to silence their expression.

The tradition of freedom of speech and the press, as inherited from England, primarily turned on the abolition of what was called "prior restraint." In other words, a publisher or writer was free to publish their ideas without prior censorship, although the writer could be punished afterwards if those expressions were found objectionable. Most states also enacted laws against "seditious libel," or written and verbal criticism of the government. Over the course of the 19th century, the Supreme Court rarely found in favor of litigants who claimed that their First Amendment rights to freedom of speech or the press had been violated by state governments. In part, this was because the Court argued that the First Amendment protected persons from congressional, but not state, interference with their speech rights. During the late 19th century, there were many who appealed for protections of their right to communicate their ideas but rarely found protections in the courts, including socialists, religious minorities, anarchists, and labor union activists. In 1925, the Supreme Court began to expand protections of free speech, first by extending those protections to the states. In the 1925 case *Gitlow v. New York,* the Court said that states, and not just Congress, were bound by the First Amendment. In the 1942 case *Valentine v. Chrestensen*, the Court identified categories of speech that were not protected, but has since gradually asserted free speech protections to many of these. For example, in *Valentine v. Chrestensen*, the Court ruled that commercial speech lacked First Amendment protections, although it now enjoys many of the protections afforded other forms of speech. Most forms of speech, excepting hard-core pornography and child pornography, are now protected from prosecution under obscenity laws. Forms of nonverbal expression have also been protected. The First Amendment protects the right to march in protest, to wear a black armband or other symbol in protest, or even to burn the flag of the United States as a protest. Neither can the government compel speech; for example, by forcing schoolchildren to say the Pledge of Allegiance, as upheld in *West Virginia Board of Education v. Barnette*.

Freedom of Assembly and Petition

Abraham Lincoln characterized the right to peaceably assemble as "the Constitutional substitute for revolution." Lincoln and the Framers of the Constitution conceptualized the right to assembly and petition largely as a political right.

However, people also experience their right to peaceably assemble when they go to a movie, have a birthday party, join a union, demonstrate publicly, or attend a sporting event. Whenever people gather together, even for nonpolitical purposes, they contribute to the creation of free society characterized by a sense of shared belonging in the life of the community. In societies characterized by repressive governments, most such assemblies are perceived as potentially subversive and necessarily surveilled. A book published in 2001 titled *Bowling Alone: The Collapse and Revival of American Community* decried the consequences of the decline of many of the ways in which Americans formerly associated.

The right to freely assemble was incorporated (extended to the states) in 1937 in *De Jonge v. Oregon*, a case involving an attendee at a Communist Party rally in Oregon who was arrested and charged with belonging to an unlawful organization because he possessed Communist Party literature. His conviction was overturned, and the Court argued that his right to peaceably assemble (no illegal activity had been advocated at the gathering) was a "right cognate to those of free speech and free press."

Second Amendment

"A well regulated Militia, being necessary to the security of a free State, the right of the people to keep and bear Arms, shall not be infringed."

The Framers believed that standing armies were most often a tool of oppression used to silence political opposition. In both English and early American tradition, professional armies were relied upon only when foreign enemies threatened. To meet other exigencies of national defense or to put down insurrections, the government relied upon militia called up from the ranks of ordinary civilians who supplied their own weaponry, and received minimal training at annual musters. The Constitution granted the federal government the authority to regulate the militia. Anti-Federalists feared that an expansive federal government could use its power over state militias in ways that would reduce the states' primary defense against either federal oppression or internal insurrection, a visceral fear in the South where slave rebellions were a perpetual worry. The Second Amendment addressed these fears, without reducing the federal government's complete legal authority over any standing armies and the militias. It did so by guaranteeing that the federal government lacked legal power to disarm the nation's citizens.

States have historically and routinely regulated guns. The Second Amendment was ruled to apply only to the federal government. In 1876, this legal position was confirmed. For example, African Americans were frequently prohibited from possessing weapons, and ownership of handguns and other types of weapons were routinely regulated. In 2008, the Supreme Court ruled by a 5–4 majority in *District of Columbia v. Heller* that a federal law forbidding most civilians from owning handguns in Washington, D.C., was unconstitutional. The majority of the court determined that individuals have a private right to own weapons, and that the Second Amendment was not simply safeguarding states' rights to arm their militia. In 2010, in *McDonald v. City of Chicago,* this interpretation was incorporated against the states, protecting private citizens from many state regulations of firearms ownership.

Third Amendment

"No soldier shall, in time of peace be quartered in any house, without the consent of the owner, nor in time of war, but in a manner to be prescribed by law."

Protections against "quartering" of troops were among the rights referenced in the English Bill of Rights, reflecting long-standing opposition to the practice of billeting soldiers in Englishmen's homes. The American colonists also raised objections to the practice. Quartering British troops in colonial Americans' homes was among the reasons given in the Declaration of Independence justifying the colonists' rebellion. The Third Amendment's wording precluded quartering troops in private residences during peacetime without the owner's consent, but allowed it during times of war (as was the case during the War of 1812 and the Civil War).

Fourth Amendment

"The right of the people to be secure in their persons, houses, papers, and effects, against unreasonable searches and seizures, shall not be violated, and no warrants shall issue, but upon probable cause, supported by oath or affirmation, and particularly describing the place to be searched, and the persons or things to be seized."

The Fourth Amendment provides the foundation of protections against overreaching police investigative powers. The Fourth Amendment restrains the government's ability to detain or search a person or their property without proper cause. The Fourth Amendment also requires that warrants be sworn out to conduct such searches or detentions.

Fifth Amendment

"No person shall be held to answer for a capital, or otherwise infamous crime, unless on a presentment or indictment of a grand jury, except in cases arising in the land or naval forces, or in the militia, when in actual service in time of war or public danger; nor shall any person be subject for the same offense to be twice put in jeopardy of life or limb; nor shall be compelled in any criminal case to be a witness against himself, nor be deprived of life, liberty, or property, without due process of law; nor shall private property be taken for public use, without just compensation."

The Fifth Amendment provides protection against over-zealous or unjust prosecutorial powers. The amendment protects against "**double jeopardy**," or being tried twice for the same crime. It protects against self-incrimination, entitling suspects to "**plead the Fifth**," or refuse to testify against themselves. The Miranda ruling that requires police officers to read a suspect their rights derives from this amendment, as do restrictions against interrogation methods used to coerce a confession.

The Fifth Amendment requires that for serious criminal charges to be brought, a **grand jury** must decide if sufficient evidence exists to try a defendant. The grand jury differs from the **petit jury** that hears evidence in criminal trials.

The **due process clause** in the Fifth Amendment derives from English legal traditions first expressed in the Magna Carta. Due process requires that no one may lose their freedom or their property as punishment for a crime unless the rules of the judicial system are followed and the rights of the individual are protected. Originally, under the Fifth Amendment, the due process standard only applied to the federal government. The Fourteenth Amendment applied it to the states as well.

Sixth Amendment

"In all criminal prosecutions, the accused shall enjoy the right to a speedy and public trial, by an impartial jury of the state and district wherein the crime shall have been committed, which district shall have been previously ascertained by law, and to be informed of the nature and cause of the accusation; to be confronted with the witnesses against him; to have compulsory process for obtaining witnesses in his favor, and to have the assistance of counsel for his defense."

The Sixth Amendment expands on the Fifth Amendment by more carefully outlining the procedures that must be followed to ensure that due process has been followed in criminal cases. This amendment codifies what was the Anglo-American common law practice of trying criminal cases through an adversarial system of jurisprudence in which the accused faces his accusers, and both sides bring witnesses who may be subpoenaed against their will, in order to present the case before a jury of their fellow citizens. This amendment also reflects the Framers' recent experience with British Admiralty Courts, in which colonists accused of violating customs laws were tried before military courts and denied jury trials.

Among the rights guaranteed the accused by the Sixth Amendment are the following:

1. Right to a speedy trial (incorporated against the states in 1967)

2. Right to a public trial (incorporated against the states in 1948)

3. Right to an impartial jury (incorporated against the states between 1966 and 1971)

4. Right to a jury from the state and district where the crime was committed (States are not required to guarantee this right.)

5. Right to be informed of accusations (incorporated against the states in 1948)

6. Right to confront accusatory witnesses (incorporated against the states in 1965)

7. Right to subpoena witnesses (incorporated against the states in 1967)

8. Right to receive legal counsel at trial (incorporated against the states 1932, 1963, and 1972)

Since 1960, the expansion of the requirement that law enforcement officers and the courts observe procedures that protect these rights illustrates the federal court system's interest in ensuring that defendants facing justice in different jurisdictions and states experience equality before the law.

Seventh Amendment

"In suits at common law, where the value in controversy shall exceed twenty dollars, the right of trial by jury shall be preserved, and no fact tried by a jury, shall be otherwise reexamined in any court of the United States, than according to the rules of the common law."

This uncontroversial amendment simply applies the principle of the right to a jury trial in federal civil cases. "Suits at common law" refers to civil rather than criminal cases. The Constitution had not originally provided for civil jury trials, even though this had been a feature of English legal traditions. Anti-Federalists saw a jury composed of residents as potentially capable of nullifying the effects of an unfair federal law.

Eighth Amendment

"Excessive bail shall not be required, nor excessive fines imposed, nor cruel and unusual punishments inflicted."

Limitations on the amount of bail that could be imposed, or the fines that could be imposed by the federal government have not proved controversial. The phrase, "nor cruel and unusual punishments inflicted," has been more difficult to precisely define. The phrase itself was found in the English Bill of Rights, and so reflects one of the "rights of Englishmen" that were incorporated into American law. Enlightenment philosophers in the second half of the 18th century also objected to the number of offenses that were capital crimes, and to the cruelty of public punishments. Furthermore, Anti-Federalists argued that the amendment was needed to prevent Congress from using torture to extort confessions and to intimidate political opponents.

Ninth Amendment

"The enumeration in the Constitution, of certain rights, shall not be construed to deny or disparage others retained by the people."

During the ratification debates over the U.S. Constitution, Anti-Federalists objected that the document lacked a Bill of Rights. Federalists responded that a listing of the rights to which American citizens were entitled would have the paradoxical effect of limiting those rights to just those that had been protected in the Constitution. The government might then feel at ease in restricting rights that had not been specified in the Bill of Rights. The Ninth Amendment was an effort to address this concern, emphasizing that the people nonetheless held rights not listed in the Constitution.

Tenth Amendment

"The powers not delegated to the United States by the Constitution, nor prohibited by it to the states, are reserved to the states respectively, or to the people."

The Tenth Amendment reaffirms the federal character of the American system of government. Powers of the federal government are limited to those granted to the federal government. For example, as the Constitution is silent on the place of education in the government—there was little in the way of public education at either state or local levels—the authority over education policy is presumed to rest with the states.

> **Competency 018 Descriptive Statement E.** The beginning teacher demonstrates knowledge of efforts to expand the democratic process in the United States and understands the contributions of significant political and social leaders (e.g., George Washington, John Marshall, Frederick Douglass, Elizabeth Cady Stanton, Franklin D. Roosevelt, Martin Luther King, Jr.).

George Washington (1732–1799)

It is difficult to distill George Washington's accomplishments and contribution to American political history in a few paragraphs. Of course, his role as commander of the Continental Army and presiding officer of the Constitutional Convention deserve mention.

In this section on American Government, however, it is best to focus attention on his role in defining the American presidency and shaping the way the new republic's institutions operated. Article II of the U.S. Constitution formally created the office of the presidency. Article II, however, provides only a bare bones structure, leaving a great deal to precedent. Because he was the first president, Washington's place in establishing precedents that would be followed by his successors was critical. The American citizenry granted to Washington a trust to shape the institution of the American presidency that they would hardly have granted to any other individual at the time.

Washington sometimes "filled in the blanks" when the Constitution offered less than clear instruction. For example, Washington established the power to remove executive branch officials from office, rejecting the view that advice and consent from the Senate was required for appointing and firing top-level government authorities. Washington also set the precedent that a president serve only two terms in office. Only Franklin D. Roosevelt overstayed that time in office.

John Marshall (1755–1835)

John Marshall was the fourth Chief Justice of the Supreme Court. He took office in 1801 on the appointment of John Adams. The Court that Marshall took over did not have a great deal of authority. It was seen as the weakest of the three branches of government. In its first decade, it had heard only 63 cases. It did not have the power of judicial review or the power to determine whether an act of Congress or the presidency was in violation of the Constitution. It was also not clear that the Supreme Court had the authority to hear cases from a single state's jurisdiction. The court also had such rapid turnover among the justices that it was difficult to carry out the court's business. When the federal government moved from Philadelphia to Washington, D.C., in 1800, no money was appropriated for the building of a Supreme Court building. The Supreme Court did not have a building of its own until 1935; until then, it met in a makeshift courtroom in the Capitol building.

It is fair to say that the Supreme Court as we know it is a creation of Chief Justice John Marshall. One simple change Marshall introduced was the wearing of black robes, a symbol of the seriousness with which he took his position. Marshall also encouraged the court to develop a sense of shared social identity as a means to overcome the partisan rivalry that characterized politics in 1801. These may seem like small things, but they created an *esprit de corps* among the justices that has continued to the present day. The most important early decision, and the one with the longest-lasting significance, was the Court's ruling in *Marbury v. Madison* that asserted the principle of **judicial review**, the principle that the federal courts had the responsibility and the right to determine the constitutionality of laws and actions of the national Congress and executive branch, as well as those of individual states. This decision, rendered in Marshall's second year in the office was an enormously brave and consequential ruling. A number of later Marshall decisions reinforced the Court's independence and authority as a coequal branch of government. The Supreme Court ruling in *Cohens v. Virginia* (1821), though less famous than the *Marbury* decision, ensured that cases from state supreme courts could be taken up by the Supreme Court. *McCullough v. Maryland* secured the principle that the Constitution granted to Congress "implied powers" to enact legislation to implement its expressed powers. The Marshall court, from 1801 to 1835, established many of the principles upon which the national government operated, and continues to operate.

Frederick Douglass (1818–1895)

Frederick Douglass was born a slave in Tuckahoe, Maryland, in 1818. At the age of 20, he escaped his master, the notorious "slave breaker" Edward Covey, and joined the famous abolitionist William Lloyd Garrison, who recognized his speaking ability and gave him a wide audience to describe the horrors of slavery. During the 1840s and 1850s, he was a renowned abolitionist and anti-slavery author. Douglass publicly agitated against slavery and took up the causes of women's suffrage, abolition of capital punishment, universal public education, and immigrant rights. He also pushed Abraham Lincoln toward declaring the emancipation of the slaves. When it became clear that the war's aims were directed to that objective, Douglass became one of the most prominent recruiters of African American soldiers into the Union army. His support for the Republican Party in the 1870s resulted in his being given a number of federal appointments. He died preparing to give a speech before the National Council of Women in 1895. While Douglass is most remembered for his activism on behalf of the progressive causes of the 19th century, he was also an important political theorist calling white America to live up to the ideals of its founding. He was also a strong supporter of the classical liberal values of self-reliance and personal responsibility united with a strong sense of the importance of community obligation and brotherhood. In combining these two stances, Douglass brought together two features of American political values that are often divided.

Elizabeth Cady Stanton (1815–1902)

Elizabeth Cady Stanton was born in 1815 to a Federalist congressman and attorney. She received a formal education at Johnstown Academy, winning awards for her academic abilities. Despite her abilities, she was unable to enroll in Union College, which only admitted male students, a slight that she would not forget. She instead went to a seminary for women in Troy, New York. While at the seminary, she was terrified by the preaching of C.G. Finney, a prominent evangelical minister, leading her eventually to reject evangelical Christianity. Instead, she turned toward social reform as a life calling, first becoming involved in the temperance movement, then abolitionism. She married Henry Brewster Stanton in 1840, making clear to him that she rejected the admonition in the wedding vows that she was, as a woman, obligated to obey her spouse. She became a part of the circle of influential reformers that included Frederick Douglass, William Lloyd Garrison, Ralph Waldo Emerson, Henry David Thoreau, and most importantly, Lucretia Mott, the Quaker feminist and abolitionist. When women who had been nominated to serve in the World Anti-Slavery Convention were refused a voice in the convention, Stanton and Mott began to focus their reforming energies on what was then called the "woman question." In 1848, she, Mott, and other prominent feminists drafted the **Declaration of Sentiments**, a declaration of women's rights modeled on the Declaration of Independence. Stanton, at the Seneca Falls Convention where the Declaration of Sentiments was drafted, met Susan B. Anthony. The two women soon began to agitate not only for women's rights within the household, but for women's rights to vote, or suffrage. The two partnered as authors and orators, with Susan B. Anthony often giving speeches that Stanton had written. The two, despite their abolitionist past, were opposed to the passage of the 14th Amendment, in large part because they viewed that this extension of the franchise as simply a further slight to women's rights to vote. As a result, she fell out with Frederick Douglass and other abolitionists. Her opposition also resulted in splits within the women's rights movement. Despite these and other splits within the African American Civil Rights movement and the Suffrage movement, Stanton is remembered as a critical voice in the expansion of the suffrage to women.

Franklin D. Roosevelt (1882–1945)

We have been introduced to Franklin D. Roosevelt on a number of occasions over the course of the previous chapters. Roosevelt served as president of the United States from 1933 until his death in 1945, and is best known for leading the nation through the Great Depression and World War II. Roosevelt's New Deal programs helped bring the country out of the Great Depression. His leadership of the nation during World War II provided a calming force during a very turbulent era. Franklin has often been credited, along with Lyndon B. Johnson, with shaping the nature of the modern presidency. In part, this resulted from the fact that he served longer than any president, remaining in office for 12 years, though he was elected four times. Following his presidency, the 22nd Amendment was passed, establishing term limits on the office. Roosevelt's New Deal and World War II policies vastly expanded the scope and size of the federal government. His use of fiscal policy (combinations of taxation and spending designed to stabilize the economy) for the first time explicitly established the government's role as a stabilizing force in the economy. Previously, presidents had hesitated to use these tools as they viewed them as unwarranted intrusions in the market economy. Such programs as Social Security, the FDIC, unemployment insurance, farm subsidies, the GI Bill, and many more became features of the relationship between the American government and its citizens. As a result of these spending programs, annual federal budget expenditures grew from just $34.9 billion in 1930 to $163 billion in 1941, the year before the start of America's involvement in World War II. During the war, federal spending increased even more, to over $900 billion.

Martin Luther King, Jr. (1929–1968)

Alongside the Framers of the Constitution and the leaders of the Revolutionary generation was a group of African American leaders almost unknown to history, who have been described as the "Black Founders." These include such figures as Lemuel Haynes, Richard Allen, Absalom Jones, and Peter Williams. Though they were not at the Philadelphia Convention, they called on the new republic in its early years to live up to the stirring sentiments of liberty and equality by putting an end to the both slavery and the slave trade, with their legacies of discrimination. Alongside these Black Founders should be added Frederick Douglass, Sojourner Truth, Harriet Tubman, and later W.E.B. Dubois and Marcus Garvey. Each of these figures again challenged Americans to live up to the better angels of their nature. Martin Luther King, Jr., has a place alongside the Black Founders, despite the fact that he lived his short life and was assassinated only a few years before the nation's bicentennial.

At the young age of 26, King found himself at the forefront of the African American Civil Rights movement. He gained nationwide fame, or notoriety, as a result of his leadership of the Montgomery bus boycott. The strength of King's appeal then and now results from his willingness to suffer for the cause of equality, economic justice, and true American idealism. He opposed violence in the face of terror and counseled forbearance when angry retaliation seemed fully justified. His iconic speeches resonate as richly among the expressions of American idealism as do the Declaration of Independence or the Gettysburg Address. He, like the other Black Founders, best expressed the true possibilities of American ideals. His contributions to changing the legal strictures of segregation and discrimination, and pressing for the right to vote for African Americans are certainly worthy of note, and were referenced earlier in this test guide. But it was his idealism, his dream, that stands out as a beacon to the country.

Barack Obama (1961–)

While it is too soon for history to give a definitive judgment on the presidency of Barack Obama, it is not too soon to reflect on its role in expanding the democratic process in the United States. For some observers, President Barack Obama, a black president, signaled an end to the racial division that has been a feature of the nation's history since Jamestown. These observers contended that his election meant that we lived in a post-racial world. For others, including the Obamas themselves, the presence of a black man and his family in the White House called the nation to a renewed reflection of and grappling with the role of race and the continuing legacy of slavery undergirding the system and symbols of American government. As Michelle Obama reminded listeners in a 2016 speech, "I wake up every morning in a house built by slaves." She made this statement as a humble acknowledgment of how much has changed in the United States, in the hope that her listeners and the nation as a whole would more clearly recognize the legacy of slavery and racism. She did not want listeners to conclude that simply because an African American was president, the legacies of slavery and racism no longer resonated.

> **Competency 018 Descriptive Statement F.** The beginning teacher demonstrates knowledge of the causes and effects of major reform movements in U.S. history (e.g., abolitionist movement, public education, temperance, women's rights, prison reform, Civil Rights movement).

Abolitionist Movement

The anti-slavery movement had deep roots before the American Revolution in England and in colonial America as Quakers, Methodists, and other religious and political figures argued that it was an inhumane institution. During the early years of the American republic, the movement seemed to stagnate. The clearest voices calling for the end of slavery came from the free African American community in Northern cities. Until the 1830s, calls for an end to slavery often emphasized the corollary that African Americans could not hope for equality or citizenship rights, and that emancipation necessitated repatriation or return to Africa. This was called the **colonization movement**. Freed blacks objected to this linkage, though Liberia was established with freed slaves. After the 1830s, abolitionism became more strident, pushed by free blacks who claimed their right to an American identity. **William Lloyd Garrison**, with a small number of other abolitionists, began the publication of Garrison's weekly abolitionist newspaper, *The Liberator*. It took a much more uncompromising stance, demanding an end to the internal slave trade and to slavery, characterizing it as the national sin. In 1833, the **American Anti-Slavery Society** was founded. Soon, Northerners were joining it and similar organizations. Many Northerners were not attracted to the radical doctrines of the abolitionists, fearing that they would lead to disruptions of the immense profits associated with slavery, particularly in banking, insurance, and commerce. But from 1830 to 1854, a growing minority of Northerners became animated by the issue of slavery and a deep desire to end its spread.

With the growth of anti-slavery fervor in the North, Southerners began to mount their own defense of the "peculiar institution." A **Pro-Slavery Ideology** emerged, which defended slavery on several fronts. Southern slavery apologists argued that: (1) Slavery was biblical; (2) Slavery was constitutional; (3) Slavery had been practiced historically in most societies, both ancient and modern; and (4) Blacks benefited from the benevolent character of American slavery, and otherwise would remain unconverted and primitive in Africa.

Public Education

American public education has its origins with the Puritans. When the Puritans first arrived on the continent, they at first did not bother with establishing school institutions. They left the education of children to Puritan parents. But then the Massachusetts Law of 1642 required all parents to find someone to teach their children how to read the Bible, how to write, and to learn the rudiments of Puritan theology and the law. In 1647, after this law had not proven sufficient, the **Old Deluder Satan Law of 1647** required that each town with 50 households had to hire a schoolteacher, and each town with more than 100 households had to build a school and hire necessary teachers. Out of these New England institutions, the first public schools in English-speaking North America developed. The New England schools were a public system of education, but were supported by tuition and fees.

In contrast to the system of grammar schools that developed in New England and in the Middle Colonies, the Southern states only belatedly developed a comparable system of schools. In part, this delay reflected the realities of the plantation system. On the plantation, sons and daughters learned from their parents, and occasionally from tutors. Enslaved Africans received no formal education; nor was there interest in using public money for the poor whites in the region. As Scots-Irish settlers moved into the Appalachian backcountry, opportunities for education were also scarce.

During the 18th century, Benjamin Franklin became one of the most vocal advocates for the education of American youth. Franklin established the American Philosophical Society and a subscription library in Philadelphia to make books and reading material available to the city's residents. Franklin also promoted the development of a secular education that combined a classical curriculum with technical skills such as surveying, navigation, and mechanical training.

The Northwest Ordinances of 1785 and 1787 laid the groundwork for public education in the Great Lakes region. The 1785 Land Ordinance specified that a one-square-mile section of land in each township be set aside to endow the building of a public school. The 1787 ordinance set aside two townships in each state for the establishment of a university. The land grants were to be rented out to fund the schools and to pay for student tuition. The practice of establishing land-grant schools provided an important model for public education in other regions.

As the U.S. Constitution did not grant to the federal government the authority over education, educational matters were reserved for the states under the 10th Amendment. Gradually, in each state lawmakers began to address the establishment of local school districts, mostly by encouraging local governments to vote support for their funding and administration. Any state aid came from sale of public land, taxes, and lotteries.

In the 1830s and 1840s, the efforts of **Horace Mann (1796–1859)** resulted in a **common school** movement of public schools. Mann argued that education was needed to develop a citizenry of thoughtful and informed people. Education thus was seen as performing a function of inculcating republican virtue in young people. These schools would also encourage students to learn a respect for property rights. Mann also emphasized that the schools provided a means for the better educated elites to exert social control over the populace. He and his colleague **Henry Barnard** proposed a system of state-funded public schools in Connecticut. The model education developed by these two reformers has persisted in many ways to the present. Each school district was to be supported by local taxes, with an elected board of trustees and a full-time administrator. Schooling would begin with a primary-school education for students from age 8 to age 12. Following this fundamental education, students would graduate to secondary schools. These would offer both a college-preparatory curriculum in the Greek and Latin classics for the more capable students, and more technical and practical education for students of lesser abilities. Though the adoption of the common school system was spotty at first, by the late 19th century many states had adopted it and were funding the schools with local property tax levies. In poorer and less populated rural areas, the one-room schoolhouse predominated. There, students were jumbled together according to ability rather than age. In the common school and in most urban districts, however, the practice took hold of placing students at grade level to allow for a more efficient passage through the curriculum.

After Horace Mann, perhaps the most influential American educational reformer was **John Dewey (1859–1952)**, a Progressive Era educator. Dewey objected to the trend of the late 19th century that sought to offer an academic education for the elites, while only a simplified vocational education for the masses. He also objected to the development of educational methods that emphasized intelligence testing and efficiency-driven management of classrooms and schools. He and other progressive educators argued that education should not be driven by utilitarian aims of creating workers or managers. Instead, he called for a holistic education of the entire person and a system of education that led to the transformation of the social order. One reform that he and others advocated was the development of "ungraded schools." During the Cold War, however, his educational ideas came to be viewed with a good deal of skepticism. As the Cold War, and then the post–Cold War, educational system began to emphasize the need for competitive science, mathematics, and technical expertise, Dewey's call for a socially transformative education fell out of fashion.

In 1983, a new wave of public education reform began, following the publication of a report entitled *A Nation at Risk: The Imperative for Educational Reform*. A blue-ribbon panel of educators considered low levels of American academic performance compared to other developed nations, high rates of functional illiteracy among American adults, and increased costs by universities, businesses, and the armed forces for remedial education and concluded that the nation's education system needed radical change. A series of reforms were proposed, and across the country, states set about assessing the levels of student performance. School spending increased, particularly for the STEM (science, technology, engineering, mathematics) fields. Under the presidency of George W. Bush, an initiative known as the No Child Left Behind (NCLB) Act, was passed with strong bipartisan agreement. The reform significantly increased federal oversight of public schools, mandating a wide range of assessment tools to measure student achievement. It also mandated that groups of disadvantaged students (English-language learners, poor and minority children, and special education students) improve their test scores and achievement. To enforce compliance, the NCLB Act threatened withdrawal of federal funding for school districts that did not make progress toward the standards the NCLB proposed. This was a significant expansion of federal intrusion into what had largely been a state prerogative.

Temperance

It may come as a surprise to learn that 19th-century Americans consumed far more alcohol per capita than do Americans today. In part, this was because transport costs for grain meant it was more profitable to distill much of it into whiskey, brandy, or gin before marketing it. In the 1830s, the average American annually consumed over seven gallons of absolute liquor. By comparison, today Americans consume 2.8 gallons of pure liquor per person per year. The impact of this consumption was felt most heavily by women and children, as men often consumed the family paycheck or came home in drunken rages. In 1825, Lyman Beecher began a campaign against the use of alcohol. The following year, evangelical Protestants created the American Temperance Society. By 1834, there were more than 5,000 state and local temperance societies. Alcohol consumption served as a symbol of a variety of social ills. The clergy declared it sinful. Physicians associated it with illness. Middle-class women attributed the abuse of women and family poverty to alcohol use. Factory owners saw it as a threat to efficiency and profits. Native-born Americans associated it with Irish and German immigrants. The temperance movement did not immediately have a great deal of influence. During the Progressive Era, the "war on alcohol" finally succeeded with the passage of the 18th Amendment, which banned the sale of alcohol nationwide between 1920 and 1933, when the amendment was repealed.

Women's Rights

In the 19th century, women could not vote. If married, they had no right to own property outright. Furthermore, they had no right to retain their own earnings. The temperance, abolitionist, Sabbatarian, and prison reform movements, however, provided opportunities for women to become involved in public political activity outside the home, while still acting within their "proper sphere." Fighting for these causes, they demonstrated their moral authority, which was said to derive from their maternal and spiritual strengths.

CHAPTER 7

Early feminists initially did not really set out to challenge restrictions to women, but their experiences within reform movements radicalized them and led them to champion women's rights. For example, women's involvement in the abolitionist movement highlighted the parallels of their own experience with the powerlessness of slaves. The discrimination they faced within the abolitionist movement led women like Elizabeth Cady Stanton and Susan B. Anthony to advocate more forcefully for their own rights. As we have already seen, Elizabeth Cady Stanton and other leading women gathered in 1848 at the Seneca Falls Convention and developed their own *Declaration of Sentiments* modeled on the Declaration of Independence. Beginning with the assertion that "all men and women are created equal," the convention passed a number of resolutions, including a call for women's suffrage.

After the Civil War, momentum for the suffrage movement initially stalled as the women's movement split over the 14th Amendment. Before 1920, as a result of the activism and legal challenges mounted by Susan B. Anthony and others, women had full voting rights in 14 states and could vote in presidential elections in 11 states. In 1920, with the passage of the 19th Amendment, women's demand for suffrage was finally granted.

Following the expansion of women's civil and political rights, women also began to push for greater economic independence and personal autonomy. The "Jazz Age" saw an increase in women in the work place, particularly younger, unmarried women. Young women also began to demonstrate more social independence. This newfound independence reflected changes in the consumer culture of the 1920s. The automobile had a significant impact on courtship practices, for example, as did other social developments of the period.

In contrast to the 1920s, women during the Great Depression who went to work were often married, slightly older, and somewhat better educated than those in the 1920s. Family hardship sometimes forced women to work. Those who already earned wages continued to work, even in poor-paying jobs. Those who didn't, began to work for the first time. Even before the beginning of World War II, women's workforce participation was much higher than it had been in the 19th and early 20th centuries. In addition to these workplace changes, Roosevelt's New Deal programs and Roosevelt's commitment to appoint women to some important government posts gave further impetus to women's issues.

World War II also contributed to the rise of the women's movement in the 20th century. Many women participated in the war effort in a variety of official roles. World War II gave women's work a certain public status that it had lacked before. Now, women who went to work did so patriotically, while they had done so defensively before. With the "Rosie the Riveter" and "Margin for Victory" public service announcements, many women took the opportunity to enter the work place. Nearly 20 million women were in the workforce in 1945, well over the 11.5 million women who were working just five years before. Additionally, women's work during the war was in higher-wage, skilled positions, giving women for the first time the experience of being principal breadwinners. One factor that resulted in a rise in feminism after the war was the fact that the government and employers considered this increase in women's employment opportunity a decidedly temporary phenomenon. When the GIs came home again, many women who had enjoyed the experience of socially and economically rewarding work resented being laid off.

Women's employment during the 1950s, though it lacked the social status and earning potential it had during the war, continued to grow. Nonetheless, many women were excluded from a wide range of professions. Moreover, the prevailing middle-class ideal emphasized women's roles as homemakers, secretaries, teachers, and other fields traditionally held for women. Many middle-class women, particularly those who had gone to college, resented their inability to advance professionally and resented the burdens of homemaking that fell almost exclusively on women.

The 1960s and 1970s saw the rise of what has been called "second-wave" feminism, differentiating it from the suffrage movement in the 19th and early 20th centuries. In 1963, Betty Friedan's publication of *The Feminine Mystique* galvanized many middle-class women to fight for equal opportunities in education, pay, and occupations. Opponents of the Civil Rights Act of 1964, seeking to derail the bill, insisted on adding prohibitions against discrimination on the basis of sex to the bill, believing that this would surely lead to such opposition that the bill would be unable to pass. This strategy backfired, as the bill passed largely as a result of women's support for the measure. The formation of the National Organization for Women (NOW) in 1966 attracted many women who had formerly been involved in the Civil Rights movement to bring many of the same methods to bear on women's issues. While the movement experienced significant successes in increasing economic opportunities and protections against discrimination, one of the more important efforts, the **Equal Rights Amendment,** has not been ratified, even though in 1973, 30 of the 38 states needed for ratification had voted in favor of the amendment.

Prison Reform

Prisons are a relatively new feature of punishment for criminal behavior. Before the early 19th century, punishments usually consisted of a combination of public humiliation, corporal punishment, banishment, or bonded labor. Often these punishments were extremely harsh. For example, a first-time convicted thief in Massachusetts would be fined, and if unable to pay the fine, would be whipped. A third-time offender faced the death penalty. There were also many more crimes that carried the penalty of capital punishment. In the 18th century, Enlightenment thinkers such as Cesare Beccaria, Voltaire, Montesquieu, and, in America, Thomas Jefferson, Benjamin Franklin, and Dr. Benjamin Rush, began to raise objections to the cruel and inhumane nature of many of these punishments. As a Virginia legislator, for example, Thomas Jefferson attempted to end the death penalty in Virginia, except in cases of murder and treason, a proposal that was only defeated by a single vote. It was largely from this sentiment that the Eighth Amendment prohibits **cruel and unusual punishment.**

In the early 19th century, a prison reform movement gathered steam. Pennsylvania, with its large population of Quakers, led the way. Already in 1786, the Pennsylvania legislature did away with the death penalty for theft and robbery cases, and then in 1794, it eliminated the death penalty entirely except for convictions for first-degree murder. Pennsylvania then adopted a **penitentiary system** to punish criminals. In 1829, Pennsylvania built its first prison, distinguished from a jail, which housed prisoners awaiting trial. Eastern State Penitentiary, which in the 20th century housed the notorious Al Capone and "Slick Willie" Sutton, at its origins represented a humanitarian alternative to the harsh physical punishments that had once been commonplace. The reformers who promoted the penitentiary movement, many of them Quakers, argued that criminal behavior resulted from corrupting social influences. The penitentiary placed prisoners in solitary confinement, often for years, where they were required to silently contemplate their crimes. The objective was for the criminal to become penitent, or truly sorry for his crimes. Prisoners were to spend their time in scriptural devotion and individual reflection. One of the leading figures in this movement was **Dorothea Dix**, who also sought to improve treatment of mental illness.

Serious questions arose in the late 19th century about the effectiveness and humaneness of these prisons. The cruel methods of ensuring silence, and the effects of prolonged periods of isolation, were questioned. Additionally, overcrowding had become a major problem. Lack of public investment in new prisons meant that most convicts were housed in dilapidated and crowded conditions. New psychological theories that explained criminal behavior by reference to psychopathology or social deviance, rather than moral failure, also encouraged new methods of punishment. Progressive reformers called for an end to corporal punishment and hard labor, and an increase in such programs as job training, literacy education, and other methods for reducing recidivism.

More recently, as a consequence of mandatory sentencing requirements and the "War on Drugs," the United States has incarcerated more of its citizens and at higher percentages than has any other country. As a result, since 2008, an increasing effort to eliminate mandatory minimums, to decriminalize marijuana usage, and to otherwise reduce the percentage of Americans in prison has gained some momentum.

Civil Rights Movement

The story of the Civil Rights movement began in earnest in the aftermath of the ***Plessy v. Ferguson*** ruling in which the Supreme Court affirmed the principle of separate but equal, opening the way for many other "Jim Crow" laws to be passed and for restrictions on black civil rights across the South and elsewhere. In 1909, the National Association for the Advancement of Colored People (NAACP) was founded to develop political and legal challenges to segregation. Many of the cases the NAACP took up gradually undermined the practice of segregation, well before the Civil Rights movement of the 1950s and 1960s galvanized the nation. For example, in ***Norris v. Alabama* (1935)** the Supreme Court questioned the absence of African Americans from juries in cases involving black defendants. In ***Gaines v. State of Missouri* (1938),** the Court ruled that the University of Missouri must allow the entry of a qualified African American entrant, as no blacks-only law school existed in the state.

World War II also contributed to the development of an African-American Civil Rights movement. Just as was the case for women, increased employment for African Americans in wartime industries had created new demands for equality and fair treatment. Additionally, more than 870,000 African Americans served in the armed forces, many with distinction, despite their service in segregated units. The irony of fighting for "liberty" while having their own civil rights denied was not lost on African American soldiers. One famously remarked, "Just carve on my tombstone, here lies a black man killed fighting a yellow man for the protection of a white man." The successes of black units, however, did encourage military and political leaders to reconsider the effects of racially discrimination in the military. In 1948, Harry Truman issued **Executive Order 9981** ending segregation in the military. The GI bill, which provided many African American veterans the opportunity to receive college educations or technical education, contributed to an increase in the number of middle-class African Americans, many of whom would take lead roles in the 1950s Civil Rights movement.

On May 17, 1954, the Supreme Court unanimously ruled in ***Brown v. Board of Education* of *Topeka*** that racially segregated schools violated the constitutional principle of equal treatment for all citizens. African American Civil Rights leaders then sought to open new fronts in the assault on segregation by using nonviolent demonstrations, such as bus boycotts, sit-ins at lunch counters, and "freedom rides" to protest segregated public accommodations. These nonviolent protests often involved liberal white activists and African Americans who took great risks in the face of police violence and vigilante attacks. A number of Civil Rights organizations formed to push for African American civil rights. Among these were the Southern Christian Leadership, the Student Nonviolent Coordinating Committee, and the Congress of Racial Equality.

The result of these group efforts and political pressure on legislatures ended *de jure* segregation in public schools. *De facto* segregation, however, remains a significant problem across the country even today. The Civil Rights Act of 1964, another significant victory of the Civil Rights movement, has opened up new legal avenues for African Americans facing discrimination, as well as for other groups who have experienced a history of legal and societal discrimination.

Competency 018 Descriptive Statement G. The beginning teacher understands civic responsibilities (e.g., jury duty), the difference between personal and civic responsibilities, and the importance of voluntary individual participation in the U.S. political process.

Key Question

The American system of liberal democracy depends on the principle of limited government. An important corollary to limited government, however, is civic participation. For a republic to function requires that citizens take seriously their many responsibilities as citizens. What are citizen responsibilities, and why are they important to the workings of the American republic?

Political Participation

Political participation takes a variety of forms, including, voting, service on jury duty, office holding, and a variety of forms of advocacy.

Voting

In 1960, 62.8 percent of Americans eligible to vote pulled the lever for either John F. Kennedy or Richard M. Nixon. Over the course of the next three-and-a-half decades, voter participation rates steadily declined. Only 49 percent of Americans of voter age chose Bill Clinton over his Republican rival, Bob Dole, and the third-party candidate, Ross Perot. In the 21st century elections, participation has risen, to nearly the heights of the 1960 election. In 2016, 60.2 percent of eligible voters turned out, compared to 58.6 percent in 2012 and 62.2 percent who chose Barack Obama over John McCain.

By comparison to other world democracies, however, the United States lags significantly behind in terms of voter participation. Voter turnout in the 2016 election ranked 27th among the most recent elections of other developed democracies. Israel, Iceland, the Netherlands, Norway, Australia, Denmark, South Korea, Sweden, and Belgium all had more than 75 percent of eligible voters cast ballots in their last national election.

Why do other countries have much higher rates of voter participation? There are a number of answers.

Some countries, Belgium for example, have compulsory voting requirements. In the United States, political participation in all forms is voluntary, and it seems unlikely that this will change, nor should it.

One answer is that in most other developed democracies, voting is encouraged in a number of ways that it is not in the United States. Many countries have made election day a national paid holiday for workers, or elections are held on weekends. These encouragements have had the effect of making voting easier for working people.

Some argue that voter registration systems in the United States are onerous and make registration difficult. Americans lag significantly behind some countries in the number of citizens who register to vote. Canada, which has comparable voting participation rates to our own, makes it much easier to register; consequently, they have nearly 91 percent registration rates, compared to only about 64 percent for the United States. One answer is to make voter registration automatic. When a citizen reaches the age for voter eligibility, they are automatically eligible. The principal impediment to such common-sense approaches in the United States has been political party resistance. Voter suppression or expansion of the voting pool benefits one party or the other; therefore, there is often little incentive to support measures that would increase this vital feature of any democracy.

Voting is not the only form of political participation asked of citizens in a liberal democracy. The following are but a few ways in which citizens have historically played a role in the civic life of the nation and of the community: (1) writing letters to local newspapers expressing an opinion on a national or local matter, (2) running for or holding local office, (3) joining a local organization championing a local cause, (4) writing or calling a congressman or senator, (5) attending political rallies or speeches, (6) attending a public meeting held on a local or school issue, (7) participating in local political party organizations, (8) volunteering on a political campaign, (8) donating to a political or social cause, (9) becoming a member and supporting a nonprofit or political interest group,

Not surprisingly, lags in voter participation have correlated to declines in other forms of political participation; since the 1970s, fewer and fewer Americans have participated in any of the above roles.

Jury Duty

In a given year, more than 3 million Americans serve on jury duty. One-third of all Americans will be empaneled on a jury during their lifetime. Often, however, the arrival of a jury summons is received as a burden. This response reveals how Americans often consider jury service as a "duty" rather than a "right."

It is important to recognize service on a jury panel not as an onerous responsibility but as a right, a right that was systematically denied African Americans until long after an 1880 case, **Strauder v. West Virginia,** which overturned a state law that excluded African Americans from juries. Despite that ruling, even as recently as the 1980s, peremptory challenges to individual African American jurors solely on the basis of their racial identity were commonplace. In 1986, in a challenge to this practice, Justice Anthony Kennedy argued that citizens are entitled to "the juror's right to sit." Kennedy described jury duty not as a responsibility or duty, but as a moment when each citizen is invested with a "kind of magistracy" or authority. Service on a jury is an educational opportunity when each citizen who participates becomes part of the government and acts to enforce and interpret the law.

COMPETENCY 019 (TYPES OF POLITICAL SYSTEMS)

The teacher understands the development of political systems and the similarities and differences among major historical and contemporary forms of government.

> **Competency 019 Descriptive Statement A.** The beginning teacher understands major political ideas in history (e.g., the laws of nature and nature's God, divine right of monarchs, social contract theory, the rights of resistance to illegitimate governments) and analyzes the historical development of significant legal and political concepts.

The ideas that helped shape the political philosophy of the Framers of the Constitution and the first generation of American leaders came from a number of traditions, including classical liberalism, republicanism, traditions of common law, Protestantism, natural rights theory, social contract theory, and many other intellectual strands. They were influenced by the writings of John Locke, Thomas Hobbes, and the English Commonwealth men (17th century proponents of limitations on monarchical government). They also found justification for the right to rebel against absolutist monarchies in the writing of 16th century French Protestant Theodore Beza and others. The ideas of Enlightenment *philosophes* from France also are evident in the structures of government put in place by the Framers. As such, the United States Constitution, and American ideals of good government have been developed from many strands of European political philosophy.

Divine Right of Kings

In establishing a republic, the American "Founding Fathers" departed fundamentally from the most common form of government in world and European history. European monarchs had, since the Middle Ages, asserted a divine right to rule. During the 16th and 17th centuries, particularly under the Stuart kings in England and Louis XIV in France, theorists of divine right monarchy emphasized the absolute authority of kings and the obligation of subjects to be obedient to their rule. Divine right theorists relied on Biblical admonitions to demand dutiful obedience to royal authority. The Biblical first man, Adam, they argued, was "declared the Lord and Sovereign of his Wife." Like a father and husband, divine right theorists argued, a king had absolute authority over his subjects, as well as a duty to protect them and discipline them. They often quoted from Paul's *Epistle to the Romans*, "Be obedient to the higher powers. For there is no authority except from God, and those which exist are from God." (Romans 13:1) Divine right theorists also used bodily imagery to explain the relationship between kings and subjects: the king was the head in relationship to arms, legs, and torso; the head directed the other bodily members, and the body could not function if the lower body began to govern the head.

The Right to Resist

The right to rebel against established authorities comes from two strands of Western thinking. The first of these strands was the theory of Protestant reformers during the Protestant Reformation that Catholic rulers unjustly oppressed the new Christian sects. In response, the Protestant reformers developed religious justifications for opposition to tyrannical rule. Some, like Jean Calvin, argued that only other rulers, themselves divinely appointed, could legally make war against tyrants. Others contended that lower officials, nobles, or town councils could legally resist injustice by tyrannical and immoral rulers. Those who claimed a right to use force to remove a tyrannical ruler nonetheless agreed that this was not a right that extended to the wider populace. When German peasants drew on Lutheran teachings to justify their rebellion against authorities in the Holy Roman Empire, Martin Luther encouraged brutal repression of the peasants. The right to rebel was later strengthened by the natural rights theories developed by Thomas Hobbes and John Locke.

Natural Law, Social Contract, and Rights Theories

The English philosophers Thomas Hobbes and John Locke developed views of government that didn't rely on religious explanations for the origins of political power and the state. Where divine right theorists had argued that political institutions had been created by God, Hobbes and Locke situated the origins of political institutions in nature. Hobbes and Locke argued that humans, before the development of social and political institutions, had existed in a "**state of nature**." In the state of nature, humans were free and equal.

Thomas Hobbes had pessimistically viewed the state of nature as characterized by a brutal equality and "war of all against all." Each individual had a natural right to anything they could take or do regardless of how this behavior affected others. In such a state of nature, individuals had the absolute right of self-defense, even against those more powerful than themselves—a justification for rebellion of a kind. In Hobbes' view, governments represented a compact among equal individuals who joined together to protect themselves and to promote peace, or at least to end war between one another. The state therefore developed from a **social contract**, and not from divine establishment.

With Hobbes, **John Locke** shared the view that government developed from a social contract established in the state of nature. Like Hobbes, Locke argued that "all Men are created equal," but he added to this equality the contention that they have certain **natural rights**, including the rights to "life, liberty and property." Humans entered into a primordial social contract that established the state, according to Locke, whose purpose was not to end a state of perpetual violence, but to protect those natural rights. Indeed, for Locke, the protection of these natural rights was the primary purpose of government. As a consequence of this contractual conception of government, Locke concluded, when the government violated the terms of that contract by threatening the life, liberty, or property of the community and thereby violating its public trust, citizens had a right to dissolve the bonds that tied individuals to the state. Locke articulated a right to rebellion, rather than resistance. Locke was not describing a right to resist, in order to bring to justice a state that had violated its contractual obligations. Instead, Locke's theory of natural rights justified the dissolution of governments that failed to protect life, liberty, and property. In short, Locke's argument justified revolution.

The Declaration of Independence reflected clearly the influence of Locke's ideas. In the second paragraph of the text, Jefferson invoked Locke's "natural" (Jefferson characterized them as "unalienable") rights: life, liberty, and (instead of Locke's "property") the "pursuit of Happiness." Jefferson contended that it was to secure these rights that governments were formed, or as he wrote: "instituted among Men." Jefferson contended that this contractual character of the establishment of governments is reflected in the fact that the government derived its "just powers from the consent of the governed."

The first paragraph of the Declaration of Independence reveals a second important influence on Jefferson, and the Framers of the Constitution as well. Jefferson references the "Laws of Nature" and of "Nature's God." This language reveals a very different conception of nature and the divine than that which sustained the Divine Right of Kings.

The Divine Right of Kings depended upon the God of the Bible that intervened in human affairs to set kings upon their thrones, who miraculously revealed himself to humankind, and who ordered obedience to earthly rulers. For Thomas Jefferson, Benjamin Franklin, George Washington, and many other early American political leaders, influenced by Locke and other 18th-century Enlightenment thinkers, Nature's God was the God of deism. This God established the laws of nature that governed the material world at the moment of creation, and then left the creation alone, like a watchmaker who fashions a timepiece, winds it up, and then lets it operate untouched. The God of Nature was evident in the creation, and in the natural laws that directed the creation. The government that the Framers established did not claim a legitimacy based on divine ordination, but depended upon the agreement of the people.

> **Competency 019 Descriptive Statement B.** The beginning teacher demonstrates knowledge of significant political documents and the philosophies of individuals in world history (e.g., Hammurabi's Code of Laws, Justinian's Code of Laws, Magna Carta, John Locke, Thomas Hobbes) and their impact on the development of political thought.

Hammurabi's Code of Laws

Hammurabi's Code of Laws is often said to be the first law code in human history. Hammurabi was the king of Babylon from ca. 1792 to 1750 BCE. Hammurabi's Code, in all likelihood, was a compilation and systematization of already existing law in the Mesopotamian region the code would have an important effect on later legal traditions. The code lists 282 laws and their punishments, covering a wide range of public and private offenses. Punishments were harsh; the death penalty was meted out for many offenses and for those that did not require death, maiming, branding, burning, whipping, and property forfeitures were commonplace. The code is often described as an example of the *Lex talionis,* or law of retaliation, in which the offense merits a comparable punishment: "an eye for an eye, and a tooth for a tooth."

Justinian's Code of Laws

Beginning in 529 CE the Byzantine emperor Justinian published a codification of Roman civil law, known as the *Corpus Iuris Civilis* or the *Body of Civil Law.* Roman laws had accumulated over time as the Roman Senate and the Roman emperors had enacted legislation, established decrees, and judged cases. Often these decisions and enactments were contradictory, confusing, or out-of-date. After all, the Roman Republic dated back more than 1,000 years from the time of Justinian. Justinian in 528 CE had ordered a team of lawyers and scholars to update and systematize Roman law. While Justinian's Code of Laws became the law of the Byzantine Empire, the recovery of the *Corpus Iuris Civilis* by Western Europeans beginning in the 12th century would inspire a reconsideration of medieval European law, which was largely reflective of Germanic custom, and the development of European legal traditions that were drawn from the ancient Roman tradition. Because England did not incorporate the Justinian Code in its traditions to the same degree as did European continental nations, the English Common Law tradition has been more influential on American jurisprudence than the Roman, and later Napoleonic Code. Only in Louisiana have the French and Spanish codes (ultimately derived from Justinian's codification) been the basis of civil law in the state.

Magna Carta

The Great Charter of the Liberties, or Magna Carta, was signed, rather unhappily, by King John I of England in 1215 CE. The kingdom's rebellious nobility had forced him to do so in exchange for ending their rebellion. The United States traces its legal traditions, as well as its Constitution and many of its federal and state statutes, to English common law. The Magna Carta contributed significantly to developments that would be important to American jurisprudence. For example, the English idea of due process was first enshrined in the Magna Carta, which states, "No freeman shall be arrested, or detained in prison, or deprived of his freehold, or outlawed, or banished, or in any way molested, . . . unless by lawful judgment of his peers and by the law of the lands." The Magna Carta also contributed to Anglo-American jurisprudence the provision that taxation be by consent. While this clause did not entirely protect against arbitrary taxation, the idea of "no taxation without representation," deemed a key English freedom, can be traced back to the Magna Carta. Magna Carta also contained provisions for a jury of one's peers (in the 13th century this was afforded only to peers or nobility); and prohibitions against the sale or delay of justice.

Thomas Hobbes (1588–1679)

As we have seen, Thomas Hobbes played an important role in the development of **social contract** theory. Hobbes, along with Niccolò Machiavelli, is often credited with applying principles of science to politics. Whereas Christian religious thinkers in early modern Europe saw the origins of politics and the law in the necessity to control sinful behavior after the "fall of man" in the Garden of Eden, Hobbes offered an explanation that did not require divine intervention or judgment. Neither was it inevitable. Instead, civil society and political institutions developed out of the decisions of free and equal individuals who entered into agreements to form social institutions, including the state, in order to gain security.

John Locke (1632–1704)

John Locke has already been referenced frequently in this and other chapters. His conception of the contractual relationship between the governed and the state strongly influenced American political thinkers like Thomas Jefferson. Locke held that the sovereign governed only with the consent of the governed, and that loss of that consent would result in the legitimate and rightful revolution or reform of that government. Locke's view of humans as being born equally and without innate knowledge, in other words as a *tabula rasa* or blank slate, contributed significantly to the view, written into the Declaration of Independence, that all "men are created equal." The idea that all humans are born without innate knowledge has also been an important argument for the necessity of public education as a means to shape citizens in a classical republic. The argument that citizens, through their representatives, should be consulted when taxation decisions are made also derives from, among other sources, Locke's view that each individual is born with a natural right to property ownership. When that property is being appropriated by the state, even for legitimate reasons, the citizenry must give their consent. Locke was the most important thinker and an influence on revolutionary Americans as they considered their right to rebel against the British crown and their right to reconstitute a new republican form of government.

> **Competency 019 Descriptive Statement C.** The beginning teacher analyzes how governments have affected and reflected cultural values and provided for social control.

Culture is a term with many meanings. It often refers to what was once called "high culture" (literature, the arts, fine wine, painting, poetry, expensive tastes in clothing, etc.). One who has a refined palate for the finer things in life has often been said to be "cultured." Popular culture—television, popular music or writing, movies, etc.—references the "culture of the masses." When anthropologists, sociologists, or political scientists use the term *culture*, they are referring to the beliefs and behavior of a population or social group, that reflect the role of such things as the meaning and place of family life, religious folkways and beliefs, economic behavior and attitudes, or political assumptions and actions. The term *culture* is thus a catch-all or umbrella term that allows social scientists to study differences between nationalities, or regional communities, or classes to determine how a battery of cultural values influence policy decisions, or vice versa.

Political culture, one dimension of the broad category of culture, incorporates the beliefs and behavior of a group or nation shares about power, politics, and government. One value shared by Americans, along with most people in the Western world, is the ideal of individual freedom. This freedom extends beyond the private sphere and includes individual freedom of political expression or belief. Liberal democracies share the conviction that individual political expression is the cornerstone of our political institutions. As a result, most Americans believe that it is reasonable for an individual to engage in peaceful protest against policies with which one disagrees. Moreover, most Americans consider it not only reasonable for individuals to protest, but also for governments to protect that right. This shared cultural conviction has been upheld in the courts. In 1977, when the National Socialist (Nazi) Party of America planned a march through the predominantly Jewish municipality of Skokie, Illinois, on the outskirts of Chicago, the city, fearing violent counter-demonstrations and property destruction, filed an injunction forbidding the Nazis from demonstrating in the town. The Supreme Court ruled that this was a violation of the Nazi Party members'

First Amendment rights. While most Americans likely agreed with the residents of Skokie in their abhorrence of Nazism, the court's decision also illustrated the importance to Americans of the right to political expression. More recently, a demonstration in Dallas in July 2016 against fatal police shootings was marred by the ambush and murder of five policemen by a sniper unconnected to the march. A large police presence was at the march not only to protect downtown properties and ensure that the rally remained peaceful, but also in large part to protect the marchers. It is poignant that five policemen gave their lives ensuring the right of marchers to peacefully express dissatisfaction, shared by a significant proportion of the Dallas community, with what they perceived as unjust use of force by the very police force that protected them from the sniper that evening. Other values shared by Americans, in addition to the right to individual political expression, are the value of **egalitarianism** (or belief in basic equality before the law) and the right of all Americans to pursue their own economic and personal interests.

While shared cultural values help provide an important cultural frame within which Americans can interact in the political sphere, competing cultural values also contribute to changes in public policy and governmental institutions. Elections in America are often less about policies, which are not well understood by the majority of the electorate, than by the ability of a politician or political party to tap into widely held cultural beliefs. Political behavior is largely mobilized as much by group identification, a feature of culture, as by individual values or beliefs.

Another way to perceive the role of culture on government is to consider the ways in which different cultural groups think about government. Sociologists have identified three categories of political culture that reflect these viewpoints: parochial, subject, and participatory cultures. People who live in **parochial** cultures emphasize a strong commitment to traditional values and perceive political, social, and economic change with suspicion. In parochial cultures, individuals prioritize their own or their family's benefit when considering their interaction with the political system. As a result, they often view government quite negatively and consequently avoid participation in or engagement with the political system. In **subject cultures,** people have a more positive, but passive, relationship to the political system and government. Subject cultures are most often associated with centralized, authoritarian political systems. In subject cultures, citizens accept the legitimacy of the state, are obedient to its authority, but do not consider it important that they play a role in shaping the law or the institutions of the state. **Participatory cultures** are composed of citizens that tend to internalize and value their roles as active participants in the political institutions of the society. They recognize the need to be active in their evaluation of policies and governmental institutions. They prioritize knowledge and understanding of politics and government. The citizen is expected to obey the law and to be loyal to the nation-state, but is also expected to knowledgeably participate in the political sphere.

People in less developed nations are often supposed to fall more into the parochial side of the political cultural spectrum and people who live in modern democracies are thought to reflect the influence of more participant cultures. People who live under more authoritarian governments are often thought to reflect the values of subject cultures. The United States, like most political cultures, exhibits evidence of all three typologies of political culture.

People in all cultures apply evaluative standards to virtually everything. These judgments, both collective and individual, reflect opinions of whether something is good or bad, beautiful or distasteful, useful or not, etc. **Social control**, broadly speaking, describes nearly all human practices or institutions that exist to ensure that people conform to socially accepted standards. Often, as is the case with law, the courts, police, and the criminal justice system, these institutions of social control are intentioned and punitively enforced. As often, social control mechanisms develop organically out of such cultural practices as childrearing, mate selection, business practices, or almost any other means of ensuring that people conform to normative practices. Social control mechanisms are virtually all practices that define and police socially deviant behavior. In this context, **deviance** is defined as any behavior that violates either formal or informal cultural norms.

Such behavior, of course, can be criminalized. Driving while intoxicated is a crime. But it was once considered a minor matter and did not occasion much social objection. Since the 1970s, legislators have strengthened the punishments for DUI offenses, and the police have increased enforcement measures to catch and punish intoxicated drivers. At the same time, driving under the influence has also become more socially unacceptable. In part, this is because of the lobbying efforts of such organizations as Mothers Against Drunk Driving (MADD), public service announcements, and the like.

Social control mechanisms need not require legislation or policing measures. There are certain words that are no longer acceptable in public, which once were widely used. It is no longer acceptable to refer to African Americans as "colored." The designation "Negro" is also unacceptable. And, of course, more objectionable epithets that were always seen as hurtful, racist, and demeaning are now unutterable in the public square. Many other examples of the evolution of language usage would apply here. What is often disparagingly termed "political correctness" is merely a means of social control that usually lacks legal or policing force. This is not to say that one uses language that deviates from the norm without consequences. These consequences may be felt in the workplace; there are certain questions asked in a hiring setting, or words used in the office, that will result in human resources investigations and potentially in loss of employment. Social control mechanisms can even take more informal forms. We learn rapidly as children from the visible reactions, facial expressions, and objections of parents or other adults what is acceptable speech, or in what contexts certain behaviors are appropriate or inappropriate.

Competency 019 Descriptive Statement D. The beginning teacher understands similarities and differences between the U.S. constitutional republic and other contemporary forms of government.

Federal Presidential Republic

The United States is a constitutional federal republic. In such a system, power is shared between a federal government and a number of state or provincial governments. The United States is not the only world government with a constitutional federal system. Mexico also has a federal presidential republic, as does Nigeria.

Presidential Republic

A presidential republic is a system of government in which the executive branch is in the hands of a president who acts as both head of state and head of government. A head of state is the public face of a nation. A head of state who is not also head of government serves as a sort of figurehead and lacks significant power over government. In a presidential republic, the executive is entirely distinct from the legislative branch.

Additionally, and quite distinct from the system in the United States, a presidential republic has a **unitary system** rather than a federal system of government. In a unitary system of government, the central or national government has supreme authority over other governmental entities that exercise only the powers delegated to them by the national government. The subnational units of government are said to be the creatures of the national government. Most states worldwide have unitary systems of government.

According to the *CIA World Factbook,* the presidential republic form of government is the most prevalent form of government in the contemporary world. It is the most frequently found form of government in Latin America, Africa, and the former Soviet Union. It is less often found in Europe. The first presidential republics were introduced in South America in the 19th century. Presidential republics have most often emerged in recently independent nation-states, most often developing in formerly colonized countries.

While many presidential republics do limit presidential authority through systems of separation of power and checks and balances, this is not always the case. For example, Turkmenistan has the form and constitution of a presidential republic, but the president of Turkmenistan is largely considered to be an authoritarian ruler who has few real limits on his power. Similarly, the nation of Rwanda has a strong presidential republic where a great deal of power has devolved to the nation's president. (Other presidential republics: Algeria, Angola, Argentina, Democratic Republic of the Congo, El Salvador, Ghana, Indonesia, Kenya, Nicaragua, Paraguay, Senegal, and many more.)

There are a number of what are called **semi-presidential republics** as well. France and Russia are the best-known examples of this type of government. In a semi-presidential system, executive power is shared, at least nominally, by both the president and a prime minister (and their ministers). The president is typically elected directly by the populace, and the people also elect the legislature. The prime minister is then selected as in the parliamentary system described below, from members of the legislative body. The president typically appoints the prime minister, but the prime minister is responsible to the legislative assembly.

Parliamentary Republic

Parliamentary republics are the second-most common form of world government, after presidential republics. In 2017, there were 49 parliamentary republics in the world. In a few cases, such as India and Germany, they are federal parliamentary republics. Canada is also a federal parliamentary democracy, though it is formally a realm of the British Commonwealth, recognizing the Queen of England as the Canadian sovereign. In most other cases, parliamentary republics are unitary governments in the form of parliamentary republics; for example, Italy, South Africa, Poland, Ireland, Israel and Greece.

Parliamentary systems of government are systems in which the citizens elect representatives to serve in a legislative parliament. Parliament then combines lawmaking and executive functions. In a parliamentary system, the parliament chooses an elected member of parliament to be prime minister to carry out the laws made in parliament. Unlike a presidential system, in which the executive and legislative functions are clearly differentiated, in a parliamentary system the prime minister is usually the leader of the political party with the greatest number of seats in parliament. In such a system, it is critical that the prime minister have the confidence of the legislators. The prime minister is typically the leader of the political party with a majority of seats in parliament. This assures that the prime minister has the authority and confidence of the parliament. If, on a major policy decision, the parliament votes counter to the wishes of the prime minister, they are often said to have "**lost the confidence**" of the parliament. This usually leads to the fall of that government and the need for new elections or the selection of a new prime minister. Additionally, if there is no clear majority party in the parliament, this is said to be a "**hung parliament,**" and the leader of the party with the most seats in parliament (even without a majority) often seeks to form a "**coalition government.**"

Absolute Monarchy

Absolute monarchies did not disappear with the French Revolution. According to the *CIA World Factbook*, there are six absolute monarchies still ruling kingdoms around the world. The six absolute monarchies are Brunei, The Vatican City, Oman, Qatar, Saudi Arabia, and Swaziland.

Absolute monarchies should not be confused with totalitarian states. Absolute monarchies do not lack constitutional or traditional limits on rulers' powers. For example, while the Pope is described by the Vatican as the absolute ruler of this religious city-state, the papacy does not operate without limits, even within the walls of the Vatican. The Kingdom of Saudi Arabia operates according to the Basic Law of Government, a form of constitution that outlines dynastic succession and other procedures of government. The king, however, rules with the help of his ministers. He is the commander-in-chief of the armed forces, with unilateral power to order troops into conflict. The Kingdom of Saudi Arabia has a legislature, known as the Consultative Assembly, and a judiciary. However, the legislature is advisory rather than an independent lawmaking body, and the judiciary has only partial independence from royal authority. As with many absolute or traditional monarchies, the Kingdom of Saudi

Arabia's ultimate check and the kingdom's fundamental constitution is the Koran and the traditions of the Prophet Muhammad. Swaziland, a small landlocked country in southern Africa, has an absolute monarchy. From 1899 until 1982, Swaziland was ruled by King Sobhuza II, making him among the longest reigning kings in world history. Sobhuza's son is the current absolute ruler of this kingdom. In Swaziland, the king and the queen mother rule together traditionally, with the queen mother acting as a check on monarchical power. In this example, while the king claims absolute power, dynastic tradition serves to restrain the use of that power.

Parliamentary Constitutional Monarchy

Today, there are 12 parliamentary constitutional monarchies: Cambodia, Denmark, Japan, Jordan, Lesotho, Malaysia, Morocco, Netherlands, Norway, Spain, Sweden, and the United Kingdom.

In most constitutional monarchies, the monarch and the royal family largely perform ceremonial duties and act as the head of state for their respective kingdoms. With the exception of the Kingdom of Jordan, each of the monarchies listed above have long histories of dynastic rule. Despite this history, in each of these countries, real power is maintained by an elected prime minister who acts as the head of government within a parliamentary system of government. Parliamentary systems of government, as we saw above, are systems in which the citizens elect representatives to serve in a legislative parliament. Parliament, then, is the ruling body of a parliamentary constitutional monarchy.

In a parliamentary constitutional monarchy, the head of government, or prime minister, is an elected member of parliament. As a member of parliament, the prime minister takes part in writing legislation, and also executes the powers granted to them by the parliament, and oversees execution of the laws passed by parliament.

Communist State

The *CIA World Factbook* lists only five remaining communist states: China, Cuba, North Korea, Laos, and Vietnam. With the exception of North Korea, which maintains a state-managed economy and a totalitarian regime, the other states have mixed economies and hardly represent clear examples of the communist regimes that ruled in many nation-states before the decline of the Soviet Union in 1989. Each of these countries, however, is governed by a single party that claims to represent the *proletariat,* or working classes. As we will see in Chapter 8, the primary characteristic of a communist state is government ownership of the primary productive resources, a centrally-planned economy, and very limited personal liberties or civil rights.

Islamic Theocratic Republic

A final system of government largely represented by the Republic of Iran, is a republic which has many of the features of presidential republican system of government, including direct elections of a representative assembly and president. The elected president and legislative organ, however, answer directly to and follows the decrees of the country's unelected Supreme Leader and head of state. The armed forces, judicial system, and media are under the Supreme Leader's control. Iran has only had two Supreme Leaders since its revolution in 1979, both of whom were chosen because they were among the most respected religious leaders of the Islamic community in Iran. As such, real power has rested in the hands of religious scholars and clerics, making Iran one of the few theocratic governments in the world today.

> **Competency 019 Descriptive Statement E.** The beginning teacher demonstrates knowledge of major forms of government in history (e.g., monarchy, authoritarian government, classical republic, liberal democracy, totalitarian government) and of the historical antecedents of major political systems.

Monarchy

Throughout human history, the most common form of government has been the monarchy. The term *monarchy* derives from the Greek word for "rule of one." A monarch is also called a *sovereign,* indicating that sovereignty or the source of all legitimate uses of power rest in the person and will of the ruler. Some monarchies have claimed absolute rule. Louis XIV of France perhaps expressed this conception most clearly. He famously remarked, *"L'état c'est moi"* (I am the state). He also is reported to have said, "It is the law because I said it," or otherwise translated, "The law proceeds from the word of my mouth." While, in fact, Louis XIV's absolutism was circumscribed by a wide range of customary and other restraints, and may have been as much wishful thinking as anything, the idea that the power and sovereignty were the possession of a single individual is common in monarchies.

Monarchies are also generally understood as a private and heritable possession. A king or queen inherits their position as part of a family bequest. An important advantage of monarchies is that, unless a king dies without an heir, there is little debate about who will succeed to power on the death of the ruler. This has the disadvantage that there is no guarantee that a king's successor will be competent, capable, morally upright, or even sane.

Most monarchies today however are **limited Constitutional Monarchies,** like the Netherlands, Great Britain, and Thailand. In most of these monarchies, real decision-making takes place in legislative assemblies. The kings or queens have ceremonial roles and public influence, but do not directly influence policy. Some monarchies, for example the Kingdom of Saudi Arabia, have both ceremonial and governmental authority, though they are restrained by law, much as Louis XIV was and cannot exercise completely arbitrary power.

Classical Republics

As we saw in Chapter 3, the term *republic* derives from the Latin, *res publica,* literally "public thing." The first indicator of the distinction between monarchy and the classical republic is the fact that where monarchy is a privately-held power, in republics, power is public and the purpose of the state is to see to the common good. Classical republicanism developed from notions developed in Ancient Greece and Rome, but also in Renaissance Italy and 17th-century England. The American Framers drew on all of these traditions when considering the form of government they would establish in 1787. Classical republicanism first begins with the conception of men (and later women) as citizens, where monarchs define residents of the kingdom as "subjects," obedient to the ruler. Classical republicanism places a premium on the active participation of individuals in the political life of the community as virtuous citizens: conscientious jury-members, educated voters, self-less office-holders, citizen-soldiers, and willing tax payers.

Direct Democracy

Most modern "democracies" are representative democracies where decisions are made by elected officials who are entrusted with representing the will of the populace. Direct democracies, sometimes called "plebiscitary democracies" enable the people to vote, or to arrive at consensus in some other fashion, making decisions directly. A plebiscite is a direct vote of an electorate. The term comes from the Latin *plebe* which designated the lower classes in Roman society. A plebiscite was a law voted on by the *plebe's* assembly. The concept therefore reflects the view that the people or the *demos* (in Greek) are expressing their wishes directly.

Historically direct democracies are quite rare. Ancient Athens, though hardly a democracy, as women, slaves, and resident non-citizens had no right to participate, has often been described as a democracy. In it, at different times in its history, all male citizens participated directly in law-making, legal decisions, and many aspects of policy administration. Cantonal government in Switzerland beginning in the 13th century also exhibited elements of a direct democracy. Switzerland, though a representative government today, still uses the referendum to both initiate constitutional change and veto parliamentary decisions. In colonial America, New England town meetings and town governments had strong traditions of direct democracy. Even today in New England, town meetings allow citizens to participate directly in budget decisions, make local ordinances, and contribute to many other day-to-day aspects of local government.

While the United States is a republic and relies on elected officials to make most policy decisions, there are a number of features of direct democracy that are employed, usually at the state and local level. Many states use **referendums**, or votes by the electorate, to ratify a decision made by the state legislature. In other instances, **ballot proposals** are placed before the electorate allowing the population of a state to vote on a proposed law. These voting practices allow the citizens of a state to directly express their wishes in a legally binding fashion.

Liberal Democracy

The term *liberal democracy* is often used interchangeably with the term *representative democracy,* and even with *republican government.* The Framers of the Constitution established a government founded on the principles of classical republicanism, which had relatively little role for "the people" in government. According to the Constitution of 1789, only the representatives to the House of Representatives (the lower chamber in Congress) were elected directly by their constituents. It was not until 1913 that all Senators faced election by the people. And, even today, the president (who is chosen by the Electoral College) and many of the federal judiciary (Supreme Court justices, court of appeals judges, and district court judges are appointed by the president and approved by the Senate) are kept at a distance from direct popular election. Use of the term *liberal democracy* does perhaps better describe the current American system of government. The American electorate has widened considerably from the first years of the republic. Today, all citizens above the age of 18 are eligible to vote and to hold most political offices.

Conservatives and Liberals

Seeing the terms *liberal* and *democracy* together in the term *liberal democracy*, however, raises questions about the common usage of these terms in today's political rhetoric. In today's heated political rhetoric "liberal" and "conservative" are often used as epithets directed at political opponents. Often, these terms are attached to such qualifiers as "radical," as in *radical liberal* or *radical conservative*. Or equally, the terms *right-wing conservative* or *left-wing liberal*. These terms have become shorthand labels used to differentiate "us" from "them." Perhaps an understanding of the origin of these terms might take some of the sting from their use.

Let us begin with the terms *liberal* and *conservative*. In the 18th and early 19th centuries, the terms *liberal* and *conservative* came into use in England primarily to distinguish political ideas and parties that either challenged or supported the system of royal government, class privilege, and traditional economic institutions. Liberals thus favored greater parliamentary power, liberalization of trade laws and an end to mercantilism, and wider suffrage and voting rights. The liberals represented the power of the rising entrepreneurial class, and the conservatives sought to conserve the power of the traditional ruling elite. Liberalism in this lexicon stood for the following beliefs: individualism, limited government, individual rights, equality under the law, free market economic assumptions, and representative government. Conservatism, by contrast, denied equality under the law, putting forth the sentiment that aristocrats are the "betters" in society. Conservatives called for a mixed constitution that combined aristocratic, monarchical, and representative forms of government. They rejected a belief in individualism (because it assumes a meritocratic reward system) and favored collective rights over individual rights (believing collective rights led to a fairer and more equitable method to dispense justice and social rewards). Conservatives, in short, wished to conserve the ancient forms.

In the 19th-century United States, where monarchical power had already been rejected and there was no tradition of an aristocratic elite, the entire spectrum of American political thinking fit neatly within the classical liberal paradigm. This is still largely the case today. Federalists and Jeffersonian-Republicans, no matter how rancorous their political rivalry, were not that different in their basic assumptions about how political power should be divided. They were both in the liberal tradition. The same could be said about the Whigs and Democrats in the Second American Political Party System. Republicans and Democrats from 1865 until the present also derive from the same **liberal democratic** tradition. So, why have the terms *liberal, democratic, conservative,* and their derivations become so freighted with hostility?

In part, the hostility reflects a divide in classical liberalism that developed in the 1930s. During the Great Depression and after the tragedy of World War I, a number of prominent liberals (John Maynard Keynes and Franklin D. Roosevelt stand out) began to argue that the *laissez-faire* economic solutions of classical liberalism were unworkable. The markets, they contended, did not provide a stable platform for growth and political development. Modern liberals still valued private property but were willing to support increased government intervention in service of individual welfare and regulation of the business cycle.

Modern conservatism (which is itself still within the tradition of classical liberalism) in the United States arose largely in response to the emergence of Keynesian and Rooseveltian government intervention in the economy and society. For much of the 20th century, from Herbert Hoover to Ronald Reagan, conservatives (present in both the Republican and Democratic Parties) stood out as a kind of loyal opposition to the dominant Roosevelt-Kennedy-Johnson strand of liberalism. These conservatives, before the rise of Ronald Reagan, shared the following basic beliefs: (1) a pessimistic view of sinful human nature and therefore the necessity of a state guided by religion, law, and tradition to restrain that nature; (2) a commitment to traditional values and limits on personal behavior; (3) a faith in free market capitalism and market mechanisms to allocate resources and wealth and a concomitant rejection of state intervention designed to accomplish those ends.

Libertarianism

Libertarianism is another expression of classical liberalism that became prominent in the late 20th century. Liberals and conservatives both tapped into or drew inspiration from libertarian positions.

Libertarians stress above all the autonomy of the individual, and reject government restraint of individual liberties. Libertarians believe that, given the uniqueness of all individuals and their moral autonomy, the individual should be free from government limitations of nearly all kinds. Libertarians emphasize the centrality of property rights to individual rights, but also contend that in matters of religion, conscience, sexuality, and all other private matters, the individual should be left to make their own decisions without governmental or societal intrusion.

Libertarians share with modern conservatives the belief that the state should limit its role in economic decision-making, reduce taxation (as a threat to private property rights), and play but a small role in providing social welfare for citizens. Libertarians differ from modern conservatives in that libertarians are as often as disdainful of traditional mores, religious restraints, and cultural conventions as they are of government restraints on individual autonomy. Thus, libertarians have supported liberalization of drug laws, which most conservatives have typically seen as necessary to restrain humans' penchant for sinful dependency and moral weakness. Libertarians have shared liberalism's suspicion of traditional communal controls, yet rejected the modern liberal's reliance on the state's coercive and regulatory power to transform society.

Totalitarian Government

Liberal democracies and representative systems of government depend upon the rule of law and constitutional procedures to ensure that government doesn't act in an arbitrary manner. While most nation-states have constitutions that purport to safeguard citizens' rights, many countries have **authoritarian governments** that gain control and institute laws and governmental systems that destroy most areas of private and public autonomy and independence. An authoritarian government need not be totalitarian. A dictator might exercise a great deal of control in some spheres of life while leaving other areas untouched. For example, a dictatorship might control the military or government, without dictating other aspects of people's lives.

Typically, however, this is not the case. **Totalitarian governments** usually share the following characteristics:

1. a single political party controlled by an authoritarian ruler or ruling group;

2. state control of media and news outlets making independent, individual judgments difficult;

3. police tactics that include near-constant surveillance, silencing of opposition parties or positions, violations of the civil and human rights of arrestees, and violations of due process;

4. government management of entrepreneurial activity and control of consumer and capital markets;

5. the cultivation of cults of personality around individual rulers, who equate their own fate with the fate of the nation and state;

6. militarization of the society;

7. use of a central ideology to legitimize power and silence opposition.

> **Competency 019 Descriptive Statement F.** The beginning teacher analyzes the process by which democratic-republican government evolved (e.g., beginnings in classical Greece and Rome, developments in England, impact of the Enlightenment).

The origins of democratic and republican systems of government are often associated with ancient Greece and Rome. A number of events around the turn of the 6th century BCE marked an important watershed in the histories of representative government. The Athenians celebrated the overthrow of a tyrannical government in 510 BCE and the establishment of the rule of the people or *demos.* Thus, Athenian democracy is then said to date from 510 BCE. The Romans dated the establishment of their *res publica*, or republic, to 509 BCE.

Americans use a political language, much of which traces its origins to the language developed in classical Greece and Rome to describe their own political institutions. Following are a list of terms and institutions with origins in classical Greece and Rome that still serve as part of the vocabulary of politics. Even the term *politics* comes from the Greek term *polis*, which means "city-state."

Democracy (*Greek*) from *demokratia*, composite of *demos* and *kratos*. *Demos* equates to "the people," and *kratos* to "power," implying that the people (defined as adult male citizens of the *polis*) share rule.

Monarchy (*Greek*) from *monarchia*, or the rule of one.

Oligarchy (*Greek*) from *oligarchia*, or the rule of the few.

Aristocracy (*Greek*) from *aristokratia*, the rule of the excellent.

Tyranny (*Greek*) from *tyrannia*, and *tyrannos*, or tyrant. It didn't have a negative connotation initially but simply suggested sole rulership. Athenian supporters of democratic governments characterized it negatively.

Republic (*Latin*) from *res publica*, literally "the public thing."

Senate (*Latin*) from *senex*, or assembly of elders, legislative and administrative assembly of the Roman Republic.

Patriarchy (*Latin*) from the word *pater*, or father.

Dictator (*Latin*) *dictatore*, a political or military leader given full authority in times of emergency.

Emperor (*Latin*) from *imperator*. Also from *imperium* which means rule or power.

Pontifex (*Latin*) meaning "bridge-builder." The *Pontifex maximus* had responsibility for a number of Roman religious duties. Among the titles of the papacy have been *pontiff* and *pontifex maximus*.

It is important to note that neither Greece nor Rome had democratic or republican institutions comparable to our own contemporary systems of government. Though at times ancient Athenians proudly proclaimed their government to be a democracy, the vast majority of Athenian residents lacked political rights. Slaves, women, and resident foreigners did not have civil or political rights. Rome established a republic in 509 BCE, but women, slaves, and most of the people of Rome (known as *plebes*) had few civil or political rights.

Following the fall of the Roman Empire, Western Europeans developed a feudal political system over the course of the Middle Ages (500 CE to ca. 1350 CE). The system was characterized by hereditary monarchies and decentralized power controlled by an aristocratic warrior class. While Europe was fragmented politically, most Europeans were united by their Christian beliefs (though there were important Jewish and Muslim minorities in some parts of Western Europe). They shared a common calendar, marked by Christian feast days and holidays; a shared liturgical, legal, and scientific language in Latin; and a culture deeply influenced by Roman, Christian, and Germanic beliefs and practices.

England, on the fringes of continental Europe, developed along slightly different lines than the rest of Europe for the first centuries of the medieval period. England was cut off earlier from Roman influence than were the areas that would become France, Spain, Italy, and Germany. After a wave of Germanic invaders (Angles, Saxons, and Jutes) settled in Britain in the fifth and sixth centuries CE, a number of Anglo-Saxon kingdoms competed to control the territory before one of these Anglo-Saxon kings, King Alfred the Great (born 849 CE, died 899 CE) managed to unify these kingdoms, creating the Kingdom of England. Shortly afterward, the Anglo-Saxon kingdom faced threats from the Danes (Norsemen) who conquered large swaths of northern and eastern England. For a period lasting nearly a century and a half, the English were more a part of the Scandinavian world than the continental European world. In 1066 CE, this changed in a stroke when both the Anglo-Saxon and Scandinavian claimants to the throne of England were defeated in battle: the Norwegian (Harald Hardrada) by the Anglo-Saxon (Harold Godwinson, often called Harold the Saxon); and the Anglo-Saxon by William the Conqueror. This victory introduced continental feudalism to England.

A critical moment in the history of the English monarchy occurred not quite 200 years later when King John I was forced to sign the *Magna Carta,* establishing an English tradition of submitting royal authority to limitations imposed by the English aristocracy and clergy. These limitations gradually developed into liberties claimed by Englishmen that included the expectation that taxes should be increased only in times of emergency, and then only with the consent of the peers of the realm; and that those charged with crimes should have their cases heard by a jury of their peers. The Kingdom of England also developed a number of important medieval institutions that would later become important features of representative government in England. For example, the King's Council, which originally had been an advisory body only, gradually developed into the British Parliament, a bicameral legislative body, with a House of Commons (its lower house) and the House of Lords. A number of other institutions, including the Exchequer (the equivalent of our Treasury Department), began a move towards a more bureaucratic and less personal set of governmental institutions.

During the 17th century, the English monarchy and English political society generally underwent a serious crisis. After the death of Queen Elizabeth I, a popular monarch who had managed to rule effectively through Parliament, but who died without an heir, the English turned to a Scottish ruling family, the Stuarts. The Stuart monarchs proved quite unpopular, and were strongly influenced by absolutist monarchies elsewhere in Europe. As a result of a combination of Parliamentary resistance to Stuart claims to absolute power and Puritan objections to the religious policies of the Stuarts, a civil war erupted in 1642. During the course of the English Civil War, King Charles I was defeated, captured, tried, and ultimately executed by the Puritan-led, Parliamentary party. This initiated a period of rule by the Puritan leader Oliver Cromwell that lasted until 1659. This period, known variously as the "interregnum," or period between the reigns, and the Commonwealth, saw the imposition of a near-theocracy in England. In the end, this proved unsatisfactory to the English, who brought back the Stuart dynasty in 1660. In 1688, when it became clear that James II, the second Stuart ruler after the restoration, was a Catholic and planned on restoring Catholicism to England, Parliamentary leaders overthrew the Stuarts in a bloodless coup that has gone down in history as the "Glorious Revolution. The English political philosophers Thomas Hobbes and John Locke developed many of their theories about the social contract between rulers and ruled, the right to rebel against tyrannical leaders, and their conception of natural rights in the context of the English Civil War and Glorious Revolution.

The Enlightenment was built on the rights theories of Hobbes and Locke, and upon the confidence in reason engendered by the Scientific Revolution. French philosophers, or *philosophes*, became the center of gravity of a movement that swept Europe and the Americas with important influences on political thought. A feature of the Enlightenment was a faith in the ability of human beings, employing their own reason, to understand their natural environments and to apply the lessons of nature to social organization. Enlightenment thinkers were confident that—with the proper application of reason—society, the economy, and governments could be improved.

Among the positions taken by Enlightenment philosophers, as we have seen, was a rejection of judicial torture as a means of questioning criminals. Philosophers like Voltaire and Cesare Beccaria, and political figures like Thomas Jefferson and Benjamin Franklin called for an end to cruel and unusual punishments and capital punishment. The ideals of religious toleration and the need for a separation between church and state also derived from the conviction of Enlightenment thinkers that each individual should be free to determine their own beliefs, dictated only by their own conscience unimpeded by church or state. Many Enlightenment thinkers, including many of the leading American intellectuals of the time, became **deists**, who believed in the existence of a creator God, but one who did not intervene in the workings of the natural world, leaving history to unfold according to the laws of nature.

French *philosophes* also challenged the absolute monarchs of France. The French philosopher, the Baron de Montesquieu, contended that the best protection against absolute power was to establish checks and balances, and to divide legislative, judicial, and executive political functions. The importance of "checks and balances" and "separation of powers" in the United States Constitution illustrates the vital importance of Enlightenment ideas on the American "Founding Fathers."

Similarly, Enlightenment thinkers argued that the kind of intervention in economic activity carried out by the mercantilist governments of Europe served to undermine the market's natural ability to best ration goods and resources and provide the greatest good for the greatest number of citizens. They espoused the ideals of free enterprise and in arguing for a *laissez-faire* approach to the economy began the emergence of the science of economics. French *Physiocrats* and leaders of the Scottish Enlightenment, such as Adam Smith, described an economic system in which the state provided a legal apparatus within which private property protections were guaranteed, but economic regulations were minimized, in order for natural market forces to flourish. Smith argued that the selfish economic behavior of individual consumers and producers, left unimpeded by government, would lead to economic expansion to the benefit of all.

CHAPTER 8

Domain VI: Economics and Science, Technology and Society

Domain VI is yet another portion of the TExES Social Studies exam that accounts for approximately 13% of the test questions, translating to perhaps 18 or 19 items that you'll see on test day. The subject matter is quite broad, crisscrossing economics and science, and technology and society. Even so, economics is the fulcrum of Domain VI. So begin by reviewing the basic vocabulary and concepts of economics. Then, be sure you are fluent in reading models, graphs, and charts particular to the discipline of economics. You will be asked to demonstrate a basic understanding of the considerations that inform the economic behavior of individuals, firms, and government entities. You will also be asked to describe the differences between various market conditions, firms or businesses, as well as the political foundations of market systems. As important as understanding these introductory elements of economic life, it will also be critical that you are able to make comparisons between the different economic systems and the ideological origins of each.

COMPETENCY 020 (ECONOMIC CONCEPTS AND TYPES OF ECONOMIC SYSTEMS)

The teacher understands basic economic concepts, major developments in economic thought and various types of economic systems:

> **Competency 020 Descriptive Statement A.** The beginning teacher demonstrates knowledge of the concepts of scarcity and opportunity costs and their significance.

Scarcity

Economics, as economists often remind us, is the "science of scarcity." Without scarcity, there would be no need for economics. Economists, therefore, characterize scarcity as a function of the human and natural condition. Scarcity is not, however, simply a function of a lack of resources, time, energy, money, etc. The Rolling Stones expressed it succinctly: "You can't always get what you want." And, you may not get what you need, either. Scarcity results from the fact that resources are insufficient to satisfy a society's wants and needs. Put another way, a resource is scarce when the many ways in which it could be put to use are greater than the amount of the resource that exists.

While every society experiences scarcity, the experience of scarcity is relative to the material conditions and expectations of a given society. Europeans encountering the !Kung people in the Kalahari Desert noted the absolute scarcity of grain crops or other plant domesticates and criticized the !Kung people for not farming. The !Kung responded by observing, "Why should we plant, when there are so many mongongo nuts in the world?" The !Kung saw abundance where Europeans saw absolute scarcity. This is not to suggest that the !Kung had solved the economic problem of scarcity. They had simply made a fundamentally logical economic choice that the time and effort that might be expended in sowing seeds, weeding, harvesting, storing, and processing grain or vegetable crops would be better spent collecting mongongo nuts, hunting, telling stories, dancing, or otherwise occupying their time.

A critical assumption of free-market or capitalistic economic theorizing is that human wants and needs are not fixed, but potentially unlimited. This presumption assumes that human nature is acquisitive; the more we have, the more we want, and our needs are infinitely expansive.

A corollary assumption follows. While the natural environment's ability to satisfy these unlimited wants and needs is limited, it also is not fixed. Human willingness to work harder, work more efficiently, develop technologically, or develop social and political organizations to maximize production can expand the capacity of the natural environment to meet our material and psychic needs. All of these decisions involve making choices.

A final assumption underlying much economic thinking is that human actors make rational decisions about how to utilize available resources in order to maximize the utility of those resources. This assumption reflects the science of economics' roots in the Enlightenment. Enlightenment thinkers had great faith in the rationality of human actors, believing that if human beings had complete access to the facts, they would make rational choices. In short, businesses would make choices that maximized efficiency and profits, and consumers would make rational choices that maximized their satisfaction at the least cost.

Factors of Production

Economists divide the resources needed for productive activity into land, labor, capital, and entrepreneurship. These are known as the **Factors of Production**.

All natural resources are grouped under the umbrella of **land**. Some resources are renewable, while others are nonrenewable. **Labor** includes all human resources that could be employed in the production of goods and services. **Capital** refers to man-made tools or materials used in the productive process. For example, a carpenter's tools; a farmer's plow, barns, or tractors; an office building's computers and desks, even the building itself, are all examples of capital. Capital can be **fixed capital**, mainly plant and equipment or other machinery that can be used over and over, or **circulating** or **working capital.** The latter circulates through the production process. Working capital includes stocks of raw materials, goods in the process of being finished, and inventories of unsold items. **Entrepreneurship** refers to the function of ownership associated with assessing risks and potential rewards and determining to establish a firm. Often entrepreneurship is associated with individuals, such as Bill Gates or Mark Zuckerberg, or, in the past, Henry Ford, Andrew Carnegie, and others who established businesses. Entrepreneurship is different from management, however. Managers are salaried employees. Entrepreneurs are the risk takers.

Opportunity Costs

To understand and study the factors underlying economic choices, it is necessary to explore the **opportunity costs** of the choices we individually or collectively make. An opportunity cost is measured by what is foregone when a particular choice is made. Here is an example from personal experience. This evening, I had a choice between watching the second game of the NBA finals while texting back and forth with my son about the game. Or, I could have continued working on this test-prep manual so I could get this chapter done under deadline. The consequences of this choice involved no monetary calculation. I chose to watch the game and experience the pleasure of bonding long-distance with my son, recognizing the cost that this would mean that I might not get the chapter done as quickly as planned, and that a number of late-night writing sessions might be a consequence.

Opportunity costs can also be measured in monetary terms. Again, a personal example might be instructive. At age 31, I decided to go back to graduate school, leaving a teaching position that paid $42,000. One opportunity cost of this decision was the forfeiture of at least $42,000 in lost salary annually that I could have earned over the six years that I was in graduate school. Over the course of the six years of graduate school, that forfeiture totaled more than $252,000. An opportunity cost of having made the choice to stay a high school teacher and coach, which is more difficult to measure financially, would have been the satisfaction of having completed a Ph.D. and later the opportunity to have a position as a tenured professor in a university. Monetarily, I doubt that I have ever made up the difference. From that standpoint, it hardly seems a rational choice. But, the opportunity benefit of an academic career and the satisfaction of completing a Ph.D. in History has had its own rewards.

Opportunity costs are also evident in national decision-making. Expenditures on the military often come at the expense of investments in education, social welfare, or infrastructure. This is the classic "guns or butter" conundrum. National policy-makers have to evaluate their opportunity costs in terms of weakened national defense that may result from increases in spending on schools, health care, or highway construction. Or, they must consider the costs of high national levels of illiteracy, infant mortality, or lost commercial growth that might result from increased spending on aircraft carriers, missile defense systems, or increased troop levels. Each choice presumes the cost of an opportunity missed.

Opportunity Costs and Production Possibilities Curves

One way that economists represent the opportunity costs of economic choices is using a **Production Possibilities Curve** or **Production Possibilities Frontier**. This model illustrates the trade-offs that occur in a simplified economy that has the capacity to produce only two kinds of goods.

For this thought experiment, imagine an economy where the land, labor, and capital available could only produce two outputs: wheat and milk. If all the resources available were devoted to growing grain 1,200 bushels of grain could be produced. This of course would mean that no milk would be produced that year. If the following year, however, a decision was made to produce 200 gallons of milk, with the available resources it would only be possible to produce 900 bushels of grain. The opportunity cost of the 200 gallons of milk would then be 300 bushels of grain. The production possibilities of this model economy could be represented in the production possibilities schedule shown in **Table 8.1** below.

Table 8.1
Production Possibilities Schedule

Grain (bushels)	Milk (gallons)
1200	0
900	200
600	400
300	600
0	800

The same data could be presented using the production possibilities frontier graph shown in **Figure 8.1** below:

Figure 8.1
Production Possibilities Frontier

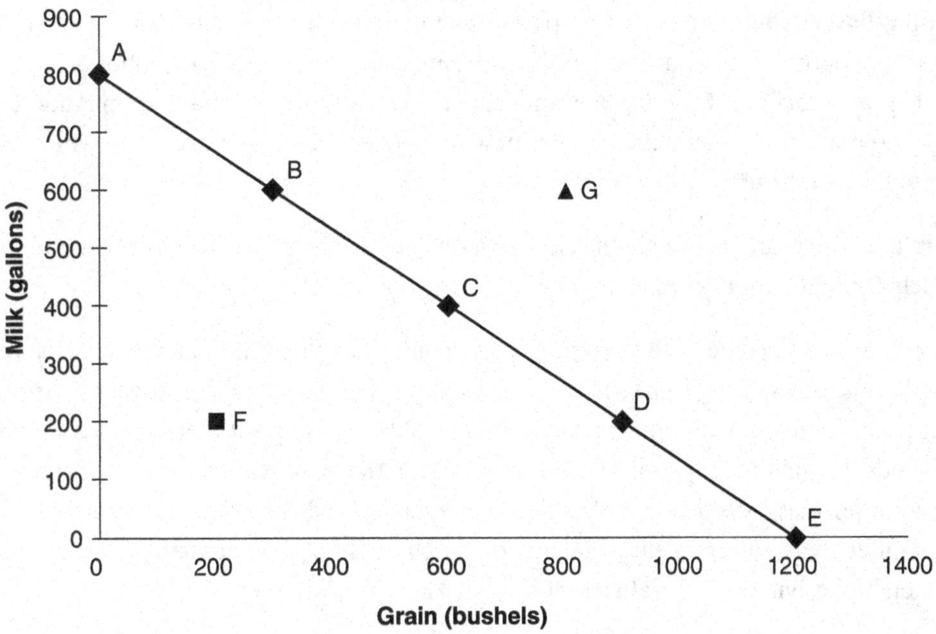

A shift along the Production Possibilities Frontier from point C to point D would result in an opportunity cost of 200 gallons of milk. Or, a shift along the Production Possibilities Frontier from E to D would result in the increased production of 200 gallons of milk, but at an opportunity cost of 300 bushels of grain. As you can also see, from **Figure 8.1**, this simplified economy could not, under present circumstances, produce at point G. In other words, without either improvements in technology or increases in available resources, this economy could not increase its production of milk and grain to 800 bushels of grain and 600 gallons of milk.

When the simplified economy in **Figure 8.1** is producing at point F (200 bushels of grain and 200 gallons of milk), the economy is said to be underemploying its resources. When an economy is operating at full employment or using its land, labor, capital, and entrepreneurship to its fullest capacity, it is said to be operating along the production possibilities frontier.

> **Competency 020 Descriptive Statement B.** The beginning teacher understands the circular-flow model of the economy.

Another way to represent the economy in a simplified form is by using a circular-flow model.

Circular-flow models are simple graphic illustrators of the workings of an economy. These models allow economists to demonstrate the movement of goods, services, labor, and resources exchanged in an economy. Circular-flow models can visually demonstrate simple and complex flows of economic activity. A simple circular-flow model describes an economy in which there are only households and firms.

Figure 8.2 is an example of a simple circular-flow model that shows the movement of resources and products through a simplified economy.

Starting on the right side of the diagram, households offer their labor and land in the resource markets to businesses willing to pay them salaries and wages, or purchase or rent their property. The households receive income in exchange. Households also deposit their savings in banks, or invest in bonds, loaning money to firms. These appear in the resource markets as capital placed at the disposal of businesses or firms. For this resource, households receive interest income. Finally, households offer their entrepreneurial talents or purchase stocks, which entitle them to a share in the ownership or entrepreneurial side of a firm. They in turn receive profits from the firms as income.

The value or price of each of these factors of production is determined in resource markets. If there is a high demand for labor relative to the supply offered by households, the price of labor or wages will be high. If not, the price of labor, or wages will be lower. Or, if household savings are high relative to the demand for capital investment, the interest rate (income for capital) will be reduced.

Businesses purchase the resources they need in resource markets. The value of the resources they are required to purchase from households is represented as the cost of doing business in **Figure 8.2**.

Firms then produce goods and services for sale in product markets to consumers, families, and individuals. The market value of these sales returns to firms in the form of revenue. The value of these private goods and services is determined by the demand for and supply of these goods and services. Households spend their disposable income to purchase goods and services in the product markets.

Figure 8.2
Simple Circular-Flow Model *without* Government

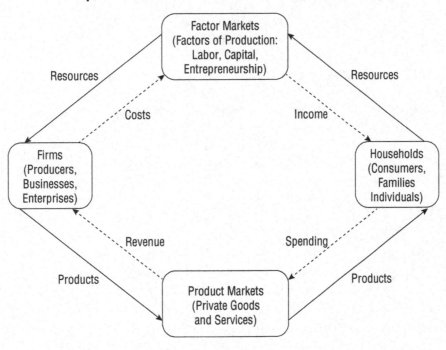

Circular-flow models can illustrate even more complex economies, as well as other economic relationships. For example, **Figure 8.3** interjects the public sector, or government, into the simple model above. Governments also spend money purchasing products and resources. When a school or state legislature purchases paper products, it does so in the product markets just as households do. Government also acquires land, labor, and capital in the resource markets. These purchases make up a portion of government spending.

Government expenditures also include such things as subsidies and transfer payments. Government transfers include all payments to private citizens that are not paid out to purchase goods and services or pay salaries. Annually, the single largest transfer is composed of Social Security payments to the elderly and disabled. Medicare and Medicaid are less clearly transfer payments because they are fees paid for medical services. Government also subsidizes firms in a variety of ways. The most obvious example of such subsidies are crop subsidies paid to farmers. There are many other examples of subsidies paid by government to encourage production.

Governments also receive revenues from firms and households in the form of corporate and business taxes, as well as individual income, sales, and excise taxes.

Figure 8.3
Simple Circular-Flow Model *with* Government

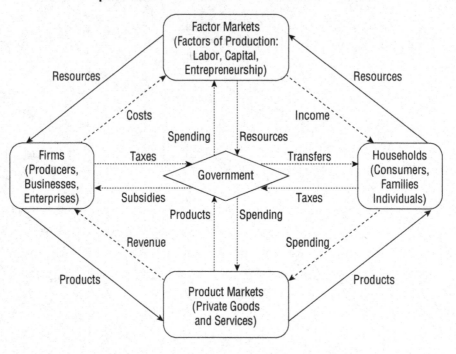

Circular flow models like those above in no way provide a complete picture of the many types of actors in a real economy or the multitude of flows of money and goods and services that circulate in a real economy. Nonetheless, circular-flow models like those above provide an important way to simplify and think about the economy.

> **Competency 020 Descriptive Statement C.** The beginning teacher analyzes interactions among supply, demand and price and factors that cause changes in supply, demand and price, and interprets supply-and-demand graphs.

Because in a free enterprise system consumer demand largely determines what will be produced, it is important to precisely define demand. **Demand** is the amount of any product that consumers are willing and able to purchase at different prices within a specific time period. All other factors being equal, when the price of a product rises, people will generally purchase less of the item, either foregoing the satisfaction they would receive from that product or substituting a similar item. Conversely, when the price of a product falls, all other things being equal, there will be a corresponding increase in consumer purchases of the product. This inverse relationship between the quantity demanded of a good and the price of that good is called the **law of demand**.

A **demand schedule** is a table demonstrating the quantity of a good or service consumers will be willing and able to purchase at different prices. A **demand curve** illustrates the information in a demand schedule in graphic form. The law of demand is demonstrated in the downward slope of the curve. Below are a demand schedule (**Table 8.2**) and a demand curve (**Figure 8.4**) for slices of pizza that a single consumer might be willing and able to purchase per week at various prices.

Table 8.2
Individual Demand Schedule for Pizza

Price per slice	Slices of pizza bought per week
$1.00	8
$1.25	6
$1.50	4
$1.75	3
$2.00	2
$2.25	1

Imagine a street vendor (let's call him Dino) situated on a corner in a commercial center that sells pizza by the slice to office workers. Let us first imagine a single customer's demand for pizza produced at this stand. According to the demand schedule above, if a slice of pizza costs $1.00, a single individual might be willing to have two slices a day for lunch on most days, eating eight slices over the course of the week. He likes pizza a lot. At $1.50 per slice, the pizza buyer may choose to forgo a slice or two of pizza for lunch, choosing perhaps to eat a taco or some other lunch fare instead. If the price of pizza rises to $2.25, this lunch-time buyer will only pamper himself with the purchase of a single slice of pizza, perhaps on Friday. At $2.25 per week, our subject may decide to make a salad or bring a sandwich on most days, or find another cheaper alternative, rather than pay the increased price for pizza.

The graph in **Figure 8.4** illustrates the data in **Table 8.2** above. The graph shows a downward-sloping curve, demonstrating the inverse relationship between the quantity of pizza that will be purchased during the workweek at prices ranging from $1.00 to $2.25 per slice.

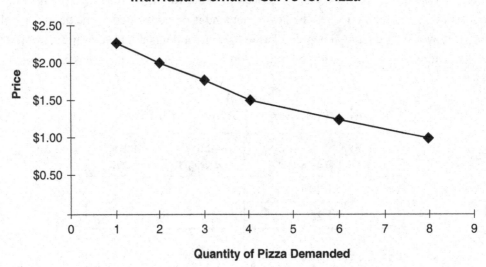

Figure 8.4
Individual Demand Curve for Pizza

The demand for pizza at this street corner vendor's pizza stand can be estimated by adding together the accumulated demand for pizza at each price point. Without being too imaginative, let us assume that there are 50 customers who regularly come to Dino's Pizza Stand on their lunch hours. And, for simplicity's sake, let us assume that each buyer has the same buying habits and budgetary constraints as our first customer. **Table 8.3** below shows the demand schedule for Dino's Pizza Stand during a typical week.

Table 8.3
Weekly Demand for Pizza at Dino's Pizza Stand

Price per slice	Slices of pizza bought per week
$1.00	400
$1.25	300
$1.50	200
$1.75	150
$2.00	100
$2.25	50

Just as the individual demand schedule could be graphically illustrated, **Figure 8.5** shows the demand curve graphically illustrating the quantity of pizza demanded at each price point for all buyers.

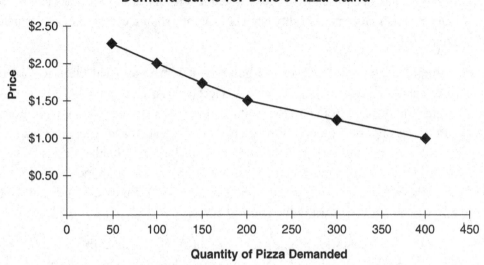

Figure 8.5
Demand Curve for Dino's Pizza Stand

Changes in Demand—Shifts in the Demand Curve

The **law of demand** refers to the inverse relationship between price and the quantity demanded of a product. When economists talk about a change in demand, they are referring to a shift in the demand curve at all possible prices. Thus, an **increase in demand** involves a shift of the demand curve to the right. And a **decrease in demand** is a shift to the left of the demand curve.

Changes in demand that shift the demand curve happen for five primary reasons.

1. **Changes in incomes.** Taking Dino's Pizza Stand again, let us consider the effect of a number of potential changes to Dino's market. If the business that Dino's Pizza Stand caters to experiences a banner year and gives significant raises to its employees, we could see Dino's customers willing to buy more slices of pizza over the coming year. This would result in a rightward shift of Dino's Pizza demand curve. Conversely, a downturn and subsequent pay reductions might see the opposite effect.

2. **Changes in the number of consumers.** Dino's Pizza Stand largely catered to the employees of one office building. If a new office building is constructed on the opposite corner, bringing additional customers into the area, Dino's Pizza Stand will see a corresponding increase in demand.

3. **Changes in tastes.** We can more easily imagine how changes in the tastes of Dino's customers might adversely affect his demand. Perhaps, after some reflection on their growing waist sizes, Dino's customers might decide that salads were in order. This would result in a decrease in demand, and a leftward shift of the demand curve. Or, if

the Centers for Disease Control announces that basil, tomato sauce, pepperoni, mush-rooms, and extra cheese lead directly to reductions in heart disease or the incidence of cancer, Dino's customers might conclude that they should eat more, rather than less, of Dino's pizza.

4. **Changes in the prices of related goods and services.** When the prices of related goods and services go up or down, the prices will have an impact on the demand for an item. In the case of Dino's Pizza Stand, an increase in the price of tacos at the taco cart on the opposite corner will have an effect on the demand for Dino's pizza. An increase in the price of a related good or service will result (all other things being equal) in a rightward shift in the demand curve for Dino's pizza, or an increase in demand. A decrease in the price of tacos will conversely lead to a decrease in demand for Dino's pizza, and a leftward shift in the demand curve.

5. **Changes in Expectation.** Expectations about future changes in prices, or about future changes in income, can affect demand schedules. Rumors about future increases in the price of Dino's pizza may induce consumers to eat more pizza today, though it seems unlikely. Here is probably where the pizza example is less than helpful. Consider instead, then, that a rumor starts that there will be sharp spikes in gas prices in the coming weeks. This might encourage car owners to go fill up their tanks immediately, rather than waiting for the price hikes to set in. This would result in a rightward shift in the demand curve for gas. Or, back to Dino's Pizza Stand, if the rumor circulated that the company Dino catered to was likely to slash its workforce in the future and cut salaries, many of Dino's customers might begin belt-tightening measures in anticipation and forgo that slice of pizza they might otherwise have purchased. **Table 8.4** shows these changes in demand.

Table 8.4
Changes in the Demand Schedule for Dino's Pizza

Price per slice	Demand 1	Demand 2
$1.00	400	700
$1.25	300	500
$1.50	200	350
$1.75	150	250
$2.00	100	200
$2.25	50	175

The information contained in **Table 8.4** is illustrated in graphic form in **Figure 8.6**.

Figure 8.6
Shift in the Demand Curve for Dino's Pizza

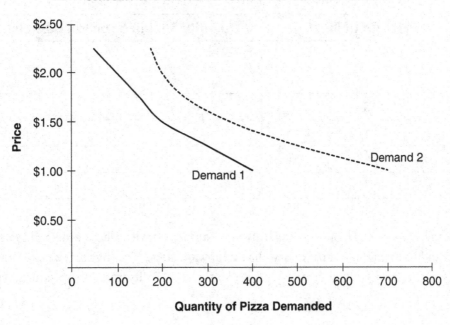

The Supply Side

Common sense will tell us that if the quantity of a product that consumers demand is inversely related to its price, the quantity of an item firms are willing to offer for sale will be directly related to changes in price. In other words, at higher prices, sellers will be happy to offer more of a good for sale; and at lower prices, sellers will offer fewer of the same item for sale. This is the **law of supply.** This is actually more than mere common sense. For firms already in an industry, higher prices will lead to greater profits and thus encouragement to produce and sell more of a commodity. Additionally, higher prices and increased profits will attract new firms to the industry, thereby increasing the supply of the good.

A **supply schedule,** much like a demand schedule, illustrates the law of supply. As evident in **Table 8.5** below, there is a direct relationship between prices and quantity of wheat supplied by farmers. The quantity of wheat that farmers are willing to supply at different price points increases with increases in prices.

Table 8.5
Market Supply Schedule for Wheat (in billion bushels)

Price (in dollars)	Quantity Supplied (billion bushels)
$6	7
$5	6.5
$4	6
$3	5
$2	4
$1	2

The same evidence can be illustrated using a **supply curve**. Where a demand curve slopes downward and to the right, a supply curve has an upward slope. The higher the price of wheat, the more wheat farmers will put on the market for sale. **Figure 8.7** illustrates an upward sloping supply curve for wheat.

Figure 8.7
Market Supply Curve for Wheat

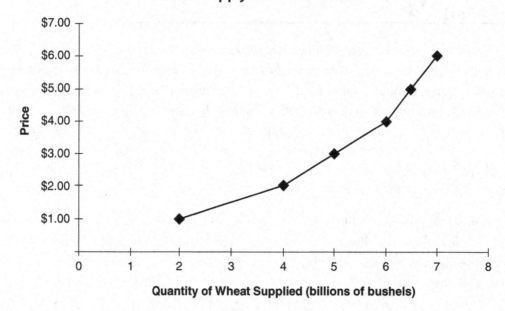

The supply curve and supply schedule represent a hypothetical market for wheat. Suppose that the price of wheat rises from $2 to $3 per bushel; the quantity of wheat that farmers are willing to sell rises from 4 to 5 billion bushels. If the price of wheat drops from $6 to $5 per bushel, farmers will reduce the quantity of wheat they are willing to sell, correspondingly, from 7 to 6.5 billion bushels.

Changes in Supply—Shifts of the Supply Curve

As was the case when examining demand curves, it is important to distinguish between movements and shifts in the supply curve. Movements along the supply curve represent responses to changes in price, whereas shifts in the supply curve represent changes in supply at all price points.

A **shift of the supply curve** is a change in the quantity supplied at any given price. An increase in supply is represented by a rightward shift in the entire curve. A decrease in supply is illustrated by a shift of the entire curve to the left.

Shifts in the supply curve for a good or service result primarily from changes in one of the following five factors.

1. **Changes in input prices.** To produce any product, you need inputs of the factors of production. To grow wheat, for example, you need fertile soil, chemical or natural fertilizers, pesticides, tractors, plows, discs, harvesters, trucks, fuel to run the machinery, storage facilities, and many other inputs. There are also labor inputs. Costs of borrowing, or interest rates, affect the production process. Whenever the price of inputs change, the changes will inversely affect the supply of an item the producer will be willing to place on the market. A decrease in the price of an input reduces the production costs for sellers, who are then more willing to supply the good at any given price point, leading the supply curve to shift to the right. For example, a decrease in the price of diesel fuel or chemical fertilizers reduces farmers' costs, encouraging them to produce more wheat. Conversely, an increase in the price of diesel fuel or chemical fertilizers will increase farmers' costs, leading them to reduce their production of wheat.

2. **Changes in the prices of related goods or services.** Like most producers, wheat farmers might use their available resources to produce a different mix of products. If the price of alfalfa, corn, cotton, soybeans, or some other agricultural product that farmers might profitably grow on their land, increases in price, farmers might be incentivized to shift some of the land, labor, and capital to growing one of these crops. This will lead the supply curve for wheat to shift to the left. If the price of soybeans, for example, skyrocketed, many wheat farmers might shift out of wheat production, causing the supply of wheat to drop at all price points. Relative decreases in the prices of these related products would see the supply of wheat increase and the supply curve for wheat shift to the right.

3. **Changes in technology.** Changes in any of the technologies or techniques used to produce a good affect the supply of a product. Improvements in any of these technol-

ogies will increase supply and consequently result in a rightward shift of the supply curve. When a better technology becomes available, costs of production are decreased and producers will supply more of the item to the market. This will cause the supply curve to shift to the right. The introduction of chemically-synthesized fertilizers, for example, vastly increased the quantity of nutrients that farmers could return to their soil, reducing the time that land had to lie fallow to restore the nitrogen in the soil. Additionally, chemically-synthesized fertilizers increased yields for most agricultural products. This led to the supply curve for wheat, corn, and other farm products to shift to the right.

4. **Changes in expectations.** Changes in the expected future price of an item may induce producers to withhold a commodity from the market in the hopes of getting a higher price in the future. Wheat farmers who have storage facilities available and who are convinced that higher prices are on the horizon may choose to put their harvest in a silo and wait until prices go up before putting their wheat on the market for sale. Conversely, farmers who hear rumors of impending drops in prices for their wheat, will likely put their wheat on the market immediately, increasing the supply of wheat for sale at all price points. This will be reflected in an inward shift of the supply curve leftward toward the *y*-axis.

5. **Changes in the number of producers.** Increases in the number of producers will clearly affect the supply of a product as well. An increase in the number of wheat farmers will have the effect of shifting the supply curve for wheat to the right. A decline in the number of wheat farmers (if all other things remain the same) will reduce the supply of wheat and shift the supply curve to the left.

Consider the following hypothetical market supply schedules and supply curves for wheat. If, for example, the price of soybeans increases, farmers producing wheat would quite likely move some of their land into soybean production, thereby decreasing the supply of wheat. The supply curve would then shift to the left, from S1 to S3, as seen in **Figure 8.8** below. Or, if the price of soybeans dropped, the supply curve would shift to the right, as farmers devoted even more cropland to growing wheat. Or, consider the consequences of the development of a new pesticide or fertilizer. This would allow farmers to either successfully protect their harvests, thereby allowing them to put more of that wheat on the market. Or, in the case of a new fertilizer, they would have higher yields, again shifting the supply curve to the right from S1 to S2. If prices, and therefore profits from wheat sales were higher than normal profits, more farmers would be interested in growing wheat and might enter the market shifting the supply curve from S1 to S2. Or, if the equilibrium price for wheat were particularly low, depressing profits, farmers might leave the market and the supply curve would shift from S1 to S3. **Table 8.6** below demonstrates how shifts in the supply curve are illustrated graphically.

Table 8.6
Supply Schedules for Wheat

Price ($)	Supply 1 (billion bushels of wheat)	Supply 2 (billion bushels of wheat)	Supply 3 (billion bushels of wheat)
$6.00	7	9	5
$5.00	6.5	8.5	4.5
$4.00	6	8	4
$3.00	5	7	3
$2.00	4	6	2
$1.00	2	4	1

Figure 8.8
Shifts in the Supply Curve for Wheat

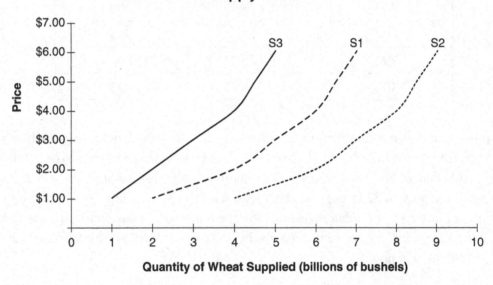

Quantity of Wheat Supplied (billions of bushels)

Supply, Demand, and Equilibrium Prices and Quantities

Having examined demand and supply and the factors that influence changes in both, it is now important to consider how analysis of supply and demand together help economists predict the market price of a commodity and the actual quantities of a commodity that will be sold.

The **equilibrium price** is the price at which the quantity supplied matches the quantity demanded of a given product. The quantity bought and sold at the equilibrium price is known as the **equilibrium quantity** of a given product. At the equilibrium price, every buyer willing to pay that price is able to find a seller willing to sell at that price. This is known as the **market-clearing price.** At the market-clearing price, every seller willing to sell at that price will find a buyer willing to pay that price for purchase of the product.

The easiest way to determine what the equilibrium price and quantity will be in a market is to combine the supply and demand schedules into a single table, and then illustrate it.

Table 8.7
Demand and Supply Schedule for Dino's Pizza

Quantity Demanded	Price per slice	Quantity Supplied
700	$1.00	100
600	1.25	200
500	1.5	300
400	1.75	400
300	2	500
200	2.25	600
100	2.5	700

In **Table 8.7** above, it is clear that at the price of $1, Dino's Pizza will be willing to sell only 100 slices of pizza. However, the office workers who frequent Dino's Pizza will want to buy 700 slices. There is a **shortage** of 600 slices of pizza. This shortage will push the price up until it reaches equilibrium. At a price of $2.50 per slice, Dino's customers will be willing to purchase only 100 slices of pizza, leaving Dino with a **surplus** of 600 slices of pizza to sell. Dino will have to lower the price of his pizza until he can be assured that he will be able to sell all he produces. That price point is the equilibrium price.

The equilibrium price, then, is the price at which the quantity demanded for a product is equal to the quantity supplied. This is best illustrated by putting the supply curve and the demand curve for Dino's Pizza on the same diagram. In **Figure 8.9**, we see that the equilibrium price for Dino's Pizza, the market-clearing price, is $1.75. At this price, Dino's customers will be willing and able to buy all of the 400 pizza slices that Dino is willing to offer for sale.

Figure 8.9
Graphing Equilibrium Price and Quantity

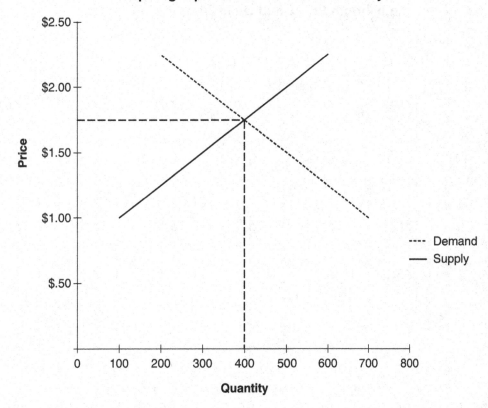

Let us now consider the consequences of a shift in the demand curve. If a new office building went up on the corner that Dino's Pizza Stand serves, the demand curve for Dino's Pizza would shift to the right, as we saw in **Figure 8.4**, and Dino could sell more slices of pizza at every price point.

Figure 8.10 below provides an illustration of the effect on equilibrium prices and quantities of Dino's pizza if there is an increase in demand. As the new office workers begin to frequent Dino's Pizza Stand, the price Dino is able to charge for his pizza increases, and the number of pizza slices he is able to sell rises as well. The new equilibrium price at which Dino can sell all the pizza he makes is now $2 and the new equilibrium quantity, or the quantity of pizza that Dino can sell at the equilibrium price, is now 500 slices of pizza.

Figure 8.10
An Increase in Demand and its Effect on
Equilibrium Prices and Quantities of Dino's Pizza

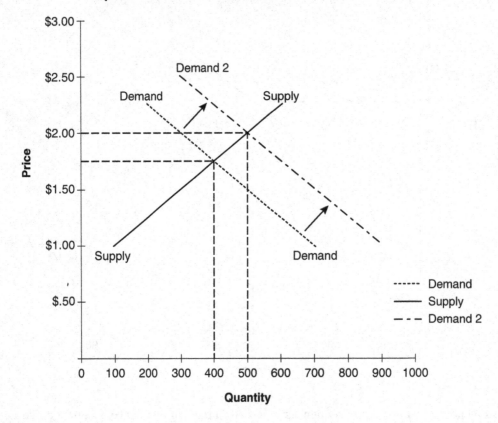

Figure 8.10 demonstrates the increase in equilibrium price and quantity that resulted from the increase in demand generated by the construction of the new office building on Dino's corner. Dino, however, has competitors who know a good thing when they see it as well. A large pizza chain decides to build a restaurant on Dino's corner, introducing a new supplier to the market for pizza. Figure 8.11 demonstrates how this new supplier shifts the supply curve to the right, representing an increase in the supply for pizza at each price point. The point where the new supply curve intersects with the second demand curve will be the new equilibrium price ($1.60) at which a slice of pizza will be sold on Dino's corner. At that market-clearing price, the number of pizza slices that will be sold (the equilibrium quantity) will be 700.

Figure 8.11
An Increase in Supply and its Effect on
Equilibrium Prices and Quantities of Dino's Pizza

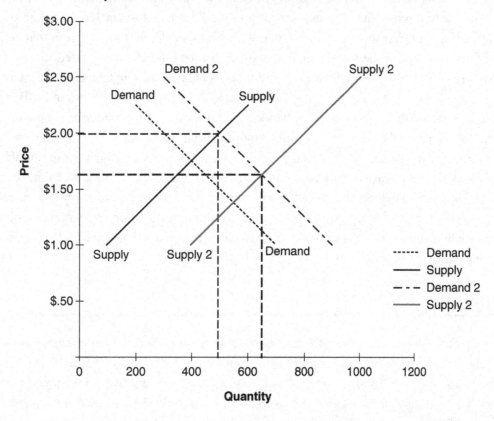

In the long run, however, we could envision other food vendors or restaurants setting up shop on Dino's corner. This would have the effect of shifting the demand curve for pizza, as alternatives to pizza become more appealing. Or, one could imagine Dino's Pizza Stand not being able to compete with the larger chain restaurant and going out of business, thereby leading to another shift in the supply curve for pizza on Dino's corner. With each shift of the supply and demand curves there will be corresponding changes in the market or equilibrium price for pizza, as well as changes in the equilibrium quantity of pizza that will be demanded and supplied.

Competency 020 Descriptive Statement D. The beginning teacher demonstrates knowledge of the historical origins of contemporary economic systems (e.g., capitalism, socialism, communism), including the influence of various economic philosophers such as John Maynard Keynes, Karl Marx and Adam Smith.

Mercantilism

An important precursor to contemporary free market economics was the theory of **mercantilism.** The leading proponent of mercantilism was the French statesman Jean-Baptiste Colbert. He and other mercantilist theorists posited that the world's wealth was a fixed sum that could be measured in the value of the world's gold and silver. Nations therefore competed to ensure that inflows of gold and silver outweighed outflows. This could be accomplished by maintaining a trade surplus. A nation that exported more than it imported experienced inflows of **bullion** (gold and silver). A nation that imported more than it exported saw its wealth in bullion flow outward. The wealth of a nation therefore was enhanced by promoting economic self-sufficiency, fostering export markets, establishing colonies, and protecting native industry and agriculture through high tariffs. The British **Navigation System** discussed in Chapter 5 of this book is an example of this policy. Though few contemporary states describe their policies as mercantilist; in fact, mercantilism is not entirely a dead letter. Arguments in favor of high tariffs to protect national industries, barriers to labor migration, or restrictions on international financial mobility harken back to the logic of mercantilism in important ways.

Capitalism

Free market theories developed at a precise moment in world history. They emerged as a way of explaining the emergence of an industrializing Europe between 1750 and 1914. The *Texas Essential Knowledge and Skills* (TEKS) insists on describing capitalism as the "American Free Enterprise System." This is a choice that reflects an association of capitalism with the development of the American political economy. Capitalism as both a theory and as an economic system, however, emerged together in Europe during the 18th and 19th centuries, in reaction to the breakdown of the medieval feudal system in agriculture and in response to the development of a growing market for agricultural, consumer, and manufactured products, which ultimately led to the Industrial Revolution.

The Physiocrats and *Laissez-faire*

In the late 17th century, the French royal financial advisor and mercantilist Jean-Baptiste Colbert asked a French merchant what the French state could do to help encourage business growth, the merchant replied, "*Nous laissez faire,*" or "Leave us alone." The French philosophical school known as the **Physiocrats**, in the middle of the 18th century, encouraged such policies as an end to France's guilds (trade organizations that kept out competitors, established prices for products, and restricted the size and number of a workshop's apprentices and journeymen laborers). They also argued for free-trade in important commodities such as grain and bread flour. They argued, before Adam Smith, that the free market would better supply a nation's populace than the tightly regulated markets of the mercantile system. The free enterprise system has consequently often been called *laissez-faire* capitalism.

Adam Smith (1723–1790)

Adam Smith is often identified as the political economist most associated with developing the theoretical underpinnings of industrial capitalism. Smith was a professor of political economy at the University of Glasgow and a key figure in the Scottish Enlightenment. His *Inquiry into the Nature and Causes of the Wealth of Nations,* usually referred to by its shortened title, *The Wealth of Nations,* was published in 1776, around the time the American colonies declared their independence from the British Empire. The *Wealth of Nations* set out to explain why some nations are wealthier than others.

Smith argued that increases in national wealth resulted from the workings of the free market. At the time when Smith wrote, most European kingdoms considered it necessary to regulate prices and supplies of food products as well as other consumer items. Governments across Europe regularly intervened in many ways in national and local economies. Smith contended instead that private individuals should be allowed to pursue their own interest in a market unhindered by government regulation. This, Smith contended, would result in the greatest economic benefit for all. Smith described how this works as follows:

> "Every individual … neither intends to promote the public interest, nor knows how much he is promoting it… he intends only his own gain, and he is in this, as in many other cases led by an **invisible hand** to promote an end which was no part of his intention."

He went on to note that butchers, brewers, and bakers do not produce our food out of their "benevolence," but out of "regard to their own interest." By freeing the marketplace of undue regulation and by permitting individuals to pursue their own self-interest, Smith argued that greater efficiencies, increased productivity, new technologies, more production, and increased national wealth would be the result. This was perhaps Smith's most important insight.

Smith contended that economic growth largely resulted from **specialization of labor** and technological efficiencies that resulted from open markets. For Smith, open competition in the marketplace resulted in an increasing division of labor. Artisanal workshops and manufacturing in the 18th century depended upon each laborer effectively learning most of the steps in the manufacturing process. A master craftsman had to demonstrate his mastery of all facets of the production process to gain the status of a master within a guild. For a pastry chef to become a master pastry chef, he had to put on a demonstration that he could make cakes, croissants, dainty cookies, meat pies, etc. Smith argued that economic growth instead resulted from increased specialization and that the process of breaking down economic tasks into ever smaller component parts (an economic practice that gave rise to the modern factory) would be the secret to economic growth and the wealth of nations.

Thomas Malthus (1766–1834) and David Ricardo (1772–1823)

Thomas Malthus was a political economist and early demographer whose study of the relationship between population and resource growth profoundly influenced the economic theories of David Ricardo. Malthus, in his *Essay on the Principle of Population*, noted that resource growth, most immediately increases in a nation's food supply, rarely resulted in sustained improvements in standards of living because population growth rapidly outstripped the capacity of the land to provide for growing populations.

David Ricardo, like Malthus, had a rather bleak view of the economic future. Ricardo believed that the "natural price of labor" corresponded with what was needed for a worker to survive. The "market price of labor," or the wage, Ricardo contended, would rarely rise far above bare subsistence level. Ricardo's conclusions were built on Malthusian population theories. Increases in wages, like increases in the nation's food supply, will simply lead to population growth, which will ultimately place downward pressure on the market price of labor, ultimately driving wages downward until they meet the subsistence needs of workers. This argument was known as the **Iron Law of Wages**. The combination of Malthusian and Ricardian theories led many 19th-century businessmen and political leaders to conclude that efforts to provide social welfare, minimum wages, old-age pensions, and other similar assistance to the working classes would ultimately prove fruitless. These policies would only have the effect of increasing population growth and distorting the marketplace, thereby putting greater pressure on natural resources and downward pressure on wages.

Businessmen and political leaders in industrializing Europe in the 19th century, despite witnessing the dislocation, poverty, and dangerous working conditions of factories in the 18th and 19th centuries, took the lessons of these classical economists as arguments against social and economic reform. Instead, they contended, like the Physiocrats, *"Laissez-nous faire."* Let market mechanisms unhindered by humanitarian concerns or governmental intervention operate, and the best interests of the society would be met.

Socialism

A number of businessmen, philosophers, and social critics, however, took a very different position. Socialism as a political and economic system emerged in response to the development of industrial capitalism as critics and even supporters of early industrialization sought to reform it, by either restraining it or ameliorating many of the human consequences of the Industrial Revolution.

19th Century "Utopian Socialists"

Critics of developing industrialization, from the early 19th century, began to develop arguments that challenged the practices of unregulated, unfettered capitalism. Many of these early critics combined under the umbrella of what would be called socialism. These socialist critics marshaled a variety of arguments against the development of industrial capitalism as it emerged in the 19th century.

Some of the earliest socialist thinkers were disparagingly called **Utopian Socialists** by later Marxist thinkers. Among them were thinkers like **Henri de Saint-Simon (1760–1825), Charles Fourier (1772–1837),** and **Robert Owen (1771–1858).** Many of their ideas were indeed fanciful but reflected a dissatisfaction with the emergence of the new industrial society of the early 19th century. Fourier, for example, condemned the deadening effect that factory labor had on individual moral and creative capacities, and argued that work should be fulfilling and varied. He rejected Smith's view that specialization and the factory would lead to growth, and instead saw the factory as destructive to the human spirit. He also objected to the individualistic ethos of emerging capitalism and sought to create communal associations—he called these phalanxes—that distributed resources and responsibilities more equitably than was the case in capitalist societies. He argued for a minimum wage to reduce the effects of poverty and an equitable sharing of a community's profits among capital, labor, and talent.

Robert Owen earned his business reputation as a textile mill owner in early 19th-century England, but observed what he perceived to be the moral degradation of workers in his mills. He determined to improve the lot of his workers by raising wages, reducing working hours, ending child labor in his mills, and providing education to his employees and their children. He believed that his program should be expanded to the entire nation, and that the British government should provide work opportunities in road construction, building, and other public works for the unemployed. By employing the poor, Owen believed they would be uplifted morally and intellectually, for the betterment of society. Owen also criticized the capitalist system's individualism, emphasis on competition and the profit motive, as well as the concentrations of wealth in the hands of a few capitalists. He also opposed such things as child labor, which was prevalent in early industrial Europe and America. He took some 80 percent of his wealth and established a utopian community in New Harmony, Indiana, an experiment in communal living and working that ultimately failed. He also began to promote trade unionism and wider societal reform.

Saint-Simon may have been the most influential of the early socialists. He coined the term "industrialism" to describe the developments of the Industrial Revolution that were shaping modern life in the early 19th century. Saint-Simon was a French nobleman who had fought in the American Revolution, and had become so inspired by the spirit of egalitarianism unleashed by the American and then French Revolutions that he renounced his noble title and began to agitate for societal reform.

Socialism as a Political-Economic System

These social reformers and idealists, however, did not have a great deal of influence in the development of socialism as it emerged as an economic and political system. Instead, socialism developed out of the political organization of labor unions and labor activists in the late 19th and early 20th centuries. In the United States, the Socialist Party, closely aligned with American workers, competed in elections across the country. In Europe, after World War I and even more clearly after World War II, socialist parties were able to successfully compete for political power at the local and national levels. As we will see in the section that follows, socialism has successfully been implemented in a variety of European nations since 1945.

Simply defined, **socialism** is a political-economic system in which the government to varying degrees owns important elements of the productive capacity of a nation; and, to varying degrees, in combination with the private sector, allocates resources in order to encourage the priorities of equality, wealth distribution, social welfare, and other societal objectives rather than prioritizing the right of individual households or firms to make these choices and to profit individually.

I emphasize "to varying degrees" here because different socialist countries have offered quite diverse answers as to how much ownership of the means of production is given over to the government, and how much government intervention is permitted in the economy. It is perhaps best to employ examples to illustrate the spectrum of socialist political and economic systems.

A number of Western European nations have adopted socialist governments and economic solutions over the course of the 20th century. Most of these have been **democratic socialist** in that they combine liberal-democratic governmental traditions (or representative democracies) and a belief in economic democracy. Democratic socialists call for a socially owned and democratically controlled economy, which they consider a means to reduce inequality, poverty, and economic exploitation. Most democratic socialist countries retain rights to private property and allow firms to operate with a good deal of freedom. In other cases, such industries as health care, public utilities, public transportation, and other industries are owned or managed by government entities.

Communism

The most adamant, and eventually most politically successful, critics of capitalism were Marxists, or Communists. Marxists called for the establishment of **revolutionary socialism**, arguing that true socialism could not coexist with the traditions of political rights common in liberal democracies or representative governments. The liberal democracies, like the United States and France, Marxists contended, protected the property rights of business owners over workers. The leading 19th-century author to develop the theories of Marxism was, of course, Karl Marx.

Karl Marx (1818–1883)

Karl Marx, a German-born philosopher and revolutionary, analyzed the development of early industrial capitalism in the nineteenth century. What he saw was unrelenting poverty and alienation of the working classes, environmental destruction, growing wealth inequalities, and political inequalities resulting from concentrations of political and economic power. Marx and his intellectual partner and patron, Friedrich Engels, developed his theories in a number of pamphlets and economic studies that represented one of the most profound critiques of Western capitalism and industrialization. The most well-known of these were *The Communist Manifesto*, published in 1848, and *Das Kapital* (translated as *Capital*), a three-volume in-depth study of capitalism.

Marx's arguments can be summarized as follows:

1. Marx argued that human history is largely defined by economic issues (rather than political, religious, or other driving forces) and by class struggle. This struggle pits the *bourgeoisie* (owners of capital, or the entrepreneurial class) against the *proletariat* (industrial workers).

2. Marx contended that economic value primarily reflected the labor time needed to produce a commodity or consumer item. This **labor theory of value** was a common-sense notion shared by many early economists. It emphasized that the real value of a commodity or manufactured item was produced by the worker who made or grew the item. Marx saw, however, that most often the beneficiary of that production was not the worker, but the owner of a factory, or the merchant who sold the item in the marketplace. For Marx, it meant that the large profits taken by business owners and merchants were immoral and represented a form of theft from the working classes.

3. According to Marx, profits represent the **surplus value** that should belong to workers rather than to employers or entrepreneurs. Capitalists are able to accumulate that surplus primarily through their control of governmental institutions, law, political power and the marketplace. It is their monopoly of power that enables them to extract inordinate profits from the productive process.

4. Marx believed that capitalism would inevitably collapse as a consequence of its own internal contradictions. He argued that as capital and wealth were increasingly consolidated in the hands of fewer and fewer capitalists, workers' wages and standard of living would be increasingly degraded (this was effectively what Ricardo had argued earlier), making it difficult for consumers to purchase the manufactured items that the economy provided. Marx also noted the instability of the business cycle in industrial societies. He saw this as a fatal flaw of capitalism. Depressions and mass unemployment would eventually lead to worker revolution and the end of capitalism.

Economists point out that Marx's labor theory of value does not describe how prices or profits are determined. Prices, they argue, are determined by the relationship between supply and demand in the marketplace. Additionally, labor is not the only factor contributing to the price of a commodity. The other factors of production, their value determined in the marketplace, also contribute to prices and profits.

Marx's predictions have also been unproven. Though the 19th and 20th centuries have been beset by moments of significant economic dislocation and unemployment (the Panic of 1893, the Great Depression, even the Great Recession of 2007–2009, for example), government fiscal and monetary policy, as well as social welfare systems and reforms of financial markets have ameliorated many of the harsher elements of the industrial capitalism that Marx witnessed in the mid-19th century.

Finally, the different attempts to put into place Marxist or Marxist-Leninist policies in the communist economies of the Soviet Union and Communist China have not been successful. Government planning and intervention of the kind seen in communist nations have led to significant shortages in consumer goods, widespread failures to meet the needs of the societies, and enormous human costs. As we will see in the next section, communism as it developed in Soviet Russia and Communist China differed in significant ways from the way in which Marx himself envisioned the workings of communism. Neither example of Marxism at work was successful.

Responding to the Business Cycle—Two Free Market Approaches

Between the two world wars, the classical theories that had guided economic policy makers came under assault as first a period of hyper-inflation in Germany threatened global markets and then as the Stock Market Crash of 1929 and the ensuing Great Depression dashed the hopes of workers and business owners alike. In response to these economic difficulties a number of prominent theorists developed policy approaches to resolve one of the most vexing and common problems associated with the free market system: the business cycle.

John Maynard Keynes (1883–1946)

Undoubtedly the most influential economist of the 20th century, John Maynard Keynes, developed his economic theories at the very lowest point in the history of world capitalism, the Great Depression. Keynes' theories received their widest acceptance in the 1930s, following publication of his *General Theory of Employment, Interest, and Money*. Keynesian theories were featured in the New Deal policies of Franklin D. Roosevelt. His theories then informed the economic policy in all the developed economies during the Great Depression and after World War II, only facing stiff criticism after the 1970s. Even in the aftermath of the 1970s, most national economies are still guided in significant ways by Keynesian ideas. While Keynes theories influenced many governments to intervene more immediately in their economies, Keynes was not a socialist, but he recognized that the sharp fluctuations of the business cycle threatened the very future of capitalism and the free market system. He believed, and demonstrated effectively, that often government efforts to bolster demand or dampen inflation were vital to the survival of capitalism. The main impact of Keynes' theories was that they supported the use of fiscal policy to reduce the wide swings common to the business cycle between 1800 and 1940. As will be discussed more fully later, Keynesian fiscal policy emphasizes the following solutions to the twin problems of inflation and unemployment: in times of recession, taxation should be reduced and government spending increased in order to bolster demand, even if this results in government deficits; and during periods of inflationary price increases, demand should be dampened by increases in taxes and reductions of government spending.

Milton Friedman (1912–2006)

More recently, Keynesian economic assumptions have been challenged by economists who contend that rather than relying on fiscal policy (government taxation and spending) **monetary policy** should be used to smooth out the ups and downs of the business cycle. The most prominent of these economists has been Milton Friedman, who published *A Monetary History of the United States, 1867–1960*, in 1963. According to Friedman's theory of **monetarism**, a nation's **Gross Domestic Product** or **GDP** will grow steadily in line with measured growth in the money supply. Recessions or economic downturns, according to Friedman, result not from too little aggregate demand in the economy, but from reductions in the available supply of money. In order for an economy to escape the downward spiral of the business cycle, it is necessary to pursue an expansionary monetary policy. In order to slow inflationary pressures on prices, the opposite tack should be taken. A tight monetary policy is then in order. Such **discretionary monetary policy** relies on the Federal Reserve System (or central banks in other nations) changing the interest rates and using other means to influence the supply of money in order to stabilize the economy.

> **Competency 020 Descriptive Statement E.** The beginning teacher understands free enterprise, socialist and communist economic systems in different places and eras.

It is perhaps best when comparing economic systems to step back from the abstract descriptions of the economic theories that underpin them and look at specific examples of free enterprise, socialist, and communist economic systems. Within any country, institutions develop within which economic choices are made. These institutions determine what will be produced and who will benefit from economic choices. Historically, these questions are answered by a mixture of public and private sector actors.

In **pure market economies** (which are an ideal and do not exist in the real world), there are two essential elements: (1) private property rights define ownership of the productive resources of the economy; and (2) decision-making is coordinated through decentralized markets in which private individuals enter into purchases, combinations, and firms with a minimum of state regulation. The choices that determine the use of resources are left to private resource owners who make decisions that benefit their own self-interest. At the other extreme are **pure command economies** (that also exist only as an ideal form and do not occur in the real world). Pure command economies feature state ownership and control of productive resources and centralized planning. The government determines what will be produced and by whom, without reliance on market mechanisms to influence those choices. Most economic systems, it must be said, lie between these two extremes and are what economists call **mixed systems.** The United States, Australia, New Zealand, Switzerland have economic systems that fall closer to pure market economies, while Cuba and North Korea are more closely associated with pure command economies.

Free Enterprise Systems

Most contemporary economies espouse to varying degrees the ideals of the free enterprise system. National economies, even those that believe in the principles of the free enterprise system, span a spectrum based on the degree to which the government provides protections in law for enterprise and property ownership, intervenes in the economy to regulate or manage outcomes, and otherwise impacts the economy. What they share, however, is that they prioritize economic freedom over social and economic equality.

In 2017, the Heritage Foundation's Index of Economic Freedom ranked Hong Kong, Switzerland, Australia, and New Zealand as the nations with the world's highest level of economic freedom. A quick look at Switzerland will illustrate why these nations were characterized as among the most economically free nations worldwide in 2017. Switzerland has an independent and fair judicial system that protects property rights and applies commercial laws equitably and consistently. Taxation rates are not onerous. The top federal income tax rate is only 11.5 percent, and government spending hovers at around 32.9 percent of gross domestic product (GDP). Annual budget deficits, according to the Heritage Foundation, average only 0.2 percent of GDP. The regulatory system serves to promote business formation and expansion, though the government does intervene to protect worker rights and to encourage competition. Switzerland also encourages imports and exports, as well as inflows of capital and investment.

The Heritage Foundation's Index of Economic Freedom ranked the United States as number 17 in its 2017 Index. The Index authors observe a number of restrictions that explain the lower ranking of the United States in comparison to the nations listed above. While rule of law and protections of property rights are strong in the United States, the ability of law enforcement agencies to seize civil assets and a significant increase in state and local licensing requirements limit Americans' property protections. Federal government regulations that limit a firm's ability to enter an industry also contribute to the lower ranking. The highest individual income tax rate in 2017 was 39.6 percent, and the top (though nominal) corporate tax rates were among the world's highest at 35 percent. Public debt amounts to 105.8 percent of GDP, an illustration of the enormous size of federal and state governments in the economy. Compare this to Switzerland, whose public debt amounts to 45.6 percent of its GDP. The Heritage Foundation's Index also observes that annually American businesses pay more than $100 billion to comply with federal regulations. Finally, more than one-third of all land in the United States is owned by the government. It was for these and other reasons that the Heritage Foundation's Index lowered the United States' ranking for 2017. While the free market system in the economies of both the United States and Switzerland prioritizes economic freedom and individual rights to make economic decisions, the role of government in their economies suggests that on a spectrum of *laissez-faire* measures, Americans are "less free" than the Swiss.

There is no need to take the Heritage Foundation's ranking at face value. The Heritage Foundation is an advocacy group with its own perspective and ranking criteria. Its ranking does illustrate that even avowed free market systems vary in the degree to which "free enterprise" characterizes the mix between government and economic activities.

Socialist Systems

Socialist systems, in contrast to free market systems, prioritize social and economic equality over economic freedom. To achieve greater social and economic equality, socialist governments engage in a degree of centralized planning and government ownership of both public services and production that is much greater than that seen in free enterprise systems. The greater government intervention and planning seen in socialist economies is often, particularly in European nations, achieved through democratic processes. Socialist governments vary significantly in the mixture of government and private sector activity.

One prominent nation with a history of socialism is Sweden, which like other Scandinavian nations in the 1950s, adopted democratic socialism. Swedish socialism is characterized by a high rate of unionization (more than 85 percent of Swedish workers are unionized, compared to fewer than 10 percent in the United States); and a strong tradition of collective bargaining. As a result of Swedish workers' political power, government involvement in social welfare is significantly greater than in most nations that pride themselves on being free enterprise systems. Swedes receive free medical care coverage, free university educations, guaranteed free housing for those who cannot afford it, subsidized child care, paid parental leave of up to 13 months, generous unemployment benefits, pensions, elder care, and many other social welfare programs. Sweden's income tax rates are substantially higher than those in the United States; its top income tax rate is 57 percent. It also has high capital gains, inheritance, and value added taxes. Government spending, not surprisingly, amounts to a much higher proportion of Sweden's GDP (51.1 percent) than is the case in the United States. Despite this, Sweden's public debt is much lower than that of the United States by comparison to its GDP. Historically, a notable feature of Sweden's economy is the large number of state-owned companies. For example, until 2009, a state-owned pharmaceutical company had a monopoly on the retail sale of medicines. Another state-owned company owns and runs the nation's railway stations. Another nationalized company owns and operates the nation's airports. Since the 1990s, a number of these have been turned over to private hands or partially privatized. Nonetheless, Sweden has a mixed economic system that remains deeply influenced by the values of socialism.

Communist Economic Systems

Today, there are few nations that claim to be communist. The People's Republic of China, North Korea, and Cuba stand out as nation-states governed by a communist party. During the Cold War, however, communism represented a substantial threat to free market economies, and to the United States and its allies. The most prominent communist nations during that period were the Soviet Union and Communist China.

The Soviet Union

The clearest example of a communist economic system was established in 1917 with the Bolshevik Revolution in Russia. Vladimir Lenin almost immediately instituted what he called "War Communism," virtually eliminating the market's role in allocating resources. As part of "War Communism," Lenin nationalized most key industries and forced farmers to supply the nation's cities at prices determined by the government. Property rights were severely curtailed and in many cases eliminated outright. This experiment ended almost immediately in disaster with widespread starvation and failing industry, forcing Lenin to liberalize the economy—in other words, to increase the role of private initiative and ownership in the economy. This policy, called the New Economic Policy, was instituted in 1921. Strikingly, with the reintroduction of market incentives and private property, Soviet Russia was again able to successfully feed its populace and began to turn its economy around. Unfortunately for millions of Soviet farmers and consumers, when Joseph Stalin took power in 1928, he steered the economy again toward a pure command economy. Between 1928 and 1991, the Soviet Union was characterized by centralized planning, few private property rights, and state-owned industries and agriculture. Under Joseph Stalin, a State Planning Commission known as *Gosplan* established production targets, which individual ministries communicated to factories and farms. State planning was not entirely unsuccessful in industrializing and militarizing the Soviet Union. By the outbreak of World War II, the Soviet Union boasted the world's second-largest industrial economy and was producing sufficient food to supply basic staples. It did so, however, by severely restricting consumer spending, denying any pretext of human rights, and absolutely repressing property rights and individual decision-making. The economy also came at a significant loss of life, as millions died under Stalin's purges, and many others died as a result of relocation done to meet government policy directives. By the 1980s, any successes that could be identified in the 1950s were long forgotten as Soviet citizens chafed under the restrictive economic system and longed for many of the consumer items that Western Europeans and Americans took for granted. The Soviet Union by the 1980s could only compete in the global economy militarily and with its vast oil and mineral resources. During the 1970s and early 1980s when oil prices were high, the communist economy was able to maintain a façade of competitiveness, but with the collapse of oil prices on the global market, the Soviet Union was no longer able to do so. Most tellingly, it could not use oil profits to maintain its military competitiveness in the face of the Reagan-era arms buildup. Faced with these twin failures, the Soviet Union's communist system collapsed between 1989 and 1992.

Communist China

Communism has also served as the ideological framework for China from 1949 to the present, although since 1978, the Chinese have followed a more liberal path to development. Before 1949, the Chinese economy was characterized by a household-based peasant agricultural society with little industry or modern manufacturing. In 1949, the People's Republic of China, as the communist government was called, followed the development strategies pursued by Stalinist Russia. Consumer spending was squeezed, and rapid industrialization and militarization took priority.

Government investment in heavy industry skyrocketed; by the 1950s, it represented one-quarter of the nation's GDP. Just as was the case with the Soviet Union, industrial output skyrocketed, growing at an average annual rate of 11.5 percent (compare this to U.S. industrial growth rates between 1920 and 2017 that averaged only 3.74 percent per year). China's planned economy successfully laid the groundwork for today's vibrant industrial economy. However, it did so at enormous human cost and privation. Since 1978, though the Chinese Communist Party has remained in control, it has abandoned much of the state planning associated with communism and adopted many features of free-market capitalism. The state still maintains ownership of significant sectors of the economy but exposes those firms to market forces that contribute to lowering costs of production and increasing efficiencies. China is still nominally a communist economy, but in many ways it has adopted the free-market mechanisms that other mixed economies exhibit.

> **Competency 020 Descriptive Statement F.** The beginning teacher understands and compares types of market structures (e.g., pure competition, monopolistic competition, oligopoly, monopoly).

Markets are not all alike. In the real world, there is a diverse variety of market conditions in which firms and households operate. Economists divide these into four basic categories: **pure competition, monopoly, oligopoly,** and **monopolistic competition**.

Pure Competition

In a marketplace characterized by perfect or pure competition, both buyers and sellers are **price-takers**. A **price-taking producer** cannot by his or her own behavior affect the market price of the goods and services they sell. A **price-taking consumer** is equally at the mercy of the market and cannot with the strength of his or her purchasing power influence the market price of the good or service he or she is interested in acquiring.

The primary characteristics of a market exhibiting the features of pure competition are the following:

1. **Many buyers and sellers.** Under conditions of pure competition, there are enough buyers and sellers that in the short run no single buyer or seller can have an impact on supply, demand, or prices.

2. **Standardized products.** In a purely competitive market, the commodity for sale cannot be differentiated from one producer to another. Consumers view it as the same good, regardless of who produced it, or where. Wheat, for example, whether it is grown in Alberta, Kansas, Argentina, or China can easily be substituted for wheat grown in any other location. As a result, farmers in Kansas will only receive for their harvest the price dictated by the global market for wheat.

3. **Complete information.** In purely competitive markets, each buyer and seller has complete knowledge of the conditions operating in an industry. This includes knowledge about the prices, operating costs, and other factors that will influence the production, sale, and consumption of a product.

4. **Freedom of Entry and Exit.** There is great variety in the ease of entry and exit into a market depending on the industry. Barriers to entry, for instance, restrict competitiveness in an industry. A requirement that barbers be licensed (though it seems a good idea) restricts entry into the business of cutting hair. This restricts competition. The requirement that public conveyances like taxis or Uber or Lyft have a city license to operate provide one mechanism to restrict competition. Patents are another potential restriction to entry in the market. Industries that require significant initial capital investment are in the short run unlikely to exhibit characteristics of pure competition. It has proven difficult for new automobile manufacturers to enter into the industry, in part because the enormous initial capital investment required, and the requirement nationally that automobile manufacturers sell their vehicles through licensed dealers.

Monopoly

A **monopolist** is a firm which is the sole supplier of a particular commodity or product that has no ready substitutes. When a firm is a monopolist, the industry is a **monopoly**. Before 1909, Standard Oil, founded by John David Rockefeller, controlled 91 percent of the United States' oil refining capacity, and thus had a clear monopoly of that industry. De Beers Diamonds, at the close of the 19th century, controlled almost all of the world's diamond mining, creating a monopoly in the diamond mining industry. Private sector monopolies, however, are usually quite rare occurrences in contemporary America, in part because of anti-trust legislation designed to break up monopolistic firms.

Monopolies form because of one or more of the following factors: control of scarce resources; increasing returns to scale (advantages gained from the size of the firm); technological advantages; and legal barriers such as patent protections, copyrights, or licensing requirements.

Monopolies may also result from unfair trade practices. Standard Oil Company in the 1890s was often accused of undercutting its competitors through unfair price-cutting and other predatory practices. Many of these practices have since been declared against the law.

Monopolies usually result in inefficient allocation of resources. A monopolist restricts production in order to raise prices and maximize profits. Monopolists, unlike producers in competitive markets, are therefore price-makers, rather than price-takers.

Oligopoly

When only a few firms compete in the same industry, the industry is known as an **oligopoly.** A firm in such an industry is an **oligopolist.** Oligopolies need not be composed of large firms. In most towns in Texas there are rarely more than two or three grocery stores, H-E-B, Walmart, or Albertsons, for consumers to choose from. Or, to take the example of another prominent industry, there are only three companies that produce the vast majority of soft drinks for American consumers: Coca-Cola, PepsiCo, and Royal Crown, or RC Cola (yes, they still exist).

Oligopolies essentially result from the same conditions that produce monopolies. The most frequent factor in the development of oligopolies are the advantages created by **increasing returns to scale**, or advantages that accrue to larger firms over smaller firms. Larger grocery stores, for example, have lower costs than mom-and-pop grocery stores.

Oligopolists, like monopolists, are price-makers. Yet, because there is competition between the two or more firms in an industry, there is tension between competition and cooperation within oligopolies. Though it is illegal in the United States, **collusion**—direct cooperation to set prices and production quotas—is one way to increase profits. **Cartels** are another way in which firms within industries avoid head-to-head and cutthroat competition that only serves to undermine their profitability. More frequently, however, oligopolistic firms will follow pricing decisions made by other firms in the industry. Oligopolies endeavor to avoid direct price competition or attempt to manage price competition. Instead, they attempt to gain market share by advertising or using their size advantages to exclude new competitors from entering the industry.

Oligopolistic industries, as with monopolies, usually result in inefficient allocation of resources. Oligopolists are similarly able to restrict production in order to raise prices and increase profits. Oligopolists, unlike producers in competitive markets, are also price makers, rather than price takers.

Monopolistic Competition

Monopolistic competition is an industry in which there are many producers. However, unlike a perfectly competitive industry, in a monopolistically competitive industry each producer has a product that is viewed as distinct from the products of its competitors, but close enough that it might be a possible substitute. My grocery store carries Bud Light, Miller Light, Coors Light, Keystone Light, Natural Light, Amstel Light, Corona Light, Heineken Light, Sam Adams Light, Kirin Light, Molson Canadian Light, and even Medalla Light from Puerto Rico. These products, while not remarkably different, can set their own prices and have some limited market power.

A key feature of monopolistically competitive markets is the importance of product differentiation. Products are differentiated, even if it is often or even primarily in the minds of consumers who have a marked preference for one brand over another. That preference, often driven by advertising and branding, will induce buyers to pay a somewhat higher price for their favorite product.

However, in a monopolistically competitive market, too great an increase in price will be greeted by the consumer shifting to another similar, but not identical, product. It turns out Amstel Light and Heineken Light are, in fact, not that different.

Monopolistic competitors, like monopolists, charge prices that are higher than those in a perfectly competitive market. Some people, after all, are firmly committed to Coors Light over Bud Light. But, the degree to which monopolistic competition misallocates resources is somewhat less than in the case of either outright monopolies or oligopolistic markets.

> **Competency 020 Descriptive Statement G.** The beginning teacher demonstrates knowledge of concepts and issues related to international trade (e.g., absolute and comparative advantage, effects of changes in the exchange rate of world currencies, free trade and the effects of trade barriers).

Political and business leaders often praise the benefits of trade. On a most basic level, we understand that without trade, even if it is only barter between two people, productivity suffers. Trade makes possible a division of labor and specialization that enables those who excel at one thing to exchange with those who excel at another so that both benefit in the process. Without trade, each of us would be dependent upon our own labor and resources, and our standard of living would fall to bare subsistence. Trade is therefore a means to encourage productivity and economic growth. This is true on both individual and international levels.

Imagine two states, the Oil-Rich State and Cotton Kingdom. Each kingdom produces both oil and cotton, but the Oil-Rich State has richer oil reserves and poorer soils for cotton, while Cotton Kingdom has richer cotton-growing lands but smaller oil reserves. Each state has equal populations and each state employs half its population in drilling for oil and half in growing cotton.

Table 8.8
Output of "Oil-Rich State" and the "Cotton Kingdom"

	Oil-Rich State	Cotton Kingdom
Oil production (barrels)	500	200
Cotton production (lbs.)	100,000	150,000

As is evident in **Table 8.8** above, the same number of oil workers in the Oil-Rich State produces two-and-one-half times as much crude oil as do the workers in Cotton Kingdom. The same number of cotton farmers in Cotton Kingdom produce double the total cotton production in the Oil-Rich State. In this example, the Oil-Rich State has an **absolute advantage** in the production of oil, and Cotton Kingdom has an absolute advantage in the production of cotton. An absolute advantage results when a country can produce more of a given product with its resources than other countries with their available resources. For example, Texas has an absolute advantage over France in producing cotton. On the other hand, France has an absolute advantage over Texas in wine production. Texas, of course, can and does produce wines. However, it has comparatively fewer areas where the soil and climate conditions are optimal for producing wine grapes. Texans are therefore better served to specialize in cotton farming and the French to specialize in viticulture (growing wine grapes).

Returning to the example in **Table 8.8,** it is evident that the Oil-Rich State and Cotton Kingdom would benefit from a trade relationship that would allow them to specialize in what they do best and trade with the other state for the item that they are less efficient at producing. If the Cotton Kingdom would shift its workers entirely into cotton production and the Oil-Rich State would shift its labor resources to the production of oil (assuming constant returns to scale) the output of the two states would look like **Table 8.9.**

Table 8.9
Output after Specialization

	Oil-Rich State	Cotton Kingdom
Oil production (barrels)	1,000	0
Cotton production (lbs.)	0	300,000

Now, consider a comparison of the total production of the two kingdoms in **Table 8.10** below. It is evident that both kingdoms gain from specialization.

Table 8.10
Gain from Specialization

	Total Production in Both Countries Mixed Specialized		Gain from Specialization
Oil production (barrels)	700	1,000	300 barrels
Cotton production (lbs.)	250,000	300,000	50,000 lbs.

No matter how gains from specialization are distributed, both nations will gain from specializing in the product in which they have an absolute advantage and trading for the item for which they do not. Were the world divided up into nations where each nation had an absolute advantage in at least one item, it would make perfect sense for each nation to do as the Oil-Rich State and Cotton Kingdom have done in the example above, specializing and trading with each to their advantage.

Unfortunately, this is not the world of international trade and commerce. Many nations do not have an absolute advantage in any single product, whereas some nations have absolute advantages in a wide range of commodities. Does this mean that there are no benefits of trade and specialization? Imagine a different scenario where the Oil-Rich State has an absolute advantage over the Cotton Kingdom in both oil and cotton production. Consider the evidence in **Table 8.11.** The Oil-Rich State produces two-and-half times the production of oil as Cotton Kingdom, and has an output of cotton that is also greater than that produced by Cotton Kingdom.

Table 8.11
Gains from Specialization and Trade

	Oil-Rich State	Cotton Kingdom
Oil production (barrels)	500	200
Cotton production (lbs.)	200,000	100,000

Will specialization and trade still be beneficial to the Oil-Rich State and the Cotton Kingdom? And, in which product should the two states specialize? The answer to the first question is still yes. And the answer to the second is that the two states should specialize in the product in which they have a **comparative advantage.**

To answer these two questions more completely, it is helpful to consider the production possibilities for the Oil-Rich State and Cotton Kingdom. **Table 8.12** describes the different production possibilities for both. From this table, it is clear that if the Oil-Rich State devotes all its labor and resources to producing oil, it will produce 600 more barrels of oil than the Cotton Kingdom will, even if the Cotton Kingdom also devotes its land and labor to oil drilling. Likewise, if the Oil-Rich State and the Cotton Kingdom decide to just grow cotton, the Oil-Rich State will out-produce the Cotton Kingdom by nearly 100,000 lbs. of cotton. If the two nations decide to forgo any trade and subsist on their own labor and resources, the Oil-Rich State will produce 300 more barrels of oil and 25,000 more lbs. of cotton than will the Cotton Kingdom on its own. What incentive then does the Oil-Free State have to trade?

Table 8.12
Production Possibilities Schedule for the Oil-Free State and Cotton Kingdom

Oil-Rich State		Cotton Kingdom	
Oil (barrels)	Cotton (lbs.)	Oil (barrels)	Cotton (lbs.)
1000	0	400	0
500	125,000	200	100,000
0	250,000	0	200,000

Specialization and trade, however, will still benefit both nations. If the Cotton Kingdom specializes in growing cotton, leaving the Oil-Rich State to specialize in drilling for oil, the two trade partners will share the production of 200,000 lbs. of cotton and 1,000 barrels of oil. The **comparative advantage** of the Oil-Rich State in oil production makes it profitable for both nations if the Oil-Rich State concentrates its labor in drilling for oil and purchases needed cotton from the Cotton Kingdom.

For a less abstract example, consider the fact that the United States purchases much of its clothing from countries like Bangladesh, the Philippines, Sri Lanka, Indonesia, India, and other nations. Why do we buy apparel from these nations? There is nothing peculiar to their climate, resources, or populations that make these areas especially good at sewing clothing items. In fact, United States manufacturers produce the same items more rapidly than do workers in these countries. The productivity of American workers in the apparel industry is greater than the productivity of workers in the countries named above. American workers in other industries (such as technology) are even more productive than their counterparts in Bangladesh, Sri Lanka, Indonesia, Guatemala, or other low-wage producers. If American workers are diverted to manufacturing apparel, this requires foregoing their production of many other items. The opportunity cost of producing clothing in these low-wage nations is thus much lower than it is in the United States. In this scenario, Sri Lanka, Indonesia, and India have a comparative advantage in producing shirts, undergarments, and other apparel; and the United States has a comparative advantage in developing computer software, pharmaceuticals, or other products that its higher worker productivity dictates the United States should concentrate on.

Free Trade

Given the advantages that accrue from the principle of comparative advantage described above, most economists argue in favor of free trade. In general, economists argue that **trade barriers** and other types of government policies that are designed to interfere with the workings of international markets are ultimately detrimental not only to individual national economies, but also to global growth.

These policies include those that are designed to encourage exports, for example subsidies given to favored economic sectors. Often, governments institute policies that are designed to exclude imports. **Protective tariffs** are taxes placed on sales of imports with the purpose of increasing the prices of imports in order to make it difficult for imports to compete with domestic products. The United States places a variety of import duties on products from across the globe. For example, in 1963, the United States levied a 25 percent tax on West German and French potato starch, dextrin, and brandy, and light trucks and vans made in Germany and France. This tariff, though modified, is still in place today. This tariff was imposed because France and (West) Germany had placed tariffs on the importation of American chickens. Today, this protection of American truck manufacturers still exists.

Economists argue that such tariffs distort global markets and undermine the comparative advantages that might develop otherwise. One way in which the tariff described above has distorted the market is that German manufacturers, like Mercedes, have imported vans built in Germany, which are disassembled before being shipped in parts to South Carolina where they are reassembled by American laborers. Presto, they are American-made and free of the tariff.

Import quotas are another form of protectionism. Import quotas limit the quantity of a particular import item. For example, to protect American sugar producers (mostly high fructose corn syrup), the United States strictly controls imports of cane and other forms of sugar. The limits reflected levels of imports established between 1975 and 1981. Sugar producers also benefit from loans, subsidies, and guaranteed minimum prices that enable American corn and sugar beet growers to compete with sugar from Brazil, China, India, and Cuba. But, if you are a fan of Mexican Coca-Cola, with its cane sugar, and disappointed at the taste of the Coca-Cola you get from the vending machine or the soda fountain, thank import quotas on imported sugar. Import quotas have also distorted the automobile market beginning in the late 1970s when import quotas were placed on the number of Japanese-made automobiles that could be sold in the United States market. From the 1960s until the late 1970s, Japanese-made cars were synonymous with cheaply-made but gas-efficient vehicles. With the imposition of quotas on Japanese vehicles, Toyota, Honda, Nissan, Subaru, and other Japanese automakers decided that to meet these quotas without suffering disastrous losses in profitability, they had to begin to sell fewer but higher quality cars that sold at higher profit margins. By the 1990s, the consequence of that strategy was that the Toyota Camry was the best-selling car for more than a decade, and Japanese vehicles had shed the reputation for being tinny, cheap, gas-sipping cars and becme known for their quality construction.

International Trade Agreements

Because protectionism harms both domestic consumers and export industries (as other nations retaliate), nations frequently enter into either bilateral (between two nations) or multilateral trade agreements. The United States in 2017 entered into bilateral trade agreements with some 20 nations. For example, the United States and Korea in 2012 signed a free trade agreement valued at approximately $84.3 billion. Multilateral treaties, such as the **North American Free Trade Agreement,** or **NAFTA**, are sometimes better known than bilateral trade agreements. Signed in 1993, NAFTA was designed to gradually remove trade barriers restricting trade between Canada, the United States, and Mexico. Another important global trade agreement is the **World Trade Organization**. It began shortly after World War II as the **General Agreement on Tariffs and Trade (GATT)**. The **GATT** talks were regularly scheduled trade negotiations designed to lower tariffs and to encourage increased international commerce. In 1994, GATT was renegotiated and the World Trade Organization formed. The organization's primary purpose is to resolve trade disputes between its 151 member states and to reduce barriers to international trade.

Effects of Exchange Rates of World Currencies

One important factor affecting global trade is currency exchange rates. In theory, when purchasing an item produced in another country, the purchase must be paid for in that nation's currency. International trade depends on foreign currency markets where currencies are exchanged for one another. The **exchange rate,** or the price of a currency in foreign exchange markets, is determined, like the price of commodities in general, by the supply and demand for that currency at a given point in time.

Buying and selling of goods, services, and assets overseas requires foreign currencies and thereby generates demand for foreign exchange. Travel and remittances, as well as investment income abroad, all contribute to demand for foreign exchange. Every time Americans purchase products from China, this generates a demand on currency markets for Chinese Yuan. And every asset purchased in the United States by Chinese citizens contributes to Chinese demand for U.S. dollars. Among the assets that are purchased by foreigners are stocks and bonds issued by American companies. Another important and safe investment (at least historically) is American treasury securities. These are bonds issued by the American government to fund its debt.

When a currency increases in value, or **appreciates**, it is said to be "strong." When a currency decreases in value, or **depreciates**, it is said to be "weak." A currency's strength or weakness is a measure of its demand in relationship to other currencies. A strong dollar is in high demand, while a weak dollar is less in demand.

What then causes a currency to appreciate or depreciate in value? Also, does it matter if the dollar is "strong" or "weak"?

Generally speaking, in global trade environments in which currencies are allowed to fluctuate freely, or **float,** without government interference, trade deficits will result in a nation's currency **appreciating** in value. For example, in the 1970s, a period of stagnant growth in the American economy, U.S. trade deficits shrank and foreign investment in the country declined. As a result, the U.S. dollar depreciated. During the 1990s, a period of significant economic growth in the American economy, trade deficits ballooned and foreign investment in American assets increased. The dollar appreciated accordingly. Since the 1990s, the United States has largely maintained policies that encourage a strong dollar. President Donald Trump, in his first months as president, in 2017, contended that the dollar was too strong, and signaled a desire to weaken the dollar on global currency markets. Why?

Which is better, a strong dollar, or a weak dollar? The answer to this question depends on whether you are Walmart or Caterpillar. Until the 1980s, Caterpillar was the world's premier maker of construction and earth-moving equipment and had few competitors around the globe. In the 1980s, the dollar was high relative to the Japanese Yen. As a result, the price of Caterpillar products around the globe was nearly 30 percent higher than the price for its primary competitor, the Japanese firm Komatsu. As an exporter, Caterpillar had difficulty competing with its Japanese rival. Even in American domestic markets, Komatsu began to sell more of its earth movers, undercutting the American company. Caterpillar was harmed by the strong dollar. By contrast, Walmart, which has been a prominent importer of Chinese products, has benefited historically from a strong United States dollar vis-à-vis the Chinese currency, the Yuan Renminbi (usually just "Yuan"). A strong dollar allows Walmart to purchase more Chinese-made goods to sell in its stores in the United

States. American consumers have also benefited from a historically strong dollar in that they have been able to afford low-priced items from abroad.

To answer the question of why President Trump would favor a weaker dollar, the examples above offer a hint. Trump famously said during his presidential campaign that he would be the "greatest jobs president God ever created." A weak dollar lowers the prices of American exports, making American manufactures more competitive on global markets. The weak dollar may therefore have the effect of increasing the number of manufacturing jobs in the nation's economy. However, the example above illustrates that increased manufacturing jobs in the nation's Rust Belt may come at the cost of increased consumer prices, and potential losses of employment in retail.

A weak dollar is also bad news for American tourists abroad or American businessmen wishing to purchase commodities in foreign markets. This is the case because a weak dollar has lower purchasing power. If you are on your European vacation, however, and the dollar is strong relative to the Euro or the British pound, then you will be able to eat better, stay longer, and buy more souvenirs. However, if you own a hotel near Disney World, a strong dollar will mean fewer foreign visitors. In other words, a strong or weak dollar (or other currency) impacts each American differently.

COMPETENCY 021 (STRUCTURE AND OPERATION OF THE U.S. FREE ENTERPRISE SYSTEM)

The teacher understands the structure and operation of the U.S. free enterprise system; the role of government, business, consumers and labor in the system; and basic concepts of consumer economics.

> **Competency 021 Descriptive Statement A.** The beginning teacher analyzes the origins and development of the free enterprise system in the United States and understands the basic principles of the U.S. free enterprise system (e.g., profit motive, voluntary exchange, private property rights, competition).

It may come as a shock to many that the terms "free enterprise system" or "capitalism" are not found in the United States Constitution or the Declaration of Independence. The Constitution of the United States did not specify which form the economic system the nation would take. This was not an oversight on the part of the Framers. The term *capitalism* did not exist yet; neither did the concepts of industrialization or industrialism, in the way we understand these terms. To speak of the 18th-century authors of these important civic documents as advocates of a "free enterprise system" is anachronistic at best. The Framers did share a range of economic ideas and concerns, though it would be a mistake to believe that they shared our economic preoccupations.

Nonetheless, it is fair to argue that the Constitution of 1789 provided for the establishment of a free enterprise or capitalistic economy. Capitalism or a free enterprise system depends upon individual private enterprise and private markets. For these to be safe from government encroachment and for them to operate effectively, they must be permitted to operate freely, and they must be protected in law. The Constitution, as written and as interpreted over time, has provided important safeguards for the free enterprise system.

The Framers shared the view that humans naturally act out of their own self-interest, a belief that capitalists from Adam Smith onward have considered natural and the basis for economic growth. Self-interested behavior in traditional Judeo-Christian thought had been seen as problematic. Though the **profit motive** is only one of the ways in which self-interested nature was expressed, the Founders did recognize that this expression of self-interest was a worthy objective and one that entrepreneurs, merchants, and businessmen could rightfully pursue without societal judgment or state prohibition. The Framers did observe the necessity of public-spiritedness for the success of a republic. Nonetheless, the role of the state remained to ensure that individuals in pursuit of their own self-interest were able to achieve their ends without trampling on the rights of others.

The Framers' attitude toward **private property** owed a great deal to their history of protecting their rights as Englishmen. The language protecting property rights in the Constitution, primarily evident in the Fifth Amendment's protections against deprivation of private property without just compensation, reflects the language in England's Magna Carta and Bill of Rights of 1689 and the traditions of English common law. In the decades after the ratification of the Constitution and in the subsequent centuries, the protections of private property have been both redefined and extended. Some Framers supported the view that the Constitution was written primarily to protect property rights. Indeed, the notion that there should be no taxation without representation followed from that view.

A private property right includes the following features: (a) the exclusive authority to make decisions on how a resource will be used; (b) an exclusive right to the benefit of the resource (such as rents, income, interest, etc.); and (c) the right to alienate or exchange the property, provided a buyer is willing.

An important but unstated property right enshrined in the Constitution, and jealously guarded from 1787 until 1861, it must be said, was the right to own property in human beings. Many of the constitutional protections of property rights implicitly protected chattel slavery. That this was the case was evident even in Abraham Lincoln's view of his authority as president of the United States, and the limits he had on the government's ability to abolish slavery.

While some of the Framers emphasized private property protections, others argued that the Constitution's primary purpose was to protect individual **liberty**, which implied not only that one's property rights were secured, but also that one had the freedom to pursue one's own happiness, primarily by being free to choose an employment, career, or business opportunity without infringement by the state. Most of the Framers nonetheless had no illusions about the risks associated with a free market. They were careful to empower states to regulate their own commerce and Congress to regulate interstate commerce. That said, what the Framers created was a customs union where commerce could cross state boundaries without internal trade barriers or tariffs. They also created a single currency system. In many ways, the real success of the American experiment was that it created a free trade zone unlike anything anywhere in the world at the time.

The principal feature of **voluntary exchange** is the assumption that the parties to an exchange both benefit from that exchange. The contracting parties enter into the agreement because they both expect to improve their situation as a result of the relationship. They may find that the exchange did not, in fact, benefit both, or either, of them. An additional feature of voluntary exchange is the presumption that Americans have the right to "freedom of contract." Contract law therefore governs the limits of voluntary exchanges.

In order for markets to work to fulfill their pricing functions and to most efficiently distribute goods and services, a degree of **competition** is required. Restraint of competition has therefore been a preoccupation of federal and state governments from the earliest days of the American republic. Among the targets of such legislation during the 19th century, as we have seen, were labor unions and organizations. State courts in the 1840s and 1850s looked unkindly on labor organizations that attempted to increase wages. Though these restrictions were ultimately overturned and labor unions permitted, many practices of union organizers have been restricted as restraint of trade. In the 1890s, the federal government and courts turned their attention to the monopolist activities of large corporations. The Sherman Antitrust Act represents the most important legislation on this score.

> **Competency 021 Descriptive Statement B.** The beginning teacher analyzes issues and developments related to U.S. economic growth from the 1870s to the present (e.g., anti-trust acts; tariff policies; the New Deal; economic effects of World War I, World War II and the Cold War; increased globalization of the economy).

Economic growth has been an almost constant feature of the American economy since the end of the American Civil War despite punctuation by cyclical crises, such as the Panics of 1873 and 1893, the Great Depression of 1929–1939, the dot-com crash of the 1990s, and the Great Recession of 2007–2009. Nonetheless, growth has been a feature of the American economy.

One measure of growth is rising life expectancy since 1870. In 1870, the life expectancy at birth for U.S. white males was 45.2 years. In 1940, it had risen to 64.2 years; by 2010, it had risen to 77.9 years.

Another measure of growth can be seen in GDP per person. In 1870, the GDP per person was $3,000. In 2016, GDP per person was $51,638, more than a seventeen-fold increase.

Growth from the "Gilded Age" to the "Roaring Twenties"

In the aftermath of the American Civil War, the United States experienced a growth surge that would continue with few interruptions to the present. Between 1870 and 1929, average annual growth rates averaged around 1.8 percent per year. During the period from 1870 to 1914 and the beginning of World War I, the federal government's stated philosophy was one of *laissez-faire* or free-market capitalism. This stated policy, however, did not reflect the actual practices of the government.

The federal government hardly took a hands-off approach to American economic growth. For example, the federal government invested significantly in "opening up" the Great Plains and American Southwest. This involved removal of the Native American and Mexican populations who stood in the way of economic expansion into the region. Additionally, the government subsidized the expansion of railroad building across the West with generous grants of public lands to railway magnates, as well as subsidies to settlers willing to homestead in Kansas, Nebraska, and other Midwestern states. The federal government also significantly expanded **protective tariffs** in the second half of the 19th century. This was done to protect American industry from foreign competition. The Republican Party generally supported tariffs, while Democrats opposed them as detrimental to agricultural interests.

According to classical free market economic theory, protective tariffs undermine growth. However, in what has been called the **Tariff-Growth Paradox**, before World War I, the United States, Japan, Germany, and other nations with protectionist trade policies experienced significant growth. The United States is perhaps the best example of this paradox, as more of its manufacturing economy was protected from competition than nearly any other economy in the world. Also, the United States experienced among the highest growth rates of any nation before World War I. Protectionist policies provided American manufacturing a window of opportunity within which to emerge as a competitor to more developed European industrial nations like Great Britain, France, and Germany. The use of protective tariffs to exclude foreign competition continued until 1929, though the Progressive Democrat Woodrow Wilson, had pushed through lower tariff rates between 1913 and 1921.

Growth and the New Deal

The Great Depression has often been seen as an era of decline and reduced growth. However, an important consensus has recently arisen around the proposition that the Depression era (1929–1941) laid the foundation for the growth that contributed to American military and economic successes in World War II and the Cold War. This seems counterintuitive because the period was characterized by high rates of unemployment, low private investment, and significant economic and demographic dislocation. Nonetheless, the combination of the New Deal policies and their resolution of a number of the bottlenecks in finance, investment, and infrastructure investment, joined with processes of innovation and invention during the period, transformed the economy of the country in critical ways that would result in growth in the ensuing period.

It is commonplace to argue that the level of public investment during the Depression was too small by comparison to levels of GDP to have really promoted growth. Frequently, economists will suggest that it was only the onset of World War II that pulled the United States economy from the Depression.

One important area where the New Deal made a significant difference in the American economy that would bear fruit in the ensuing years was in highway construction and transport. The boom in automobile sales and production of the 1920s had vastly outstripped the ability of the nation's road system to accommodate traffic. It was primarily during the Great Depression, thanks to the Public Works Administration and Works Progress Administration, that the nation's first road network was constructed. Though the Interstate Highway Act of the 1950s would significantly improve on this network, the roads built in the 1930s would substantially improve the nation's productivity.

The establishment of the Federal Deposit Insurance Corporation (FDIC), another New Deal program, must also be credited with having a long-term impact on investment growth. The FDIC did a great deal to encourage private saving before the war and since. As small savers put their money in banks with the conviction that they were not going to be left penniless at the first financial panic, a much wider pool of savings was made available for loans and other investments.

New Deal programs also established programs like Social Security that kept income levels up, even during future downturns in the business cycle. These and other transfer payments reduced the depth of economic recessions by keeping aggregate demand from falling too far.

World War II

World War II encouraged economic growth first and foremost, simply as a consequence of the vast increase in government spending. Total federal military spending during the period topped $296 billion between the start of the war in December 1941 and the end of the war in 1945. Federal spending as a percentage of the national economy during the war years reached levels not approached since. Federal spending neared 46 percent of GDP. By comparison, during the Great Depression, even with the New Deal programs, federal expenditures never reached 15 percent of GDP. The expansive government investment in the economy not only enabled the nation to fight and win a war in the Pacific and Europe, but also propelled the economy into a period of long-term growth.

World War II contributed to long-term growth in a number of ways. Perhaps the most important contribution of the war to long-term growth was the many technological advances that occurred during the war, which would be employed in civilian uses after the end of hostilities. Radar, microwave technology, atomic energy, improvements in metalworking, and many other technologies would later transform the world economy, pushing outward future production possibilities frontiers.

Additionally, many advantages that accrued from economies of scale were for the first time realized in a number of industries. For example, Americans developed the organizational apparatus to produce enormous quantities of ships, aircraft, synthetic rubber, weaponry, and fuel, and workers learned lessons along the way about how to most efficiently produce these technically sophisticated goods efficiently in great quantities. Many of the plants that produced these items were rapidly transformed without reductions in size to produce similar products for civilian markets. There were also a number of immediate transfers from war production with immediate impacts. For example, the wartime production of munitions left a surplus stock of materials that could be used as chemical fertilizers. The price for these fertilizers dropped by over 90 percent in the postwar period initiating a "green revolution" in the American Midwest which later spread to Mexico, India, and other developing countries.

The war effort also drew into the industrial workplace an army of African American, Latino/a, and women workers who had previously been underutilized as a labor resource. The diversion of 12 million or more men into the military wasted an important productive resource, and cost these men (without referencing loss of life or limb) dearly in terms of education, income-earning opportunities, and training.

Globalization

Globalization has been underway since the end of World War II, though often it hasn't been recognized as such. From the 1950s to the 1990s, a series of international institutions led by the United States have contributed to growing integration of the world economy. Institutions and large-scale initiatives like the International Monetary Fund (IMF), which stabilized global financial markets; the World Bank, which fostered investment in developing countries; the Marshall Plan; the Global Agreement on Tariffs and Trade (GATT), which would later become the World Bank; the European Union; the North Atlantic Treaty Organization (NATO); and even the United Nations created a system of international institutions that reduced international conflict and encouraged economic growth. These institutions set rules of the game that allowed globalization to take off between 1945 and 1989. The period of time since 1989, however, is most often seen as the period of world economic globalization.

In 1989, the political scientist Francis Fukuyama published a paper entitled *The End of History*. The publication date was important because in 1989, the Berlin Wall was torn down; Eastern Europe was convulsed with a series of mostly peaceful revolutions that overthrew the communist regimes that had governed the region since the end of World War II; and not long after 1989, the Soviet Union collapsed, leaving the United States and Western-style capitalism no rival on the global stage. The end of the Cold War signaled the end of the polarized political and economic rivalry that had characterized the previous 45 years. Many political leaders, economists, and business leaders in the West saw the moment as an auspicious time to transform the world in ways that had been impossible during the Cold War. They imagined that with the end of the Soviet Union, the world was embarking on a "global democratic revolution" characterized by the victory of liberal democratic institutions around the world. Another feature of this revolution was the belief that the spread of liberal democracies would be accompanied by a reduction of barriers to the spread of trade, financial resources, and populations. According to this "neoliberal consensus" this opening of barriers would lead to growth not only in the previously repressed economies of India, China, Latin America, and Africa, but also in developed economies. The argument was that as the economies of Asia, Latin America, and Africa opened up their borders to trade, and the West opened its borders to population and capital transfers, growth in the developing world would lead to increased job opportunities and investment opportunities in both developed and developing countries. In short, the end of the polarized rivalry of the Cold War, coupled with the spread of democratic and capitalist values, would lead to a new age of global openness, economic growth, and international cooperation.

A number of policy prescriptions were proposed to ensure that this global growth took place. The proposals reflect what has become known as the **Washington Consensus**. These included recommendations to developed and developing countries alike to institute **"austerity measures"** (reductions of fiscal deficits by lowering government spending on social welfare, health care, and public education); tax reforms that lowered tax rates on the wealthy; liberalized trade (cutting tariffs, licensing requirements, and subsidies for agriculture and manufacturing industries); privatizing state-owned industries; selling off state-owned resources; and reducing occupational, environmental, financial, and consumer protection regulations.

Globalization has seen significant changes in individual national economies and in international trade. China, for example, massively transformed over the course of the period after the Cold War, with a remarkable impact on the global economy. In 1980, when the Chinese premier Deng Xiaoping began to liberalize the Chinese Communist government's economic policies, per capita incomes in China were the equivalent of those in the United States at the time of the American Revolution. By 2010, per capita incomes in China had risen to the equivalent of those in the United States in the 1930s.

Living standards elsewhere have also improved significantly. In 1990, the World Bank described an income of $1 a day or less as the threshold of absolute poverty. In 1990, 36 percent of the world's population lived on $1 or less a day. Adjusted for inflation, in 2011, only 15 percent of the world's population lived on $1.25 or less per day. This represented a 58 percent reduction in 21 years. In 2017, with a metric of $1.90 (the equivalent of $1 a day in 1990) only 9.6 percent of the world's population lives at or below this level of absolute poverty. Globally, and in most developing nations, the share of the population living in conditions of poverty has been reduced significantly over the period of globalization.

One effect of globalization has been the opening up of financial markets to easy transfers of capital across international borders. This has contributed to easing investment in developing countries (witness the many American companies that have moved manufacturing operations to

Mexico, the Philippines, El Salvador, or anywhere else where lower wages or relaxed regulatory climates enable the American companies to profit).

Another effect of globalization has been the vast increase in the cross-cultural influences of international commerce. Think simply of the ways in which diets and food offerings have changed since the 1970s. Towns of nearly all sizes in the United States reflect foreign influences. For example, many boast a Mexican restaurant, a Chinese restaurant, Thai food, a Vietnamese restaurant, Indian food, etc.

Another effect of globalization is significant migratory movements. Much of the growth in the West has been driven by the arrival of immigrants. Since 2010, as the baby boom generation in the United States has moved into retirement, for the United States economy to continue to grow at even a 3 percent rate would require a replenishment and even growth of the working population. Given current low birth rates, growth of the United States economy at a 3 percent annual rate over the next 10 years would require a 40 percent increase in immigration of younger workers. One of the reasons that Japan has not seen significant growth rates during the period of globalization is its very restrictive immigration policies.

In short, since 1989, globalization has contributed to both significant economic growth, as well as political and social instability in many countries around the world.

> **Competency 021 Descriptive Statement C.** The beginning teacher understands and compares types of business ownership (e.g., sole proprietorships, partnerships, corporations).

Economists call business enterprises "**firms**." A firm may be as small as a food cart, a handyman's business, or a family farm. It may also be as large as Walmart, Inc., with its many shopping outlets across the country. The decision-making function of firms is known as **entrepreneurship**. Entrepreneurs determine when to open a firm, what goods to produce or sell, how and where the firm's financing will be acquired, at what prices goods or services will be sold, whether or not to expand the firm, and many other decisions.

In the example of the food cart owner-operator, the *entrepreneur* is the proprietor. They decide where to locate their cart (limited of course by local ordinances), and whether to sell hot dogs, tacos, gyros, or some other item. They decide how to price their product. The entrepreneur of a multi-national corporation is more difficult to identify. Is it the CEO? Is it the board of directors? Is it the hundreds of thousands of shareholders who own the company's stock?

The buildings, machinery, or fixed equipment that compose the physical space where production or sales take place is called the **plant**. In the case of a Ford dealership, the plant is fairly easily identified: the car lot, service bays, showroom, and offices compose the plant of the dealership.

An **industry** often is used to imply all the producers of a particular commodity. A taxi driver is part of the transportation industry. A cotton farmer is in the cotton industry. A banker is in the finance industry. A cotton farmer who also grows sorghum is simultaneously in both the cotton and sorghum industries.

The form that businesses take is largely defined by legal and economic factors. Economists divide firms among those that are sole proprietorships, partnerships, and corporations.

Sole Proprietorships

Firms in which individuals put up their own money or borrow the needed financing to establish a business, run it themselves, and receive the profits or bear the losses themselves are **sole proprietorships.** The large majority of firms in the American and global economy are sole proprietorships.

Partnerships

As greater capital is needed, or when the requirements of a firm involve the need to bring together very different management or technical skill sets, entrepreneurs may wish to form **partnerships**. Partnerships diffuse ownership or the entrepreneurial function among two or more people. Partners to an enterprise bear joint financial responsibility, share liability, divide the profits, and divide management functions of a firm. Partnership arrangements have significant advantages over sole proprietorships, particularly in the ability of a partnership to raise start-up funds. Nonetheless, partnerships are usually unable to accumulate sufficient financial capital to support really large-scale businesses. Additionally, just as the sole proprietor is personally liable for the debts of the firm, the partners in a firm are also personally liable. In most cases, this liability is an **unlimited liability,** in which each partner in a firm is personally liable for all the deeds of the other partners. While partnerships exist in many industries, some firms that are commonly organized as partnerships include doctor's offices, law firms, etc. There are far fewer partnerships in the American economy than there are sole proprietorships.

Some partnerships are organized as **limited liability companies** or **LLCs.** LLCs combine characteristics of partnerships or sole proprietorships and corporations. LLCs are often formed when a group of owners or a sole owner create a barrier between their own private wealth and the wealth of the company.

Corporations

Corporations were conceived to limit the liability of ownership, and to meet financial and managerial demands of large-scale enterprises. The term **corporation** derives from the French term *corps*, or body. A corporation is a social body that takes on a life of its own and can persist long after the deaths of its founders and first shareholders. The earliest corporations in Europe were not business enterprises *per se* but social entities that were formed for a variety of reasons.

The first universities were corporations of teachers and students who were granted a charter and legal identity that allowed them to collectively rent or purchase buildings and land, and to establish standards and curricula.

The first business enterprises organized in corporate fashion were the **joint-stock companies** that were organized to facilitate long-distance trade and exploration. For example, the Virginia Company of London, which set out to explore and settle the Chesapeake Bay area, was such a corporation. Purchasers of a share of stock in the company became part owners of the company, entitled to a share of the profits in the company. In such a risky venture, however, few of the stockowners would have been willing to place themselves at risk to bear the burdens of all the potential losses that a company like the Virginia Company might have generated. A corporation thus limits liability.

A **corporation** is thus a "legal person" distinct from the individuals who own it (stockholders) and the individuals who control it (the managers and board of trustees). Corporations can conduct business in the name of the company, engage in contracts, sue others for contractual violations, be sued by individuals and other firms, borrow, lend, purchase or lease property, lobby for political or social change, support political candidates, and in other ways act as a person within the civil society.

Advantages of a corporation are many, which perhaps explains their prominence in modern capitalism. These advantages are the following:

1. Shareholders have no personal liability for corporate debts or decisions. Shareholders can only lose their initial investment, or the value of their stocks.

2. Corporations can gain nearly unlimited funding by selling shares of stocks (which increases the pool of owners) or issuing bonds (borrowing from private investors who expect a regular return as part of the cost of doing business).

3. Stockholders elect the board of directors charged with oversight of the company's management. Management of the corporation is delegated to a board of directors who oversee salaried employees, including the Chief Executive Officer, Chief Financial Officer and others who oversee day-to-day operations.

4. Corporate securities (shares of stock) are heritable or easily sold, allowing the ownership of the company to survive long after the death of the original shareowners.

Corporate Finance

Corporations raise funding by selling stocks and bonds. Investors who buy **stocks** purchase an ownership share, however small, in the corporation. Investors who purchase **bonds** loan money to the corporation.

Common **stockholders** have an ownership share. They participate in the election of boards of directors. If the corporation is dissolved, they are entitled to a share of the assets of the corporation, if any remain after all the creditors are paid. The shareholders are the first to gain when profits are high, and the first to lose if the company is not doing well. Profits are distributed to shareholders in the form of **dividends.** A corporation may decide, however, not to distribute the profits but to reinvest or plow them back into the company.

Bondholders are creditors. Corporations wishing to borrow large sums for significant capital investment often issue bonds for sale to private buyers or institutions. Bonds are repaid over time at a set rate of interest. Bondholders have no ownership stake in the corporation. They do not have the right to participate in the selection of board members. Bondholders are not also entitled to the profits of the company. However, bondholders are paid first in the case of corporate liquidation.

> **Competency 021 Descriptive Statement D.** The beginning teacher demonstrates knowledge of the role of financial institutions in saving, investing and borrowing.

Households do not spend all their disposable income on consumer items, housing, and services. Typically, households set aside a portion of their income as **private savings.** Historically, Americans have not had high personal savings rates by comparison to households in other countries. The personal savings rate of Americans was only 5.7 percent in 2016. Thus, for every $100 in after-tax income Americans earned, they set aside only $5.70.

Household or private saving is one of the main sources for public borrowing and private investment. Private savings are placed into financial institutions and markets where individuals, banks, and other institutions purchase stocks and bonds, and make loans.

Households are not the only savers in an economy. The government can save (a rare occurrence in recent American history) when it collects more tax revenues than it spends. This is called a **budget surplus**.

A nation's **national savings rate** is the sum of private and public savings. It equals the nation's income minus total consumption and government expenditures. National savings rates are one measure of the health of an economy.

An important fact to keep in mind when discussing private and public savings is that savings and investment spending are always equal. This is known as the **savings-investment spending identity**. For an economy as a whole, once net inflows into the economy from foreign investors and net outflows from the economy measured by investment abroad are considered, savings always equals investment spending. Savers and investors, however, are not always the same people.

Modern economies depend on a number of financial instruments to ensure that savings are fluidly made available for investment spending. There are four primary kinds of financial assets that are held by businesses, government, and households: bank deposits, loans, bonds, and stocks.

Banks

A properly operating financial system brings together savers and investors. Perhaps the best-known institutions within modern financial systems are banks. Banks work by accepting funds from depositors. A depositor who opens a checking account or savings account and deposits their money into that account is essentially loaning money to the bank. I imagine this is not how you feel about the relationship. The rising cost of fees for services such as the availability of an ATM, checks, debit cards, and other services suggest that the depositor is paying for the privilege of putting his or her money in a local bank. Depositors are paying a price to have their money readily available or **liquid**. A saver might put their money in other less liquid assets—stocks, bonds, real estate, etc.—but would not be able to quickly convert that asset into cash. Savings accounts more clearly reflect the depositor's relationship as a bank's creditor. A savings account usually pays an interest rate (though that rate has been historically quite low) to the depositor. This interest represents the price paid by the bank to the depositor for the privilege of holding his or her money.

Banks keep only a fraction of their depositors' money on hand as cash. Banks loan out many times the amount of their total deposits to businesses, homebuyers, and other borrowers. Borrowers pay back the value of their loans, plus the accumulated interest (the price for borrowing) over long periods of time. In this way, the "liquid assets" of depositors are made available for the long-term and often illiquid assets of borrowers.

Banks depend on the fact that only a small number of their depositors will on a given day come to withdraw from their accounts. American banks are also protected from "runs" by the **Federal Deposit Insurance Corporation (FDIC)**, which guarantees depositors' individual bank accounts up to $250,000.

Loans are one of the most familiar categories of financial assets/liabilities. A loan is a liability to the debtor, but an asset for the creditor. The most common loans are those taken out to purchase a home or a car, or to finance one's higher education. Most small businesses also take out bank loans to finance business expansions or purchases of new equipment.

Bonds provide a more efficient means for large borrowers, whether corporations or government entities, to finance their operations. Bonds are simply promises to pay a fixed annual interest payment and to repay the principal borrowed from the owner of the bond at some fixed future date. The bond owner purchases the bond from the borrowing entity, a corporation or government organization that issues and sells the bonds to whomever will buy them under the terms specified with the bond issue.

Loan-backed Securities (also called Asset-backed Securities)

During the recession of 2007–2009, loan-backed securities came to most Americans' attention for the first time. Banks, credit card companies, auto finance companies, and consumer finance companies pool loans and offer them to financial institutions that turn these loans into securities, which can be bought and sold like stocks or bonds. The most frequently referenced loan-backed securities are mortgage-backed securities, but student loans, automobile loans, and other loans have been similarly securitized.

Stocks

Stocks are shares of ownership in a corporation. Stocks are sold to raise capital and to spread the risks of ownership. Most large companies sell stock. Stockholders are allowed to vote for the board of directors and occasionally on other matters. They are often also allowed to attend the shareholders' meetings and voice concerns. A share of stock can be bought and sold by its owners, one way of gaining value from the ownership of stock. Another way shareholders benefit is by receiving dividends, or shares of the company's profits.

Mutual Funds

Ownership of a stock exposes the owner to risks if the company goes bankrupt or its value decreases. One way to diversify and diminish risk is to own shares in a mutual fund. A mutual fund pools a group of stocks or other assets and creates a fund in which investors can purchase shares. This allows investors with relatively small amounts of money to invest in a portfolio of stocks or other assets.

> **Competency 021 Descriptive Statement E.** The beginning teacher analyzes the role of government in the U.S. free enterprise system (e.g., significance of government rules and regulations, impact of fiscal and monetary policy decisions, role and function of the Federal Reserve System, relationship between government policies and international trade).

While the free enterprise system celebrates private entrepreneurialism and individual choice, the free enterprise system also depends upon a scaffolding of federal and state government institutions to protect private property, to provide a legal framework within which contracts are secured, to ensure fair and competitive markets, and to provide the infrastructure that makes commerce and industry possible.

Government Rules and Regulation

In the United States, government rules and regulation fall into six broad categories: (1) regulations designed to restrict unfair or monopolistic trade practices; (2) regulations designed to protect against fraud and unfair business practices; (3) regulations of labor and labor conditions; (4) regulations designed to protect the health and safety of consumers; (5) regulations of education and social welfare; and (6) regulations designed to protect the environment.

Before the 1890s, industrialists faced few restrictions when they engaged in monopolistic practices or unfair trade practices designed to limit competition in American marketplaces. In 1890, Congress passed the Sherman Antitrust Act. Trusts were stock arrangements that pooled resources in major industries in order to control those industries and destroy competition. One of the most significant early antitrust suits was directed against the Standard Oil Company. The case, decided in 1911, would eventually lead to the breakup of the company. Exxon, Mobil, Amoco, and Chevron are oil companies that were hived off of Standard Oil. Another prominent suit that resulted in a similar breakup was a suit against Bell Telephone in the 1980s. Microsoft, more recently, was found in 2000 to have constituted a monopoly and to have used its monopoly power to undermine competitors including Apple, Lotus Software, Linux, and other firms.

Competitive markets require that consumers make decisions on the basis of accurate and full knowledge of their purchases, and that businesses operate in good faith. Consumer fraud is a purposeful effort to deceive, manipulate, or make false representations. Businesses and consumers alike depend upon state and federal government rules against fraud and enforcement of these sorts of crimes. Annually, fraud costs U.S. businesses more than $600 billion a year, and consumers more than $30 billion a year.

Government regulations have been vital to the improvement of labor conditions and wages in the United States. During the 19th century, there were few state or federal regulations protecting workers and worker rights. Free market advocates and business leaders in the 19th century argued that such regulations undermined market mechanisms, and that the market should determine wages and working conditions. The result was long workweeks (three-quarters of U.S. workers worked more than 54 hours per week), with workers in many industries on the job 12 hours a day for 6 to 7 days a week). Industrial accidents were commonplace. In the 1910s, more than 25,000 American workers died in workplace accidents annually; and more than 700,000 each year missed a month's work due to their workplace injuries. Annually, 1 in 300 coal miners died in mining accidents. In the early 20th century, there was no federal minimum wage. In 1910, a family of five needed an annual income of $800 to maintain a minimum standard of living. More than two-thirds of American families, even with women and children working, earned less. The average worker was also unemployed (with no unemployment benefits) between one-sixth and one-third of the year. Additionally, workplace discrimination on the basis of race, religion, gender, and nationality were commonplace features of the labor environment.

In response to these conditions, labor unions, progressive political and business leaders, and the courts developed a number of protections for workers. These included minimum wage laws, regulations limiting the work week (with premiums for weekend, holiday, and overtime work), child labor laws, and abolition of payment in scrip. Many workers were paid in scrip, basically coupons that could only be redeemed in the company store or by participating merchants. This reduced worker mobility. Antidiscrimination legislation, culminating in the Civil Rights Act of 1964, provided protections against workplace and hiring discrimination on the basis of race, color, creed, sex, sexual orientation age, gender identity, religion, veteran status, and national origin. Economists argue that antidiscrimination laws increase competition in labor markets and have the positive effect of reducing stickiness in wage markets. (Sticky wages, as Renee Haltom of the Richmond Fed has written, "are when workers' earnings don't adjust quickly to changes in labor market conditions.") Social welfare regulations are another category of federal and state government regulation that impact the marketplace. Examples include unemployment insurance, workers' compensation, health insurance, and old-age insurance. Unemployment insurance, health insurance, and old age insurance operate on the rationale that individuals have difficulty saving on their own for an unexpected layoff, a disabling injury, or aging. Unemployment insurance underwritten by state and federal governments provides workers a window of time in which they may search for work when they have been laid off. All employed persons pay into this insurance fund, just as they pay into Medicare or Social Security. Workers' compensation funds are similar social insurance programs that provide a safety-net for workers disabled on the job. While these programs provide individual benefits, they also serve a macroeconomic function, benefiting the entire economy. Social Security, health insurance, and unemployment benefits permit workers who are either laid off or no longer at their peak productivity to continue purchasing goods and services they would otherwise have to forgo, thereby sustaining aggregate demand in the economy.

Federal and state governments have since the early 1900s been active in legislating important consumer protections. For example, under Theodore Roosevelt, the Meat Inspection Act (1906) and Pure Food and Drug Act (1906) were passed to protect consumers. The Meat Inspection Act reformed the meatpacking industry and created a government regulatory body to inspect livestock feedlots, slaughterhouses, and meat processing plants. The Pure Food and Drug Act created the Food and Drug Administration (FDA), which still exists, to investigate adulteration and misbranding of food and drugs. In the Great Depression, additions to this act made it illegal to make false or misleading statements about foods, drugs, cosmetics, and other consumables. Since the 1960s, a variety of consumer protection agencies at the federal and state levels have been established to protect consumers.

Environmental quality has only recently become a matter of significant concern to federal and state officials. In 1969, Congress passed the National Environmental Policy Act which was signed into law by Richard Nixon. The following year, the Environmental Protection Agency (EPA) was established to carry out the primary functions of this legislation. The National Environmental Policy Act made the prevention and reduction of environmental damage a priority of the federal government. Though it is not a Cabinet level position, the agency reports directly to the president and administers regulations to ensure air and water quality.

Government Fiscal and Monetary Policy

The federal government has since the early twentieth century become increasingly involved in developing policies designed to stabilize the economy and reduce the unpredictability and human suffering associated with swings in the business cycle. These predominantly take the form of fiscal and monetary policy.

Fiscal Policy

Fiscal policy is a combination of tax and spending measures designed to ensure that the American economy is operating at its optimal level. Classical economists argued that when an economy experienced high rates of unemployment or inflation, the market would in the long run achieve equilibrium and balance out on its own. During the Great Depression, as we have seen, the theories of John Maynard Keynes captured the attention of policy makers around the world, including in the United States, encouraging government decision-makers to rely more explicitly on fiscal policy to stabilize national economies.

In periods when economic growth has stagnated and unacceptable levels of unemployment occur, governments often resort to **expansionary fiscal policy** to prime the pump and increase aggregate demand in an economy. Expansionary fiscal policy is a combination of decreased taxes, increased government spending, and increased transfer payments. Transfer payments are payments such as social security spending, welfare payments, farm or corporate subsidies, and other direct payments from the government to citizens. When the government reduces tax rates or provides a one-time tax rebate, it increases disposable income which can be used to purchase consumer items. This, in turn, will encourage increased production and employment of a nation's workforce (as well as its other productive resources). Similarly, increases in government spending on goods and services or on transfer payments also increases employment and aggregate demand.

Contractionary fiscal policy is called for to slow economic growth and reduce inflationary pressures in the economy. Contractionary fiscal policy is a combination of increased tax rates, decreased government spending, and reduced transfer payments. A contractionary fiscal policy will have the effect of lowering economic output and reducing increases in prices. When the federal government raises taxes, it decreases the amount of disposable income an individual has, which in turn causes decreases in the production of consumer goods. This slows the economy and helps reduce inflation. Similar effects result from decreasing government expenditures on goods and services and from reductions in the disbursal of transfer payments.

Monetary Policy

The amount of money in an economy is the responsibility of a nation's central banking system. In the United States the central bank is the **Federal Reserve System**, established with the Federal Reserve Act of 1913. The Federal Reserve System uses **monetary policy** to influence interest rates, which are the price of money. The Fed, as it is often called, also determines the quantity of money and the rate of the money supply's growth or reduction. The primary goal of monetary policy is to maintain stability of the money system, though the Federal Reserve System also has the goal of using monetary policy to achieve low unemployment in the American economy.

The Federal Reserve System influences the supply and growth rate of money as well as interest rates by using a number of monetary policy tools. First, the Fed can raise or lower the **discount**

rate, which is the interest rate it charges to banks that borrow from it, mostly in overnight loans used to make sure banks have enough money in reserve.

Second, the Fed can raise or lower the **reserve rate,** which is the amount of money that banks have to maintain in their vaults or in reserve. Banks loan out most of their deposits to borrowers, but must keep a certain fraction of their deposits in reserve in case there is a "run" on their bank. Raising or lowering the reserve rate influences the amount of money that banks can loan to their customers. Loans in effect create money and expands the money supply, while calling in loans constricts the money supply.

Third, and the most frequently employed tool of monetary policy, are purchases of federal government securities (bills, notes, and bonds) on the open market. These **open market operations**, whether purchases or sales of government securities, influence the interest rates the banking industry charges. Purchases of government securities put money into circulation in the economy. Selling government securities that the Fed owns, takes money out of circulation.

The Federal Reserve System can use the tools of monetary policy to stimulate demand and expand the economy when it is in a recession or depression and experiencing high rates of unemployment. This is called **expansionary monetary policy** because it expands the supply of money in the economy. The Fed accomplishes this by lowering the discount rate, reducing the reserve rate, or buying U.S. securities. The Federal Reserve System can also use the tools of monetary policy to dampen demand and contract the economy when it is experiencing unacceptable rates of inflation. This is called **contractionary monetary policy**. The Fed reduces aggregate demand in the economy by tightening the money supply by raising the discount rate, increasing the reserve rate, and selling U.S. securities. Each of these strategies contracts the supply of money in circulation and reduces demand.

> **Competency 021 Descriptive Statement F.** The beginning teacher demonstrates knowledge of the goals of economic growth, stability, full employment, freedom, security, equity and efficiency as they apply to U.S. economic policy.

Recently, it was reported that North Koreans are on average three inches shorter than their South Korean counterparts. The difference cannot be explained by genetics because the two populations are essentially the same; neither nation has experienced significant immigration that would have changed the population's genetic makeup. Much of this differential can be explained by the comparative wealth of the two neighboring states. What then explains the difference in comparative wealth between the two countries? The easy answer is that since the end of World War II, North Korea has been under a totalitarian communist dictatorship, while South Korea has encouraged the growth of a free enterprise system. While this answer is easy, it is not entirely complete. The explanation of South Korea's differential development is its encouragement of economic growth. Why economic growth occurs is one of the most important questions economists and political leaders endeavor to answer. Encouraging economic growth has also become among the most important functions of government, even for the most determined of free market advocates.

So, how do economists account for and explain economic growth? One way that economists represent growth is to use production possibilities schedules, or production possibilities frontiers. **Figure 8.1** at the beginning of this chapter described a simplified economy that could produce only milk and grain. When this model economy was producing at its maximum capacity it produced along the curve of PPF 1 as seen below in **Figure 8.12.** If this model economy were producing at below capacity, say at point A in the graph, it would be underutilizing its factors of production (land, labor, capital, and entrepreneurship). This would be an indicator that the economy was not operating at full capacity. If the economy began to produce at full capacity, it would shift to a point on the curve PPF 1. Were this economy to experience growth, that growth could be represented by an outward shift of the production possibilities frontier, perhaps to PPF 2. Growth occurs in this simplified economy with either increases in inputs (the factors of production) or increases in the efficiency with which those factors of production are employed.

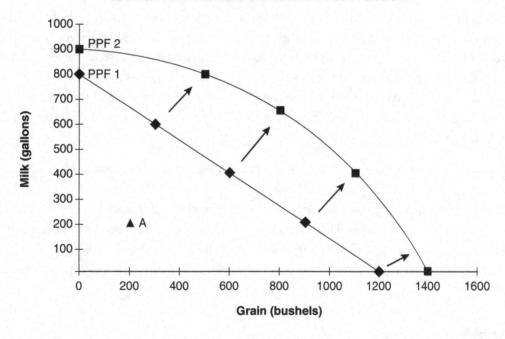

Figure 8.12
Growth and Production Possibilities Frontiers

Economic Growth and Productivity

Classical economists had a simple answer to the question, "What causes economic growth?" Economic growth depended on increases in the productive factors: entrepreneurial activity, land, labor, and capital. To encourage economic growth, they argued, the productive capacity of the economy must be increased. This was accomplished by increasing the numbers and capabilities of the workforce, improving the social and economic organization of the society, and diverting resources from the satisfaction of immediate consumer demands towards savings and investment that would increase capital, research, infrastructure, and other goods that contributed to long-term growth.

Ultimately, however, long-run economic growth depends primarily on rising **productivity**, when the output produced by the average worker increases. Of course, an economy can experience growth in the short term by putting more of its population to work (as for example happened during World War II when many women were drawn into the industrial workforce), or by putting more land into productive use. Over the long run, however, both of these strategies will experience diminishing returns.

The most important ways in which sustained economic growth takes place are by improving the productivity of land, labor, and capital. Productivity is improved by expanding the **physical capital** available for labor. Physical capital includes such manufactured resources as machinery, buildings, and other technologies. A farmer with a tractor and a plow can cultivate far more corn than a farmer with a horse-drawn plow. The average American worker has far more physical capital available to them today than they did 50 or 100 years ago, and far more than workers in most other countries. Workers also must have the knowledge to use the mix of technologies or physical capital available to them. This knowledge is called **human capital.** Productivity growth is closely tied to increases in human capital. Educational attainment levels of a given population are more important to long-term growth than even increases in physical capital. The most important determinant of long-term growth, however, is **technological progress**. Technological improvements of all kinds drive economic growth. In other words, increases in physical capital, improvements in technology, or higher levels of knowledge, all push the production possibilities frontiers outward.

Public policy decisions and entrepreneurial choices clearly foster, or alternately, diminish possibilities for growth. Public investment in higher education, scientific research, and technological innovation, for example, bear fruit in increased human capital and technological progress. High levels of government regulation and high tax rates, conversely, have been shown to undercut entrepreneurial incentives and to discourage technological innovation. Patent protections and protections of private property rights are often seen as critical to encouraging scientific and technological invention.

Economic Stability

While economic growth is an important objective of public and private policy decisions, and is particularly important in the long term, economic stability is also a desirable goal of policy makers. Over the long run, the American economy has experienced consistent growth, but in the short run, **business cycles**, characterized by periods of unacceptable levels of **unemployment** or **inflation,** have resulted in considerable hardship.

Unemployment

Unemployment of men or machinery means that an economy is operating below the capabilities of its production possibilities frontier. It also means both in the short term and the long term that there will be fewer consumer items and capital goods produced. An economy experiencing high levels of unemployment will watch its workforce and capital stock decline. It may also experience a great deal of human misery and potentially social and political upheaval. The United States government therefore has a statutory obligation to seek to address high levels of unemployment.

In June 2017, the unemployment rate in the United States was reported at 4.3 percent with 6.9 million Americans listed as unemployed. The United States Bureau of Labor Statistics regularly reports these and other closely-watched labor-related statistics. What do they mean?

The **unemployment rate** is arrived at by determining the ratio of unemployed workers to the size of the labor force. The **labor force** is composed of all people who are currently working (even if only part-time) and all the people currently looking for work. The unemployment rate provides one indicator of the health of an economy. When unemployment rates are low (and 4 percent is low) almost everyone who wants a job is able to find one. When the unemployment rate is high (historically, unemployment rates in the United States above 7 percent are considered high) even well-qualified workers are without work and have difficulty finding employment.

There are four types of unemployment: **structural unemployment, cyclical unemployment, frictional unemployment,** and **seasonal unemployment**.

1. Seasonal unemployment is an expected level of unemployment that reflects predicted increases and decreases in workforce participation. For example, during the summer months construction work, agricultural labor, and other jobs affected by the weather will see increases.

2. Frictional unemployment is unemployment due to time workers spend looking for work. Many of the workers counted as "frictionally unemployed" are entering the workforce (high school or college graduates looking for their first job) or re-entering the workforce after planned or unplanned absences from the workforce. Some level of frictional unemployment is expected.

3. Cyclical unemployment results from downturns in the business cycle and is an unwelcome event. Cyclical unemployment reflects a general decline in overall demand (economists call this **aggregate demand**) and is an indicator of the ill health of the economy.

4. Structural unemployment reflects a persistent surplus of laborers in particular sectors of the economy that results from a gap between the skills workers have and the demands for that labor in the economy. For example, in the so-called "Rust Belt" of industrial cities in the American Midwest and Northeast from the 1980s to the present,

there have been high rates of structural unemployment as steel workers and coal miners were laid off as steel mills and mines closed or relocated. Mechanization, robotics, and artificial intelligence all threaten to increase structural unemployment in such fields as manufacturing, truck driving, etc.

Each of these causes of unemployment requires different public policy solutions. High rates of structural unemployment may require retraining programs designed to retailor worker's skills to a changing economy, or perhaps relocation support for workers who find their skills in low demand in one area but whose skills are in demand elsewhere. For example, skilled automobile workers may not have opportunities in Michigan, but could use their skills in new automobile plants in North Carolina or Texas.

Full employment

Full employment is not, despite what it sounds like a situation where everyone has a job, or where the unemployment rate reaches or approaches zero. Full employment is reached when there is no cyclical unemployment. The full-employment unemployment rate has varied over time. In the 1950s and 1960s, economists usually said that the economy had reached full employment when the unemployment rate was between 3 percent and 4.5 percent. More recently full employment in the United States has been said to exist when the unemployment rate is between 4 and 6.4 percent.

Economic Stability

In the long run, economists argue that the economy regulates itself. But, as John Maynard Keynes said, "In the long run we are all dead." To reduce the human dislocation of the business cycle and to reduce the degree of oscillation in the business cycle, most economists argue for the necessity of fiscal and monetary policies that stabilize the economy.

John Maynard Keynes, as we have seen, argued that fluctuations in aggregate demand was the primary driver of the business cycle. A **recession** (technically two successive quarters without economic growth) or a **depression** (a longer-lasting and deep recession), according to Keynes, resulted from too little demand for consumer items, housing, capital goods, and other goods and services. Periods of excessive price increases, or **inflation**, were the result, generally, of too great a demand for consumer goods, services, etc.

Keynes' observation describes a "trade-off" between inflation and unemployment. In other words, the lower the level of unemployment, the greater likelihood that there will be generalized price increases, or inflation.

Stabilization policies include fiscal policies (taxation and government spending) designed to either dampen demand, in the case of inflation, or increase demand, in the case of a recession. During recessions, the federal government is often called upon to institute stimulus plans to bolster demand. Perhaps the best example of such a stimulus package was developed during the presidency of Franklin D. Roosevelt during the Great Depression. The Civilian Conservation Corps was a program that put young men to work, put money in their pockets, and pumped money into the economy. The Works Progress Administration pursued a similar end. Other government spending programs, for example military spending before and after World War II, had the same economic impact as the stimulus packages of the Great Depression, priming the pump of economic demand. Social insurance programs like Social Security, while they were developed to meet the needs of the elderly and disabled, also have a stimulatory effect on the economy by providing income stabilization to seniors, and by increasing aggregate demand.

Other stabilization policies rely on tax policies. During times of recession or high unemployment, reductions in taxation are often called for as a way of stimulating demand. The exact mix of tax cuts to encourage economic growth and aggregate demand is often debated. Supply-side supporters contend that tax cuts for the wealthiest Americans will encourage investment and job creation, indirectly promoting growing demand. Others contend that tax cuts to the middle class have the greatest and most immediate influence on rates of aggregate demand.

Public policy decisions designed to ensure economic stability, foster growth, and address chronic unemployment or inflation must also take into consideration competing objectives of freedom, security, equity, and efficiency.

> **Competency 021 Descriptive Statement G.** The beginning teacher understands the rights and responsibilities of consumers, labor, and business in the U.S. free enterprise system.

Unlike many of the world's constitutions, the United States Constitution does not explicitly identify any economic or social rights to which American citizens are entitled. The Constitution specifically enumerates a number of prohibitions against government interference with individual behavior (these are negative rights) but does not list governmental obligations to provide some form of individual or collective benefit (these are positive rights). As such, many of the rights that consumers, workers, and businesses claim are rights that have accumulated as a result of legislation, government regulation, and practice. Additionally, often the assertion of worker rights and consumer rights confront competing claims of property rights made by business or property owners.

Consumer Rights and Responsibilities

Consumers represent the backbone of the free market system in that their choices direct the production of the marketplace. Consumer spending represents two-thirds of America's GDP. Despite this fact, claims of consumer rights have not had a long history. For much of our history the axiom *caveat emptor,* or "let the buyer beware," largely defined American views of consumer rights. In 1962, President John F. Kennedy outlined in an address to Congress the need to secure the basic rights of consumers. Kennedy defined four broad categories of consumer rights: (1) the right to safety, (2) the right to be informed, (3) the right to choose, and (4) the right to be heard.

Though a Consumer Advisory Council was established as an outgrowth of this speech, Kennedy's rights were mostly aspirational. Unlike rights enshrined in the United States Constitution, these "rights" are largely extended as protections legislated by the federal and state governments.

State and federal governments maintain offices or bureaus of consumer protection where consumers have the opportunity to report fraud, concerns about a product's safety, or products that fail to live up to an advertiser's billing. The most prominent consumer protection guardians in the federal government are the Consumer Product Safety Commission, which has the authority to establish standards for consumer safety and the power to take off the market items that are unsafe. The Federal Trade Commission addresses fraud, price fixing, false advertising, credit abuse, and monopolistic behavior. The Food and Drug Administration, U.S. Postal Service, and the U.S. Office of Consumer Affairs all share the responsibility of protecting consumers.

Labor Rights

The Constitution says nothing about the protections afforded laborers per se in the United States. Quite unlike the situation in England and other European nations, employer-worker relations in early America were not (with the exception of slavery and indentured servitude) marked by statutory regulation. Workers could organize and strike, and had a freedom of mobility that European workers could rarely claim. With the development of an industrial economy, however, many of these freedoms were reduced. For example, when workers sought to limit the length of the workday, state and federal courts found that freedom of contract prevented states from limiting the maximum number of hours workers could be asked to work each week. U.S. state courts in the early nineteenth century found that trade unions were, in effect, criminal conspiracies designed to raise their members' wages. Only after 1880 was this "conspiracy doctrine" overturned. With workers free to organize, state governments then sought to protect the property of business owners and their right to continue operation of their firms, as well as to protect strike breakers from intimidation by union workers by issuing injunctions restraining workers right to strike.

Only in the midst of the Great Depression did the federal government enter into labor relations in a significant fashion. In 1935, the **National Labor Relations Act (NLRA)** (also known as the Wagner Act) began a pattern of federal government intervention in labor-management relations that has continued to the present. One of the features of the NLRA was the affirmation that wage earners had the right to **collective bargaining**. The law also pledged the government's "aid to employees in securing independent organizations, free from employer interference." Workers were entitled to organize to negotiate with their employers, and employers were required to negotiate with workers in good faith. The NLRA also prohibited a number of practices that were defined as unfair labor practices. These included any business owner's attempt to interfere with workers "freedom of association" by dominating their labor organizations, refusing to hire or keep a worker as a way of discouraging union membership, or discriminating against any employee who filed charges or testified to a violation of the Wagner Act. In 1947, the **Labor Management Relations Act,** also known as the **Taft-Hartley Act**, represented a business response to the Wagner Act. It restricted many practices of labor unions, including wildcat strikes, political strikes, closed shops, and most importantly allowed states to pass **right-to-work laws**. Twenty-eight states, including Texas, are "right-to-work" states. Right-to-work laws, despite how they sound, are not guarantees of employment to workers. Instead, these laws forbid "union," "closed" or "agency" shops, which require a worker to join a union as a condition of their employment with a company. They also forbid requirements that workers pay union dues or fees. Right-to-work advocates contend that these laws are not "anti-union" but simply an affirmation of individual freedom.

Not all worker rights fall under the umbrella of collective bargaining rights. Workers are protected by other legislation and regulations.

For example, under the **Equal Employment Opportunity Act of 1972**, enforced by the Equal Employment Opportunity Commission, it is illegal to discriminate against job applicants or employees because of a person's race, color, religion, sex (including pregnancy), national origin, age, disability or genetic information. Neither may an employer retaliate against a person who has complained about or filed a charge of discrimination.

In 1938, another worker right that has gradually been extended was enacted with the **Fair Labor Standards Act of 1938**. The federal law established the 40-hour workweek, established a minimum wage, and guaranteed time-and-a-half for overtime in many jobs, while prohibiting child labor. In 1938, the federal minimum wage was only 25 cents. In 2009, the federal minimum wage was increased to $7.25 per hour.

The **Occupational Safety and Health Act (1970)** was passed to "assure ... every working man and woman... safe and healthful working conditions. . . ." In the decade before passage of this act, over 14,000 Americans died annually in workplace accidents, and millions more were maimed. In 2015, the last year statistics are available, 4,836 workplace fatalities took place in an economy with more than double the number of workers.

Business Rights and Responsibilities

For a free enterprise system to function properly, a combination of individual and business rights must be secure. Additionally, though it is common to consider business firms as operating in an amoral sphere where the profit motive, unrestrained by ethical or moral considerations, guides business decisions, nothing could be further from the truth.

Among the basic business and individual rights necessary for free enterprise to function are the following:

1. Individuals and business enterprises must have secure property rights, which include the right to alienate or sell that property without interference from the state as well as the right to pass on property to heirs. Without such rights, business owners have little incentive to work or save.

2. Businesses must have the right to profit and to determine to what uses those profits will be put. These decisions, of course, are constrained by law, ethical principles, and societal expectations.

3. While government regulation exists to protect individuals and society from unlimited powers of business owners, the owners and managers of businesses must have the right to determine the priorities and choices individual firms pursue. The regulatory apparatus exists to establish the "rules of the game" and to ensure fairness, but within those parameters, in the U.S. free enterprise system we err on the side of freedom of business owners to make their own decisions.

4. Businesses have the right to mobility, to choose where they do business, what resources they will use, what wages they will pay for labor, etc.

These rights ensure that entrepreneurs are free to pursue their own self-interest, and are incentivized to fulfill the demands of the marketplace. Businesses, however, do not operate without legal, ethical, and moral restraints.

Business firms have a variety of responsibilities beyond the economic responsibility of earning a profit. If a business fails in this responsibility, it will be unable to stay in business and unable to fulfill its other duties.

Businesses have legal responsibilities. Labor laws, environmental laws, securities regulations, and criminal law all have a bearing on business decision making. While legal responsibilities have priority, most businesses also have ethical and social obligations as well as philanthropic interests in their communities.

> **Competency 021 Descriptive Statement H.** The beginning teacher demonstrates knowledge of basic concepts of personal financial literacy and consumer economics (e.g., factors involved in decisions to acquire goods and services, means by which savings can be invested, and risks and rewards of various investment options).

Personal financial literacy and education are becoming ever more important given the effect of a number of demographic, economic, and policy changes that have taken place in the past three decades. Consumers today have a wider range of choices and greater access to a diversity of credit and savings choices. The advent of online tools for banking and investment have made it easier (and sometimes riskier) for individuals and families to plan and save for the future. Changing pension and retirement options increasingly require workers to be responsible for saving for their retirement and managing their retirements. Most workers are ill-equipped to make many of these choices. Longer life spans are at the same time making it imperative that people plan for longer years in retirement. Uncertainty attached to health care prices and availability make saving even more imperative.

Choices

As we saw at the beginning of this chapter, choice is the dominant feature of the study of economics. The realm of personal financial literacy depends on a careful understanding of the variety of choices that financial consumers face. Even such simple decisions as what kind of checking or savings account one should have are increasingly more complex. Some savings accounts pay interest with no fees. Others limit the number of transactions allowed. The range of investment options are also expanding. When selecting from an array of mutual funds for a retirement account, employees are faced with international funds, growth funds, income funds, and tax-free funds, to name only a few of the possibilities.

Income and Benefits

Personal financial literacy begins with an understanding of the forms of income and benefits that individuals may expect over the course of their working and non-working lives.

Earned income comes in a variety of forms; many employees earn an hourly wage, while others contract for an annual salary. Others receive an important part of their income in the form of commissions, tips, or bonuses. Professionals like doctors or lawyers earn income in the form of professional fees. Self-employed workers receive self-employment income, which represents a cost to their business. There are also a number of forms of unearned income, often received by the upper end of income earners. These include interest income from savings, dividends from stocks or capital gains from the sale of assets. A final form of income comes in the form of transfer payments from government. Veterans' benefits, social security, workers' compensation, and unemployment compensation are but a few of the variety of transfer payments that Americans receive.

Full-time employees often also receive a range of benefits in addition to their wages or salaries. Benefits provide a way for employers to compete for talent without relying on wage competition. Benefits include such things as life and health insurance, paid vacation, vehicles, phone service, and stock options, to name only a few. Many employers also contribute in whole or in part to workers' retirement or pension plans. Since the 1970s, most workers have not received fixed benefit pension plans and are instead enrolled in 401(k) plans that return a benefit dependent on returns of the financial markets. Workers are not taxed on benefits, though usually workers contribute to their own health or life insurance plans.

Taxation

Taxation takes a variety of forms as well. The most commonly paid categories of taxation are income taxes, property taxes, payroll taxes, consumption taxes, and user fees. Taxes are often evaluated by the degree to which they are progressive, neutral, or regressive.

Progressive taxes fall more heavily on higher income earners than on lower income earners. In other words, richer people pay a higher percentage of their income in taxes.

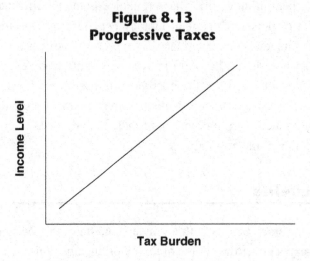

**Figure 8.13
Progressive Taxes**

The federal income tax is a progressive tax that falls more heavily on higher income earners than on wage earners with lower incomes. In 2017, workers who earned less than $9,325 a year were taxed at a 10 percent rate, while the highest wage earners were taxed at the marginal tax rate of 39.6 percent. Most, but not all, state income taxes are also progressive taxes, though the rates are substantially lower than federal tax rates. Texas is one of six states that do not have a state income tax.

Because most wage earners have their income taxes withheld from their gross earnings, the income tax is often conflated with other withholding taxes. These include the **payroll taxes** collected by employers on behalf of employees to fund Medicare and Social Security. These taxes are also known as the **Federal Insurance Contributions Act (FICA)** tax.

Regressive taxes fall more heavily on lower income earners. If poor people pay higher percentages of their income in a particular tax than do more wealthy Americans, then the tax is said to be a **regressive tax**. Below is an illustration of the relationship between the tax burden and income levels in a regressive tax.

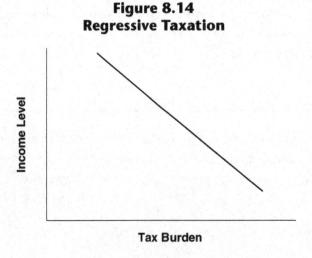

**Figure 8.14
Regressive Taxation**

Sales taxes are one example of taxes that generally fall more heavily on lower income earners. They are therefore usually considered a regressive form of taxation. Forty-five states collect state-wide sales taxes, while 38 states have local sales taxes as well. State and local sales taxes in Texas total as much as 8.05 percent, the 12th-highest sales tax rate in the country.

The FICA taxes are also partially regressive in nature, though the argument is often made that these taxes are eventually paid back to taxpayers in the form of Social Security payments and Medicare payments. Payroll taxes are progressive (the higher your income the greater a percentage of that income is paid in the tax) from the bottom 20th percentile of income earners to the 90th percentile of income earners. For the upper 10 percent of income earners, however, the tax becomes increasingly regressive as incomes rise. The bottom 20 percent of income earners pay only 7.3 percent of their income on average in payroll taxes. The middle classes (from the 40th percentile to the 90th percentile) pay around 10.2 percent of their income in payroll taxes. Payroll taxes then decline from 9.3 percent to below 2 percent for the upper 10 percent of income earners. The richest 0.1 percent of Americans pay less than 1 percent of their income in withholding taxes. The FICA taxes may therefore be described as having an upside-down U-shaped curve, falling more heavily on the middle class.

Some taxes fall instead on users only in an effort to have the beneficiaries of a government service pay the costs of the benefit. User fees include such government charges as taxes charged construction firms or developers for building permits, tolls for the use of roads, tuition at public schools or colleges, and licensing fees. Ultimately, however, these fees are often passed on to consumers as well in the form of higher prices. For example, if a state or local government established a toll for travel on a roadway, trucking firms and grocers would, if possible, pass the increased costs of transport on to their consumers.

Banking, Investment, and Saving

Savings is money set aside to meet future needs. Savings should be in a form that is easily available in case of emergency. Economists describe assets that are easily transformed into cash as *liquid*. A savings or checking account is more liquid, for example, than stocks, bonds, or real estate. The latter are said to be **illiquid**. Certificates of deposit provide an intermediary form of savings, as they pay higher interest but are not immediately transferable to cash. Savings and checking accounts are the safest form of savings in that they are insured by the Federal Deposit Insurance Corporation (FDIC). In 2016, it was reported that nearly 70 percent of Americans had less than $1,000 in their savings and checking accounts, leaving nearly three-quarters of Americans extremely vulnerable to any personal or financial crisis. Nearly half of Americans had no retirement savings. Most financial advisors contend that individuals and households should maintain in savings a total of between three and six months of living expenses.

Investments are savings that provide for longer-term planning for the future. Investments have greater risks of loss, but investments also pay higher interests rates than do more liquid forms of saving. Investments take a variety of forms. **Bonds** are one form of investment. They are issued by corporations and governments. As described earlier, bonds are a way for governments and firms to raise funding. For the bond issuer, they are a debt. For the bond purchaser, they are a credit. Some bonds are sold at *face value.* These bonds pay the face value to the bondholder when the bond comes due. Series EE Savings Bonds sold by the federal government are an example of a bond sold at a face value. These bonds were once sold by banks, but they can now only be bought online through the Treasury Department. These bonds earn interest for up to 30 years. The minimum purchase of a series EE savings bond is $25. The face value of a $25 bond is $50, meaning that when the bond reaches its maturity date, it is redeemable for $50. These are very safe, tax-exempt ways to invest by loaning the federal government money it needs to fund day-to-day operations. Other bonds are sold at variable rates and fluctuate with the market value of the company or of the bond itself. These are riskier forms of investing. Bonds are issued by states, cities, counties, and other government entities. Bonds are used to fund building projects or other public projects. Corporate bonds are usually issued to fund business expansions, refinance debt, or support capital improvements.

A medium-risk investment, often found in retirement plans, are investments in **mutual funds**. Mutual funds are diversified combinations of stocks, bonds, and other forms of investment that lower risk. Each mutual fund pursues a different investment strategy and combines different mixtures of investments. Each mutual fund also has a different level of risk. Purchasing mutual funds allows investors to indirectly own shares of stock in companies, as the mutual fund purchases corporate stocks, while the owner of a share in a mutual fund does not own the company stock. This allows the risk of stock ownership to be diffused.

Many jobs include a variety of pension and retirement options among their benefits. These include **defined-benefit plans** in which retired employees receive a predetermined payment or monthly benefit depending on the workers' length of employment or wages. These are becoming increasingly rare. Instead, most employers now offer more **market-oriented defined-contribution plans**, such as 401(k)s. During the 1950s, in an effort to reduce competition for workers that would drive up wages, the federal government encouraged corporate employers to offer **pensions** that provided a secure retirement as a benefit. In the 1980s corporations shifted increasingly to riskier market-oriented defined contribution plans where employees and employers contributed to retirement accounts which were then invested in mutual funds or other investment instruments.

Investors may also buy **corporate stocks**, investing directly in a firm, becoming a stockholder who owns shares in a company. Shareholders, as already discussed, benefit either from the receipt of dividends (shares of corporate profits) or by the sale of the stock at prices higher than those originally paid for the stock. Stocks are purchased through stockbrokers. Investors may also purchase **futures contracts** or **commodities**. The former are contracts binding purchasers to buy or sell a commodity at a set price or a future date. Commodities are such things as gold, silver, cattle, coffee, corn, pork-bellies, etc. These investments carry substantially more risk than do mutual funds.

COMPETENCY 022 (SCIENCE, TECHNOLOGY AND SOCIETY)

The teacher understands major scientific and mathematical discoveries and technological innovations and the societal significance of these discoveries and innovations.

> **Competency 022 Descriptive Statement A.** The beginning teacher demonstrates knowledge of how major scientific and mathematical discoveries and technological innovations have affected societies throughout history.

This descriptive statement provides an extremely broad scope for preparation. The Economics TEKS also does not offer a great deal of guidance. To prepare for this particular descriptive statement, it is recommended that TExES Social Studies 7–12 test-takers review both the World History (Chapter 3) and United States History (Chapter 4) chapters in this test guide.

The descriptive statement asks beginning teachers to reflect on the impact of scientific, mathematical, and technological discoveries on societies. In this section, a selection of scientific, mathematical, and technological changes have been examined with reference to the social changes that followed. In sections that follow, there are also references to the social and economic impact of other technologies, such as the cotton gin, the automobile, and electricity, to name a few.

Stone Age Technology and Knowledge (before 4000 BCE)

By 70,000 years ago, *homo sapiens* had left East Africa and driven other hominid species into extinction, spreading across Afro-Eurasia. This expansion reflected what historian Yuval Harari has called a "cognitive revolution." It was accompanied by the development of an array of technologies: boats made of skin and wood, bone and wood hooks, needles, nets for carrying infants and collected foods, stone axes, throwing sticks, blades, bows and arrows with stone-tipped arrowheads, rudimentary pottery, and many other technologies. Even earlier, human forebears had employed fire to drive herds before them, and then learned to process foods, allowing humans to digest foods that would otherwise have been difficult to process. It is perhaps comforting to believe that modern humans are vastly more knowledgeable than the earliest *homo sapiens*. However, it is likely that the understanding of pre-agricultural human individuals of their own immediate surroundings, and the uses that could be made of their natural resources, was in some ways more complete than our own, as individuals. Collectively, thanks to the development of scientific knowledge and literacy, we have a much greater and more complex understanding of the natural world. Nonetheless, the technology developed by Stone Age peoples enabled them to conquer their evolutionary competitors and to spread around the world.

The transition to agriculture, which occurred at different times around the globe, as we have seen, represented a critical watershed in human knowledge and technological development. Some 11,000 years ago, domestication of plant and animal varieties initiated a second revolution, the Agricultural Revolution. While early humans exploited novel technologies to adapt to their environments, the earliest farmers developed a wide range of new technologies and knowledge as they transformed nature to suit their presence, rather than the reverse. The technologies associated with the Neolithic or Agricultural Revolution were many. While they still used stone tools, Neolithic tools were often polished smooth, making them less prone to breaking. Digging sticks, stone-blade hoes, storage baskets, pottery, grinding stones, and stone sickles, made it possible to plant, harvest, and process the new staple grains. Spindles were used to make thread from hemp, flax, and cotton fibers or from wool. The first looms date from around 6000 BCE. Humans could now clothe themselves in lighter fabrics. Neolithic peoples, like their predecessors, employed technology to express themselves symbolically. Construction of stone monuments, like Stonehenge, are seen across the Neolithic world. The first temples date from this era as well.

What were the social consequences of the technological and knowledge revolution associated with the transition to agriculture? The social consequences of this transition were many and varied, but it is clear that social hierarchies became more pronounced and gender distinctions more rigid. At the same time agriculturalists were required to work harder to provide the surpluses upon which divisions of labor depended.

The Stirrup and Medieval Feudalism

Feudalism, as described in Chapter 3, was a political and military system that emerged during the European Middle Ages in part as a response to the endemic violence of the age. Lynn White, Jr., a historian of medieval technology, argued that the development of feudalism and the introduction of the stirrup in Western Europe were closely linked. Though there is ancient evidence of the stirrup in Assyria, China, India, Korea, and Japan before 700 CE, it appears in European sources only in the late seventh or early eighth centuries.

Carolingian armies in Europe were the first to employ the stirrup to its full advantage. The stirrup allowed men anchored on horseback to use the momentum of their charging animals to drive spears or long swords into their enemies without being propelled from the horse. Carolingian, and later European cavalrymen, began to use long swords (rather than the Roman short-bladed sword) and spears with a metal cross-wing projection that stopped the blade from penetrating so deeply that it couldn't be easily withdrawn. The lance, long sword, and other weapons, coupled with armored men on horseback, gave the cavalry an advantage over the infantry forces that had characterized Greco-Roman armies. Cavalrymen, however, required a lengthy and costly training—at least two years, compared to the 12 weeks required for infantrymen—and the expense of maintaining at least four warhorses. An army composed primarily of armored horsemen was significantly more costly than the infantry armies of the Roman Empire.

The Carolingian state was chronically short of the necessary gold and silver to pay men-at-arms. This would be the case throughout the medieval period for most European states. The answer was to diffuse control of land and governance to the warrior caste, "those who fought," who would become the warrior aristocracy of medieval and early modern Europe. With the fragmentation of the Carolingian Empire after the ninth century, the necessity of dispersing political and economic power became ever more pressing. The feudal aristocracy were then given charge of manorial estates that provided them the needed economic resources to maintain their mounts and pay for their military needs. The peasants who resided on these estates would be enserfed, or bound to the land as the ready labor force needed to work the land that provided these knights with their maintenance.

The Gunpowder Revolution

Between 1300 and 1600 CE from China to Western Europe, nation-states confronted the significance of gunpowder as a military technology. Gunpowder, made from saltpeter, sulfur, and charcoal, was discovered in China, spread by Song Dynasty armies, and then introduced by the Mongols to the Arabs and Europeans. The first known illustration of its use in Europe dates to 1327 CE. Its use in warfare in Europe was as a siege weapon, rather than a personal firearm. One consequence of the introduction of gunpowder was a construction boom as cities and fortifications were rebuilt to adapt to the new threat. In the 15th century Italian city-states pioneered the *trace italienne*. These new fortifications relied on low stone walls (rather than the high walls of medieval castles) supported by packed earth embankments, organized to maximize angles of fire on advancing armies. These new fortifications were costly and necessitated significant increases in municipal or royal taxation. When personal firearms became more accurate, armies adapted by relying on larger numbers of paid mercenaries who fought in organized infantry units. The age of the aristocratic knight as the ideal warrior was over. Infantry armed with guns and cannons were more expensive than a smaller cavalry force. Kings began to develop new fiscal measures to raise the money to fund either mercenary or conscript armies. As a result, wherever gunpowder technology was adopted, the powers of kings increased, along with their powers of taxation and reliance on bureaucratic institutions.

The Print Revolution

Printing with movable, metal type was perfected in Germany about 1450 by Johannes Gutenberg. Gutenberg's revolution was not immediately apparent. The earliest printed books were made to closely resemble manuscript books. Additionally, for some time, armies of copyists had been reproducing books in a sort of assembly line. What, then, was the wider social impact of printing and the printed word upon ways of knowing, thinking, etc.?

Print quickly transformed learning. Previously, learning occurred largely in an oral environment, whether it was an apprentice at the knee of a master craftsman, or a student listening to their teacher. The word "lecture," from the medieval Latin word for reading, described the dominant pattern of learning at a medieval university, where the master read to students from books. Printing permitted students to escape the master's monopoly of learning, allowing them to learn a skill or master a body of knowledge on their own. Learning changed as well. Learning before had been memorizing. Printing freed the memory. There was less need to keep a fact in mind if it could be more easily found on a shelf. Printing also reduced the power of visual representation. The interiors of Gothic cathedrals were covered with painted imagery depicting the Biblical story, primarily to visually communicate to congregants moral messages that they could not read. After the print revolution, words had greater solidity to literate populations. Images and icons no longer had the authority they once commanded. There was a transformation from an "image culture to a word culture." The printing press made it possible to exactly duplicate texts over and over, giving the printed word an authority it previously lacked. It is no surprise that in the aftermath of the print revolution, Europeans began to develop written constitutions. Rising literacy rates resulted not unexpectedly from the growth of printed material. Literacy in the 16th century was probably less than 30 percent for men, much less for women. By the middle of the 18th century, this had probably reached 65 percent for men and nearly 30 percent for women. As growing numbers of people learned to read, we notice a number of changes. The first was "private reading." More people began to read silently, rather than out loud to others. Reading, therefore, increasingly became a private act. Silent reading reflects the degree to which learning became a more intimate, private activity, a personal confrontation with written texts or scientific knowledge. It also made possible a more personal form of private devotion and a relationship with a sacred object away from the eye of community or Church. The printed word increased the possibility of holding "private" ideas—heretical, erotic, critical, etc. It is hard to imagine the development of the Protestant Reformation, the Scientific Revolution, the Enlightenment, or the French or American Revolutions without the print revolution that preceded them.

Chemical Fertilizer

The biological limitations of the pre-industrial world were conditioned by the fact that food production reduced the nutritional quality of the soil. Population growth, whether sooner or later, inevitably pushed a society toward the limits of its production possibility frontier. Sales of food to city dwellers, the surplus population of the fertile countryside, transferred nutrients from the countryside to the city. To rejuvenate the soil, farmers could turn to animal fertilizers. However, each head of livestock needed to manure their farm acreage also consumed the nutrients of the soil, in the form of silage, grain, or grass. In the urban hinterlands, farmers often contracted with the cities for their human and animal waste. Cities accumulated large quantities of human and animal waste. Industrial cities, however, rapidly overwhelmed these systems for returning sewage to the farms. Instead, particularly in European cities, human waste was washed into the rivers, spreading microbial diseases and wasting the valuable nitrogen that might otherwise have rejuvenated the surrounding countryside. In the 19th century, bat and bird guano had been mined in Peru and Chile to supply European and American farms. But, this had proven a short-lived solution. In 1913, Fritz Haber and Carl Bosch developed the process for producing artificial nitration fixation whereby atmospheric nitrogen is converted into nitrogen fertilizers. The Haber-Bosch process produces approximately 97 percent of all nitrogen fertilizers produced today. In fact, the Haber-Bosch process puts more nitrogen into the environment than all natural processes combined. The effect of this technological process has been a staggering outward shift of the global production possibilities frontier, enabling an agricultural growth that in the United States has meant that fewer than 2.5 percent of the American population remain employed in agricultural production. Still, the total output of American agriculture is enough to help feed the U.S. population and export a large quantity as well.

The Pill

In 1956, scientific experimentation with hormonal prevention of ovulation and pregnancy resulted in the development of an oral contraceptive. The pill was first sold in the United States in the early 1960s. The pill is often said to have had a radical impact on sexual mores, family life, and women's employment. Perhaps the most often observed social influence of the pill is its place as a symbol of the sexual revolution of the 1960s and 1970s. The pill, however, may have had its greatest impact in playing a role in the "demographic transition" in the West. In the early 20th century, Europeans and Americans began to experience marked declines in mortality rates due to increased caloric intake and improved medical care. Without a corresponding decline in fertility, population growth was inevitable. In 1800, the global population reached 950 million souls. By 1900, it had nearly doubled. In the West, however, after 1900, fertility began to stabilize. Most of the world's population growth since 1900 has been in Asia, Africa, and Latin America. In part, declining fertility in the West resulted from improved birth control measures. The pill was an important feature of that demographic transition. The contraceptive revolution had important effects on women's control of their own fertility. Women could space their children more predictably, delaying childbirth until they had satisfied other life goals. Women could also restrict family size. It also allowed many women to choose to remain childless.

Containers and Global Trade

Since the end of World War II, the world has experienced an economic boom that is without parallel. Much of this growth has resulted from ever-tightening commercial connections that bind the world together. Reduced tariffs and trade barriers, and improvements in communication and transport have enabled cheap, bulk items to circle the globe in search of the best markets. Similar ease in the circulation of financial wealth has also contributed to the world's economic boom. A rather modest technology has been a contributing factor: the shipping container. Developed by a North Carolina trucker named Malcom McLean, this simple metal box, sturdy and uniform in size, has allowed shipping companies to vastly reduce transport costs and labor requirements. Container ships are built to maximize the number of containers they can carry above and below decks. Cranes quickly load and unload shipping cargo containers, easily transferring them to trains or trucks without the need to repackage their contents. This simple technology has reduced the cost of shipping. Transport costs between Asia and the United States have since 1972 fallen by more than 66 percent in inflation-adjusted terms. It is now often cheaper to transport goods from China to markets in the United States than it is to ship them within the country. To no small degree, we may thank Malcom McLean for the proliferation of Walmarts, Best Buys, and other big box stores that dot the landscape and have transformed our lives.

> **Competency 022 Descriptive Statement B.** The beginning teacher traces the origin and diffusion of major ideas in mathematics, science, and technology that occurred in river valley civilizations; classical Greece, Rome, and India; the Islamic Caliphates between 700 and 1200; and in China from the Tang to Ming dynasties.

Early River Valley Civilizations (4000 BCE–600 BCE)

Early river valley civilizations emerged across the globe after 4000 BCE. These civilizations featured new forms of technology and knowledge, which rightly could be called science and mathematics. For the first time, this knowledge was communicated by what many have identified as the most important of human technologies: writing. Writing permits the storage and transmission of knowledge, making possible more complete cross-generational learning.

In conjunction with the development of literacy, ancient river valley civilizations also developed early mathematics. Before 3200 BCE in ancient Mesopotamia, token-based accounting was used to make simple calculations. By 3000 BCE, Mesopotamian scribes were carrying out sophisticated calculations and quantitative planning exercises. As early as 2050 BCE, a sexagesimal (base 60) numeral system had been developed for measuring time and angles. The Greeks would later apply this system to geographic coordinate systems. Egyptians were also developing complex mathematics, though perhaps somewhat later. The predictability of Nile flooding led Egyptian scribes to devise a 365½-day calendar. Egyptian records include manuals for scribes instructing them in techniques ranging from simple calculations using fractions, to more complex solutions involving linear and quadratic equations. Most mathematical calculations in early river civilizations were directed at mercantile and tax accounting; however, the pyramids, irrigation networks, and early road systems are evidence of these early civilizations use of complex mathematics.

Early civilizations depended upon complex irrigation systems to feed the growing populations that amassed in these urban societies. To build their cities and monumental architecture, ancient civilizations used kiln-fired bricks and quarried limestone, marble, and granite. The potter's wheel was developed in Mesopotamia as early as the fifth millennium, and the wheel used in transport soon followed.

Chinese and Egyptian civilizations developed the ability to produce fine cloths of silk and linen.

Metallurgy, beginning with the more easily worked copper, and then mixing copper with softer metals to form alloys, led successive ancient civilizations to develop bronze from copper and tin. Across Afro-Eurasia, bronze was associated with the development of more advanced civilizations.

Ancient Empires and Classical Civilization (600 BCE–600 CE)

Iron would be the technology most closely associated with the rise of the great ancient empires. The Hittites, from ancient Anatolia, were the first to smelt iron. Iron smelting was a more exacting science than that required to produce copper or bronze. Iron ore, however, is found more or less equally across the globe and is easy to acquire. Blacksmiths could produce tools for peasants and craftsmen as well as weapons of war. The harder, more durable metal would lead to outward shifts of the production possibilities frontiers of every country that adopted the technology. Iron axes made it possible to settle previously uninhabitable forest land. Iron plows and hoes opened up new agricultural land with soils too thick for the scratch plows or digging sticks previously employed. As we saw in Chapter 3, the Bantu migration was made possible by the adoption of iron tools and weaponry.

Iron weaponry and horse-drawn chariots resulted in the beginnings of a new age of warfare. Nomadic horsemen, using iron weaponry, attacked settled agriculturalists across Eurasia. Nomads invaded Egypt, southern Russia, and the Ganges River Valley. The Zhou Dynasty, nomads with iron weapons, conquered the Huang He River in China. The Dorians destroyed the first Greek civilization. New empires such as the Assyrians arose using the new complex of weaponry. Classical Greece, Rome, the Persians, Mauryan India, and the Han Dynasty in China represented the apogee of social and political organization that developed out of Iron Age technology.

These classical empires, however, developed other noteworthy technology. Rome, for example, supplied its cities with aqueducts that carried water as far as 300 miles to fill baths, fountains, and private pools. Chinese, Roman, and Persian societies also developed a variety of types of water wheels to grind grain and power trip hammers and bellows in iron forges.

Romans also were the first to use cement to construct walls and structures, many of which are still standing. The Chinese were no less capable engineers, carefully supervising the building of canals to transport food stuffs, terraces to improve rice harvests, and massive earth-tamped walls. Each of the ancient empires interlinked their populations and city centers with complex road systems. Many Roman and Chinese roads and bridges built during this time are still in use today. These are only a few of the many technologies that transformed the ancient world, raising standards of living for the vast majority of the Earth's population.

Post-Classical and Medieval Scientific and Technological Revolutions (600 CE–1450 CE)

Often the period between the end of the Roman Empire and the beginning of the Renaissance has been characterized as a "Dark Age": a period of economic and technological decline. This is an unfortunate disparagement that fails to recognize the significant scientific, technological, and mathematical developments of the world outside Western Europe, and ignores important changes that occurred in medieval Europe as well.

Agricultural innovation across Afro-Eurasia resulted in a population explosion and period of mercantile and urban growth from the eighth century to the mid-14th century. These innovations were most evident in Song China. There, Champa rice seeds, which originated in Vietnam, were imported and intensively cultivated in rice paddies across southern China. The technologies that developed around Champa rice cultivation are noteworthy. Moldboard plows pulled by water buffalo, weeding rakes, the use of human waste, ashes, and silt as fertilizer all increased Champa rice yields. The "dragon-backbone machine," a waterwheel turned by men or animals on a treadmill, made it possible to drain paddies and divert water to other fields. The Chinese also instituted agricultural education to encourage peasants to adopt new techniques. A simple yet enormously important labor-saving device developed in China was the wheelbarrow. The Arab and Persians also developed advanced systems of water control, including the *qanat*, tunnels that transported water long distances. Commerce resulted in a widespread interchange of agricultural products. Arab and Persian traders spread cultivation of oranges, lemons, sugar cane, cotton, melons, spinach, and coffee to the Mediterranean world.

Technologies also spread within the Islamic world system. Paper, the compass, gunpowder, crossbows, printing, the heavy-plow, horse collar, and the stirrup all were diffused from East and Central Asia across the Islamic world and belatedly to Europe. Arab scientists and mathematicians had significant impacts as well. Arab mathematicians took both the concept of zero and the Indian numeral system from India (we know them as "Arabic" numerals), and passed them on to the West. An Arab mathematician in his book titled *Kitab al-Jabr* systematized the principles of algebra. Similarly, the study of chemistry and advancements in medical knowledge owe a great debt to Arab scientists. Many new drugs and surgical techniques were developed in the medieval Islamic world. Arabs also developed water clocks to tell time on cloudy days or at night, employing elaborate gearing mechanisms to ring bells or chimes to mark the hours.

Medieval Europeans, though they lagged significantly behind the Chinese and the Islamic world, also benefited from important technological innovations and knowledge. The moldboard plow, or heavy plow, adapted from Chinese models made it possible to cultivate the heavy soils of northern Europe. A system of three-field crop rotation was adopted in the period enabling Europeans to increase yields and rejuvenate their soils. Horseshoes and horse collars made it possible for Europeans to use the animal more effectively in warfare and as a beast of burden. The stirrup, it has been argued, made it possible for cavalry to so dominate infantry forces in Europe that a feudal society developed to supply needed horses and horsemen in a money-starved economy. Europeans also adapted windmills and watermills to more effectively use their abundant wind and water resources. The water clocks designed by Arabs were later adopted by Europeans.

East Asian ironworkers improved on ancient smelting techniques, building enormous blast furnaces that could produce as much as 125,000 tons of iron a year. This cheap iron made it possible to supply an army of over 1 million soldiers, with suits of armor, spears, and iron tipped arrows. Much of this inexpensive iron was also put to agricultural use or exported to the Mongols and other central Asian peoples. The Chinese specialized in producing cheap, mass-produced iron and cast-iron implements, while Arab, Persian, and Indian craftsmen became adept at making fine steel swords and even scientific instruments.

Chinese maritime technology must also be mentioned here. Long before the Portuguese navigated the shores of Africa to make their way to India, the Chinese had made their way across the Indian Ocean and down the eastern shores of Africa. In 1405 CE, Admiral Zheng He began a series of voyages from China to demonstrate China's political and technological superiority to its neighbors. Eventually, Zheng He sailed as far west and south as Mozambique on the East African coast. Zheng He's tribute ships dwarfed the size of the Spanish and Portuguese caravels that would soon ply the Indian and Atlantic Oceans. Though a recent historian, Gavin Menzies, has claimed that Zheng He's voyages may have reached the coast of the Americas, most historians believe Menzies' argument is not supported by the evidence. Nonetheless, Zheng He's fleet is but one indication of Chinese organizational and technological advantages over European and Islamic competitors in the fifteenth century. It would not be until the late 18th and early 19th century that the Chinese economy would begin a decline relative to the West that it is only now escaping.

> **Competency 022 Descriptive Statement C.** The beginning teacher demonstrates knowledge of the contributions of significant scientists and inventors (e.g., Copernicus, Galileo, Isaac Newton, Marie Curie, Thomas Edison, Albert Einstein).

An important feature of the modern economy is its dependency on science and systematic research and development.

Nicholas Copernicus (1473–1543 CE)

In 1543, Nicholas Copernicus, in his *On the Revolution of the Heavenly Spheres*, was the first to suggest that the Earth, and the other planets, revolved around the Sun. In his *heliocentric* cosmology, he proposed that the Earth revolved on its own axis and orbited the Sun once a year. Before Copernicus, the dominant theory situated the Earth at the center of the cosmos. After Copernicus, the *geocentric* Ptolemaic system began to crumble under the accumulation of data that began to corroborate Copernicus's ideas. Most importantly, Copernicus began a Scientific Revolution that transformed our understanding of nature and our approach to the power of human reasoning. Economically, Copernicus's discoveries would have little immediate impact.

Galileo Galilei (1564–1642)

Galileo Galilei provided important support for Copernicus's *heliocentric* theory. In 1608, Galileo heard about a "toy" telescope and understood immediately its possibilities as a scientific instrument. His first telescope was an eight-power telescope, but he soon had telescopes with 20- and

30-power magnifications. Using his study of optics, Galileo developed a compound microscope. Using his telescope, he identified mountains on the moon. He discovered moons orbiting around Jupiter and observed and analyzed sunspots. Galileo developed precursors to the thermometer, studied tidal patterns, and recognized that the Milky Way was composed of multiple stars. He also improved on geometric and military compasses, improving artillery accuracy.

Isaac Newton (1642–1727)

The next important piece of the planetary puzzle was provided by the English scientist Isaac Newton. Newton's work provided an explanation for the elliptical orbits of the planets in the theory of universal gravitation. Newton's view that the heavens and the Earth were distinct, and that the motion of heavenly bodies was governed by natural laws, not supernatural forces, was truly revolutionary. Newton's universe was one that did not require a divine explanation for its normal operation. It was a universe that, like a machine, was self-regulating. Furthermore, knowledge of the universe could be arrived at through observation. Newton's influence on science is clear.

Newton's impact on economics as a science was also significant. Newton described nature as a self-regulating system governed by clear scientific laws. Classical free market economists applied Newton's insights to the economy. The Laws of Supply and Demand are equivalent in the field of economics to the Laws of Thermodynamics in physics. Additionally, just as Newton imagined that the natural world operated without divine intervention, naturally finding its own equilibrium, the economy, without government intervention, would also seek an equilibrium.

The question of Isaac Newton's immediate economic impact is more difficult to determine. Newton in 1680 proposed a steam carriage mounted on four wheels that was propelled by steam power. This may have been one of the earliest suggestions of using the force of steam for transport. Newton's idea was not put into practical effect until more than a century later, but his interest in steam power may have had an impact on James Watt's development of a steam engine. More directly, Newton's scientific discoveries laid the groundwork for a scientific world view that has over time contributed to increased innovation by scientists and engineers.

Marie Curie (1867–1934)

Marie Curie was born Maria Sklodowska in 1867 in Warsaw, Poland, to a family of schoolteachers. After studying mathematics and physics in Paris, she met Pierre Curie, a French scientist. The two married and with her help, Pierre completed and defended his thesis. After earning her teacher's certificate in 1896, Marie set out to earn a doctorate of her own. Marie discovered the radioactive element that she named *polonium* (after her homeland). During the course of her research, she and her husband both suffered from radiation exposure. Inadvertently, the discovery of the physical damage caused by radiation exposure led to the idea of using radiation to attack cancerous cells. In 1903, Curie shared the Nobel Prize in Physics with her husband and Antoine

Henri Becquerel for their work in discovering radioactivity. She received a second Nobel Prize in 1911 for discoveries that would revolutionize chemistry.

Thomas Edison (1847–1931)

Thomas Alva Edison is perhaps best known for his development in 1879 of the incandescent light bulb.

His electric lamp produced more than 100 times the power of the candle. The light bulb is certainly an important technological advance, and evidence of Edison's genius. The real importance of electricity was not its function of lighting but in delivering a regular, measurable source of power to run streetcars, assembly lines, etc. Developing electricity provided businesses the possibility of moving away from water where steam power and waterwheels had tied them. Perhaps Edison's greatest significance was his establishment of a research lab in Menlo Park, New Jersey (in today's Edison Township), staffed with an array of engineers and scientists who set about to resolve a host of practical problems. Edison promised to his investors and the public that his lab would produce "a minor invention every 10 days and a big thing every six months." His lab got results. In addition to improvements in electrical lighting, Edison developed electrical motors, storage batteries, an electric locomotive, the phonograph, the mimeograph (an early form of copying machine), and many more inventions. Additionally, Edison was able to marshal the capital investment to develop the infrastructure for many of his innovations. Edison's genius included not only inventing new technologies but also the business acumen to manufacture and market his technologies while developing the necessary infrastructure to make these items household technologies.

Albert Einstein (1879–1955)

We live in a world made possible in many ways by Albert Einstein. Nuclear energy, as well as nuclear weaponry, depend upon Einstein's scientific discoveries, of course. But, the impact of Einstein on our daily life is even more pervasive. When you are awakened at 5:30 a.m. by your phone's alarm clock, or when you change time zones and your phone readjusts the time exactly, it is able to do so with precision thanks to Albert Einstein. Your phone's clock is synchronized through global positioning satellites with the government's atomic clocks. These satellites, circling rapidly around the globe, automatically correct for the effects of relativity, without which the data relayed to your phone would be so error-prone as to make the clocks useless. Einstein also used atomic theory to accurately calculate the movements of molecules immersed in liquids. Cell phones, microwave ovens, burglar alarms, computers and semi-conductor technology, the lasers used to read UPC symbols at the grocery store, PET scans and many other technologies owe their development to Einstein's calculations and physics discoveries. It may be fair to say that no single individual has done as much to push the production possibilities frontiers of the human race further to the right than did Albert Einstein.

> **Competency 022 Descriptive Statement D.** The beginning teacher understands how major scientific and mathematical discoveries and technological innovations have affected societies from 1750 to the present.

Early Modern Interactions (1450–1750 CE)

In the period from 1450 to 1750 CE, advances in Western Europe would allow what was once a backward and underdeveloped region of the world begin to advance into the ranks of the other world regions as a competitor. Western European conquest of the Americas and dispossession of the Amerindian populations there, coupled with their ability to harness the labor of Africa to exploit lands in the Americas would provide the West with the leg up it would need by the 1750s to become the core of the global economy.

One technology critical to European successes was the caravel, a small ship that used lateen sails (an Indian Ocean innovation) that allowed Portuguese and Spanish explorers to traverse the Atlantic and circumnavigate the Cape of Good Hope and reach Asian ports. Earlier European vessels were square-masted and less seaworthy on ocean voyages. The caravel also had a shallow draft that allowed it to sail into coastal waters and up rivers to explore and trade. Armed with Europe's advanced mounted cannons, the ships also were an efficient way for European states to exert power over maritime trade routes. The compass and astrolabe as well as maritime charts allowed Europeans to improve their navigation abilities. European maritime developments allowed them to reach far shores, but did not give them an insurmountable advantage except in the Americas. European guns and iron weaponry did not give them a significant advantage over Asian or African kingdoms, but they proved vital in the conquest of the Americas. Critical to Portuguese and Spanish maritime exploration were also increases in knowledge of the sea and wind currents in the Atlantic.

As described in Chapter 3, the Columbian Exchange, an exchange of Old World and New World crops, disease pathogens, and animals, transformed both the Americas and Afro-Eurasia. For both world regions, the exchange represented an explosion of botanical and zoological knowledge that expanded production possibilities frontiers throughout the world. World populations grew as these new crops were incorporated into agricultural regimes. In 1500, estimates are that the world's population was around 425 million. By 1600, world population had grown to around 545 million. Between 1700 and 1800, when the full possibilities of the Columbian Exchange were being felt, world populations rose from 610 million to 900 million.

European use of paper and printing technology represented a cultural borrowing from the Chinese (via the Arabs) that would have enormous consequences for Europeans. Between 1453, when Gutenberg first developed movable type, and 1600, perhaps as many as 220 million books had been printed. This represented an explosion of knowledge and ideas that transformed religion, scientific understanding, and political life.

Industrial Revolutions (1750–1900)

The combination of scientific and technological developments that resulted in the Industrial Revolution have been covered in some detail in the earlier chapters on World History and United States History. A number of observations here are nonetheless in order.

First, it is important to realize that industrialization (beginning in Great Britain and spreading to northern Europe and then the Americas) reversed what had until the mid-18th century been the dominance of China and India in the global economy. Second, the industrialization begun in Great Britain resulted from both a favorable combination of natural resources, British commercial traditions and values, and a favorable tax and regulatory climate, as well as advantages accruing from colonization and the slave trade.

The first series of technological innovations to trigger this rightward shift in Britain's production possibilities frontier were centered in the textile industry. These included the spinning jenny and water frame, which could harness water and later steam power. With a glut in spun thread, water power and then steam power were employed to drive looms to weave the thread into cloth. Then, in 1793, the cotton gin unleashed the potential of the American South's land and enslaved its labor force, providing the vital raw material that the mechanized textile factories (themselves a new form of production) so desperately needed. Technological improvements in iron and steel refining and coal mining then combined to further extend the growth potential of Britain's industrial economy. The iron and coal industry were also intimately tied to the development of the steam engine. The steam engine then provided a new source of power, reliant for the first time on fossil fuels, and made possible a veritable transportation revolution across Europe and the United States. These technologies and organizational systems in the textile mills, coal mines, steel and iron foundries, and railroads represented a great leap forward in the production possibilities of Great Britain, then continental Europe and the United States, followed by Japan and Russia. Wherever this complex of industrial technologies flourished, a new industrial capitalism emerged; and where it did not, nations like China and India that had once been at the forefront of the global economy, soon found themselves increasingly marginalized.

In part, this resulted from the fact that these technologies also provided their adopters with important military and strategic advantages. Ironclad British steamships sailed up the Pearl River in southern China in the 1840s Opium Wars, and the Chinese had little recourse but to accept the humiliating trade terms that the British then imposed. Similar British advantages made possible the conquest and colonization of India. Railroads extended European power into the interior of Africa and India. The early machine gun, coupled with anti-malarial medicine, made it possible for English, French, Belgian, and later German colonizers to divide Africa.

The pace of these changes only accelerated after 1860 in what has often been described as the "Second Industrial Revolution." Railroads, steamships, and submarine telegraph cables linked Europe and the United States with markets across the globe, making possible their market penetration and access to hitherto unreachable natural resources.

The Second Industrial Revolution, unlike the first century of industrialization, depended more directly on science, advanced mathematics, and engineering. Tinkerers, artisans, and mechanics developed most inventions in the early modern period and from 1750 to 1860. There was little systematic and self-sustaining innovation during this period. But since the 1860s, engineering as a field has only grown. Research and development funded by corporate and public institutions has become commonplace and contributed to a process of progressive technological innovation. Thomas Alva Edison's Menlo Park, New Jersey, lab is only one of the many examples of institutions intentionally developed to resolve scientific and technical bottlenecks that reduced efficiency and growth. A list of the many inventions from the latter half of the 19th century would be long indeed. Consider this partial listing: the telephone, typewriter, adding machine, storage batteries, cash register, stock ticker, celluloid (an early plastic), the camera, incandescent light bulb, phonograph, the escalator, elevators, maxim gun, smokeless powder, electric iron, the radio, automobile, motorcycle, dynamite, the revolving door, refrigeration, refrigerated rail cars, and don't forget blue jeans and potato chips. If we contemplate only the impact of the typewriter, adding machine, and telephone on business productivity and record keeping it is clear that the latter half of the 19th century had a transformative effect on commerce in the United States and worldwide.

20th Century Growth

In 1914, European nations went to war. Though World War I only lasted until 1918, the conflict begun in 1914 would not come to a definitive end until 1945. Even the peace that followed World War II would be an uneasy one, as the threat of thermonuclear war and the tensions of the Cold War cast their pall. These persistent overt and latent conflicts, however, powerfully influenced scientific and technological developments over the course of the short mid-20th century (1914–1989). It is perhaps fair to say that many of the most important 20th-century technological and scientific developments owe their origins to the violent struggle for power that characterized one of the most violent centuries in human history.

World War I saw the use of submarines, chemicals, advanced explosives, radio, airplanes, machine guns, and the tank, to name only a few of the military uses of the Second Industrial Revolution's inventions. During World War II, each of these technologies saw advances, and new technologies saw military use. Nuclear weapons, radar, ballistic missiles, and jet aircraft were all introduced in World War II. One measure of the importance of conflict to 20th-century technological and scientific developments is reflected in the fact that almost all technologies developed after World War I have originated in the United States, the Soviet Union, Germany, Japan, or Great Britain, the chief belligerents in the wars of the 20th century.

Not all of the wartime innovations increased death rates. Computers also were used for the first time during the war. Mathematicians and scientists played important roles in the war efforts of each of the belligerents. British and German mathematicians designed computers to encode messages and to crack codes, to calculate trajectories of artillery shells, and to manage the incredible logistical challenges of the war. The computer, known as ENIAC, or Electrical Numerical Integrator and

Calculator, was a computational machine that could be used for a variety of tasks. Antibiotics were put to use during the Second World War, though penicillin had been discovered earlier, in 1928, by Alexander Fleming. Both the British and American general staffs purchased stockpiles of penicillin sufficient to protect their troops from the infections that had ravaged armies in earlier conflicts. The Cold War brought an increased investment in science and technology. Although the nuclear arms race is the clearest example of this competition, nuclear power and ballistic missile technology also had important civilian uses. The first nuclear power plants opened in Russia and Great Britain, followed by the United States, France, India, and China. The Soviet Union's launch of the Sputnik satellite inaugurated a space race that ultimately has seen the United States and the Soviet Union (and now the Russian Federation) significantly expand human knowledge of the cosmos. Although most of the satellites launched since 1957 are spy satellites, others have made possible vastly improved communications, astronomy, surveying, and cartography. Our cell phones' use of global positioning systems is now one of the most obvious links to that technology.

> **Competency 022 Descriptive Statement E.** The beginning teacher demonstrates knowledge of how specific developments in science, technology, and the free enterprise system have affected the economic development of the United States (e.g., cotton gin, Bessemer steel process, electric power, telephone, railroad, petroleum-based products, computers).

Cotton Gin (1793)

It could be argued that the cotton gin made possible the boom in cotton production that provided the principal raw material of the Industrial Revolution. Cotton comes tightly attached to its seed and seed pod. To extract the cotton fibers from the seed and seed pod before the development of the cotton gin (gin is short for engine) was a very labor-intensive process. Before, the invention of the cotton gin, West Indian cotton growers had used a device modeled on a South Asian device called a *churka,* which cleaned cotton between two rolling pins. Additionally, the variety of cotton produced in Mexico and in the American South, upland cotton, proved more difficult to clean than the cotton varieties used in India. It took a single individual, most often an enslaved person, eight hours to produce one pound of cleaned cotton fiber, extracting the seed and pod by hand. Eli Whitney was granted a patent for the cotton gin in 1793. Whitney's cotton gin sped up the process immediately. The earliest, hand-cranked cotton gin could clean 50 pounds of cotton in eight hours. Whitney also developed a cotton gin that could be turned by animal or water power.

The cotton gin had a number of economic effects beyond its importance in improving the efficiency of cleaning cotton. The cotton gin made possible the expansion of cotton production using enslaved labor across the American South. After 1793, there was a rapid increase in American cotton production, increases in the property values of land in the American South that could be devoted to cotton farming, and increases in the demand for slaves in Georgia, Louisiana, Mississippi, South Carolina, Alabama, and eventually Texas. The cotton gin also tightly linked United

States cotton planters to the textile industry in Great Britain that was undergoing industrialization at the time. By 1860, nearly 80 percent of Great Britain's raw cotton came from the American South. Fully two-thirds of the value of American exports in 1860 was cotton produced by enslaved African Americans in the American South.

Railroads

The first railways were used in mining operations in Germany and Britain in the 16th and 17th centuries, where small handcarts pushed along wooden tracks to haul coal or iron ore from the interior of mines. The rails allowed horses to pull heavier loads. By the early 18th century iron rails replaced wooden rails. In 1804, **Richard Trevithick** was the first to employ a steam engine to haul iron ore and people. His steam locomotive, however, only traveled at five miles per hour. Improved locomotives were developed. By 1852, locomotives could travel at 50 miles per hour.

Railroads had numerous and varied impacts on the culture and economy of Europe, the United States, and everywhere else they were introduced. Railroad demand for steel, coal, and iron fueled expansion in each of these industries, while also enabling that expansion. Railroads needed steel for the engines and rails and coal as a fuel for the steam engine. The expansion of rail lines enabled coal and iron ore to be extracted from distant coal and iron fields. Railroads also significantly reduced costs of transportation, and thereby the costs of consumer items. Transporting a commodity overland in early 19th-century America cost 30 cents per ton-mile. In 1860, to transport a commodity by rail in the United States cost 3 cents per ton-mile. Railroads thus opened up markets for goods and raw materials across the world. Railroads were critical to opening up colonial markets. By the early 20th century, railroads crisscrossed Africa, Asia, and South and Central America.

Railroads had enormous cultural impact as well. Perceptions of time and space changed. Physical barriers that had formerly proven insurmountable were now breached. Railroad schedules changed perceptions of time as it became necessary to standardize schedules to be sure that trains did not crash. Railroads created their own time zones, eventually agreeing in the United States to four standard time zones.

The Telegraph

Samuel F.B. Morse was an artist without any scientific or engineering background. He was barely able to earn a living painting portraits. After his wife and father died suddenly, he lived for two years as a homeless drifter and was only able to escape this life by a fortuitous marriage. A chance discussion in 1832 with a fellow traveler who explained that electricity passed instantaneously through any length of wire led Morse to leap to the conclusion that "intelligence," or information, might also be able to be transmitted by electricity. Between 1832 and 1835, he scraped together bits and pieces of clock mechanisms, wire, and batteries, and experimented unsuccessfully with trying to transmit information using electrical impulses. By 1837, however, he had solved the technical difficulties and was ready to seek a patent for his invention, in addition to recruiting partners who could supply the needed capital to set up a telegraph system. In 1840, he was able to secure a patent, but had difficulty financing his enterprise. In March of 1843, he was saved by the appropriation of $30,000 by the U.S. Congress to develop a demonstration line between Baltimore and Washington, D.C. When his initial idea of burying the cables underground in lead pipes failed, Morse decided to hang them overhead. On May 24, 1844, Morse sent his famous first message, "What hath God wrought?," from the Capitol building (an illustration of the federal government's involvement) to Baltimore, where his partner returned the message. A boom in telegraph construction began immediately as Morse sold licenses to use his product to other entrepreneurs. Soon, other businessmen developed competing designs. By 1850, there were more than 22,000 miles of telegraph lines stretching the length of the country. Stock traders and newspapermen who needed real-time information were the first to adopt its use. The telegraph, however, also made possible the expansion of the vast merchandising enterprise of Richard W. Sears, founder of the mail-order catalogue company Sears, Roebuck and Company. Many other late 19th-century fortunes were made possible by the development of this vital communication device.

The Bessemer Steel Process

In 1855, Henry Bessemer patented the Bessemer process for producing steel in England. Before the invention of the Bessemer Furnace, steel was expensive and difficult to produce in large quantities. Before developing this process, Bessemer had a reputation as an inventor, developing a hydraulic press for sugar cane, patenting a process for compressing graphite for use in wooden pencils, and inventing the artillery shell in the early nineteenth century. The kind of hardened steel needed for artillery shells at the time, however, could only be made in small batches.

Iron is a chemical element found abundantly throughout the world. Steel, however, is composed of a mixture of iron and carbon. A mixture of 0.2 percent to 2.1 percent carbon and iron produces hardened steel. Bessemer's process blew air over the surface of molten iron to produce the desired mixture of carbon and iron. Bessemer's furnace produced steel much faster and with a far smaller fuel requirement than earlier processes. The Bessemer furnace produced 30 tons of steel in a half-hour, compared to previous methods that took many hours for an output of less than 50 pounds of steel.

The Bessemer process became vital to the industrialization of Europe and the United States. It was particularly useful for producing bulk steel for use in rail lines, bridges, building, and other uses where cost and quantity were more important than the quality of the steel. In the United States, Andrew Carnegie was the entrepreneur to use the Bessemer process to greatest advantage. He built his first furnace in 1875 near Pittsburgh, Pennsylvania, to produce steel rails. By 1895, Carnegie Steel Company produced over 1 billion tons of steel annually using Bessemer's method.

Urbanizing Technologies

Four urbanizing technologies have shaped American commerce and cultural development and should be understood in connection with one another. Just as the steam engine, railroad, and new iron and steel smelting processes combined to produce a revolution in industry and commerce in the first half of the 19th century, electrification, the telephone, radio, and the automobile combined to have a transformative effect on the global economy and cultures across the world. All of these technologies were invented in the latter decades of the 19th century; however, they had their most widespread impact in the 20th century, after 1920.

Electrical Power

Electricity depended on a number of previous discoveries including Benjamin Franklin's discovery of electricity's positive and negative charges and conductivity as well as Allesandro Volta's electrical battery. Early uses of electricity in the telegraph, for example, were then reliant on batteries. In Europe, during the 1870s, practical electric generators called dynamos were developed for use in electroplating. Other uses for these dynamos were soon developed, including street lighting using arc lighting. In 1879, Charles Brush, an American entrepreneur introduced an arc lighting system to light the streets of San Francisco. At the time, there were more than 400 gas lighting companies around the country. Soon, Brush's technology was displacing these gas lighting companies in New York, Boston, and Philadelphia. Since arc lighting was too bright for use indoors, **Thomas Alva Edison** developed the incandescent light bulb in 1878 and founded the **Edison Electric Lighting Company** to distribute electricity. George Westinghouse and the Westinghouse Electric Lighting Company offered a competing method, **alternating current,** which proved a more efficient means of generating and distributing electricity. Westinghouse's innovation allowed for centrally located power generation capable of generating enormous quantities of electrical power.

These new power generators were first employed in transportation. Public transportation in American and European cities in the 1870s and 1880s was largely horse-drawn streetcars or steam-powered railways. Both had significant environmental disadvantages. By 1900, the vast majority of urban public transport was electrified streetcars. Westinghouse, in 1892, hired Nikola Tesla to build electric motors capable of using alternating current power. These small motors were soon used in telegraph machines, radios, telephones, motion pictures, electric washing machines, refrigerators, and many other household utensils. During the 1920s and 1930s, electrical power generation and rural electrification spawned a vast grid of electrical wires that connected Americans to one another, creating whole new generations of consumers of electrically powered tools, household items, etc.

Electricity also made possible a new organization of the workplace. Before electric lighting, shift work had typically been divided into 12- to 15-hour shifts, dependent upon the length of daylight hours. With electricity, an additional shift, the night shift, was possible, allowing factories to produce around the clock.

With the electrification of rural areas in the 1920s and 1930s, thanks in part to such federal programs as the Tennessee Valley Authority, an entirely new marketplace for consumer items such as washers, dryers, radios, telephones, and, later, televisions, was created. This made possible the integration of the American economy.

The Telephone

The telephone was one of the most important innovations in the development of the modern capitalist economy. **Alexander Graham Bell** in 1876 developed the device as a means to transmit speech along electrical wires. Bell's invention, along with the telegraph and radio, rapidly sped up communications between distant parts of the planet. The telephone, however, did not immediately have much impact. Like electricity and the automobile, the telephone required a vast infrastructure and significant capital investment. To raise the necessary funds, Bell formed a joint-stock company, the **Bell Telephone Company,** to profit from his patent. It later merged with a sister company formed by his father-in-law. Bell publicized his invention at expositions and world's fairs. The network of telephone lines grew slowly, at first providing only local service. It was a novelty in the beginning and only gradually drew interested subscribers. In rural areas, farmer's co-ops would often be encouraged to subscribe and fund the running of wires to connect a rural network. Sometimes, municipal governments would franchise their operation by local companies. The Bell Telephone Company eventually became part of a larger conglomerate known as American Telephone & Telegraph that was for some time the world's largest telephone company, effectively maintaining a monopoly over phone service in the United States and Canada. It bought up smaller telephone companies and telegraph services, eliminating or consolidating most of its potential competitors. In 1984 was AT&T's monopoly broken up as the result of a Justice Department antitrust suit.

Initially, the telephone was primarily utilized for business purposes. It was only in the 1920s that the telephone became an important part of American social life. Rural women were among the first to make social use of the telephone. In cities, middle-class women visited in person. Rural women were able to make their visiting rounds "virtually" through the telephone. Women also found an important occupational niche in the telephone industry. From the outset, women were most often the telephone operators who "manned" the banks of switchboards necessary to connect subscribers to the telephone network. People who picked up the phone to dial came to expect a woman's voice to be on the other end of the line to direct their call to its destination.

The Automobile

The automobile has been among the most transformative technologies in American history. Many inventors in the United States and Europe experimented in the late 19th and early 20th centuries to improve the internal combustion engine and employ it in transportation. **Henry Ford (1863–1947)** is rightly credited with many of the changes in the automobile that would have the greatest effect on the American economy.

In 1913, Ford established a gigantic assembly-line, mass production manufacturing plant in Highland Park, Michigan, to produce his Model T Ford. Where once cars were built by skilled labor, Ford used semi-skilled and unskilled factory workers who repeated simplified tasks over and over. At first, there was massive labor turnover since few workers enjoyed the rigor and repetitive nature of the assembly line. In response, Ford began to pay his workers double the prevailing wage for the time. This had the unforeseen consequence of providing a ready market for his product, his own workers, and workers in surrounding industries whose wages were increased to compete with Ford's wage rates. Additionally, the advantages afforded by efficiencies and returns to scale significantly lowered the cost of the automobile in the United States. The cost of the Model T dropped from $850 in 1908 to $300 by 1925 (the equivalent of a reduction from $18,000 to $4,240 in 2017 dollars).

The expansion of the automobile industry had an immediate effect on other areas of the American economy. From the 1920s until World War II, even during the Great Depression, automobile ownership in the United States continued to grow. And with it, so did steel production, plastics, rubber, gasoline, road construction, and other related industries. The automobile also opened up new areas to suburban building. When streetcars and rail lines had been the primary commuter vehicles, suburbs built up along rail and streetcar lines in what were called "finger cities," with the city center representing the palm of a hand with the suburbs hugging the rail and streetcar lines extending outward. The automobile made it possible for rural land between the rail and streetcar lines available for suburban growth. Along America's roads, particularly after World War II, a network of motels and hotels, drive-in movies, drive-in restaurants and fast-food stands, gas stations, and other places of employment flourished. In 1956, President Dwight D. Eisenhower pushed through the Interstate Highway Act, which funded nearly 90 percent of a massive interstate highway system. This highway system provided a massive publicly-funded jobs program, which further expanded the networks connecting the American commercial system.

Petroleum-based Products

The American economy has, since at least the 1930s, been tied together by petroleum. It was only in 1950 that petroleum surpassed coal as the leading source of the nation's energy. American dependence upon oil goes far beyond its use in our cars. Oil has changed the American diet, our clothing, where and how our houses and neighborhoods are built, our leisure time, and our jobs. There is not an aspect of American life that is not shaped by our reliance on petroleum and petroleum by-products. American consumer culture depends on cheap crude. Between 1945 and 1970, the price per barrel remained below $20, and Americans had a stable supply of inexpensive petroleum. Since the 1970s, that stability has diminished. Nonetheless, crude oil at the time this is being written is priced at $44.62 per barrel (worth less than $6 in 1960 prices). Despite that instability, American and global dependence on petroleum and petrochemicals has only increased.

One way to conceptualize the way in which petroleum and petrochemicals are employed is to imagine a single barrel of about 45 gallons of refined crude oil. Of that, 37 gallons will be burned for heating or transportation. The remainder will be used to make plastics, pharmaceuticals, synthetic fibers and fabrics, detergents, soaps, synthetic rubber, asphalt, squeeze bottles, garbage pails, and any number of a thousand products you find around your home or in your workplace.

One obvious link between cheap oil and our consumer culture is the connection between our diet and petroleum-powered transportation and technology. We are likely to think first about the link between fast food and the automobile. The first McDonald's restaurant was purposely situated just off Route 66 in southern California. The lesson learned from that success has resulted in the proliferation of burger places, diners, motels, and strip malls scattered across the American landscape.

The American diet has also been transformed in other ways by petroleum products. Beginning in the 20th century, chemists relied on petroleum and natural gas to create synthetic fertilizer to significantly enhance soil fertility. Pesticides used to protect American crops are also petroleum by-products. The use of chemical fertilizers and pesticides resulted in a green revolution both in the United States and abroad. Coupled with petroleum-powered tractors, harvesters, and trucks, American agribusiness became dependent upon oil. With this "green revolution" built on the foundation of cheap oil, the American diet was also transformed, in part by an abundance of corn that flourished with the green revolution. High-fructose corn syrup sweetens and flavors sodas, toothpaste, salad dressings, and all manner of foods; corn is present in hot dogs, buns, and the mustard, mayonnaise, and ketchup that dress them; and corn feeds the chickens, pigs, cattle, fish, and other livestock Americans consume. For every three bushels of corn grown and marketed, one gallon of oil is needed. The American diet and consumer lifestyle is impacted by petroleum in ways we don't often imagine.

Computers

One contemporary technology that has significantly changed the lives of 21st-century Americans is the computer. The computer as we know it was made possible by a number of interlocking mathematical and technological innovations. One of these was the Hungarian-American mathematician John von Neumann's development of the stored program, a program that allowed computers to perform different tasks without being reprogrammed by engineers for each task. This allowed software designers to design a host of programs without required hardware modifications. Beginning in the 1950s, International Business Machines (IBM) began to develop mainframe computers for business uses. Soon, banks, retail firms, and government agencies began to use computers to carry out many of the calculations needed in business and government. Mainframe computers in the early 1970s faced competition from a surprising source: amateurs like Stephen Wozniak and

Steve Jobs, who began to use microchips to design computer circuit boards. In 1977, Jobs and Wozniak developed a desktop computer they called Apple II and targeted small businesses as a potential market. The Apple II captured the small business and educational markets. IBM followed suit with its own desktop computers, using Intel chips and an operating system designed by Bill Gates and Paul Allen.

> **Competency 022 Descriptive Statement F.** The beginning teacher analyzes moral and ethical issues related to changes in science and technology.

Consider briefly the economy depicted in **Figure 8.13** below. This hypothetical economy has the land, labor, capital, and entrepreneurial capacity to produce two products: poison gas and green vegetables. The society may choose to devote its entire productive capacity to growing 25,000 tons of broccoli, chard, lettuce, bok choy, and asparagus. Or, it can choose to use these same resources and produce as much as 3,000 pounds of mustard gas, nearly 18,000 lethal doses of the poison.

Figure 8.13
Production Possibilities Frontier

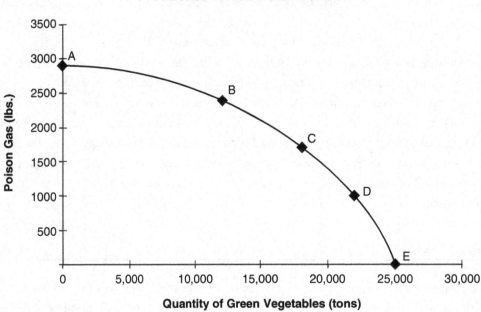

In the hypothetical economy depicted in **Figure 8.13**, we see a stark ethical choice. The society can choose to produce a deadly gas, which may bring far greater income to the society than the vegetables would (were it able to market the poison gas), or it could grow healthful, organic foods that would sustain life.

Though the choices are not typically so harsh, economic choices often entangle individual entrepreneurs, firms, workers, and political leaders in just such ethical dilemmas. The ethical dimension of technological and scientific change, is not merely a matter of choosing between life and death as in the example above. Human beings face ethical and moral decisions with each set of choices. Technological and scientific change bring with them a number of risks that must be considered.

The first is the risk of catastrophic existential threat. Since the 1750s, our consumption of fossil fuels, which has at once enriched our lives and fostered enormous economic growth, has the potential to prove in the near term likely to have catastrophic consequences for our weather patterns, food supplies, and demography. During the Cold War, the potential that choices made by political leaders might lead to global destruction appeared quite clearly within the realm of possibility. Nuclear technology promised the possibility of unlimited supplies of energy, but it also offered the equally real likelihood of nuclear reactor meltdowns and nuclear warfare, both of which could threaten life on the planet. Despite the unwillingness of many political and economic actors to acknowledge the possibility, climate change is upon us and poses a number of critical economic and ethical questions. Is the disruption caused by a retooling of the American economy away from oil, natural gas, and coal consumption warranted? There are those, particularly within the state of Texas, who would argue against such a strategy, given the prominence of the oil and natural gas industries in the state. If those judgments are wrong, or based on flawed scientific conclusions, the consequences will not just have a negative bearing on Texas, but on the entire globe.

Other economic decisions pose existential challenges to a narrower range of the population. For example, the driverless vehicle, a technology that seems inevitably on its way into our lives, threatens to put out of business a whole population of laborers. According to the Bureau of Labor Statistics, in Texas alone during 2016, there were 175,000 truck drivers in the state. Truck drivers may very well be displaced by the development of driverless vehicles. However, if economic history is any measure, technological change often opens up new avenues of employment. For example, in 1985, the first computerized spreadsheet was introduced. Before Dan Bricklin and Bob Frankston developed VisiCalc for the Apple II computer, spreadsheets were sheets of lined paper spread out over a table. Changes in one square required the accountant or bookkeeper to use his calculator to re-calculate each affected row or cell. This was a time-consuming process that required hours and many bookkeepers or accountants. Bricklin and Frankston's invention changed all that, threatening the occupations of millions of paper pushers. In fact, however, the development of the spreadsheet has actually increased employment of bookkeepers and accountants.

A second area of moral and ethical consideration is the problem of inequality. The benefits of technological innovation are not always evenly distributed across the population or across the globe. In Europe and the United States, cell phone penetration (with an average of 118 and 121 cell phone subscriptions per 100 residents respectively) is substantially higher than cell phone penetration in sub-Saharan Africa (at 76 per 100 residents). In the United States, there is a divide between rural and urban communities in terms of broadband Internet access. While only 10 percent of Americans in 2016 lacked access to high-speed Internet connections, fully 39 percent of rural residents were unable to connect to broadband Internet access. Given the importance of Internet access to economic growth and development in the 21st century, this gap poses a critical moral and ethical quandary to policy makers.

A third ethical challenge posed by scientific and technological innovation reflects the ways in which technology and science change the meaning of nature and humanity. For much of human history, technology and science have been employed to relieve human beings of the drudgery of labor or the suffering from disease and death. Economists have long recognized the role of the corporation in prolonging human life. Of course, the founders of a corporation did not have eternal life. But their creations, as a legal and practical matter, did.

Modern science and technology has similarly begun to move beyond alleviating the human condition to actually replacing humans in many facets of life. Within the past decade, economists have begun considering the possibility that soon humans will require a **universal basic income** to which they are entitled as citizens or human beings, without any relationship to their labor productivity, simply because so many of the tasks formerly carried out by men and women will be conducted by machines. Economists are asking: what "full employment" will mean in an age when most routine and many complex tasks are completed by artificially intelligent machines?

While human labor is potentially threatened by increasingly complex machinery, nature itself is being transformed by science. Genetically modified or GMO crops are plants that have been modified using DNA from another species inserted in their own DNA in order to acquire beneficial traits of the inserted DNA. For example, genetic modifications have been used to make crops more resistant to dangers such as disease, drought, and insects, and even herbicides. The first GMO procedure was done in 1983 by Monsanto Corporation. Today, more than 90 percent of the soybean and 80 percent of the corn crop grown in the United States is genetically modified. Critics of the practice see genetic modification as a kind of Frankenstein experiment with global food supplies. Scientists who promote the GMO crops see genetic modification as simply an extension of breeding practices that have modified plants and animals since the beginning of the agricultural revolution. Farmers and American agribusiness argue that genetic modification will improve efficiency and yields, to the benefit of both the consumer and the producer.

Each of these three challenges emphasizes the degree to which economic choices are never simply matters of efficiency, productivity, and optimizing resource use. Economic choices and the development of new technologies or scientific methods almost always engage consumers, producers, and policy makers in ethical and moral debates.

> **Competency 022 Descriptive Statement G.** The beginning teacher analyzes the impact of scientific discoveries, technological innovations, and the free enterprise system on the standard of living in the United States (e.g., radio, television, automobile, vaccines).

American standards of living have changed remarkably since the end of World War II. Most of the changes identified in this descriptive statement are postwar changes that impacted the American economy.

Radio and Television

Radio and television have been closely related with two periods of economic growth and rising standards of living in America: radio in the 1920s, and television in the 1950s. While other factors contributed to increased growth in these two eras, the most notable are the role of the radio in the "Jazz Age" of the 1920s, and the importance of television to growth and rising living standards in the 1950s.

The radio was the result of a combination of inventions between 1886, when Heinrich Rudolph Hertz demonstrated the ability to transmit electromagnetic (radio) waves through the air, and 1920, when the first radio program was broadcast from a station in Detroit, Michigan. One question that required resolution, however, was: who owns the airwaves? Almost immediately, large corporations like AT&T, RCA (Radio Corporation of America), Westinghouse, and General Electric had sought to secure control of the airwaves and profit from the lucrative possibilities of providing commercial programming. Radio's importance for naval and defense purposes as well as fears of broadcast monopolies resulted in regulations stipulating that maritime radio, amateur (often called ham radio), and government radio operations were relegated to certain radio wavelengths, while commercial broadcast stations were limited to other wavelengths and broadcasting power. Larger corporations controlled the more powerful broad bands, while smaller, locally-owned or independent stations had less lucrative spots on the dial. In the 1920s, many of the corporate-owned radio stations then united into networks. The first of these networks was the National Broadcasting Company (NBC), created by RCA, GE, and Westinghouse. NBC had two network distribution systems, NBC Red and NBC Blue. Not long after the establishment of NBC, the Columbia Broadcasting System (CBS) entered the fray. A third network, the Mutual Broadcasting Network unsuccessfully sought to compete, ultimately filing suit against NBC for unfair competition. As a result, in part, of that suit, RCA sold off NBC Blue, eventually leading to the creation of the American Broadcasting Company (ABC). These three, NBC, CBS, and ABC, dominated radio and television broadcasting until the 1980s, when cable television emerged.

One goal of NBC at its founding was to sell radio hardware; RCA produced and sold radios. Sales of radio sets were one of the consumer items that figured in the Jazz Age consumer spending boom. In 1923, there were only 400,000 radio owners in the country. By 1930, that number had grown to more than 13.75 million. It was also immediately apparent that programming attracted advertisers interested in reaching consumers. The broadcast networks soon drew most of their revenues not from sales of their hardware, but from ad agencies and businesses eager to sell their products. Radio programming allowed businesses to target their advertising in new ways, directing their pitches toward specific audiences. Radio offered a unique opportunity to appeal to the emotions of buyers and to shape their tastes. Additionally, radio, unlike catalogs or door-to-door salesmen, invaded the home uninvited, creating a national marketplace of listeners who could be appealed to at the same time, providing the first mass medium. By the 1930s, food, drug, and personal and household product industries, along with tobacco companies, had reached into nearly every American home, sponsoring "soap" operas (so-called because they advertised soap or hygiene products), vaudeville acts, musical concerts, and many other programs.

Television developed initially in the 1920s and 1930s, but the technology had little impact until after World War II. Television followed the same pattern that had emerged with the development of radio. The emerging TV medium organized its markets and viewers by adapting the laws, regulatory policies, and marketing systems that had developed to shape the radio waves. The "Big Three" radio networks, NBC, CBS and ABC, shifted easily to dominance in the new mass medium. Many radio programs were simply adapted to television. Game shows, like *The $64,000 Question,* were modeled on the CBS radio quiz show *Take it or Leave It.* The program *Amos 'n' Andy,* which ran from 1928 to 1960 on radio, was adapted to television in 1951. The *Texaco Star Theatre,* a vaudeville variety show on radio starring Milton Berle and sponsored by the Texaco oil company, was transformed into a similar variety show for television audiences. The show opened with a jingle sung by service station attendants (before self-service was the norm) who encouraged viewers to "join the ranks of those who know, and fill your tanks with Texaco." These commercials and program sponsorships transferred easily from radio to television, encouraging American consumers across the country.

To no small degree, radio and television broke down market barriers that separated consumers across the country. This meant that consumers in California, Texas, Florida, and Wisconsin could be appealed to at the same time and by the same advertisers, fostering demand growth across the country. The emergence of cable and satellite television set in motion a fragmentation of that unified marketplace, a process that has only been increased with the internet and social media networks that fit consumers into ever more finely-narrowed niches.

Television was not just a medium for programming and advertising. It was also one of the most important consumer purchases of the 1950s and 1960s. Before 1945, there were only 7,000 television sets owned by American homeowners. Almost all these sets were owned in the New York area, which as late as 1948 was one of the few urban areas with multiple television stations. By 1959, more than 67 million television sets had been sold. By 1970, more than 99 percent of all American households had at least one television set in their home.

One factor related to the spread of television ownership was the television's connection to the baby boom. Much of the earliest programming was directed at children. Children in the 1950s and 1960s became an important "emerging" market for advertisers and television producers. Families with children were the first to purchase television sets, while childless couples often were among the last, a trend repeated with VCRs and DVD players. Shows like *Howdy Doody Time, Captain Kangaroo,* or *Kukla, Fran, and Ollie* provided mothers with an entertainment device (although it is perhaps fair to call it a babysitting aid) at a time when middle-class women's household work demands increased despite the widespread use of electric ranges, irons, washer-dryers, and other "time-saving" devices. For advertisers, children represented an important and growing market. As the baby-boom generation grew up, became teenagers, entered the workforce, and are now retiring, they have driven consumer culture in the country in important directions. They bought

Davy Crockett coonskin caps, moccasins, toy rifles, and other toys largely at the instigation of television shows. They purchased rock-and-roll albums, bell-bottomed jeans, and Ford Mustangs, again shaped by the consumer culture of television. Their adult aspirations and consumer choices were similarly influenced by a shared television culture, as adult baby boomers gathered around the proverbial water cooler to discuss the previous evening's sitcoms. Now, though the market has fragmented to some degree, their tastes are similarly being shaped as they head into retirement.

The Automobile and American Living Standards

The automobile, as we have seen, had a transformative effect on the American economy and culture. In 1910, the United States had the most developed system of public transportation, railroads, subways, elevated trains, and streetcars in the world. Since the 1920s, however, 80 percent of public investment in transportation has been spent on roads, highways, bridges, tunnels, and other construction designed to facilitate automobile and truck transport. The massive road-building project that begun in the 1950s, coupled with low-cost gasoline and American auto purchases, has had the following direct economic impacts:

- Interstate highways lowered transport costs by 17 percent over those of other highways, and have been linked to a 25 percent increase in productivity of American manufacturers and retailers between 1956 and 1996 (the peak of the highway-building boom). Warehousing costs were reduced, improving manufacturing efficiency and reducing delivery times. The interlocked interstate trucking and highway system lowered product prices, saving Americans more than $1 trillion between 1956 and 1996.

- More than $1 of every $9 spent by American consumers is directly related to automobile transportation. The automobile has been an engine of growth and consumer spending since its development.

- Americans have experienced increased employment opportunities since the 1920s as a result of the automobile. One example is in restaurant employment. Between 1956 and 1996, employment in fast-food and other restaurants increased seven times more than the rate of population growth.

- Americans have experienced greater employment freedom as a result of the automobile and highway system. This reduces "stickiness" in unemployment rates, allowing Americans to move more easily to take advantage of job opportunities. This has been particularly important in the migration of rural residents to urban centers as farm employment declined (think "Okies" migrating in the Great Depression, or the Great Migration of African American sharecroppers to Northern cities during and after World War II). Fluid worker migration is also seen in the movement of unemployed residents from areas with fewer economic opportunities to more prosperous areas (consider the migration of laid-off autoworkers and steel workers from the "Rust Belt" to the "Sunbelt").

Automobiles have contributed in many other ways to the economic growth of the United States and to American standards of living.

Vaccines

Vaccines have a longer history than often suspected. Immunization began in China and India as healers practiced "variolation," or inoculation of healthy subjects with the smallpox virus. Edward Jenner developed the practice of vaccination in Western Europe in 1796. Jenner used a vaccination from less virulent and life-threatening cowpox, reducing the rates of occasional mortality common with the variolation used in Africa and Asia. Using Jenner's techniques, smallpox has gradually been eradicated globally. Vaccinations have been developed for a wide variety of formerly debilitating or life-threatening diseases, including chicken pox, diphtheria, hepatitis, human papillomavirus (HPV), influenza, measles, polio, rabies, rubella, tetanus, tuberculosis, typhoid fever, and yellow fever. Today, more than 120 different vaccines are currently available.

Vaccines have clearly had an impact on human health and longevity. Most importantly, vaccines have contributed to what demographers call the **demographic transition**. Most developed countries have seen a transition from high birth rates and high death rates to low birth rates and death rates. Vaccinations and improved diet began in the early 20th century to reduce infant and child mortality. As a result, households began gradually to reduce family sizes. In the early stages of the demographic transition, the lag between declines in birth rates (which fell at lower rates) and death rates resulted in natural increases (as opposed to those from immigration) resulted in rapid population growth. Later in the demographic transition, as households sought to decrease family size through family planning and birth control, birth rates fell, more closely approximating death rates. As a result, populations stabilized at lower levels of natural growth. This has happened wherever birth control, vaccination, improved diets, and improvements in female income have occurred.

Though it is difficult to differentiate cause and effect, vaccines and lower infant mortality rates, coupled with smaller family sizes, have been associated with increases in female income levels and workforce participation. Freeing women's talents for the labor force and increasing women's opportunities for higher educational levels has unleashed economic growth in the United States and elsewhere in the developed world. Much of the growth of the American labor force since the 1950s has been the result of an influx of women into the workplace.

Domain VII: Social Studies Foundations, Skills, Research, and Instruction

Domain VII, the focus of Chapter 9, differs significantly from the content covered in the previous six domains. Instead of asking readers to engage the subject matter and content of the different disciplines of history and the social sciences, this domain requires prospective teachers to demonstrate knowledge of the methods of teaching in the social studies classroom and to show an understanding of the underlying principles that guide the social sciences. The TExES Social Studies 7–12 test devotes 18 to 20 questions of its 140 items to testing this domain—by now a familiar apportionment to you since Domain VII is one of five domains to which the test devotes roughly 13 percent of its coverage. In preparing you for this portion of the test, this test guide examines the philosophical and methodological underpinnings of the social sciences but also attempts to outline useful strategies for engaging students with the subject matter of history and the social studies disciplines. Future teachers should, after studying this chapter, be able to articulate justifications for social studies in the classroom and society at large. They should be able to identify what kinds of evidence are most appropriate for use in classroom settings as well as how to use such evidence to encourage inquiry learning and understanding. By the time you have reached this point in your preparation with this book, you should have a strong foundation in the content and the central questions that are taught in Texas secondary school social studies classrooms. In this chapter, you will be asked to reflect on the best methods to make this subject matter come alive to the students you will be asked to teach.

COMPETENCY 023 (SOCIAL STUDIES FOUNDATIONS AND SKILLS)

The teacher understands social studies terminology and concepts; the philosophical foundations of social science inquiry; relationships among and between social science disciplines and other content areas; and skills for resolving conflicts, solving problems, and making decisions in social studies contexts.

The social studies provide students opportunities to explore the contemporary world around them and to situate themselves within the changing global social environment. They also provide students opportunities to understand the history of the world and their individual place in that history.

According to the National Council for the Social Studies, social studies is defined as:

> the integrated study of the social sciences and humanities to promote civic competence. Within the school program, social studies provides coordinated, systematic study drawing upon such disciplines as anthropology, archaeology, economics, geography, history, law, philosophy, political science, psychology, religion, and sociology, as well as appropriate content from the humanities, mathematics, and natural sciences. The primary purpose of social studies is to help young people develop the ability to make informed and reasoned decisions for the public good as citizens of a culturally diverse, democratic society in an interdependent world.

> **Competency 023 Descriptive Statement A.** The beginning teacher demonstrates knowledge of the philosophical foundations of social science inquiry.

During the Scientific Revolution of the 1600s and early 1700s, when people talked about the sciences, they didn't much use the term "science." Instead, they combined all the studies of the natural world and natural history under an umbrella term called **natural philosophy.** Only in the later years of the Enlightenment did "science" begin to take on its more contemporary usage. In the 19th century, the first modern disciplines began to appear: chemistry, physics, mathematics, biology, and geology. Terms like "biology" or "chemistry" emerged with the development of these separate studies. Only in the 19th century did the term "scientist" begin to be used as we mean it today.

The social sciences as distinct disciplines emerged from natural philosophy. Philosophers had long asked questions about human behavior and actions; inquired into the soul, mind, and morals of human beings; and taken interest in social questions like the nature of politics, trade, money, etc. With the emergence of natural philosophy and then the natural sciences, the "science of society" and the study of human behavior also developed. In the Enlightenment, thinkers like Adam Smith, the Baron de Montesquieu, Auguste Comte, and others sought to apply the methods of the natural sciences to human behavior, and social relations in the hopes of reforming society. It was only during the 19th century, when the disciplines of the natural sciences developed their own academic practitioners, scientific journals, and specialized subject matter, that the social sciences began gradually to emerge as professional disciplines.

In the 19th century, social scientists also began to conceptualize the social sciences as a pragmatic set of tools that could be applied to rationalize administration, economic institutions, and social organizations. In concert with the professionalization of medicine and the development of professional engineers and engineering schools, social scientists and historians began to increasingly professionalize their disciplines. Professional organizations developed, such as the National Association for the Promotion of Social Science (Great Britain), which was formed in 1857. The American Social Science Association, founded eight years later, was modeled on its British counterpart. In the universities, first in Germany, then France, and finally the United States, the social sciences became academic disciplines, with their own departments, journals, graduate programs, and tenured faculty.

One school of thought prominent among 19th-century social scientists was **positivism.** Positivists argued for the application of natural science methods to the social sciences and conceived the social sciences as akin to the natural sciences. Positivism begins with the assumption that knowledge of human behavior and social relations can be understood with the same certainty as the natural sciences, and that general laws of human and social behavior can be developed from empirical research in the same way that they can be in physics, mathematics, or chemistry.

Positivism in the social sciences shares the following basic assumptions with the natural sciences.

1. **Scientific method:** The natural sciences and social sciences both share a reliance on the scientific method. For positivists, science offered the scholar a means to describe reality.

2. **Naturalism:** The natural sciences assume that the scientist studies a natural reality that is outside of himself or herself, and that the scientist can objectively observe natural phenomena and scientifically reduce the complexity of natural phenomena to terms that can be readily understood and explained. Positivists make a similar assumption about their relationship to social phenomena.

3. **Empiricism:** Science depends upon observation and verification. The experimental method makes this possible in the natural sciences. Positivists shared a similar belief in the ability of social behavior to be empirically analyzed through experimental observation. From these observations, causal laws and explanations could be identified and verified.

4. **Value neutrality:** Science does not pass judgment. Scientists observe without judging their subjects according to social mores or ethical values. When chimpanzees kill rivals that enter their territories, Jane Goodall does not find them wanting morally or ethically. Positivism similarly emphasizes the responsibility of social scientists to remain value neutral in relation to their subjects. In pursuit of scientific truths and knowledge, the social scientists must be a neutral observer.

5. **Instrumentalism:** Though the "pure sciences" or "pure mathematics" pride themselves on seeking knowledge for knowledge's sake, and not for practical reasons, often science is motivated by the pursuit of technically useful knowledge. Positivists emphasize this in particular.

In contrast to positivism, some social scientists argue instead for a more **interpretive approach** to social and human relations. Where positivist scholars saw social conditions as a meaningful and objective reality, the interpretive tradition emphasized the ways in which social conditions are constructed in part by the interpretation of the social scientist. For this reason, the interpretive approach has often been characterized as a **constructivist** approach. This tradition shares a number of assumptions that differ markedly from those that guide positivist social scientific approaches. Most importantly, where positivists see the natural world and social phenomena as independent of the scientist's mind but available for analysis as an objective reality apart from the thought processes of the scholar, constructivists argue that knowledge of the natural or social sciences requires the construction of mental frameworks within which to explain and make sense of sensory experience, whether of the natural world or of social conditions. Constructivists share a number of the following assumptions:

1. **Anti-scientism:** Constructivist or interpretive approaches argue that there is a clear distinction between the human and natural sciences.

2. **Interpretation:** Social realities are too complex, constructivists argue, to be understood through simple observation. The founder of history as a professional discipline, Leopold von Ranke, very much in the positivist vein, said that the historian's responsibility was to describe the past "essentially as it actually happened." Von Ranke taught that historians can approach primary sources in an empirical fashion, like a scientist does the natural world, and describe the past as it actually was. Historians from more interpretive schools of thought argue that a realistic representation of social conditions requires instead that the historian interpret the data (or facts) in order to give meaning to the past. Similarly, the framework through which an economist studies the behavior of firms, consumers, or governmental actors in an economy will shape (whether they recognize that fact or not) the realities they attempt to study or make sense of.

3. **Relativism:** Just as the natural scientist and positivist social scientist refuse to interject moral criticism or ethical evaluation of his or her subject matter, constructivist scholars argue that the social scientist should remain values free when studying social, economic, political, and cultural phenomena. Both positivist and constructivist scholars reject the argument that the social sciences provide a means for attaching moral or ethical judgment to the behavior of individuals, social groups or institutions in the past or in contemporary situations.

4. **Humanism:** Constructivists accept that differences exist across time and across culture in the values and behavior of different cultures and societies, but they argue that human

nature provides an underlying meaning that remains constant. One feature of constructivist theories of the social sciences is the importance of a humanist search for the ways in which individuals and societies create meaning. This extends to constructivist approaches to teaching, which emphasize student-centered learning.

5. **Language and meaning:** For constructivists, language is seen as central to structuring society. For positivists, more often language is seen as deriving from the underlying realities of physical, economic, political, and other conditions. For constructivists, language and its changes, as well as the ways in which language shapes social relations, are the critical focus of the social sciences.

Against the positivists and the constructivists, another philosophical school of the social sciences is represented by the **Marxist approach to social theory.** Constructivists have focused on shared meanings within cultures (as well as the ways in which dominant systems of meaning are contested), and positivists have sought to identify the objective realities that explain the development of social and cultural differences. By contrast, the Marxist social sciences, which have had wide influence on many scholars who are not Marxist politically, have concentrated on the role of conflict within societies as the primary driver shaping the development of economies, social relations, culture, and political institutions. Marxists and other "social conflict theorists" focus on the role of class and class conflict, whereas constructivists are more often interested in cultural ideas, language, religion, etc. Additionally, Marxists argue that the social sciences should not simply seek to explain society for its own sake. In this, they contrast significantly with positivists, who see the social scientist's responsibility from a position outside the society, somewhat akin to a scientist who peers through a microscope at his subject matter. Marxist social scientists (and constructivists as well) consider this both an impossibility and a mistaken objective. Instead, knowledge must be used to critique the existing social order and to reveal systems of social domination and control. Marxist social sciences consider their purpose to be a critique designed to encourage social emancipation. In this, Marxist social theorists share a good deal with liberal and conservative social scientists, who perceive the proper role of social science as encouraging the improvement of social institutions and who argue that the social studies have as a central purpose the goal of creating politically active and knowledgeable citizens.

> **Competency 023 Descriptive Statement B.** The beginning teacher uses social studies terminology correctly.

Social knowledge and the social studies generally depend upon shared usage of terminology and concepts that allow students, teachers, and researchers the ability to both communicate with one another and to argue with one another about the knowledge claims that they can make using the facts, evidence, and theories of the social sciences. Without a shared terminology, it is impossible to make claims or arguments about an issue, policy, or social phenomenon that can be heard and either agreed to or challenged by others.

The social studies build upon a hierarchy of terms and concepts that extend across the social studies disciplines and that allow knowledge to build. Facility with the vocabulary of the social sciences allows students and teachers to build a common language with social scientists and historians.

Facts

At the most basic level, the social sciences depend upon factual knowledge: data about events, objects, people, or other phenomena. Facts can be presented in a myriad of forms. Tables, charts, graphs, texts, images, reference books, institutional reports, and many more. Facts are the data themselves. **Facts, however, do not speak for themselves.** Whenever the observer of facts compiles and selects facts (and excludes some facts over others), discovers trends, makes comparisons, or infers conclusions from the facts, the observer **interprets** the data. Furthermore, unless a student (or anyone else for that matter) uses data to help them to develop concepts, generalizations, and theories, or to identify questions, problems, issues, or policies, the facts are effectively meaningless.

Concepts

A concept is an abstract term that makes possible the classification or categorization of phenomena. Concepts help reduce the complexity of data by allowing one to sort and situate disparate facts into manageable and ordered groupings. Concepts vary in the degree to which they are inclusive. For example, consider the decreasing numbers of individual concepts in this list of animal categories: animal, vertebrate, mammal, carnivore, canines. Each category subsumes an ever-smaller number of individual concepts that themselves contain other categories and concepts. Concepts also differentiate between the simple and the complex. Consider the increasing complexity of the following concepts: family, community, society, nation. Concepts also vary in terms of their concrete or abstract character.

Below is a list of key concepts in the social studies that are employed in each discipline and across all grade levels. The list is an old one, derived from the *Taba Social Studies Curriculum*, developed in the 1970s. However, it still provides a list of concepts that apply broadly to the social studies.

Causality: Events can often be explained by reference to antecedent events. Causation is rarely the result of a single factor. Usually there are multiple causes for any single event. It is also useful to think of ultimate and proximate causes, or long-term and immediate causes for events.

Conflict: Conflict takes many forms and need not always result in overt violence. Tensions between social groups or individuals involve struggles to control resources, legitimacy, meanings, or political power. Conflict is often a driving force for societal and civilizational development. It has as often been a factor explaining societal or civilizational decline or under-development. Conflict is a central focus of many of the social sciences.

Cooperation: Complexity requires cooperation. Cooperation need not always be the result of joyful unity of purpose. Often, cooperation presumes some level of coercion. Nonetheless, every civilization depends on a wide range of cooperative behaviors.

Cultural change: Cultures, even those declared to be "traditional," do not remain unchanged. The speed of change varies and is accelerated by cross-cultural interaction, commerce, demographic mobility, or changes in knowledge.

Theories of change vary. Human development may be understood as a part of **evolutionary processes.** Organic processes of evolution, of course, produced *homo sapiens.* Social and cultural evolution has also made it possible for human populations to adapt to specific niches in natural habitats. Social scientists and theorists, particularly in the 19th century, espoused a **progressive theory** of social change. Adam Smith, Auguste Comte, Herbert Spencer, Emile Durkheim, Max Weber—the leading social theorists of the era—were agreed in the view that sociocultural development essentially is a process of successive improvement. These Europeans, perhaps not surprisingly, believed that people who shared modern Western culture found themselves at the peak of that progressive development. Among these theorists, there was disagreement between those who saw this progress developing in a **linear evolution** and those who contended for a **dialectical** or **cyclical progression.** Karl Marx, for example, saw this progress deriving from a dialectic or "success-leads-to-failure" paradigm. Socio-cultural change occurred then in a step-like process.

Obviously, social scientists who came from Asia, Africa, or Latin America did not share the view that social progress was inevitable, nor that European society stood at the pinnacle of that success.

Difference: Variation in the physical, social, and biological features of any population is central to social science analysis. These differences ensure the survival of the species. Yet, difference is also often the defining axis of conflict and inequity. Difference, however, is not entirely "natural." Often, differences are socially constructed in ways that naturalize or make them appear to be the result of innate realities.

Diffusion (sometimes called **Social diffusion** or **Cross-cultural conversion**): Societies and cultures are always interconnected. The assumption that we as individuals exist in an isolated space, disconnected culturally from other cultures and societies, underpins identity politics and claims of the "otherness" of those who differ. However, from the beginning of human history, cross-cultural interaction and conversion are features of the human condition. Diffusion, or cross-cultural conversion, provides useful terms for describing the ways in which cultural traits are transferred from one people to another. Cultural traits, consumer items, religious belief, and any other cultural feature, however, are never transmitted from one society to another without a process known as **syncretism.** Syncretism speaks to the ways in which the receiving society or culture attaches new meanings, or uses, to the received cultural trait.

Interdependence: Interdependence occurs in multiple dimensions. Populations are interdependent geographically and economically; they are interdependent politically and culturally, if only as foils against which to define their own identities. Social interdependence is fundamental to human existence. **Positive interdependence** is exhibited when individuals and societies work together promoting common success. **Negative interdependence** is apparent when oppositional interaction is characteristic.

Modification: Human beings and human societies modify their environments and are modified by them. Modification references the ways in which individuals and societies transform their surroundings in an adaptive fashion.

Power: Power can be either legitimate or illegitimate. Power considered to be legitimate is accepted as such by those who exercise it and by those who are subjected to it. Individuals and institutions vary in terms of their ability to exert legitimate power. The desire to acquire and exert power often underlies social and political conflict. Study of power relationships and exertions of power is central to most of the social sciences.

Societal control: All societies exert measures of social control over their members. The degree of such control varies significantly from one society to another. The mechanisms of social control also differ significantly. Some societies emphasize punishment, legal restrictions, and coercion. Others rely on a mix of market mechanisms, public pronouncements, role models, etc. Also important is the role given to different institutions. How families, schools, places of employment, the courts, and police are involved in ordering society are critical variables to understanding mechanisms of social control.

Tradition: The degree to which societies are open to change and adaptation, and the degree to which they are resistant and dependent upon timeworn values, organizations, and folkways is an important focus of the social sciences. Understanding both the traditional ways of doing things and the forces that are exerted upon those traditions provides a means to understand processes of change and continuity.

These broad concepts serve as a few categories of analysis that extend across the social sciences. The vocabulary of the subject matter, however, is expansive. Below are terms that test-takers should be able to readily employ. Note that these include terms that might be used more often in some disciplines than in others.

Terminology

Alienation	Class	Communism
Behaviorism	Cognitive dissonance	Conservatism
Bureaucracy	Collective	Culture
Capital/capitalism	Colonization	Culture element
Civilization	Commodification	Deductive/inductive reasoning

Democracy	Idealism	Political Culture
Determinism	Ideology	Positivism
Developed/developing countries	Imperialism	Prejudice/discrimination
	Individualism	Protestant ethic
Deviant behavior	Industrialization	Rationalism
Dialectic	Legitimacy	Realism
Diffusion	Liberalism	Relativism
Division of labor	Marginalization	Revolution
Egalitarianism	Marxism	Sanction
Empiricism	Materialism	Social Darwinism
Ethnocentrism	Methods	Social mobility
Ethnography	Micro-/macroeconomics	Social stratification
Fascism	Modernism/postmodern	Socialism
Feminism	Modernity	Socialization
Functionalism	Multiculturalism	State
Fundamentalism	Nationalism	Status
Globalization	Norms	Syncretism
Hegemony	Other	Totalitarianism
Historical materialism	Paradigm	Urbanization
Historiography	Patriarchy	Utilitarianism
Human/social ecology	Personality	Values
Id/Ego/Superego	Pluralism	

The concepts above reflect only a small, but significant, sampling of the terms and concepts that are used frequently in the social sciences. Still, they provide a useful repertoire of terms that a teacher conversant with the social studies should be able to recognize and use in context.

The social sciences, like the natural sciences, are not just bodies of knowledge or a collection of concepts and terms. The social sciences endeavor to develop theories and laws that help explain the way human and social relations operate.

Theories

Theories are systematic explanations of social phenomena and behavior. Each discipline develops a variety of theories that help guide research and analysis of social relations. For example, in psychology, *cognitive dissonance* theory offers an explanation of how people react when their perceptions of an event differ sharply from what they expected of that event. In economics, there are a number of theories that are drawn upon to help explain macroeconomic and microeconomic phenomena. For example, the *quantity theory of money* (QTM) posits that price levels of goods and services are directly proportional to the quantity of money in circulation. *Keynesian economic theory* argues that QTM explains long-term relationships between prices and the money supply, but fail to offer solutions to short term problems. Historians have also relied upon a number of theories to explain past events. The "Great Man" theory once helped explain the development of history. Certain archetypical great men were offered as the propelling forces in human history. Historians focused their attention on lawgivers like Hammurabi, Moses, and Solon; or conquerors like Alexander, Caesar, or later Napoleon; republican heroes like Washington, Simon Bolivar, and the "founding fathers." Indeed, it is not difficult to see in the TEKS and in this book the continuing influence of this view that what should be taught by historians are the stories of "Great Men" and a few "Great Women." The point here is not to identify the many theories that guide or divide the social sciences. But it is worthwhile to recognize the ways that social scientists build theories from facts and concepts. And, conversely, historians and social scientists also use theories to make sense of concepts and facts.

Laws

Natural science practitioners are fond of saying that the social sciences are not true sciences because there are few assertions in the social sciences with which social scientists are so confident that they proclaim them laws. Social scientists have only a few "laws" they can point to in response to this complaint. Economists would reply that the Law of Supply and Demand has been demonstrated so often and sufficiently that it might be placed alongside the Three Laws of Thermodynamics. The truth, however, is that social systems often have such complexity, and the variables are so numerous that it is difficult to isolate social phenomena in order to confidently demonstrate causal relationships or clear and predictive laws.

> **Competency 023 Descriptive Statement C.** The beginning teacher knows how knowledge generated by the social science disciplines affects society and people's lives, understands practical applications of social studies education, and knows how to use social studies information and ideas to study social phenomena.

What can anthropology, history, economics, political science, geography, sociology, or the other social science disciplines possibly have to say about our day-to-day lives? What relationship is there between these scholarly fields and more mundane concerns? And what practical applications result from social science research? The social sciences inform the teaching of the social studies in Texas and classrooms nationally from K–12. The range of subjects that the social sciences engage are practically unlimited, and the impact of social science research on our daily life is impossible to reduce to a short survey of this sort.

Historical Thinking

Pope Francis in January 2016 said, we live "not merely in an Era of Change, but a Change of Era." Alvin Toffler, a futurist popular in the 1970s and 1980s, commented often about the pace of change in the late 20th century and spoke about its unsettling nature: "Future shock is the shattering stress and disorientation that we induce in individuals by subjecting them to too much change in a short time." Do we live in an era of unprecedented change? Are we undergoing a faster pace of change than the Romans did in 410 CE or the Bedouins of the Arabian Peninsula did around 650 CE? History provides perspective on such wild claims. Journalists have repeated recently the view that Americans are in an unprecedented period of political rancor and partisanship. Really? Historians might point them to the beating Senator Charles Sumner, a Massachusetts anti-slavery politician, received on the floor of the Senate chambers by a member of the House of Representatives from South Carolina named Preston Brooks. Or, they might direct them to the summer of 1968 when protesters at the Democratic National Convention fought running battles with police along Chicago's waterfront hotel district in plain view of news media cameras.

History also gives students thinking skills that will help them understand their own place in society, as well as their place in history. History provides much of the raw material for any discussion about current policies, issues, problems, etc. There can't be a meaningful debate about contemporary inequalities of income without discussion of historical events as far afield as the Gilded Age, Franklin Roosevelt's New Deal policies, the growth and decline of union organizing between 1935 and the present, Ronald Reagan-era tax policies, and the economic collapse of 2007–2009. Neither is it possible to discuss what should be done about climate change in the 21st century without some understanding of the role of coal, steam, and petroleum as historical sources of energy. If you want to be a knowledgeable participant in local, state, national, or global affairs, you have to have a historical context and the historical thinking skills to engage the present in meaningful ways.

The Social Studies and the World Around Us

Social studies teaching and learning helps explain the world we live in. Geography classrooms give students windows on places around the world to which most students will never travel. Geography teaches students about the different ways in which people farm, build, and otherwise shape their environments. As students explore the world around them, they encounter cultural differences and solutions to problems we all share but which are solved in different ways around the world.

The variety of ways in which others around the world resolve social problems, political divisions, and other issues provide students and teachers with models for problem solving that might not have been considered without the social sciences. The social sciences also challenge commonly shared assumptions and provide teachers and students experiences of cognitive dissonance that lead to learning.

The Social Studies and Civic Life

The social studies are intended to prepare citizens and to encourage them to engage in their communities, to vote, and to otherwise participate as active contributors to the republic. It is in the primary grades that students are first introduced to the influence of government on their lives, in the most practical and immediate way. Public schools are, after all, government institutions, a fact that is often not well understood by parents, teachers, and students alike. When students cheer for their school, they are expressing a civic pride in one of the first government agencies they will consciously encounter. The social studies curriculum from K–12 is designed to gradually provide students with a mature understanding of both the problems faced by our society and the institutions that have developed over time to address these issues. Students study the electoral process and the branches of government in order to be better informed about their electoral decisions. They study other types of governmental institutions outside the United States in order to both appreciate freedoms granted to American citizens and to understand how other democratic societies have developed their own liberal institutions.

Civics lessons are by necessity multi-disciplinary. Economics, history, geography, political science, and sociology provide the raw material for the well-educated, engaged citizen.

Public policy decisions when thoughtfully implemented rely on a range of social science disciplines. Nearly every public policy decision must begin by considering the problem to be solved in its historical context. Then, a range of social science methods are often employed to gauge the extent of the problem and the solutions that will best solve the social problem. The nature of the problem will undoubtedly affect the different social science disciplines that will be used to study the problem and propose solutions.

Social Studies and Making a Living

Economic themes are intertwined in all social studies classrooms. Students in social studies classes explore the concepts and processes at work in global, national, and local economies. Social studies enables students to understand issues of production, distribution, and consumption in Texas, the United States, and the globe. Only with an understanding of the history and contemporary context of our economic system and how it operates can students understand the issues of their own personal financial decisions and the ways in which wider economic forces will shape their personal possibilities frontiers.

> **Competency 023 Descriptive Statement D.** The beginning teacher understands how social science disciplines relate to each other and to other content areas.

Like most fields of knowledge, the rapid growth in information and the technical nature of much social science research has resulted in many social science researchers and teachers narrowing their study to ever more arcane and limited subject matter. Because each social science discipline has its own specialized body of knowledge, its own methods of study, and its own organizing concepts, theories, and interests, it is easy for scholars and teachers in each discipline to retreat into their own separate corners and remain in dialogue only with like-minded thinkers. Social scientists fragment the world in the hopes of being able to study it more effectively. These disciplines, however, all intersect in important ways.

One way of conceptualizing the relationship between the social studies disciplines is to think of them as a web that extends outward from the self. Each of the disciplines provides insights and appropriate content for each age group and for each of the social relationships in which we are all embedded.

**Figure 9.1
The Web of the Social Sciences**

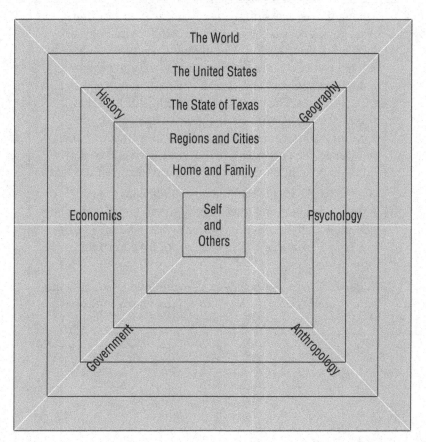

Another way is proposed by the National Council for the Social Studies, which likens the social studies disciplines to an orchestra:

"Consider a musical ensemble such as an orchestra (the social studies program) as it performs a specific musical composition (a grade level or specific course within the curriculum). At certain times, one instrument (a discipline such as history) takes the lead while others (such as geography and economics) play supporting roles. At other times, several instruments (history, geography, economics) play together on an equal basis to explore the composer's thematic aims."

By imagining the social science disciplines in this fashion we can see the ways in which the organizing concept of each discipline and the objectives of the different social sciences contribute to an integrated study of social relations and social institutions.

Table 9.1
Organizing Concepts of the Social Science Disciplines

Organizing Concept	Objectives of the Discipline	Social Science Discipline
The Self and Society	Among the basic assumptions of our civic society and of social sciences is the presumption that individuals are decision-making (rather than instinctual) actors capable of rational choice. Our educational, political, and economic systems presume a "self" capable of self-knowledge and self-awareness. The educational system is designed to inform that "self" with content knowledge and skills necessary to transform the individual into an active and knowledgeable participant in the workplace and society. Psychology is the study of how the individual self develops.	Psychology
	Many of society's most intractable challenges—crime, poverty, violence, prejudice—may be studied by reference to human attitudes, values, and behavior. The science of psychology provides an important tool for approaching these issues.	
	Understanding voter behavior, consumer behavior, and the actions of political leaders, both currently and in the past, are informed by psychological study.	

Organizing Concept	Objectives of the Discipline	Social Science Discipline
The Role of Space and Place	Every member of society is to varying degrees "geo-literate." We naturally situate ourselves within space (the abstract coordinates and area in which we find ourselves) and place (the meaning we associate with those coordinates). Human beings situate themselves in space and place and understand their own individual and social identity within those geographic coordinates. Academic geo-literacy—the kind we hope students develop in social studies classes—provides tools with which to approach questions in the other disciplines. For example, without a rudimentary geo-literacy it is impossible to understand many historical, economic, or political issues. More advanced geo-literacy allows one to understand the connections between human and physical systems. Geo-literacy also allows the individual to make thoughtful decisions about individual, workplace, and civic choices that affect human and natural sustainability.	Geography
Scarcity and Interdependence	Each society resolves three related economic problems that stem from the fact of scarcity and individual and social group interdependence. These are what to produce, how to produce, and for whom shall they be produced. Economics bears directly on people's roles as consumers and producers. Economic literacy is also imperative to citizenship education as economic issues frequently influence voters in national, state, and local elections. Understanding economics is critical to understanding public policy decisions at the local, state, national, and international level. A well-informed economic understanding allows citizens to function more effectively in a democratic market economy.	Economics

(continued)

Organizing Concept	Objectives of the Discipline	Social Science Discipline
Culture and Meaning	Every society exists within a web of shared understanding and contested meanings. The artifacts, beliefs, and behaviors that provide the material with which a society both expresses that meaning and shapes its environment and social relations makes up the culture of that society. The methods of cultural analysis used to study anthropology encourage habits of mind that allow students to reflect on their own beliefs and cultural assumptions. Studying other cultures enables students to escape momentarily the conviction of the singularity of their own ways of doing things. Within the anthropology class it is possible to have cross-cultural experiences without the travel expense. Anthropology allows students to understand the beauty and diversity of human experience. It encourages an empathy towards other cultures and contributes towards the creation of a more peaceful world. In this sense it leads to a global civic-mindedness.	Anthropology
Social Interaction and Organization	Most human behavior is social. We are not isolates. Sociologists investigate social life, social change, and the social causes (as opposed to psychological) and consequences of human behavior. Because we are social beings, family life, religious traditions, racial, gender, and class identities are key subjects of sociology. Civic education benefits from a study of the social dimensions of problems such as poverty, violence, crime, and climate change. The quantitative and qualitative tools employed in sociology also serve as useful skill sets to bring to bear in the other social sciences and history.	Sociology

Organizing Concept	Objectives of the Discipline	Social Science Discipline
Power and Authority	Each society authorizes certain individuals or groups to make decisions and develop processes for making decisions and allocating resources that have legitimacy within the society. Political science provides the tools to analyze who makes these decisions and how. The study of political science in the Texas classroom has civic education as one of its goals. The objective of civic education is the development of competent and informed citizens committed to fundamental values of American constitutional democracy. Responsible citizen behavior requires the acquisition of both a body of content knowledge and a range of participatory skills. Civic education cannot merely inculcate a body of knowledge and skills. Civic education also has an affective aim. Civic education seeks to develop certain dispositions and character traits.	Political Science
Change and Continuity	Without a mature historical sensibility, a society has no common memory of where it has been, what continuities bind its citizenry to their heritage and past, what core values unite them, or how past decisions account for the society's present conditions. History provides many of the raw materials with which we can effectively test the theories and assumptions of the other disciplines. As such, history provides much of the data necessary to a full understanding of the other disciplines. Additionally, each of the other social science disciplines provide useful approaches within which to frame the study of the past. History provides the precondition of civic education. Effective participation by an informed, thoughtful citizenry interested in resolving political, social, or moral issues in society is impossible without a mature historical knowledge. George Orwell's warning, "He who controls the past, controls the future. He who controls the present controls the past," illustrates the importance of history for civic engagement and civic responsibility.	History

> **Competency 023 Descriptive Statement E.** The beginning teacher knows how to use problem-solving processes to identify problems, gather information, list and consider options, consider advantages and disadvantages, choose and implement solutions, and evaluate the effectiveness of solutions.

Problem-Solving: A Model of Social Inquiry

The social sciences engage in social science inquiry largely to find solutions to current problems. In doing so, they engage in research designed to formulate the theoretical knowledge and data necessary to provide policy makers with a range of solutions and with tools to evaluate which solutions best resolve the matter. In this sense, a social science discipline is not just a **body of knowledge** but a **process of knowing** peculiar to that discipline. Each of the disciplines have their own methods of data collection and their own analytical tools with which they approach that data. Nonetheless, each follows a basic inquiry process. The differences between the disciplines turn on the kinds of questions they ask, the concepts and theories they test, and the vocabulary they use to express their findings.

The Scientific Method and the Social Sciences

Regardless of the social science, there are steps common to all social science disciplines as to how the scientific method is applied:

1. Making observations—literature survey

2. Defining the problem

3. Proposing hypotheses

4. Gathering evidence or collecting data

5. Evaluating and analyzing the data (testing the hypothesis)

6. Interpretation of results and conclusions

Let's look at each in turn.

Observation

The social sciences are empirical sciences in much the same way as are the natural sciences. This means that they stem from observable data and from observation. Observation in the social sciences, just as in the natural sciences, however, is not simply a matter of the scientist peering out over the natural or social environment as if from a tower overseeing the surrounding world.

Social scientists observe the environment from a perspective informed by the literature in their own fields and by their philosophical or theoretical perspective. They also make their observations with an eye towards publication, and not merely because publication leads to promotion. Science is public. It is meaningless as private thought or meditation. This is critical because a social scientist builds on and confronts other scholars and policy makers. The observational period then involves an immersion in the literature surrounding a social problem, historical subject, economic issue, or policy matter. It also involves observation of a wide range of data, facts, etc.

Problem Formulation

Identifying and stating a specific and clear question is the first step before a social scientist or historian can begin studying any problem or issue. The problem to be studied must be clearly defined and the question to be resolved must be **complete, precisely stated,** and **researchable**. It is often difficult to develop such precise and researchable questions. For example, a historian interested in the question "How did the presence of Africans in colonial America influence the culture of early Americans?" must further narrow this question to make it an effective and researchable question. Proceeding from the question above, the researcher might have the line of inquiry with questions like these: "What African terms and language entered into English usage?" or "What food-ways were evident in the cuisine of Southern plantation owners?" or "What patterns of social interaction between white adults and children show evidence of African childrearing practices?"

It is critical at an early stage in research to carefully define the terms that will be used to define the problem, formulate a hypothesis, and identify the necessary data to test the hypothesis. A sociologist interested in exploring the role of class in American education should carefully identify what is meant by social class. The term, like many other social science concepts—think "popular culture" or "partisanship," for example—can be subject to different interpretations and understanding. The social scientist must clearly define the terms to ensure that a research question and data yield meaningful results.

Formulation of Hypotheses

With a precise, complete, and researchable question in hand, the social scientist must formulate a tentative statement or proposition to direct his research. Good hypotheses must stem from a combination of empirical observation, deductive reasoning, prior knowledge, and existing theories. Good hypotheses do not appear as if by magic in the mind of the researcher. They are reflections of the researchers' immersion in the literature and study of the subject matter. Many hypotheses are developed from existing theories. A Keynesian economist may wish to test the impact of certain levels of government spending on economic growth, for example. This will lead to a very different hypothesis than the hypothesis likely generated by an economist from the monetarist school.

Collection of Data

Social scientists use a diverse array of methods to acquire necessary data. The range of different types of data that can be used by social scientists to develop theories is also very wide.

Physical scientists have the advantage of conducting lab experiments within controlled environments where they limit the variables under study. Moreover, physical scientists can repeat their experiments, and other scientists can replicate the experiments. Social scientists usually examine problems that involve large groups of people, often taking an entire society as a subject of study. Controlled experiments are therefore virtually impossible for most social scientists. Additionally, the number of variables that impact social phenomena or policy—for example, the effects of tax policy on economic growth—are so great that it is often difficult to single out the relationships that are most important.

Social scientists, however, can apply the scientific method to data collection and analysis. Economists may, for instance, collect data about consumer buying patterns, information about prices, business firms' pricing, production costs, advertising strategies, and tax records. This data can be observed and analyzed. The observations of this data can provide evidence against which to test theories about the effects of prices on consumer purchasing habits, or business decisions.

Anthropologists and sociologists often use ethnographic data gathered by observation to test their hypotheses. Psychologists, economists, sociologists, and political scientists use sample surveys, case studies, and other evidence. Historians collect and analyze documents, material evidence, and other sources.

Evaluation and analysis of data (testing the hypothesis)

A researcher must evaluate the information and data collected alongside the methods used to gather it to understand the shortcomings or limits to that data. The historian must evaluate the biases or point of view of the sources. Social science researchers must also test their original hypothesis to see if that original hypothesis can be verified given the data the researcher has collected.

Interpretation of results and conclusions

The interpretation of results and conclusions drawn enters the researcher into further dialogue with other researchers. Conclusions and interpretation are published or presented to other scholars to further the debate and to provide new directions for further inquiry.

> **Competency 023 Descriptive Statement F.** The beginning teacher knows how to use decision-making processes to identify situations that require decisions, gather and analyze information, identify options, predict consequences, and take action to implement decisions.

The social studies disciplines, unlike most other academic disciplines, have as a central goal the development of thoughtful citizens, even student-citizens, who are unable at this stage in their lives to vote or hold public office. In most disciplines, students are tasked with accumulating information, grasping the concepts and terminology of a discipline, and developing an introductory understanding of the disciplinary methods of the subject-matter. In the social studies, content and methods are coupled with the development of decision-making capabilities that are crucial to citizenship. It is in this way that the social studies are connected to real-life applications.

Students should not merely be acquiring knowledge and skills for the sake of passing tests or statewide assessments. Students should be encouraged to see the ways in which the knowledge and skills of the social studies allow them to test the truth claims made by politicians, civic and social leaders, opinion shapers, news media, Facebook posts, internet trolls, and even teachers and school administrators. They should also be allowed to develop issues-centered decision-making processes so that they can begin to consider, evaluate, and propose solutions to problems.

Models for issues-based decision-making processes abound. John Dewey, who was perhaps the most influential public educator of the 20th century, in 1933 offered a problem-solving model that still serves as a useful approach. Dewey is often quoted as saying, "Learning is learning to think." Dewey also observed that "the origin of thinking is some perplexity, confusion, or doubt." All thinking—or as he phrased it: "reflection"—is guided by the demand for a solution to a "perplexity," or problem. His model, modified below by Anna S. Ochoa-Becker, outlines a process for identifying and developing solutions for policy issues.

1. Recognizing a predicament.

2. Defining or stating the issue.

3. Gathering and evaluating data that might constitute evidence.

4. Hypothesizing alternate solutions.

5. Predicting possible consequences.

6. Deciding on and justifying a preferred solution.

7. Acting to implement the solution.

Dewey's problem-solving model, like most such models, presupposes that a number of other questions associated with problem-solving must also be addressed. These include some, but not all, of the following questions.

1. What issues deserve attention?

2. What data, facts, and information are needed to prioritize the issues that require attention?

3. In prioritizing and solving issues, what values should be pursued?

4. What actions should be taken by individuals, social groups, institutions, businesses, and public officials?

5. What public policies should be supported? Questioned? Resisted?

6. What are our individual obligations and responsibilities to act? How should that action be carried out? What are the risks of personal action?

Using Real-World Problems in Instruction

Effective social studies instruction employs real-world problems rather than hypotheticals as its primary framework for teaching problem solving skills. Real-world problems are not riddles or mathematical word problems. Real-world problems do not have an answer that can be looked up at the back of the book. It is fair to say that teachers do not have solutions to real-world problems. These problems can be intractable macro-social problems, like "How can we help the homeless?" Or they can be local problems, like "How can we reduce bullying in our school?"

Real-world problems and problem-solving serve two important roles in instruction: (1) motivation and (2) civics education. When students can see how their social studies classroom knowledge can be applied to contemporary problems, they are often more motivated to learn and engage the material. Additionally, when students see the connections between their own civic engagement and problem solving of real-world problems, they are more likely to become participants as readers, voters, activists, etc.

COMPETENCY 024 (SOURCES OF SOCIAL STUDIES INFORMATION; INTERPRETING AND COMMUNICATING SOCIAL STUDIES INFORMATION)

The teacher understands sources of social studies information and knows how to interpret and communicate social studies information in various forms.

> **Competency 024 Descriptive Statement A.** The beginning teacher demonstrates knowledge of characteristics and uses of primary and secondary sources (e.g., databases, maps, photographs, documents, biographies, interviews, questionnaires, artifacts).

Social studies teachers, like biologists, chemists, and the other natural science educators, depend upon evidence to support their observations, theories, and arguments. This evidence is divided between primary and secondary sources.

Primary Sources

Primary sources are materials from the time period under study. Primary sources are most often described as first-hand or eyewitness accounts. Primary sources include such varied evidence as interviews, surveys, polls, questionnaires, experiments, oral histories, diaries, journals, newspapers, speeches, manuscripts, paintings, cartoons, photographs, governmental documents, or physical artifacts like tools, weapons, roads, buildings, or consumer items.

Primary sources may also be reflections of a scientist, journalist, fiction writer, or anyone else writing a diary or letter about an event or issue taking place in their lifetime.

This is the narrowest definition of a primary source in that it implies that the historian or student is able to understand the unfolding of a historic event through the experience of the author of a primary source in the same way that one hears the experience of an eyewitness to a contemporary event. When reading a diarist's account of life on the front in World War I, for instance, it is easy to imagine employing the source in much the same way that its author intended its use, as a record of their experience in this traumatic moment. One can imagine, with enough eyewitness accounts, that it might be possible to recreate what exactly happened. This is similar to how a trial lawyer hopes to accumulate evidence to convince a jury that the many eyewitnesses to a crime provide evidence beyond a reasonable doubt that the crime unfolded in the way that the case suggests.

Primary sources may also include institutional records that were created for very different purposes than those for which a historian might use them. For example, beginning in the 12th and 13th centuries in medieval Europe, parishes began to record baptisms. They did so to ensure that parents had properly thought about the salvation of a child's soul. Later, marriage and burial records were kept. The Roman Catholic Church did not initiate this practice to help later generations of historians. These records were kept to ensure that parish residents were living up to their sacramental responsibilities.

Historians, however, have taken these records and put them to very different uses. With these records, a demographic history of villages in the 14th or 15th century can be constructed. Parish registries, for example, make it possible to answer questions such as: At what age did men and women marry? How soon after marriage did women typically give birth to their first child? The discovery that in 18th-century England that as many as 37 percent of all first-born children were the product of premarital conceptions raised other questions about courtship rituals, attitudes toward premarital sex, and community moral standards in rural villages. Parish registries allowed historians to estimate infant and child mortality rates, as well as the average life span for adults. Since parents and godparents were required to sign if they could read and write, or leave their mark in the presence of witnesses if they could not, historians were able to gauge the levels of literacy in medieval and early modern towns and villages. Parish registries are just one of many types of institutional documents that could be important primary sources for a historian to use. Other possible primary sources include criminal court testimony, wills, marriage contracts, business records—

the possibilities are endless. It often requires only creativity and effort on the part of an enterprising student, teacher, or scholar to extract meaning and understanding from a primary source.

Words and texts are not the only primary sources. Material objects may also be primary sources. Objects provide important evidence of other complex social relationships. For example, on the coast of East Africa, cemented in the coral walls of merchants' homes from the 13th to the 19th centuries were porcelain plates clearly made in China. The presence of these plates provides evidence of trade relationships that extended across the Indian Ocean. They also illustrate how elite Swahili families projected their status and wealth with trade goods acquired from Arab and Indian traders. Similarly, an entire array of consumer items developed alongside the interconnected trade in slaves, tobacco, and sugar. The proliferation of pipes, snuffboxes, silverware, teacups, serving spoons, tea trays, tea cozies, and other consumer items are primary sources that speak volumes about the relationships between consumer culture in Europe and the enslavement of Africans between 1600 and 1800. Our smartphones, laptops, televisions, t-shirts, baseball caps, and other material artifacts of our contemporary lives are primary sources for present-day social scientists and scholars.

Art, music, literature, film, theater, and other representational media provide another range of primary sources. Literature, movies, art or other similar media tell us a great deal about the time in which they were written or produced. The murals of Diego Rivera, for example, tell us a great deal about the politics and social criticism of the 1930s. Anyone wishing to write a definitive history of the Elizabethan period in England would do well to immerse themselves in the language of Shakespeare or the King James Bible. A historian who 50 years from now writes a history of post-9/11 America could hardly do so without referencing television shows, movies, literature, and other cultural products of our era.

To this point, this discussion of primary and secondary sources has been carried out with reference to the kinds of sources that historians use. Other social scientists, however, also analyze primary sources in order to answer research questions, and publish their works in secondary sources (journal articles, monographs, textbooks, and other media) where they interpret their findings and conclusions. Primary sources in the social sciences other than history are original, uninterpreted information. Selecting the appropriate primary source is dependent on what the scholar intends to study and in what discipline they are working. They can include such varied things as datasets, field notes taken by a sociologist, anthropologist, economist, or political scientist, recordings of interviews with subjects, photos, manuscripts, physical artifacts, government reporting data, and many other items.

An economist, for example, might wish to study changing prices and price levels to assess how and why prices have risen in the way that they have. Recently, economists have noticed an increase in many of the costs of parenting. One sign of this has been an increase in the amount the "tooth fairy" leaves under pillows. Delta Dental Insurance Company conducts polling to gauge how much tooth fairies give children. This poll is a primary source of a whimsical sort that provides a small window into changing prices associated with child-raising. If you are interested, the amount of the tooth fairies' payout has risen at a much faster rate over the previous two decades than the general rate of inflation. The Delta Dental poll also provides a picture of regional costs of living. Tooth fairies in the Northeast give substantially more for teeth than do the tooth fairies of the Midwest. An economist interested in explaining why prices had increased faster for children's lost teeth than for other goods would need to rely on a whole range of other primary data. For example, the economist might ask, "Have prices for children's candy, toys, and other things that a newly gap-toothed child might spend the tooth fairy's generosity on risen in price?" This information would require analyzing price data from a number of industries, either by surveying toymakers, candy companies, or examining government data on the subject. Or, an economist might ask, "Are children valued more today than they were in the past?" How they answered that question would require examining another series of data sources. When an economist then attempts to make sense of why the tooth fairy's gifts have increased, the product of that analysis is a secondary source. The data that the economist uses in the article they publish to explain the phenomenon is, however, a primary source.

Anthropologists have traditionally immersed themselves in the culture of a "primitive" ethnic or tribal population to understand from the inside how that culture operates, what it values, etc. An anthropologist's field notes, interview transcripts, and other observations then become primary sources that can be analyzed to draw conclusions about their subject matter.

One example of a collection of primary sources that could be used by an anthropologist interested in the culture of the people of the Himalayas would be the database called the **Digital Himalayas.** In this collection, an anthropologist could access census data and query that data about demographic or economic conditions in specific villages in the Himalayas. In the same collection, it is possible to view a series of short films demonstrating, step-by-step, without dialogue or narration (and hence the interpretation of the filmmaker) an exorcism ritual carried out in a village in Chinese Himalayas. The anthropologist could also listen to songs of the Laya people in another region of the Himalayas.

Secondary Sources

Secondary sources are often more difficult to precisely define. They are a resource that comments on or analyzes something, not written by someone directly involved. They are accounts of an event recorded with the benefit of historical distance or time. How much time or distance is not always immediately obvious. One important defining characteristic of a secondary source is that it relies on primary sources and evidence to comment on or interpret a past event, time period, or historical personage. Or it relies on primary data to draw conclusions about an event, time period, etc.

Secondary sources, though traditionally they have been most often written texts, need not be. For example, the film *Braveheart* is a secondary source (not a great one, I will add) for the life and story of William Wallace. The painting *The Death of Socrates* is similarly a secondary source, an interpretation of the death of Socrates nearly 2,300 years earlier.

Documentary films are, of course, secondary sources as well. The documentary film *Black Is . . . Black Ain't* (1994), for example, is an insightful sociological study of African American identity. It relies on interviews with numerous African Americans of all ages and from many parts of the United States. The interviews, uncut and unmediated by the filmmaker (which, of course, we are not likely to see unless they are collected and archived) are the primary sources from which this secondary source was constructed.

Secondary sources range in terms of reliability and recognized authority. Academic researchers distinguish between scholarly and non-scholarly secondary sources.

Simultaneous Primary and Secondary Sources

Sources can be both "primary sources" and "secondary sources" at the same time. Many artistic or cultural images rely on the past as their subject matter. They then become both "primary" and "secondary" sources. The power of these images or texts often lead their consumers (students, readers, film viewers) to perceive these sources as a kind of evidence of that past. They are not. In this they are secondary sources. Of course, a film or documentary about the Vietnam War produced in the 1960s is a primary source for the history of that war. But, movies, historical fiction, or other representations of the Vietnam War, such as the films *Platoon, We Were Soldiers Once . . . and Young,* and *Good Morning, Vietnam,* are not primary sources of the Vietnam War. It is easy to see these representations of the past as secondary sources. They are, however, also primary sources for the time period and culture in which they were produced. The films *Platoon, We Were Soldiers Once . . . and Young, Saving Private Ryan, Glory,* or *Braveheart* each take up historical subject matter. They are also primary sources, but not about their subject matter, which includes the Civil War, Vietnam War, World War II, or the life of the Scottish hero William Wallace. They are primary sources in that they provide insights into the preoccupations of the 1980s and 1990s when the films were made. Similarly, Jacques-Louis David's famous painting, *The Death of Socrates,* painted in 1787, tells us little about the actual death of the philosopher, but offers an important primary source for the Enlightenment period and the period preceding the French Revolution.

The same could be said of historians' and social scientists' scholarly productions, or even textbooks. A textbook produced in 1900 will have a very different interpretation of the relationship between European settlers and the Native American inhabitants of North America than will one produced in 2017. This is not simply a consequence of the accumulation of new knowledge and facts. It reflects the time in which the text was produced.

Scholarly Research and Secondary Sources

Published or unpublished working papers. Frequently, scholars present their research at conferences where the research is critiqued by fellow specialists in a discipline. Occasionally these are published in **Conference Proceedings** or made available on the internet for wider dissemination. These are usually provisional findings which are important early indicators of the direction of research.

Scholarly sources. These distinguish between refereed and non-refereed secondary sources. A refereed journal or book is one that has been reviewed before publication by a team of scholars who accept the methods and conclusions of the author as reputable, even if they do not necessarily agree with their arguments. These sources include:

- **Scholarly journal articles.** These are written for audiences of fellow specialists. These usually reflect the most recent research on a subject but often take for granted the reader's familiarity with the jargon or specialized vocabulary of the discipline.

- **Monographs.** A monograph is a book written on a single subject, often deriving from a Ph.D. thesis. These are also directed at audiences of scholars. The focused subject matter and disciplinary language make them less accessible to the wider public. Monographs are drawn from the primary research of a scholar.

- **Surveys or textbooks.** Usually, these books are written for an audience of non-specialists, or specifically for audiences of lower-level undergraduates (in the case of textbooks) and upper-level undergraduates or graduate students (in the case of surveys). Surveys and textbooks rely mostly on other secondary sources (monographs, journal articles, and reference books).

- **Reference Works and Encyclopedias.** Encyclopedias, dictionaries, and other reference material provide important sources of secondary information which teachers with general background knowledge need as they begin to engage in a more specialized study of a subject matter.

Non-Scholarly Secondary Sources

Examples of non-scholarly secondary sources include:

- Books or articles written by professional writers who are not experts in the field.

- Books or articles that rarely cite or offer information about the sources being used.

- Books, journals, or websites.

- News sources, newspapers, and other primarily journalistic sources.

- Advocacy or opinion-based sources: editorials, letters to editors, reviews of books, movies, plays, etc.

- Data and statistical publications and compilations.

- Trade and professional magazines.

- Websites, blogs, movies, videos, etc.

> **Competency 024 Descriptive Statement B.** The beginning teacher evaluates the validity of social studies information from primary and secondary sources and identifies bias (e.g., assessing source validity on the basis of language, corroboration with other sources, and information about the author).

Analyzing social studies information using an inquiry method requires the development of critical faculties of analysis. Too often, students—and adults for that matter—are mere consumers of information. When approaching the many different kinds of information found in social studies classes it is important to develop habits of critical consumption of information. Students and teachers would do well to keep the following questions in mind as they encounter information found in surveys, polls, editorials, policy reports, historical accounts, etc.

Surveys and Polls

Sociologists, political scientists, and other social scientists often use surveys and polls. These represent one form of primary source. Below are some of the questions that social scientists often ask when evaluating polls and surveys.

- What was the **sample size**? Was the sample size large enough? Was the sample randomized? How was the sample size arrived at? Would the conclusions of the survey be more complete with a larger sample population?

- Did the **sample population** include a diverse enough representation of the population? Were there more males than females, or more females than males? How might gender imbalance in the survey have skewed results? How was the age distribution of the survey or poll sample decided on? Did the researchers select only certain populations for the survey? Why might they have done so?

- Did the questions have **validity**? In other words, did the survey or poll questions provide the answers to the research questions outlined in the survey? What questions might alternatively have been asked or excluded?

- Are the results **reliable**? Would the same results occur if the survey or poll were taken a second time? Or, if the poll is designed to show changes over time in the answers of the populace, were the questions effectively posed in ways that would allow for reliability over time?

- Is there **bias** evident in the survey or poll? Do the questions lead to biased results? Did the researchers ask questions that were looking for particular kinds of answers? Did the researchers start with a predetermined answer and use leading questions to arrive at those results? Did the researchers only report some of the answers or emphasize some over others?

Using primary sources in inquiry-based social studies education provides opportunities for students to develop and practice the skills of the social studies.

Textual Sources

When evaluating primary sources in history and other disciplines, it is useful to keep in mind a simple process in evaluating and analyzing the document.

Step One: Decide what you are looking at.

1. What type of document is the source?

2. For whom was the document produced?

3. Why was the document produced?

4. Who created the primary source?

5. Does the creator of the source have firsthand knowledge of the event being described?

6. When was the source produced? How soon after the events being described?

Step Two: How is point of view or bias reflected in the primary source?

When a researcher has determined what the source is by answering the questions in step one, it is important to ask how the factors above inform the point of view of the document. Authorship, audience, the form of the document, and the distance between the author and his or her subject matter all affect the point of view or biases of the source. It is preferable to examine a source for point of view, without necessarily impugning bias or a negative motivation to an author of a source.

Step Three: Closely examine (and re-examine) the source.

Written documents, visual imagery, reports, charts, graphs, databases, and, indeed all sources require a deep investigation and careful observation to determine what details are most important to extract from a source. How a source is read or an image interpreted or a report analyzed is influenced by the research focus and interests of the student. It is important to approach the document with research questions in mind. *Primary sources do not speak for themselves.*

Historians and social scientists give meaning to the primary source. When reading or examining a primary source, not only should the historian or social scientist pose their own questions of the source, but they should be open to new questions that are revealed in the process of analyzing the evidence.

Step Four: Compare with other sources.

It is never sufficient to rely on a single primary source. Any investigation of contemporary issues or historical events will be more interesting and more accurate if students are able to compare a wide variety of perspectives. It is not true that the more sources that are examined, the clearer the picture will be; instead, because historical or contemporary events have multiple actors, audiences, and perspectives, the more a student engages multiple perspectives, the more complex their understanding of the historical event or social issue will become. Students need to grow accustomed to multiple and diverse perspectives. Primary sources also raise new questions that often require answers from other documentary evidence.

Step Five: Analyze secondary sources, alternative interpretations, and yourself.

Throughout Steps One to Four, it is important to be informed using secondary sources or alternative interpretations of the evidence or context of the primary source. If you are reading, for example, an interview conducted by the Federal Writers' Project with former slaves, it is critical that the context of those interviews and the context of the interviewers be well understood. The sources provide rich evidence from the recollections of slaves about their lives many decades before. Other historians, anthropologists, and scholars have written extensively about the meaning that can be extracted from transcripts of these interviews. It is vital that researchers and students learning to research use reliable secondary sources and alternative interpretations to more fully understand the multiple perceptions of an event, study, or concept.

It is also important for the researcher to be alert to the ways that they themselves also bias their reading of the facts. *Facts do not speak for themselves.* Moreover, facts are often understood through prisms of the observer's own experiences and point of view. This five-step approach should not be understood as a linear process. Think of it instead as an iterative process where each step is informed by the other steps.

Competency 024 Descriptive Statement C. The beginning teacher assesses multiple points of view and frames of reference relating to social studies issues and knows how to support a point of view on a social studies issue or event.

An important role of the social studies teacher is to guide students to mature and complex understanding of the ways in which bias, point of view, and divergent frames of reference shape both social studies information and the study of the social sciences. This is even more important when students are learning about historical or contemporary issues where sharp divisions of opinion and perspective are evident. For example, when I teach the history of slavery, it comes as no small surprise to my classes that slavery had strong apologists who defended it on biblical, scientific, economic, and racial grounds. Juxtaposing the voices of abolitionists with the writing of pro-slavery apologists is discomforting to students, who experience a level of cognitive dissonance as their view of the absolute evil of slavery as an institution comes face-to-face with the opinions of otherwise respected religious, political, and economic leaders who did not share that perspective.

Similar opportunities to model approaches to differing points of view and frames of reference abound in the social studies classroom. Government classes provide a setting where contemporary political debates can be carried out, hopefully with less rancor and bitterness than one sees on the public stage. Psychology classes offer an opportunity for very different theories about human motivation and behavior to be examined.

Though teachers must be careful not to silence student voices by their own advocacy for political positions or their perspective on historical or contemporary issues, it is nonetheless important for teachers to also model the thoughtful commitment to principled positions. This requires a delicate balancing act. Nonetheless, not only is it impossible to maintain complete objectivity in the classroom, students benefit from teachers who express opinions and support those opinions with data, evidence, and reason while also respecting their students right to their own intellectual positions, similarly defended with data, evidence, and reason.

> **Competency 024 Descriptive Statement D.** The beginning teacher organizes and interprets information from outlines, reports, databases, narratives, literature, and visuals including graphs, charts, timelines, and maps.

Using Literature in the Social Studies Classroom

Literature adds depth and empathic understanding to the social studies classroom. Textbooks and monographs often make more clear and concise arguments, but literature allows students to engage the individual human experience that is often aggregated in much of the teaching material of the social studies. The variety of literary sources (biographies, autobiographies, historical fiction, poetry, fables, folktales) that can be used in social studies instruction is abundant. Using literature allows students to learn in a natural way, through stories, myths, and legends. Narratives attach to something primal in our character. Stories allow us to make associations with our own lives. Literature helps social studies students to put themselves in the experiences of others from the past or from our own contemporary era. Literature also enhances the ability to reflect on moral issues and values.

Databases

Databases allow students to manipulate and query information as they carry out authentic social studies research. Social sciences databases provide classrooms with collections of secondary sources and primary sources and data. Each social science discipline has its own specialized databases with which teachers should become familiar. Learning how to search, sort, and filter data requires students to develop meaningful research queries. Using databases effectively will require mastery of many basic skills of computer literacy. Often, we assume that children who have grown up in the age of the internet are adept at these tasks. In fact, this is rarely the case. Students can also examine databases for such things as bias, currency of the information, omissions, errors, and value judgments. Students may also use databases to organize information they have collected.

Organizing Ideas and Data

Social studies teachers and researchers use a number of common organizational elements in presenting their materials that students should become familiar with. These include the following:

Graphics and visual organizers

- Maps

- Graphs

- Timelines

- Photos

- Drawings

Textual organizers

- Boxed or shaded text

- Bulleted or numbered lists

- Highlighted materials

- Chapter introductions identifying key topics

- Chapter summaries recalling conclusions

- Questions to consider

Social studies texts, lectures, reports, and papers follow certain predictable patterns. It is important to recognize the features of these patterns.

- Chronological order

- Cause and effect

- Compare and contrast

- Main idea and details

Maps

Maps are perhaps the most common graphic encountered by social studies teachers and students. Maps simplify and represent three-dimensional space on the plane of the page. Most often, reference maps are used to identify such spatial markers as landforms, waterways, continents, political boundaries, cities, and many other places. Maps come in numerous forms, including most recently computerized electronic versions of maps. The key features of the map include, the compass rose, its legend or key, distance indicator or scale, labels attached to specific places, captions. The ability to read a map for direction, time, distance, etc., is an important skill that social studies teachers and students must master. There are a variety of maps: relief maps, flat maps, and sketch maps are a few examples.

A beginning social studies teacher should be familiar with the following basic map-reading skills:

- Orienting the map and noting direction

- Understanding map scale and computing distances using the scale

- Locating places on maps and globes

- Reading map symbols

- Comparing maps

Charts, Graphs, Timelines, and Outlines

Charts, graphs, and timelines are common graphic organizers encountered in social studies texts.

Charts

Charts make possible easy visualization of relationships between important facts and ideas. There are a number of prominent types of charts. The following are the most common charts used in the social studies:

1. **Genealogy charts.** Most often, these charts represent the blood and marital relationships within a dynasty, or empire. They may also be useful in anthropology or sociology to illustrate marriage patterns.

2. **Flow charts.** Flow charts can be used to demonstrate relationships between different functions or actors in an organization. They are also useful in demonstrating processes or, like the circular flow charts used in economics, to illustrate circulation of real goods and money.

3. **Tabulation charts.** Tabulation charts merely provide a format for compiling and tabulating data. These charts allow data to be grasped at a glance.

4. **Chronology charts.** Chronology charts put information in chronological form allowing students to see the relation, for example, between such things as religious developments, political changes, or technological and economic changes in one or more time periods.

Graphs

Graphs are useful visual tools for making comparisons or showing developments over time. There are many different graphing tools for showing data in the social studies. The most commonly used are listed below. In each case, the graph will illustrate data from the following chart of the categories of revenue received from taxpayers by the federal government between 1960 and 2015.

Categories of Federal Revenue	1960	1980	2000	2015
Individual Income Taxes	40.7	244.1	1,004	1,541
Corporate Income Tax	21.5	64.6	207.3	343.8
Social Insurance Taxes	14.7	157.8	652.8	1,065
Excise	11.7	24.3	68.9	98.3
Other	3.9	26.3	91.7	202
Total	92.5	517.1	2024.7	3249.9

1. **Line graphs** are the most commonly used graphs. Timelines on one axis are one sort of line graph. More common are line graphs with two axes. The supply and demand graphs used in economics are just one example. On the *x*-axis is the quantity measured, and on the *y*-axis is the corresponding value. Line graphs are particularly useful in showing change over time.

Total Revenues U.S. Government (in billions $)

2. **Circle graphs (pie charts)** are most useful when a teacher seeks to show the relationship of individual variables to the whole. The parts (slices of the pie) usually represent a percentage of the whole. One of the common uses of circle graphs is to illustrate the differing proportions taken up by each category of public spending or revenue source.

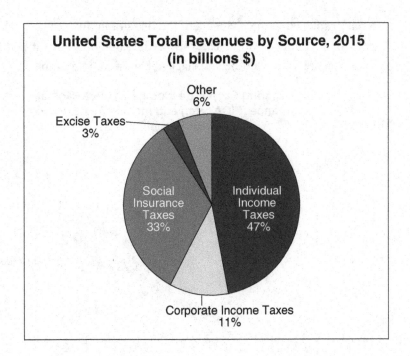

3. **Bar or column graphs (stacked or clustered)** present information similarly to how line graphs do, with the exception that they use a horizontal or vertical bar rather than a point on the graph. The bar graph can also present proportions within the bar that are similar to the information presented in a pie chart, while at the same time making possible comparisons over time, as seen in the example below.

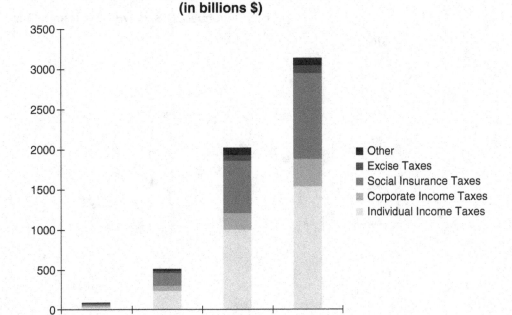

6. **Area graphs** combine elements of the line graph, for example, showing changes over time for a number of variables, while at the same time permitting the kinds of comparisons that are seen in circle and stacked bar or column graphs.

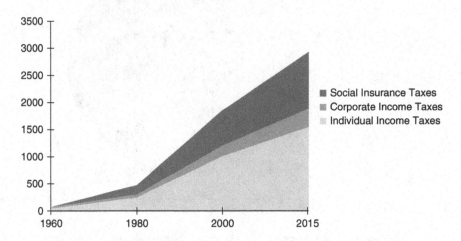

Comparing Corporate Income Taxes to Social Insurance (FICA, etc.) and Income Tax Burden, 1960–2015 (in billions $)

7. **Scatter graphs** graph pairs of numerical data, with one variable on each axis, in order to determine the relationship between the two variables. If the variables are correlated, the points will fall along a line or curve. The greater the correlation, the closer the points will be to the line. Below is a scatter plot showing the relationship between home prices and the distance to the city center.

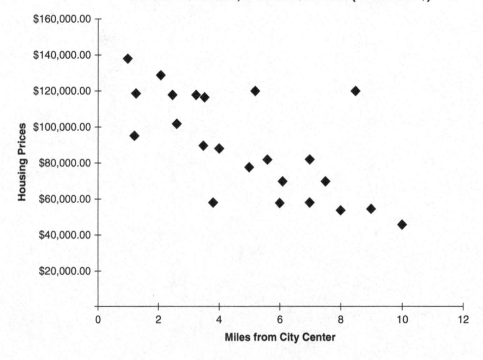

Total Revenues, U.S. Government (in billions $)

Timelines

Timelines are graphic organizers that show time on a spectrum with important dates or events listed.

Outlines

Outlines serve as organizers for writing, oral presentations, and simplified and succinct presentation of information. Outlines can be formal or informal. In the social sciences and in social studies education, effective outlines often make it possible for writers, researchers, and teachers to separate their arguments from the subordinate points or evidence that sustains that argument. Using outlines as note-taking devices and prewriting tools is also important.

Competency 024 Descriptive Statement E. The beginning teacher knows how to use maps and other graphics to present geographic, political, historical, economic and cultural features, distributions, and relationships.

Maps and graphics, as discussed earlier in this chapter, provide handy tools for showing relationships and illustrating data. They can be read uncritically, as we have seen, and understood at face value. The skill of map reading is an important one and should be an important objective in a social studies classroom. But, cartographic literacy is much more than merely reading the surface of the map.

Maps are too often taken as "facts" and are not critically interpreted. Instead, they should be understood as "value-laden images" that contribute to constructing spatial and social relationships and telling stories of their own. Teachers must model for students the skill of reading maps just as critically as they read other primary or secondary sources.

Maps can be important sources for cultural study. Primary source maps provide a visual image of a culture and the culture's values. Maps illuminate a culture in ways that other documents may not. Maps therefore require a more careful reading than is often given.

Maps also have a point of view and, like narratives, include some "facts" and exclude others. Maps mediate a host of differing worldviews. Making a map is a subjective act. What projection is used, how a map is oriented, and the scale of the map all reveal the point of view of the cartographer and the culture. Mercator projections, for example, were for a long time the dominant map projections for maps used in schools. The Mercator projection also enhanced the significance of Europe and the United States, not so subtly illustrating Europe and North America's power and economic supremacy. Often, Mercator projection maps used in schools placed the Atlantic at their center, further emphasizing the United States and Europe as the core of the world economy and political system.

Maps also reflect political contexts. Maps have also been important tools for statist and imperial projects. Surveyors and mapmakers went hand-in-hand with the *conquistadors* who claimed Texas (see Alonso Álvarez de Piñeda, who mapped the coastline of Texas, in Chapter 5) or the Europeans who claimed African colonies. The habit of reading a map as one would another primary source is therefore an important social studies skill.

Using maps as primary sources is increasingly possible, given the many digitized historic maps that are available online. Other digital tools allow students to zoom in on details that would otherwise be inaccessible. GIS (Geographic Information Systems) maps allow vast quantities of geographic information to be mapped. Maps can provide a visual representation of vast databases. However, just as maps drawn by early explorers reflected the imperialist objectives of the mapmakers and their societies, GIS-derived maps or imagery can also show bias and must be studied with that in mind.

Photography

Photographs have become a feature of our daily life to a degree that those who have grown up with cell phones take for granted. Facebook, Snapchat, and other social media platforms permit a record of our daily lives, children, food, cats, etc., that could hardly have been imagined not so long ago. These visual images and photographs, however, just like other primary sources, do not speak for themselves. Photographs are not simply mirrors of reality; they construct a realistic image, but one that is no less subject to the kinds of analysis that the social studies teach. Just as a diary or a written report reflects the author's purpose, point of view, historical and personal context, audience, etc., a photograph has similar authorial intent, perspective, contextual influences, and audience influence. Photographs, like maps, therefore must be looked at through these lenses.

> **Competency 024 Descriptive Statement F.** The beginning teacher uses maps to obtain and analyze data for solving locational problems and to answer questions, infer relationships, and analyze spatial change.

Maps are important communications tools for teachers. *Graphicacy,* or the ability to understand and present information using photographs, maps, plans, charts, graphs, etc., is—alongside numeracy, literacy, or oral communication—central to social studies education. Maps illustrate relations between people and the world around them. As a result, mastering an ability to read and communicate with maps is critical to the social studies. Students and teachers should be able to make, use, and interpret maps.

Characteristics of Maps

Understanding the basic characteristics of maps is important to the development of mapping skills. Let's look at each skill in turn.

Plan View

Maps represent three-dimensional space from a bird's-eye view, permitting the viewer to see things that would be impossible from ground level. This perspective does not follow naturally for all students. Aerial photographs, satellite images from Google Earth, and other representations of familiar images from a perspective above an area enable students to prepare for the more abstract map. Students need to also be familiarized with ways in which maps attempt to reintegrate height or slope on the two-dimensional map. Contours are one way this is done, but contour maps are often the most difficult for even experienced social studies teachers and their students to read.

Arrangement

Maps permit readers to locate landmarks, either absolutely (by reference to longitude, latitude, or other grid systems) or in relation to other landmarks. Similarly, directions can be absolute or relative to one's position. An important feature of what teachers must be able to aid students in understanding are the ways in which map readers use maps to guide their movement through space and how mapmakers draw maps to illustrate movement through space (for example, historical maps that show troop movements).

Proportion

Maps rely on scale to reduce the size of objects for representation on a smaller, two-dimensional form. These reductions result in distortions, biases, and omissions that also must be recognized. Teachers must also be able to model for students how to both properly read scale and distance on a map, and how to recognize the bias, distortion, and omission common to maps.

Map Language

Just as written texts rely on signs and symbols to communicate, maps employ signs, symbols, words, letters, and numbers, all of which serve as a code accessible only to those familiar with decoding and interpreting these visual representations of spatial patterns.

> **Competency 024 Descriptive Statement G.** The beginning teacher communicates and interprets social studies information in written, oral, and visual forms and translates information from one medium to another.

Writing, oral communication, and visual presentation are all important tools for communicating social science knowledge and assessing student progress. It is imperative, therefore, that teachers both model effective communication strategies and use written, oral, and visual communication in their classrooms.

Teachers should model and encourage expository writing as a vehicle for exploring ideas, developing organized and systematic thought, and communicating arguments and information with their classmates. Written communication requires a process including the following steps:

- **Prewriting** (listing, brainstorming, literature review, outlining)

- **Writing a draft** (more free-form and expansive than a final draft)

- **Revision**

- **Editing** (grammar, mechanics, spelling, and punctuation issues are resolved)

- **Final draft**

There are many varieties of writing assignments that work well in social studies classes. **Journaling** in social studies classes increases student interest and improves their writing abilities. Allowing students to tap into their own prior knowledge and engage their own interests has a positive impact on student motivation. There are many journal prompts. Sharing journal entries is a useful way for students to share their ideas and receive feedback from their peers. Encouraging students to share with a partner, a small group, or the whole class offer opportunities for informal feedback and shared learning.

Oral communication (and not just by the teacher) enhances content learning, improves skills acquisition, and provides other avenues for learning for students who are not able readers or writers. There are a variety of oral communication platforms that allow students to share their knowledge in an unwritten form. For example, students might be asked to create a concept map from an assigned textbook section and present their understanding to the class. They might be asked to give a brief talk to the class on related social studies topics. A persuasive speech offers another vehicle for students to gain confidence as communicators.

Visual communication is also important in the social studies classroom. Teachers should model using a variety of visual aids, pictures, symbols, and methods to communicate meaning and to support arguments. Pictures, diagrams, models, graphs, charts, and other imagery improves language acquisition and improves students' abilities to connect ideas and concepts to their base of knowledge.

> **Competency 024 Descriptive Statement H.** The beginning teacher analyzes various economic indicators to describe and measure levels of economic activity.

Social studies teachers should be familiar with the economic vocabulary commonly employed in national economic and political discourse. These terms are frequently thrown about by politicians, newspaper editorialists, and others to make policy arguments.

Unemployment Rate

The unemployment rate in the United States is defined by the Bureau of Labor Statistics as the "total unemployed, (or those who are actively looking for work but aren't currently unemployed) as a percent of the civilian labor force (the total of people over the age of 16 who are either employed or currently looking for work)." The unemployment rate can be determined using the following formula:

$$\text{Unemployment rate} = \frac{\text{Labor force}}{\text{population age 16 or older}} \times 100$$

Unemployment rates in the United States have varied since 1945, but they have seldom fallen below 4 percent (which is usually understood to be at or around full employment) and rarely risen above 10 percent. Since the end of World War II, only in the early 1980s under President Ronald Reagan and then in October 2009 under President Barack Obama, have U.S. unemployment rates risen to 10 percent or above. Below is a chart indicating the monthly unemployment rates from January 2007 to June 2017, as reported by the U.S. Bureau of Labor Statistics.

Table 9.2
Monthly Unemployment Rates (2007–2017)

Year	Jan	Feb	Mar	Apr	May	Jun	Jul	Aug	Sep	Oct	Nov	Dec
2007	4.6	4.5	4.4	4.5	4.4	4.6	4.7	4.6	4.7	4.7	4.7	5.0
2008	5.0	4.9	5.1	5.0	5.4	5.6	5.8	6.1	6.1	6.5	6.8	7.3
2009	7.8	8.3	8.7	9.0	9.4	9.5	9.5	9.6	9.8	10.0	9.9	9.9
2010	9.8	9.8	9.9	9.9	9.6	9.4	9.4	9.5	9.5	9.4	9.8	9.3
2011	9.1	9.0	9.0	9.1	9.0	9.1	9.0	9.0	9.0	8.8	8.6	8.5
2012	8.3	8.3	8.2	8.2	8.2	8.2	8.2	8.1	7.8	7.8	7.7	7.9
2013	8.0	7.7	7.5	7.6	7.5	7.5	7.3	7.3	7.2	7.2	6.9	6.7
2014	6.6	6.7	6.7	6.2	6.3	6.1	6.2	6.2	5.9	5.7	5.8	5.6
2015	5.7	5.5	5.4	5.4	5.5	5.3	5.2	5.1	5.0	5.0	5.0	5.0
2016	4.9	4.9	5.0	5.0	4.7	4.9	4.9	4.9	4.9	4.8	4.6	4.7
2017	4.8	4.7	4.5	4.4	4.3	4.4						

The unemployment rate understates the true level of unemployment in a number of ways. **Discouraged workers** (individuals who would like a job but have given up looking for work), **marginally attached workers** (people who have looked for work in the recent past but during the reporting period did not look for work), and the **underemployed** (workers who would like a full-time position, but have had to settle for part-time work) are not counted as unemployed. The unemployment rate also disguises the differential impact on different racial, ethnic, and age groups.

Inflation and Inflation Rate

Inflation is a rise in the overall level of prices. The **inflation rate** is the annual percent change in a price index that measures changes in the prices of a basket of goods over time. The most frequently used price index is the *consumer price index* (CPI). While overall level of prices for most of the post–World War II period has been rising, the inflation rate has both risen and fallen during the period.

Table 9.3
Consumer Price Index (1980–2015)

1980	82	1992	140	2003	189
1981	91	1993	145	2005	196
1982	97	1994	148	2006	202
1983	100	1995	152	2007	207
1984	103	1996	157	2008	215
1985	107	1997	161	2009	214
1986	109	1998	163	2010	219
1987	113	1999	167	2011	224
1988	118	2000	172	2012	230
1989	124	2001	177	2013	233
1990	130	2002	180	2014	237
1991	136	2003	184	2015	237

Using the CPI above, it is possible, using the formula below, to calculate the inflation rate from year to year, or for a defined period of time.

Thus, the inflation rate between 1983 and 2015 could be calculated as follows:

$$\text{Inflation rate} = \frac{\text{Price index in year 2} - \text{Price index in year 1}}{\text{Price index in year 1}} \times 100$$

Thus, the overall level of prices has risen 137.97 percent since 1983. Consequently, while the prices for some things are actually less in real terms than they were in 1983, the overall level of prices more than doubled between 1983 and 2015.

While it is useful to be able to use an index like the one above to measure rates of change in price levels, it is also possible to determine the difference between the **real price** (after accounting for inflation rates) and the **money** or **nominal price** of a good. The Bureau of Labor Statistics provides a handy CPI inflation calculator at its website: *www.bls.gov/data/inflation_calculator.htm.*

Gross Domestic Product (GDP)

One of the terms that is frequently employed in news accounts of the health of the economy, or in comparisons of national economies, is the term **GDP** or **gross domestic product**. GDP is the total *value* of all *final goods and services* produced in an economy in a given period, most often a year. GDP as a measure dates only to the 1930s and was devised by U.S. government economists as a tool to help government planners better manage the economy during the Great Depression.

There are a number of ways to measure GDP, but the easiest way to remember how this number is arrived at is through the following formula: **GDP = Consumption + Investment + Government Spending + Net Exports (Imports – Exports).** Economists represent this equation as follows:

$$Y = C + I + G + NX.$$

Table 9.4
GDP of the United States in 2016 by Component

Component	Amount (trillion dollars)	Percent
Personal Consumption	$13.01	69%
Business Investment	$3.10	16%
Net Exports	(–$.55)	(–3%)
Government	$3.30	18%
TOTAL GDP	$18.87	100%

GDP gives us a measure of the size of the national economy and allows us to make comparisons over time, and with reference to other national economies. It also provides a means to make comparisons among individual states' economies. At the close of 2016, Texas' economy had a GDP of $1.587 trillion, ranking it second behind California in the nation for GDP. In fact, Texas' economy would rank it 10th in the world, close behind Italy and Brazil, and just above Canada.

While GDP measures the *size* of an economy, it is less helpful as a measure of the overall *health* of an economy, which includes many other factors than just GDP. Although GDP is a major determinant of an economy's health, it is not the only one. Also, because of inflation, the increase in the *size* of the GDP doesn't accurately reflect its *growth*. For example, when making year-to-year GDP comparisons, it is important to remember that the measure of GDP includes inflationary changes in the monetary values of goods, services, business investment, and government expenditures—all of which follow the price increases for goods and services. For example, U.S. GDP was $6.657 trillion in 1997 and in 2017 is now $18.87 trillion. But this tripling of the *size* of the GDP does not imply a tripling in the *growth* of the GDP. Because of inflation, our economy has not actually tripled since 1997. In 1997 dollars, the U.S. GDP in 2017 amounts to $12.46 trillion, which represents a doubling, not a tripling, of the size of the GDP. This growth reflects the fact that during this period, prices doubled, rising by 50 percent. Therefore, taking inflation into account, the economy has only *doubled* in growth, not *tripled*, in the past 20 years. Another problem with GDP as a measure of the nation's health is that it does not provide a qualitative measure of the goods and services produced in the economy. It could be argued that an economy that produces a GDP made up of a heavy reliance on military weaponry is not as healthy as an economy that produces mostly durable and non-durable consumer items. Or, an economy that is dependent, as the U.S. economy is, on personal consumption is not as healthy in the long term as an economy that has a higher investment in capital (which will increase productivity and production in the long term).

Lastly, GDP as an economic measure, on its own, provides little indication of the productivity of the economy, which is a better gauge of an economy's long-term sustainability.

GDP per capita

An important measure of the economy's health, and perhaps a more critical statistic to track, is **real GDP per capita,** or real GDP divided by population size. Real GDP, of course, is in constant dollars. Table 7.5 shows the growth of real GDP since 1950. It also shows the percentage growth of real GDP per capita since 1950.

Table 9.5
Per Capita Real GDP since 1950

	Per Capita GDP	Percentage of 1950 real GDP per capita	Percentage of 2016 real GDP per capita
1950	13,346	100%	26%
1960	17,223	129	33
1970	23,159	174	45
1980	28,775	216	55
1990	35,419	265	68
2000	44,654	335	86
2010	46,941	352	95
2016	51,849	388	100

Table 9.5 shows that the U.S. economy produced 129 percent more per person in 1960 than it did in 1950. Or, in 2016, the economy produced nearly 388 percent more per person than it did in 1950. This nearly fourfold increase in real per capita GDP represents a significant growth over the period. Similarly, we can recognize that in 1950, the U.S. economy only produced just over one-quarter of what the U.S. economy produces today in real per capita terms. This growth in per capita wealth is supported by other measures. For example, in 1950, the average size of a single-family dwelling was only 983 square feet. By 2010, the average size of a single-family home was 2,169 square feet. The average American home has nearly three televisions today, whereas in 1950, only 3.8 million out of 43 million households had a television.

> **Competency 024 Description Statement I.** The beginning teacher uses economic models such as production possibilities curves, circular flow charts, and supply-and-demand graphs to analyze economic concepts or issues.

Economists use a variety of models, graphs, and charts to illustrate in simplified form the complexities of the economy. Among these are production possibilities curves, circular flow models, and supply-and-demand graphs. We have already described these in some detail in Chapter 8.

Production Possibilities Curves

Economists use production possibilities curves (or frontiers) to illustrate the problem of scarcity and the opportunity costs faced by economies that must make choices about the optimal use of scarce resources. **Figure 9.2** below provides an example of a production possibilities curve. A production possibilities curve illustrates points along the curve where the economy is producing efficiently and is not wasting resources. The outward-bowing curve in **Figure 9.2** also illustrates the diminishing returns that occur as you move along the curve. For instance, if you start at point A in **Figure 9.2**, where you are producing 700 watermelons but no cantaloupes, to point B, the opportunity cost in reduced watermelons for the 300 cantaloupes grown is only 20 watermelons. However, when you move from point B to point C, the opportunity cost of producing more cantaloupes is a much greater number of watermelons, 60 to be precise. The production possibilities curve also allows economists to represent both underemployment of resources and growth. For example, if you are producing at point G, well within the frontier of possibilities, the economy is not using its resources efficiently. Conversely, if new agricultural techniques, seeds varieties, or other improvements are introduced, the production possibilities curve will shift outward. Point H is a point where the economy cannot produce given the present state of technology, resources, and other factors of production.

Figure 9.2
Production Possibilities Curve

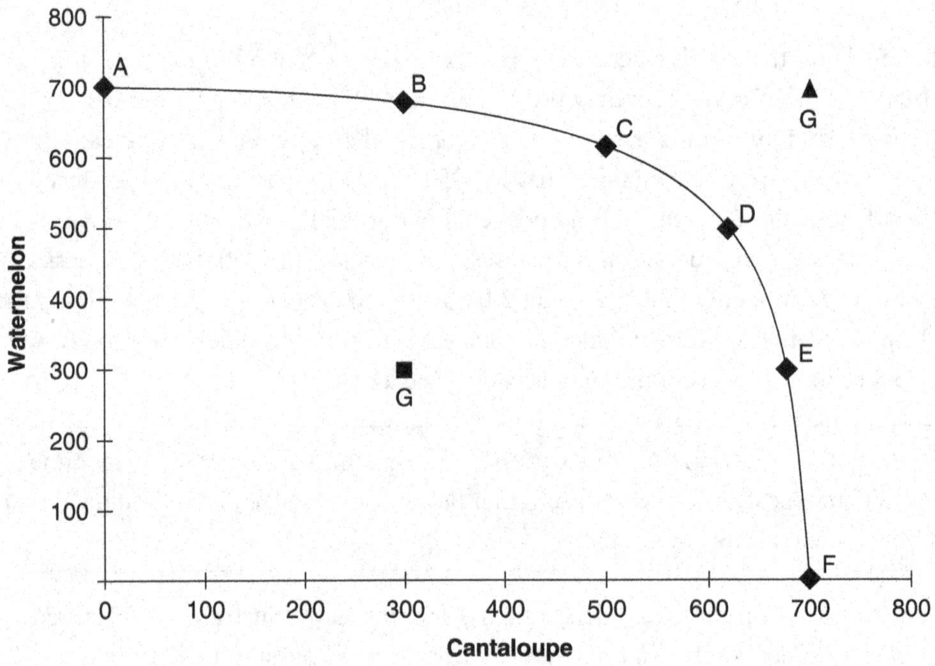

Circular Flow Models

A second important economic tool with which economists represent simplified economic relationships are circular flow models, also known as circular flow charts. Circular flow models trace the flows of income, goods and services, and factors of production between households, firms, and government.

The simple circular flow model in **Figure 9.3** illustrates the exchange between households and firms. From households, firms acquire land, labor, capital investment. In return firms pay rent, wages, and interest. Investment equals the savings of households. Savings receive interest in exchange for their use by firms. Firms then turn these factors of production into goods and services that are purchased by households.

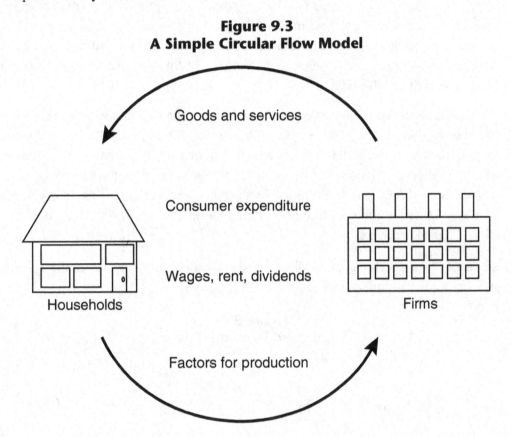

Figure 9.3
A Simple Circular Flow Model

Goods and services

Consumer expenditure

Wages, rent, dividends

Households

Firms

Factors for production

Circular flow models may also serve to illustrate the GDP equation, $Y = C + I + G + NX$.

Supply-and-Demand Graphs

Perhaps the most frequently employed graphs in economics are those that illustrate supply and demand, and changes in both.

Supply-and-demand curves illustrate the following:

- The Law of Demand: The quantity demanded of a good or service is inversely related to the price of the good or service.

- The Law of Supply: The quantity that will be supplied of a good or service is directly related to the price of the good and service.

- An increase in supply is represented by a rightward shift of the supply curve indicative of a willingness of firms to supply more of a good or service at all the possible price points. A decrease in supply is demonstrated graphically by a shift of the supply curve to the left, indicating that firms will offer less of the good or service at all price points.

- An increase in demand is represented by a rightward shift of the demand curve as consumers are willing and able to purchase more of the good or service at each of the possible price points. Conversely, a decrease in demand is illustrated by a rightward shift of the demand curve, demonstrating that consumers are willing and able to purchase less of the good or service at each possible price.

- Where the supply curve and the demand curve meet is the equilibrium, or market price for a good or service. At that price the seller is able to clear his inventory. Where the demand and supply curve intersect will also be the equilibrium quantity of the good or service for sale. At this price, every consumer who is willing and able to purchase the good and service will do so. This is the market-clearing price for a good or service. Shifts of the supply or demand curve will have the effect of raising or lowering the equilibrium price and equilibrium quantity of a good or service.

Figure 9.4 illustrates shifts of both the demand and supply curves as well as the new equilibrium prices and quantities of the product.

Figure 9.4
Supply and Demand Curves

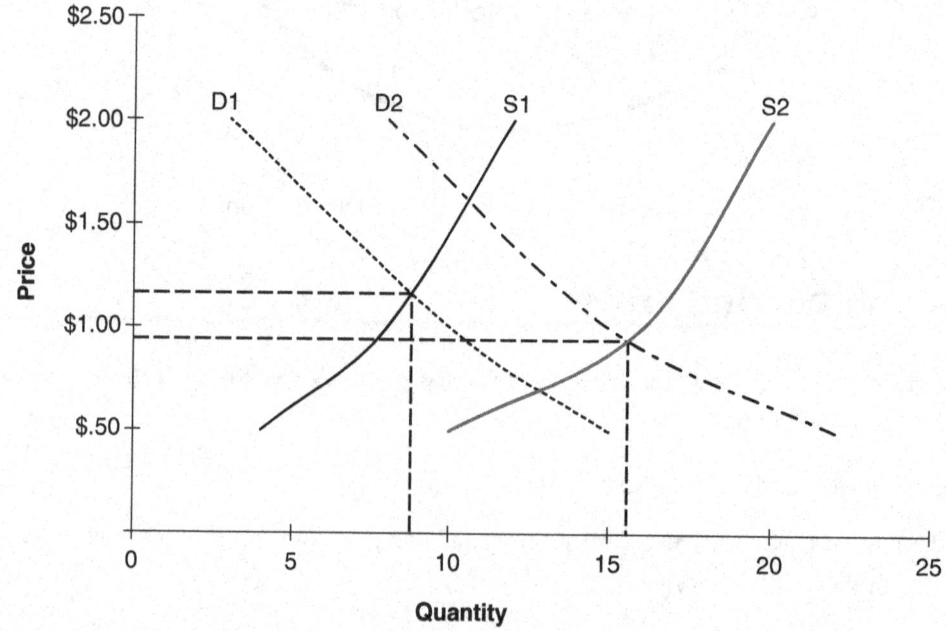

COMPETENCY 025 (SOCIAL STUDIES RESEARCH)

The teacher understands social science and historical research methods, including procedures for formulating research questions and for organizing, analyzing, evaluating, and reporting information.

Competency 025 Descriptive Statement A. The beginning teacher knows how to formulate research questions.

What Makes a Question a Research Question?

Not all questions are social science research questions. Some questions are "unresearchable." For a question to be a research question, a scholar must be able to answer the question, or at least address it through empirical research. Some questions are obviously unanswerable and fall into the realm of the theological or philosophical. For example, the following are fascinating questions, but they are not research questions.

- Is it immoral or sinful to lend money at interest? Did a creator make the cosmos? Are such reproductive strategies as contraception, artificial insemination, and surrogate parenting ethical? Many of the questions that are asked in English Literature classes are not "researchable" in the way that social scientists and historians mean the term. For example, consider the following questions:

  ▶ What makes the protagonist sympathetic or unsympathetic?

  ▶ Why do certain characters act the way they do?

  ▶ How does the arrangement of a book, essay, or poem help or detract from the ideas the literary work contains?

Each of these questions is important to literary scholars. But, they are unanswerable in the way that social scientists or historians formulate and answer research questions.

What Types of Research Questions Can Be Asked?

There are a wide variety of research questions that are asked within the social sciences.

Descriptive questions

A study that seeks to describe existing conditions. Other descriptive questions might start with "how often?," as in: How often do marriages end in divorce among populations of Evangelical Christians? Or: How often do marriages end in divorce among other ethnic, religious, or demographic groups? Other descriptive questions often start with "how much?," as in: "How much do those in the upper 20th percent of income earners make per year compared to income earn-ers in the lowest 20th percent. For a historian, a most basic descriptive question might start with "What happened?" For example: "What happened when the American troops landed on Normandy beaches on D-Day?" Descriptive questions are the most basic building block of research and the answers often lead to other questions.

Comparative questions

Descriptive questions are often said to be "first-order" questions, whereas comparative ques-tions are often described as "second-order" questions. Comparative questions presuppose descrip-tive questions and their answers. Taking the descriptive questions above, it is easy to imagine a series of comparative questions that would follow. "How do the divorce rates among Evangelical Christians differ from those of Christians in mainstream denominations? Or: "How do the divorce rates of Evangelical Christians differ from those among Orthodox Jewish populations?" An econo-mist who has described the differences in shares of income claimed by each quintile of the Ameri-can population might ask, "How do these income distributions compare with income distributions in other developed countries?" Or, a historian might ask, "How did casualty rates on Normandy beaches compare to those in North Africa, or Italy, during World War II?"

Explanatory questions

Perhaps the most immediate question that follows from answering a descriptive question begins with "why?" For example: "Why did the Americans have such high casualties on Omaha Beach?" Or, "Why do populations of Evangelical Christians in the United States have such high divorce rates by comparison to other religious groups?" Or, "Why has the share of national income claimed by the upper 20th percent of Americans grown so significantly since the early 1970s?" Explanatory research questions lead to studies that are designed to try to explain why a particular social phenomenon occurs.

Causal questions

A causal research study seeks to determine the relationship between two or more phenomena. For example, economists have sought to explain the falling crime rates that have been a feature of American society since the late 1990s. The economist Rick Nevin asked the question, "Was there a relationship between the rise and fall in violent crime and the use of leaded gasoline in cars?" The economists and legal scholars John J. Donohue and Steven D. Levitt asked a different but related research question. They asked, "Was there a causal relationship between the legalization of abortion in the 1970s and the sharp decline in violent crime in the 1990s?" Each of these questions sought to determine the relationship between a phenomenon (like falling crime rates) and other phenomena.

Predictive questions

Predictive questions try to determine whether one or more variables can be used to predict an outcome. Predictive questions generally look something like this: "Does x (a cause) lead to or create y (an outcome)? Predictive research questions move beyond descriptive, explanatory, causal, or analytical questions. An economist might pose the following question: "Will an increase in population growth rates necessarily result in increases in farm land rents?" A more complex version of this question might ask: "Given population growth and increases in economic growth (with accumulation of capital, skills, technological improvements, etc.), will farmland rents increase or decrease?" A political scientist might have a different interest. For example, a political scientist interested in predicting congressional voting behavior on specific areas of legislation might test the predictive value of their constituents' attitudes, the views of their fellow legislators, the amount of money donated to them by interest groups, political party platforms, etc. A political scientist might ask, "Does the high rate of constituent support for health care reform by voters in a representative's district predict that congressman's likelihood to vote in support of a health care plan?" Or, "Does the position of a representative's party leaders predict how the congressman will vote on a bill?"

Normative questions

Normative questions are often contrasted with descriptive and analytical questions (comparative, causal, explanatory, or predictive). Whereas the latter attempt to answer *what is*, normative questions ask *what should be*. In short, normative questions are *evaluative*. Normative questions and normative statements are more than just opinions. Normative questions and statements are subject to empirical testing. For example, a normative question might ask, "Should handguns be more tightly regulated?" Or, "Should a more redistributive progressive income tax be instituted?" The answers to these questions would be determined by empirical research designed to evaluate the varied impacts of the suggested changes in policy.

Where Do Research Questions Come from?

Research questions reflect a scholar's interests, values, curiosity, and world view. I was attracted to the study of the way poor people worked because I grew up in Central Africa where I saw whole populations cobbling together a living in the most creative ways.

Often, research questions come from a scholar's political or philosophical positions. Marxist historians and socialist scholars have historically been much more interested in economic and specifically class relations and their impact on social and cultural developments than have classical liberal or neoliberal scholars. Instead, these scholars have been more attentive to such things as the role of individuals (particularly powerful men and women, entrepreneurs, politicians, etc.) in shaping the history and development of social institutions. They have also emphasized the progressive and liberalizing effect of government, global economic forces, etc.

Scholars' research agendas also reflect their historical, material, and social context. During the Cold War, researchers were often drawn to ask questions about the nature of communism, totalitarian states, or international relations between the Soviet Union and the United States. Since 1992, there has been comparatively less interest in Russia, communism, or totalitarianism as a political system. Instead, China, its history, social conditions, political structures, and economic policies have attracted much wider scholarly interest.

It is worthwhile whenever teachers employ secondary sources as teaching tools to carry out a bit of research on the factors that influenced the researcher to make the choices they did. It is worth paying the same kind of attention to textbooks and other teaching materials.

> **Competency 025 Descriptive Statement B.** The beginning teacher uses appropriate procedures to reach supportable judgments and conclusions in social studies.

Social studies teachers must model for their students how to support claims and draw conclusions from disparate and often contradictory information. While emphasis is often placed on teaching content, concepts, and skill development, students learn as much from the ways in which teachers come to their own judgments and conclusions and the ways in which they share these conclusions with their students. Teachers should therefore model the following in their teaching.

Literature-based Instruction

The social sciences are constructed from the scholarly efforts of researchers who publish their findings in peer-reviewed journals. Teachers should be conversant with the literature of the social sciences, and particularly with the literature of social studies pedagogy. To expect colleagues and students to respect the teaching profession, social studies teachers must do the work to remain current in their fields. Just as one would expect a physician to remain up-to-date on the most recent surgical techniques or diagnostic methods, teachers should also maintain their currency through a regular professional development plan.

Use Reliable Sources and Model Critical Analysis

Teachers should model thoughtful analysis of primary and secondary sources as they prepare their own lectures and lesson plans. Students must see their teachers wrestle with the reliability of the primary sources, secondary literature, newspaper columns, editorials, or other materials they use.

Model the Scientific Method

The social studies class must effectively demonstrate how analysis necessarily enters into the development of content knowledge. Though content knowledge is important, it is not sufficient. In both geography and history courses, students need to learn how and why social scientists reached their conclusions. Teachers should consistently and frequently model the analytical skills needed to develop and support claims about history, economic conditions, government, or geographic knowledge.

Defending Arguments

Social studies education is characterized less by widely-held and shared belief than by shared arguments. It is important that the social studies are not thought to be a closed circle, but open for discussion and debate. Using these debates to encourage discussion and to develop the skills of open dialogue will go a long way towards encouraging the civic involvement that the social studies curriculum is intended to foster.

> **Competency 025 Descriptive Statement C.** The beginning teacher understands social studies research and knows how social scientists and historians locate, gather, organize, analyze, interpret, and report information using established research methodologies.

Researchers in the social sciences and history use a wide variety of research methodologies and an even wider range of sources of information.

Quantitative versus Qualitative Methods

Social scientists employ both quantitative and qualitative methods in their research. Rather than seeing them as polar opposites, however, it is important to see that social scientists will usually employ both qualitative and quantitative research. **Quantitative methods** collect numerical data and draw their conclusions from numerical or statistical analyses. **Qualitative methods** examine non-numerical information, such as literary sources, oral interviews or other verbal information, visual imagery or pictorial records, etc. Qualitative methods rely on non-numerical and non-statistical analysis. Each social studies discipline has practitioners or sub-disciplines that rely more heavily on either quantitative or qualitative approaches. For example, economic and social historians have been more likely to use quantitative and statistical methods of analysis and research. Cultural historians and historians of religion tend to rely more on non-statistical analysis and rely more on literary evidence.

Archival Research

Each of the social studies disciplines, to varying degrees, rely on archival research. Archival research involves investigation of data from the records of governmental, institutional, and even private archives. U.S. census data, criminal court records, church records, business records, and virtually any sort of documentary evidence that has been collected are held in a repository that is available for use by researchers and scholars from any social science discipline. Scholars approach archival sources much as they would other written documents, identifying collections with relevant documents, carefully reading the documents, taking notes and often making copies or taking photographs for later analysis. Historians perhaps are the most likely to rely on archival sources. Though quantitative data can be derived from archival research, most frequently, archival studies tend towards the qualitative.

Case Studies

Case studies are most often used in psychology, anthropology, sociology, and political science. Case studies are in-depth studies of complex issues or objects. Unlike surveys, case studies typically do not produce quantitative results, as they lack a large enough data sample size. Case studies are often designed to test the validity of more extensive quantitative claims. Case studies most often require collecting data in the field. For example, anthropologists stay with populations in other countries or with subgroups within the United States to allow the anthropologists to develop a richer picture of a culture than would a number of statistical surveys. The data collected in case studies often consists of field notes, databases, testimonies, recordings of oral interviews, etc.

Content Analysis

Content analysis is a research method for analyzing written and oral communication. Content analysis can be both quantitative and qualitative in its findings. A quantitative content analysis of political messaging, for example, might examine to what degree American politicians emphasize character issues when compared to policy proposals in their political campaigns. Such a study might count the number of times debates, speeches, or advertisements mention policy proposals and compare that to the number of times a candidate's character strengths or their opponent's character flaws are mentioned. Qualitative content analysis emphasizes study of the meanings evident in communication; for example, the ways words are used, rather than the number of times those words are used. My daughter, for example, a few years ago did a senior thesis where she analyzed the ways in which evangelical Christian language and messaging was used in the speeches of Jimmy Carter, Ronald Reagan, George W. Bush, and Barack Obama. Content analysis is most often done by psychologists, anthropologists, historians, political scientists, and sociologists.

Experimental Research

Experimental research is most often associated with the natural sciences. Experimental research seeks to understand how or why something happens. In other words, experimental research is most often used to determine cause-and-effect relationships. Social scientists also use experiments to test hypotheses in their own fields. Laboratory experiments occur in controlled environments, while field experiments are conducted in real-world contexts. Social groups—the focus of much social science research—are too complex to be easily studied in controlled and measurable ways. Psychologists, geographers, and economists are thus more likely to use experimental methods.

Economists often use games, learning experiments, and other similarly controlled environments to determine how individuals will react to certain economic conditions.

Interviews

Interviews with human subjects are an important source of data for social scientists. Interviewing can be used as a research tool in all of the social sciences. The data collected usually lends itself to qualitative research, though there are occasional quantitative studies that rely on interviewing techniques. Interviews involve the researcher asking questions of his or her subjects. The data collected usually takes the form of field notes or tape recordings, which are either coded or qualitatively analyzed for meaning.

Modeling (Computer Simulation)

Mathematical modeling, now most often relying on computers, is used to make projections about economic or political conditions. For example, an economist might create a simulation or model that takes historical data, or projected data and establishes certain parameters that will guide the computational mathematics that enable the model to be predictive. Economists frequently do this to determine what the effect of tax policy, changes in spending patterns, or other variables might have on an industrial sector or the wider economy.

Surveys

One of the more frequently-used methods of social science research is the survey. Surveys use quantitative methods to identify a sample population which is surveyed using questionnaires. Statistical surveys do not rely on polling an entire population, but in taking a representative sample and drawing inferences from the results. Public opinion polls, market research surveys, government surveys, and censuses provide data for psychological, political science, sociological, and economic research. The criteria for identifying the sample population, the ways in which questions are framed, whether the survey is conducted in person, by phone, online, etc., and the ways in which the data are analyzed will all have important impacts on the kinds of conclusions that can be drawn from the survey.

All the methods described above are the research methods most frequently employed in the social sciences. Providing students the opportunity to participate in research using these varied methods will help students better understand the processes of research and data collection used in the social sciences, as well as the limitations of these research methods.

> **Competency 025 Descriptive Statement D.** The beginning teacher knows how to analyze social studies information by sequencing, categorizing, identifying associations, and cause-and-effect relationships, comparing and contrasting, finding the main idea, summarizing, making generalizations, and drawing inferences and conclusions.

Analysis in the social sciences involves breaking down complex material into component parts and explaining the relationship of the parts to the whole. Analysis is one of the important skills that social studies teachers must encourage in their students. It is a varied skill that includes a number of ways to divide complex material into manageable explanatory components.

Finding the Main Idea

To effectively analyze any reading passage, or to analyze primary source documents, it is imperative that students find the main ideas and distinguish them from subordinate arguments and relevant details. When teaching note-taking, reading content, and writing, teachers should both model these skills and encourage the basic analytical skill of finding the main idea.

Sequencing

The analytical skill of sequencing involves identifying the *chronological* or *logical* sequence of events that explains a concept, event, or social phenomenon. For example, an analysis of the Civil Rights Movement might explain its emergence by reference to a chronological sequence of earlier events. This is a common narrative form of explanation. It is useful, however, to remember the classical logical fallacy known as *post hoc ergo propter hoc*, or "Since Y came after X, X must have caused Y." The fact that one event followed another should not be taken as conclusive evidence that the former caused the latter.

Categorizing

Another form of analysis involves categorization or classification. One way of making sense of data is to categorize it or divide it into groups or conceptual categories. From these categories, it is then possible to proceed to theories. For example, students might be asked to identify characteristics of political systems that are associated with liberal democracies, monarchies, theocracies, totalitarian dictatorships, etc. They might then be asked to identify either world regions or historical eras when prominent examples of each of these political structures existed. From this, they might then develop a theory for how and why these systems of government developed.

Identifying Associations

A critical analytical strategy is to identify associations between two or more phenomena. Social studies analysis depends upon drawing connections between often very disconnected phenomena. It is perhaps easiest to illustrate the ways in which social scientists identify associations by giving an example. What connection could possibly be drawn between differences between European and Asian wage levels in 17th- and 18th-century Asia when compared to wages in European cities, and differences between European and Asian waste removal regimes? In fact, there is a connection. Chinese and Indian cities did not dump their human waste into the rivers that provided their water supply, as the European city dwellers did. They transported the human urine and feces to nearby vegetable and rice farmers, who used it to fertilize their crops. Most Europeans were quite late to the practice of fertilizing their fields. As a result, farm yields in China and India vastly outstripped the yields in most European farming. These high yields lowered the typical expenses needed by an Asian laborer's family. As a result, Chinese and Indian manufacturers paid wages well below those demanded by European artisans without significantly reducing standards of living for Asian workers. As a result, producers of high-quality Chinese and Indian cotton and silk textiles were able to undercut European production until European inventors and entrepreneurs developed new technological means to increase efficiencies and break free of dependence on Asian textiles.

Cause-and-Effect Relationships

Establishing the causes of historical and social changes or identifying the effects of technological change, policy decisions, or many other changes are central analytical skills that must be developed in the social studies classroom. Each of the social science disciplines that are introduced in the classroom endeavors to explain cause-and-effect relationships. Student-led and inquiry-based learning afford the teacher numerous opportunities to examine causes of a wide variety of social, economic, political, and historical phenomena and provide students the opportunity to predict likely effects of policy proposals and the like.

Comparing and Contrasting

Social studies classrooms are also enriched by the frequent and capable employment of comparative approaches. These can be developed for every subject matter. Comparisons across time can be especially useful. For example, you might compare events, such as the war in Iraq with that in Vietnam. You might also compare policy choices, such as approaches to health care among various developed nations, or gender and ethnic differences between countries, or even within a country.

Classrooms that enable student development of complex analytical skills and teachers that model these abilities take students beyond vocabulary development and simple content knowledge and encourage the kind of critical thinking that will help students more easily transition to college and university classrooms and the workplace.

> **Competency 025 Descriptive Statement E.** The beginning teacher analyzes social studies data using basic mathematical and statistical concepts and other analytical methods.

Students and teachers should be familiar with a range of quantitative methods for analysis of social studies problems. The statistical and mathematical methods most often used in social studies classrooms to analyze social science data include both descriptive and inferential statistics.

Descriptive statistics serve basic descriptive functions. Descriptive statistics allow students and teachers to present and simplify large amounts of data in manageable forms.

Inferential statistics are quantitative analyses that help the researcher draw conclusions from that data. Descriptive statistics allow researchers to describe what is happening in their data sets, and inferential statistics allow researchers to reach conclusions beyond what their immediate data is telling them. In social studies classrooms (though not in social science research), the latter are less often seen and are probably less likely to be required of either teachers or students. Inferential statistical analysis include such tools as the T-Test, Dummy Variables, General Linear Model, Randomized Block Analysis, Regression-Discontinuity Analysis, and many other tools. It is unlikely that test-takers will be asked to wrestle with these complicated tools.

To illustrate the ways in which descriptive statistics might be used in the social studies, the following fictional classroom will be used.

Table 9.3
Classroom Data for the Fictional Classroom of Mr. Green and his Colorful Students

Student	Party Affiliation	Grade Level	Class Grade
Apricot, Alice	Democrat	9	65
Black, Jack	Republican	12	77
Crimson, Chuck	Democrat	11	78
Denim, David	Independent	10	85
Eggplant, Elisa	Green	10	95
Fuchsia, Felix	Socialist	10	80
Gold, Ari	Republican	11	65
Heliotrope, Helen	Republican	12	63
Ivory, Iran	Libertarian	10	85
Jade, Jerry	Republican	11	97
Khaki, Kelly	Democrat	12	77
Lavender, Leroy	Democrat	11	73
Maroon, Mitchel	Green	10	64

Student	Party Affiliation	Grade Level	Class Grade
Navy, Noelle	Republican	9	84
Orange, Olivier	Democrat	9	95
Plum, Peter	Green	11	69
Quartz, Quashie	Libertarian	12	70
Russet, Russel	Socialist	11	72
Salmon, Salvatore	Independent	10	77
Tangerine, Theresa	Democrat	9	79
Ultramarine, Ulysses	Republican	10	82
Violet, Vince	Democrat	12	75
White, Lawrence	Democrat	11	61
Xanthic, Xavier	Republican	10	99
Yellow, Yesenia	Libertarian	9	65
Zucchini, Zed	Green	12	77

Descriptive Statistics

- **Central tendency (mean, median, mode)**

  ▸ **Mean**—the sum of all values in a data set divided by the total number of values. In the classroom set above, the mean (or average) grade is 77.23.

  ▸ **Median**—a value that divides a data sample into two halves. In the sample above half of the students received a grade of 77 or higher. Half of the students earned a grade below 77.

  ▸ **Mode**—the value in a data set that received the highest number of occurrences. In the data set above, the mode for the class grade is a 65, and the mode for grade level is 10. In other words, there are more 10th graders in Mr. Green's classroom than there are freshmen, juniors, or seniors.

- **Frequency distribution.** A frequency distribution presents how many or what proportion of a number of cases fell within a particular category of analysis. For example, Mr. Green might identify the frequency distribution of party affiliation of his students or the frequency of their grade distribution. The following charts graphically illustrate first the frequency distribution of party affiliation in Mr. Green's classroom.

Figure 9.5
Frequency Distribution: Party Affiliation (Mr. Green's Classroom)

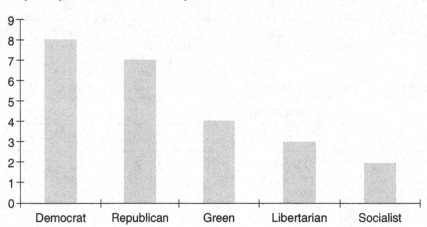

- **Dispersion (range, standard deviation)**

  ▸ **Range**—the difference between the largest and smallest values in a data set.

  ▸ **Standard deviation**—a measure of the spread of scores within a data set. Low standard deviations indicate that most of the numbers are bunched around the mean, while a high standard deviation indicates that the data is widely spread. Standard deviation is not as often used in journalistic or textbook accounts of data. Without standard deviation, it is difficult to compare two sets of statistical information. For example, if you are told that the average salary for beginning teachers at both Corpus Christi I.S.D. and Calallen I.S.D. is $42,000, you have only part of the relevant information you might need as you decide where to seek a job. Suppose you hear that at CC I.S.D. the standard deviation is $7,000 and at Calallen I.S.D. the standard deviation is only $1,000. You can be more assured of earning a salary at or around the $42,000 average at Calallen I.S.D. At Corpus Christi I.S.D. you may have an outside chance of earning substantially more than at Calallen, but you may also have a reasonably good chance of earning much less. In short, you are better able to predict what your likely salary is going to be from the data you have from Calallen.

- **Correlation**—correlation is a very useful and common statistical analysis. A correlation is a single number that describes the relationship between two variables. Using the information from Mr. Green's social studies classroom above, is it possible to test if there is a correlation between class grade and political affiliation, or between grade level and political affiliation? As it turns out, based on this small sample, the correlation between class grade and political affiliation was not clear. There was, however, a reverse correlation between class grade and grade level. In other words, ninth graders did better in Mr. Green's class than did 12th graders.

How a Researcher Might Design a Study for Statistical Analysis

Research question: Do gun control laws lower or increase the rates of violent crime? Is there a greater relationship between other factors (law enforcement, urbanization, poverty rates, income inequality) and crime rates than between gun control laws and crime?

1. **Hypothesis.** Gun control laws lead to reductions of violent crime rates.

2. **Variables to be studied.**

   • Crime rates (based on the FBI's annual Uniform Crime Reports)

   • Gun control regulations (based on the Bureau of Alcohol, Tobacco, Firearms, and Explosives listings of state and local gun control laws).

   • Number of law enforcement officers

   • Degree of urbanization

   • Poverty rates

   • Rates of economic inequality

3. **Statistical analysis.** Using regression analysis (a statistical process that estimates the relationship between variables), analyze the relationship between crime rates and gun control regulations. Do the same for crime rates and number of law enforcement officers in a state, rates of urbanization, poverty rates, or levels of income inequality. Determine if states with more stringent gun control regulations have lower or higher crime rates. Determine what relationship exists between crime rates and levels of police enforcement, urban populations poverty rates, or economic inequality.

4. **Draw conclusions.**

Percentages, percentiles, quintiles, deciles, etc.

These terms are used frequently in the social studies and should be understood. A **percentage** is a ratio expressed as a fraction of 100. In 2015, for example, 35% of Texans had an associate degree or higher. **Percentile** ranks a score according to the percentage of scores that are equal or lower than the given score. For instance, if you score in the 94th percentile on the GRE test, it would mean you scored higher than 94 percent of test-takers. Or, in Texas if you annually earn $194,900, you are at the 95th percentile of income earners in the state. If you earn $65,100, you are in the 60th percentile of income earners. A **decile** is one of 10 equal groups of a population divided according to a selected variable. For instance, income earners can be divided into 10 equally divided sets.

The average income of income earners in the lowest decile, or bottom 10 percent, in 2016 earned on average $9,516 per year. Those in the top decile earned on average $104,982 per year. Similarly, we can divide populations into **quartiles** (25 percent) or **quintiles** (20 percent).

COMPETENCY 026 (SOCIAL STUDIES INSTRUCTION AND ASSESSMENT)

The teacher understands the Texas Essential Knowledge and Skills (TEKS) in social studies; knows how to plan and implement effective social studies instruction, including helping students make interdisciplinary connections and develop relevant reading skills; and knows procedures for assessing students' progress and needs in social studies.

> **Competency 026 Descriptive Statement A.** The beginning teacher knows state content and performance standards for social studies that comprise the Texas Essential Knowledge and Skills (TEKS) and understands the vertical alignment of social studies in the TEKS from grade level to grade level, including prerequisite knowledge and skills.

Each of the social studies content areas is vertically aligned from kindergarten to the high school end-of-course exam. The state-mandated content and standards can be found in the **Texas Essential Knowledge and Skills (TEKS)** for K–12 education. The TEKS are descriptions of the learning objectives for classroom teachers and the content students will be held accountable for on state assessments.

The TEKS for K–12 social studies can be found at the Texas Education Agency website at *http://ritter.tea.state.tx.us/rules/tac/chapter113/ch113c.html.*

The Texas Education Agency (TEA) also provides a lengthy document that outlines the vertical integration of the social studies from kindergarten to end-of-course exams in each of the high school social studies classes. This document puts in one place the key TEKS and the expected grades where they will be addressed. The document can found at *http://tea.texas.gov/student. assessment/special-ed/staaralt/vertalign/.*

> **Competency 026 Descriptive Statement B.** The beginning teacher selects and uses developmentally appropriate instructional practices, activities, technologies, and materials to promote student knowledge, skills, and progress in social studies.

The TEA has created standards for beginning educators. These can be found at its website: *http://tea.texas.gov/Texas_Educators/.*

Adolescent Development and Social Studies Instruction

Middle schools and high schools are populated with children and young adults who differ enormously in their physical and mental development. This is true, of course, across grade levels, but also quite frequently, even within grade levels. According to Glenda Beamon, adolescents exhibit a number of contradictory characteristics that are both an opportunity and a hindrance to classroom teachers. According to Beamon:

- Adolescents are at ease with technology (often more so than their teachers), but do not have the organizational, analytical, or evaluative skills to critically use technology in sophisticated ways.

- Adolescents are used to having information at their fingertips, yet are quickly distracted and often fail to follow through with tasks.

- Adolescents are often independent-minded and attuned to exerting that independence, but are at the same time prone to pressure from peers.

- Adolescents are frequently intellectually able to perform at the highest levels, yet they are not often required to move beyond lower-order thinking skills to such cognitive tasks as application, analysis, synthesis, or evaluation, nor even exposed to these cognitive tasks.

Scholarship shows that the successful middle school and high school classroom teacher:

- Places students at the center of the learning process.

- Develops lessons and learning activities that are designed to appeal to young adolescents.

- Encourages and incorporates into teaching student-generated questions and concerns.

- Accommodates and builds upon diverse learning styles, abilities, and prior knowledge.

- Cultivates multiple forms of intelligence.

- Presents a challenging and relevant curriculum that develops students' ability to hypothesize, organize data to solve issues and answer questions, and encourages sophisticated but varied student expressions of their learning.

Secondary social studies classrooms are particularly suited to the development of civic education as students increasingly are being asked to assume responsibility for themselves and to be aware of their social and interpersonal relations. Fostering this civic education involves allowing students to debate, role-play, discuss, and examine their own and society's values and expectations. Studies show that reliance on traditional teaching methods results in students who are primarily involved in lower-level thinking.

Bloom's Taxonomy

When considering the fashioning of developmentally-appropriate social studies lessons, it is important to recall Benjamin Bloom's hierarchy of thinking and reasoning skills. Studies show that the bulk of middle school and high school social studies teaching relies heavily on traditional methods of instruction (lecture and guided discussion). Moreover, too much instruction remains directed at lower-order thinking skills. While at all grade levels it is possible, indeed vital, to engage students at all levels of Bloom's taxonomy, in the middle school and high school social studies classroom the opportunity to reach students with lessons that move beyond the lower-order thinking skills is vital to the successful classroom and teacher.

Knowledge. Simple recall or recognition of learned material. **Student action:** Identify, define, list, label, describe.

Comprehension. Moving beyond memorization. **Student action:** Explain, rewrite, paraphrase, summarize.

Application. Taking learned material and using to accomplish an objective. **Student action:** Use, operate, solve, show, prepare, determine.

Analysis. Breaking down complex material into component parts and explaining their relationship to the whole. **Student action**: Distinguish, separate, break down, compare, show cause-effect, analyze.

Synthesis: Combining previous knowledge to form new wholes. **Student action:** Compose, organize, arrange, construct, plan, design.

Evaluation. Making judgments on the value of an idea, approach or solution to a problem. **Student action:** Appraise, justify, critique, evaluate.

Bloom's Taxonomy can serve as a guide for planning developmentally-appropriate lessons for social studies teachers.

> **Competency 026 Descriptive Statement C.** The beginning teacher understands the appropriate use of technology as a tool for learning and communicating social studies concepts and provides instruction on how to locate, retrieve and retain content-related information from a range of texts and technologies.

Technology is developing at a rapid pace. Much of this technological evolution carries great promise for teachers and students.

Information Technology and Inquiry-Based Learning

Inquiry-based learning in the social studies classroom has been enormously enhanced by the availability of the Internet and the wealth of primary and secondary sources that are easily accessible.

For the history teacher, a wealth of online sources can be brought into the classroom. For example, a collection of Thomas Jefferson's papers are accessible from the Massachusetts Historical Society at *https://www.masshist.org/thomasjeffersonpapers/*. There a teacher could have students compare a manuscript copy of the Declaration of Independence with the published version. Or, students could be directed to *Jefferson's Farm Book* at the following site: *https://www.masshist. org/thomasjeffersonpapers/farm/*. The *Farm Book* offers an opportunity to explore the lives of Jefferson's many enslaved African Americans. A tool that provides a wealth of primary sources that students and teachers can access is Google Books Advanced Search engine. A large number of books published before the 1920s are available through this site. The number of primary sources that modern information technology makes available allows teachers to increasingly escape the textbook and engage students directly with inquiry-based learning.

Economics classes can also draw on the voluminous quantity of local, state, and federal government reporting data to engage real-world issues in economics. Government teachers who are not guiding their students through current political leaders' use of Twitter, Facebook, and other social media platforms to get their message out are missing a golden opportunity to engage their students with primary sources that political scientists will be studying for generations to come. And this includes much more than just the president's tweets. Tracking local or national government officials' or institution's Twitter feed engages students directly in the national political dialogue in ways that were impossible only a few years ago. Twitter and Facebook also provide platforms for students to express their civic sensibilities.

By using spreadsheet software, such as Excel, students can be drawn into real-world analyses of economic problems and issues. For example, students might be given the data for a supply schedule or a demand schedule, which they could enter into an Excel spreadsheet before using its graphing functions to develop supply and demand curves. Similarly, government students should be encouraged to develop research questions that can be tested using student-developed spreadsheets, databases, etc.

Geography classrooms may also draw on the wide range of information technologies available to enhance student inquiry. For example, students might be asked to collect weather data from the National Oceanic and Atmospheric Administration (NOAA) website or from more local weather sites. A spreadsheet can be used to compile and graph data. Geographic Information System (GIS) mapping programs can be used to allow students to plot the results of any number of studies and to create maps of their findings.

Information Technology and Acquiring Secondary Source Material

Up-to-date information in newspapers, statistical analyses, reports, and images are widely available through Google Books, Google Scholar, and local university and public libraries. Reliable news sources and scholarly material have never been more accessible. Of course, the teacher's responsibility to prepare students to evaluate sources critically for bias, distortion, and outright fabrication has never been greater. The days are thankfully over when a term paper required only six to 10 sources and students had only the public library or their own school library as resources.

YouTube may be one of the most striking educational platforms, if used carefully. Most of us have by now learned a recipe from YouTube, or followed the instructions on a YouTube video to fix a car or complete a do-it-yourself home project. The same skills training is available for social studies teachers and their students. The "Crash Course" video series is only one of the many videos that provide content materials for the classroom. Podcasts also provide outstanding sources of content material. World history teachers would be well-advised to subscribe to the BBC Channel 4's "In Our Time" podcasts. These secondary sources should, however, be approached with the same critical thinking skills that are applied to other materials.

Communication Technologies and Feedback

Information technologies provide new tools for encouraging interaction within and beyond the classroom. They also provide new means for informal assessment and immediate feedback. Social media platforms like Twitter and Facebook are two tools that can be used in this fashion.

Twitter can also provide a place for teachers to assess and receive feedback from students about their learning. At the conclusion of a class, for example, students might be asked to type a very brief summary of their learning or pose questions they might have not had the opportunity or confidence to pose aloud.

There are numerous apps that teachers can use for acquiring feedback from students. A partial list includes Poll Everywhere, Polldaddy, Doodle, Plickers, Socrative, and Google Forms. Feedback can be gathered mid-class, or assigned at the end of class time or as homework. In most of these platforms, teachers or other users can create questions in a variety of formats, get answers in real time, and, if desired, project student responses as a tool to elicit further discussion. Some of these platforms require subscriptions, while some are free. Many offer paid versions with more features.

Internet Literacy

While today's middle school and high school students are at ease with their smartphones, tablets, and computers and are used to finding information on the internet, they often lack sophistication in their ability to conduct internet searches or to evaluate sources and sites. This is perhaps one of the most pressing demands of today's secondary schoolteachers: helping students evaluate websites and carry out effective searches for good sources of information.

According to Andrew P. Johnson, a Minnesota educator, there are six types of websites: informational sites, news sites, advocacy sites, business or marketing sites, resource sites, and personal websites. Regardless of their purpose, Johnson argues that students need to learn to assess the quality and credibility of the information they find there. This is accomplished by evaluating the authority (expertise, experience, and credibility), accuracy, objectivity, currency (how recent is the information), and coverage (completeness) of the site.[1]

> **Competency 026 Descriptive Statement D.** The beginning teacher uses a variety of instructional strategies to ensure all students' reading comprehension of content-related texts, including helping students link the content of texts to their lives and connect related ideas across different texts.

Too often, reading instruction is thought to be the responsibility of elementary school educators, rather than those at the middle school or secondary school level. Reading is also mistakenly thought to be a skill that is disconnected from subject matter. Social studies teachers often assume that their responsibility is to teach content, not literacy. When students fail to understand their textbooks or fail to work their way through primary or secondary sources, often middle school and high school teachers (and college professors, to be fair) point a disapproving finger at parents and elementary school teachers, or at English teachers, blaming them for this failure. Too often, students are prepared only for leisure or pleasure reading. After they leave elementary school and certainly in their adult lives, estimates are that only 10 percent of reading is done for pleasure or as a leisure-time pursuit. Instead, informational reading makes up the vast majority of reading that high school and college age readers will do. This makes learning to read social studies materials (or other content area texts) critical to lifelong learning.

Reading experts agree that successful reading in the content area requires instruction in reading strategies that address:

1. the reader and his or her background experience, prior knowledge of the subject matter, and such things as motivation, mental imagery, goal-setting, metacognition, etc.;

2. the learning context and environment (i.e. atmosphere, comfort, cooperative learning, tasks, etc.); and

3. the text itself, its characteristics, structure, and other features.

---

[1] Andrew P. Johnson, *Making Connections in Elementary and Middle School Social Studies* (Los Angeles: Sage, 2010), pp. 304–306.

Preparing Learners

Many psychologists argue that learning takes place when learners are able to relate new information to already known information by situating that new information in a mental blueprint or map that learning theorists call a **schema** (plural, **schemata**).

Effective readers of social studies content bring their existing knowledge to bear to make sense of their reading. They draw inferences, generate questions, and make predictions about what they are reading. They situate what they are reading within schemata or patterns of thought that organize information and the relations between that information. To enable students to incorporate the new vocabulary and concepts they encounter in textbooks or in other reading material, social studies teachers must help students activate their prior knowledge, personal experiences, prior reading, and other contexts that have already been incorporated into their respective schemata.

Social studies teachers must also be aware of which students have low background knowledge of the material before students are asked to engage textual material. This will enable teachers to help students build a frame within which to place new and unfamiliar information. Incorrect prior knowledge must also be identified and responded to before students will be capable of effectively learning from new materials.

To prepare learners for reading new material a number of the following strategies can be used.

- Brainstorming ideas associated with a topic

- Surveying a passage or text, noting cues to the meaning of the text including headings, bold print, definitions, images, etc.

- Framing questions about the topic to be read

- Identifying problems or issues in a text that require decision-making or problem-solving responses

- Developing organizers for use in reading and note-taking (outlines, content maps, information webs, etc.)

To improve students' interaction with texts requires not only engaging students' background knowledge, but also a conscientious effort to **build background knowledge**. There are a number of methods that will help accomplish this objective.

- **A multi-text strategy.** Using a variety of texts and trade books that are matched to students reading abilities to introduce textbook material has the benefit of tailoring reading assignments to student abilities. It also has the advantage of providing different perspectives on the same subject matter to students.

- **Rewrites.** Before students read an assigned text, a short rewrite or summary of the text done by the teacher will provide students with a capsule of the longer document or source. This rewrite or summary is particularly useful when teachers are using longer primary source materials that contain antiquated or technical language. Preparing this rewrite or summary is obviously time-consuming, but even a short summation or bulleted list that students can use to build connections will yield dividends.

- **Graphic organizers.** Graphic organizers promote visual literacy as well as textual literacy. Such tools, whether developed by the teacher, the whole class, or students (in group work), can aid students as they work their own way through unfamiliar or difficult texts. Graphic organizers can include concept maps, outlines, and other similar tools.

Motivation

An important factor in successful reading of social studies content is the level of motivation or interest students have in the material. Even capable readers are less able to understand and think about a subject they are not interested in.

Climate for Reading

For active, critical reading to be successful, teachers must foster a climate where students are encouraged to participate not just in reading, but in discussions of the reading as well. Classroom settings are also important. Room temperature, lighting, furniture arrangement, etc. all impact the learning and reading process. Creating a sense of acceptance to promote learning even by small things like classroom arrangement will contribute significantly to learning.

Cooperative learning groups, whether informal, formal, or base groups, encourage interdependence of readers, group processing, and individual and group accountability that encourage students to approach a text with less intimidation. Comprehension and learning are not simply individual processes, but take place in social contexts. Groups that allow students to articulate ideas and construct meanings will result in greater learning and comprehension of reading.

Text Structure and Organization

Reading comprehension is enhanced when teachers help students understand how texts are organized or presented. Unpacking a text's structure and organization are vital steps to successful reading of social studies content.

Effective social studies readers are adept in all of the following skills:

- Locating key information, discriminating between important and unimportant information

- Recalling relevant information from elsewhere within the text or from other sources

- Connecting new information with prior knowledge

- Reframing new knowledge in old schema or revising schema to adapt to new knowledge

- Recalling information previously read

Teachers can assist students in improving their ability to read effectively by helping them know the difference between narrative texts and informational texts, and how each typically organizes information.

Narrative texts, not surprisingly, tell a story (either fictional or fact-based). Narratives are most often written sequentially, though literary devices such as flashbacks may alter that sequential nature. History texts, for example, are often written in narrative form. Biography, autobiography, firsthand narratives, and period literature provide teachers with materials that are useful to teach reading of narrative texts.

Informational texts or expository texts such as newspaper articles, editorials, textbook chapters, scholarly articles, and other informational texts are usually written to inform or argue a particular position. Informational texts follow a number of predictable patterns. Students who recognize the organizational pattern of a text will be better able to extract meaningful information from them.

These patterns include the following:

- **Chronological sequencing.** Texts are structured in chronological or logical order.

- **Analysis.** Analysis investigates the relationship between *superordinate information,* such as a higher-order concept, theory, or idea, with *subordinate information,* such as facts or evidence that support that higher order or superordinate point.

- **Comparison/contrast.** Texts are structured to emphasize similarities or differences among facts, events, concepts, authors, or other pertinent factors.

- **Concept-definition.** Texts are structured to explain the meaning of a concept. This requires using synonyms, analogies, etc.

- **Description.** Descriptive writing is a listing or compilation of facts or events (subordinate information) that serve to characterize a concept, individual, event, etc.

- **Analogy or example.** Often texts use analogy or example to establish a preparatory set for readers. Social studies texts commonly use this technique. An example or analogy (the subordinate information) is used to signify a wider argument.

- **Generalization/principle.** Much expository writing in the social sciences establishes a theory, generalization, or principle. The superordinate information or theoretical position is explained and supported by subordinate information.

- **Cause-Effect.** Cause-and-effect writing proceeds from a cause or an effect, the superordinate information, and relates either to subordinate information, either the consequences of a cause, or the causes of an event or condition.

The most common textual structures in the social studies are cause/effect, description, comparison/contrast, and analysis. Not all social studies disciplines rely on these text structures to the same degree. For example, world history texts emphasize chronological sequencing, comparison/contrast, analysis, and cause-effect writing. United States history texts will have more chronological sequencing, analysis, description, and cause-effect writing. Economics textbooks will emphasize concept-definition, cause-effect, analogy or example, and generalization/principle structures. It is important for students and teachers to recognize the structures most common to each discipline and to recognize them when they encounter them in the course of a reading.

Approaching the Text

Students need to understand not only how expository or informational texts are structured, but how content is organized in these kinds of texts. Where narrative texts generally lead the reader sequentially through a series of events, expository writing depends upon the presentation of **superordinate information** supported by **subordinate information.** A traditional essay format, for example, begins with an introductory paragraph in which a **thesis** is identified and subordinate arguments that support that thesis are listed. The body paragraphs of the essay then restate the subordinate argument or points and support them with evidentiary statements. These evidentiary statements are merely the building blocks that sustain the subordinate points, which in turn support the thesis. Book-length expository writing builds a more extensive argument on a similar but expanded scaffold.

Teaching students to "unpack" the superordinate and subordinate information and identify the thesis or overarching argument and distinguish it from the supporting arguments and the evidence is critical to successful reading (and writing) in the social studies.

This can be accomplished using a number of tools:

- **Concept mapping.** This is a useful tool for helping readers distinguish superordinate points from subordinate points, and evidence from argument. The following is one model for constructing a concept map of a text:

  ▶ Identify the main idea of a content passage and summarize that idea, writing it in the center of a piece of paper.

  ▶ Circle that restated main idea.

  ▶ Identify and note subordinate points. (In textbooks, these are often subheadings).

  ▶ Connect the subordinate arguments to the main idea.

  ▶ Identify supporting details or evidentiary statements and note them on the same paper (whiteboard, etc.)

- **Formal or Informal Outlines.** Formal and informal outlines, like concept mapping, help readers differentiate between main ideas, subordinate points, evidence, and conclusions.

- **Directed Reading-Thinking Activities** (or SQRRR——that is, **s**urvey, **q**uestion, **r**ead, **re**cite, and **r**eview—method).

  ▸ **Survey** or preview a segment of text. (Titles, Introductions, Subtitles, Pictures, Charts, Maps, Graphs, Sidebars, Vocabulary, Summary or Conclusion, and End-of-chapter questions.

  ▸ **Question**.

    — What do students know after surveying the text?

    — What do they need to learn?

    — What kind of expository writing form is being followed?

    — Transform superordinate and subordinate points into question form and posit possible answers.

    — What kinds of evidence might be needed to prove superordinate points? Subordinate points?

  ▸ **Read.** Either individually or in groups, read selected sections of the text.

  ▸ **Recite.** Determine answers to the questions raised. Have students defend their inferences by citing references to the text.

  ▸ **Review (or Reflection).** Both within the classroom and outside of it, teachers need to model reflection and review of information and concepts encountered in primary or secondary sources. This is where students become lifelong learners, active readers, and critical thinkers.

Competency 026 Descriptive Statement E. The beginning teacher provides instruction on how to locate the meanings and pronunciations of unfamiliar content-related words using appropriate sources, such as dictionaries, thesauruses, atlases, and glossaries.

Social studies literacy requires the development of a content area vocabulary that enables increasingly sophisticated understanding of the concepts and skills of the social studies. In middle school and then high school social studies classrooms, literacy instruction transitions from language learning and basic vocabulary to the development of language skills necessary to the understanding specialized concepts and content. The language-learning strategies students have employed in early grades do not always transfer to content-area vocabulary acquisition and reading. Students who do not become proficient in content-related vocabulary acquisition will struggle gaining comprehension from textbooks and social studies materials.

Acquisition of content-area vocabulary is strongly associated with reading comprehension. A reader who knows more vocabulary from economics, sociology, geography, or the other social studies is likely to be better able to read and comprehend social studies texts. A reader who lacks that vocabulary, or struggles with it, will be less able to comprehend texts and even less likely to learn new content-area vocabulary.

When using a textbook, students of course can take advantage of vocabulary that is bolded with definitions located in the sidebars of a chapter's pages. Rather than introduce these separately or without context, it is useful to group them in ways that bring out connections and connect them to prior knowledge. Concept maps are useful ways to illustrate these connections. Relating new words to already familiar concepts and vocabulary is vital to students' ability to build content-area vocabulary. As often, however, in the social studies, students will come even to college or high school classes with little background knowledge.

Vocabulary of Scholarly Argument

Content-related texts are typically written to inform or persuade. Usually, such texts are organized along a number of predictable lines. There are a number of clue words that students should recognize as signals. It is useful for students to not only recognize their use in others' writing, but also to begin to employ these signal words in their own writing.

1. **Chronological sequence.** These texts structure their narratives in logical sequences, most often in chronological order. **Cues:** *after, afterward, as soon as, before, during, finally, first, following, immediately, initially, later, meanwhile, next, not long after, now, on (date), preceding, second, soon, then, third, today, until, when*

2. **Comparison/contrast.** Comparative writing juxtaposes two or more topics and highlights similarities and/or differences. **Cues:** *although, as well as, as opposed to, both, but, compared with, different from, either...or, even though, however, instead of, in common, on the other hand, otherwise, similar to, similarly, still, yet.*

3. **Concept/Definition.** Social studies texts often introduce new terminology or concepts and endeavor to define their use. **Cues:** *for instance, in other words, is characterized by, put another way, refers to, that is, thus, usually*

4. **Description.** Social studies questions often elicit descriptive answers. **Cues:** *above, across, along, appears to be, as in, behind, below, beside, between, down, in back of, in front of, looks like, near, on top of, onto, outside, over, such as, to the right/left, under*

5. **Generalization/Principle.** Social scientists often scaffold their arguments around the establishment of a generalization or principle that explains data or phenomena they are studying. **Cues:** *additionally, always, because of, clearly, conclusively, first, for instance, for example, furthermore, generally, however, if . . . then, in fact, it could be argued that, moreover, most convincing, never, not only . . . but also, often, second, therefore, third, truly, typically*

6. **Process or Cause-Effect.** Social studies writing frequently outlines processes or cause-effect relationships. **Cues:** *accordingly, as a result of, because, begins with, consequently, effects of, finally, first, for this reason, how to, how, if . . . then, in order to, is caused by, leads or is lead to, may be due to, next, so that, steps involved, therefore, thus, when . . . then.*[2]

Understanding what the purpose of a passage is by recognizing the kind of language used in different types of expository writing is an important way for students to make sense of their reading.

Context Clues

How do students figure out the meanings of words they have not encountered before, or don't know? Often, they must rely on context clues that are within the text itself. The most common context clues include the following:

- **Definition.** Often when writers introduce terms that readers might find unfamiliar, they include a brief description or definition. *Example*: The Roman *spata,* or broadsword, was the principal weapon of the Roman army's legions.

- **Synonym or Antonym.** (Comparison/Contrast). New vocabulary is often accompanied by either a synonym or an antonym. *Example:* The Republican Party of the 1890s favored strong protective tariffs, while the Democrats objected to high import taxes.

- **Description.** Often, sentences following an unfamiliar word will provide a brief description of the meaning of the word. *Example*: Rates of *consanguinity* in early modern French villages were often so high that most marriages had to receive clerical approval before they could take place. Until the 13th century, the Roman Catholic church forbade marriages between kin separated by as much as seven degrees of kinship.

- **Summary.** Occasionally, unfamiliar words are followed by a list that is subsumed in the category of the vocabulary item. Often, these clues begin with words like "such as," "like," or "include." *Example:* The most famous *obelisks* include the obelisk in Florence's Villa Medici, the Luxor obelisk in the Place de la Concorde in Paris, and the Washington Monument in Washington, D.C. Students who know the Washington Monument now know what an obelisk is.

Before students turn to dictionaries, they should attempt to use as many of the context clues as they can. It is important for teachers to teach these clues and model their use.

Dictionary Skills

Recognizing the context clues when encountering new vocabulary, however, only takes a student part of the way to understanding. Dictionaries are important reference tools that students

---

[2] Rachel Billmeyer and Mary Lee Barton, *Teaching Reading in the Content Areas: If Not Me, Then Who?* 2nd Edition. (Aurora, Colorado: McREL, 1998), p. 36.

should be familiarized with early on in their social studies education. Dictionaries provide the following information:

- Definitions

- Pronunciation guides

- Etymology or word origin and history

- Synonyms and antonyms

- Word usages

- Idiomatic uses

Glossaries

Glossaries serve largely the same function as dictionaries, with the exception that they are usually found in textbooks or manuals, and are intended specifically to assist readers when they encounter what the book's authors already recognize are likely unfamiliar or specialized terms. Students should be encouraged to take full advantage of this support.

Thesaurus

A thesaurus, like a dictionary, uses individual words as an entry into wider vocabulary-building. A thesaurus is best used in conjunction with writing, as it helps students build a richer range of terms with which to communicate. Like a dictionary, a thesaurus lists its base words in alphabetical order. Students should use a thesaurus when they need a more appropriate word, or when they want to add variety to their word usage. Students should be made aware of one caution when using a thesaurus: they should be sure they know the word and are certain of its appropriateness to the context for which they are writing. Otherwise, they may choose a two-dollar word to replace a five-cent word, only to find that they have not impressed their readers.

> **Competency 026 Descriptive Statement F.** The beginning teacher knows how to provide instruction that makes connections between knowledge and methods in social studies and in other content areas.

Social studies instruction benefits from being about individual behavior, human social interaction and human societies. What belongs under the umbrella of the social studies classroom? *Everything.* Academics, business leaders, and political figures often decry what has recently been called the "siloed" nature of modern institutions. When an institution is said to be "siloed," it is being described as composed of isolated departments, separated by tall institutional walls that make it difficult for individuals in the business or university to communicate with one another and to integrate their activities in meaningful ways. Social studies education (even though in high schools and colleges there are also "siloes") is an antidote to this phenomenon. Creative social studies teachers make use of music, the visual arts, drama, literature, mathematics, and the sciences in their classrooms.

Language Arts and Literature

The knowledge and skills acquired in language arts classes go hand in hand with the content and skills of the social studies. Social studies and language arts are naturally integrated. Many of the products of the social studies classroom are also useful language arts activities.

- Support-a-statement

- Oral presentations

- Oral interviews

- Essays

- Poetry

Literature addresses more clearly the ways in which humans in social situations feel, how they imagine their condition, and what they think about the world around them. Literature provides insightful primary sources for historical periods or contemporary issues. Social studies texts are most often structured as expository or persuasive materials, whereas literature allows teachers to expose students to more affective sorts of information.

Mathematics

Mathematics offers important analytical tools for each of the social studies courses and can be used to examine social studies data. Students should frequently be asked to describe ideas, concepts, ideas, or events in numerical terms, rather than simply in words or images.

Mathematics allows students and teachers to quantify ideas and to provide precise support for arguments. Inquiry exercises that require students to collect numerical data and use it to look for averages or other statistical trends that enable students to see how real-world social science research is undertaken. Developing word problems to allow students to test theories, hypotheses, or concepts from the social studies are another useful way to integrate mathematics and the social studies. The answers to mathematical problem sets that integrate social science data allow students to develop their own theories, hypotheses, or conceptual frameworks.

Natural Sciences

The natural sciences, or physical sciences, are intimately intertwined with the social studies. World history, geography, psychology are more evidently reliant on content knowledge from the sciences. World history requires that students understand the evolutionary theories that explain the development of *homo sapiens* as well as theories about the origins of agriculture. The importance of scientific understanding in ancient Greece, the Islamic world, and ancient China are also considered important areas where world history directs attention at scientific questions. Similarly, the Scientific Revolution of the 17th and 18th centuries are important touchstones in the world history curriculum.

> **Competency 026 Descriptive Statement G.** The beginning teacher provides instruction that models and promotes understanding of various points of view.

Learning in the social studies requires momentarily suspending one's own often deeply held convictions and commitments, and considering others' behavior, beliefs, actions, values, and experience on their own terms. An anthropologist who parachutes into a foreign culture and immediately begins to pass judgment on the beliefs and practices of this society will no doubt soon be unwelcome in that society. If the anthropologists' purpose is to widen his own and others' knowledge of the culture under study, that judgmental approach will make it difficult for them to understand that culture in its richness and complete context. The same can be said of the past. As the British novelist L.P. Hartley wrote, "The past is a foreign country: they do things differently there." To understand how the author of the Declaration of Independence could have written the words, "We hold these truths self-evident, that all men are created equal, that they are endowed by their Creator with certain unalienable Rights, that among these are Life, Liberty, and the pursuit of Happiness," while at the same time denying over 200 men and women these very same rights, the historian must suspend judgment in order to maximize understanding. Notice I used the words "suspend judgment." Social scientists and historians are not bound to discontinue their moral or ethical standards in order to study contemporary or past societies. Neither must teachers and students. However, in order for real learning about the past or about contemporary economic, social, and political cultures, it is vital that students and teachers briefly, to the best of their ability, step outside of their own cultural, class, racial, and religious perspective in order to understand and teach the other.

It is important to distinguish between point of view, values, and perspectives. A point of view is a position, viewpoint, opinion, preference, or argument made in support of or in opposition to an issue or policy proposal. The following statement expresses a **point of view**. "I am strongly in favor of the passage of a reparations bill that remunerates African American descendants of enslaved persons for their deprival of wages and opportunities during the 245 years of legalized slavery in territories and states of the United States of America."

Values explain why someone holds a particular point of view. Values reflect beliefs about moral, social, cultural, aesthetic, economic, environmental, or political rights and wrongs. For example: support for the reparations bill described above might result from a number of value propositions. The demand for reparations might reflect a conviction that resolution of moral wrongs cannot be accomplished without some form of restitution, and the belief that a republic cannot thrive without addressing a history of discrimination.

Perspectives are the factors that shape values. It is perhaps easiest to observe that Franklin Roosevelt supported the establishment of a social welfare net for American citizens that included a national health care system and social security. The values underlying that position are evident in many of the things that Roosevelt wrote and said during his presidency. It is clear, though, from his speech on the "Four Freedoms," given in January 1941, that Roosevelt's values were informed by his desire to sustain democracy during a historical period when totalitarian dictatorships were threatening the globe. Though other factors informed Roosevelt's point of view and values, this context must be seen as one of the perspectives that gave rise to Roosevelt's commitment to social welfare and health care.

Point of View in the Classroom

Teachers need to carefully develop lesson plans that allow students to explore points of view, values, and perspectives of historical figures, politicians, other societies, etc. Below are some suggestions on how to do this.

1. Select primary sources that reflect diverse perspectives on the topics being studied. When examining primary sources, keep in mind the discussion above in Competency 24.A and 24.B about how to approach primary sources.

2. Provide prompts that focus students' attention on words, ideas, concepts, or attitudes that historical or contemporary figures use to convey their point of view and values. Graphic organizers can be used to illustrate and record the ideas and language being used. These can be developed by students or teachers.

3. For students to understand the underlying values or perspectives of the primary source or its author will require further reading, either in classroom texts, handouts, or on the internet. Teachers will need to guide students to appropriate secondary or contrasting primary sources.

Diversity in the Classroom

Social scientists must be conscious of the point of view of their subjects and of the factors influencing their own point of view. Social studies teachers have as critical a responsibility to model and promote understanding of diverse points of view within their own classrooms. Within every classroom is a diverse population of ability, belief, learning styles, religious convictions, class and ethnic background, sexual orientation, etc. The public education classroom is a laboratory of democracy. If students do not learn to understand and even appreciate the varieties of points of view, values, and perspectives evident in their classrooms, they will be unlikely to be able to do so when they are asked to do so as adult voters and citizens.

There have historically been two schools of thought regarding how to teach culturally diverse populations: assimilation and cultural pluralism. **Assimilation** encourages students to abandon their own cultural heritage and values and assimilate into the dominant culture. The objective is to create a homogeneity. The alternative, **cultural pluralism**, emphasizes cultural diversity and heterogeneity and the embrace of others' traditions, values, and beliefs without a corresponding rejection of one's own. This is accomplished by matching teaching styles to students' learning styles, creating a classroom that values all cultures, and being attentive to students' racial, ethnic, class, and religious attitudes that might be exclusionary, while gently seeking to modify these prejudices.

How are these objectives accomplished in practice? Below are a few suggestions.

1. Use instructional materials that are gender-fair, racially and ethnically diverse, and accepting. Often, primary sources, particularly historical documents, are illustrative of past perspectives. Be sensitive to their use and incorporate them thoughtfully as "teachable moments."

2. Model and use language that is inclusionary and does not limit the possibilities of different genders, racial, ethnic, linguistic, or other groups. Be attentive to changes in such terminology. To point this out to students, ask them to think of recent controversies in the world of sport over the use of "posse" and "thug." These terms that once had little racist connotation have been called out as objectionable. If students object to the spread of "political correctness," ask them to think of how language limits the frontier of possibilities for many people and signals a lack of inclusiveness on the part of those who are not sensitive to the use of language.

3. Physically organize classrooms and select cooperative groups in ways that are inclusive and break down barriers, rather than in ways that exclude or perpetuate social barriers.

4. The social studies provide opportunities to recall historical or contemporary role models or exemplars. Be sure to select role models from different genders and sexual orientations, as well as from a diversity of racial, ethnic, and linguistic communities. Whenever possible, bring in these perspectives to the classroom.

5. Establish zero-tolerance for sexual harassment; racial, ethnic, or linguistic belittlement; or verbal bullying.

Competency 026 Descriptive Statement H. The beginning teacher demonstrates knowledge of forms of assessment appropriate for evaluating students' progress and needs in social studies.

In the ideal classroom, **assessment** is a continuous cycle of activities designed to discover students' strengths and weaknesses. The assessment cycle must also be designed to evaluate your own teaching. Assessment involves the collection of data to see how well students are doing and how well the teacher is doing in helping students learn.

Written tests include the **standardized tests** employed by the state to assess student success and the performance of teachers and school districts. Standardized tests include **norm-referenced tests**, which describe student performance relative to a group norm, and **criterion-referenced tests**, which measure a student's performance in comparison to predetermined curriculum standards. Advanced Placement exams, the SAT, LSAT, ACT, GRE, and other similar tests are norm-referenced. The **TExES 7–12 Social Studies exam** is a **criterion-referenced test,** as are the STAAR exams taken by Texas schoolchildren. The STAAR tests determine how well students meet the curriculum standards in the Texas Essential Knowledge and Skills (TEKS).

There are a variety of ways for teachers to assess student performance besides relying on standardized tests. Classroom assessment may be divided into three broad categories of evaluation: diagnostic assessment, formative assessment, and summative assessment.

Diagnostic Assessment

Teachers cannot fly blind in the classroom. They need to have an understanding of what content students already know, what skills they possess, and what teaching strategies would best enable their students' success. Assessment that serves diagnostic or needs-assessment purposes is critical to meeting students where they are.

Formative Assessment

Classroom assessment of a formative nature focuses on improving student motivation and learning. Formative assessment tools provide teachers with a check for student understanding that helps them make decisions about their own teaching strategies. The teacher is therefore one important audience for formative assessment. Students must also be made to understand that formative assessment allows them to evaluate their own learning to see where their own strengths and weaknesses lie. Formative assessment works best when it occurs soon after the learning process (usually within one to two days), when it gives feedback on students' work, and when it measures an identifiable criterion or standard.

Summative Assessment

Summative assessment examines a student's level of achievement of desired learning goals and standards. Summative assessment usually occurs at the end of an instructional unit or period. Summative assessment also is an effort to document the degree to which students have learned the assigned content. Most often summative assessments are tests, quizzes, reports, projects, or other written assignments.

Summative assessments should provide the teacher with useful information tied to the learning objectives of the class that provide meaningful assessment of the students' mastery of critical concepts and skills. The best summative assessments measure what they are supposed to measure. Testing students' understanding of changing boarders, for example, by asking them to draw a map, may reflect less their understanding of the territorial changes than their ability to draw. Multiple-choice exams as often test students' ability to read or their deductive reasoning and persistence than their mastery of the desired content. Summative assessments must also be reliable and fair.

Teacher Reflection on Social Studies Assessment

In the social studies classroom, assessment should reflect thoughtful answers to the following questions:

1. Does my assessment test what is really important for students to know and be able to do?

2. Are my assessments mere measures of student recall of facts, or do they help students demonstrate mastery of social studies skills?

3. Are my assessment tools providing a more full and real-world measure of student ability, knowledge, motivation, and skills than that provided by multiple-choice exams and quizzes?

4. Do my assessment tools motivate students (and more as a carrot than a stick)?

5. Do assessments help students learn to reflect on their own learning and consider how to improve their work and produce higher-quality products?

6. Are my assessments there to fill a gradebook, or are they designed to hold students accountable for quality work?

Authentic Assessment

Authentic assessment refers to assessment tools that require students to demonstrate their mastery of skills and content knowledge in real-world ways. Such assessment requires collecting a variety of data from students, rather than single snapshots. Authentic assessments are undoubtedly more time-consuming to maintain and evaluate. They include such things as anecdotal records or written observations or field notes that describe what a teacher is seeing in their classroom. Keeping a journal of observations of students as they work in small groups might be one form of authentic assessment. Authentic assessment methods also incorporate checklists and/or rubrics.

Portfolios

As mentioned earlier in this chapter but worth repeating here, the educational reformer John Dewey famously said, "Learning is learning to think." Learning to think is rarely demonstrated in multiple-choice tests. Social studies learning, just as clearly as learning in mathematics and the natural sciences, should be guided by a spirit of inquiry, problem-solving, and decision-making. One of the important tools of "authentic assessment" is the portfolio, which documents student performance on real-world tasks; demonstrates how students solve problems; illustrates both students' individual and group products; and permits students to demonstrate their abilities and mastery in a variety of forms.

Portfolios generally include a collection of students' actual work over time. This enables students to put together full records of their own products that demonstrate growth and learning over time. How such portfolios are evaluated and what exactly is included in a portfolio will vary with the classroom and discipline.

Checklists provide another means of collecting data about student behavior and skill acquisition. These can also allow students to reflect on their own learning and skill development. For example, students can use a checklist (perhaps combined with a rating scale) that allows students to reflect on their level of skill competency or mastery of content knowledge. Having students complete such checklists encourages students to be more self-reflective of their learning. Teacher-completed checklists are another tool that can be used to assess student learning and give feedback.

Rubrics

Rubrics are also vital to competent assessment. A rubric is a scoring guide that identifies the specific skills or attributes a teacher hopes to see from students. A rubric is particularly useful for improving consistency in grading. It also provides students more feedback than do checklists, though at a cost in time spent constructing clear and well-framed rubrics. There are many rubrics available online, which can be relatively quickly adapted to specific skills and assignments.

"I-Learned" Statements

"I-learned" statements involve the surprisingly simple assessment tool of just asking students what they learned about a particular topic. These can be collected at the end of each class period or unit. These statements can also be graphically illustrated or through "I-learned" concept maps that allow students who better express their learning visually to do so.

Performance-based learning

Performance-based learning requires that students demonstrate mastery of a set of skills. This method of assessment is most useful in evaluating such things as students' abilities to read a graph, chart, or map, or to demonstrate other social studies skills. Performance-based assessment should not be used as a measure of prior knowledge, but should be employed once a teacher has taught and given students opportunities to practice a skill. Teachers may use such things as a product, performance, or ratings checklist to evaluate a student's mastery of the skill. For example, an economics teacher interested in students' ability to graph supply and demand curves or production possibilities curves might construct an assignment where students are given pricing and quantity data for a given product. The students demonstrate their mastery of the skill by developing a supply schedule and a demand schedule, and then graph this data using an Excel spreadsheet. Their ability to accomplish this task would be a performance-based assessment of that skill mastery.

Competency 026 Descriptive Statement I. The beginning teacher uses multiple forms of assessment and knowledge of the TEKS to determine students' progress and needs and to help plan instruction in social studies (e.g., Freedom Week).

The State of Texas Assessments of Academic Readiness (STAAR) is the state's current assessment program (initiated in the 2011–2012 school year) used to measure student progress and knowledge of the TEKS. Every STAAR question is directly aligned to the TEKS for the grade/ subject or course being assessed. The STAAR includes the operational STAAR test, a STAAR test for Spanish-language speakers, a linguistically-accommodated version, and one for students who require other accommodations.

The STAAR for middle school social studies students is administered at the end of grade 8 and includes questions principally from United States history before 1877.

The only social studies course with a required end-of-course (EOC) exam is the United States History STAAR for high school students. Unlike the AP exams, the History STAAR assesses student understanding of United States history since 1877. Released tests for each of these exams can be found at the TEA website.

The questions in these released exams are not only a good resource to teachers interested in helping their students do well on the test; they are also likely to provide additional refreshers for prospective teachers readying themselves to take the TExES Social Studies 7–12 test. For the STAAR tests, students are evaluated on their ability to meet the performance standards established in the TEKS. Students are identified as follows:

- Masters Grade Level

- Meets Grade Level

- Approaches Grade Level

- Did not meet Grade Level

For Language Arts and Mathematics for the lower grades, there are benchmark tests or pre-assessments that serve diagnostic purposes and provide teachers with opportunities to reteach or tailor their lessons to specific classroom or individual weaknesses. However, nothing exists with the same function for the Social Studies STAAR or the United States History End-of-Course exam.

Teachers must therefore develop a number of effective assessment measures and mechanisms to evaluate the progress of their students. These require that teachers carefully address the TEKS in their teaching and integrate the TEKS in their unit objectives, lesson planning, and review strategies.

Freedom Week

"Freedom Week" is an official holiday celebrated by Arkansas, Florida, Kansas, Oklahoma, and Texas. Kansas and Texas commemorate this holiday during the week of September 17, the date the United States Constitution was signed. The placement of this commemoration in the curriculum is designed specifically to single out the country's origins through the use of the nation's founding documents.

TExES Social Studies 7–12
Practice Test 1

Practice Test 1 Answer Sheet

1. Ⓐ Ⓑ Ⓒ Ⓓ
2. Ⓐ Ⓑ Ⓒ Ⓓ
3. Ⓐ Ⓑ Ⓒ Ⓓ
4. Ⓐ Ⓑ Ⓒ Ⓓ
5. Ⓐ Ⓑ Ⓒ Ⓓ
6. Ⓐ Ⓑ Ⓒ Ⓓ
7. Ⓐ Ⓑ Ⓒ Ⓓ
8. Ⓐ Ⓑ Ⓒ Ⓓ
9. Ⓐ Ⓑ Ⓒ Ⓓ
10. Ⓐ Ⓑ Ⓒ Ⓓ
11. Ⓐ Ⓑ Ⓒ Ⓓ
12. Ⓐ Ⓑ Ⓒ Ⓓ
13. Ⓐ Ⓑ Ⓒ Ⓓ
14. Ⓐ Ⓑ Ⓒ Ⓓ
15. Ⓐ Ⓑ Ⓒ Ⓓ
16. Ⓐ Ⓑ Ⓒ Ⓓ
17. Ⓐ Ⓑ Ⓒ Ⓓ
18. Ⓐ Ⓑ Ⓒ Ⓓ
19. Ⓐ Ⓑ Ⓒ Ⓓ
20. Ⓐ Ⓑ Ⓒ Ⓓ
21. Ⓐ Ⓑ Ⓒ Ⓓ
22. Ⓐ Ⓑ Ⓒ Ⓓ
23. Ⓐ Ⓑ Ⓒ Ⓓ
24. Ⓐ Ⓑ Ⓒ Ⓓ
25. Ⓐ Ⓑ Ⓒ Ⓓ
26. Ⓐ Ⓑ Ⓒ Ⓓ
27. Ⓐ Ⓑ Ⓒ Ⓓ
28. Ⓐ Ⓑ Ⓒ Ⓓ
29. Ⓐ Ⓑ Ⓒ Ⓓ
30. Ⓐ Ⓑ Ⓒ Ⓓ
31. Ⓐ Ⓑ Ⓒ Ⓓ
32. Ⓐ Ⓑ Ⓒ Ⓓ
33. Ⓐ Ⓑ Ⓒ Ⓓ
34. Ⓐ Ⓑ Ⓒ Ⓓ
35. Ⓐ Ⓑ Ⓒ Ⓓ

36. Ⓐ Ⓑ Ⓒ Ⓓ
37. Ⓐ Ⓑ Ⓒ Ⓓ
38. Ⓐ Ⓑ Ⓒ Ⓓ
39. Ⓐ Ⓑ Ⓒ Ⓓ
40. Ⓐ Ⓑ Ⓒ Ⓓ
41. Ⓐ Ⓑ Ⓒ Ⓓ
42. Ⓐ Ⓑ Ⓒ Ⓓ
43. Ⓐ Ⓑ Ⓒ Ⓓ
44. Ⓐ Ⓑ Ⓒ Ⓓ
45. Ⓐ Ⓑ Ⓒ Ⓓ
46. Ⓐ Ⓑ Ⓒ Ⓓ
47. Ⓐ Ⓑ Ⓒ Ⓓ
48. Ⓐ Ⓑ Ⓒ Ⓓ
49. Ⓐ Ⓑ Ⓒ Ⓓ
50. Ⓐ Ⓑ Ⓒ Ⓓ
51. Ⓐ Ⓑ Ⓒ Ⓓ
52. Ⓐ Ⓑ Ⓒ Ⓓ
53. Ⓐ Ⓑ Ⓒ Ⓓ
54. Ⓐ Ⓑ Ⓒ Ⓓ
55. Ⓐ Ⓑ Ⓒ Ⓓ
56. Ⓐ Ⓑ Ⓒ Ⓓ
57. Ⓐ Ⓑ Ⓒ Ⓓ
58. Ⓐ Ⓑ Ⓒ Ⓓ
59. Ⓐ Ⓑ Ⓒ Ⓓ
60. Ⓐ Ⓑ Ⓒ Ⓓ
61. Ⓐ Ⓑ Ⓒ Ⓓ
62. Ⓐ Ⓑ Ⓒ Ⓓ
63. Ⓐ Ⓑ Ⓒ Ⓓ
64. Ⓐ Ⓑ Ⓒ Ⓓ
65. Ⓐ Ⓑ Ⓒ Ⓓ
66. Ⓐ Ⓑ Ⓒ Ⓓ
67. Ⓐ Ⓑ Ⓒ Ⓓ
68. Ⓐ Ⓑ Ⓒ Ⓓ
69. Ⓐ Ⓑ Ⓒ Ⓓ
70. Ⓐ Ⓑ Ⓒ Ⓓ

71. Ⓐ Ⓑ Ⓒ Ⓓ
72. Ⓐ Ⓑ Ⓒ Ⓓ
73. Ⓐ Ⓑ Ⓒ Ⓓ
74. Ⓐ Ⓑ Ⓒ Ⓓ
75. Ⓐ Ⓑ Ⓒ Ⓓ
76. Ⓐ Ⓑ Ⓒ Ⓓ
77. Ⓐ Ⓑ Ⓒ Ⓓ
78. Ⓐ Ⓑ Ⓒ Ⓓ
79. Ⓐ Ⓑ Ⓒ Ⓓ
80. Ⓐ Ⓑ Ⓒ Ⓓ
81. Ⓐ Ⓑ Ⓒ Ⓓ
82. Ⓐ Ⓑ Ⓒ Ⓓ
83. Ⓐ Ⓑ Ⓒ Ⓓ
84. Ⓐ Ⓑ Ⓒ Ⓓ
85. Ⓐ Ⓑ Ⓒ Ⓓ
86. Ⓐ Ⓑ Ⓒ Ⓓ
87. Ⓐ Ⓑ Ⓒ Ⓓ
88. Ⓐ Ⓑ Ⓒ Ⓓ
89. Ⓐ Ⓑ Ⓒ Ⓓ
90. Ⓐ Ⓑ Ⓒ Ⓓ
91. Ⓐ Ⓑ Ⓒ Ⓓ
92. Ⓐ Ⓑ Ⓒ Ⓓ
93. Ⓐ Ⓑ Ⓒ Ⓓ
94. Ⓐ Ⓑ Ⓒ Ⓓ
95. Ⓐ Ⓑ Ⓒ Ⓓ
96. Ⓐ Ⓑ Ⓒ Ⓓ
97. Ⓐ Ⓑ Ⓒ Ⓓ
98. Ⓐ Ⓑ Ⓒ Ⓓ
99. Ⓐ Ⓑ Ⓒ Ⓓ
100. Ⓐ Ⓑ Ⓒ Ⓓ
101. Ⓐ Ⓑ Ⓒ Ⓓ
102. Ⓐ Ⓑ Ⓒ Ⓓ
103. Ⓐ Ⓑ Ⓒ Ⓓ
104. Ⓐ Ⓑ Ⓒ Ⓓ
105. Ⓐ Ⓑ Ⓒ Ⓓ

106. Ⓐ Ⓑ Ⓒ Ⓓ
107. Ⓐ Ⓑ Ⓒ Ⓓ
108. Ⓐ Ⓑ Ⓒ Ⓓ
109. Ⓐ Ⓑ Ⓒ Ⓓ
110. Ⓐ Ⓑ Ⓒ Ⓓ
111. Ⓐ Ⓑ Ⓒ Ⓓ
112. Ⓐ Ⓑ Ⓒ Ⓓ
113. Ⓐ Ⓑ Ⓒ Ⓓ
114. Ⓐ Ⓑ Ⓒ Ⓓ
115. Ⓐ Ⓑ Ⓒ Ⓓ
116. Ⓐ Ⓑ Ⓒ Ⓓ
117. Ⓐ Ⓑ Ⓒ Ⓓ
118. Ⓐ Ⓑ Ⓒ Ⓓ
119. Ⓐ Ⓑ Ⓒ Ⓓ
120. Ⓐ Ⓑ Ⓒ Ⓓ
121. Ⓐ Ⓑ Ⓒ Ⓓ
122. Ⓐ Ⓑ Ⓒ Ⓓ
123. Ⓐ Ⓑ Ⓒ Ⓓ
124. Ⓐ Ⓑ Ⓒ Ⓓ
125. Ⓐ Ⓑ Ⓒ Ⓓ
126. Ⓐ Ⓑ Ⓒ Ⓓ
127. Ⓐ Ⓑ Ⓒ Ⓓ
128. Ⓐ Ⓑ Ⓒ Ⓓ
129. Ⓐ Ⓑ Ⓒ Ⓓ
130. Ⓐ Ⓑ Ⓒ Ⓓ
131. Ⓐ Ⓑ Ⓒ Ⓓ
132. Ⓐ Ⓑ Ⓒ Ⓓ
133. Ⓐ Ⓑ Ⓒ Ⓓ
134. Ⓐ Ⓑ Ⓒ Ⓓ
135. Ⓐ Ⓑ Ⓒ Ⓓ
136. Ⓐ Ⓑ Ⓒ Ⓓ
137. Ⓐ Ⓑ Ⓒ Ⓓ
138. Ⓐ Ⓑ Ⓒ Ⓓ
139. Ⓐ Ⓑ Ⓒ Ⓓ
140. Ⓐ Ⓑ Ⓒ Ⓓ

Practice Test 1

TIME: 4 hours and 45 minutes
140 multiple-choice questions

Directions: Read each item and select the correct response or responses.

---

1. Which of the following would NOT have been a feature of hunter-gatherer societies before the Neolithic revolution?

   (A) Fishhooks and harpoons

   (B) Nets and carrying slings

   (C) Digging sticks

   (D) Grindstones

2. Ancient Mesopotamian texts were written on clay tablets using a reed stylus. Because of the wedged-shaped marks the reeds made, the writing became known as which of the following?

   (A) Hieroglyphic

   (B) Ideographic

   (C) Cuneiform

   (D) Codices

3. Which of the following best explains the legal principles underlying Hammurabi's Code?

   (A) Punishments were designed to encourage penitence, feelings of remorse for immoral behavior.

   (B) Punishments for crimes varied depending on the status of both the victim and the perpetrator.

   (C) Laws reflected the will of the people expressed by their representatives.

   (D) Laws represented the divine authority of a monotheistic deity.

Read the following excerpt from Xenophon and answer Question 4.

As for the constitution of the Athenians, their choice of this type of constitution I do not approve . . . *First* of all, then, I shall say, that at Athens the poor and the commons seem to have the advantage over the well-born and wealthy; . . . It may be said that they ought not to have allowed everyone in turn to make speeches or sit on the Council, but only those of the highest capability and quality.

Xenophon, *On the Polity of the Athenians*, ca. 424 BCE

4. Which of the following paired political systems is Xenophon referencing in the passage above?

   (A) Tyranny . . . Oligarchy

   (B) Republic . . . Dictatorship

   (C) Democracy . . . Aristocracy

   (D) Theocracy . . . Monarchy

5. In what way was Christianity's spread into Western Europe similar to Buddhism's spread into China after the second century CE?

   (A) Both took advantage of instability resulting from the weakening of the Han Empire and the Roman Empire.

   (B) Both were spread by a combination of military conquest and political coercion.

   (C) Christians appealed to traditional Roman family values while Buddhism appealed to Han China's Confucian emphasis on family loyalty.

   (D) Because both Buddhists and Christians preached the coming of a heavenly kingdom, the religions appealed to societies in transition.

6. Trade between the west coast of India and the east coast of Africa before 1450 CE was facilitated by which of the following?

   (A) The caravel sailing ship

   (B) Monsoon winds

   (C) El Niño ocean currents

   (D) Chinese tribute ships

Use the graph below to answer questions 7 and 8.

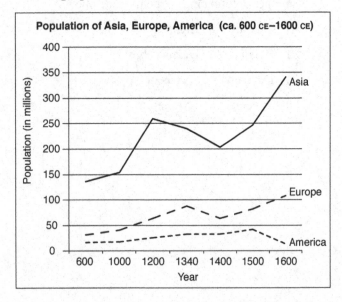

7. Which of the following best explains the changes in Asian and European population between 600 CE and 1300 CE?

   (A) Reduced levels of violence and conflict

   (B) A global warming trend and improved agricultural techniques

   (C) Improved medicine led to lower mortality rates and increased fertility

   (D) The spread of Islam increased global commercial integration and trade

8. Which of the following best explains the decline in Asian and European population between 1200 and 1400 CE?

   (A) The spread of gunpowder technology increased the lethality of warfare.

   (B) A global warming trend resulting in widespread drought and famine.

   (C) The spread of epidemic diseases including the bubonic plague.

   (D) The collapse of the Han, Gupta, and Byzantine empires created global instability.

9. Which of the following medieval European institutions were self-governing organizations that regulated labor conditions, guaranteed quality control, and limited admission to trades and commerce?

   (A) Communes

   (B) Guilds

   (C) Monasteries

   (D) Manors

10. Which of the following figures is most often described as the prototypical "Renaissance" man?

    (A) Henry VIII

    (B) Thomas Aquinas

    (C) Leonardo da Vinci

    (D) Martin Luther

11. Which of the following consequences of the development of the printing press in the middle of the 15th century contributed most to the Protestant Reformation and the Scientific Revolution?

(A) Mnemonic devices and memorization became less important to learners as education became more a matter of reading than listening.

(B) Reading became a more private and intimate practice that allowed greater independence of thought.

(C) Europeans became more confident in written texts with print's more accurate reproduction of texts.

(D) As books became a commonplace consumer item, interest in secular subject matter increased and religious devotion waned.

12. Which of the following Old World crops contributed most to the emergence of the transatlantic slave trade?

(A) Tobacco

(B) Indigo

(C) Cotton

(D) Sugar

Use the timeline below to answer Question 13.

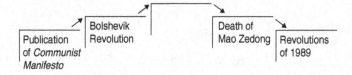

13. Which of the following best completes the timeline above showing the rise and fall of communism?

(A) Rise of the Nazi Party in Germany

(B) Chinese Revolution of 1949

(C) Lenin establishes the New Economic Policy (N.E.P.)

(D) The Korean War

Use the following excerpt to answer Question 14.

Declaration of the Rights of Man and the Citizen
(Approved by French National Assembly, August 1789)

Article I. Men are born and remain free and equal in rights. Social distinctions may be founded only upon the general good.

Article II. The aim of all political association is the preservation of the natural and imprescriptible rights of man. These rights are liberty, property, security, and resistance to oppression.

Article X. No one shall be disquieted on account of his opinions, including his religious views, provided their manifestation does not disturb the public order established by law.

Article XI. The free communication of ideas and opinions is one of the most precious of the rights of man. Every citizen may, accordingly speak, write, and print with freedom, but shall be responsible for such abuses of this freedom as shall be defined by law.

14. Article I and Article II of the *Declaration of the Rights of Man and the Citizen* are most like which of the following?

(A) Article I of the United States Constitution

(B) The English Bill of Rights

(C) The preamble of the American Declaration of Independence

(D) The Articles of Confederation

Use the timeline below to answer Question 15.

Timeline of Innovation in the Textile Industry

1733: John Kay's Flying Shuttle
1764: James Hargreaves' Spinning Jenny
1771: Richard Arkwright's Water Frame
1783: Richard Arkwright opens first steam-powered textile mill
1784: Edmund Cartwright's Power Loom
1793:

15. Which of the following would best complete the above timeline of developments in the textile industry?

    (A) James Watt's steam engine

    (B) Eli Whitney's cotton gin

    (C) Joseph Marie Jacquard's punchcard loom.

    (D) Lewis Paul's carding machine

16. Which of the following had the greatest role in turning the assassination of the heir to the throne of Austria-Hungary into a war involving all the great powers of Europe?

    (A) Competition for colonial territory between France, England, Germany, and Russia

    (B) Increases in military spending by European powers between 1871 and 1914

    (C) The growth of nationalistic fervor across Europe over the course of the 19th century

    (D) A system of alliances and joint defense agreements that divided the great powers

17. Which of the following international incidents during the Cold War seemed most likely to result in a nuclear exchange between the United States and the Soviet Union?

    (A) the Soviet blockade of Berlin (1948–1949)

    (B) the Korean War (1950–1953)

    (C) the Cuban Missile Crisis (1962)

    (D) the Soviet Union forcibly putting down Czechoslovakia's Prague Spring (1968)

Use the map below to answer Question 18.

Cold War Alliances (1975)

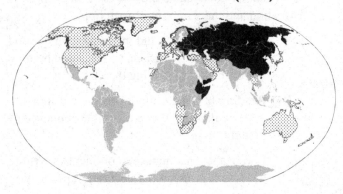

18. The countries shaded in gray in the map above represent

    (A) non-aligned nations.

    (B) capitalist nations supporting the United States.

    (C) communist nations largely favoring the Soviet Union.

    (D) nations with predominantly Muslim populations.

19. Which of the following best explains why the colony of South Carolina was founded in 1663?

    (A) To cut the French off from an important supply of furs

    (B) As a haven for England's persecuted Roman Catholic minority

    (C) To provide Barbados and other sugar islands with corn, rice, and other supplies

    (D) As a way station for ships sailing between Africa and New England

20. The oldest continuously occupied European settlement in what would become the United States is located in which of the following?

    (A) St. Augustine, Florida

    (B) Plymouth, Massachusetts

    (C) Roanoke Island, North Carolina

    (D) Santa Fe, New Mexico

21. Dissatisfied with the way in which Puritan leaders imposed their view of a Biblical Commonwealth on the Massachusetts Bay Colony, Roger Williams

    (A) charged the Puritan ministers with preaching a "covenant of works" rather than a "covenant of grace."

    (B) so criticized Massachusetts' leaders that he was finally banished to the island of Barbados, starting a wave of English settlement in the West Indies.

    (C) abandoned Massachusetts Bay Colony and fled to live among the Iroquois with whom he had long cultivated good relations.

    (D) founded the settlement of Providence Plantation (later Rhode Island) where he advocated greater religious tolerance and no established state church.

Use the excerpt below from George M. Whitefield's journal to answer Question 22.

. . . Preached to about 15,000 people in the Morning, and observed a great Melting to follow the Word.

. . . Went twice to Church, and heard myself tasked by the Commissary [representative of the Bishop of London responsible for supervising the Church of England in the American colonies] . . . who . . . exclaimed loudly against me in the Pulpit. . . . After he had done, I preached my Farewell Sermon to I believe very nearly 20,000 hearers.

The poor People were much concerned at my bidding them Farewell. And after I had taken my leave, oh how many came to my lodgings, sorrowing most of all that they were likely to see my Face no more for a long Season.—I believe 50 Negroes came to give me Thanks under God, for what had been done for their Souls."

George M. Whitefield's *Journal*, 1741.

22. Which of the following claims about the Great Awakening could be inferred from the passage in George Whitefield's journal?

    (A) The Great Awakening was the first movement to have an impact across all of the thirteen British colonies in North America.

    (B) The Great Awakening was largely a movement that appealed to urban residents.

    (C) The Great Awakening encouraged colonial Americans to challenge authority.

    (D) The Great Awakening contributed to the development of racial animosity within the colonies.

23. Conditions for agricultural success in New England differed from those in the Middle Colonies primarily in that

    (A) New England's many seaports made commercial agriculture more profitable.

    (B) New England had a larger supply of young, single male laborers and therefore reduced costs.

    (C) its rocky soils and shorter growing season resulted in poorer harvests.

    (D) the high mortality rates of New England's indentured workforce cut into agricultural profits.

24. Which of the following developments resulted most immediately from the egalitarian spirit unleashed by the American Revolution?

    (A) Inheritance laws favoring firstborn sons were abolished across the 13 original states.

    (B) The right to vote was extended to all white males regardless of their property holdings.

    (C) Bicameral legislatures were established in all states in order to reflect the interests of the populace more effectively.

    (D) Northern states immediately made the ownership of enslaved persons illegal.

Use the table below to answer Question 25.

New Jersey Plan	Virginia Plan
• Unicameral legislature	• Bicameral legislature
• Equal representation in Congress	• Representation in Congress based on population
• Supported by smaller states	• Supported by larger states

25. Which of the following best describes the compromise that was reached to settle the differences between the two plans in the table above?

   (A) The enslaved population of each state would be counted as three-fifths of their total for purposes of representation.

   (B) A Congress composed of two houses with equal representation in the upper chamber and representation determined by population in the lower.

   (C) A bicameral legislature with the Senate chosen by state legislatures and the House of Representatives chosen by direct popular vote.

   (D) The establishment of three separate branches of government with sufficient checks and balances to reduce the likelihood of a tyranny of the larger over the smaller states.

26. Thomas Jefferson argued that the only powers the federal government could legally exercise were those explicitly granted to it in the U.S. Constitution. This view of the Constitution is known as

   (A) strict constructionism.

   (B) judicial activism.

   (C) liberalism.

   (D) fundamentalism.

27. This pamphlet published in 1776 was perhaps the most widely-read appeal for American independence:

   (A) John Dickinson's *Letters from a Pennsylvania Farmer*

   (B) Benjamin Franklin's *Join or Die*

   (C) Thomas Paine's *Common Sense*

   (D) Henry W. Longfellow's *Paul Revere's Ride*

28. John Hancock, Patrick Henry, and Samuel Adams opposed the ratification of the United States Constitution largely because

   (A) they feared that the Constitution gave too much power to voters.

   (B) they argued that the Constitution protected the interests of plantation owners over mercantile or manufacturing interests.

   (C) they favored a parliamentary democracy with a more vigorous party system.

   (D) they argued that state and local governments had lost too much power to the national government.

29. James Madison and Thomas Jefferson compromised with Alexander Hamilton during Washington's first term in office, agreeing to accept Hamilton's banking and debt-assumption program in exchange for

   (A) extending the deadline to end the transatlantic slave trade.

   (B) agreeing to move the nation's capital from Philadelphia to Washington, D.C.

   (C) an agreement to support the later purchase of the Louisiana Territory from France.

   (D) support for the Alien and Sedition Acts.

Use the chart below to answer Question 30.

• 1803: Louisiana Purchase
• 1819: Treaty of Adams Onis

• 1845: Annexation of Texas
• 1846: _____

• 1848: Treaty of Guadalupe Hidalgo
• 1853: Gadsden Purchase

30. Which of the following correctly completes the timeline above?

(A) The Webster-Ashburton Treaty

(B) The Russo-American Treaty

(C) The Alaska Purchase

(D) The Oregon Treaty

31. "Manifest destiny" refers to the belief that

(A) humans are predestined by God to either salvation or damnation.

(B) the United States Constitution reflects the God-given wisdom of the Founding Fathers.

(C) the United States had a "civilizing mission" akin to that claimed by Europeans in their colonization of Africa and Asia.

(D) the United States had a God-given right to expand across the North American continent.

32. In the *Dred Scott* decision (1857) the Supreme Court determined that the plaintiff had no standing to sue for his freedom even though he had lived for some time in territories where slavery had not been permitted because

(A) he had no citizenship rights in the United States and Congress had no authority to outlaw slavery in the territories.

(B) the status of slavery in the territories had to be decided by a vote of each territory's residents.

(C) slavery was an immoral but Constitutionally permissible institution.

(D) slavery was a biblically ordained and benevolent labor system that was supported by history and custom.

33. Which of the following was the first Southern state to secede from the Union?

(A) Texas

(B) Virginia

(C) South Carolina

(D) Kentucky

34. After several earlier commanders, Lincoln turned the war effort over to this general whose successes on the war's western front suggested a strategy that would lead to victory.

(A) William Tecumseh Sherman

(B) George B. McClellan

(C) John Bell Hood

(D) Ulysses S. Grant

35. Following the abolition of slavery, most white landowners employed which of the following approaches to acquiring sufficient labor to work their land?

(A) Convict labor

(B) Sharecropping

(C) Serfdom

(D) Indentured servitude

36. With the outbreak of World War I in Europe, Woodrow Wilson and most Americans

    (A) saw Germany, the Ottoman Empire, and Austria-Hungary as natural American allies given the large number of Central and Eastern European immigrants in the United States.

    (B) believed that the United States should remain neutral.

    (C) believed that the United States should provide assistance to England and France, America's historic allies.

    (D) were fearful the United States' large German population would prove to be a disloyal group that would threaten Americans domestically.

37. Which of the following was not a feature of Woodrow Wilson's Fourteen Points?

    (A) The League of Nations

    (B) National right to self-determination

    (C) Reduction of trade barriers

    (D) A German "war guilt" clause

Use the image below to answer question 38.

38. The preceding cartoon image, from the 1952 film *Duck and Cover*, warned children of the necessity to find shelter in case of

    (A) tornados.

    (B) chemical mishaps.

    (C) Soviet nuclear attack.

    (D) German air raids.

39. In the aftermath of the Soviet Union's development of an atomic bomb and the "fall" of China to communism, this Wisconsin Senator sought to root out Communist sympathizers in Hollywood, universities, and government agencies.

    (A) Ronald Reagan

    (B) Whittaker Chambers

    (C) J. Edgar Hoover

    (D) Joseph McCarthy

40. Which of the following has NOT contributed to growing interconnectedness of the global economy since 1989?

    (A) Reduction of regional trade restrictions through such institutions as NAFTA and the European Union

    (B) Increased cell phone use and the spread of the internet as commercial tools

    (C) The use of cargo containers in transoceanic shipping

    (D) Reduction of international flight times with increased adoption of supersonic transport

41. Which of the following New Deal programs brought electricity to rural communities, thereby allowing them to enter into American consumer society in earnest?

    (A) Civilian Conservation Corps (CCC)

    (B) Tennessee Valley Authority (TVA)

    (C) Works Progress Administration (WPA)

    (D) The Federal Emergency Relief Administration (FERA)

42. Inspired by the African American Civil Rights movement's methods, in 1963 César Chávez set out to organize Mexican Americans

    (A) to fight against school districts that segregated Mexican American students from Anglo-American children.

    (B) to unionize and use the boycott to improve working conditions, living conditions, and wages for Mexican-American farm workers.

    (C) to object to the dependence of the American military in Vietnam on Hispanic soldiers.

    (D) to demand voting rights for Mexican Americans denied the suffrage across the American South.

43. Which of the following Native American tribes only migrated into Texas in the late 17th and early 18th centuries?

    (A) The Karankawa

    (B) The Caddo

    (C) The Jumanos

    (D) The Comanche

44. Which of the following was NOT a feature of Spanish settlement of Texas in the late 17th and early 18th centuries?

    (A) The establishment of Catholic mission stations

    (B) The chartering of *villas* or settled towns

    (C) Building a fortress or *presidio*

    (D) The establishment of a *Cortes generales* or representative assembly

45. Which of the following was the immediate cause of increased Spanish settlement interest in Texas in the 1690s?

    (A) The establishment of Sieur de la Salle's short-lived French colony on Matagorda Bay and growing French presence along the Mississippi

    (B) Requests from the Caddo Indians for religious teaching from missionary priests

    (C) The legend of El Dorado, which led to expeditions into Texas in search of a city of gold

    (D) The need to pacify the Comanche who had begun to raid across the Texas frontier

46. Which of the following was the first Anglo-American to be granted a contract to settle 300 families in the Mexican state of Texas, though he never lived to see his contract fulfilled?

    (A) Sam Houston

    (B) Moses Austin

    (C) Quanah Parker

    (D) William Barret Travis

Use the excerpt from the *Texas Constitution of 1836* to answer the question that follows.

Texas Constitution of 1836

SEC. 9. All persons of color who were slaves for life previous to their emigration to Texas, and who are now held in bondage, shall remain in the like state of servitude, provide the said slave shall be the bona fide property of the person so holding said slave as aforesaid. Congress shall pass no laws to prohibit emigrants from the United States of America from bringing their slaves into the Republic with them, and holding them by the same tenure by which such slaves were held in the United States; nor shall Congress have power to emancipate slaves; nor shall any slave-holder be allowed to emancipate his or her slave or slaves, without the consent of Congress, unless he or she shall send his or her slave or slaves without the limits of the Republic. No free person of African descent, either in whole or in part, shall be permitted to reside permanently in the Republic, without the consent of Congress, and the importation or admission of Africans or Negroes into this Republic, excepting from the United States of America, is forever prohibited, and declared to be piracy.

47. Which of the following best describes the context of Section 9 of the *Texas Constitution of 1836*?

   (A) Texans' desire to improve on the United States Constitution's failure to abolish slavery

   (B) Texans' desire to end the domestic and international slave trade

   (C) The Mexican government's efforts before 1835 to abolish slavery

   (D) The Mexican government's efforts to confiscate property of Anglo-Americans in Texas

48. The Mexican-American War (1846-1848) was in part triggered by territorial disputes over which of the following?

   (A) The Big Bend region and its mineral resources

   (B) The Llano Estecado region on the border with *Nuevo México*

   (C) The Nueces Strip between the Nueces and the Rio Grande rivers

   (D) The Red River and Sabine River watersheds

49. African Americans in Texas celebrate "Juneteenth," commemorating which of the following events?

   (A) The passage of the 13th Amendment formally putting an end to slavery in the United States

   (B) Abraham Lincoln's signing of the Emancipation Proclamation in 1863

   (C) The birthday of Joshua Houston, Sam Houston's slave, who became a prominent African American politician during Reconstruction

   (D) The day that enslaved persons in Texas were informed that they were no longer legally the property of their owners

50. What Comanche warrior led the most significant post–Civil War resistance against white encroachment on Comanche lands?

   (A) Sitting Bull

   (B) Geronimo

   (C) Quanah Parker

   (D) Blue Duck

51. The Texas economy before 1900 depended primarily on which of the following commodities?

   (A) Cattle and cotton

   (B) Sugar and rice

   (C) Wheat and oil

   (D) Hides and fisheries

52. In addition to cotton, the Texas Panhandle region depended upon which of the following cash crops?

    (A) Corn

    (B) Wheat

    (C) Rice

    (D) Alfalfa

53. Texas suffragettes, like Jane McCallum, believed that women voters would

    (A) fundamentally challenge the Democratic Party's stranglehold on political power in Texas.

    (B) support other reforms like prohibition, an end to child labor laws, and educational improvements.

    (C) back political candidates that favored racial equality and integration.

    (D) not have much interest in issues outside of their traditional domestic and marital concerns.

Use the photograph below to answer Question 54.

"Wendy Welder" at the Richmond Shipyards, Richmond, California (Wikimedia Commons)

Source: https://commons.wikimedia.org/wiki/File:
Wendy_Welder_Richmond_Shipyards.jpg

54. The preceding image of a woman welding an airplane wing in a plant near Houston illustrates which of the following?

    (A) Greater independence of "flapper girls" during the Roaring 20s

    (B) The growth of women's employment in traditionally male jobs during the Great Depression

    (C) The importance of women's work to the American war effort during World War II

    (D) The importance of commercial airline growth during the 1950s

55. Consider these cases originating in Texas: *Del Rio v. Salvatierra* (1930), *Mendez v. Westminister* (1945) and *Minerva Delgado v. Bastrop ISD* (1948). Which of the following best illustrates what ties all three together?

    (A) They overturned the system of "separate but equal" established in *Plessy v. Ferguson* (1896).

    (B) They resulted in widespread desegregation of Texas public schools before the 1960s.

    (C) They challenged the segregation of Mexican-American school children well before *Brown v. Board of Education of Topeka, Kansas* (1954).

    (D) They guaranteed the right of migrant workers' children to expect education in local school districts.

56. Which of the following figures was NOT a prominent Texas political figure of the 1960s?

    (A) Lyndon B. Johnson, President of the United States

    (B) James Farmer, founder of the Congress of Racial Equality (CORE)

    (C) Henry B. Gonzalez, member U.S. House of Representatives

    (D) Kay Bailey Hutchison, U.S. Senator

57. The primary invasive species threatening Texas's cotton farms in the early 20th century was the

    (A) Asian Gypsy Moth

    (B) Fire Ant

    (C) Boll Weevil

    (D) Asian Longhorn Beetle

58. Which of the following terms did NOT originate in the cattle culture of the *vaqueros* of Mexico and Texas?

    (A) Lariat

    (B) Cowboy

    (C) Bandanna

    (D) Chaps

59. Which of the following has no impact on climatic conditions?

    (A) Ocean currents

    (B) Longitude

    (C) Elevation

    (D) Latitude

60. Which of the following Middle Latitude climate types is the result of the influence of ocean currents and the presence of mountains?

    (A) Marine West Coast

    (B) Humid Subtropical

    (C) Mediterranean

    (D) Tropical Wet Dry

61. Which type of cultural diffusion would most likely be the result of human migration?

    (A) Contagious Diffusion

    (B) Relocation Diffusion

    (C) Expansion Diffusion

    (D) Hierarchical Diffusion

Use the photograph below to answer Question 62.

62. The landform shown above was likely the result of which of the following?

    (A) Volcanic activity

    (B) Subduction

    (C) Wind and water erosion

    (D) Rifting or separation of tectonic plates

63. According to the theory of plate tectonics, which of the following is true? Select *all* that apply.

    (A) The matching coastlines that form the Earth's continental boundaries are evidence of an earlier supercontinent known as Pangaea.

    (B) Glacial drift is best explained as a feature of the gradual movement of continental land masses.

    (C) Volcanic activity along plate boundaries contributes to the creation of mountains and mountain ranges.

    (D) Most of the major continental mountain ranges are the product of a process of subduction.

64. What is the characteristic that marks modern developing countries in stage two of the demographic transition model?

   (A) Slow, stable decline in population growth

   (B) Slow, stable growth in population

   (C) Rapid decline in population growth

   (D) Rapid increase in population growth

65. What artificial waterway was instrumental in connecting Asian trade with European trade during the 19th century?

   (A) Panama Canal

   (B) Grand Canal

   (C) Suez Canal

   (D) Elbe-Lubeck Canal

66. What is a direct result of the annual movement of the earth in its orbit around the sun?

   (A) Global warming

   (B) Water evaporation in the hydrological cycle

   (C) Loss of biodiversity in the biosphere

   (D) Seasonal climate variation

67. What are the three main climate zones of planet Earth?

   (A) Cold, Hot, Wet

   (B) Tropical, Temperate, Polar

   (C) Moderate, Dry, Humid

   (D) Arid, Continental, Arctic

68. Which of the following is NOT an example of the impact of the Columbian Exchange on the Texas environment?

   (A) Honeybees

   (B) Longhorn cattle

   (C) Sugarcane

   (D) Chili peppers

69. Which of the following New World crops contributed most to population growth in Europe and Asia in the 18th and 19th centuries?

   (A) Corn

   (B) Wheat

   (C) Potatoes

   (D) Beans

70. Which of the following belief systems has sought to achieve social harmony by situating each individual within a fixed caste, closely linking status and occupation?

   (A) Confucianism

   (B) Zoroastrianism

   (C) Buddhism

   (D) Hinduism

71. Which of the following would be an example of a historical migration driven primarily by "push factors"?

   (A) Italian migration to 19th-century American cities in search of manufacturing jobs

   (B) Irish migration to 19th-century America in response to the potato famine

   (C) Germanic migrations into the western Roman Empire in the fourth century CE in search of plunder

   (D) Arab migrations from the Arabian Peninsula across North Africa in the seventh century CE

72. The popularity of American fast food restaurants in countries such as South Korea and Japan is an example of which of the following kinds of diffusion.

   (A) Contagious Diffusion

   (B) Hierarchical Diffusion

   (C) Relocation Diffusion

   (D) Stimulus Diffusion

73. Auguste Comte, the 19th-century scholar often called the founder of modern sociology, would have been most associated with which of the following statements?

    (A) "The history of all hitherto existing societies is the history of class struggle."

    (B) "Masculine and feminine roles are not biologically fixed but socially constructed."

    (C) "Each branch of knowledge passes through three different theoretical conditions: the theological, the metaphysical, and the scientific or positive."

    (D) "Every individual . . . intends only his own gain, and he is in this, as in many other cases, led by an invisible hand to promote an end which was no part of his intention."

Use the chart below to answer Question 74.

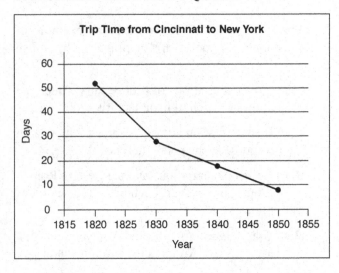

74. Which of the following best explains the changes in travel time evident in the chart above?

    (A) Steamships, canal networks, and railroads

    (B) Clipper ships and coal-powered steamships

    (C) The National Road and the interstate highway system

    (D) Keelboats, stagecoaches, and the Pony Express

75. The 14th Amendment

    (A) reserves for the states the right to decide who is entitled to citizenship and who is not.

    (B) ensured that former slaves would have the right to vote.

    (C) requires that states uphold the principle of equality before the law.

    (D) protects property owners from loss of property without due process of law.

76. In the landmark court case *Marbury v. Madison* (1803), Chief Justice John Marshall confirmed the principle of

    (A) implied powers.

    (B) strict constructionism.

    (C) dual federalism.

    (D) judicial review.

77. Which of the following methods for amending the United States Constitution has been most often used?

    (A) When the legislatures of two-thirds of the states request that a constitutional convention be called.

    (B) When a two-thirds majority of the voting population of the United States requests that a constitutional convention be called.

    (C) When two-thirds of both houses of Congress vote to propose an amendment to the Constitution.

    (D) When three-quarters of state ratifying conventions approve of an amendment.

Read the excerpt below and answer Question 78.

Does the Constitution of the United States act upon him whenever he shall be made free under the laws of a State, and raised there to the rank of a citizen, and immediately clothe him with all the privileges of a citizen in every other State, and in its own courts? The court thinks the affirmative of these propositions cannot be maintained. And, if it cannot, the plaintiff . . . could not be a citizen of the State of Missouri, within the meaning of the Constitution of the United States, and consequently, was not entitled to sue in its courts.[. . .]

78. The decision above, written by Chief Justice Taney in the Supreme Court case *Dred Scott v. Sandford*, had which of the following effects?

(A) It denied African Americans the right to United States citizenship and ensured that slaves who were transported to states where slavery was illegal were nonetheless not emancipated.

(B) It created a system of "separate but equal" in public accommodations and education, and legalized the suppression of African American votes across the South.

(C) It overturned the Missouri Compromise's provision that slavery would be allowed in Missouri.

(D) It forbade states to pass laws freeing the slaves as this violated the private property rights of slave owners.

79. Which of the following is NOT a power delegated to the President of the United States?

(A) The power to protect the nation from threats of domestic insurrection

(B) The authority to appoint ambassadors and to negotiate treaties with foreign powers

(C) The power to pardon people and commute sentences for federal crimes

(D) The power to declare war

80. Every president since Franklin D. Roosevelt has sent American troops into combat without meeting which of the following Constitutional provisions?

(A) Congressional declaration of war

(B) Congressional authorization of use of force

(C) Senate advice and consent

(D) Compliance with the War Powers Resolution

81. Concurrent powers are powers that are shared by both the state and national government. Which of the following is NOT a concurrent power?

(A) Providing for public safety

(B) Establishing courts

(C) Regulating interstate trade

(D) Levying taxes

82. In 1824 and 1876, the presidential election returned no electoral college winner. What is the process outlined in the Constitution if no candidate wins an electoral college majority?

(A) State legislatures each vote separately with the candidate who wins the most contests taking the presidency.

(B) The Supreme Court determines the winner after careful deliberation.

(C) The candidate with the popular vote majority wins the election.

(D) The election is determined in the House of Representatives with the winner being the candidate who receives the vote of the most state delegations.

83. Which of the following was the PRIMARY reason for the inclusion of the Second Amendment in the Bill of Rights?

   (A) To enable private citizens to resist the power of tyrannical governments

   (B) To ensure that private citizens were able to defend themselves against crime

   (C) To ensure that states could maintain a militia as a defense against federal oppression or internal insurrection

   (D) To ensure that Americans were able to feed their families in an era when hunting was critical to survival

84. Because of the vague nature of the Constitution's description of the office of the presidency, most of the ways in which presidents have exercised the powers of their office

   (A) have been established by Congressional enactment.

   (B) have resulted from precedents set by early presidents like George Washington.

   (C) were the consequence of efforts by presidential opponents to reign in executive power.

   (D) have been put in placement through the amendment process.

Use the outline below to answer Question 85.

   I. _____

   A. FERA and WPA mandate new state government institutions.

   B. Federal government accepts responsibility for fiscal stimulus of economy.

   C. Federal expenditures increase from $34.9 billion to $163 billion.

   D. Roosevelt's policies require states to eliminate racial and ethnic preferences to receive federal funding.

85. Which heading would best complete the outline above?

   (A) New Deal overturns President Hoover's market-based economic policy.

   (B) New Deal expands scope and size of federal government.

   (C) Great Depression threatens American confidence in government.

   (D) New Deal policies address causes of the Great Depression.

Use the following excerpt from the *Declaration of Independence* to answer Question 86.

   We hold these truths to be self-evident, that all men are created equal, that they are endowed by their Creator with certain unalienable Rights, that among these are Life, Liberty and the pursuit of Happiness. That to secure these rights, Governments are instituted among Men, deriving their just powers from the consent of the governed. That whenever any Form of Government becomes destructive of these ends, it is the Right of the People to alter or to abolish it . . .

86. The views expressed in the preamble to the Declaration of Independence, quoted above, best reflect the political philosophy of which of the following?

   (A) Thomas Hobbes

   (B) Karl Marx

   (C) John Locke

   (D) Adam Smith

87. England's Parliament and the United States Congress share which of the following characteristics?

    (A) Separation between the legislative and executive branches

    (B) An upper chamber representing the interests of the aristocracy

    (C) The power to override the veto of the nation's head of state

    (D) A bicameral structure

88. The United States Constitution

    (A) was amended to allow for political parties.

    (B) expressly forbade the development of political parties.

    (C) was silent on the place of political parties in American government.

    (D) called for a two-party system.

89. Which of the following statements most clearly describes the difference between the United States system of government and that of most parliamentary systems of government.

    (A) Parliamentary systems typically do not have a strong executive independent of the legislature.

    (B) Parliamentary systems have a unitary system rather than a federal system of power sharing.

    (C) Parliamentary systems are most often found in monarchies rather than republics.

    (D) Parliamentary systems reduce popular influence over the legislature unlike the United States system.

90. A government with political power in the hands of religious leaders is known as a(n)

    (A) oligarchical system.

    (B) theocracy.

    (C) Caesaro-papist system.

    (D) feudal system.

91. Which of the following personal choices best illustrates the concept of opportunity cost?

    (A) A student pays high rates of tuition in order to attend a prestigious college.

    (B) A student cancels a spring break trip in order to study for an upcoming exam.

    (C) A student takes out a loan to pay for a car needed to get to his or her job.

    (D) A student changes majors to prepare for a more lucrative career.

Use the chart below to answer Question 92.

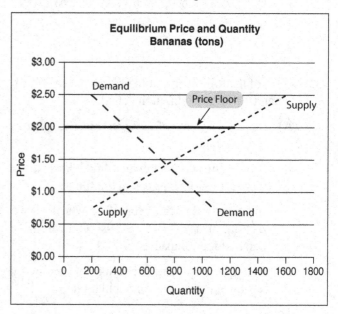

92. If the federal government were to set a price floor at $2.00 per ton of bananas, which of the following would be expected results?

    (A) There would be a surplus of bananas.

    (B) There would be a shortage of bananas.

    (C) The demand curve for bananas would shift to the right.

    (D) The supply curve for bananas would shift to the right.

Use the chart below to answer Question 93.

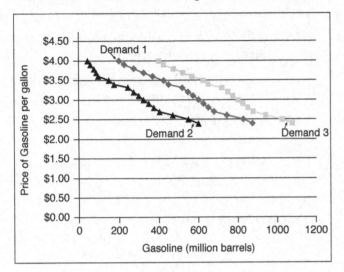

93. Which of the following would explain the shift from Demand 1 to Demand 2 in the chart above?

   (A) Increasing costs of storage batteries used in electric cars

   (B) Rumors that conflict in the Middle East would increase gasoline prices in the future

   (C) Increased demand for four-wheel drive pick-up trucks and SUVs compared to demand for compact cars

   (D) Rising unemployment and loss of income by a growing sector of the population

94. Which of the following technological innovations had the most immediate impact on the spread of slavery into Alabama, Mississippi, Arkansas, and Texas?

   (A) Spinning jenny

   (B) Sugar mill

   (C) Cotton gin

   (D) Steamship

95. Which of the following theorists is most often associated with the development of socialism?

   (A) John Maynard Keynes

   (B) Adam Smith

   (C) Karl Marx

   (D) John Locke

96. In 2008, during the height of the economic recession, President Barack Obama pushed through Congress a stimulus plan designed to increase government spending on infrastructure and other internal improvements. This policy most reflected which of the following?

   (A) John Maynard Keynes's argument that deficit spending should be employed during times of reduced aggregate demand.

   (B) Adam Smith's arguments encouraging faith in the market's ability to right the economy during economic downturns.

   (C) Milton Friedman's contention that gradual increases in the money supply provide the best strategy for achieving long-term economic stability.

   (D) Support for David Ricardo's contention that population growth will ultimately undermine prospects for wage growth and higher standards of living.

97. Samuel has been laid off because the economy is experiencing a recession. The kind of unemployment Samuel is experiencing is known to economists as

   (A) structural unemployment.

   (B) cyclical unemployment.

   (C) frictional unemployment.

   (D) seasonal unemployment.

Use the chart below to answer Question 98.

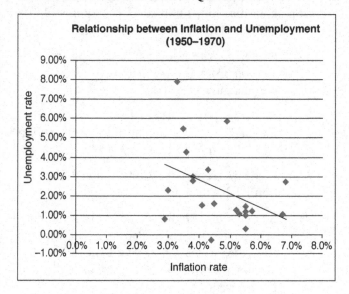

98. The chart above suggests that there is what relationship between inflation and unemployment?

    (A) A direct relationship

    (B) An inverse relationship

    (C) A proportional relationship

    (D) A normal relationship

99. Wheat farmers, soybean farmers, coffee growers, dairy farmers, and other producers of agricultural commodities are most often found in which of the following market structures?

    (A) Pure competition

    (B) Oligopoly

    (C) Monopoly

    (D) Monopolistic competition

100. A partnership or sole proprietorship that creates a legal barrier between the private wealth of the owners and the debts of the firm is known as a

    (A) joint-stock company.

    (B) corporation.

    (C) limited liability company (LLC).

    (D) cooperative.

101. Which of the following groups of firms or individuals would benefit from the appreciation of the U.S. dollar?

    (A) American workers in firms that export goods and services

    (B) Tourists visiting the United States

    (C) Banks that hold large gold reserves

    (D) American consumers who purchase imports

Use the following excerpt from the *United States Constitution* to answer Question 102.

Article I. Section 8, Clause 8 of the United States Constitution.

"The Congress shall have the power . . . to promote the progress of science and useful arts, by securing for limited times to authors and inventors the exclusive right to their respective writings and discoveries."

102. Which of the following resulted from this clause in the Constitution?

    (A) The Sherman Antitrust Act

    (B) The Interstate Commerce Commission

    (C) United States Patent and Trademark Office

    (D) The Food and Drug Administration

103. Which of the following best describes how the Federal Deposit Insurance Corporation (FDIC) contributed to increased capital investment in the 1940s and 1950s?

    (A) It encouraged increased private saving.

    (B) It provided the funding for the Social Security System.

    (C) It stabilized exchange rates and strengthened the value of the dollar.

    (D) It reduced mortgage costs and encouraged home construction.

104. What is the difference between a bondholder and a stockholder?

    (A) The owner of a share of stock has part ownership of a corporation, whereas a bondholder is merely a creditor of the company.

    (B) A bondholder is not taxed on interest earned from ownership of a bond, while a stockholder is taxed on dividend income.

    (C) Stocks can be sold, but bonds cannot.

    (D) When a company goes bankrupt, stockowners are paid first before bondholders.

105. Frequently, retirement or pension accounts are composed of a group of stocks or other assets that are pooled to allow retirement accounts to reduce risks and ensure a regular source of income later in life. These kinds of accounts are known as

    (A) Mutual funds

    (B) Asset-backed securities

    (C) Bonds

    (D) 501(c)(3)s

106. Which of the following individuals was largely responsible for developing the telegraph?

    (A) Richard Arkwright

    (B) Robert Fulton

    (C) Samuel F.B. Morse

    (D) Samuel Slater

107. Which of the following best illustrates how a lesson about the Constitutional Convention could be designed to reflect inquiry-based learning?

    (A) Students write a journal describing the convention from the perspective of one of the participants.

    (B) Students draw a cartoon that reflects the opinion of Federalists or anti-Federalists during the ratification process.

    (C) Students reenact the Constitutional Convention's debates in class.

    (D) Students use Madison's notes from the convention, the Federalist Papers, and transcripts from the ratification debates to develop a thesis about the factors leading to the calling of the Convention.

108. Which of the following most depends upon the utilization of critical thinking skills?

    (A) Memorizing the Gettysburg Address for a re-enactment

    (B) Researching the role of Congressional committees in the legislative process

    (C) Recalling the names and locations of European capital cities for a map test

    (D) Listening to a presentation by a local politician

109. Content knowledge in which of the following social science disciplines would prove most helpful to an economist interested in theorizing about the relationship between technological change and economic growth in 1750?

    (A) Geography

    (B) History

    (C) Anthropology

    (D) Sociology

Use the flow chart below to answer Question 110.

Define a sociological problem.

Review the secondary literature.

?

Design a research program and collect data.

Evaluate and analyze the data.

Interpret the results and draw conclusions.

110. Which of the following research steps would best complete the flowchart above?

(A) Conduct a literature survey to identify scholarly approaches to the problem.

(B) Develop a hypothesis.

(C) Acquire funding for the research proposal.

(D) Present research to other scholars and publish findings.

Use the chart below to answer Question 111.

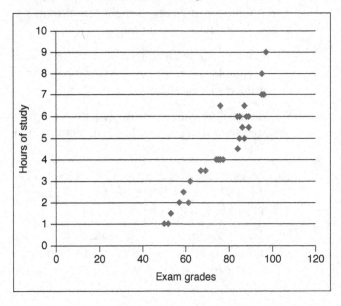

111. The scatter plot above illustrates which of the following relationships between hours of study and exam grades?

(A) A positive correlation between hours of study and exam grades

(B) A causative relationship between number of hours spent studying and exam grades

(C) A perfect positive correlation between hours of study and exam grades

(D) A negative correlation between hours of study and exam grades

112. Which of the following assignments would be most likely to engage students in higher-level thinking, as defined by Bloom's taxonomy?

    (A) A map assignment where students must identify the locations of key Civil War battles and properly locate them

    (B) An assignment requiring students to write a summary of a historical documentary seen in class

    (C) An assignment requiring students to evaluate the accuracy of Ralph Nader's criticism of auto safety in the 1960s

    (D) An assignment requiring students to develop a timeline of the important events leading up to the American Civil War

113. Which of the following signal words are **incorrectly** linked with the kind of argument being developed?

    (A) Chronological reasoning: *first, following, then, when, before*

    (B) Comparative reasoning: *additionally, but also, often, generally, if . . . .then, therefore*

    (C) Cause-effect reasoning: *as a result of, consequently, leads to, may be due to*

    (D) Concept or definition: *in other words, refers to, usually, put another way*

114. Which of the following is an example of a causative relationship?

    (A) Levels of educational attainment and income levels

    (B) Low rates of unemployment and high rates of inflation

    (C) Development of settled agriculture and increases in population density

    (D) Rates of voter participation and protections of individual freedoms

115. Which of the following classroom assignments would best encourage an understanding of the ways in which social science disciplines interact?

    (A) Developing a Venn diagram showing the differences between the French and Russian revolutions

    (B) Developing a Production Possibilities Curve to illustrate the role of scarcity in making economic choices

    (C) Writing a report that explains the process for passing legislation

    (D) Researching the factors that contribute to different land use and development decisions

116. Social science research methods include which of the following? Select *all* that apply.

    (A) Surveys

    (B) Diagnostic analysis

    (C) Case studies

    (D) Interviews

117. Which of the following is an example of a primary source used in the social sciences? Select *all* that apply.

    (A) The movie *Selma* (2014) used by a historian studying changing views of the Civil Rights movement since the 1950s.

    (B) Field notes taken and interviews done by an anthropologist studying a Polynesian island community.

    (C) A U.S. Labor Department report on labor force characteristics and earning patterns by race used by an economist studying American labor force participation.

    (D) A letter from George Washington to Alexander Hamilton for a political scientist interested in the history of the American presidency.

118. Which of the following assessment tools provides a more "authentic assessment" of student abilities?

    (A) National or state-designed criterion-based multiple-choice tests

    (B) "I-learned" statements that capture student self-awareness

    (C) Portfolios that document student performance on a variety of learning tasks

    (D) Teacher-designed tests that evaluate student understanding of in-class learning

119. Which of the following would be an appropriate instructional differentiation for a student with a reading disability in a U.S. History classroom?

    (A) Fewer choices on a multiple-choice test

    (B) Paired partner reading where the students read and retell the text

    (C) Provide the student with a copy of the teacher's lecture notes to follow along during lesson

    (D) Extended time to complete an assignment

120. Which of the following graphic organizers would best enable students to develop an understanding of key social studies terminology?

    (A) Venn diagram

    (B) Timeline

    (C) Concept map

    (D) Story map

121. A glossary differs from a dictionary in that

    (A) it does not typically include the etymology or history of the word.

    (B) it usually is included in a text or manual to specifically assist readers with unfamiliar terms.

    (C) it is more complete and expansive than a dictionary.

    (D) it provides a pronunciation guide for the included words.

122. Which of the following social studies lessons most clearly reflects the inquiry-based learning approach encouraged by constructivist educational theory?

    (A) A lecture on the differences between communism and capitalism

    (B) A shared reading exercise using the Texas Declaration of Independence to guide students to the causes of the Texas Revolution

    (C) A small-group exercise where students speculate about the consequences of current population growth trends and develop a chart of likely effects

    (D) A vocabulary square exercise in which students dissect a word, its etymology, definition, and use in order to master course-relevant terminology

123. Which of the following social groups took the lead in the Latin American Wars for Independence?

    (A) *Peninsulares*

    (B) *Creoles*

    (C) *Mestizos*

    (D) Native Americans

124. Which of the following Asian nations, after 1868, joined Western Europeans and the United States as industrial and imperialist powers?

    (A) Qing China

    (B) Mughal India

    (C) Meiji Japan

    (D) Qajar Persia

125. The Industrial Revolution began in which of the following countries?

    (A) Germany

    (B) United States

    (C) Great Britain

    (D) France

126. Which of the following was the Soviet leader who in the late 1980s argued that the Soviet Union needed a new approach characterized by *glasnost* (openness) and *perestroika* (reform)?

    (A) Boris Yeltsin

    (B) Nikita Khrushchev

    (C) Mikhail Gorbachev

    (D) Vladimir Putin

127. Which of the following was the Confederate Army's leading general throughout the Civil War?

    (A) Jefferson Davis

    (B) Thomas "Stonewall" Jackson

    (C) Nathan Bedford Forrest

    (D) Robert E. Lee

128. Even before the Mexican-American War had been decided, this Pennsylvania congressman had introduced a "proviso" into legislation that demanded that slavery not be allowed into territory taken from Mexico.

    (A) William Lloyd Garrison

    (B) David Wilmot

    (C) Thaddeus Stevens

    (D) Stephen A. Douglas

129. The "Double V" campaign led by A. Philip Randolph reflected

    (A) minority rights groups' insistence that the war against racism abroad should be accompanied by an end to segregation at home.

    (B) the commitment by American minority groups to victory over both Germany and Japan.

    (C) African American fears that Mexican immigrants would take jobs in wartime manufacturing.

    (D) Fears that the war effort against the Axis powers would become an excuse to restrict minority rights in the United States.

130. Since the 1960s the "Solid South" began to shift its support from the Democratic Party to Republican candidates in a major party realignment. Which of the following best explains that shift?

    (A) The Democratic Party's abandonment of labor and working-class interests.

    (B) Evangelical Christian's objections to Supreme Court decisions like *Roe v. Wade* and *Engel v. Vitale.*

    (C) Southern white voters' dissatisfaction with Democratic Party support for the Civil Rights movement and integration.

    (D) The appeal of candidates like Jimmy Carter and Bill Clinton to fellow Southerners.

131. Which of the following was the first African American woman elected to Congress from a Southern state?

    (A) Barbara Jordan

    (B) Lulu Belle Madison White

    (C) Oveta Culp Hobby

    (D) Jane McCallum

132. What climate type is found in tall mountains or elevated plateaus?

    (A) Tundra

    (B) Arid

    (C) Highland

    (D) Humid Continental

133. Japan, where the birth rates have fallen below death rates, would be considered in which stage of the demographic transition model?

    (A) Stage Two

    (B) Stage Three

    (C) Stage Four

    (D) Stage Five

134. The movement of tectonic plates away from each other, above the ocean, results in the formation of what type of landform?

(A) Trenches

(B) Mountain ranges

(C) River valleys

(D) Rift valleys

135. What are the main characteristics upon which culture regions are organized and recognized?

(A) Adaptations to environment

(B) Standards of living

(C) Human beliefs and activities

(D) Religious ideas

136. Texas city governments are divided between smaller city and town governments and larger cities with a degree of self-government that are known as

(A) single-purpose governments

(B) general-law governments

(C) home-rule governments

(D) council-manager governments

Use the chart below to answer Question 137.

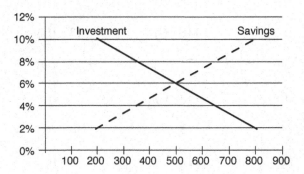

137. All other things being equal, what will the interest rates for savers and investors be based on the chart above?

(A) 2%

(B) 4%

(C) 6%

(D) 8%

138. Which of the following forms of taxation is most regressive?

(A) The United States income tax

(B) The FICA tax

(C) State sales taxes

(D) Capital gains taxes

139. When students are asked to demonstrate mastery of a set of skills by producing a product or carrying out a task, this is known as which of the following?

(A) Critical thinking

(B) Performance-based learning

(C) Deductive reasoning

(D) Metacognition

140. Social scientists who see their disciplines as akin to the natural sciences would most likely agree with which of the following statements?

(A) Human behavior can be effectively described using empirical observation and experimental observation.

(B) Because social realities are so complex, social scientists' primary responsibility is to interpret rather than simply describe their subject matter.

(C) The most important focus of the social sciences must be on the ways in which human social groupings construct meaning using language, beliefs, and culture.

(D) Social scientists, despite their efforts to the contrary, are unable to separate themselves from their own cultural and class biases in order to study social relations objectively.

Practice Test 1 Answer Key

1. (D)	25. (B)	49. (D)	72. (B)	96. (A)	118. (C)
2. (C)	26. (A)	50. (C)	73. (C)	97. (B)	119. (B)
3. (B)	27. (C)	51. (A)	74. (A)	98. (B)	120. (C)
4. (C)	28. (D)	52. (B)	75. (C)	99. (A)	121. (B)
5. (A)	29. (B)	53. (B)	76. (D)	100. (C)	122. (C)
6. (B)	30. (D)	54. (C)	77. (C)	101. (D)	123. (B)
7. (B)	31. (D)	55. (C)	78. (A)	102. (C)	124. (C)
8. (C)	32. (A)	56. (D)	79. (D)	103. (A)	125. (C)
9. (B)	33. (C)	57. (C)	80. (A)	104. (A)	126. (C)
10. (C)	34. (D)	58. (B)	81. (C)	105. (A)	127. (D)
11. (B)	35. (B)	59. (B)	82. (D)	106. (C)	128. (B)
12. (D)	36. (B)	60. (D)	83. (C)	107. (D)	129. (A)
13. (B)	37. (D)	61. (B)	84. (B)	108. (B)	130. (C)
14. (C)	38. (C)	62. (C)	85. (B)	109. (B)	131. (A)
15. (B)	39. (D)	63. (A), (C),	86. (C)	110. (B)	132. (C)
16. (D)	40. (D)	and (D)	87. (D)	111. (A)	133. (D)
17. (C)	41. (B)	64. (D)	88. (C)	112. (C)	134. (D)
18. (A)	42. (B)	65. (C)	89. (A)	113. (B)	135. (C)
19. (C)	43. (D)	66. (D)	90. (B)	114. (C)	136. (C)
20. (A)	44. (D)	67. (B)	91. (B)	115. (D)	137. (C)
21. (D)	45. (A)	68. (D)	92. (A)	116. (A), (C),	138. (C)
22. (C)	46. (B)	69. (C)	93. (D)	and (D)	139. (B)
23. (C)	47. (C)	70. (D)	94. (C)	117. (A), (B),	140. (A)
24. (A)	48. (C)	71. (B)	95. (C)	(C), and (D)	

Practice Test 1: Detailed Answers

1. (D)

Grindstones were developed to process grains and thus represent a technology of agricultural societies. **Option A is incorrect.** Fishing served as a significant source of calories for hunter-gatherer societies. Harpoons made from fire-hardened wood and fishhooks fashioned from bone fragments were common to many hunter-gatherer societies. **Option B is incorrect.** Among the earliest technologies developed by human beings were technologies used to carry fruits and berries, or to allow mothers to carry their infants. **Option C is incorrect** as hunter-gatherer societies developed digging sticks to dislodge tubers or other foods. **(Domain and Competency I.001.A. Skill: Content knowledge, Contextualization)**

2. (C)

Cuneiform is the Latin term meaning "wedge-shaped." **Option A is incorrect.** Hieroglyphic writing was employed in ancient Egyptian culture, but not in Mesopotamia. **Option B is incorrect.** Ideographic writing employs a graphic symbol to represent an idea or concept while Mesopotamian writing used an alphabet of symbols that represented either concepts or phonetic sounds, and could therefore be employed by different languages. **Option D is incorrect.** *Codices* is the plural for *codex*, the Latin word for a book composed of multiple sheets. Many of the Mayan and Aztec writings are recorded in codices. **(Domain and Competency I.001.A. Skill: Content knowledge)**

3. (B)

Hammurabi's Code is known for its draconian punishments, but the social hierarchy of Mesopotamian society was reflected in the different punishments enforced depending on the status of perpetrators and victims. **Option A is incorrect** because penitence or remorse, which implies the possibility of the criminal's reform, was not the objective of punishment under Hammurabi's Code. **Option C is incorrect** because the principle of popular sovereignty and representative institutions was not a feature of Mesopotamian notions of justice. These ideals would develop during the Enlightenment in Western Europe and the United States. **Option D is incorrect** because while Hammurabi claimed a divinely legitimized authority, Mesopotamian religion was polytheistic. **(Domain and Competency I.001.B. Skill: Contextualization)**

4. (C)

Xenophon objected to commoners' influence in Athens' democracy, contending that those with the highest capability and quality should rule. Aristocracy, from the Greek word *aristokratia*, means "rule of the best." **Option A is incorrect.** The Greek concepts of tyranny and oligarchy describe respectively the power of an absolute ruler unrestrained by law and the rule of the few.

Option B is incorrect. Republic and dictatorship were Latin political terms. Xenophon objects mostly the power of the commons and offers the rule of the best instead. A dictatorship refers to the Latin grant of power to a single individual during a time of crisis. **Option D is incorrect.** A theocracy is a system of government in which religious leaders rule based on the authority of God or a god. **(Domain and Competency I.001.B. Skill: Analysis)**

5. (A)

Christianity's spread into Western Europe benefited from the demise of classical Rome, while Buddhism spread into China as the Han Empire declined, benefiting from the breakdown of order in China. **Option B is incorrect** because neither Buddhism nor Christianity's early spread were accomplished by conquest or coercion. **Option C is incorrect** because both Christianity and Buddhism fundamentally challenged the traditional family models of ancient Rome and China. **Option D is incorrect** because while the Christian message of a heavenly kingdom, which appealed to many Romans, had no parallel in Buddhism. **(Domain and Competency I.001.C. Skill: Comparison)**

6. (B)

Knowledge of the monsoon wind patterns enabled merchants from India and the Arabian Peninsula to transport trade goods from China, India, and the Islamic world to East Africa on the outward voyage, while they waited for the winds to change to return from Africa with ivory, incense, gold, and slaves. **Option A is incorrect** because the caravel ship was used by European merchants and explorers in the 15th and 16th centuries to enter into Indian Ocean trade networks. **Option C is incorrect** because the El Niño ocean currents are found in the Pacific Ocean, rather than the Indian Ocean. **Option D is incorrect** because the Chinese tribute fleet led by Zheng He traveled along the coast of the Indian Ocean in the beginning of the 15th century. Additionally, the Zheng He expedition had less to do with trade than with Chinese diplomatic overtures. **(Domain and Competency I.002.A. Skill: Causation)**

7. (B)

From about 950 to 1250 there was a warming trend, followed by what has often been called the "Little Ice Age." Additionally, such technologies as the heavy plow, three-field crop rotation, Asian use of animal and human waste as fertilizer increased crop yields. **Option A is incorrect.** Raids by Norsemen, expansion of the Arab Caliphates, the Crusades, the An Lushang rebellion in Tang China, the Mongol conquests suggest that violence had not subsided significantly. **Option C is incorrect.** Small improvements in medical knowledge in China and the Islamic world may have had a small impact on mortality rates, but not enough to explain this growth in population. **Option D is incorrect.** Islam's spread did create a unified global trade system, which contributed to commercial and economic growth. This growth, however, was likely also influenced by growing populations resulting from increased agricultural yields. **(Domain and Competency I.002.B. Skill: Causation, Graph Reading)**

8. (C)

With the expansion of the Mongol Empire, epidemic diseases spread along the trans-Eurasian trade routes. The most spectacular example of this was the Black Death that struck Europe from 1348 to 1351. **Option A is incorrect.** Gunpowder technology spread with the Mongol conquests;, however, early gunpowder weaponry was not remarkably more lethal than existing forms of warfare. Long-bows and cross-bows were as lethal as many early guns. Guns were most important in breaking sieges. **Option B is incorrect.** Instead of global warming, this period was characterized by a global cooling trend. **Option D is incorrect.** The Han and Gupta Empires collapsed between the third and sixth centuries CE, and the Byzantine Empire was still intact, though declining, in this period. **(Domain and Competency I.002.B. Skill: Causation, Graph reading)**

9. (B)

Guilds were organizations of merchants or craftsmen in medieval and early modern Europe. **Option A is incorrect.** Communes (and not the kind where hippies went in the 1960s) were chartered towns in medieval and early modern Europe. **Option C is incorrect.** Monasteries were self-governing religious institutions where the regular clergy (those who lived according to a rule) lived and worshipped. **Option D is incorrect.** Manors were self-contained agricultural systems governed by the lord of the manor and worked by serfs, or peasants bound to the land. **(Domain and Competency I.002.C. Skill: Content knowledge)**

10. (C)

Leonardo da Vinci was an accomplished painter, sculptor, engineer, scientist, and humanist. A "Renaissance" man was imagined to be an individual who excelled in a wide range of areas. **Option A is incorrect.** Henry VIII was King of England from 1509 to 1547. He is best known for his decision to lead England away from Roman Catholicism in his desire to divorce his first wife Catherine of Aragon. **Option B is incorrect.** Thomas Aquinas was a characteristic medieval scholar, focusing narrowly on the study of religion and philosophy. **Option D is incorrect.** Martin Luther is best known for his role in beginning the Protestant Reformation. **(Domain and Competency I.003.A. Skill: Content knowledge)**

11. (B)

As Europeans began to read more in private and own libraries of their own, they were able to develop heretical or religiously controversial ideas, and to develop new perceptions of the world around them. **Option A is incorrect.** It is true that mnemonic devices and memorization became less important to the educational process, but the decline in these practices did not lead to new ways of thinking about science and religion. **Option C is incorrect.** It is true that Europeans gained confidence in written texts as they came to trust that print reproduced texts more faithfully than did scribes. However, this did not result in the development of ideas that contradicted the views of authorities. **Option D is incorrect.** Contrary to this claim, the increased availability of printed material actually corresponds with an increase in religious devotion and publications of religious tracts and literature. Only gradually and much later did purchases of secular literature begin to outstrip sales of religious materials. (**Domain and Competency I.003.C. Skill: Causation**)

12. (D)

Sugar was first cultivated in Southeast Asia, then spread to India and finally to the Mediterranean. In the 15th century, Portuguese slavers were the first to acquire slaves as a labor force for sugar cultivation. The vast majority of enslaved Africans were transported from West Africa to the Caribbean and Brazil to work on sugar plantations. **Option A is incorrect.** Tobacco was an American crop. Tobacco cultivation, moreover, never required the kind of labor demands as sugar cultivation. **Option B is incorrect.** Indigo was an Old-World crop that would become an important slave-grown crop in the Americas. However, far fewer Africans were employed in its cultivation than they were in growing sugar. **Option C is incorrect.** Cotton had varietals original to both the Old World and the New. Cotton became the predominant crop produced by enslaved Africans in the American South, but only in the 19th century after the transatlantic slave trade had been outlawed. (**Domain and Competency I.003.D. Skill: Causation**)

13. (B)

The victory of the Chinese Communists in 1949 represented a high point in the spread of communism. **Option A is incorrect.** The rise of Nazism represented the victory of the antithesis of Communism. **Option C is incorrect.** Lenin's New Economic Policy was an acknowledgment that his policies of war communism had failed. The New Economic Policy was an economic program that adopted markets and private ownership. **Option D is incorrect.** The Korean War, a hot war in the middle of the Cold War, ultimately ended in lasting stalemate rather than a decisive result for or against communism. (**Domain and Competency I.004.A. Skill: Chronological reasoning**)

14. (C)

The Declaration of Independence stresses rights to liberty, equality, and the pursuit of happiness, while proclaiming the right to resist oppression. **Option A is incorrect.** Article I of the United States Constitution outlines the structure and powers of the United States Congress. **Option B is incorrect.** The English Bill of Rights did not assert social or political equality but instead emphasized the rights of Englishmen to be protected from unjust uses of royal power. **Option D is incorrect.** The Articles of Confederation stressed the rights and sovereignty of the individual states of the new United States. (**Domain and Competency I.004.B. Skill: Comparison**)

15. (B)

The development of the flying shuttle, spinning jenny, water frame, steam engine, and power loom vastly increased demand for raw cotton. The bottleneck in cotton textile production then was the fact that it was so time-consuming to clean raw cotton. Whitney's cotton gin increased the speed of cleaning raw cotton by a factor of 50 and made possible the expansion of cotton cultivation across the American South. **Option A is incorrect.** James Watt's steam engine was developed between 1765 and 1781. Its impact on cotton textile production was muted in the 18th century as most textile mills were positioned near streams and powered by water wheels. **Option C is incorrect.** The Jacquard loom made it possible to produce intricate designs on woven cloth but the technique was only developed in 1804 and used initially primarily in silk manufacturing. **Option D is incorrect.** Carding is the process of aligning cotton or woolen fibers so they can be rolled into yarn and then spun into thread. Paul's carding machine was developed in 1748. **(Domain and Competency I.004.D. Skill: Causation Chronological reasoning)**

16. (D)

Each of the distractors reflect conditions that contributed to the outbreak of a global conflict, but only the alliance system can be blamed for causing a conflict between Serbia (allied with Russia) and Austria-Hungary (allied with Germany) into a Europe-wide and then worldwide war. **Option A is incorrect.** Imperial competition had been present from the end of the Middle Ages. **Option B is correct.** European powers increased military spending by 400 percent between 1871 (the end of the Franco-Prussian War) and 1914, but increases in military spending do not necessarily result in the opening of hostilities. **Option C is incorrect.** Nationalistic jingoism had been growing since the French Revolution and Napoleonic Wars, but patriotism does not always lead to war. **(Domain and Competency I.004.F. Skill: Causation)**

17. (C)

While at each of these historical moments, nuclear war was a possibility, it was the Soviet Union's attempt to place nuclear missiles on the island of Cuba that most threatened to erupt in a nuclear exchange. **Option A is incorrect.** The Soviet blockade of Berlin led to nearly a year-long airlift to resupply the city. Both sides took care not to trigger a war at this point, and the Soviet Union had not yet acquired nuclear weaponry, so only the United States had the atomic bomb. **Option B is incorrect.** There were several moments during the war when American leaders contemplated using nuclear weapons on the Chinese who had entered the war to stop the entire peninsula from becoming a western stronghold, but all these suggestions were quickly dismissed. **Option D is incorrect.** The United States and NATO largely did nothing to stop Soviet aggression in Czechoslovakia, considering it within the Soviet sphere of interest and not of vital American national interest. **(Domain and Competency I.004.G. Skill: Chronological reasoning)**

18. (A)

Though each of the nations shaded in gray on occasion favored one side or the other in the Cold War, for the most part they endeavored to remain non-aligned. **Option B is incorrect.** Most of the nations in gray traded with and had diplomatic relationships with the United States but sought to remain independent of American influence. **Option C is incorrect.** Most of the nations in gray traded with and had diplomatic relationships with the Soviet Union but sought to remain independent of Soviet influence. **Option D is incorrect.** While North Africa, the Middle East, and South Asia had significant Muslim populations, sub-Saharan Africa and Latin America did not. **(Domain and Competency I.004.G. Skill: Comparison)**

19. (C)

Many of the early founders had sugar plantations in Barbados and were interested in supplying their sugar islands with provisions so that the land there could be devoted to the more lucrative sugar trade. **Option A is incorrect** because the center of the French fur trade was in the Northeast and Midwest. **Option B is incorrect** because Maryland had been established as a haven for Catholics and South Carolina was Anglican. **Option D is incorrect** because sailing vessels traveling from New England to West Africa would follow the trade winds and ocean currents. **(Domain and Competency II.005.A. Skill: Cause/Effect)**

20. (A)

St. Augustine, Florida, is the longest-lasting Spanish settlement in the United States. It was established in 1565. **Option B is incorrect.** The Plymouth Rock settlement was established in 1620. **Option C is incorrect.** The British settlement at Roanoke predated other English settlements, but it was short-lived, lasting only two years from 1585-1587. **Option D is incorrect.** Santa Fe, New Mexico, was established in 1610, only three years after the founding of Jamestown. **(Domain and Competency II.005.A. Skill: Content knowledge)**

21. (D)

Roger Williams founded the colony of Rhode Island in 1636 shortly after falling out with Puritan religious leaders in Massachusetts. **Option A is incorrect.** Anne Hutchinson is known for making these charges against the Puritan clergy. She was forced to leave Massachusetts and ultimately settled in Rhode Island alongside Roger Williams. **Option B is incorrect.** The island of Barbados was originally settled by English privateers (pirates) and other ne'er-do-wells who sought to profit from raids on Spanish shipping. **Option C is incorrect.** Williams did not flee to the Iroquois, though he did advocate fairer treatment of the Native American population. **(Domain and Competency II.005.A. Skill: Causation)**

22. (C)

The Great Awakening drew most of its followers from younger, poorer Americans (even many of African descent) who began to question the authority of clergy they felt did not have the true spirit of religious revival. **Option A is incorrect.** While this statement is true, it cannot be inferred from this passage. **Option B is incorrect.** Many urban residents were attracted to Whitefield's sermons, but his crowds came from widely scattered areas. Moreover, nothing about the rural or urban origins of his crowds can be inferred from this passage. **Option D is incorrect.** The Great Awakening saw racially mixed crowds worshipping together (as seen in this passage) and therefore, briefly, black and white Americans shared the experience of religious revivalism. **(Domain and Competency II.005.B. Skill: Analysis of evidence)**

23. (C)

New England had poor soils and, because it was further north, a shorter growing season. **Option A is incorrect.** New England had a number of important seaports, but New England's agricultural markets were largely local and most farmers did not grow significant surpluses. **Option B is incorrect.** New England had an age-normal distribution of settlers, actually having a smaller proportion of young, single males than did most other colonial regions. **Option D is incorrect.** New England's mortality rates were not substantially different from those in the Middle Colonies, and New England had fewer indentured servants than was the case in New York, Pennsylvania, and New Jersey. **(Domain and Competency II.005.E. Skill: Content knowledge)**

24. (A)

Primogeniture, or laws favoring the firstborn sons, were important features of aristocratic societies. Americans adopted equal inheritance instead. **Option B is incorrect.** Though in most states property requirements for voting were lowered, most states felt that universal white male suffrage was too wide an expansion of the suffrage. **Option C is incorrect.** Bicameral legislatures are usually seen as a method for limiting the power of the populace. **Option D is incorrect.** While Northern states did begin eliminating the practice of slavery, ownership of slaves in the North persisted well into the 19th century. **(Domain and Competency II.006.A. Skill: Causation)**

25. (B)

The so-called "Great Compromise" established the Congress as currently comprised, with the number of seats in the House of Representatives based on state population, and with equal membership in the Senate. **Option A is incorrect.** This is what is called the Three-Fifths Compromise that settled how population would be counted for purposes of representation. **Option C is incorrect.** Each of the statements in this distractor is correct. However, this was not the Great Compromise. **Option D is incorrect.** While the Constitution established a separation of powers, the Great Compromise was instead an agreement that settled the differences between small and large states. **(Domain and Competency II.006.D. Skill: Analysis, Content knowledge)**

26. (A)

Jefferson argued that the powers not explicitly granted to the federal government were held by the states. He contended that such proposals as the establishment of a National Bank were powers that were not specifically granted to the federal government in the Constitution, and were thus unconstitutional. This position became known as strict constructionism. **Option B is incorrect.** Judicial activism is a charge often laid at the feet of judges whose opponents contend are too broadly interpreting the law. **Option C is incorrect.** Liberalism is a political doctrine that seeks to protect and enhance the freedom of the individual. **Option D is incorrect.** Fundamentalism is a form of religion (Islam or Protestant Christianity, for example) that upholds a belief in the strict, literal interpretation of scriptural texts. **(Domain and Competency II.006.E. Skill: Content knowledge)**

27. (C)

Thomas Paine's pamphlet was a widely-read call for American independence, with over 150,000 copies sold in the colonies. **Option A is incorrect.** Dickinson's *Letters* did not call for American independence, but constituted an important document in the development of an American sense of cultural identity separate from their Britishness. **Option B is incorrect.** Benjamin Franklin published this famous cartoon image depicting the colonies as a snake cut into pieces with the slogan "Join or Die." It was widely seen, but had less impact than Paine's *Common Sense.* **Option D is incorrect.** Longfellow's poem memorialized Paul Revere's ride to Lexington and Concord, but was written well after the American Revolution. **(Domain and Competency II.006.B. Skill: Causation)**

28. (D)

Each of these Revolutionary War era heroes feared that state power would be undermined by a powerful central government. **Option A is incorrect.** The voters were only the determinative voice in elections for the House of Representatives, so the Constitution limited the power of the population rather than expanded it. **Option B is incorrect.** The opponents of the Constitution instead feared that private interests of all sorts would be strengthened over the interests of the nation as a whole. **Option C is incorrect.** Anti-Federalists instead wanted a republic and were deeply suspicious of party politics, which had a long tradition in the English parliamentary system. **(Domain and Competency II.006.D. Skill: Contextualization)**

29. (B)

Madison, Jefferson, and Hamilton agreed to a compromise that would geographically separate the seat of federal political power (Washington, D.C.) from the centers of financial and economic power (Philadelphia and New York, in exchange for the bank and debt assumption plan of Alexander Hamilton. **Option A is incorrect.** The deadline to end the slave trade was constitutionally established as no earlier than 1808. While it could have been extended by Congress, Madison and Jefferson, as Virginia slave holders with surplus slaves, had a financial interest in maintaining the 1808 date, rather than extending it. **Option C is incorrect.** At the time this compromise was made, Jefferson had no plans to purchase the Louisiana Territory from France. **Option D is incorrect.** At the time that Madison and Jefferson agreed with Hamilton on this compromise, the Alien and Sedition Acts had not been enacted yet. They were features of John Adams' administration. **(Domain and Competency II.006.E. Skill: Content knowledge)**

30. (D)

   The United States resolved conflicting claims to the Oregon Territory (Oregon, Washington, and parts of Idaho, Wyoming, and Montana) with Great Britain. Test-takers should recognize that the Annexation of Texas and the acquisition of Oregon was a key campaign platform of James K. Polk in the 1844 election. **Option A is incorrect.** The Webster-Ashburton Treaty settling the boundaries between Canada and the United States was signed in 1842. **Option C is incorrect.** The Russo-American Treaty was signed in 1824 and actually recognized Russian territorial claims in the American Northwest. **Option D is incorrect.** The Alaska Purchase was finalized in 1867. **(Domain and Competency II.007.B. Skill: Chronological reasoning)**

31. (D)

   Manifest Destiny advocates considered American liberty, progress, democratic institutions, and Protestant Christianity as legitimizing westward expansion. **Option A is incorrect.** This is known as the doctrine of "double predestination," a position held by some Calvinists. **Option B is incorrect.** There were those who held the divine inspiration of the American Constitution, but this was not what Manifest Destiny meant. **Option C is incorrect.** The "civilizing mission" of European imperialists had parallels with American Manifest Destiny, but American Manifest Destiny emphasized land acquisition more than a sort of burden for the resident populations of conquered areas. **(Domain and Competency II.007.C. Skill: Contextualization)**

32. (A)

   Dred Scott, like other African Americans, the decision argued, had not been intended for citizenship by the founding fathers. Furthermore, Congress lacked the authority to legislate slavery's illegality, as each American property owner was entitled to move to the Western territories without fear of losing their property rights, including those in slaves. **Option B is incorrect.** Stephen A. Douglas had proposed that territories be granted the right to determine by majority vote whether they would permit slavery, but this was not the rationale of the decision. **Option C is incorrect.** This is a statement that many on the court would have agreed with; however, it was not the basis of a legal argument because the Court had to explain why slavery was Constitutionally permissible, not morally permissible. **Option D is incorrect.** This was a commonly-held position of pro-slavery apologists; however, it is not a legal argument but rather a historical and religious argument. **(Domain and Competency II.007.E. Skill: Causation)**

33. (C)

   South Carolina, long a haven of states' rights support, seceded in December 1860, shortly after Lincoln's election. **Option A is incorrect.** Texas was the sixth state to vote to secede. **Option C is incorrect.** Virginia wavered, originally voting against secession, but when Lincoln ordered up troops to put down the rebellion in South Carolina, Virginia joined the Confederacy. **Option D is incorrect.** Kentucky, along with Missouri, Maryland, West Virginia, and Delaware, remained in the Union despite being a slave-owning state. **(Domain and Competency II.007.F. Skill: Content knowledge)**

34. (D)

Ulysses S. Grant gained a reputation for being willing to use strategies of total warfare to defeat his enemies through costly attrition. This strategy ultimately brought the South to surrender. **Option A is incorrect.** William T. Sherman was one of Grant's subordinates and the commander most associated with carrying out Grant's strategy. **Option B is incorrect.** Lincoln settled on Grant after relying on McClellan, who turned out to be a bitter political rival and opponent of Lincoln's war-fighting strategy. **Option C is incorrect.** John Bell Hood was Texas' best-known Civil War general. **(Domain and Competency II.007.F. Skill: Content knowledge)**

35. (B)

Sharecropping satisfied landowners' need for labor without their giving up ownership of land. It also permitted former slaves to work family farms they rented from white landowners, rather than working as gang labor as they had on the plantation system. **Option A is incorrect.** Convict labor persisted well into the 1950s; however, it did not provide a sufficient or predictable supply of labor for most landowners. **Option C is incorrect.** Serfdom was used in the Middle Ages to bind peasant farmers to the land. **Option D is incorrect.** Indentured servitude was used during the colonial period to acquire labor, but it was not used in the postbellum South. **(Domain and Competency II.007.G. Skill: Content knowledge)**

36. (B)

Wilson urged Americans to be neutral in fact as well as in deed, an admonition most Americans were happy to heed. **Option A is incorrect.** Wilson and most Americans were uneasy with supporting either of the imperial powers on both sides of the conflict. **Option C is incorrect.** Only as the war progressed did Wilson and leading American politicians come to support England and France. With the withdrawal of Russia from the war in 1917, Wilson could promote the war as a war to save democracy. **Option D is incorrect.** German Americans only were stigmatized once the United States entered the war. **(Domain and Competency II.008.A. Skill: Contextualization)**

37. (D)

Wilson had hoped to soften the Allies' anger at Germany, but France and England sought to punish Germany and forced them to accept the "War Guilt" clause in the Treaty of Versailles. **Option A is incorrect.** The League of Nations was a centerpiece of Wilson's proposal. **Option B is incorrect.** Wilson viewed the immediate cause of the war as resulting from unsatisfied national aspirations in the Balkans. **Option C is incorrect.** Wilson believed that protectionism had contributed to the underlying causes of the war. Moreover, the United States, as the world's most productive economy, would benefit from the opening of international trade. **(Domain and Competency II.008.B. Skill: Content knowledge)**

38. (C)

The propaganda film taught Americans about the ways to survive a nuclear holocaust. **Option A is incorrect.** Tornados were a natural disaster that Americans in the Great Plains and in tornado alley prepared for, but this refers to preparations to survive a nuclear attack. **Option B is incorrect.** Sheltering in place was an important response to chemical plant hazards, but this is not what this image refers to. **Option D is incorrect.** By 1952, Germany had ceased to be a threat to American interests or safety. **(Domain and Competency II.008.C. Skill: Contextualization)**

39. (D)

Joseph McCarthy was the most prominent anti-communist in Congress. He used smear tactics to discredit potential communists. The term "McCarthyism" has been used to describe the use of unsubstantiated accusations to smear political opponents with charges of communist sympathy. **Option A is incorrect.** Ronald Reagan as President of the Screen Actors Guild during much of the 1950s had been an FBI informant earlier, giving names of actors he believed were pro-communist. Reagan then appeared before the House Un-American Activities Committee (HUAC) and testified about the influence of communists in the movie industry. **Option B is incorrect.** Whittaker Chambers had been a member of the Communist Party in the 1920s and worked as a Soviet spy from 1932 to 1938. In 1948, he testified against Alger Hiss, a State Department official who was charged with espionage. **Option C is incorrect.** J. Edgar Hoover was the long-term director of the FBI and directed many of the bureau's resources toward rooting out Soviet spies in the United States. **(Domain and Competency II.008.E. Skill: Content knowledge)**

40. (D)

Though SSTs (supersonic transports) like the Concorde and other jets were a dream of the 1970s, they did not materialize as a real competitor to slower air transport. **Option A is incorrect.** NAFTA, MERCOSUR (a common market for South America), the eurozone, ASEAN, and other transnational economic organizations have reduced tariffs and trade restrictions, encouraging widespread interregional trade. **Option B is incorrect.** Cell phone penetration and the widespread availability of internet access have opened up enormous commercial opportunities. **Option C is incorrect.** "Containerization" has reduced the costs of consumer transport by over 60 percent since the 1960s. **(Domain and Competency II.008.F. Skill: Causation)**

41. (B)

The TVA created a network of hydroelectric dams that enabled the electrification of many rural areas in Tennessee, Kentucky, Arkansas, Georgia, and Alabama. As a result poor rural residents were able to then begin purchasing radios, electric ranges, and other consumer items. **Option A** is incorrect. The CCC provided work clearing brush, planting trees, and building roads, trails, ranger stations, etc. **Option C is incorrect.** The WPA was a public works program providing jobs to unemployed. **Option D is incorrect.** The FERA provided welfare to families without employment and also provided a jobs program. (**Domain and Competency II.009.B. Skill: Content knowledge**)

42. (B)

César Chávez was primarily a labor activist, though his interests and significance did extend more broadly to expansions of Mexican-American rights. **Option A is incorrect.** Segregated schools that denied Mexican Americans were an important issue in the struggle for Mexican American rights. However, Chávez was more involved in organizing farm workers. **Option C is incorrect.** Though Hispanics fought in Vietnam in significant, though not disproportionate, numbers and Chávez opposed the war, the war was never his primary focus. **Option C is incorrect.** Hispanics were often discriminated against because of language requirements demanded of voters. This was a secondary concern of Chávez. (**Domain and Competency II.009.D. Skill: Content knowledge**)

43. (D)

The Comanche emerged as an identifiable ethnic group only in the 1600s and gradually expanded into the Great Plains, and Texas during the later 1600s. **Option A is incorrect.** The Karankawa presence on the Gulf Coast long predated European arrival. They were first recorded by the shipwrecked Spaniard, Álvar Núñez Cabeza de Vaca in the 1530s. **Option B is incorrect.** The Caddo presence in Texas predated the arrival of Europeans in the Americas. **Option C is incorrect.** The Jumanos settled in the trans-Pecos region before the middle of the 15th century. (**Domain and Competency III.010.A. Skill: Comparison**)

44. (D)

While there were institutions for local government, Texas did not have its own General Assembly. **Option A is incorrect.** An important feature of Spanish settlement in the Americas was the establishment of mission stations that sought to convert, and civilize, the Native American populations. **Option B is incorrect.** There were a number of chartered *villas* in Texas, including San Antonio de Béxar. **Option C is incorrect.** Wherever Spanish settlement spread in the Americas the Spanish extended military control and defense of their settlements with the building of forts. (**Domain and Competency III.010.B. Skill: Contextualization**)

45. (A)

De la Salle's expedition to Texas and settlement on the Texas coast alarmed the Spanish authorities, who had to that point paid relatively little attention to Texas. **Option B is incorrect.** The Jumano (not Caddo Indians) had requested religious teachers be sent to them as early as 1629.

Franciscan friars had established missions to the Jumano in response, but there had been little expansion into the rest of Texas. **Option C is incorrect.** The legends of El Dorado had contributed to expeditions across Texas in the 1540s, but by the 1690s these fables were largely discredited. **Option D is incorrect.** At the time the Spanish began to show increased interest in Texas, the Comanche were not yet a significant threat to settlers. **(Domain and Competency III.010.C. Skill: Causation)**

46. (B)

Moses Austin first acquired a land grant to settle in Missouri in 1795 in what was then Spanish territory. In 1820, he requested the right to settle in Texas and was granted an empresario contract. He died before he was able to move, and his contract was taken up by his son, Stephen F. Austin. **Option A is incorrect.** Sam Houston was a hero of the Texas Revolution who served both as the president of independent Texas and its governor. However, he was a latecomer to Texas, only arriving in 1832. **Option C is incorrect.** Quanah Parker was a Comanche leader, son of the Comanche chief Peta Nocona and Cynthia Ann Parker, an Anglo-American who had been kidnapped as a child and raised as a Comanche. He was a key leader of the Comanche during the Red River War in the 1870s. **Option D is incorrect.** William Barret Travis died at the Alamo after having fled a disastrous domestic and business past in the United States. He arrived in Texas in 1831 and purchased land from Stephen F. Austin. **(Domain and Competency III.010.D. Skill: Content knowledge)**

47. (C)

The Guerrero Decree of 1829 had alarmed Texans by abolishing slavery in the Mexican republic. The law had not been enforced in Texas. Nonetheless, the possibility of Mexico's abolition of slavery was a grave concern and an underlying cause of the Texas Revolution. **Option A is incorrect.** The U.S. Constitution did not mention slavery, in part because it provided important guarantees of the right to own slaves. The Texas Constitution wanted to make these guarantees explicit. **Option B is incorrect.** Section 9 forbade the African slave trade, but guaranteed the rights of Texans to import slaves from elsewhere. **Option D is incorrect.** The Mexican government did not aim to confiscate the property of Anglo-Americans in Texas, because the Mexican government had similar guarantees of private property as the Texas Constitution of 1836. **(Domain and Competency III.011.B. Skill: Analysis, Contextualization)**

48. (C)

Mexico argued that the southern border of Texas was the Nueces River. The United States and Texans claimed all the way to the Rio Grande River. **Option A is incorrect.** The Big Bend was not understood to have large mineral resources at the time. It was not particularly coveted territory. **Option B is incorrect.** The *Llano Estacado* was effectively Comanche country. **Option D is incorrect.** The Red River and Sabine River watershed boundaries had been settled in the aftermath of the Louisiana Purchase. **(Domain and Competency III.011.C. Skill: Causation)**

49. (D)

Union soldiers landing in Galveston, Texas, on June 19, 1865, signaled the Emancipation Proclamation to enslaved African Americans in Texas. **Option A is incorrect.** Slaves were informed of the Emancipation Proclamation of 1863. The 13th Amendment would not be ratified until December 18, 1865. **Option B is incorrect.** Though the Emancipation Proclamation was signed in January 1863, it had little effect on areas that were outside Union control; therefore, Texas slaves were only informed of their freedom in June 1865, well after Lincoln's executive order. **Option C is incorrect.** Joshua Houston was Sam Houston's slave, and he did rise to political prominence during Reconstruction, but this was not the point of Juneteenth. **(Domain and Competency III.011.E. Skill: Content knowledge)**

50. (C)

Quanah Parker, son of a Comanche leader and a hostage Anglo woman, was an important leader of the Comanche "Red River War." **Option A is incorrect.** Sitting Bull was the Sioux leader at the Battle of the Little Big Horn. **Option B is incorrect.** Geronimo was a Chiricahua Apache who led an Apache rising against forcible removal to a reservation from the mid-1870s until 1886. **Option D is incorrect.** Blue Duck was a notorious Cherokee bandit who was sentenced to death by the "Hanging Judge" Isaac Parker in 1884. **(Domain and Competency III.011.F. Skill: Content knowledge)**

51. (A)

Before the discovery of Texas oil reserves, cattle and cotton were most important. **Option B is incorrect.** Sugar and rice were important, but secondary commodities. **Option C is incorrect.** Wheat would emerge as an important commodity in the 1880s and oil in the early 1900s, but before 1900 neither were significant as cotton and cattle ranching. **Option D is incorrect.** Leather products and fisheries were not insignificant, but they trailed cotton and cattle for Texas' economy. **(Domain and Competency III.011.F. Skill: Content knowledge)**

52. (B)

Many of the settlers in the Panhandle left Indiana, Illinois, and Kansas. They brought with them skills at winter wheat cultivation. Many were Germans, Russians, and Ukrainians. The southern Great Plains proved a profitable place to grow winter wheat. **(Domain and Competency III.011.H. Skill: Content knowledge)**

53. (B)

Advocates of women's suffrage saw women as important allies in these other progressive reform movements. **Option A is incorrect.** Though nationally, the Republican Party was most strongly supportive of women's suffrage of the two parties; in Texas, the suffrage movement sided with more progressive voices within the Democratic Party, rather than switching its allegiance to the Republican Party. **Option C is incorrect.** Women's suffrage advocates were not strong advocates of African American rights and equality, fearing that binding the demands for women's voting rights to integration would reduce the chance for women's voting rights to be passed. **Option D is incorrect.** Women activists in favor of women's right to vote felt that women's unique domestic vantage point and maternal instincts would provide a new moral authority for wider reforms of the society. **(Domain and Competency III.012.A. Skill: Contextualization)**

54. (C)

"Wendy the Welder" was a less-well-known counterpart to "Rosie the Riveter." **Option A is incorrect.** Flappers were young women in the 1920s known for their socializing and free spirits, but not for their labor in factories. **Option B is incorrect.** Women were drawn into wage work in the 1930s, but not so clearly in these traditionally male occupations. **Option D is incorrect.** Commercial airlines were of growing importance in the 1950s, but by then, much of the work was being done again by men. **(Domain and Competency III.012.B. Skill: Contextualization)**

55. (C)

These cases, illustrating the leadership of LULAC, served as important precedents to the *Brown v. Board of Education* decision. **Option A is incorrect.** The doctrine of "separate but equal" was only overturned with *Brown v. Board of Education*. **Option B is incorrect.** The desegregation of Texas schools would not be fully realized (in law) until after the late 1970s and early 1980s. **Option D is incorrect.** These cases did not address migrant workers' children's educational rights. **(Domain and Competency III.012.A. Skill: Causation)**

56. (D)

Kay Bailey Hutchinson was the first Texas woman to serve in the U.S. Senate, but she did so between 1993 and 2013. **(Domain and Competency III.012.C. Skill: Content knowledge)**

57. (C)

The Boll Weevil in some years destroyed one-third of the state's cotton crop. **Option A is incorrect.** The Asian Gypsy Moth was introduced into the Pacific Northwest in the 1990s and threatens hardwood forestry in the area. **Option B is incorrect.** Millions of acres in Texas are infested with fire ants. They annually cost Texas $1.2 billion in damage and control costs. **Option D is incorrect.** The Asian Longhorn Beetle is an invasive species that threatens Texas's hardwood trees and timber industry. **(Domain and Competency III.012.D. Skill: Content knowledge)**

58. (B)

The term *cowboy* was first used in colonial South Carolina to refer to African slaves who herded cattle in the open range herding system. **Option A is incorrect.** The term *lariat* comes from *la riata,* or rope. **Option C is incorrect.** *Bandanna* (or *bandana*) was worn by *vaqueros* to cover their faces during dust storms, or soaked in water to cool their heads in the heat. The term comes from a South Asian term introduced by the Portuguese into Spanish. **Option D is incorrect.** The term *chaps* comes from *chaparajos,* which were leggings used to protect a *vaquero's* legs and lower garments. **(Domain and Competency III.010.F. Skill: Content knowledge)**

59. (B)

Longitude does not impact climatic conditions. **Option A is incorrect.** Ocean currents regulate climate by transporting warm water and precipitation towards the poles and returning cold water towards the equator. **Option C is incorrect.** Higher elevations have colder climates. The closer a region is to sea level the warmer its average temperature. **Option D is incorrect.** Locations at higher latitudes receive less sun than those closer to the equator and thus have colder climates. **(Domain and Competency: IV.013.A. Skill: Content knowledge)**

60. (A)

The Marine West Coast climate is found on the west coast of continents and generally is marked by limited temperature fluctuation with cool (but not cold) winters and relatively cool summers. It also features high precipitation. **Option B is incorrect.** Tropical air masses dominate in humid subtropical climates, resulting in relatively high temperatures and evenly distributed precipitation year-round. **Option C is incorrect.** Characterized by long summers and mild winters, the Mediterranean climate type experiences changes in seasonal temperatures and precipitation as a result of changes in ocean currents and water temperatures. **Option D is incorrect.** Tropical Wet Dry climates are known for distinctive wet and dry seasons. Most precipitation occurs during the high-sun season, with a dry season that becomes longer the farther one moves from the equator. **(Domain and Competency: IV.013.E. Skill: Content knowledge)**

61. (B)

Relocation Diffusion is the direct result of the movement of people from one location to another. As they move they bring their own culture that then spreads throughout the new area in which they have relocated. **Option A is incorrect.** Contagious Diffusion occurs as a result of an innovation spreading from person to person within a culture. **Option C is incorrect.** Expansion Diffusion occurs when ideas spread form one culture to another of close proximity. **Option D is incorrect.** Hierarchical Diffusion is the result of culture moving from more influential and powerful cultures to less powerful or influential cultures.**(Domain and Competency: IV.014.B. Skill: Content knowledge)**

62. (C)

The landform is a mesa, which is formed by the effects of erosion. **Option A is incorrect.** Volcanic activity occurs in regions where tectonic plates are in collision and usually indicate the presence of newer mountains or ranges that have not had as lengthy exposure to erosion. **Option**

B is incorrect. Subduction creates mountain ranges as tectonic plates collide driving one plate upward to form mountains and mountain ranges. **Option D is incorrect.** Rifting occurs when tectonic plates drift apart resulting in rift valleys. **(Domain and Competency: IV.013.B. Skill: Analysis)**

63. (A), (C), and (D)

The theory of plate tectonics explains the matching continental coastlines noticed by 19th century geologists and geographers. Volcanic activity and uplift continental mountain ranges are both explained by the movement along the boundaries of continental plates. **Option B is incorrect.** Glacial drift reflects changing climates and global temperatures rather than the movement of continental plates. **(Domain and Competency: IV.013.B. Skill: Content knowledge)**

64. (D)

In stage two, the death rates drop while birth rates remain high, and rapid population growth occurs. **Option A is incorrect.** Decline in population growth occurs in stage five in a few modern nations as fertility decreases to below replacement levels. **Option B is incorrect.** A slow stable growth occurs after a country proceeds from stage two to stage three and into stage four. Fertility rates are stable but sufficient to more than replace populations experiencing low mortality rates. **Option C is incorrect.** Rapid decline in population occurs in times of demographic crises such as famine, disease, and war. The decline usually represents only a momentary demographic shock as populations usually grow in the aftermath of such crises. **(Domain and Competency: IV.014.E. Skill: Content knowledge)**

65. (C)

The Suez Canal connects the Red Sea with the Mediterranean Sea, and thus connects European and Asian trade. **Option A is incorrect.** The Panama Canal crosses the Isthmus of Panama and connects the Pacific and Atlantic Oceans. It was only opened in the 20th century. **Option B is incorrect.** The Grand Canal links the Yangtze and the Huang He Rivers in China and fostered trade within China. **Option D is incorrect.** The Elbe-Lubeck Canal connects the North and Baltic seas, and thus facilitated trade in northern Europe. **(Domain and Competency: IV.015.D. Skill: Content knowledge)**

66. (D)

The seasons, which vary from climate to climate—some with two different seasons, and some with four—are a direct result of the Earth's annual movement, or revolution, around the sun. **Option A is incorrect.** "Global warming," or climate change since the beginning of the Anthropocene period, is the result of man-made pollution and greenhouse gases and is not a result of the earth's revolution around the sun. **Option B is incorrect.** Evaporation is a step in the hydrological cycle resulting from the sun's energy, but it is not a direct result of the Earth's revolution. **Option**

C is incorrect. Loss of biodiversity, much like the processes of global warming, is the result of man-made pollution and human changes to the earth's environments. (**Domain and Competency: IV.013.C. Skill: Causation**)

67. (B)

The three main zones are Tropical, Temperate, and Polar. They are divided by lines of latitude. From the equator to 23.5 degrees north or south are the tropics. From 23.5 to 66.5 degrees north or south are the temperate regions. And from 66.5 to 90 degrees north or south are the polar regions. **Options A, C, and D are incorrect.** All of these terms describe general climate subtypes. (**Domain and Competency: IV.013.A. Skill: Causation**)

68. (D)

Chili peppers were a crop grown in Mesoamerica and the Caribbean before 1492. **Option A is incorrect.** Honeybees came with Europeans after 1492 and soon spread across the continent. **Option B is incorrect.** Cattle including longhorn cattle were introduced from Europe after 1492. **Option C is incorrect.** Sugar cane originated in Southeast Asia, spread from there to India and the Mediterranean, from where Europeans brought the crop to the Americas. (**Domain and Competency III.010.E. Skill: Analysis**)

69. (C)

Potatoes provided a rich source of calories and nutrients on small plots of land, allowing Europeans to marry at younger ages as a family required less land to be sustainable. Earlier marriage ages increased women's fertile lifespan, thereby increasing European population. **Option A is incorrect.** Corn had an important effect on African populations and Asian populations, but not until the 19th and 20th centuries. **Option B is incorrect.** Wheat was an Old World crop, originating in the Fertile Crescent. **Option D is incorrect.** Beans, though increasingly important to diets in Africa, never became as critical to populations in Europe and Asia. (**Domain and Competency I.003.D. Skill: Causation**)

70. (D)

Hinduism developed a system of social ranks that were closely linked to one's occupation, making social mobility difficult. **Option A is incorrect** because, while occupation and status were linked within Confucianism, social hierarchy was not fixed and opportunities for social mobility were available. **Option B is incorrect.** Zoroastrianism, while it had remnants of a caste system, most notably elevating priests and warriors, exerted social control largely through the priestly class's management of the ritual calendar. **Option C is incorrect** because Buddhism rejected the moral authority of caste identity. (**Domain and Competency I.001.C. Skill: Content knowledge**)

71. (B)

Push factors are factors that push people to leave their place of origin. Famines, war, and over-population are often considered push factors. **Option A is incorrect.** The primary factors encouraging Italian migration to the United States in the 19th century were the abundance of jobs in manufacturing, rather than the dismal conditions in the Italy. **Option C is incorrect**. Germanic migration into the Roman Empire (with the exception of those driven there by the arrival of the Huns) was largely a result of the attractiveness of opportunities for plunder in the Roman Empire. **Option D is incorrect.** Arab migration across North Africa was less a result of conditions in the Arabian Peninsula than the weakness of North Africa in the face of the rising force of Arab warriors motivated by the desire to spread Islam and acquire territory. **(Domain and Competency IV.014.E. Skill: Content knowledge)**

72. (B)

Hierarchical diffusion describes the spread of a cultural practice from a politically or economically dominant region to a region under its control. The spread of American food ways into South Korea and Japan resulted largely from the stationing of troops in both countries in the aftermath of World War II and the Korean War. **Option A is incorrect.** Contagious diffusion spreads from person to person in a contiguous fashion. For example, Buddhism's original spread within the Indian sub-continent. American food ways were adopted as a result of the power and influence of American institutions in the post-war period. **Option C is incorrect.** Relocation diffusion occurs as a result of the migration and settlement of a population outside their homeland, with a consequent spread of the cultural practice. The spread of Judaism within the Mediterranean region during the period before and after the destruction of Jerusalem in 70 CE would be an example. **Option D is incorrect.** Stimulus diffusion refers to the spread of a new cultural practice or idea, but with the new idea being changed by the adopting culture. An example of this would be the spread of McDonald's in India, where vegetarian and other culturally appealing options were substituted for McDonald's burgers. **(Domain and Competency IV.014.B. Skill: Content knowledge)**

73. (C)

Comte argued that the study of society could be as rigorous and empirically driven as the natural and physical sciences. He thus argued for a scientific study of society. **Option A is incorrect.** This statement reflects the views of Karl Marx who saw the history of social development as explicable by reference to class conflict. Comte instead saw society developing in stages from societies driven by religious explanations, to those that sought more abstract, philosophical explanations, to finally the modern scientific mindset. **Option B is incorrect.** This statement reflects modern constructivist arguments rather than positivist arguments such as those Auguste Comte offered to explain social phenomenon. **Option D is incorrect.** These are the words of Adam Smith. "Invisible hand" should be the giveaway. **(Domain and Competency IV.016.D. Skill: Content knowledge)**

74. (A)

Before the 1830s, the most important transportation improvements were related to the adaptation of the steam engine to shipping and the growth of canal networks, particularly in the Northeast. After 1830, railroads became ever more important to reducing transport times. **Option B is incorrect.** The clipper ship was most important in the China trade and in transportation between East Coast cities and the West Coast. But the heyday of the clipper ship was after 1830. Steamships were important to the opening up of trade along the Mississippi and Ohio Rivers. But, the real decreases in transport times after 1830 were the result of the expansion of railroad networks. **Option C is incorrect.** The National Road, which was begun in 1816, did improve transport times significantly, but not so much as did the steamship and the canal system. The heyday of the canal was in the 1820s and 1830s. After 1840, the railroad was much more significant. The interstate highway system was not put in place until the 1950s. **Option D is incorrect.** Keelboats were critical to opening up the Mississippi before the 1820s. However, after the arrival of the steamboat, which had the same operating costs and speeds going up-river or down-river, the steamboat rapidly replaced keelboats. Stagecoaches were most important in the American West, particularly after 1850. They were not widely used in the East. The same could be said for the Pony Express. **(Domain and Competency IV.015.B. Skill: Chart reading, Causation)**

75. (C)

The "equal protection clause" of the 14th Amendment has been the basis of important expansions of equal rights in the United States. **Option A is incorrect.** The 14th Amendment makes clear that "all persons born or naturalized in the United States are citizens of the United States, and of the state in which they reside." **Option B is incorrect.** This right was declared in the 15th Amendment, though voter suppression has been applied to African American voters in many ways since the ratification of that amendment. **Option D is incorrect.** Property protections are established in the Fourth Amendment. **(Domain and Competency V.017.G. Skill: Content knowledge)**

76. (D)

The system of judicial review entitles the federal courts to determine the constitutional validity of a legislative act or administrative decision. It was not immediately clear that the Supreme Court had this role. This case confirmed that responsibility in the hand of the federal court system. **Option A is incorrect.** Article I of the Constitution grants Congress powers that are not explicitly enumerated in the Constitution, so long as they are "necessary and proper" to implement the powers listed in the Constitution. These powers are said to be implied powers. **Option B is incorrect.** A strict constructionist interpretation of the Constitution requires the federal government to only act in ways that are specifically granted in the text of the Constitution. In short, it severely limits the implied powers of the Congress. **Option C is incorrect.** Dual federalism is a federal system with clearly demarcated differences between federal and state government powers and institutions. **(Domain and Competency V.017.F. Skill: Change over time)**

77. (C)

Most of the Constitutional amendments have been proposed by Congress and ratified by the state legislatures. **Option A is incorrect.** While option A is one of the ways in which constitutional amendments may be proposed, this method has not been often used. **Option B is incorrect.** The US Constitution does not allow for a plebiscite (popular vote) of this kind to propose or ratify amendments. **Option D is incorrect.** This is one of the way in which amendments can be ratified, but it has not been used since the original ratification of the Constitution itself. **(Domain and Competency: V.017.C. Skill: Process knowledge)**

78. (A)

The decision denied that African Americans were entitled to citizenship rights in the United States regardless of their rights within their individual state, and made it clear that slave owners' rights to their slaves extended to states where slavery was outlawed. **Option B is incorrect** because the doctrine of "separate but equal" was established by *Plessy v. Ferguson.* **Option C is incorrect** because while the Missouri Compromise's principle of restricting the northward expansion of slavery within the Louisiana Territory was overturned, the Missouri Compromise had permitted slavery in Missouri and this principle was not at issue. **Option D is incorrect** Chief Justice Taney accepted the contention that slaves were free to legislate the freedom of slaves within their own territory. **(Domain and Competency V.017.H. Skill: Causation, Analysis of evidence)**

79. (D)

The power to declare war is held exclusively by the Congress. **Option A is incorrect.** The president has the responsibility to use the power of the executive branch to put down uprisings or domestic threats. **Option B is incorrect.** Most of the powers relating to foreign policy are within the purview of the president. **Option C is incorrect.** The president is granted the power to pardon and commute sentences, but only for federal crimes. **(Domain and Competency V.017.B. Skill: Content knowledge)**

80. (A)

Since World War II, presidents have claimed wide latitude to use the American military to respond to a number of international threats. According to Article II, Section 8, Clause 11, Congress alone is charged with the right to authorize a war. **Option B is incorrect.** Even though there have not been formal declarations of war, presidents have requested, and most often received, congressional authorizations of use of force. **Option C is incorrect.** The president is required to seek the advice and consent of the Senate for treaties, but the whole Congress is required to declare war. **Option D is incorrect.** The War Powers Resolution was passed in 1973 over Richard Nixon's veto. It required that presidents report to Congress within 48 hours of sending troops into combat and gave presidents a time limit before which Congressional authorization or declaration of war had to be received. **(Domain and Competency V.017.F. Skill: Process knowledge)**

81. (C)

Only the federal government can regulate interstate and international trade. **Option A is incorrect.** Both federal and state governments maintain law and order and provide for public safety. Consider the policing function of the federal Drug Enforcement Agency or FBI. **Option B is incorrect.** Both state and federal governments are authorized to create courts and staff them. **Option D is incorrect.** Federal and state governments both tax. We pay federal income taxes, state sales taxes, and local property taxes, for example. **(Domain and Competency V.017.I. Skill: Comparison)**

82. (D)

The election is "thrown" into the House of Representatives. There, rather than a vote by each member, as is the case on all other matters before the House, the Constitution calls for each state delegation to receive one vote. **Option A is incorrect.** Representation in the House of Representatives is based on a state's population, but each state has two senators regardless of a state's population size. **Option B is incorrect.** If this were the case, Alaska would have more electoral college votes than Texas. It has three electoral votes. **Option D is incorrect.** This would be an interesting idea. Rather than suppressing the vote, it might encourage states to do their utmost to get the vote out. Alas. **(Domain and Competency V.018.B. Skill: Content knowledge)**

83. (C)

Many states had included this right in their own Bills of Rights, and limited rights to bear arms had been among the rights of Englishmen listed in the English Bill of Rights. However, the debates in state ratifying conventions, and the first clause of the amendment, make clear that the right was principally a right of the states for the purpose of maintaining a militia. **Option A is incorrect.** While the Framers viewed rebellion as a justified response to tyrannical governments, having just done so, the amendment makes it clear that the purpose of the amendment was in order to maintain state militias. **Option B is incorrect.** Only with the case *District of Columbia v. Heller* in 2008 did the Supreme Court rule that laws forbidding civilians from owning handguns were unconstitutional. Prior to that decision, states and local governments routinely regulated ownership of handguns and other types of weapons. **Option D is incorrect.** Most Americans did not rely on hunting to feed their families, even in the colonial period. **(Domain and Competency V.018.D. Skill: Causation)**

84. (B)

Such precedents as the president's title (Mr. President), the tradition of two-term presidencies (later enforced by the 22nd Amendment to the Constitution), and the president's right to fire executive branch officers, to name only a few, were put in place by Washington (and later presidents), and became the practice for successive presidents. **Option A is incorrect.** Though congressional legislation has contributed, the power of precedent has been critical to the developing institution of the presidency. **Option C is incorrect.** Limitations on the power of the presidency have resulted in changing the office of the presidency, but the most important factor in shaping the presidency has been the traditions established by its earliest holders. **Option D is incorrect.** The amendment process has limited the length of presidential service, but beyond that there have been relatively few amendments that have shaped the behavior and practices of the presidency. **(Domain and Competency V.018.E. Skill: Causation)**

85. (B)

Each of the subordinate points illustrate ways in which the New Deal increased the scope and reach of the federal government vis-à-vis the states. **Option A is incorrect.** While the New Deal increased the governmental role in the economy, Roosevelt's policies were designed to save capitalism rather than to overturn it. Moreover, each of these points illustrate ways in which federalism was changed by New Deal policies. **Option C is incorrect.** None of the subordinate points of the outline speak to American fears or lack of confidence in government during the Great Depression. **Option D is incorrect.** Not all of the subordinate points of the outline (most notably choice D) speak to ways in which the New Deal addressed the causes of the Great Depression. **(Domain and Competency V.017.E. Skill: Argumentation)**

86. (C)

John Locke argued that governments were formed from a social contract for the purposes of protecting these natural rights, and that when governments failed to meet their obligations to do so, the people of the nation had the right to overthrow and refashion that government. **Option A is incorrect.** Thomas Hobbes argued that government originated in a social contract, but not one designed to protect natural rights. Instead, according to Hobbes, the social contract was formed to end the violence of all against all of primordial society. The sovereign state represented a bulwark against that violent reality and should not be overthrown, as society would then return to its original state of violent competition. **Option B is incorrect.** Karl Marx saw government as reflective of the class interests of the economic system and its beneficiaries. Marx argued that "natural rights" doctrine sustained the interests of the *bourgeoisie*. **Option D is incorrect.** Adam Smith would have likely accepted many of Locke's assumptions, but as Adam Smith published his treatise *The Wealth of Nations* in 1776, his philosophy likely had little direct impact on Thomas Jefferson or the other drafters of the Declaration of Independence. **(Domain and Competency V.019.B. Skill: Contextualization)**

87. (D)

Bicameralism refers to a two-chamber legislature. **Option A is incorrect.** England's parliamentary system relies on an executive that is drawn from the legislature rather than separated from it. **Option B is incorrect.** While the U.S. Senate is often considered the more stable, less democratic branch of the legislature, it is not composed of an aristocracy. None exists in the United States. **Option C is incorrect.** The American president has the power to veto, but Congress can override that veto. The British head of state—the Queen or King—has the veto power in name only, but in fact has no power to halt legislative enactments. **(Domain and Competency V.019.D. Skill: Content knowledge)**

88. (C)

The Constitution did not provide for political parties, as the Framers were suspicious of them. **Option A is incorrect.** While the Constitution did not address parties, it was also not amended to allow them. **Option B is incorrect.** The Framers did not abolish parties. **Option D is incorrect.** The "first-past-the-post" voting system (or simple plurality or winner-take-all system) that developed in the United States has resulted in two-party dominance in American politics, but this was not written into law as an aim of the Framers. **(Domain and Competency V.017.E. Skill: Content knowledge)**

89. (A)

Most parliamentary systems have an executive or prime minister chosen from the ranks of the legislature. **Option B is incorrect.** Some parliamentary systems have federal power sharing with state or provincial governments while others are organized into unitary governments. **Option C is incorrect.** While parliamentary systems originated in monarchies, there are parliamentary republics. Israel, for example, is a parliamentary republic, as is Greece, Germany, and many others. **Option D is incorrect.** Most parliamentary systems have proportional systems of representation that increase the opportunity for minority parties to influence political decision-making. **(Domain and Competency V.019.D.1. Skill: Comparison)**

90. (B)

A theocracy involves clerical leaders controlling the levers of power. **Option A is incorrect.** An oligarchy is the rule of the few, usually the wealthy. **Option C is incorrect.** Caesaro-papism involves the secular ruler exercising both predominant political power and religious authority. **Option D is incorrect.** Feudal systems are decentralized and personalized systems of government. **(Domain and Competency V.019.D.2. Skill: Comparison)**

91. (B)

Though there is no monetary price associated with this choice, the student is choosing to use a resource (their time) in one way rather than another in order to accomplish different goals. **Option A is incorrect.** This reflects the monetary price or cost of a choice, but not its opportunity cost. An opportunity cost is incurred when one makes a choice between two alternatives uses of one's resources. **Option C is incorrect.** Acquiring a loan to purchase a vehicle makes it possible for the student to spread out the monetary costs of their purchase, but is not an example of the opportunity cost. **Option D is incorrect.** The choice to change majors is not an example of an opportunity cost. **(Domain and Competency V.020.A. Skill: Contextualization)**

92. (A)

The quantity of bananas supplied at $2.00 would be greater than the quantity of bananas demanded. Suppliers would be encouraged to produce and sell more bananas than buyers would be willing to purchase at that price. **Option B is incorrect.** At $2.00, consumers would be unwilling or unable to purchase the quantity of bananas sellers would be willing to sell. **Option C is incorrect.** Price floors do not have an impact on movements in the demand curve. Demand curves shift as a result of changes in the number of buyers, changes in the price of related products, changes in the incomes of consumers, changes in consumer tastes, or changes in expectation about future changes in prices. **Option D is incorrect.** Price ceilings do not have an effect on movements of supply or demand curves. Changes in the supply curve result from changes in input prices, changes in the prices of related goods or services, changes in technology, changes in expectation, or changes in the number of producers. **(Domain and Competency VI.020.C. Skill: Causation, Chart reading)**

93. (D)

Changes in incomes affect demand. In this case, falling income levels will reduce demand, leading the demand curve to shift to the left. **Option A is incorrect.** Changes in the prices of related goods and services result in changes in demand. Increasing costs of storage batteries will increase the prices of electric cars, reducing their demand, and increasing the demand for gasoline vehicles. **Option B is incorrect.** Changes in expectations affect demand curves. Fears that gasoline prices will rise in the future will result in an increase in demand and a rightward shift of the demand curve. **Option C is incorrect.** Increased demand for SUVs and four-wheel drive trucks will result in greater gas consumption and increasing demand for gasoline. This will result in the demand curve shifting to the right rather than to the left. **(Domain and Competency VI.020.C. Skill: Causation, Chart reading)**

94. (C)

Before the cotton gin, it was not profitable to use slave labor to grow cotton, as the time spent by an enslaved person processing the raw cotton was a costly use of enslaved labor. **Option A is incorrect.** The spinning jenny vastly increased the demand for raw cotton thread. This had an indirect impact on the demand for cotton, but the cotton gin was a more immediate factor. **Option B is incorrect.** Sugar mills were important to processing sugar cane, and there were sugar plantations in Mississippi before the expansion of the cotton economy. But real settlement in the trans-Appalachian Southeast was really only triggered by the growth of cotton production. And the cotton gin made that possible. **Option D is incorrect.** The steamship made it possible for cotton growers to ship their cotton from the interior of the South. However, this was a later contributing factor to the expansion of cotton plantations after 1793. **(Domain and Competency VI.022.E. Skill: Causation)**

95. (C)

Karl Marx's theories were important to the development of socialist governments, and the rise of communist states as well. **Option A is incorrect.** John Maynard Keynes' ideas about the role of government intervention in the economy with the purpose of reducing business-cycle fluctuations were designed to save capitalism rather than introduce socialism. **Option B is incorrect.** Adam Smith is most often associated with the rise of *laissez-faire,* or free market economics. **Option D is incorrect.** John Locke's writings were largely devoted to analyzing law and political systems and had much less influence on the study of economics. **(Domain and Competency VI.020.D. Skill: Content knowledge)**

96. (A)

John Maynard Keynes argued that during recessions, governments should increase spending, particularly on projects that put people back to work, in order to prime the pump of the economy. This is best done without corresponding increases in tax burdens. **Option B is incorrect.** Adam Smith and his adherents emphasize the market's self-correcting abilities and discourage such projects as government building or job-creation proposals. **Option C is incorrect.** Friedman's contention that monetary policy is best used to correct inflationary or recessionary trends in the economy is not reflected in Obama's policies described in the question, which are examples of fiscal policy (government taxing and spending proposals) and not monetary policy. **Option D is incorrect.** The Obama policy prescription neither reflects nor supports Ricardo's arguments. **(Domain and Competency VI.21.F. Skill: Contextualization)**

97. (B)

Cyclical unemployment refers to unemployment that results from fluctuations in aggregate supply and demand. **Option A is incorrect.** Structural unemployment refers to unemployment that occurs when a worker's skills do not match the skills demanded by businesses, usually because of some technical or technological change. **Option C is incorrect.** Frictional unemployment refers to those workers who are unemployed because they are new entrants into the job market, or voluntarily transitioning between jobs. A certain level of frictional unemployment is seen as both inevitable and a positive sign of a vibrant economy. **Option D is incorrect.** Seasonal unemployment refers to workers who are out of work because the industry in which they work does not need them year-round. This is often the case in construction, some agricultural labor, and retail. **(Domain and Competency VI.021.F. Skill: Content knowledge)**

98. (B)

With a few exceptions, between 1950 and 1970, inflation and unemployment were inversely related, as predicted by the Phillips curve, named after William Phillips. **Option A is incorrect.** A downward-sloping trend line suggests an inverse (or indirect) relationship, rather than a direct relationship. **Option C is incorrect.** A proportional relationship would suggest that the inflation and unemployment would always change proportionally. Thus, if the inflation rate was 1.5 percent and unemployment rate was 3 percent in 1950, if the inflation rate rose to 2 percent in 1951, unemployment would rise to 4 percent. **Option D is incorrect.** A normal relationship or distribution is described by a bell curve. **(Domain and Competency VI.021.E. Skill: Chart reading)**

99. (A)

Markets for most agricultural products exhibit the features of pure competition: many buyers and sellers, standardized products, complete information, and ease of entry and exit. As a result, farmers are price takers, not price makers. **Option B is incorrect.** Oligopolies are composed of two or three firms in the market, whereas most farmers are one of thousands of producers in the same industry. **Option C is incorrect.** A monopoly is characterized by only one producing firm in the market. **Option D is incorrect.** Monopolistic competition has many firms competing with one another. However, these firms have a product that is distinguished from those of its competitors giving each producer somewhat greater market power than is the case in a perfectly competitive marketplace like that faced by most farmers. **(Domain and Competency VI.020.F. Skill: Contextualization)**

100. (C)

While all corporate structures reduce the liability of the owners, the partnership or sole proprietorship that forms an LLC protects the owners' or the partners' assets from creditors and legal liability. **Option A is incorrect.** Joint-stock companies were simply the earliest forms of corporations. **Option B is incorrect.** Corporations are liable for the firm's debts and for lawsuits against the corporation; however, the owners of a corporation are shielded from such liability. Corporations are not partnerships or proprietorships. **Option D is incorrect.** Cooperatives may be LLCs and are organized as partnerships, but cooperatives do not necessarily have to form LLCs to protect their assets. **(Domain and Competency VI.021.C. Skill: Content knowledge)**

101. (D)

The appreciation or strengthening of the U.S. dollar will result in cheaper imports from foreign countries. As a result, American businesses that import goods from abroad will be able to purchase more imports and sell them at lower prices in the United States. **Option A is incorrect.** American firms that produce goods for sale abroad suffer from increases in the value of the U.S. dollar. As a result, they will likely have to lay off American workers. **Option B is incorrect.** Tourists interested in visiting the United States benefit from the strengthening of their own currencies vis-à-vis the American dollar. Thus, if the dollar increases in value, foreign tourists will be less able to stay longer, eat better, or enjoy more purchases. **Option C is incorrect.** Gold's value fluctuates largely on the strength or weakness of the American dollar, as it is traded mainly in U.S. currency. When the dollar depreciates, foreign investors often look to invest in gold rather than dollars, thus driving up the price of gold. A bank with large gold reserves therefore will see the value of its holdings rise when the dollar is weak and fall when the dollar is strong. **(Domain and Competency VI.020.G. Skill: Causation)**

102. (C)

This clause authorized the United States government to establish patents, trademarks, copyrights, and limited monopolies for inventors, writers, etc. **Option A is incorrect.** The Sherman Antitrust Act was passed by Congress claiming its right to restrict the size and growth of private monopolies as part of its responsibility to regulate interstate commerce. **Option B is incorrect.** The Interstate Commerce Commission also reflected Congressional claims to the authority to regulate interstate commerce. **Option D is incorrect.** The Food and Drug Act that authorized the establishment of the FDA was carried out under the auspices of the interstate commerce clause of the constitution. **(Domain and Competency VI.021.A. Skill: Content knowledge)**

103. (A)

With savings guaranteed by the federal government, more Americans put their nest-eggs in banks, making those savings available for loans to firms and homeowners. **Option B is incorrect.** There is no connection between the FDIC and FICA (Federal Insurance Contributions Act) taxes for Social Security. **Option C is incorrect.** Exchange rates refer to the price of currencies on international currency markets. The FDIC has little impact on these values. **Option D is incorrect.** The FDIC only indirectly reduces mortgage costs by increasing the pool of savings that can be made available to homebuyers. **(Domain and Competency VI.021.B. Skill: Causation)**

104. (A)

Stocks entitle the holder to a share of company ownership, while a bond signifies money loaned to the company at interest. **Option B is incorrect.** Bond holders pay taxes on interest earned and stock owners pay capital gains taxes when a stock is sold, or pay income taxes on dividend income. **Option C is incorrect.** Both stocks and bonds are sold on the open market. **Option D is incorrect.** Stockholders as owners of the company are paid after the company's creditors, some of whom are bondholders. **(Domain and Competency VI.021.C. Skill: Content knowledge)**

105. (A)

Mutual funds pool assets into less risky combinations of assets than if one were to purchase stocks or bonds in individual companies. **Option B is incorrect.** Asset-based securities are stocks or securities that are composed of collections of loans issued by banks for student loans, homes, automobiles or other purchases. These are bought and sold by brokers who are betting on the likelihood that the loans will be paid off. **Option C is incorrect.** Bonds are simply loans given to the government or to private corporations with a promise of repayment at a later date with interest. **Option D is incorrect.** A 501(c)(3) is a nonprofit corporation under the U.S. tax code. A 501(c)(3) is not to be confused with a 401(k), another term for a stock-based or bond-based retirement account. **(Domain and Competency VI.021.D. Skill: Content knowledge)**

106. (C)

Samuel F.B. Morse developed the telegraph in the early 19th century. The code used to communicate using the telegraph machine is known as the Morse Code. **Option A is incorrect.** Richard Arkwright was an English entrepreneur of the 18th century whose innovations, including the spinning jenny, revolutionized the textile industry. **Option C is incorrect.** Robert Fulton is known primarily for his improvements of the steamship. **Option D is incorrect.** Samuel Slater was the first American entrepreneur to develop a textile factory in the United States. **(Domain and Competency VI.022.E. Skill: Content knowledge)**

107. (D)

Inquiry-based learning requires students to pose their own questions, develop their own hypotheses, and test these hypotheses using primary and secondary source data. Each of the other distractors require students to individually or collectively put themselves in the shoes of a historical actor and acquire an empathy (different from sympathy) for that actor's historical situation. That is not inquiry. **Option A is incorrect.** This task does not require inquiry but empathy. In effect, it is an evaluative task, not an exploratory task. **Option B is incorrect.** This task requires students to attempt to recreate attitudes or opinions from the past, not to develop their own theory about the events of that past. **Option C is incorrect.** Re-enactment of a historical event, while it might require research and careful study, has as its aim not the development of the student's own theory about the event, but the recreation of that event. **(Domain and Competency VII.023.A. Skill: Analysis)**

108. (B)

Conducting research involves both identifying sources of information, reading and comprehending that information, and analyzing that information. It therefore involves a number of higher order thinking skills. **Option A is incorrect.** Memorization involves mastering the recollection of information, but not higher order or critical thinking. **Option C is incorrect.** Identifying and recalling names and locations of cities is mere recall. **Option D is incorrect.** Listening is an important skill, but it primarily involves comprehension rather than critical thinking processes. **(Domain and Competency VII.023.F. Skill: Comparison)**

109. (B)

History is a discipline that most clearly examines change over time. An economist interested in this question would be required to take a historical perspective. **Option A is incorrect.** Geography as a discipline will be less applicable to these kinds of technological questions and analysis of growth in productivity over time. **Option C is incorrect.** Anthropology is more interested in cultural questions and in the development of "primitive" societies. **Option D is incorrect.** Sociology emphasizes the study of social relations rather than economic change over time. **(Domain and Competency VII.023.D. Skill: Comparison)**

110. (B)

In order to develop a research program and collect data, a hypothesis is needed. **Option A is incorrect.** Literature surveys are useful for developing hypotheses and identifying what evidence might be useful. **Option C is incorrect.** Acquiring funding is a feature of academic research today, but need not be a requirement of scientific research. **Option D is incorrect.** Presenting the conclusions to other scholars or publishing findings is an important final part of the scientific and academic endeavor but not necessary to the scientific method. **(Domain and Competency VII.023.E. Skill: Contextual knowledge)**

111. (A)

The scatter plot shows a positive correlation as generally, though not in each case, the more students studied, the better their exam grade. **Option B is incorrect.** Scatter charts such as this are used to illustrate correlation, not causation. **Option C is incorrect.** A perfect positive correlation would indicate that for each hour of increased study a student's grade would improve by the same amount. **Option D is incorrect.** If there were a negative correlation between hours of study and exam grade, the more a student prepared, the lower their grade would be. **(Domain and Competency VII.024.D. Skill: Analysis, Chart reading)**

112. (C)

An assignment like this involves not only comprehension of Nader's criticism, but also evaluation, a higher-order thinking skill. **Option A is incorrect.** This reflects simple recall knowledge. **Option B is incorrect.** This assignment requires only comprehension. **Option D is incorrect.** This assignment requires recall, but not higher-order thinking. **(Domain and Competency VII.026.C. Skill: Analysis)**

113. (B)

The signal words associated with comparative reasoning include the following: *although, as well as, as opposed to, both, but, compared with, different from, either . . . or, even though, however, instead of, in common, on the other hand, otherwise, similar to, similarly, still, yet.* **(Domain and Competency VII.026.E. Skill: Analysis)**

114. (C)

Wherever settled agriculture developed throughout history, population densities increased. Agriculture made possible, and indeed required, greater population density. **Option A is incorrect.** Higher levels of educational attainment correlate positively with increased incomes, but do not necessarily cause them. **Option B is incorrect.** There is a correlation between lower rates of unemployment and higher rates of inflation, but the two do not have a causative effect. **Option D is incorrect.** The highest rates of voter participation, in fact, are often found where individual freedoms are most severely restricted. **(Domain and Competency VII.023.B. Skill: Content knowledge)**

115. (D)

Understanding the factors that contribute to land use and development requires the use of the following disciplines: economics, geography, sociology, anthropology, etc. **Option A is incorrect.** This comparative assignment is a historical assignment alone. **Option B is incorrect.** A Production Possibilities Curve is an assignment that requires only economics. **Option C is incorrect.** This is an assignment that requires only political science knowledge. **(Domain and Competency VII.023.D. Skill: Analysis)**

116. (A), (C), and (D)

Options A, C, and D are correct. Surveys are commonly used as social science research tools. Case studies are commonly used in sociology, political science, and economics. And interviews are frequently used in anthropology, sociology, political science, and other disciplines. **Option B is incorrect.** Diagnostic analysis implies a pathology requiring a cure. Social science research does not begin with such a presumption. **(Domain and Competency VII.023.E. Skill: Analysis)**

117. (A), (B), (C), and (D)

Options A, B, C, and D are correct. A historian interested in contemporary views of the Civil Rights movement would use the movie *Selma* as a primary source. Field notes are primary sources in ethnological research undertaken by anthropologists. Economists often rely on governmental reports as primary sources for their research. A letter from George Washington to Alexander Hamilton would be an important primary source of information about the history of the American presidency. **(Domain and Competency VII.024.A. Skill: Content knowledge)**

118. (C)

Authentic assessment means are used to evaluate students' ability to demonstrate their learning using a variety of tasks and across a variety of skills. **Option A is incorrect.** National and state-designed criterion-based multiple-choice tests are useful as measures of student abilities, but they don't offer as wide a range of tests of real world skills. **Option B is incorrect.** I-learned statements are useful ways to informally evaluate student understanding of a lesson but do not provide as wide a range of opportunities for students to demonstrate competence and understanding. **Option D is incorrect.** Teacher-designed tests provide one means of evaluating student learning, but do not necessarily test students' real-world skills and understanding. **(Domain and Competency VII.026.H. Skill: Evaluation)**

119. (B)

The student will be able to read and follow along with his partner and have the opportunity to demonstrate comprehension by retelling what might otherwise have been too difficult to read alone. **Option A is incorrect.** This does not represent a differentiation in instruction. This is assessment. Moreover, it merely improves the student's chances for success without differentiating assessment to best evaluate learning. **Option C is incorrect.** A student with a reading disability would have similar difficulties comprehending the lecture notes. Moreover, when the student has the lecture notes they are less likely to engage in classroom learning. **Option D is incorrect.** Extended time to complete an assignment, while perhaps appropriate for other reasons, is not an example of good differentiated instruction. **(Domain and Competency VII.026.B.1. Skill: Application)**

120. (C)

A word web (concept map) allows students to create associations between their existing vocabulary and unfamiliar social studies terms. **Option A is incorrect.** A Venn diagram is best used to identify similarities and differences. **Option B is incorrect.** A timeline is best used to engage students understanding of chronological reasoning. **Option D is incorrect.** A story map enables students to simplify and conceptualize complex narratives by identifying characters, narrative arcs, etc. **(Domain and Competency VII.026.D. Skill: Content knowledge)**

121. (B)

The purpose of the glossary is to identify and explain potentially unfamiliar terms used in a text. **Option A is incorrect.** Glossaries and dictionaries may both include etymological information. **Option C is incorrect.** Glossaries are usually less complete. **Option D is incorrect.** Typically both dictionaries and glossaries provide pronunciation advice. **(Domain and Competency VII.026.E. Skill: Content knowledge)**

122. (C)

Inquiry-based learning depends upon students' questioning and upon their developing their own conclusions. **Option A is incorrect.** Teacher lectures are useful for many elements of teaching social studies curriculum, but lectures do not reflect an inquiry-based learning model. **Option B is incorrect.** Shared reading in this example is being used to guide students (rather than students directing the analysis of the document). **Option D is incorrect.** A vocabulary square exercise requires little in the way of student inquiry and questioning. **(Domain and Competency VII.023.A. Skill: Application)**

123. (B)

Creoles were colonists of Spanish descent but born in Latin America. They resented the power of Spanish colonial government that was dominated by the *peninsulares*, who were sent from Spain to govern the colonies. **Option A is incorrect.** Spanish colonial government was controlled by the *peninsulares*, who were sent from Spain to govern the colonies, thus making them the target of independence movements. **Option C is incorrect.** *Mestizos* were of mixed ethnic and racial parentage, and were important to the success of Latin American independence movements, but they did not have the same wealth and political influence as the *creoles*. **Option D is incorrect.** Native Americans made up significant populations with identified grievances at Spanish rule, but their complaints were largely ignored by the independence movements. **(Domain and Competency I.004.B. Skill: Content knowledge)**

124. (C)

Following the "Meiji Restoration" in Japan, Japan opened up to western influences and adopted industrial manufacturing and parliamentary institutions, soon expanding into Korea, Manchuria, and elsewhere in Asia. **Option A is incorrect.** China was victimized by "unequal treaties" during this period and was unable to reach the heights of its economic and political success of the previous centuries. **Option B is incorrect.** The last Mughal ruler in India had been deposed in 1857 and Great Britain had taken direct control over the South Asian subcontinent. **Option D is incorrect.** Persia under the Qajars in the 19th century did experience a degree of constitutional reform and territorial expansion, but it never rose to the ranks of Europe, the United States, or Japan as imperial powers. **(Domain and Competency I.004.C. Skill: Comparison)**

125. (C)

The complex developments known as the "Industrial Revolution" began in Great Britain in the middle decades of the eighteenth century. **Option A is incorrect.** Germany as a nation-state did not exist until the mid-19th century, and so came late to industrialization. However, the "Second Industrial Revolution" would see Germany rapidly catch up. **Option B is incorrect.** The United States lagged behind Great Britain in industrialization until after the Civil War. **Option D is incorrect.** France remained more agricultural and less industrially innovative until well after the French Revolution. France's highly regulated pre-revolutionary economy did not encourage technological or organizational efficiencies. **(Domain and Competency I.004.D. Skill: Comparison)**

126. (C)

Mikhail Gorbachev set out on a reform of the Soviet Union that would ultimately lead to the breaking apart of the Soviet Union. **Option A is incorrect.** Boris Yeltsin succeed Mikhail Gorbachev. **Option B is incorrect.** Nikita Khrushchev repudiated the abuses of Joseph Stalin in 1953 and began a process of liberalizing the Soviet Union. This did not last and Khrushchev's reign as Soviet premier was not a long one **Option D is incorrect.** Vladimir Putin came to power in 1999 and has been Prime Minister and President of the Russian Federation. **(Domain and Competency I.004.G.4. Skill: Content knowledge)**

127. (D)

Robert E. Lee commanded the Army of Virginia but had overall command over the Confederate military only late in the war. **Option A is incorrect.** Jefferson Davis was the President of the Confederate States of America and the strategic commander of the Southern armies for most of the war, but was not a general. **Option B is incorrect.** Stonewall Jackson was an iconic figure in the Confederate army but was shot in May 1863 and died shortly after. **Option C is incorrect.** Nathan Bedford Forrest, ancestor and namesake of the fictional Forrest Gump, was accused of war crimes at Fort Pillow, Tennessee. He later was an early organizer of the KKK. **(Domain and Competency II.007.F.4. Skill: Content knowledge)**

128. (B)

"Wilmot's Proviso" was an enormously divisive measure designed to eliminate slavery in territories taken from Mexico. **Option A is incorrect.** William Lloyd Garrison was an abolitionist who opposed the expansion of slavery, but he was not a member of the legislature. **Option C is incorrect.** Thaddeus Stevens was a tireless congressional opponent of slavery, a "Radical Republican" during Reconstruction, and a Pennsylvanian, but he did not author "Wilmot's Proviso." **Option D is incorrect.** Stephen A. Douglas was a United States senator from Illinois who argued that the decision of where and whether slavery should be allowed to expand into territories where it did not exist should be left to the votes of territorial citizens. **(Domain and Competency II.007.E.1. Skill: Content knowledge)**

129. (A)

The "Double V" campaign called for victory in the war against Nazi racism, but also for victory in the war against segregation at home. **Option B is incorrect.** American minority groups including African Americans were strongly supportive of the war effort, but this was not the aim of the "Double V" campaign. **Option C is incorrect.** African Americans and Mexican immigrants were largely competing in different occupational sectors, with most Mexican immigrants brought through the "Bracero" program working in agricultural labor. **Option D is incorrect.** The war effort required increased African American participation and involvement and was thus seen as a largely liberating force, rather than the reverse. **(Domain and Competency II.008.C. Skill: Contextualization)**

130. (C)

Though *Roe v. Wade* and *Engel v. Vitale* alarmed Evangelical Christians, who made up an important blocs of Southern voters, the predominant concern of Southern voters that shifted from the Democratic Party in the 1960s and 1970s was the Democratic Party's alignment with Civil

Rights and anti-segregationist policies. **Option A is incorrect.** The Democratic Party in the 1990s and 2000s supported policies like NAFTA and bailouts of the financial sector that lost them support of the labor unions and working classes. However, this has mostly been felt in the shift of blue collar voters in "Rust Belt" states from the 1980s to the present. **Option B is incorrect.** Though *Roe v. Wade* and *Engel v. Vitale* alarmed an important bloc of Southern voters, the most prominent reason for Southern flight from the Democratic Party stemmed from its support for integrationist laws and enforcement of Civil Rights. **Option D is incorrect.** Jimmy Carter (from Georgia) and Bill Clinton (from Arkansas) did manage to attract significant minorities of Southern voters. However, they were both Democrats and did not stem the tide of the party realignment. **(Domain and Competency II.009.A. Skill: Analysis; Causation)**

131. (A)

Barbara Jordan was the first African American woman elected to Congress from the South. She was also the first woman to give a keynote address at a national political convention. **Option B is incorrect.** Lulu B. White was active in the Texas NAACP and fought against segregation and white supremacy in the state, but was never elected to public office. **Option C is incorrect.** Oveta Culp Hobby, wife of the Texas governor, William Hobby, served in a number of political posts but never won a contest for elected office. **Option D is incorrect.** Jane McCallum was a prominent Texas progressive, suffragist, and temperance advocate at the turn of the 20th century. **(Domain and Competency: III.012.C. Skill: Content knowledge)**

132. (C)

Highland climates are found on elevated mountains and elevated plateaus. There are no seasons in highland climates; elevation determines precipitation, temperature and vegetation. **Option A is incorrect.** Tundra climate is found in the northern hemisphere and has two seasons, cold harsh winter and cool summers. **Option B is incorrect.** Arid climate is a subcategory of dry climates, which are found along 30 degrees latitude both above and below the equator. **Option D is incorrect.** Humid continental climate is a subcategory of continental climates. These are found from 30 to 60 degrees latitude in the northern hemisphere, and have four distinct seasons. **(Domain and Competency IV.013.E. Skill Comparison)**

133. (D)

There are five stages to the Demographic Transition Model. The newest and last stage (Stage 5) occurs in a society when the birth rates fall below the death rates, which results in a negative natural increase. Japan is one such example. **Option A is incorrect.** In Stage 2, birth rates stay high and death rates plummet, resulting in rapid population growth. **Option B is incorrect.** In Stage 3, birth rates start to drop to come closer to death rates, and natural increase becomes more stable and slow. **Option D is incorrect.** Stage 4 reflects stable birth and death rates and slow natural increase. **(Domain and Competency IV.014.F. Skill Comparison)**

134. (D)

Divergence of tectonic plates above the ground results in rift valleys such as Olduvai Gorge in Africa. **Option A is incorrect.** Trenches are also the result of plate divergence, but are found only on the ocean floor, underneath the water. **Option B is incorrect.** Mountain ranges are the result of plate convergence. **Option D is incorrect.** River valleys are the result of erosion over many years. **(Domain and Competency IV.013. Skill: Causation)**

135. (C)

Human beliefs and activities. Culture regions are made of common beliefs and activities in general. **Options A, B, and D** are subcategories, or characteristics, of human beliefs and activities, and are used to help create culture regions based on wealth, religion, or environmental adaptations. **(Domain and Competency: IV.014.A. Skill: Content knowledge)**

136. (C)

Home-rule cities are cities or towns with over 5,000 residents granted a charter and certain rights to self-government. **Option A is incorrect.** Single-purpose districts include such government entities as water districts, school districts, community colleges districts, etc. **Option B is incorrect.** General law governments are towns with fewer than 5,000 residents that lack a charter and may carry out functions only as authorized by the state. **Option D is incorrect.** Council-manager governments are a progressive reform that combines an elected council and a professional manager with administrative experience. **(Domain and Competency V.017.J. Skill: Comparison)**

137. (C)

6% represents the equilibrium price of investment and saving which will be the market interest rate. **Option A is incorrect.** A 2% interest rate would discourage household saving and result in households spending rather than saving. It would also encourage firms to borrow. **Option B is incorrect.** Interest rates at both 2 and 4% would be below the equilibrium rate of interest. **Option D is incorrect.** At 8% interest rates, households and firms would be encouraged to save, while lenders would find it difficult to attract borrowers.**(Domain and Competency: VI.021.D Skill: Supply and demand graph reading)**

138. (C)

State sales taxes are usually considered the most regressive of taxes. **Option A is incorrect.** The U.S. income tax is progressive with lower rates of taxation paid by lower paid workers and higher rates paid by higher income earners. **Option B is incorrect.** The FICA taxes fall more heavily on middle-income earners than on the poor or wealthy. **Option D is incorrect.** Capital gains taxes, which in the United States are proportionally levied on income received from the sales of assets, are disproportionately paid by those who have significant assets. **(Domain and Competency VI.021.G. Skill: Content knowledge)**

139. (B)

Performance-based learning requires students to demonstrate their ability to do specific tasks. **Option A is incorrect.** While performance-based learning may require critical thinking, it is not necessarily the case. **Option C is incorrect.** Deductive reasoning is a logical thought process rather than a skill. **Option D is incorrect.** Metacognition is a student's awareness and understanding of his or her own thought processes. (**Domain and Competency: VII.026.H. Skill Level: Comparison**)

140. (A)

Positivistic social sciences argued that the scientist can distance him or herself from the subject being studied in order to describe that phenomena. **Option B is incorrect.** The sciences are said to emphasize description and prediction rather than interpretation and meaning. Positivist social scientists believe that this is possible for the social sciences as well. Constructivists question this assumption. **Option C is incorrect.** Constructivist social sciences emphasize this approach, in contrast to positivists who see the social sciences as akin to the natural sciences. **Option D is incorrect.** Natural scientists assume that they are distinct from their subject matter and able to study it by being apart from what they're studying and thereby attaining objectivity. This is more difficult in the social sciences. Nonetheless, positivist social scientists maintain their ability to use their discipline to objectively investigate social phenomena using scientific research methods. (**Domain and Competency VII.023.A. Skill Level: Analysis**)

SELF-ASSESSMENT GUIDE FOR PRACTICE TEST 1

Practice Test 1 questions are sorted here by domain. To get an idea of your level of mastery, check the box under the question numbers that you answered correctly.

Domain I: World History—approx. 15% of the test

1	2	3	4	5	6	7	8	9
10	11	12	13	14	15	16	17	18
69	70	123	124	125	126			

Total: __/24

Domain II: U.S. History—approx. 20% of the test

19	20	21	22	23	24	25	26	27
28	29	30	31	32	33	34	35	36
37	38	39	40	41	42	127	128	129
130								

Total: __/28

Domain III: Texas History—approx. 13% of the test

43	44	45	46	47	48	49	50	51
52	53	54	55	56	57	58	68	131

Total: __/18

Domain IV: Geography, Culture and the Behavioral and Social Science—approx. 13% of the test

59	60	61	62	63	64	65	66	67

72	73	74	81	132	133	134	135

Total: __/17

Domain V: Government and Citizenship—approx. 13% of the test

75	76	77	78	79	80	81	82	83

84	85	86	87	88	89	90	91	136

Total: __/18

Domain VI: Economics and Science, Technology and Society—approx. 13% of the test

92	93	94	95	96	97	98	99	100

101	102	103	104	105	106	137	138

Total: __/17

Domain VII: Social Studies Foundations, Skills, Research and Instruction—approx. 13% of the test

107	108	109	110	111	112	113	114	115

116	117	118	119	120	121	122	139	140

Total: __/18

Index

A

Abbasid Dynasty, 39
Abolitionism, 154
Abolitionist movement, 412–413
Abortion, 385–386
Absolute advantage, 476–477
Absolute monarchies, 430–431
Acculturation, 313
Achaemenid Empire, 25–26
Adams, John, 141–142
Adams, Samuel, 139
Adams-Onís Treaty, 224
Adaptation, cultural, 313
Addams, Jane, 199
Afghanistan, 184
Africa
    Atlantic Slave Trade, 70
    during early modern period, 56
    Empires during Middle Ages, 42
    Scramble for Africa, 78
    Swahili coast and Southern Africa,
      42
African Americans
    Black Codes, 161, 249–250, 377
    Buffalo Soldiers, 254
    Civil Rights movement and,
      208–209
    cultural contribution 1821–1900, 260
    holding office during Reconstruction
      era, 251
    Ku Klux Klan, 162
    WWII and, 170–171, 268
Age of Empires, 25
Agricultural Adjustment Act (AAA),
    194–195
Agriculture
    Aztec civilization, 57
    chemical fertilizer, 514–515
    Columbian Exchange, 70

    commercial agriculture in Texas
      1900–present, 278–280
    in early Texas, 228, 229
    Neolithic agricultural revolution,
      14–17, 333–334, 336–337
    New Deal legislation during
      Depression, 194–195
    populism, 189–190
    Russia and communism, 87
    scientific revolution and, 83–84
    sharecropping system, 251, 252, 279
    in US since 1877, 188–189
Akhenaten, 20
Akkadians, 18
Aksum, 21
Alamo, Battle of, 237
Alaska, 164
Alexander the Great, 26, 28, 32
Alfred the Great, 40
Alien and Sedition Acts (1798), 142
Alliance system, cause of World War
    I, 89
Allied Powers, 91, 167
Al-Qaeda, 98, 208
Al Shabab, 98
Alternating current, 528
Amendments. *See individual*
    amendments
America First movement, 169
American Anti-Slavery Society, 154,
    412
American Federation of Labor (AFL),
    187
American Indian movement, 210
American Indians. *See* Native
    Americans
American Revolution and early
    Republic, 124–146
    Articles of Confederation, 137–138
    Boston Tea Party, 132

    British policy after 1763, 129–134
    Declaration of Independence,
      133–134
    Enlightenment ideas, 125–126
    First Continental Congress, 133
    government investment and
      economic growth, 144–145
    Indian removal, 145–146
    Intolerable Acts, 130–132
    mercantilism and British
      imperialism, 128–129
    military action and battles of,
      134–136
    No Taxation without Representation,
      131
    overview of, 124–125, 140
    Philadelphia Constitutional
      Convention, 138–139
    political parties during, 140–144
    religious toleration, 127
    slavery during, 127–128
    social and political culture during,
      125–128
    voting rights in, 126
American Revolution era, 74
American System, 145
Americas
    early civilizations in, 23–24
    during early modern period, 56
    origins of agriculture, 17
Amorites, 18
Ancient World Civilizations (8000 BCE–
    3000 BCE), 13–37
    classical civilizations, 24–37
    early civilizations, 17–24
    hunter-gatherers, 14
    Neolithic agricultural revolution,
      14–17
Animism, 328
Anthony, Susan B., 192

Anthropomorphic gods, 19
Anti-Federalists, 139, 355
Anti-scientism, 542
Apache, 214–215
Appalachian Divide, 293
Appalachian Mountain System, 318
Appeasement, 91
Appomattox Court House, 160
Aquatic biome, 299
Archival research, 591–592
Area graph, 574
Aristocracy, 437
Arms race, cause of World War I, 89
Art
    of Renaissance, 61–62
    time period created in, 331–332
Articles of Confederation, 137–138,
    349–350
Ashoka, 32–33
Assembly, freedom of, 403–404
Assessment, 617–622. *See also* Social
    studies instruction and
    assessment
Asset-backed securities, 493–494
Assimilation, 313, 617
Association, identifying, 594–595
Assyrians, 18–19
Atahualpa, 58
Athens, 27
Atlantic Coastal Plain and the Gulf
    Coastal Plain, 318
Atlantic revolutions, 74
Atlantic Slave Trade, 70
Atmosphere, 294–295
Augustine, St., 103
Austerity measures, 488
Austin, 286–287
Austin, Moses, 224–225
Austin, Stephen F.
    brief biography, 225
    role in early years of Republic of
        Texas, 239–240
Authentic assessment, 619
Authoritarian governments, 436
Automobile
    economic impact of, 537
    as urbanizing technology, 529–530
Axis, Earth's, 297
Axis Powers, 91
Aztec civilization, 24

during early modern period, 57
during middle ages, 44

B

Background knowledge, 606–607
Bacon, Nathaniel, 114
Bacon's Rebellion, 114
Ballot proposals, 433
Bank holiday, 193
Banking industry, New Deal reforms,
    193–194
Bank of the United States, 140
Banks, 493
Bantu migrations, 21
Bar graphs, 573
Barnard, Henry, 414
Basins, 290
Bastille, 75
Bays, 294
Behavioral learning theory, 345
Bell, Alexander Graham, 529
Bell Telephone Company, 529
Benefice, 46
Berlin Airlift, 179
Bessemer steel process, 527
Bicameralism, 358–359
Bicameral legislature, 138
Bill, journey of, to become law, 365–
    367
Bill of Rights, 139, 401–408
    comparing Texas to U.S.
        Constitution, 391–392
Bills of attainder, 355
bin Laden, Osama, 98, 184, 208
Biomes, 299–307
Biosphere, 295
Birth rates, 323
Bishop of Constantinople, 48
Bishop of Rome, 48, 49
Black Codes, 161, 249–250, 377
Black Death, 41, 54–55
Black Shirts, 85
Blanket primaries, 398
Bleeding Kansas, 156
Bloom's taxonomy, 602
Boko Haram, 98
Bolívar, Simón, 76
Bolshevik Party, 77
Bonds, 491–492, 493, 509–510

Boston Massacre, 132
Boston Tea Party, 132
Bourbon Reforms, 219
Bourgeoisie, 47
Bracero program, 171
Brahe, Tycho, 66
British East India Company, 78, 79
British Empire, 79
British Royal Society, 84
*Brown v. Board of Education of Topeka,
    Kansas,* 208, 263, 264, 378,
        383–384, 419
Bryan, William Jennings, 190
Bubonic plague, 41
Buddhism, 33–34, 44
Budget surplus, 492
Buffalo, 227, 229
Buffalo Soldiers, 254
Bullion, 462
Burghers, 47
Burton, Richard, 79
Bush, George H.W., 183
Bush, George W., 184
    brief bio, 275–276
Bush Doctrine, 208, 373
Business
    reforms during Progressive era, 191
    rights and responsibilities of,
        505–506
Byzantine Empire, 48–50
    fall of Constantinople, 55

C

Cabeza de Vaca, Álvar Núñez, 222–223
Cabinet, 363
Caddo
    overview of, 213–214
    trade routes and mound building, 227
Caesar, Augustus, 30
Caesar, Julius, 29
Caesaro-papism, 48
Calvin, Jean, 63
Canals, 291
Canon, 31
Capital, 443, 500
Capitalism
    history of, 462
    not mentioned in Constitution, 357
Caravel, 68, 522

Caribbean, as cultural region, 314
Carnegie, Andrew, 198
Carolinas, 107, 116–117
Carolingians, 39, 45, 46
Cartel, 475
Carthage, 29
Case studies, 592
Caste system, 22, 32
Castro, Fidel, 182
Categorizing, 594
Catholic Church. *See* Roman Catholic Church
Cattle ranching
    Spanish influence on, 230–231
    in Texas 1821–1900, 257
    in Texas 1900–present, 280–281
    Texas environment and, 229
Caucuses, 398
Causality, 544
Causal questions, 588
Cause-and-effect relationships, 595
Cause-effect organization, 608, 611
Central America, as cultural region, 314
Central Asia, as cultural region, 315
Central Plains of Texas, as cultural region, 322
Central Powers, 89
Chandragupta, 34
Chandragupta Maurya, 32
Charlemagne, 39
Charter of Liberty, 110
Charts, 571
Chávez, César, 201–202
Chavín society, 23
Checks and balances
    Texas Constitution, 389
    U.S. Constitution, 353
Cherokee Nation v. Georgia, 381
Chesapeake Bay colonies, 112–115
China
    collapse of Han Dynasty, 35–37
    communist economic systems, 472–473
    communist reform movement, 96
    early civilizations in, 22–23
    during early modern period, 58–59
    Han Dynasty, 35
    Mandate of Heaven, 23
    during Middle Ages, 43
    Ming Dynasty, 58–59

    Nixon and, 177
    origins of agriculture, 16
    Qin Dynasty, 34–35
    Qing Dynasty, 58–59
    Shang Dynasty, 23
    Silk Road, 41
    Song Dynasty, 43
    Sui and Tang Dynasties, 43
    Warring States Period, 23
    Zhou Dynasty, 23
Chinampas, 57
Chinese Exclusion Act, 207
Christianity, 30, 328
    Crusades, 52–53
    Eastern Orthodox Church and Byzantine Empire, 48–49
    Jesus of Nazareth, 30
    medieval Christianity, 48–50
    Paul of Tarsus, 31
    persecution and triumph of, in Rome, 31–32
    Roman Catholic Church and Western Christendom, 49
    schism between Eastern Orthodoxy and Roman Catholicism, 50
Chronological sequence, 608, 611
Churchill, Winston, 93
Church of England, 331
Circle graph, 572–573
Circular-flow model of economy, 446–448, 584–585
Circulating capital, 443
Cities/towns
    Austin, 286–287
    Dallas-Fort Worth, 284
    in early Texas, 229
    Houston, 284–285
    largest, 202–203
    rise of, during Middle Ages, 47
    urbanization, 202–203
Citizenship
    Bill of Rights, 401–408
    double jeopardy, 405
    due process clause, 406
    Electoral College, 398–399
    establishment clause, 401–402
    freedom of assembly and petition, 403–404
    freedoms of speech and press, 403
    free exercise clause, 402–403

    in Greece, 26
    interest groups, 396–398
    jury duty, 421
    political parties, 395–396
    political systems, 421–440
    primaries and caucuses, 398
    reform movements, 412–419
    significant political and social leaders, 408–412
    voting, 420–421
Citizenship clause, 377
Civilian Conservation Corps (CCC), 194
Civil Rights Act of 1964, 205–206
Civil Rights interest groups, 397
Civil Rights movement
    African American, 208–209
    American Indian, 210
    early efforts, 192–193
    Hispanic, 209
    history of, 418–419
    important Texan figures in, 261–264
    King and, 200–201
    Malcolm X, 201
    reforms and reaction to, 195–196
Civil War
    abolitionism, 154
    Bleeding Kansas, 156
    Confederate States of America, 157–158
    Davis, 158
    Dred Scott decision, 156
    Emancipation Proclamation, 159–160
    Fugitive Slave Act, 155
    Grant and, 159
    Lee and, 158, 160
    Lincoln and, 158–159
    Missouri Compromise, 154–155
    reconstruction, 160–162
    Secession, 157
    sectional division and slavery, 153–154
    Texans role in, 246–248
    Texas secession, 245–246
    wartime policies and government changes, 370–371
Classical civilizations, 14, 24–37
    as Age of Empires, 25
    Buddhism, 33–34

Christianity, 30
classical Greece, 26–27
decline and fall of classical empires, 35–37
Han Dynasty, 35
Hellenistic Empire, 28
Mauryan and Gupta India, 34
overview of, 24–25
Paul of Tarsus, 31
Persian Empire, 25–26
Punic Wars, 29
Qin Dynasty, 34–35
Roman Empire, 29–30
Roman Republic, 28–29
science and technology, 517
Sparta and Athens, 27
Clay, Henry, 145
Climate patterns, 297–299
Climates, types of, 304–307
Clinton, Bill, 183
Closed primaries, 398
Coahuiltecan Indians, 213
Coal, industrial Revolution and, 82–83
Coastal Plains of Texas, as cultural region, 321
Code of Hammurabi, 18
Coercive Acts, 132–133
Cognitive learning theory, 345
Cold War
    Berlin Airlift, 179
    communist reform movements, 96–97
    containment, 176
    Cuban Missile Crisis, 182
    Domino Theory, 176
    Korean War, 96, 180
    Marshall Plan, 178–179
    McCarthyism, 179–180
    miracle year of 1989, 97
    North Atlantic Treaty Organization (NATO), 179
    overview, 95–96, 178
    periods of, 177–178
    space race, 181
    spread of communism, 95
    Texans and, 268–269
    Vietnam War, 96, 180–181
Collective bargaining, 504
Collusion, 475
Colonial America

Carolinas, 116–117
Chesapeake Bay, 112–115
early settler colonies, 104–107
English settlers relationship with Native Americans, 104–107
frontier and American individualism, 111–112
geographies influence, 121–122
Georgia colony, 118
Glorious Revolution, 120
Great Awakening, 110
indentured servitude, 114
integration of colonies and Atlantic economy, 110–111
Massachusetts Bay colony, 116
Middle Colonies, 109–110, 117–118
New England colonies, 115, 116
religious fervor and American exceptionalism, 108–109
religious tolerance, 109–110
self-rule in, 118–121
slavery and racial hierarchies, 122–123
spatial exchange, 123–124
triangular trade in, 111
Colonization, 77–80
    British Empire, 79
    European in Africa and Asia, 78
    European in Americas, 103–105
    Japanese, 80
Colonization laws, 225
Colonization movement, 154, 412
Columbian Exchange, 70
    Texas and, 227–228
Columbus, Christopher, 69
Column graph, 573
Comanche
    Council House fight, 244
    grassland ecology and, 226–227
    overview of, 214–215
    Quanah Parker, 254
Command economies, 326
Commercial revolutions, during Middle Ages, 47
Common school movement, 414
Common Sense (Paine), 133
Communism. See also Cold War
    communist economic systems, 471–473
    communist states, 431

containment, 176
Domino Theory, 176
Marx and, 466–468
miracle year of 1989, 97
Red Scare, 169
reform movements, 96–97
Russian Revolution, 76–77
Second Red Scare, 172
spread of, during Cold War, 95
Stalin and, 87
Communist states, 431
Comparative advantage, 478–479
Comparative questions, 588
Comparison-contrast organization, 608, 611
Competition
    in free enterprise system, 484
    monopolistic competition, 475–476
    pure, 473–474
Compromise of 1850, 155
Computers, 531–532
Computer simulation, 593
Concept-definition organization, 608, 611
Concept mapping, 609
Concord, Battle of, 134
Concurrent powers, 388
Confederacy, 354
Confederate States of America, 157–158
Conflict, 544
Confluence, 293
Confucianism, 23, 328
Congress, U.S.
    committees of, 359–360
    journey of bill to become law, 365–367
    presidential powers and, 361–362
Congressional committees, 359–360
Connecticut, 116
Conquistadors, Age of, 216–219
Conservatives, 434–435
Constantine, 31
Constantinople, 53, 55
Constitution, of Texas. See Texas Constitution
Constitution, of United States. See also individual amendments
    amendments to, 376–380
    Articles of Confederation, 137–138

beliefs and principles of, 350–356
Bill of Rights, 139
checks and balances, 353
compared to Texas Constitution, 391–392
federalism, 353–354
individual rights, 355–356
judicial review, 374
Philadelphia Constitutional Convention, 138–139
political parties and, 140
Popular sovereignty, 350–351
public policy process, 399–401
ratification of, 139
Republicanism, 351–352
separation of church and state, 354–355
separation of powers, 352
steps in amending, 364–365
strict constructionist interpretation, 141
words missing from, 356–357
Constitution of 1824, 232
Constructivist approach, 542–543
Consuls, 28
Consultation of 1835, 236
Consumers
protection reforms during Progressive era, 191
rights and responsibilities, 503–504
Contagious diffusion, 312
Containment, 176
Content analysis, 592
Context clues, 612
Continental climate, 306
Contraception, 515
Contractionary fiscal policy, 497
Contractionary monetary policy, 498
Convention of 1836, 237
Convergence, plate tectonics, 296
Cooperation, 545
Copernicus, Nicholas, 66
contributions of, 519
Córdova Rebellion, 243
Corporate colony, 115
Corporations, 198, 490–492
Correlation, 598
Cortés, Hernán, 58, 216
Cotton economy, 146, 148
after Civil War, 256

slavery and, 255–256
in Texas 1821–1900, 255–256
Cotton gin, 82, 146, 148, 525–526
Council House fight, 244
Council of Nicaea, 31
Council of Trent, 65
Count, 51
Court-packing, 375
Courts
court-packing, 375
federal court system, 364
judicial power of president relative to judiciary, 362–363
judicial review, 374, 380
Cradle of Civilization, 336
Creeds, 31
Cross-cultural conversion, 545
Cruel and unusual punishment, 417
Crusades, 52–53
Cuba, 182
Platte Amendment, 166
Spanish-American War, 165–166
Cuban Missile Crisis, 95, 182
Cultural change, 545
Cultural pluralism, 617
Cultural universals, 308–309
Culture, 307–325
art and time period of, 331–332
cultural universals, 308–309
defined, 308, 426
government and role of, 426–428
growth and distribution of population, 323–325
innovation and diffusion, 311–313
language and, 309–310
place and, 329–330
political, economic and social processes and, 325–328
political systems and, 310
religion and, 310, 328–329
world cultural regions, 314–322
Curie, Marie, 520–521
Currencies, exchange rate effects on, 480–482
Cuzco, 330
Cyclical progression, 545
Cyrillic alphabet, 48
Czar, 49

D

da Gama, Vasco, 69
Dallas-Fort Worth, 283–284
Daoism, 23, 329
Darwin, Charles, 99
Databases, 569–570
da Vinci, Leonardo, 55, 61–62
Davis, Jefferson, 158
Death rates, 323
Debs, Eugene V., 187–188
de Champlain, Samuel, 103
Decile, 599
Declaration of Independence, 74
natural rights and, 423–424
overview, 133–134, 348–349
Declaration of Sentiments, 410, 416
Declaratory Act, 131
De facto discrimination, 209
Defined-benefit plan, 510
De jure discrimination, 209
de León, Juan Ponce, 103
Dell, Michael, 286–287
Dell Computer, 286–287
Deltas, 291
Demand, law of, 448, 451
Demand curve, 449–453, 585–586
Democracy
defined, 437
direct, 27
direct democracy, 433
liberal democracy, 433–434
origins and evolution of, 436–440
Democratic Party
Dixiecrats, 196
establishment of, 143–144, 368
political party alignment since 1877, 186
Democratic principles. *See* Government, democratic principles
Democratic-Republicans, 141–142
Democratic socialist, 466
Demographic transition, 324, 538
Demography, 323
Demokratia, 27
Demotic script, 20
Depression, 502–503
Description organization, 608, 611
Descriptive questions, 587–588
Descriptive statistics, 596, 597–598

Desert Biomes, 302–303
Deserts, 291
de Soto, Hernando, 217
Détente, 177
Developing countries, 327
Deviance, 428
Dewey, John, 414
Dharma, 33
Diagnostic assessment, 618
Dialectical progression, 545
Dias, Bartolomeu, 69
Diaspora, 19
Dictator, 437
Dictionary skills, 612–613
Diet of Worms, 63
Difference, 545
Diffusion, 545
   culture and, 311–313
Digital Himalayas, 563
Dillon Rule, 392
Direct democracy, 27, 433
Directed Reading-Thinking Activities, 610
Direct primary, 398
Direct tax, 130, 131
Discount rate, 497–498
Discouraged workers, 579
Discretionary monetary policy, 469
Discrimination, 209
Diseases
   Black Death, 41, 54–55
   decline of classical empires and epidemic disease, 36
   European expansion and spread of, 70
   Native American and exposure to Europeans, 102
Dispersion, 598
Divergence, plate tectonics, 296
Diversity, in classroom, 616–617
Dividends, 492
Divides, 293
Divine Right of Kings, 422, 423–424
Dix, Dorothea, 418
Dixiecrats, 196
Domesday Book, 40
Dominion of New England, 120
Domino Theory, 176
Double jeopardy, 405
Double V campaign, 171

Douglass, Frederick, 409–410
Dred Scott v. Sandford, 156, 377, 381–382
Drought, 334
Dry climate, 306–307
DuBois, W.E.B., 193
Due process clause, 377, 406
Duke, 51
Dunmore, Lord, 134–135
Dust Bowl, 205, 336
Dutch East India Company, 78
Dutch settlement, 104

E

Early civilizations, 14, 17–24
   in Americas, 23–24
   ancient nomadic charioteers, 18–19
   China, 22–23
   Indus River valley civilization, 21–22
   Mesopotamia, 17–18
   Mesopotamian religion, 19
   Nile River valley, 20
   origins of Judaism, 19
   science and technology, 516–517
   sub-Saharan Africa, 20–21
Early Modern Period (1450–1750 CE), 54–71
   Africa, 56
   Americas, 56
   Aztec civilization, 57, 58
   Black Death, 54–55
   China, 58–59
   da Vinci as Renaissance Man, 55
   Enlightenment, 67
   European expansion, 68–71
   fall of Constantinople, 55
   Inca Empire, 57
   Japan, 59
   Martin Luther, 55
   Mayan civilization, 56, 58
   Middle East, 58
   overview, 54, 60
   Protestant Reformation, 60, 63–65
   Renaissance, 60–62
   science and technology, 522
   Scientific Revolution, 65–66
Earthquakes, 334
East Asia, as cultural region, 316

Eastern Continental Divide, 293
Eastern Orthodox Church, 48–50
   schism with Roman Catholic Church, 50
East Texas Indians, 213–214
Economic activities, 326
Economic concepts. *See also* Economy
   absolute and comparative advantage, 476–479
   Adam Smith and, 463
   business ownership, 489–492
   capitalism, 462
   circular-flow model, 446–448, 584–585
   communism, 466–468
   consumer, labor and business rights/responsibilities, 503–506
   demand, 448–452, 585–586
   economic stability, 500, 502–503
   effect of exchange rates on world currencies, 480–481, 482
   equilibrium price and quantities, 457–461
   factors of production, 443
   financial institutions for savings/borrowing, 492–494
   financial literacy, 506–510
   fiscal policy, 497
   free trade, 479–480
   government rules and regulations, 494–496
   GPD per capita, 582–583
   Gross Domestic Product (GDP), 581–582
   inflation and inflation rate, 580–581
   international trade, 476–479
   international trade agreements, 480
   John Maynard Keynes, 468–469
   Malthus and Ricardo, 464
   Marx, 466–468
   mercantilism, 462
   Milton Friedman, 469
   monetary policy, 497–498
   monopolistic competition, 475–476
   monopoly, 474
   oligopoly, 475
   opportunity costs, 443–445
   physiocrats and laissez-faire, 462
   production possibilities curves, 444–445, 583–584

productivity and economic growth, 499–500

pure competition, 473–474

scarcity, 442

socialism and, 464–466, 471

supply, 453–457, 585–586

unemployment and full employment, 501–502, 579–580

Economic interest groups, 397

Economy. *See also* Economic concepts

communist economic systems, 471–473

comparing Roman Empire to Medieval Europe, 51

free enterprise systems, 470–471, 482–484

Gilded Age to Roaring Twenties growth, 485

globalization and growth, 487–489

New Deal and growth of, 485–486

socialist systems, 471

Texas 1900–present, 278–288

WWII growth and, 486–487

Ecosphere, 295

Edison, Thomas A., 197, 528

contributions of, 521

Edison Electric Lighting Company, 528

Edo, 59

Education

integration in Texas, 264

public, 413–415

Edwards, Haden, 234–235

Edward VI, English king, 64

Egalitarianism, 126, 427

Egypt, Nile River valley and early civilization, 20

Eighth Amendment, 407, 417

Einstein, Albert, 521

Eisenhower, Dwight, 180

Electoral College, 139, 143

overview of, 398–399

Electrical power, 528–529

El Niño/La Niña, 298, 334

Emancipation Proclamation, 159–160

Embargo, 142

Emergency Banking Relief Act, 193

Emergency Quota Act, 207

Emigration, 325

Emperor, 437

Empire of Liberty, 149

Empiricism, 541

Employment

industrial workforce and American industrialization, 198

labor movement, 187–188

New Deal legislation during Depression, 194

during WWII on home front, 170–171

Empresario contracts, 225–226

Enabling Act, 86

Engel v. Vitale, 384

England. *See also* Great Britain

American colonies, 104–107

democracy and origins/evolution of, 438–439

Magna Carta, 40

Norman Conquest, 39–40

English Bill of Rights, 120–121, 348

Enlightenment, Age of, 67, 74

American Revolution and, 125–126

democracy and origins/evolution of, 439–440

Entrepreneurship, 443, 489

Enumerated powers, 387–388

Episcopal organization, 31

Equal Employment Opportunity Act, 505

Equal inheritance, 126

Equal protection clause, 377–378

Equal Rights Amendment, 417

Equilibrium price, 457–461

Erie Canal, 147

Escandón, José de, 224

Establishment clause, 354–355, 401–402

Estates General, 75

Estevanico, 223

Ethnic group, 340

Ethnic religions, 310, 328

Etruscans, 28

Europe, as cultural region, 315

European expansion, 68–71

European imperialism, 78

Evangelical Christians, 186

Evolutionary processes, 545

Exchange rates, effect on world currencies, 480–482

Executive Office of the President (EOP), 363, 369

Executive Order 9981, 419

Expansionary fiscal policy, 497

Expansionary monetary policy, 498

Expansion diffusion, 312

Experimental research, 592–593

Explanatory questions, 588

Exploration

European, in Texas, 220–222

European expansion, 68–71

Extinction, cultural, 313

F

Face value, 510

Factories, 82

Factors of production, 443

Fair Employment Practices Committee, 171

Fair Labor Standards Act, 505

Family, structures of, 343

Fannin, James W., 238

Farmer, James, 270–271

Fascism, in Italy, 85

Fealty, 46

Federal court system, 364

Federal Deposit Insurance Corporation (FDIC), 194, 493

Federal Emergency Relief Administration (FERA), 194

Federal government, spending in Texas, 392–393

Federal Insurance Contributions Act (FICA) tax, 508–509

Federalism

Texas Constitution, 389–390

U.S. Constitution, 353–354, 387–388

Federalist Papers, 139, 357–358

Federalist Party, 140

Federalists, 354

Federalist system, 354

Federal presidential republic, 428–429

Federal Reserve System, 497

Federal Trade Commission, 191

Feminine Mystique, The (Friedan), 202

Ferdinand, Franz, Archduke, 88

Fertile Crescent, 336

Fertilizer, 514–515

Feudalism, 46

stirrup and Medieval feudalism, 512–513

Fief, 46
Fifteenth Amendment, 378
Financial literacy, 506–510
Firm, 489
First Amendment, 401–403
First American Party System, 143
First Continental Congress, 133
First Political Party System, 368
First-world countries, 95
Fiscal policy, 497
Fixed capital, 443
Florida, acquisition of, 150
Flying shuttle, 82
Folkways, 341
Foothills, 291
Ford, Henry, 197, 199–200, 530
Foreign policy, American
    American rise to world power
        (1890–1914), 163–167, 173–177
    failure to take leadership during
        interwar years, 168–170
    key figures in, 173–177
    key schools of thought influencing,
        172–173
    presidential powers over, 361
Forest biomes, 300–301
Formative assessment, 618
Four Freedoms, 200
Fourier, Charles, 465
Four Noble Truths, 34
Fourteen Points, 90, 168, 174
Fourteenth Amendment, 161, 377–378
Fourth Amendment, 405–406
France
    colonization in Americas, 103–104
    encroachment in Texas, 218–219,
        222
    French Revolution, 74–75
    Napoleon Bonaparte, 75
Franklin, Benjamin, 125
Fredonian Rebellion, 234–235
Freedmen's Bureau, 250
Freedom Week, 622
Free enterprise systems, 482–484
    economies and degree of, 470–471
    not mentioned in Constitution, 357
Free exercise clause, 402–403
Free trade, 479–480
French and Indian War, 107, 129
French Revolution, 74–75

Frequency distribution, 597–598
Freshwater biomes, 299
Friedan, Betty, 202
Friedman, Milton, 469
Frontier Thesis, 163
Fugitive Slave Act, 155
Fundamental Orders of Connecticut,
    120
Futures contract, 510

G

Gadsden Purchase, 152
Gaines v. State of Missouri, 418
Galilei, Galileo, 66
    contributions of, 519–520
Galveston, Battle of, 247
Gandhi, Mohandas, 79, 99
Ganges River, 330
Gaozu, 35
Garcia, Hector P., 263
Garrison, William Lloyd, 154, 412
Gender, defined, 340
General Agreement on Tariffs and Trade
    (GATT), 176, 480
Generalization-principle organization,
    608, 611
General Welfare, 141
Genghis Khan, 40–41
Gens, 50
Geography
    biomes, 299–303
    climate, 304–307
    culture, 307–332
    Earth-Sun relationship, 297–299
    geographic features of Earth,
        290–295
    growth and distribution of
        population, 323–325
    human, 308
    human interaction with physical
        environment, 333–339
    landforms, 303–304
    natural disasters, 334–335
    plate tectonics, 296–297
    world cultural regions, 314–322
Geography of Texas
    American Indians and influence of,
        226–227
    North Texas, 258

    overview of, 226
    Panhandle, 258
    Southeast Texas, 257
    South Texas, 258–259
Georgia colony, 118
Germanic tribes, 36
Germany
    Hitler and, 86
    Holocaust, 86
    Nazi Germany, 86
    terms imposed on after WWI, 90–91,
        168
Gettysburg Address, 159
Ghana, 42
GI Bill, 205
Glasnost, 97
Glass-Steagall Banking Act, 193–194
Globalization, 325
    American foreign policy and, 173
    economic growth and, 487–489
    free trade and, 183
    in post-Cold War, 97–98, 182–183,
        207
    shipping container and, 515–516
Global War on Terror, 373
Glorious Revolution, 60, 64, 81, 120
Glossaries, 613
Gold standard, 189
Goliad, 219, 229
    surrender at, 238
Gonzales, Battle of, 236
Gonzales, Manuel C., 262–263
González, Henry B., 271
Good Neighbor Policy, 175
Gorbachev, Mikhail, 97
Government, democratic principles,
    347–395
    American party systems, 367–369
    Articles of Confederation, 349–350
    bicameralism, 358–359
    bill, journey to become law, 365–367
    checks and balances, 353
    Declaration of Independence,
        348–349
    English Bill of Rights, 348
    federal court system, 364
    federalism, 353–354
    Federalist Papers, 357–358
    individual rights, 355–356
    judicial review, 374

New Deal legislation, 369–370

political systems, 421–440

Popular sovereignty, 350–351

powers of federal and state government, 387–388

presidential powers, 360–363

Republicanism, 351–352

separation of church and state, 354–355

separation of powers, 352

steps for amending Constitution, 364–365

Supreme Court landmark decisions, 380–387

wartime policies and, 370–373

words missing from Constitution, 356–357

Government interest groups, 397

GPD per capita, 582–583

Grand jury, 406

Grant, Ulysses S., 159

Graphic organizers, 570–571

Graphs, 572–574

Grassland biomes, 301–302

Grasslands, Plains Indians and ecology of, 226–227

Great Awakening, 110

Great Britain. *See also* England

American Revolution, 74

British Empire, 79

Glorious Revolution, 81

Industrial Revolution and, 80–82

mercantilism and American colonies, 128–129

policy towards American colonies, 129–134

Great Compromise, 138

Great Depression

agriculture in Texas and, 279–280

New Deal legislation, 193–195

in Texas, 266–267

weaknesses in economy and, 203–205

Great Man theory, 68

Great Plains of Texas, as cultural region, 322

Great Society programs, 273–274

Great Wall, 35

Great Western Divide, 293–294

Greco-Persian Wars, 27

Greece

Athens, 27

classical, 26–27

Hellenistic culture, 28

Hellenistic Empire, 28

Solon, 27

Sparta, 27

Gregory VII, Pope, 49

Grenville, George, 130

Gross Domestic Product (GDP), 327, 469, 484

elements of, and measuring, 581–582

Gross National Product (GNP), 327

Guam, 166

Guantanamo Bay, 166

Guerrero, Vicente, 232–233, 235

Guerrero Decree, 235

Guild, 47

Gulf Coast Indians, 212–213

Gulf of Tonkin Resolution, 181

Gulfs, 294

Gunboat diplomacy, 164

Gunpowder, 68

Gunpowder revolution, 58, 513

Gutenberg, Johannes, 62

H

Haitian Revolution, 75

Hamilton, Alexander, 138, 139, 140

First Political Party System, 368

Hammurabi's Code of Laws, 18, 424

Hancock, John, 139

Han Dynasty, 35

Hannibal, 29

Han Wudi, 35

Harappan civilization, 22

Hart-Cellar Act, 207

Harvey, William, 66

Hastings, Battle of, 40

Hawaii, acquisition of, 165

Hayes, Rutherford B., 162

Haymarket Square, 187

Hays, Jack Coffee, 244–245

Headright system, 113

Hellenistic Empire, 28

Henry, Patrick, 139

Henry IV, Holy Roman Emperor, 49

Henry "the Navigator," Portugal prince, 69

Henry VII, English king, English reformation and, 64

Hernandez v. Texas, 209

Hidalgo, Francisco, 218, 232

brief biography, 223

Hierarchical diffusion, 312

Hieroglyphics, 20

Highland climate, 307

Hills, 291

Hinduism, 22, 34, 44, 328–329

Hiroshima, 94

Hispanics

Civil Rights movement and, 209

LULAC and, 263

WWII and, 170–171

Hiss, Alger, 172

Historical thinking, 549

History. *See* Texas history; U.S. History; World history

Hitler, Adolf, 86, 91

Hittite Empire, 18

Hobbes, Thomas, 423, 425

Hobby, Oveta Culp, 262

Ho Chi Minh, 96, 180

Hogg, James S., 261

Holocaust, 86

Holy Roman Empire, 39, 64

Home front, during WWII, 170

Hood, John Bell, 247

Hoover, J. Edgar, 179

Hoplite, 26

Horizontal integration, 198

House Committee on Un-American Activities (HUAC), 172

House of Representatives, committees of, 359–360

Houston

history of, 284–285

as hub for aerospace, aviation and health care, 287–288

Houston, Joshua, 242

Houston, Sam

Battle of San Jacinto, 238–239

brief bio, 240–242

Runaway Scrape, 238

Hull House, 199

Human capital, 500

Human geography, 308

Humanism, 61, 542–543

Hung parliament, 430

Huns, 36
Hunter-gatherers, 14
Hurricanes, 334–335
Hutchinson, Anne, 109
Hutchison, Kay Bailey, 275
Hydrological cycle, 298
Hydrosphere, 295
Hypotheses, 557

I

IBM, 286
Idealism, 329
    American foreign policy and, 173
Ideological interest groups, 397
Ignatius of Loyola, 65
I-learned statements, 620
Immigration, 325
    European to Texas, 259–260
    history of American restrictions,
        206–207
    Red Scare and, 169
    in Texas, 277
Immigration and Nationality Act, 207
Imperialism
    America's rise as world power, 163
    British Empire, 79
    European, 78
    Japanese, 80
    Manifest Destiny and, 163
Imperium, 50
Import quotas, 480
Impressment, 141
Inca Empire, 57
Incorporation, 401
Indentured servants, 114, 127
Independence movements, 73–77
India
    British imperialism, 79
    Buddhism, 33–34
    caste system, 32
    collapse of Gupta empires, 35–37
    as cultural region, 316
    Gupta Dynasty, 34
    Hinduism, 34
    Indian Rebellion of 1857, 77, 78
    Mauryan Empire, 32–33
    during Middle Ages, 43–44
    Vedic Age, 32
Indian Rebellion of 1857, 77, 78, 79

Indians. *See* Native Americans
Indirect tax, 131
Individual rights
    Texas Constitution and, 391
    U.S. Constitution, 355–356
Indo-Aryan warriors, 22
Indus River valley, 21–22
Industrialization
    America's rise as world power, 163
    causes and effects of, in U.S.,
        197–199
    in U.S. during WWII, 170
Industrialized countries, 327
Industrial Revolution
    America's rise as world power, 163
    England and causes of, 81–82
    Factories, 82
    first, 80
    iron, coal and steam, 82–83
    science and, 81, 83–84
    second, 81, 83, 523–524
    technological developments in,
        523–524
    textiles, 82
Industry, 489–490
Infant mortality, 327–328
Inferential statistics, 596
Inflation, 502–503, 580–581
Influence of Sea Power on History,
    1660–1783, The (Mahan), 173
Innovation, culture and, 311–313
Inquiry-based learning, 603
Institutional racism, 209
Instruction. *See* Social studies
    instruction and assessment
Instrumentalism, 542
Interdependence, 545–546
Interest groups, 396–398
International Monetary Fund, 94, 176
International trade, 476–479
Internet literacy, 604–605
Interpretation, 542
Interpretive approach, 542
Interviews, for research, 593
Investiture Controversy, 49
Investments, 509–510
Invisible hand, 463
Iraq, 184–185
Iron, Industrial Revolution and, 82–83
Iron Law of Wages, 464

Iron metallurgy, 18
Iroquois Confederacy (Iroquois
    League), 119–120
Irrigation canals, 228
Islamic Caliphate, 38–39
Islamic State in Iraq and Syria (ISIS),
    98, 185
Islamic theocratic republic, 431–432
Islam/Islamic world
    Crusades and, 52–53
    culture and, 322, 329
    fundamentalism and rise of
        terrorism, 184–185
    Islamic Caliphate, 38–39
    Islamic theocratic republic, 431–432
    during Middle Ages, 42–43
    Muhammad, 38
    Ottoman expansion, 71
    radical Islamic fundamentalism, 98
    rise of, 38
    Shi'ites and Sunni Muslims, 39
Isolationism
    American foreign policy and,
        172–173
    during interwar years, 169
Istanbul, 71
Italian Renaissance, 61
Italy, fascism and Mussolini, 85, 92

J

Jackson, Andrew, 142–143, 145, 151,
    368
James II, English king, 60, 64, 120
Jamestown, 105, 113
Janissary Corps, 58
Japan
    during early modern period, 59
    Japanese imperialism, 80
    during Middle Ages, 44
    Tokugawa Japan, 59
    Warring States era, 59
    World War II and, 92–93
Japanese American, internment during
    WWII, 171
Jefferson, Thomas, 125, 141, 142
    Empire of Liberty, 149
    First Political Party System, 368
    Louisiana Purchase, 150
Jerusalem, 19, 330

Jesuits, 65
Jesus of Nazareth, 30
John I, King (England), 40
Johnson, Andrew, 159, 161
Johnson, Eddie Bernice, 274
Johnson, Lyndon B., 181, 209
   brief bio, 271–274
   Great Society programs, 273–274
Joint-stock companies, 491
Joint stock company, 112–113
Joliett, Louis, 103
Jordan, Barbara, 270
Judah, kingdom of, 19
Judaism/Jews
   culture and, 329
   Holocaust and, 86
   origins of, 19
Judicial review, 142, 364, 374, 380,
   409
Jumano Indians, 215–218
Juneteenth, 249
Jungle, The (Sinclair), 191
Jury duty, 421
Justinian, Code of Laws, 424–425

K

Kansas-Nebraska Act, 155
Karankawa, 212
Karmic behavior, 33
Kennan, George F., 176
Kennedy, John F., 181
Kepler, Johannes, 66
Keynes, John Maynard, 468–469
Kiddoo, Joseph B., 250–251
King, Martin Luther, Jr.
   brief biography, 200–201
   contributions of, 411–412
King Philip's (Metacom's) War, 106
Kissinger, Henry, 177
Knight, 46, 51
Knights of Labor, 187
Kongo, Kingdom of, 69
Korean War, 96, 180
   Texans and, 269
Korematsu v. United States, 171
Khrushchev, Nikita, 87
Ku Klux Klan, 162
Kush, Kingdom of, 21
Kuwait, 183

L

La Bahia, 229
Labor
   industrial workforce and American
      industrialization, 198
   new regime in Reconstruction era,
      251–252
   in Revolutionary Era, 127
   rights and responsibilities, 504–505
   sharecropping system, 251, 252
   specialization of, 463
Labor Management Relations Act,
   504–505
Labor movement, 187–188
Labor theory of value, 467
Laissez-faire, 462
Lakes, 291, 299
Lamar, Mirabeau Buonaparte, 242–243
Land, 443
Landforms, 303–304
Language, culture and, 309–310
La Raza Unida Party, 209
Laredo, 229
Lateen sail, 68
Law of April 6, 1830, 235
Laws
   enforcing cultural rules, 341
   Hammurabi's Code of Laws, 18,
      424
   journey of bill to become, 365–367
   of social science, 548
League of Nations, 90, 169
League of United Latin American
      Citizens (LULAC), 171, 263
Learning theory, 345
Lee, Robert E., 158, 160
Legalism, 23
Lend-Lease Program, 175, 372
Lenin, 87
Lenin, Vladimir, 472
Lepanto, Battle of, 71
Levitt, William, 206
Levittown, 206
Lexington, Battle of, 134
Liberal democracy, 433–434
Liberal revolutions
   American Revolution, 74
   Atlantic revolutions, 74
   first wave of, 73–77

French Revolution, 74–75
Haitian Revolution, 75
Latin American independence
   movements, 76
Russian Revolution, 76–77
Liberals, 434–435
Liberator, The, 154, 412
Libertarianism, 435–436
Liberty, 483
Life expectancy, 327
Limited constitutional monarchy, 432
Limited government, 325
   Texas Constitution, 389
Limited liability companies (LLCs),
   490
Lincoln, Abraham, 152, 370
   Emancipation Proclamation, 159–
      160
   Gettysburg Address, 159
   leadership in Civil War, 158–159
   Second Inaugural Address, 159
Linear evolution, 545
Line graph, 572
Literacy rates, 327
Literature, 332
Lithosphere, 295
Livingstone, David, 79
Loan-backed securities, 493–494
Loans, 493
Lobbying, 396
Locke, John, 67, 125, 423
   contributions of, 425–426
Lords, 46
Lost Colony, 105
Louisiana Purchase, 150
Louisiana Territory, 142
Louis XVI, French king, 75
Louverture, Toussaint, 75
Loving v. Virginia, 378, 387
Loyalists (Tories), 135–136
Luther, Martin, 55, 63

M

Macedonia, 28
Madison, James, 138, 139, 141
Magna Carta, 40, 53, 118, 425
Magruder, John B., 247
Magyars, 46
Mahan, Alfred Thayer, 173

Majoritarianism, 351

Malcolm X, 201

Mali, 42

Malthus, Thomas, 464

Managerial revolution, 198

Mandate of Heaven, 23

Mandate system, after WWI, 91

Mandela, Nelson, 99–100

Manifest Destiny
    America's rise as world power, 163
    westward expansion and, 149

Mann, Horace, 414

Manorialism, 46–47, 51

Mansa, Musa Keita I, 42

Manufacturing, in Texas 1900–present, 283

Mao Zedong, 99, 172

Maps
    characteristics of, 576–577
    information conveyed by, 575–576
    map-reading skills, 571

Marbury v. Madison, 142, 374, 380, 409

Marine biomes, 300

Market-clearing price, 458

Market economies, 326

Marquette, Jacques, 103

Marshall, George, 178

Marshall, John, 380
    contributions of, 409

Marshall, Thurgood, 383–384

Marshall Plan, 94, 178–179

Marshes, 292

Marx, Karl, 95, 466–468
    approach to social theory, 543

Maryland, 115

Massachusetts Bay Colony, 106, 116

Massachusetts Body of Liberties, 119

Massanet, Fray Damián, 223

Mauryan Empire, 32–33

Maverick, Mary, 242

Maxim gun, 78

Mayan civilization, 24
    during early modern period, 57
    during middle ages, 44

Mayflower, 115

Mayflower compact, 119

McCallum, Jane, 261–262

McCarthy, Joseph, 179–180

McCulloch v. Maryland, 380–381

M.D. Anderson Foundation, 288

Mean, median, mode, 597–598

Meat Inspection Act, 191

Mecca, 330

Mehmed II "the Conqueror," 71

*Mendez, et al. v. Westminster School
    District of Orange County,* 209

Mercantilism, 462

Meroe, 21

Mesoamerica, during Middle Ages, 44

Mesopotamia
    Hammurabi, 18
    overview of, 17
    religion of, 19
    Sumer, 18

Mesosphere, 295

Meuse-Argonne offensive, 167

Mexican Cession, 151, 152

Mexican War, 152, 231–233

Mexico
    Aztec and Inca Empires, 57–58
    as cultural region, 314
    Latin American independence
      movements, 76

Michelangelo, 61

Micro-habitat exploitation, 102

Middle Ages (600–1450 CE), 37–53
    African Empires, 42
    Battle of Tours, 39
    Charlemagne, 39
    China after fall of Han Dynasty, 43
    commercial revolutions and rise of
      towns, 47
    comparing Roman Empire to society
      of, 50–51
    Crusades, 52–53
    feudalism and feudal society, 46
    India during, 43–44
    Islamic civilizations, 42–43
    Japan during, 44
    Magna Carta, 40
    manorialism, 46–47
    medieval Christianity, 48–50
    medieval political and social
      systems, 45
    Mesoamerica and South America, 44
    Mongol conquest, 40–41
    Norman conquest, 39–40
    overview of, 37
    rise of Islam and development of
      Islamic World, 38–39

science and technology, 517–519

Silk Road, 41

Spanish Reconquista, 53

stirrup and Medieval feudalism,
    512–513

Viking, Magyar, and Muslim
    invasions, 45–46

Middle Colonies, 121–122
    establishment of, 117–118
    religious tolerance in, 109–110

Middle East, during early modern
    period, 58

Midwest region of US, as cultural
    region, 319

Migration
    defined, 324
    Puritans to Massachusetts, 116
    Rust Belt to Sunbelt, 277–278

Miller, Dorrie, 268

Ming Dynasty, 58–59

Minorities
    in Texas during Great Depression,
      266
    WW II and, 170–171

Minutemen, 134

Miranda v. Arizona, 384–385

Missionaries
    as factor in rise of American
      international involvement, 164
    Texas geography's influence, 228
    in Texas history, 217–218, 220, 221

Missouri Compromise, 154–155

Mita, 57

Mixed economic systems, 469

Mixed economies, 326

Model T, 200

Moderate (temperate) climate, 305

Modern Period (1750–present), 72–100
    Cold War, 95–97
    first wave of liberal revolutions and
      independence movements, 73–77
    industrialization and global
      integration, 77–80
    Industrial Revolution, 80–84
    key individuals, 99–100
    overview, 72–73
    post-Cold War, 97–100
    rise of totalitarian states, 84–87
    science and technology development,
      524–525

World War I, 88–91
World War II, 91–94
Modification, 546
Monarchy, 422
  absolute monarchies, 430–431
  defined, 437
  limited constitutional monarchy,
    432
  overview of, 432
  parliamentary constitutional
    monarchy, 431
Monetary policy, 469, 497–498
Mongols, 40–41
Monopolistic competition, 475–476
Monopoly, 474
Monotheistic faith, 19
Monroe, James, 165
Monroe Doctrine, 165
  Roosevelt Corollary to, 174
Monsoons, 335
Montesquieu, 67, 352
Montezuma, 58
Montgomery bus boycott, 200
Moon, 297
Moral Majority, 186
Mores, 341
Morgan, J.P., 197, 198
Morrill Act, 371
Morse, Samuel F.B., 526–527
Mother Teresa, 100
Motivation, 346
Mound building, 227
Mountains, 292
Mountains and Basin region of Texas, as
  cultural region, 322
Muckraker, 191
Muhammad, 38
Muslims. *See* Islam/Islamic world
Mussolini, Benito, 85, 92
Mutual funds, 494, 510
Mutually Assured Destruction (MAD),
  95, 171–172

N

Nacogdoches, 229
Nagasaki, 94
Napoleon Bonaparte, 75
National American Woman Suffrage
  Association (NAWSA), 192

National Association for the
  Advancement of Colored People
  (NAACP), 193
National debt, WWII and, 170
National Industrial Recovery Act
  (NIRA), 195
National Interstate Highway System,
  206
Nationalism, cause of World War I,
  88–89
National Labor Relations Act (NLRA),
  504
National Organization for Women
  (NOW), 202
National Origins Act, 207
National Road, 147
National savings rate, 492
National Women's Party (NWP), 192
National Youth Administration, 194
*Nation at Risk: The Imperative for
  Educational Reform, A,* 414–415
Nation-state, 310
Native Americans
  American Indian movement, 210
  Apache, 214–215
  Caddo, 227
  Coahuiltecan Indians, 213
  Comanche, 214–215, 226–227
  in early Texas history, 212–216, 221
  East Texas Indians, 213–214
  Gulf Coast Indians, 212–213
  Indian Removal, 145–146, 253–254
  Jumano Indians, 215–216
  Karankawa, 212
  Plains Indians, 214–216
  population before European arrival,
    102
  Quanah Parker, 254
  relationship with English settlers,
    104–107
  Texas geography's influence on,
    226–227
Natural disasters, 334–335
Natural gas industry, in Texas, 281–283
Naturalism, 541
Natural law, 423
Natural philosophy, 540
Natural resources, American
  industrialization and, 197
Natural rights, 423

Navigation Acts, 110–111
Navigation System, 110–111, 128, 462
Navy, U.S., buildup of, 164
Nazi Germany, 86
Necessary and proper clause, 380–381
Negative interdependence, 546
Neo-Babylonians, 19
Neolithic agricultural revolution,
  333–334
  impact on development of first
    civilizations, 336–337
  independent origins and diffusion of
    agriculture, 14–17
New Deal legislation, 193–195, 200,
  369–370
  economic growth and, 485–486
New England colonies, 115, 116, 121
  geographic influences, 121
  slavery in, 122
New England town meetings, 119
New France, 103–104
New Guinea, 16
New Hampshire, 116
New Jersey colony, 117
New Jersey Plan, 138
New Netherland, 104, 109–110, 117
Newton, Isaac, 66, 520
New York colony, 104, 109–110, 117
Niagara Movement, 193
Nile River valley, 20
Nineteenth Amendment, 203, 379
Ninth Amendment, 407–408
Nixon, Richard, 172, 181, 186
  influence on American foreign
    policy, 177
Nomadic chari-teers, 18–19
Nomination process, 398
Non-Importation Agreements, 131
Normative questions, 589
Norris v. Alabama, 418
Norte Chico civilization, 23
North Africa, as cultural region, 315
North America, as cultural region, 314
North American Free Trade Agreement
  (NAFTA), 183, 339, 480
North Atlantic Treaty Organization
  (NATO), 95, 179
North Carolina, 116
Northeast region of US, as cultural
  region, 317–318

North Korea, 498
North Texas, 258
Northwest Ordinances, 137, 147
No Taxation without Representation, 131
Nuclear age, 94
Nuclear weapons
    Cold War, 171–172
    World War II, 171
Nucleated villages, 116

O

Obama, Barack, 412
Obergefell v. Hodges, 377, 387, 392
Occupational Safety and Health Act, 505
Oceana, as cultural region, 317
Oceans, 292
Octavianus, Gaius Julius Caesar, 29–30
October Revolution, 77
Ogallala Aquifer, 295
Oil. *See* Petroleum industry
Old Deluder Satan Law of 1647, 413
Oligarchy, 437
Oligopoly, 475
Olmec civilization, 24
Open-Door Policy, 164
Open market operations, 498
Open primaries, 398
Opium Wars, 79
Opportunity costs, 443–445
Oregon Territory, 151
Original Jurisdiction, 364
Orogeny, 296
Ottoman Empire, 58
    Ottoman expansion, 71
Outlines, 575, 609
Owen, Robert, 465
Ozone layer, 295

P

Pacific Coastal Region of US, as cultural region, 320–321
Pacific Railroad Act of 1862, 371
Paine, Thomas, 133
Palastine, 19
Palmito Ranch, Battle of, 247–248
Panama Canal, 166, 336

Panhandle, 258, 266
Panic of 1893, 163–164
Parker, Quanah, 254
Parliamentary constitutional monarchy, 431
Parochial cultures, 427
Participatory cultures, 427
Partnerships, 490
Patriarchy, 437
Paul of Tarsus, 31
Payroll taxes, 508
Peace dividend, 183
Peace of Augsburg, 64
Pearl Harbor, 92, 169, 176
Peasants, 46–47
Peloponnesian War, 27
Penitentiary system, 418
Penn, William, 107, 110, 118
Pennsylvania, 110
Pennsylvania Colony, 117–118
Pensions, 510
People's Party, 189
Pequot War, 106
Percentage, 599
Percentile, 599
Perception, 346
Perestroika, 97
Performance-based learning, 620–621
Perot, Ross, 196
Persian Empire, 25–26
Personality, 346
Personality learning theory, 345
Perspectives, 616
Perspective technique, 61–62
Petition, freedom of, 403–404
Petit jury, 406
Petroleum-based products, 530–531
Petroleum industry, in Texas, 281–283
Phalanx, 26
Pharaoh, 20
Philadelphia Constitutional Convention, 138–139
Philip II, Macedonian King, 28
Philippines, 166
Photography, 576
Physical capital, 500
Physiocrats, 462
Pie charts, 572–573
Piedmont Region, 318
Pilgrims, 115

Pill, The, 515
Pineda, Alonso Álvarez de, 222
Pippin "the Short," 39
Pizarro, Francisco, 58, 216
Place, culture and, 329–330
Plains, 292
Plains Indians, 214–216
Plant, 489
Plateaus, 292
Plato, 27
Platte Amendment, 166
Plead the Fifth, 405
Plessy v. Ferguson, 193, 209, 263, 378, 382–383, 418
Plymouth Colony, 115
Plymouth Rock, 106
Pocahontas, 105–106, 113
Point of view considerations, 615–616
Polar climate, 306
Polis, 26, 50
Political culture, 426–428
Political interest groups, 396
Political parties
    alignment of, since 1877, 186
    American party systems, 367–369
    Constitution and, 140
    Democratic Party, 143–144
    Democratic-Republicans, 141–142
    during Early Republic, 140–144
    Federalist Party, 140
    First American Party System, 143
    not mentioned in Constitution, 356
    Populist Party, 189–190
    realignments, 368–369
    role of, 395–396
    Second American Party System, 143–144
    third parties and independent candidates since 1980, 196
    Whig party, 144
Political systems, 421–440
    absolute monarchies, 430–431
    classical republics, 432–433
    communist states, 431
    comparing Roman Empire to Medieval Europe, 50–51
    conservatives and liberals, 434–435
    culture and, 310
    democracy and origins/evolution of, 436–440

direct democracy, 433
Divine Right of Kings, 422
federal presidential republic, 428–429
government and culture, 426–428
Hammurabi's Code of Laws, 424
Islamic theocratic republic, 431–432
Justinian's Code of Laws, 424–425
liberal democracy, 433–434
libertarianism, 435–436
Magna Carta, 425
monarchy, 432
natural law, social contract, and rights theories, 423–424
parliamentary constitutional monarchy, 431
parliamentary republics, 430
presidential republic, 429
right to resist, 422–423
totalitarian governments, 436
types of, 325–326
Polk, James K., 151, 152
Polls, 566–567
Poll tax, 379
Polytheism, 19
Polytheists, 20
Ponds, 299
Pontiac's Rebellion, 107
Pontifex, 437
Pope, 31, 39, 48, 49
Popular sovereignty
Texas Constitution, 390–391
U.S. Constitution, 350–351
Population, Texas
in 1777, 230
1950–1990, 285
Populism, 189–190
Populist Party, 189–190
Portfolios, 619–620
Portugal, 69
Latin American independence movements, 76
Positive interdependence, 546
Positivism, 541–542
Post-Cold War
globalization, 97–98, 182–183
global war on terrorism, 184–185
peace dividend and global hotspots, 183–184
radical Islamic fundamentalism, 98

Power, 546
Power loom, 82
Powhatan, 105
Predictive questions, 589
President, of United States, 360–363
cabinet and executive agencies, 363
immunities and privileges, 362
powers over foreign affairs, 361
powers relative to judiciary, 362–363
powers vis-à-vis the Legislative Branch, 361–362
protective powers, 362
War Powers Act and, 375–376
Presidential Reconstruction, 161, 248
Presidential republic, 429
Presidio, 103, 218
Texas geography's influence, 228
Press, freedom of, 403
Price-taker, 473–474
Primaries, 398
Primary sources, 561–563
evaluating, 567–568
Primogeniture, 126
Printing press, 62, 68, 513–514
Printing revolution, 513–514
Prison reform, 417–418
Private property, 483
Problem-solving process, 556–559
Proclamation Act of 1763, 130
Production possibilities curves, 444–445, 498–499, 583–584
Productivity, 500
economic growth and, 499–500
Profit motive, 483
Progressive movement
governmental reforms, 190–191
in Texas, 261–264
Progressive taxes, 508
Progressive theory, 545
Proprietary colony, 115
Pro-Slavery Ideology, 154, 413
Protective tariffs, 479, 485
Protestant Reformation
Henry VIII and English reformation, 64
Jean Calvin, 63
Martin Luther, 63
overview, 60
religious warfare, 64

Psychology
principles and processes of, 345–346
theoretical foundations of, 344–345
Public education, history of, 413–415
Public interest groups, 397
Public policy process, 399–401
Puerto Rico, 166
Pull factors, 325
Punic Wars, 29
Pure command economies, 469
Pure competition, 473–474
Pure Food and Drug Act, 191
Pure market economies, 469
Puritanism, 115, 331
Push factors, 325

Q

Qin Dynasty, 34–35
Qing Dynasty, 58–59
Qin Shi Huangdi, 35
Quakers, 331
Pennsylvania colony, 117–118
relationship with Native Americans, 107
Qualitative methods, 591
Quantitative methods, 591
Quartile, 600
Quinine, 78
Quipu, 57

R

Race
defining, 340
human geography and, 308
Radical Reconstruction, 161, 248
Radio, 535–536
Railroads
impact of, 526
Scramble for Africa and, 78
in Texas, 256–257
westward expansion and, 147
Rainforest, 300
Raleigh, Walter, 105
Randolph, A. Philip, 171
Range, 598
Reading skill development, 605–611
Reagan, Ronald, 97, 186
Realignments, 368–369

Realism, 329
    American foreign policy and, 173
Recession, 502–503
Reconstruction
    African American office-holding,
        251
    Black Codes, 249–250
    Freedmen's Bureau, 250–251
    white resistance to, 249
Reconstruction era
    Juneteenth, 249
    new labor regime, 251–252
    Presidential Reconstruction, 161,
        248
    Radical Reconstruction, 161, 248
    white Southerners' reaction to, 162
Redeemers, 162
Redemption period of Reconstruction,
    248
Red Scare, 169, 207, 269
Referendum, 433
Reform Party's, 196
Refugee, 325
Regents of the University of California
    v. Bakke, 386–387
Regressive taxes, 508–509
Regular clergy, 48
Regulations, governmental
    history of, 494–496
    New Deal legislation during
        Depression, 195
Reign of Terror, 75
Relativism, 542
Religion
    in American colonies, 108–110
    Buddhism, 33–34, 44
    Christianity, 30, 31–32
    comparing Roman Empire to
        Medieval Europe, 51
    culture and, 310, 328–329
    establishment clause, 401–402
    free exercise clause, 402–403
    Great Awakening, 110
    Hinduism, 22, 34, 44
    Islam, 42–43
    Jesus of Nazareth, 30
    Mesopotamian, 19
    missionary impulses, 164
    monotheistic faith, 19
    origins of Judaism, 19

polytheism, 19
polytheists, 20
puritanism, 115
radical Islamic fundamentalism, 98
Vedic religion, 33
way of life in colonial America,
    330–331
Zoroastrianism, 26
Religious interest groups, 397
Relocation Diffusion, 312–313
Renaissance, 332
    art of, 61–62
    humanism, 61
    Italian Renaissance, 61
    northern, 62
    overview, 60
    printing press and print revolution, 62
Renaissance Man, 55, 61
Representative democracy, 433–434
Republic, 437
Republicanism
    Texas Constitution, 389
    U.S. Constitution, 351–352
Republican Party
    establishment of, 156, 368
    political party alignment since 1877,
        186
Republic of Fredonia, 234
Republic of Texas
    Córdova Rebellion, 243
    Council House fight, 244
    important figures in, 239–245
    Santa Fe Expedition, 243–244
Republics, 126, 432–433
Research. See Social studies research
Research question, 587–590
Reserved powers, 388, 390
Reserve rate, 498
Resources
    conflict over control of, 338–339
    patterns of settlement and, 335
Res publica, 28, 50
Revolution, Earth's, 297
Revolutionary era. See American
    Revolution and early Republic
Revolutionary socialism, 466
Revolutions
    American Revolution, 74
    Atlantic Revolutions, 74
    French Revolution, 74–75

Haitian Revolution, 75
Latin American independence
    movements, 76
Russian Revolution, 76–77
Rhode Island, 109, 116
Ricardo, David, 464
Richard II, "the Lionhearted," 40, 53
Rights
    of consumers, 503–504
    labor, 504–505
    natural, 423
    to resist, 422–423
Right-to-work laws, 505
Riis, Jacob, 191
Rivers, 293, 299
Roanoke Island, 105
Robinson, Jackie, 195, 208
Rockefeller, John D., 198
Rocky Mountains region of US, as
    cultural region, 320
Roe v. Wade, 186, 385–386
Rolfe, John, 113–114
Roman Catholic Church
    Council of Trent, 65
    Ignatius of Loyola, 65
    Protestant Revolution, 55, 63–65
    schism with Eastern Orthodoxy, 50
    Western Christendom and, 49
Roman Empire
    fall of Constantinople, 55
    rise of, 29–30
Roman Republic, 28–29
Rome, 28–29
    Augustus Caesar, 29–30
    comparing Roman Empire to
        Medieval society, 50–51
    decline and fall of Roman Empire,
        35–37
    Julius Caesar, 29
    persecution and triumph of
        Christianity in, 31–32
    Punic Wars, 29
    Roman Empire, 29–30
    Roman Republic, 28–29
Roosevelt, Franklin D., 93, 372
    brief biography, 200
    contributions of, 410–411
    court-packing, 375
    influence on American foreign
        policy, 175–176

New Deal legislation, 193–195
Roosevelt, Theodore
    influence on American foreign
        policy, 173–174
    Spanish-American War, 166
Roosevelt Corollary to the Monroe
    Doctrine, 174
Rosenberg, Julius, 172
Rotation, Earth's, 297
Rough Riders, 165
Rubrics, 620
Runaway Scrape, 238
Russia
    Eastern Orthodox Christianity and,
        48–49
    Russian Revolution, 76–77
Russian Revolution, 76–77
Rust Belt, migration to Sunbelt,
    277–278
Rwanda, 183

S

Safavid Persian empire, 58
Sahel, origins of agriculture, 17
Saint-Simon, Henri de, 465
Saint Sophia Cathedral, 71
Saladin, 52
Salas, Juan de, 221
Salem Witch Trials, 108–109
Sales tax, 509
Samoa, 164
Samurai, 44
San Antonio, in early Texas, 229
San Antonio de Béxar, 219
San Jacinto, Battle of, 238–239
Sans-culottes, 75
Santa Anna, Antonio López de, 235–
    236
    Battle of Alamo, 237
    Battle of San Jacinto, 238–239
Santa Fe Expedition, 243–244
Saratoga, Battle of, 135
Sargon, 18
Savannas, 301
Savings, 492–494, 509–510
Savings-investment spending identity,
    492
Scarcity, 442
Scatter graph, 574

Schema, 606
Schenck v. U.S., 383
Scholarly research, 565
Science and technology
    ancient empires and classical
        civilizations, 517
    automobile, 529–530, 537
    Bessemer steel process, 527
    chemical fertilizer, 514–515
    computers, 531–532
    contraception, 515
    cotton gin, 82, 146, 148, 525–526
    Early Modern Period, 522
    Early river valley civilizations, 516
    electrical power, 528–529
    ethical issues of, 532–534
    gunpowder revolution, 513
    Industrial Revolution, 523–524
    Industrial Revolution and, 81, 83–84
    petroleum-based products, 530–531
    Postclassical and Middle Ages,
        517–519
    printing revolution, 513–514
    radio, 535–536
    railroads, 526
    shipping container and global trade,
        515–516
    significant scientist and inventors,
        519–521
    social studies instruction and,
        603–605
    stirrup and Medieval feudalism,
        512–513
    Stone Age technology and
        knowledge, 511–512
    technological progress and economic
        growth, 500
    telegraph, 526–527
    telephone, 529
    television, 536–537
    twentieth century growth and,
        524–525
    urbanizing technologies, 528–530
    vaccines, 538
Scientific method, 541
    model, 590–591
    steps of, 556–559
Scientific Revolution, 65–66
Scramble for Africa, 78
Seas, 294

Seasoning time, 114
Secession, 157, 246–248
Second Amendment, 404
Second American Party System,
    143–144
Secondary source
    finding with information technology,
        604
    non-scholarly, 565–566
    scholarly research and, 565
Secondary sources, 563–564
Second Great Awakening, 149
Second Inaugural Address, 159
Second Political Party System, 368
Second Red Scare, 172
Second-world countries, 95
Secular clergy, 48
Seguín, Juan N., 239
Selective Service Act of 1917, 371
Semi-presidential republics, 429
Senate, 437
    committees of, 359–360
    Roman, 28, 29
Sensation, 345
Separation of church and state, 354–355
Separation of powers
    Texas Constitution, 390
    U.S. Constitution, 125, 352
Sepoy Mutiny, 77
Sequencing, 594
Serbia, 183
Serfs, 46
Settler colonies, 78
Seventeenth Amendment, 378–379
Seventh Amendment, 407
Seven Years' War, 107, 129
Seward, William, 164
Shang Dynasty, 23
Sharecropping system, 251, 252, 279,
    280
Shays' Rebellion, 138
Sherman Antitrust Act of 1890, 191
Shi'ites Muslims, 39
Shintoism, 329
Shipping container, global trade and,
    515–516
Shogun, 59
Shortage, 458
Shrine of Guadalupe, 330
Siddhartha Gautama, 33–34

Silk Road, 35, 41
Sinclair, Upton, 191
Single-issue interest groups, 397
Sixth Amendment, 406–407
Slaves/slavery
    abolitionism, 154
    abolition of, in North, 127–128
    in American colonies, 122–124
    Atlantic Slave Trade, 70
    Bacon's Rebellion, 114
    Bleeding Kansas, 156
    Carolinas, 116–117
    colonization movement, 154, 412
    Compromise of 1850, 155
    Constitution and, 139
    Dred Scott decision, 156
    expansion of slavery in early
        Republic, 146
    Fugitive Slave Act, 155
    Haitian Revolution, 75
    indentured servitude, 114
    Missouri Compromise, 154–155
    not mentioned in Constitution,
        356–357
    during Revolutionary Era, 127–128
    role in Texas Revolution, 234, 235
    Roman Empire, 30
    sectional division and slavery, 153–154
    in Texas and cotton, 255–256
    thirteenth amendment, 376
    Underground Railroad, 155
Smith, Adam, 67, 125
    contributions of, 463
Smith, John, 106, 113
Social contract, 423
Social control, 428
Social diffusion, 545
Social institutions, 342
Socialism, 187–188
    defined, 466
    as political-economic system,
        465–466
    socialist economic systems, 471
    Utopian Socialists, 464–465
Socialization, 343
Social learning theory, 345
Social Security Act, 195
Social studies foundations and skills
    civic life and, 550
    concepts of, 544–547

facts, 544
historical thinking, 549
laws, 548
making a living with, 550
multiple points of view and, 568–569
organizing concepts of, 552–555
philosophical schools of, 540–543
problem-solving process, 556–559
scientific method and, 556–559
terminology, 546–547
theories, 548
web of concepts, 551
in world around us, 549–550
Social studies instruction and
        assessment
    adolescent development and, 601
    assessment, 617–622
    Bloom's taxonomy, 602
    charts, graphs, timelines and
        outlines, 571–576
    context clues, 612
    databases and, 569–570
    defending arguments, 591
    dictionary, glossaries, thesaurus
        skills, 612–613
    diversity in classroom, 616–617
    economic indicators, 578–586
    feedback and communication
        technology, 604
    graphic and visual organizers,
        570–571
    I-learned statements, 620
    inquiry-based learning, 603
    interdisciplinary connections for,
        613–615
    Internet literacy, 604–605
    literature-based instruction, 590
    maps, 571, 575–576, 576–577
    model scientific method, 590–591
    performance-based learning,
        620–621
    photography, 576
    point of view considerations,
        615–616
    portfolios, 619–620
    reading skill development, 605–611
    scholarly argument vocabulary,
        611–612
    use reliable sources and critical
        analysis, 590

using literature in classroom, 569
using technology for, 603–605
writing and oral communication,
    577–578
Social studies research
    analyzing information for, 594–595
    archival research, 591–592
    Case studies, 592
    content analysis, 592
    experimental research, 592–593
    interviews, modeling and surveys,
        593
    primary sources, 561–563, 567–
        568
    quantitative vs. qualitative methods,
        591
    research question, 587–590
    scholarly research and secondary
        sources, 565
    Secondary sources, 563–564
    simultaneous primary and secondary
        sources, 564
    statistical analysis for, 595–600
    surveys and polls, 566–567
    textual sources, 567–568
Societal control, 546
Sociology, 339
    maintaining expected cultural
        behavior, 341–342
    social stratification, 342
Sole proprietorships, 490
Solon, 27
Somalia, 183
Somerset v. Stewart, 132
Song Dynasty, 43
Songhai, 42
Sons of Liberty, 131
South America
    as cultural region, 314–315
    during Middle Ages, 44
South Asia, as cultural region, 316
South Carolina, 116
Southeast Asia
    as cultural region, 316–317
    origins of agriculture, 16
Southeast region of US, as cultural
    region, 318
Southeast Texas, 257–258
Southern Christian Leadership
    Conference (SCLC), 201

Southern Colonies
    geographic influences, 116–117, 118, 122
    slavery in, 123
Southern roots, in Texas, 259
South Korea, 498
South Texas, 258–259
Southwest Asia
    as cultural region, 315
    origins of agriculture, 15–16
Southwest region of US, as cultural region, 319–320
Soviet Union
    Cold War and, 178–182
    communist economic systems, 472
    communist reform movement, 97
    Stalin and, 87, 93
    World War II and, 93
Spain
    colonization in Americas, 103
    conquistadors, 58, 216–219
    exploration and colonization of Texas, 216–222
    influence on early Texas, 229–231
    Latin American independence movements, 76
Spanish-American War, 165–166
Spanish Reconquista, 53
Sparta, 27
Spatial diffusion, 311
Spatial exchange, 123–124
Specialization of labor, 463
Speech, freedom of, 403
Spinning jenny, 82
Spoils system, 143
Sports, integration in Texas, 264
Sputnik I, 181
SQRRR method (survey, question, read, recite, review), 610
Squanto, 106
Square-rigged sails, 68
Stabilization policies, 502–503
Stalin, Joseph, 93, 472
Stamp Act, 130–131
Stamp Act Congress, 131
Standard deviation, 598
Standard Oil, 198
Standards of living, 310, 326–327
Stanton, Elizabeth Cady, 410
State government

powers of, 387–388
structure and function of Texas, 392
Texas revenue and spending of, 392–394
State of nature, 423
State of Texas Assessments of Academic Readiness (STAAR), 620–621
Statistical analysis, 595–600
Steam, Industrial Revolution and, 82–83
Steamboat, 147
Steffens, Lincoln, 191
Steppes, 301
Stimulus diffusion, 312
Stocks, 491–492, 494, 510
Stone Age technology, 511–512
Stratosphere, 295
Strauder v. West Virginia, 421
Streams, 293, 299
Strict constructionist interpretation, 141
Stupas, 33
Subculture, 309
Subduction, plate tectonics, 296
Subject cultures, 427
Subordinate information, 609
Sub-Saharan Africa
    as cultural region, 315
    early civilizations, 20–21
Suburbanization, 206
Sudan, 21
Suez Canal, 336
Sugar Act, 130
Sui Dynasty, 43
Sumer, 18
Summative assessment, 618–619
Sunni Muslims, 39
Superordinate information, 609
Supply, law of, 453
Supply curve, 454–457, 585–586
Supremacy clause, 389–390
Supreme Court, of United States
    judicial review, 374, 380
    landmark decisions of, 380–387
Surplus, 458
Surplus value, 467
Surveys, 566–567, 593
Swahili, 42
Swamps, 292
Sweatt, Heman Marion, 263–264
Sweatt v. Painter, 263
Syncretism, 311, 545

Syria, 184

T

Taft-Hartley Act, 188, 504–505
Talas River, Battle of, 43
Tang Dynasty, 43
Taoism, 329
Tarbell, Ida, 191
Tariff-Growth Paradox, 485
Tariffs, 479, 485
Taxes
    direct and indirect, 130, 131
    No Taxation without Representation, 131
    paying for WWII and, 170
    in Texas, 392–393
    types of, 508–510
Tea Act, 132
Technology. *See* Science and technology
Telegraph, 526–527
Telephone, 529
Television, 536–537
Temperance movement, 415
Tennessee Valley Authority (TVA), 194
Tenochtitlán, 57, 58
Tenth Amendment, 408
Territorial acquisitions, 150–153
Terrorism
    global war on, 184–185
    overview of, 207–208
    in post-Cold War era, 98
    war on, and government changes, 373
Tet Offensive, 181
Texas
    annexation of, 150–151
    Columbian Exchange and, 227–228
    cultural regions of, 321–322
    local government structure and function, 392
    state revenue and spending, 392–394
Texas Constitution
    checks and balances, 389
    federalism, 389–390
    individual rights, 391
    limited government, 389
    popular sovereignty, 390–391
    republicanism, 389
    separation of powers, 390

Texas Essential Knowledge and Skills (TEKS), 600
Texas history, 211–288
    American Indian groups in, 212–216, 221
    cattle ranching, 257
    Civil War and, 245–248
    Cold War, 268–269
    Conquistadors, Age of, 216–219
    cotton and slavery, 255–256
    cultural diversity 1821–1900, 259–260
    economy 1900–present, 278–288
    European exploration and colonization of, 216–222
    geographic feature influence on Indians and settlers, 226–229
    Great Depression, 266–267
    immigration, 277
    important figures 1950–present, 270–276
    important figures in early history, 222–226
    important figures in Progressive and Civil Rights movement, 261–264
    important figures in Republic of Texas/early statehood, 239–245
    Indian Removals, 253–254
    integration in education and sports, 264
    Mexican War of Independence, 231–233
    overview, 211–212
    Progressive movement, 261–265
    Reconstruction era, 248–252
    Rust Belt to Sunbelt migration, 277–278
    settler and Native American conflicts, 252–255
    Texas Revolution, 233–239
    Texas secession, 245–246
    Vietnam War, 269–270
    World War I, 265
    World War II, 267–268
Texas Instruments, 284, 286
Texas Rangers
    historical overview, 254–255
    role in United States–Mexican War, 245
Texas Revolution, 233–239

    Anglo-American immigration and cultural differences, 233–234
    Antonio López de Santa Anna, 235–236
    Battle of Gonzales, 236
    Battle of San Jacinto, 238–239
    Battle of the Alamo, 237
    causes of, 233
    Consultation of 1835, 236
    Convention of 1836, 237
    Fredonian Rebellion, 234–235
    Guerrero Decree, 235
    Juan N. Seguín, 239
    Law of April 6, 1830, 235
    Runaway Scrape, 238
    slavery and, 234
    surrender at Goliad, 238
    William B. Travis, 237–238
TExES Social Studies 7–12 (232) test
    content and format of, 3
    online prep for, 1–2
    practice tests for, 2–3
    prep schedule for, 6–7
    registering for, 5–6
    scoring, 6
    test day tips, 7–8
    test-taking tips, 9–12
    types of questions, 4–5
    when to take, 5
Textiles, 82
Text structure and organization, 607–609
Thanksgiving, 106
Theories, social science, 548
Thermopylae, 27
Thesaurus, 613
Thesis, 609
Third Amendment, 405
Third parties, 196
Third Political Party System, 368–369
Third-world countries, 95
Thirteenth Amendment, 376
Thoreau, Henry David, 152
Three-Fifths Compromise, 139
Thurmond, Strom, 196
Tigris river, 17
Timelines, 575
Tithe, 47
Tojo, Hideki, 92–93
Tokugawa Ieyasu, 59

Toltecs, 44
Torah, 19
Tories, 135–136
Tornadoes, 335
Totalitarian governments, 436
Totalitarian states
    defined, 85
    Hitler in Germany, 86
    Mussolini in Italy, 85
    overview, 84–85
    Stalin in Soviet Union, 87
Total War, 90
Tours, Battle of, 39
Townshend Acts, 131
Trade
    Caddo trade routes, 227
    in early Texas history, 221
    free trade, 479–480
    international trade, 476–479
    international trade agreements, 480
Trade barriers, 479–480
Trade unions, 187
Trading-post empires, 78
Tradition, 546
Traditional economies, 326
Transportation
    automobile, 529–530, 537–538
    government investment in early Republic, 144–145
    highway system, 206
    Industrial Revolution and, 82
    integration of American economy, 148–149
    patterns of settlement and, 335
    in Texas 1821–1900, 256–257
    westward expansion and, 147–148
Travis, William B., 237–238
Treaty of Guadalupe Hidalgo, 151
Treaty of Paris (1763), 129
Treaty of Paris (1783), 136
Treaty of Versailles (1919), 85, 86, 90, 168
Trench warfare, 89–90
Trevithick, Richard, 526
Triangular trade, 111
Tributary, 293
Triple Entente, 89
Tropical climate, 304–305
Tropical forest biomes, 300–301
Troposphere, 295

Truman, Harry, 171, 419
    influence on American foreign
        policy, 176
    Red Scare and, 172
Truman Doctrine, 176
Trustbuster, 191
Trusts, 198
Tundra, 303
Twenty-fourth amendment, 379
Twenty-sixth amendment, 379–380
Tyranny, 437

U

Umayyad Dynasty, 39
Underemployed worker, 579–580
Underground Railroad, 155
Unemployment, 501–502
    rate of, 579–580
Unicameral legislature, 138, 358
Unions
    labor movement, 187–188
    trade, 187
Unitary government, 390
Unitary system, 429
Unitary systems, 354
United Farm Workers Association
    (UFW), 201
United Nations, 94, 176, 339
United States, cultural regions of,
    317–322
United States history, 101–210
    Civil War and Reconstruction,
        153–162
    colonial America, 112–124
    European exploration and
        colonization, 101–112
    political, economic and social
        developments 1877–present,
        185–210
    Revolutionary era and early years of
        Republic, 124–146
    United States as world power,
        162–185
    westward expansion, 146–153
United States-Mexican War, 245
Universal basic income, 534
Universalizing religions, 310, 328
University of Texas, 286
Unlimited government, 326

Urban II, Pope, 52, 53
Urbanization, 202–203
    technologies of, 528–530
USA PATRIOT Act, 208, 373
Utopian Socialists, 464–465

V

Vaccines, 538
Valley Forge, 135
Valleys, 294
Value neutrality, 541
Values, 615
Van Buren, Martin, 143, 151
Vassal, 46
Vedic Age, 22, 32
Vedic culture, 22
VENONA Files, 172
Verdun, Treaty of, 45
Vertical integration, 198
Veterans Administration Housing
    Loans, 205
Veto power, 361
Viet Cong, 180
Vietnam War, 96, 180–181
    Texans and, 269–270
Vikings, 45–46
Virginia Company of London, 112–113
Virginia House of Burgesses, 119
Virginia Plan, 138
Visual organizers, 570–571
Voltaire, 67
Voluntary exchange, 484
Voting rights
    age for, 379–380
    poll tax and, 379
    in Revolutionary Period, 126
    voting as political participation,
        420–421
    women's right to, 192, 203, 379,
        415–416
Voting Rights Act of 1965, 206

W

Wagner Act, 188
Wallace, George, 196
War of 1812, 142
War on Terror, 373
War Powers Act of 1973, 375–376

Warring States era, 59
Warring States Period, 23
Warsaw Pact, 95, 179
Wartime policies, 370–373
Washington, Booker T., 193
Washington, Craig Anthony, 276
Washington, George, 140
    accomplishments of, 408
Washington Consensus, 183, 488
Water frame, 82
Watt, James, 83
Wealth of Nations, The (Smith), 126,
    463
Weimar Republic, 86
Wells, Ida B., 193
West Africa, origins of agriculture, 17
Western Civilization, 322–323
Western Front, 89
Westward expansion, 146–153
    cotton economy and, 146
    Empire of Liberty, 149
    Gadsden Purchase, 152
    integration of American economy,
        148–149
    Manifest Destiny, 149
    Mexican Cession, 151
    Northwest Ordinances, 147
    territorial acquisitions, 150–153
    transportation revolution, 147–148
Wetland regions, 299–300
Whig party, 144, 368
White, Lulu Belle Madison, 262
White House Office, 363
White racial supremacy, 79
White resistance, to Reconstruction, 249
Whitney, Eli, 146, 148, 197
William III, English king, 120
William of Normandy, 40
Williams, Roger, 109
Wilmot, David, 155
Wilson, Woodrow, 191
    Fourteen Points, 90, 168, 174
    influence on American foreign
        policy, 174–175
    League of Nations, 169
    role in WWI, 167
Winthrop, John, 108
Woman's Christian Temperance Union,
    192
Women

right to vote, 203, 379, 415–416
suffrage movement, 192
Temperance movement, 192
in Texas during Great Depression, 266–267
women's rights movements, 192, 210, 415–417
working during WWII, 170
Worcester v. Georgia, 145, 374
Working capital, 443
Works Progress Administration (WPA), 194
World Bank, 94, 176
World history, 13–100
    Ancient World Civilizations (8000 BCE-3000 BCE), 13–37
    Early Modern Period (1450–1750 CE), 54–71
    Middle Ages (600–145 CE), 37–53
    Modern Period (1750–present), 72–100
World Trade Organization, 176, 183, 480
World War I
    causes of, 88–89
    effects of, 90–91

initial neutrality of U.S., 166–167
mandate system, 91
redrawing map of Europe after, 90–91
Texas and, 265
Treaty of Versailles, 90, 168
U.S. role in, 166–167
warfare technology and tactics in, 89–90
wartime policies and government changes, 371–372
Wilson's Fourteen Points, 90, 168
World War II, 91–92
    atomic bomb, 171
    causes of, 91–92
    economic growth and, 486–487
    effects of, 94
    home front during, 170
    human costs of, 94
    Japanese American internment, 171
    key figures of, 92–93
    minorities and, 170–171
    overview of, 91
    reasons for U.S. involvement, 169
    Texas and, 267–268

wartime policies and government changes, 372–373
Writing
    cuneiform writing, 18
    Cyrillic alphabet, 48
    demotic script, 20
    in early China, 23
    hieroglyphics, 20
Writs of Assistance, 130

X

Xiongnu, 35, 36

Y

Yellow journalism, 165
Yorktown, Battle of, 136

Z

Zavala, Lorenzo de, 240
Zheng He, 59
Zhou Dynasty, 23
Zoroastrianism, 26